Perspectives on Persuasion, Social Influence, and Compliance Gaining

John S. Seiter

Utah State University

Robert H. Gass

California State University, Fullerton

PEARSON

Boston   New York   San Francisco
Mexico City   Montreal   Toronto   London   Madrid   Munich   Paris
Hong Kong   Singapore   Tokyo   Cape Town   Sydney

*To my friend, Kirk Knalson, for proving the person who claimed
"blood is thicker than water" wrong.*

—John Seiter

*To my wife, Susan, who has put up with me for 25 years now, and to
my parents, who have put up with me for 50 years.*

—Robert Gass

Executive Editor: *Karon Bowers*
Editorial Assistant: *Jennifer Trebby*
Marketing Manager: *Mandee Eckersley*
Production Administrator: *Anna Socrates*
Composition Buyer: *Linda Cox*
Manufacturing Buyer: *JoAnne Sweeney*
Editorial Production Service: *Susan McNally*
Electronic Composition: *Peggy Cabot*

For related titles and support materials, visit our online catalog at www.ablongman.com

Between the time Website information is gathered and then published, it is not
unusual for some sites to have closed. Also, the transcription of URLs can result
in unintended typographical errors. The publisher would appreciate notification
where these occur so that they may be corrected in subsequent editions.

Library of Congress Cataloging-in-Publication Data

Perspectives on persuasion, social influence, and compliance gaining / edited by John S.
Seiter and Robert H. Gass.

p. cm.

ISBN 0-205-33523-3

1. Persuasion (Psychology).   2. Influence (Psychology).   3. Manipulative behavior.
I. Seiter, John S.   II. Gass, Robert H.

BF637.P4P415 2003
153.8'52—dc21

2003050028

Printed in the United States of America

10 9 8 7 6 5 4 3 2   08 07 06 05 04

Contents

Preface

For the last several years we have had the privilege of directing a short course at the annual meeting of the National Communication Association, aimed at helping others teach classes on the topic of persuasion, social influence, and compliance gaining. As part of each course, we typically include a discussion on available textbooks, encouraging others to ask questions or offer evaluations of books they have used themselves. If not for some of the comments we have received at such courses, this reader might never have been published. As an example, some of our "short coursers" had used our textbook, *Persuasion, Social Influence, and Compliance Gaining,* and wondered if we had plans for putting together a collection of readings to accompany it that might be used by advanced students. Others told us they did not like using traditional textbooks and wondered if we might suggest an alternative list of recommended readings that represented the scope, depth, and richness of the field. Still others encouraged us in this venture, but for different reasons, noting that at the time there were few, if any, current, edited texts of readings on topics related to persuasion, even though a good number of universities offer upper-division and graduate-level courses in this area. In short, we got the push, or perhaps more truthfully, the nudge, we needed. We won't pretend it was a tough sell. The thought of such a project intrigued and excited us.

Even so, there were difficult decisions. For example, the field of persuasion is hefty—an enormous amount of research and theory has already been published on this topic—and it is constantly changing. With that in mind, our first task was to generate and refine a list of topics. Of course, when asked to choose the most important topics, every scholar probably shows some bias. Who doesn't have favorites? This book certainly reflects some of ours. Even so, we think that most scholars in this field would find considerable overlap among their lists. Certainly, a number of topics make an appearance in practically every book written on the subject of persuasion. That said, this book represents "our list." Even so, it is not a patchwork quilt of topics that were thrown together because we found them interesting. The chapters are systematically organized and designed to provide a balanced view of the field. Though many collections of readings reprint already-published articles, we solicited original chapters so that the material would be up to date and so that the authors could in many cases reflect on the recent development of theory or research—where it is going, and where it has been.

Consequently, compared to lower-division books, this reader provides depth in specific topic areas. This, we hope, will enable instructors to augment texts from use in lower-division courses to upper-division or graduate-level courses. In addition to serving as a supplementary reader, this book is, in our opinion, perfectly suited for use as a stand-alone text. For those who wish to use it as such, we have provided a good deal of background information. Thus, in addition to selecting chapters that represent a wide variety of topics, we have written a couple of "groundwork" chapters ourselves. Each unit in the reader is preceded by a brief overview that frames the material for students who may be less familiar with the field of persuasion.

We hope that others as well may find the topics covered in this collection useful. For example, those who teach persuasion primarily from a rhetorical perspective but would also like their students to understand social scientific approaches to the field should find it possible to marry a rhetorical text to a set of readings such as those represented in this book. Likewise, teachers who approach the field from the perspectives of mass media or public persuasion might use these readings to complement their approach by providing students with an understanding of face-to-face persuasion and recent research on compliance gaining.

After generating a list of topics that would accomplish such goals, our next task was to locate and invite scholars to contribute chapters to the reader. We set about this task in the same way a sports organization might go about selecting the best possible team. We generated a list of "superstars," that is, theorists and researchers who could "play their positions" extraordinarily well. We had no idea how lucky we would be. Indeed, a quick glance at our list of contributors (pages ix–xv) demonstrates that we succeeded in creating a "dream team" of persuasion scholars. These contributors have made significant, lasting contributions to theory and research in the field of persuasion. Most are prodigious scholars who have written their own books and published dozens of articles. We think that students will not only benefit from insights "straight from the horse's mouth" but will also appreciate the multidisciplinary approach of this book. Our authors come from a wide variety of disciplines, including communication, psychology, and business. We hope this breadth not only provides students with a more panoramic view of persuasion but also broadens this collection's appeal to readers in related disciplines.

We are confident that students will learn a great deal about persuasion from this book, because we have learned so much in the process of editing it. We have also asked our own students to test-read the chapters and have received very positive responses. While some of the chapters are more challenging than others, all of them, as we've noted, should be accessible to upper-level undergraduate and graduate students, and all of them are well worth the read.

Acknowledgments

We are delighted to see this reader published and are grateful to all of those who helped us along the way. First and foremost, we want to thank the chapter contributors, for they are the real writers of this volume. Thank you all for being generous enough to contribute your time and knowledge. Second, we want to thank our students, both undergrads and grads alike, who reviewed early drafts of the chapters and told us what they liked, what they disliked, what kept them awake, and what put them to sleep. Third, we are indebted to Karon Bowers and Jennifer Trebby at Allyn & Bacon. Thank you for being patient with us, for answering all of our pesky questions, and for always being a pleasure to work with. We don't know how she does it, but Karon is able to answer an e-mail before it has even been sent. Jennifer is a wizard at details and knows how to follow through on tasks to completion. We also cannot forget our colleagues: Harold Kinzer, Jennifer Peeples, Jeanine Congalton, Rich Wiseman, Bill Gudykunst, and Elizabeth Mechling. You folks offered helpful insights into the editing process, useful suggestions on different aspects of the chapters themselves, and much-needed comic relief from our occasional frustration. We appreciate all of your sage advice and the time you devoted to listening and supporting us through our editing ordeals. We would also like to thank the following reviewers: Jean DeHart, Appalachian State University; Steve Duck, University of Iowa; Elaine Jenks, West Chester University; Michelle Mazur, University of Hawaii; Lynnette Mullins, University of Minnesota–Crookston; Sabrena Parton, Kennesaw State University; John Kares Smith, SUNY–Oswego; and Elena Strauman, Auburn University. Finally, and most important, we are grateful to our families—Debora, Christian, Susan, Jordan, and Graham—for tolerating time away, piles of papers, crankiness as deadlines approached, and two absent-minded professors.

Contributors

Peter A. Andersen (Ph.D., Florida State University) of the School of Communication at San Diego State University has authored over 100 book chapters, research papers, and journal articles. He has received recognition as one of the 100 most published scholars in the field of communication. Dr. Andersen has consulted for dozens of school districts, child-care centers, health organizations, political campaigns, universities, and business organizations. He is currently coinvestigator on a project funded by the National Cancer Institute. He has served as the President of the Western Communication Association, director of research for the Japan-U.S. Telecommunications Research Institute, and editor of the *Western Journal of Communication*. He teaches courses in many areas of interpersonal and mass communication. He is the author of three recent books: *The Handbook of Communication and Emotion* (1998, with L. Guerrero, Academic Press), *Nonverbal Communication: Forms and Functions* (1999, McGraw-Hill), and *Close Encounters: Communicating in Relationships* (2001, with L. Guerrero and W. Afifi, McGraw-Hill).

Leslie A. Baxter (Ph.D., University of Oregon, 1975) is F. Wendell Miller Distinguished Professor of Communication Studies at the University of Iowa. Author of over 90 articles, book chapters, and books, her research interests concentrate on the study of communication in personal relationships and family relationships.

William L. Benoit (Ph.D., Wayne State University, 1979) is professor of communication at the University of Missouri. He has published seven books and over 100 articles and book chapters. His book, *Accounts, Excuses, and Apologies,* was selected as an Outstanding Scholarly Book for 1995 by *Choice*. He received a grant from the National Institute of Mental Health for a study of resistance to persuasion. In 2000, he was given the American Communication Association's Award for Excellence in Teaching at the Doctoral Level.

George Bizer earned his B.A. at Indiana University and his Ph.D. in social psychology at Ohio State University in 2001. He is currently assistant professor of psychology at Eastern Illinois University in Charleston, Illinois. The bulk of Dr. Bizer's research is focused on two areas. One involves the relation between framing of attitudes and the strength of those attitudes, while the other examines the underlying structure of the features of strong attitudes. He has published several articles and chapters on these topics. At Eastern Illinois, he primarily teaches introductory psychology and social psychology.

David B. Buller (Ph.D., Michigan State University) holds the Harold Simmons Chair in Health Communication at the Cooper Institute. He also is the director of the Cooper Institute-Denver and the institute's Center for Health Communication. He has authored over 80 books, book chapters, and articles related to nonverbal communication, social influence, and health communication. Dr. Buller's research on deception has been supported by extramural grants from the Department of Defense. His research on health communication has been supported by extramural grants from the National Institutes of Health, the U.S. Centers for Disease Control and Prevention, the Robert Wood Johnson Foundation, and the Cancer Research Foundation of America. Dr. Buller is a member of the Governor's Scientific Advisory Committee for the Colorado Tobacco Research Program. He has consulted with numerous government agencies and university research groups on communication processes in disease prevention.

Judee K. Burgoon (Ed.D., West Virginia University) is professor of communication, professor of family studies and human development, and director of human communication research for the Center for the Management of Information at the University of Arizona. She has authored seven books and monographs and nearly 200 articles, chapters, and reviews related to nonverbal and relational communication, interpersonal relationship management, dyadic interaction patterns, deception, computer-mediated communication, research methods, and public opinion toward the media. Her research on deception has been supported by extramural grants from the Department of Defense. Her awards and honors include the National Communication Association's Distinguished Scholar Award, Golden Anniversary Monographs Award, and Charles H. Woolbert Research Award for Scholarship of Lasting Impact, the International Communication Association's B. Aubrey Fisher Mentorship award, election as a fellow of the International Communication Association, and election to membership in the Society for Experimental Social Psychology.

Michael Burgoon (Ph.D., Michigan State University, 1970) is professor of medicine, public health, and family and community medicine at the University of Arizona College of Medicine. He has published numerous articles and 16 books. He has acted as a consultant to both government and industry and has received grants from the National Cancer Institute, the National Institutes of Child Health and Development, and the National Institutes on Drug Abuse. When asked for a brief biography, he modestly reported that "he has done some work in the area of social influence." Given his record of scholarly accomplishments, this statement, in the editors' opinions, is akin to saying, "Michael Jordan has played a little basketball."

Carma L. Bylund (Ph.D., Northwestern University, 2001) is an assistant professor at the University of Iowa, holding a joint appointment in the Department of Communication Studies and the Department of Community and Behavioral Health. Her research interests include family communication and health communication.

John T. Cacioppo received his B.A. at the University of Missouri-Columbia and his Ph.D. in social psychology from Ohio State University in 1977. Since then he has been on the faculty at the University of Notre Dame, the University of Iowa, and Ohio State University. He is currently the Tiffany and Margaret Blake Distinguished Service Professor of Psychology at the University of Chicago. His current work focuses on affect, emotion, and social behavior, with an emphasis on integrating biological, behavioral, and social levels of analysis to develop more comprehensive theories of human behavior. He is the author of nine books and over 270 articles and chapters. Among his awards are the National Academy of Sciences Troland Research Award, the Society for Personality and Social Psychology's Campbell Award for Distinguished Scientific Contributions, and the Society for Psychophysiological Research's Award for Distinguished Scientific Contributions. Most recently he received the American Psychological Association's Distinguished Scientific Contributions Award. He is past editor of the journal *Psychophysiology.*

Linda L. Carli is an associate professor of psychology at Wellesley College. She received her Ph.D. in psychology from the University of Massachusetts at Amherst. Her published research includes articles and chapters examining the effects of gender on group interaction, communication, and influence, as well as papers on reactions to adversity and victimization. Currently, she is involved in research examining children's use of gender as a status characteristic. In addition to her teaching and research, she has developed and conducted negotiation and conflict resolution workshops for women leaders and has lectured to business organizations on sex discrimination and the challenges faced by professional women.

Hyunyi Cho (Ph.D., Michigan State University) is assistant professor in the Department of Marketing Communication at Emerson College. Her research interests center on the examination of impacts and implications of health communication campaigns. Most recently, she is investigating ways of promoting self-efficacy perceptions over the Internet for disease prevention and management.

Robert B. Cialdini, Ph.D., is a Regent's Professor of Psychology at Arizona State University. He has extensive scholarly training in the psychology of influence, together with over 25 years of research on the subject. His book *Influence: The Science of Persuasion* is the result of years of studying the reasons that people comply with requests in business settings. Dr. Cialdini received graduate training at the University of North Carolina and Columbia University. He has held visiting scholar appointments at Ohio State University, the University of California, the Annenberg School for Communication, and the Graduate School of Business at Stanford University. Additionally, Dr. Cialdini has been elected president of the Society for Personality and Social Psychology.

Michael J. Cody is professor of communication at the Annenberg School for Communication at the University of Southern California. Trained in psychology and philosophy at California State University, Sacramento, and Tel Aviv University (1973), Dr. Cody received his Ph.D. in communication from Michigan State University in 1978. He specializes in health communication, persuasion and campaign communication, and interpersonal communication. He teaches doctoral, master's, and undergraduate courses at USC, where he has worked since 1982. In recent years he has worked on projects to train older adult learners to use new technologies, studied how tobacco companies have exploited the Internet to portray positive images of tobacco, and examined family communication patterns about health beliefs and practices among minority members. Recognized as one of the most widely published writers in the field of communication, he is the author of numerous books, chapters, and articles focusing on the process of social influence.

James Price Dillard (Ph.D., Michigan State University, 1983) is professor of communication arts at the University of Wisconsin. His research interests revolve around interpersonal influence, emotion, and persuasion with an emphasis on the communication of risk, threat, and fear. The majority of his published work appears in *Human Communication Research, Communication Monographs,* and *Communication Research.* He is the editor of *Seeking Compliance: The Production of Interpersonal Influence Messages* (1990) Scottsdale, AZ: Gorsuch Scarisbrick Publishers, and the first recipient of the John E. Hunter Award for Meta-Analysis.

Robert H. Gass (Ph.D., University of Kansas, 1984) is a professor at the College of Communications at California State University, Fullerton. He has authored more than 70 journal articles, book chapters, and professional papers. He teaches courses in argumentation, persuasion, and research methods. Most recently, his research interests have focused on visual persuasion and compliance gaining and compliance resisting. He and John Seiter are coauthors of another text, *Persuasion, Social Influence, and Compliance Gaining* (Second Edition, 2003 Allyn & Bacon).

Rosanna E. Guadagno, M.A., is a doctoral candidate in social psychology working with Dr. Cialdini at Arizona State University. She first discovered her love of research while earning her B.S. in psychology at Santa Clara University. During her senior year she ran her first foot-in-the-door study as part of an upper-division research practicum, and from then on she became fascinated with the question of why people comply. She went on to further her training in the study of compliance and other social influence issues while pursuing a graduate education at Arizona State University. Additionally, she is a former NSF fellow and has authored several articles on social influence.

Randy Hirokawa (Ph.D., University of Washington) is professor and chair of the Department of Communication Studies at the University of Iowa. He is recognized for his work on the role of communication in group decision-making processes and also has strong secondary interests in the study of social influence processes in groups and organizations. Professor Hirokawa has published over 50 journal articles and book chapters, is the coeditor with Marshall Scott Poole of *Communication and Group Decision Making,* now in its second edition, and has given numerous invited lectures—including the Van Zelst Lecture at Northwestern University, the Scheidel Lecture at the University of Washington, and the Fisher Lecture at the University of Utah. He is the former editor of *Communication Studies,* and has served on the editorial board of five journals.

Renee Storm Klingle (Ph.D., University of Arizona, 1994) is currently associate professor in the Speech Department at the University of Hawaii at Manoa. Her areas of specialty are persuasion and health communication. Her publications can be found in *Human Communication Research, Communication Research, Health Communication, Communication Studies, Addictive Behaviors, Journal of Behavioral Medicine,* and *Evaluation and the Health Professions.* Since 1996 she has been actively involved in projects investigating adolescent substance use and the risk and protective factors associated with substance use.

Daniel J. O'Keefe (Ph.D., University of Illinois) is Professor in the Department of Speech Communication at the University of Illinois at Urbana-Champaign and has taught at the University of Michigan and Pennsylvania State University. He has received the National Communication Association's Charles Woolbert Research Award and its Golden Anniversary Monograph Award, the American Forensic Association's Outstanding Monograph Award, the International Communication Association's Division 1 John Hunter Meta-Analysis Award, and teaching awards from the Central States Communication Association and the University of Illinois.

Richard E. Petty received his B.A. at the University of Virginia and his Ph.D. in social psychology from Ohio State University in 1977. After an initial position at the University of Missouri-Columbia, he returned to Ohio State, where he is currently Distinguished University Professor of Psychology. His current work focuses broadly on the situational and individual difference factors responsible for changes in beliefs, attitudes, and behaviors. His topics of special interest include understanding the role of meta-cognitive as well as implicit factors in persuasion and resistance to change. He is the author of seven books and about 200 articles and chapters. Among his awards are the Society for Personality and Social Psychology's Campbell Award for Distinguished Scientific Contributions and the Society for Consumer Psychology's Award for Distinguished Scientific Contributions. Recently, Petty served as president of the Midwestern Psychological Association. He is past editor of the *Personality and Social Psychology Bulletin.*

Michael Pfau (Ph.D., University of Arizona) is professor and chair of the Department of Communication at the University of Oklahoma. Previously he was professor and director of graduate studies in the School of Journalism and Mass Communication at the University of Wisconsin-Madison. Pfau's research interests concern resistance to influence and mass media influence, particularly in a political context. He has conducted a number of studies on the relative influence of various communication forms or modalities in election campaigns. He won the Rose B. Johnson Award for an essay published in *Southern Communication Journal.* Pfau has coauthored/edited six books and is now working on a seventh. His authorship/coauthorship of more than 75 journal articles and book chapters earned him a ranking of 26th in the last (1995) national assessment of active scholars in communication.

Andrew S. Rancer (Ph.D., Kent State University, 1979) is a professor in the School of Communication at the University of Akron. He teaches courses in interpersonal communication, nonverbal communication, training methods, and communication theory. He has published his research on the aggressive communication traits of argumentativeness and verbal aggression in numerous national and regional communication journals, and his research has been featured on *Good Morning America.* He is coauthor with Dominick Infante and Deanna Womack of the widely used textbook, *Building Communication Theory* (3rd ed., 1997) Prospect Heights, IL: Waveland Press. Dr. Rancer also presents training programs on managing conflict productively to organizations and educational institutions.

Derek Rucker received his B.A. at the University of California, Santa Cruz, and is currently a Ph.D. candidate in social psychology at Ohio State University. Derek is primarily interested in the study of attitudes and social cognition. Currently, he is examining what effects distinct processing strategies have on persuasion. This research examines how objective versus biased processing of a persuasive message, and different types of biased processing such as counterarguing and bolstering, affect subsequent attitudes and attitude strength. In addition to this research, Derek has published on the topics of emotion and persuasion, the use of accusations as an influence tactic, and methodological techniques in the social sciences.

John S. Seiter (Ph.D., University of Southern California, 1993) is associate professor of speech communication at Utah State University, where he teaches courses in social influence, interpersonal communication, theories of communication, and intercultural communication. His published research includes articles investigating persuasion in selling contexts, nonverbal influence, and perceptions of deceptive communication. He has received six "Top Paper" awards for research presented at professional conferences. Together with Robert Gass, he wrote the book *Persuasion, Social Influence, and Compliance Gaining*. His teaching has been recognized with awards at both the University of Southern California and Utah State University.

Jason T. Siegel (M.A., University of Arizona, 2000) is a senior research specialist with the Health Informatics Program at the University of Arizona, where he is also a doctoral candidate in the Department of Educational Psychology. He is concerned with the testing and application of social science theory in the context of health promotion and disease prevention. He is currently working on several projects that use interdisciplinary approaches to increase the ability of health campaigns to assist depressed adolescents, increase organ donor registration, and reduce adolescent substance use.

Alan Strathman (Ph.D., Ohio State University, 1992) is a social psychologist at the University of Missouri. He is interested generally in the area of communication and persuasion, and specifically in research using the Elaboration Likelihood Model. In addition, he is involved in research examining the extent to which individuals are influenced by the immediate or distant consequences of their behavior. He is the author of numerous journal articles and book chapters.

Erin Alison Szabo (Ph.D., University of Wisconsin-Madison, 2000) is assistant professor of communication at St. John's University/College of St. Benedict. Her research interests include persuasive processes, resistance to influence, psychological reactance to influence attempts, and media effects, with particular influence on adolescents and risk behaviors.

Amy E. Wagner (M.A., UNLV) is a doctoral candidate in the Department of Communication Studies at the University of Iowa. Her research interests are in the areas of interpersonal communication and family communication. She is currently working on her dissertation, focusing on communication in marital couples who take a hiatus.

Kim Witte (Ph.D., University of California) is a professor in the Department of Communication at Michigan State University. She is working as a senior program evaluation officer at the Center for Communication Programs, Johns Hopkins University, where she is providing technical assistance with conceptualization, design, evaluation, and analysis of international health communication research projects. Her current research focuses on the development of effective health risk messages for members of diverse cultures and on gender equality and domestic violence educational projects. Dr. Witte is immediate past chair of the Health Communication Division of the International Communication Division and a past chair of the Health Communication Division of the National Communication Association. She sits on ten editorial boards and has served as a consultant to the National Libraries of Medicine, the Centers for Disease Control and Prevention, the National Institute of Occupational Safety and Health, and others. Dr. Witte has received funding from the Centers for Disease Control, the National Institute of Occupational Safety and Health, the American Cancer Society, and elsewhere. Her work has been recognized by over a dozen "Top Paper" awards at both national and international conferences, as well as by the "Distinguished Article Award" from the Applied Communication Division of the National Communication Association. In 1997 Dr. Witte received the Teacher-Scholar Award from Michigan State University. Recently, Dr. Witte was named the Lewis Donohew *Outstanding Scholar in Health Communication.* She is the lead author of *Effective Health Risk Messages: A Step-by-Step Guide* (2001, Sage Publications), and was awarded the 2001 Distinguished Book Award by the Applied Communication Division of the National Communication Association.

1

A Rationale for Studying Persuasion

John S. Seiter and Robert H. Gass

Some time ago, one of the authors was invited to his son's second grade classroom to talk about "persuasion," the subject the author teaches and researches at a university. The second graders, the author was told, were having "career year," and parents with all sorts of professions were making appearances. The author said he would be happy to do it, though privately he had his doubts. Perhaps he'd seen too many movies with "career day" scenes—featuring overzealous parents speaking to classrooms of squirmy, fidgety children. Whatever the case, he was sure about one thing: He was going to have to adapt to an audience prone to "ants in the pants."

On presentation day, after a quick definition of persuasion (involving a chocolate bribe for all those who listened closely), the author and second graders tried a few simple experiments. In one, they watched commercials that made certain products (e.g., dolls, cars, cereal) appear much more dazzling and irresistible than they were when seen or tasted in the classroom. One ad featured a child who, immediately after eating a particular brand of cereal, became popular, hairy, and skilled at skateboarding. But when several of the second graders sampled the cereal themselves, none seemed hairier (as if they would want to be!) and none was able to replicate the skateboard stunts. The author was pleased with his results. The second graders seemed to understand that there were a lot of sneaky ways people try to persuade them. So, after warning them about a few other messages they should watch out for (e.g., those involving drugs and cigarettes), the author passed out Snickers and went on his way, convinced he'd done a fine job.

It did not take long to discover he was mistaken. Just a few days later, in fact, a fishing trip with his son turned into a discussion of mosquitoes, flies, bullies, and *persuasion,* all of which had made his son's list of "bad things." That was when the author realized he might have spent too much of his presentation time on entertainment and snacks while neglecting to discuss the good things persuasion can accomplish. He also wondered about his reputation. After all, if persuasion were "bad" and he taught it, what kind of a villain did his son think he was? Of course, if his son or classmates had been thinking such thoughts, they wouldn't be the first. Indeed, from time to time, those who study and teach social influence have been criticized harshly. In the fifth century B.C., for example, Plato derided the first teachers of persuasion for "making the worse appear the better reason" (Corbett, 1971, p. 598). Later, in the mid-1970s, Simons (1976) noted:

> From a number of quarters these days, persuasion is under attack for being a manipulative activity. Its highest critics equate not just some persuasion, but all persuasion with deception and role-playing, domination and exploitation. (p. 35)

More recently still, feminist scholars have characterized traditional rhetoric, that is, persuasion, as a type of communication that devalues the lives and perspectives of others, and a means by which persuaders attempt to feel good about themselves by denigrating others. By way of example, Foss and Griffin (1995) wrote:

> The value of the self for rhetors in this rhetorical system comes from the rhetor's ability to demonstrate superior knowledge, skills, and qualifications—in other words, authority—in order to dominate the perspectives and knowledge of those in their audiences. . . . The act of changing others not only establishes the power of the rhetor over others but also devalues the lives and perspectives of others. (p. 3)

With such criticisms in mind (and reputations at stake!), we thought it essential that the introductory chapter to this text set forth a rationale for studying persuasion as well as provide a brief ethical backdrop for examining such a study. Before we do so, however, we think it important to address two related issues. First, considering that critics of persuasion seem to emerge and reemerge with some regularity, you might be wondering whether the study of persuasion has suffered as a result. At first glance, one might be tempted to conclude that this is the case. When examining this issue, for example, Miller and Burgoon (1978) initially noted:

> While it would be hyperbolic to state that the guns are silent on the persuasive battleground, their roar has grown sporadic and muted. No longer are the pages of journals glutted with the results of persuasion studies. . . . As a result of these disciplinary trends, bedrock pessimists proclaim that persuasion research is a dying enterprise, while skeptics content themselves with the observation that it has become an area of limited, secondary import. (p. 29)

Though observations such as these paint a grim picture, such skeptics and pessimists are mistaken. To be certain, upon further inspection, Miller and Burgoon (1978) concluded that the study of persuasion has not wavered; it has simply changed focus and direction. Thus, while traditional studies examining linear, "one-to-many" persuasive attempts are less in evidence now, you'll find a host of studies on new persuasion topics, including those on compliance gaining and deception. In other words, skeptics concluding that persuasion research has diminished were looking in the wrong places. Persuasion is a dynamic area of study. On the one hand, scholarly interest in topics may change as a result of social, personal, or political climates—hence the large amount of research on mass persuasion and propaganda during the 1940s, especially in World War II, followed by examinations of social protest and resistance to persuasion during the 1960s, when there was a great deal of political unrest and distrust of government. On the other hand, scholarly interest in specific topics may not fade forever. Instead, interest in various aspects of persuasion may be cyclical. This ebb and flow of interest is evidenced by research on cognitive dissonance, which flourished in the 1950s and 1960s, entered a period of the doldrums in the 1970s and 1980s,[1] and then reemerged as a vital theory with important implications for persuasion in the 1990s. At one point, Leon Festinger, who created Cognitive Dissonance Theory, stopped conducting research on the theory altogether. In a transcription of his remarks at a 1987 symposium (cited in Harman-Jones & Mills, 1999), he said, "I ended up leaving social psychology. . . . I left and stopped doing research on the theory of cognitive dissonance because I was in a total rut. The only thing I could think about was how correct the original statement had been" (p. 383). In a recent volume by Harmon-Jones and Mills (Eds.) devoted to cognitive dissonance, however, Aronson (1999) underscored the importance of the theory and "its reemergence in the 1990s as a powerful means of predicting and changing human behavior in a variety of areas, including those that have abiding social importance" (p. 103). In short, then, despite what skeptics and pessimists might say, persuasion research has never gone out of fashion; it has just changed its style and has on occasion brought back into fashion styles of old.

In addition to noting the unwavering nature of interest in persuasion research, a second point we would like to make before offering our rationale for studying persuasion is that we do not disagree with all that critics of persuasion have to say. That is, we agree that plenty of people have used persuasion for the wrong reasons, sometimes with tragic consequences. Focusing on such instances alone, however, strikes us as seeing the glass half empty. Think, for example, as the author and his son did for the rest of their fishing trip, of all the good things that persuasion might accomplish. Without persuasion, how does a physician urge a diabetic patient to lay off sweets or get more exercise? How does a friend get her drunken buddy to accept a ride rather than drive himself home? How does a mother warn her five-year-old child never to take rides from strangers? How do civil rights activists speak out against racism or world leaders lobby for peace agreements? We hope you see our point. The list of good things that can be accomplished through persuasion is endless.

The arguments of some critics, however, focus less on the ends of persuasion and instead point accusing fingers at the means by which persuasion is accomplished. For example, the feminist scholars we mentioned earlier take issue with traditional persuasion because it embodies an adversarial view of communication encounters in which one person is trying to do something *to* another. In contrast, their approach, an "invitational approach" to rhetoric, emphasizes cooperation and dialogue. One person is trying to communicate *with* another.

We respect this point of view. Indeed, we would be among the first to acknowledge that in our patriarchal society, people often fail to recognize incentives for cooperative communication. They presume that communication encounters are competitive or adversarial in nature. They overlook their interdependence and view communication as a win-lose process. They neglect shared or communal approaches to problem solving and decision making.

While cooperative, dialogic encounters may be the ideal to which we should all aspire, we believe that there are many situations in which people have to roll up their sleeves and persuade.[2] Imagine, for example, that you observed an injustice being committed by one person against another. You could begin by inviting the aggressor to engage in a dialogue in the hope of arriving at a mutually satisfactory outcome. But what if the aggressor spurned your invitation? Would you simply say, "Oh well, I tried" and resign yourself to the fact that the world is full of injustices? We think it would be better to resort to persuasion, to engage in an active effort to change the mind of the aggressor. We see dialogue and persuasion as complementary, not antithetical, forms of communication. There are times, we submit, when *one has a moral obligation to try to change others' minds and behavior.* And as we've argued elsewhere (Gass & Seiter, 2003), we think the motives of persuaders have as much to do with the ethical defensibility of their influence attempts as the means of persuasion used. The women's suffrage movement was a persuasive campaign. So was the women's rights movement that began in the 1970s. So are the efforts to secure basic human rights for women throughout the world. We don't think that women who toil in sweatshops, or who live in poverty, or who are denied the most basic educations or medical care, or who are forced to marry against their will, mind too much if others use persuasion to try to improve their lot in life. Persuasion is essential precisely because dialogue sometimes fails.

From an ethical standpoint, then, we side with Plato's student, Aristotle, who had this to say about persuasion:

> If it is urged that an abuse of the rhetorical faculty can work great mischief, the same charge can be brought against all good things (save virtue itself), and especially against the most useful things such as strength, health, wealth, and military skill. Rightly employed, they work the greatest blessings, and wrongly employed, they work the greatest harm. (1355b)

In other words, we take the position that persuasion is amoral, or as McCroskey (1972, p. 269) called it, "ethically neutral." Persuasion, much like any tool, can be used for good or bad. It all depends on the motives of the tool user—Hitler versus Gandhi, Osama bin Laden versus Martin Luther King, Jr., Jim Jones versus Mother Teresa. In short, the glass is neither half empty nor half full—it's both.

Although we believe that this point addresses the previously mentioned criticisms of persuasion, there are additional and perhaps even more compelling reasons for reading a book such as this. First, critics who argue against the study of social influence by pointing their fingers at unethical persuaders provide what we consider one of the best reasons for studying persuasion: self-defense. The fact that unethical persuaders are lurking around corners, plying their trade on unsuspecting targets, is no reason to stop studying persuasion. On the contrary, we believe that such a response only makes them more successful. Instead, by learning the tricks of their trade, we are in a better position to defend ourselves against unethical persuaders. This, of course, was what the author was trying to accomplish with his second-grade audience. By exposing some of the bells and whistles advertisers use to appeal to children, he hoped to make the children more critical consumers of the persuasive messages they receive. What better way to disarm those who might try to manipulate or coerce us into doing something that's not in our best interest? Learning about persuasion is an excellent defense!

We realize, of course, that by studying persuasion people may become more effective persuaders themselves. This, we believe, is another valuable reason for studying social influence. While some critics might shudder at this prospect, we view the ability to influence others as a fundamental ingredient of communication competence. And we are not alone. For example, in an extensive review of communication competence research from multiple fields, Spitzberg and Cupach (1984) reported that an individual's ability to adapt effectively in order to achieve goals is perhaps the most universally accepted aspect of communication competence. This ability, they noted, is a crucial part of being well adjusted that, when absent, "is often associated with abnormal or even pathological orientations" (Spitzberg & Cupach, 1984, p. 36). Competent communicators are persuasive. They know how to adapt successfully in order to achieve their goals.

With the above in mind, it makes no sense to us to suggest that the study of such an important communication ability be avoided. Imagine, for example, a communication teacher telling a student, "I want you to be able to organize your ideas; use solid reasoning and evidence; have good command of language; and use movement, gestures, and eye contact effectively—*but not if you are going to persuade anyone of anything!*" Imagine a teacher telling a class, "You need to be able to engage in active listening, to paraphrase others' ideas, to engage in perception-checking, to self-disclose in the here and now—*but not if you're trying to convince someone of something!*" Being an effective persuader is part and parcel of being a competent communicator.

Having made our bias clear, we feel it's important to pause for a moment to point out, as others have (see Kellerman, 1992; Spitzberg & Cupach, 1984), that competent communicators are not only effective in achieving their goals but also do so in appropriate ways. Here, we emphasize the word *appropriate*. While we have no qualms about teaching students to become more effective persuaders, we believe that the power to persuade carries with it an obligation to persuade ethically.

Happily, there seems to be increasing and continued interest in ethical issues surrounding persuasion. By way of example, Robert Cialdini (1999) has compared ethical persuaders to "sleuths." Unlike "bunglers," who use ineffective strategies, or "smugglers," who rely on unscrupulous tactics, "sleuths" study a persuasive situation in order to develop the most effective tactics, yet they also make sure that the tactics they use are ethical. Similarly, Brockriede (1974) compared ethical persuaders (or arguers) to "lovers." Unlike "seducers," who use trickery and deceit to achieve their goals, or "rapists," who use threats or force, "lovers" respect others' dignity, are open to others' arguments, and strive for equality. Finally, as we've already noted, persuasion itself is amoral. This suggests to us that decisions regarding how right or wrong any given influence attempt is depend largely on the nature of the situation and on the motives of the persuader.[3] Even so, we believe that a few general guidelines apply to almost every influence attempt. We cannot overemphasize, for example, the importance of respecting others and looking out for their welfare, especially when they are more vulnerable than others (e.g., children). We believe that persuasion is generally more ethical when people are made aware that they are being influenced and when they have unconditional freedom to say "no" to influence attempts.

In addition to its defensive and instrumental benefits, there is another reason for studying persuasion. Before offering our final reason, though, we wish to point out one more thing about persuasion's detractors. Specifically, those who argue against the study of persuasion are themselves committing a *tu quoque* fallacy, that is, accusing another of a similar wrong. In the process of criticizing persuasion, such critics are relying on persuasion themselves. They would like to persuade you *not* to study persuasion, not to use persuasion, or to use persuasion less. This approach raises an interesting dilemma: How can one communicate one's beliefs, opinions, values, views, positions, preferences or 'druthers *without* employing persuasion?[4]

We have noted elsewhere (Gass & Seiter, 2003) that influence attempts, whether implicit or explicit, are ubiquitous. Look around you. Each day you are bombarded with messages, advertisements, logos, and countless other influence attempts. Consider, for example, some of the following figures:

- More than $200 billion per year is spent on advertising in the United States (Berger, 2000).
- If all the money spent on advertising were divided up, it would work out to about $800 per person in the United States per year (Berger, 2000).
- The average person in the United States is exposed to more than 3,000 advertising messages per day (Borchers, 2002; Dupont, 1999; Simons, 2001; Woodward & Denton, 1999).

Besides that, think of the other contexts in which you are exposed to influence attempts. Persuasion is an obvious and indispensable component in a number of professions, including counseling, law, management, politics, sales, social work, teaching, and the ministry. It can be found abundantly in the sciences, the arts, interpersonal interactions, and second-grade classrooms, just to name a few. Moreover, depending on the way one defines persuasion (see chapter 2), it may be virtually impossible *not* to influence others. Appearances, for example, even if unintentionally communicated, can be influential. Thus, baby-faced people tend to be perceived as honest (Brownlow, 1992), and bald candidates are less likely to get elected than those with a full head of hair (Sigelman, Dawson, Nitz, & Whicker, 1990). People who use a lot of eye contact tend to be more persuasive (Segrin, 1993), and attractive people are more believable than unattractive ones (Seiter & Dunn, 2000). Heavier people are less likely to earn high salaries than slim people (Argyle, 1988), and tall people are more likely than short people to get jobs (Argyle, 1988). In short, avoiding persuasion would be difficult, if not impossible. Even critics of persuasion cannot avoid it. Clearly, engaging in persuasion is an inextricable part of being human.

This statement, to us, provides the most compelling reason for studying persuasion. Specifically, if we humans ever hope to understand ourselves, how can we ignore one of the major underlying impulses for human communication? Studying persuasion can and does tell us a great deal about how humans produce, shape, perceive, interpret, and respond to messages. It provides insights into the social and cultural forces that give rise to influence attempts, among them presidential debates, social protests, religious cults, and health campaigns. It dispels various "common sense" assumptions about the ways in which persuasion "really" works. In short, as Miller and Burgoon (1978) argued:

No matter how fervently some well-meaning individuals try to deny or wish the fact away, questions concerning control and influence will remain an integral aspect of humanity's daily communicative activities. Given the centrality of these questions, it seems both foolhardy and fruitless to assume that our understanding of human communication can go on advancing without continued research attention to the persuasion process. (p. 45)

It is in this spirit that we present and hope you will approach this collection of readings. It contains what we believe are some of the finest ideas from some of the most important persuasion scholars of our time. The collection is organized into four parts.

1. Part I lays the groundwork for study by examining conceptualizations of persuasion, the history and nature of the field, and the ways in which persuasion functions.
2. Part II examines important variables in the process of persuasion. Specifically, it discusses communicator characteristics—source credibility, argumentativeness, verbal aggressiveness, and gender—and how they affect the creation, sending, and receiving of persuasive messages. This section also examines elements of persuasive messages themselves, both verbal and nonverbal.
3. Part III explores the strategies and processes by which people seek and resist compliance. It includes a theoretical discussion of how compliance-gaining messages are produced, as well as an exploration of sequential persuasion tactics, fear appeals, deception, and inoculation.
4. Part IV examines social influence in several contexts. Specifically, it analyzes persuasion as it takes place between doctors and patients, in interpersonal relationships, and between employees, buyers, and sellers in organizational contexts.

Despite its critics, persuasion, as you will see, is a study with a rich past, a promising future, and widespread contemporary interest. We hope we have convinced you that it is a topic well worth studying. We also hope you find the topic of persuasion as fascinating as we do and that you enjoy reading this collection as much as we enjoyed editing and compiling it.

Notes

1. In 1978, Miller and Burgoon argued that attribution and equity theories had ended the reign of cognitive dissonance and other cognitive consistency theories.

2. In fairness, we should note that some feminist scholars admit that persuasion is sometimes necessary (Foss & Griffin, 1995).

3. Clearly, the number of persuasive situations that could be debated is endless and could fill volumes. Though we do not have room to consider such situations here, for a more detailed discussion, see Gass & Seiter (2003), chapter 16.

4. Again, to be fair, we should note that some feminist critics (see Foss & Griffin, 1995) say that their approach, known as invitational rhetoric, is not designed to "change" anything (indeed, that would be persuasion). Instead, they say:

Although invitational rhetoric is not designed to create a specific change, such as the transformation of systems of oppression into ones that value and nurture individuals, it may produce such an outcome. (p. 16)

Moreover, while such critics claim they are not attempting to characterize traditional approaches to rhetoric (i.e., persuasion) as "misguided," one has to wonder whether some of the language they use to characterize persuasion, for example, that it "devalues lives and perspectives" (p. 3), "infringes on others' rights to choose" (p. 3), constitutes "a kind of trespassing on the personal integrity of others" (p. 3), and leads to the "denigration" of others' perspectives (p. 6)—is persuasive, whether it was intended to be or not.

References

Argyle, M. (1988). *Bodily communication* (2nd ed.). Madison, CT: International University Press.

Aristotle. (1932). *The rhetoric* (L. Cooper, trans.). Englewood Cliffs, NJ: Prentice-Hall.

Aronson, E. (1999). Dissonance, hypocrisy, and the self-concept. In E. Harmon-Jones & J. Mills (Eds.), *Cognitive dissonance: Progress on a pivotal theory in social psychology* (pp. 103–126). Washington, DC: American Psychology.

Berger, A. A. (2000). *Ads, fads, and consumer culture.* Lanham, MD: Rowman and Littlefield.

Borchers, T. A. (2002). *Persuasion in the media age.* Boston: McGraw-Hill.

Brockriede, W. (1974). Arguers as lovers. *Philosophy and Rhetoric, 5,* 1–11.

Brownlow, S. (1992). Seeing is believing: Facial appearance, credibility and attitude change. *Journal of Nonverbal Behavior, 6,* 253–259.

Cialdini, R. B. (1999). Of tricks and tumors: Some little-recognized costs of dishonest use of effective social influence. *Psychology & Marketing, 16*(2), 91–98.

Corbett, E. P. J. (1971). *Classical rhetoric for the modern student* (2nd ed.). New York: Oxford University Press.

Dupont, L. (1999). *Images that sell: 500 ways to create great ads.* Ste-Foy, Quebec, Canada: White Rock Publishing.

Festinger, L. (1999). Reflections on cognitive dissonance: 30 years later. In E. Harmon-Jones & J. Mills (Eds.), *Cognitive dissonance: Progress on a pivotal theory in social psychology* (pp. 381–385). Washington, DC: American Psychology.

Foss, S. K., & Griffin, C. L. (1995). Beyond persuasion: A proposal for an invitational rhetoric. *Communication Monographs, 62,* 2–18.

Gass, R. H., & Seiter, J. S. (2003). *Persuasion, social influence, and compliance gaining* (2nd ed.). Boston: Allyn & Bacon.

Harmon-Jones, E., & Mills, J. (1999). *Cognitive dissonance: Progress on a pivotal theory in social psychology.* Washington, DC: American Psychology.

Kellerman, K. (1992). Communication: Inherently strategic and primarily automatic. *Communication Monographs, 59,* 288–300.

McCroskey, J. C. (1972). *An introduction to rhetorical communication* (2nd ed.). Englewood Cliffs, NJ: Prentice-Hall.

Miller, G. R., & Burgoon, M. (1978). Persuasion research: Review and commentary. In B. R. Ruben, (Ed.), *Communication yearbook 2* (pp. 29–47). New Brunswick, NJ: International Communication Association.

Segrin, C. (1993). The effects of nonverbal behavior on outcomes of compliance gaining attempts. *Communication Studies, 44,* 169–187.

Seiter, J. S., & Dunn, D. (2000). Beauty and believability in sexual harassment cases: Does physical attractiveness affect perceptions of veracity and the likelihood of being harassed? *Communication Research Reports, 17* (2), 203–209.

Sigelman, L., Dawson, E., Nitz, M., & Whicker, M. L. (1990). Hair loss and electability: The bald truth. *Journal of Nonverbal Behavior, 14,* 269–452.

Simons, H. W. (1976). *Persuasion: Understanding, practice, and analysis.* Reading, MA: Addison Wesley.

Simons, H. W. (2001). *Persuasion in society.* Thousand Oaks, CA: Sage.

Spitzberg, B. H., & Cupach, W. R. (1984). *Interpersonal communication competence.* Beverly Hills, CA: Sage.

Woodward, G. C., & Denton, R. E. (1999). *Persuasion and influence in American life* (3rd ed.). Prospect Heights, IL: Wadsworth.

Part I

Preliminaries

Definitions, Trends, and Theoretical Underpinnings in the Field of Persuasion

Like most "part 1s," this first section sets the stage for all that follows. It does so by addressing some preliminary questions involving the study of persuasion—questions of the "what?," "when?," "where?," "why," and "how?" variety. We hesitate, however, when calling these questions "preliminary." Indeed, to us the term *preliminary* implies the technical and detailed material that one must labor through before getting to the "good stuff," in much the same way that one needs to finish one's spinach or broccoli before enjoying dessert.

Contrary to such connotations, we find the material covered in this section appealing and fascinating. Thus (at the risk of pushing metaphors too far), rather than think of this section's chapters as "warm-up acts" or "appetizers" we consider them "main events" or "main courses" in and of themselves. And (at the risk of mixing metaphors), we view this section as the first reel of a movie that grabs one's attention and lays out the basic characters and foundations for the plot that follows. Although on the one hand the chapters in this section provide a background for understanding material later in the book, they address issues that not only continue to intrigue (and vex) persuasion scholars but in many ways, dictate the ways in which research and theorizing about persuasion are done.

As we've already noted, each chapter in this section addresses basic questions about persuasion, social influence, and compliance gaining. Chapter 2 examines the "what" of persuasion. As the saying goes, "Before beginning a hunt, it is wise to ask someone what you are looking for before you begin looking for it" (Milne, 1995, p. 55). This chapter, then, addresses questions about "the nature of the beast." In short, it offers a definition of persuasion and related terms such as influence and compliance gaining. As you will see, the study of persuasion has undergone a dramatic transformation in the last few decades. This chapter argues that such changes invite a reexamination of how persuasion is conceptualized. It focuses specifically on two criteria—whether persuasion is intentional, and whether it is successful—that scholars have used to define persuasion. It also discusses the implications of using or not using such criteria to limit what is studied in the field. After reading the chapter, we think you will see that understanding "what" persuasion is involves a lot more than consulting a dictionary. We also hope the chapter will help you better understand the terms "persuasion," "social influence," and "compliance gaining" when you encounter them later in the text.

If chapter 2 is the "what" chapter, chapter 3 is the "when and where" chapter. In it, Daniel O'Keefe provides a roadmap for research and theory in persuasion, explaining when and where the field got its start, where it has been, and where it may be heading. Besides showing us "the lie of the land," we think this chapter is important because it invites us to explore the ways in which the field has expanded and how we have as a result developed new understandings about persuasion. At the same time, this chapter places the complexity of variables related to persuasion into perspective and underlines the importance of understanding how specific contexts influence the process of persuasion—concepts that, as you will see, become important later in this text. Although the "trends" and "prospects" laid out in this chapter represent just one author's perspective on the field, we like this portrayal and find it a compelling and informative journey.

Finally, chapters 4 and 5 focus on theories of persuasion or, more specifically, the "how" and "why" questions of social influence. What is a theory? According to Littlejohn (1996), in its broadest sense, a theory is simply an explanation of a phenomenon. Theories are comprised of a set of related concepts or propositions that help us understand how something functions or why it works the way it does (Infante, Rancer, & Womack, 1997). Theories not only explain how or why persuasion works, they also offer the prospect of prediction and control. By way of illustration, Kim Witte's theory and model of fear appeals, described in chapter 13, not only explains how fear appeals function but also predicts the specific circumstances in which they will or will not be effective and offers insights into controlling their use for maximum persuasive effect. In addition, good theories are heuristic—they generate research, aid in discovery, and are "vital to the growth of knowledge" (Littlejohn, 1996, p. 32).

The theories presented in chapters 3 and 4 meet all of these criteria. Chapter 3 provides a brief overview of some of the most influential theories in the discipline, whereas Richard E. Petty, Derek Rucker, George Bizer, and John T. Cacioppo, devote chapter 4 entirely to one theory, the Elaboration Likelihood Model (ELM), which is arguably one of the most important contemporary theories of persuasion. The scope of its influence is reflected in the number of places where it is cited in the other chapters of this book. The ELM helps us understand the ways in which multiple variables (such as communicator characteristics, credibility, message factors, the nature of context, and so forth) come into play in the process of persuasion. As you'll see, persuasion is rarely a simple, linear process, like a cue ball knocking an eight ball directly into a corner pocket. Instead, persuasion involves interactions among a number of variables, like pool balls banking off the cushions of a pool table or ricocheting off one another before finally dropping into a pocket. This chapter not only demonstrates such complexity, it lays out the key propositions of the ELM, and also addresses recent criticisms of the theory.

We hope you find the chapters in this part informative and enlightening. After reading them, you should have a much better understanding of what persuasion is, where it stands, and how it functions. Moreover, although we said earlier that we would like you to consider this section more of a main course than an appetizer, we hope that this first batch of chapters will whet your appetite for all those that follow.

References

Infante, D. A., Rancer, A. S., & Womack, D. F. (1997). *Building communication theory* (3rd ed.). Prospect Heights, IL: Waveland Press, Inc.

Littejohn, S. W. (1996). *Theories of human communication* (5th ed.). Boston: Wadsworth Publishing Company.

Milne, A. A., (1995). *Pooh's little instruction book*. New York: Dutton Books.

2

Embracing Divergence

A Definitional Analysis of Pure and Borderline Cases of Persuasion

Robert H. Gass and John S. Seiter

Scholars in various disciplines devote considerable attention to defining their terms. Consider the field of communication, for example. Dance and Larson (1976) reported well over 100 different definitions of the term "communication" in the literature. Much of the wrangling over what constitutes communication has centered on issues such as intentionality (Is communication necessarily intentional?), symbolicity (Is communication limited to symbolic action?), and the number of participants required (Does communication require two or more persons?).

Similar concerns have surrounded definitions and conceptualizations of the term "persuasion," though admittedly on a lesser scale. More than a dozen and a half definitions of persuasion have appeared in writing over the last two decades (see table 2.1). Yet although articles addressing the merits of competing definitions of communication have appeared with regularity in communication journals (e.g., Andersen 1991; Bavelas, 1990; Beach, 1990; Clevenger, 1991; Cronkhite, 1986; Dance, 1970; Gerbner, 1966; Miller, 1980; Motley, 1990a, 1990b, 1991; Shepherd, 1992), few or no recent articles have addressed issues related to defining and conceptualizing persuasion or its closely related terms, influence and compliance gaining (Dillard, 1988). This is hardly because the issue has been settled. To the contrary, many current definitions of persuasion are incompatible. It appears that as persuasion research has evolved over the last two decades, notions about what constitutes the study of persuasion have become less and less distinct.

Still in evidence are "traditional" studies of persuasion, typified by public or one-to-many investigations aimed at belief, attitude, or behavior change. Such traditional studies are apparent in health awareness campaigns designed to reduce smoking, increase seat belt usage, promote safe sex, or prevent drug use (see for example, Pfau, Kenski, Nitz, & Sorenson, 1990; Pfau, Van Bockern, & Kang, 1992; Pfau & Van Bockern, 1994; Witte,

TABLE 2.1   *Assorted Definitions of Persuasion over the Past Three Decades*

"A conscious attempt by one individual or group to change the attitudes, beliefs, or behavior of another individual or group of individuals through the transmission of some message."

Bettinghaus, E. P., & Cody, M. J. (1994). *Persuasive communication* (6th ed.). Fort Worth, TX: Harcourt Brace, p. 6.

"Persuasion is the coproduction of meaning that results when an individual or group of individuals uses language strategies and/or visual images to make audiences identify with that individual or group."

Borchers, T. A. (2002). *Persuasion in the media age.* Boston: McGraw-Hill, p. 15.

"Persuasion is the name we give to the type of communication that brings about change in people."

Bostrum, R. N. (1983). *Persuasion.* Englewood Cliffs, NJ: Prentice-Hall, p. 8.

"We define persuasion as a conscious symbolic act intended to form, modify, or strengthen the beliefs, opinions, values, attitudes, and/or behaviors of another or ourselves."

Burgoon, M., Hunsaker, F. G., & Dawson, E. J. (1994). *Human Communication* (3rd ed.). Thousand Oaks, CA: Sage, p. 177.

"Persuasion is intended communication that affects how others think, feel, and/or act toward some object, person, group or idea."

Cegala, D. J. (1987). *Persuasive communication: Theory and practice* (3rd ed.). Edina, MN: Burgess International, p. 13.

"Persuasion is the process by which language and symbolic actions influence choice-making by others."

Cooper, M., and Nothstine, W. L. (1992). *Power persuasion: Moving an ancient art into the media age.* Greenwood, IN: Educational Video Group, p. 2.

"Persuasion involves one or more persons who are engaged in the activity of creating, reinforcing, modifying, or extinguishing beliefs, attitudes, intentions, motivations, and/or behaviors within the constraints of a given communication context."

Gass, R. H., & Seiter J. S. (2003). *Persuasion, social influence, and compliance gaining* (2nd ed.). Boston: Allyn & Bacon/Longman, p. 34.

"Persuasion takes place when a motivator is able to either change or confirm an existing attitude in the minds of listeners."

Hazel, H. (1998). *The power of persuasion* (2nd ed.). Dubuque, IA: Kendall-Hunt, p. 2.

"Persuasion is a transactional process among two or more persons whereby the management of symbolic meaning reconstructs reality, resulting in a voluntary change in beliefs, attitudes, and/or behaviors."

Johnston, D. D. (1994). *The art and science of persuasion.* Madison, WI: William C. Brown, p. 7.

"Persuasion is the co-creation of a state of identification or alignment between a source and a receiver that results from the use of symbols."

Larson, C. U. (2001). *Persuasion: Reception and responsibility* (9th ed.). Belmont, CA: Wadsworth, p. 9.

TABLE 2.1 *Continued*

"Persuasion is a complex, continuing, interactive process in which a sender and receiver are linked by symbols, verbal and nonverbal, through which the persuader attempts to influence the persuadee to adopt a change in a given attitude or behavior because the persuadee has had his perceptions enlarged or changed."

O'Donnell, V., & Kable, J. (1982). *Persuasion: An interactive-dependency approach.* New York: Random House, p. 9.

"A successful intentional effort at influencing another's mental state through communication in a circumstance in which the persuadee has some measure of freedom."

O'Keefe, D. J. (2002). *Persuasion: Theory and research* (2nd ed.). Newbury Park, NJ: Sage, p. 17.

"Persuasion is an activity or process in which a communicator attempts to induce a change in the belief, attitude, or behavior of another person or group of persons through the transmission of a message in a context in which the persuadee has some degree of free choice."

Perloff, R. M. (1993). *The dynamics of persuasion.* Hillsdale, NJ: Erlbaum, p. 15.

"We use the term persuasion to refer to any instance in which an active attempt is made to change a person's mind."

Petty, R. E., & Cacioppo, J. T. (1981). *Attitudes and persuasion: Classic and contemporary perspectives.* Dubuque, IA: William C. Brown, p. 4.

"We define [persuasion] as the shaping, changing or reinforcing of receivers' responses, including attitudes, emotions, intentions, and behaviors."

Pfau, M., and Perot, R. (1993). *Persuasive communication campaigns.* Boston: Allyn & Bacon, p. 6.

"Persuasion is, in all cases, the activity of demonstrating and attempting to change the behavior of at least one person through symbolic interaction. It is conscious and occurs (a) when a threat to at least one person's goals is observed and (b) when the source and degree of this threat are sufficiently important to warrant the expenditure of effort involved in persuasion."

Reardon, K. K. (1981). *Persuasion: Theory and context.* Beverly Hills, CA: Sage, p. 25.

"The phrase 'being persuaded' applies to situations where behavior has been modified by symbolic transactions (messages) which are sometimes, but not always, linked with coercive force (indirectly coercive) and which appeal to the reason and emotions of the person(s) being persuaded."

Roloff, M. E., and Miller, G. R. (1980). *Persuasion: New directions in theory and research.* Beverly Hills, CA: Sage, p. 15.

"Persuasion is human communication designed to influence the autonomous judgments and actions of others."

Simons, H. W. (2001). *Persuasion in society.* Thousand Oaks, CA: Sage, p. 7.

[Persuasion is] "any message that is intended to shape, reinforce, or change the responses of another, or others." (based on Miller's 1980 definition)

Stiff, J. B., & Mongeau, P. A. (2003). *Persuasive communication.* New York: Guilford Press, p. 4.

(continued)

TABLE 2.1   *Continued*

Without offering a specific definition, Trenholm states that persuasion embodies the following characteristics: Persuasion is "symbolic and noncoercive," it "creates, reinforces, or changes responses," it is "transactional," and it is "ubiquitous."

Trenholm, S. (1989) *Persuasion and social influence.* Englewood Cliffs, NJ: Prentice-Hall.

"Persuasion encompasses the processes by which language and actions influence the choice-making of ourselves and others."

Williams, M. R., & Cooper, M. D. (2002). *Power persuasion: Moving an ancient art into the media age* (3rd ed.). Greenwood, IN: Educational Video Group, p. 4.

"Persuasion is the process of preparing and delivering verbal and nonverbal messages to autonomous individuals in order to alter or strengthen their attitudes, beliefs, and behaviors."

Woodward, G. C., & Denton, R. E. (1992). *Persuasion and influence in American life* (2nd ed.). Prospect Heights, IL: Waveland, p. 21.

1994, 1995). Overlaying such traditional investigations are more recent, "nontraditional" studies of persuasion, emphasizing interpersonal or face-to-face influence. The wealth of studies on compliance gaining, compliance resisting, deception, and deception detection reflect this recent trend, which can be characterized as a watershed era in persuasion research. As Boster (1995) commented, "arguably, in the last 15 years the study of compliance-gaining message behavior has held the attention of communication scholars as much as, if not more than, any other single topic in the discipline" (p. 91). More recently, Wilson (1998) noted that scholarly interest in compliance gaining "is very much alive" (p. 273).

This evolution, or divergence, in research interests has served only to muddy the definitional waters. Thus, it remains unclear whether studies of compliance gaining and deception represent an extension of persuasion research or separate lines of inquiry altogether (Burgoon & Dillard, 1995). This lack of clarity is unfortunate when one considers the importance of definitions to theory building and scholarly inquiry. In this regard, Dance (1970) noted that in the process of constructing theories, a definition determines the behavioral field observed, which in turn affects the principles derived, the hypotheses generated, and the system of laws stated. George Gerbner (1966) similarly argued that "the choice of a problem for study and research, the allocation of resources, and the assessment of the relevance of contributions, depend upon definitions" (p. 99).

The fact that persuasion research has undergone a major transformation, and that a divergence in research methods and foci has developed, invites a reexamination of how persuasion should be defined and conceptualized. Because definitions limit what is studied in a field, they may also limit variables that are given attention and in turn the ways in which we think and build theories of communication. As Burke (1966) noted, one's choice of terminology not only reflects attention, it selects and deflects attention as well (p. 45).

To this end, we provide an analysis of two fundamental criteria upon which prevailing definitions of persuasion are based, illustrated by an accompanying diagrammatic representation, and suggest useful ways in which persuasion may be distinguished from closely related concepts such as influence, or social influence as it is often called, and compliance gaining.

Boundaries and Limiting Criteria

We wish to acknowledge from the outset that we maintain no illusions about there being a "correct" definition of persuasion. Various scholars and researchers conceptualize persuasion differently and therefore subscribe to varying definitions of the term. And although there are *some* commonalities among *some* definitions, there are as many differences as there are similarities. The current transition from "public" persuasion to "interpersonal" persuasion has done little to clarify boundaries. Rather, as Boster (1995) noted, the emphasis on compliance-gaining research has had the effect of broadening the focus of study. Studies on the use of touch as a compliance-gaining strategy, for instance, have broadened the persuasion construct to include nonverbal behavior, as opposed to more traditional studies focusing on language and discursive symbols. Studies on deception have similarly examined the behavioral and physiological correlates of deception, rather than symbolic forms of influence. The emergence of such nontraditional research interests has had the effect of expanding the swath of human activities that potentially may be regarded as "persuasion."

Pure versus Borderline Cases of Persuasion

Our position is that many of the definitional vagaries can be clarified, if not resolved, by focusing on two considerations. The first is whether a given scholar or researcher is attempting to define "pure" persuasion—what Simons (1986) and O'Keefe (1990) have labeled "paradigm" cases of persuasion—versus *all* of persuasion, including its periphery, which we term "borderline" cases of persuasion. By pure persuasion, we refer to clear-cut cases on which almost all scholars in communication and related disciplines would agree. As examples, nearly everyone would include a presidential debate, a television commercial, or an attorney's closing remarks to a jury as instances of persuasion.

Other instances, though, lie closer to the boundary of what we normally think of as persuasion. Not everyone would agree that a derelict's mere appearance "persuades" passersby to keep their distance. Nor would everyone agree that when city planners install speed bumps on a street where speeding is common, they are "persuading" motorists to slow down. Such cases are less clear-cut. Much of the disparity in definitions, then, is rooted in the fact that some scholars and researchers are concerned with "pure" persuasion, whereas others are concerned with borderline cases as well. The perspective, shown in figure 2.1, illustrates this distinction.[1] As the gradation or shading in the figure suggests, the threshold between pure and borderline persuasion is fuzzy rather than distinct.

What implications does the shift in emphasis from traditional to nontraditional research interests have on "pure" versus "borderline" conceptualizations of persuasion? Among other things, there appears to be a need to expand the scope of persuasion to encompass nonverbal behavior and implicit social cues that accompany face-to-face encoun-

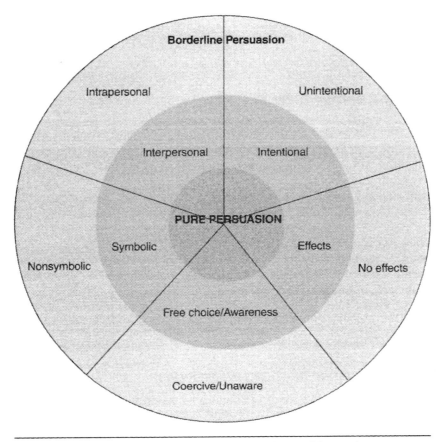

FIGURE 2.1   *A Model of Pure versus Borderline Cases of Persuasion*

ters. Because a good deal of what happens in interpersonal encounters occurs at a low level of awareness (Langer, 1989a, 1989b), we suggest, as has Roloff (1980), that much of the influence that takes place operates at a similarly implicit level. As an illustration, cultural factors may influence an individual's choice of compliance-gaining strategies without the individual's conscious awareness (Wiseman, Sanders, Congalton, Gass, Sueda, & Ruiqing, 1995). As deception detection research has shown, nonverbal cues, such as blinking or smiling, may also affect perceptions of veracity (Feeley & Young, 1998; Hale & Stiff, 1990; Seiter, 1997; Vrij, 2000), even though a good deal of nonverbal behavior is nonmindful. If these kinds of studies are to be included within the purview of persuasion, then the definition must be broadened accordingly.

Choice of Limiting Criteria

A second consideration in defining and conceptualizing persuasion involves the limiting criteria that form the basis for a given definition. Elsewhere we have identified five key criteria that constitute the basis for nearly all definitions of persuasion (Gass & Seiter, 1997; 2003). These are (1) whether persuasion is intentional or unintentional, (2) whether persuasion must be effective or successful, (3) whether free will or conscious awareness must be involved, (4) whether persuasion necessarily occurs via language or symbolic action, and (5) whether persuasion can be intrapersonal as well as interpersonal. In this chapter, we focus on two of these five criteria in an effort to differentiate the types of influence studied in our field. Although each limiting criterion is discussed separately for convenience's sake, many definitions incorporate both criteria simultaneously.

Intentionality and the Issue of "Accidental" Persuasion.　Many definitions adopt a "source-centered" view by focusing on the sender's intent as a defining feature of persuasion. Bettinghaus and Cody (1994), Burgoon, Hunsacker, and Dawson (1994), Cegala (1987), O'Keefe (1990), Perloff (1993), Petty and Cacioppo (1981), Reardon (1981), Stiff (1994), and Woodward and Denton (1992) all adhere to this requirement, making it the most common characteristic of standard textbook definitions (see table 2.1).

Certainly, "pure" persuasion would seem to fall into this category. When one considers traditional cases of persuasion, one tends to think of conscious, intentional efforts, along the lines of the classic fear arousal studies. Compliance gaining, too, would appear to satisfy this requirement, to the extent that compliance gaining is conceived of as planned, goal-directed communication (see Dillard, 1989, 1990; Dillard, Segrin, & Harden, 1989). But what about other borderline cases of persuasion? We suggest that "accidental" influence often takes place with little or no conscious awareness on the part of the influential individual. Appearance cues, for instance, may affect credibility judgments, without the source's awareness that he or she is conveying such impressions to others. Research on social modeling (Bandura, 1977) illustrates this phenomenon as well. As just one example, parents commonly instill beliefs, impart values, and model behavior for their children. Yet as any parent can attest, many of the lessons parents "teach" their children are completely unintended.

Even when persuasion is intentional, many of the cues conveyed by a source may be unintentional, such as the appearance of nervousness or the use of a powerless language style. Such unintended cues nevertheless carry considerable persuasive weight. In this regard, Cooper and Nothstine (1992) have commented that "those we try to influence through our persuasion may well respond to aspects of our persuasive actions that we are not aware of" (p. 3). This certainly holds true for research on nonverbal and physiological correlates of deception. It is precisely those cues over which deceivers have little conscious control that may serve as the most reliable indicators of deception.

Another way in which an "intent" criterion is troublesome involves the prospect of unintended receivers. Two studies (Greenberg & Pyszczynski, 1985; Kirkland, Greenberg, & Pyszczynski, 1987) clearly demonstrate the operation of the "unintended receiver effect." In these studies the researchers created a situation in which third parties overheard ethnic slurs directed against African Americans. The results of both studies revealed that the slurs they overheard led the third parties to evaluate the individuals at whom they were directed less favorably. Of course, even traditional, public persuasion can involve unintended audiences. An advertising campaign might target one group of consumers but provoke a backlash among nontargeted consumers. Traditional laboratory studies, though, have typically relied on clearly defined target audiences and carefully constructed messages in the form of stimulus videos or booklets, thereby affording few or no opportunities for unintended receivers to be affected. This lack of emphasis on unintended receivers, however, can be seen more as a limitation of traditional research paradigms than a rationale for restricting the scope of persuasion.

Basing a definition of persuasion on intentionality makes good sense if one wishes to focus primarily on "public" persuasion. From an "interpersonal" perspective, however, such a limiting criterion implies a rather linear view of communication. An intent requirement is problematic insofar as compliance gaining is concerned, because compliance gaining in the interpersonal arena is mutual or bilateral. Berger and Burgoon (cited in Burgoon & Dillard, 1995) have underscored this point in criticizing some researchers for "their failure to acknowledge the reciprocal nature of social influence processes in interpersonal communication" (p. 398). Interpersonal Deception Theory (Buller & Burgoon, 1996; also see chapter 14 of this volume) also stresses the importance of acknowledging the transactional nature of deceptive communication. Where influence is reciprocal, whose intent counts? Do both parties' influence attempts have to be intentional? Does compliance *resisting* constitute a persuasive intent? Standard textbook definitions that are based on an intent criterion do not provide clear-cut answers to these questions. In fact less than a third of the definitions listed in table 2.1 explicitly acknowledge the reciprocal nature of persuasion. In order to accommodate nontraditional persuasion studies, some clarification or modification of the intent requirement would seem to be in order. At a minimum, adherents to an intent requirement should explain how the requirement is to be applied in two-way, transactional settings.

We suggest that one pragmatic approach toward clarifying the situation and establishing some modest boundaries is to use the term "persuasion" to refer solely to intentional efforts and the term "influence" to refer to either intentional or unintentional outcomes. Thus, conscious modeling of behavior constitutes persuasion, while unconscious modeling should be considered a form of influence. According to this scheme, "influence" can be understood as an umbrella term that encompasses any and all forms of persuasion, whether pure or borderline.[2] "Persuasion" should thus be considered a special case of influence that satisfies an intent requirement.

This conceptualization is useful because it preserves the intent requirement embodied in many definitions of persuasion, while simultaneously acknowledging that at times beliefs, attitudes, and behaviors can be modified accidentally. Although this distinction may seem obvious, it is worth noting that most scholars and researchers use *persuasion* and *influence* interchangeably. Few of the standard textbook definitions make any distinctions whatsoever between these terms.

This distinction still leaves open the question of whether compliance gaining is best thought of as a part of persuasion or social influence. We tend to favor Dillard's conceptualization of compliance gaining as a type of planned, goal-directed communication (Dillard, 1990; Dillard, Segrin, & Harden, 1989). At the same time, however, we can envision situations in which one person gains another's compliance without intending to do so. For example, a shopper might decide to buy a specific brand because she/he observed another attractive shopper selecting that brand. A pedestrian who crosses the street when the light is red may encourage other pedestrians to follow, based on status cues associated with the first individual's dress or appearance. The most practical way to resolve this ambiguity, we suggest, is to return to the distinction between pure and borderline cases of persuasion made earlier: In its purest form, compliance gaining is an intentional, effortful activity. "Typical" compliance gaining can thus be conceptualized as a subset of persuasion, a subset that takes place in face-to-face settings. In some borderline instances, however, compliance may be secured unintentionally or accidentally. In those "nontypical" instances, compliance gaining can be conceptualized as a subset of influence that takes place in face-to-face settings. Intentional compliance gaining should therefore be considered part of persuasion, whereas unintentional compliance gaining should be regarded as an aspect of influence.

Effects and the Issue of Unsuccessful Persuasion.   In addition to, or instead of, adopting an intent requirement, some scholars and researchers have opted for a "receiver-oriented" definition by restricting persuasion to situations in which receivers are somehow changed, altered, or affected. The definitions by Bostrum (1983), Cegala (1987), Cooper and Nothstine (1992), Johnston (1994), Larson (1995), O'Keefe (1990), and Pfau and Perot (1993) embody this requirement in varying degrees (see table 2.1). An effects requirement would seem part and parcel of compliance gaining as well. The very term *compliance gaining,* suggests that a persuasive outcome is being sought—although the form the compliance must take is less readily apparent. In fact, if one wishes to focus on pure cases of compliance gaining, it seems sensible to combine both an intent *and* an effects criterion: The prototypical case of compliance gaining is a planned, purposeful effort to secure compliance, usually in the form of behavioral conformity, in response to a request or other message recommendation.

Despite the intuitive appeal of the above, we cannot help mentioning one or two reservations about restricting *all* compliance gaining, both pure and borderline cases, to an effects criterion. We submit that a person can be engaged in an activity, whether or not he or she is performing the activity well. A salesperson, for example, could be engaged in selling without necessarily closing a deal. A parent might try to persuade a child to say no to drugs but might fail in the effort. Similarly, we suggest that a person can be engaged in the activity of persuasion even if it is ineffective persuasion. The difference in approaches hinges on whether one's focus is on persuasion and/or compliance gaining as an *outcome*, or as a *process*. This distinction mirrors the discussion some years ago about the conceptualization of argument as a product (argument[1]) versus argument as a process (argument[2]) (O'Keefe, 1976).[3] If persuasion or compliance gaining is viewed as an outcome, then limiting the use of either term to successful influence attempts makes perfect sense. If, however, one is interested in studying the process or activity of persuasion, such a limitation is questionable.

Consider the wealth of studies on compliance-gaining strategy selection, which we believe tell us a great deal about persuasion. Granted, the seeming preoccupation with strategy selection studies, at the expense of studies focusing on actual compliance, has been rightly criticized (Dillard, 1988). Nevertheless, investigations into the dynamics of the persuasion process, such as failed or foiled persuasion, serve a legitimate research purpose. For instance, Ifert and others (Ifert & Bearden, 1998; Ifert & Roloff, 1996; Neer, 1994), examined how sources respond when targets resist initial influence attempts. And any number of studies on compliance resisting have focused specifically on how targets avoid complying altogether (see for example, Kazeoloas, 1993; Kearney, Plax, & Burroughs, 1991; O'Hair, Cody, & O'Hair, 1991). It would be an odd state of affairs, indeed, if successful compliance gaining were considered a bona fide area for persuasion research but successful compliance resisting were not. Nor does it help to argue that successful resistance is in itself a type of effect. Because successful compliance resisting implies unsuccessful compliance gaining, virtually every compliance-gaining encounter could be construed as a success for one side or another.

Much the same may be said about research on deception and deception detection. Vrij (2000), for instance, has criticized others' definitions of deception as incomplete for failing to include unsuccessful as well as successful attempts at deception. Based on an effects criterion, successfully duping someone would clearly seem to constitute not only deception but persuasion as well; it is purposeful, and it achieves its intended effect. But what about successful deception detection? Success in detecting deception spells failure for the deceiver. Hence, reliance on an effects criterion would exclude studies on deception detection from the scope of persuasion, even though such studies make up a significant portion of the literature (Miller & Stiff, 1993). Such a limitation appears to "cut the baby in half," in Solomonic fashion, by focusing on only half of the deception–deception detection equation. In fact, taken to its extreme, an effects criterion would seem to exclude from the scope of persuasion all efforts at studying ways to increase targets' awareness of, and resistance to, influence attempts, since such efforts tend to decrease rather than increase persuasion's effectiveness. Strict adherence to an effects criterion would thus appear to rule out "defensive" studies of persuasion, despite the fact that nearly every persuasion text published in the last two decades touts greater knowledge of how to resist influence attempts as one of the chief benefits of learning about the subject.

Another reservation we have about relying exclusively on an effects criterion echoes our earlier concern with an intent requirement: Both embody a linear view of persuasion. In face-to-face encounters influence peddling is commonly a two-way street. Do effects have to be observed in only one or in both interactants? And who decides if the effort was a success? Moreover, compliance is rarely an all-or-nothing affair. The participants may succeed in some respects but fail in others, or succeed only partially. The difficulties are compounded when one is faced with participants whose goals may be multiple, sketchy, and changing, and whose willingness to accept various outcomes or compromises may fluctuate during the communication encounter.

In the case of research on deception or deception detection, it seems much more practical to include all such investigations under the rubric of persuasion. In fact, we believe the case has already been made, rather convincingly, that deception is a form of persuasive activity (Stiff, 1995). Deliberate falsifications, omissions, or distortions all satisfy an intent requirement, and the goals of deceivers correspond with those traditionally associated with persuasion, for example, affecting beliefs, attitudes, and behaviors. Although hypothetically some forms of deception, such as unconscious omissions, may be unintentional, virtually all of the deception literature to date has focused on deception as conscious, effortful activity.

A Graphic Representation of Persuasion

The preceding discussion leads us to the diagram of persuasion shown in figure 2.2, which encompasses research on compliance gaining, compliance resisting, deception, and decep-

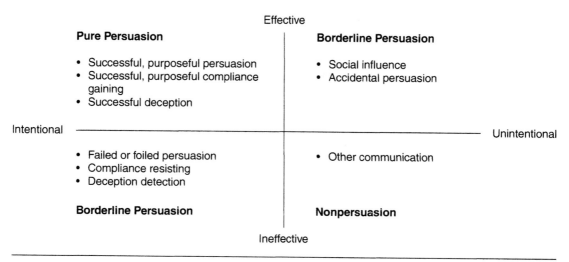

FIGURE 2.2 *Four Quadrants Model of Persuasion, Based on Intentionality and Effectiveness*

tion detection. The model consists of four quadrants, segmented according to the two limiting criteria we have presented; intentionality and effects. The upper left quadrant represents pure persuasion, or persuasion in its most prototypical form. Pure persuasion, as we noted earlier, satisfies both an intent and an effects requirement.

The upper right and lower left quadrants represent borderline persuasion, or more "iffy" instances of persuasion. The upper right quadrant, labeled "influence," reflects those situations in which persuasion "succeeds without trying," that is, where there are unintended effects. Influence here includes unintentional social modeling, nonverbal, or appearance cues that are conveyed without conscious awareness, as well as other forms of "accidental" influence. As per our earlier discussion, we've classified all such unintentional alterations of beliefs, attitudes, and behavior under the umbrella term "influence."

The lower left quadrant represents unsuccessful persuasion or, conversely, successful attempts at foiling persuasion. Thus, successful compliance resisting and successful deception detection are included here. Although one could argue that success in resisting compliance or detecting deception qualifies as pure persuasion, we believe there is merit in distinguishing between proactive and reactive influence attempts, with compliance resisting and deception detection representing the latter. An admitted weakness of our figure, however, is that the physical separation of the quadrants implies that activities taking place in one quadrant are somehow separate and distinct from those taking place in another quadrant. Conceptually, and in practice, interpersonal persuasion is transactional; interactants are operating in several quadrants simultaneously. Thus, interactant A may be actively engaged in attempting to persuade interactant B, while at the same time trying to resist being persuaded by B.

The lower right quadrant represents "nonpersuasion," that is, words or deeds that neither seek to persuade nor manage to influence. Since every definition of persuasion included in table 2.1 includes either intentionality or effects as a requirement for persuasion, it seems safe to say that communication that fails to satisfy either of these tests should not be considered part of persuasion, or influence, or compliance gaining. Communication that was neither planned nor goal-directed, for instance, and had no effect on another's beliefs, attitudes, or behavior would fall into this category. A good deal of noncommmunicative behavior would fall into this category as well.

Discussion and Implications

This approach, we believe, offers a practical, workable scheme for conceptualizing persuasion and its related terms. We acknowledge that it represents *an* approach toward conceptualizing persuasion, not the *only* approach. Nevertheless, we suggest that conceiving of persuasion in this manner offers a number of benefits. First, this approach makes meaningful distinctions between the terms *persuasion, influence,* and *compliance gaining*. Based on criteria central to most definitions of these terms, our conceptualization clarifies where one concept leaves off and another begins. Hitherto, these terms have been used with considerable ambiguity, often interchangeably, and often with different or even contradictory meanings even within the same article or text. This approach makes it relatively easy to classify most investigations as falling primarily into one of the four quadrants we've identified.

Second, this approach accounts for and integrates both traditional and nontraditional approaches to studying persuasion. The role and relationship of more traditional "public persuasion" studies to more nontraditional "face-to-face" research on compliance gaining is clarified: If both are intentional and successful, they are one and the same thing according to our conceptualization (the upper left quadrant). However, if compliance is secured unintentionally rather than as a form of planned, goal-directed activity, it is better classified as a form of influence rather than persuasion (the upper right quadrant). If compliance gaining is intentional but unsuccessful, the event may be better thought of as successful compliance resisting (the lower left quadrant). Finally, this approach clearly identifies what *isn't* persuasion: communication or behavior that neither seeks to, nor succeeds in, moving another person to think or do something.

The graphic representation we've offered is subject to some limitations. One such limitation, mentioned previously, is that persuasion, especially face-to-face persuasion, often operates in several quadrants simultaneously. A persuasive interaction also might begin in one quadrant and end in another. Because persuasion is a dynamic process, this is to be expected. Our conceptualization incorporates this overlap, but the figure cannot.

Another limitation with our figure is that the boundaries between the quadrants don't represent distinct categories so much as characteristics that are matters of degree. It isn't really the case that a given interaction is or isn't persuasion. Rather, a given interaction possesses more or fewer of the characteristics that persuasion comprises. This is especially true insofar as an effects criterion is concerned. Persuasion is rarely wholly successful or unsuccessful. Usually, there are degrees of success or failure. A persuader might succeed in changing another's attitudes, but not as much as she/he intended. Or a persuader might change another's attitudes, but not the other's behavior. And whenever an effects criterion is in use, it raises the question of when, or at what point, the effects should be measured. Some effects may be short-term, some long-term, and some hoped-for effects may never materialize. We would thus suggest that the two criteria that make up the quadrants, intentionality and effects, be viewed as dimensions along a continuum rather than as discrete characteristics. Some persuasive intentions may be more clear-cut or obvious, while others may be less carefully formulated or planned. Some persuasive effects may be easily measured or quantified, whereas others may be more subtle or difficult to detect.

A third limitation with the figure is that compliance-gaining studies focusing on "strategy selection" or "strategy preferences," and using hypothetical scenarios, are still difficult to classify according to this scheme. While such studies involve intentional efforts to persuade, inasmuch as strategy selection entails conscious planning, they include no measurable, discernible outcomes. The goal of strategy selection is compliance, but in many studies success in achieving the goal is never measured. Should such investigations be classified as part of pure persuasion, given that the objective is to secure compliance, even if success in achieving this objective is never considered? We submit that the problem in classifying such studies resides not in our approach to conceptualizing persuasion but rather in the inherent ambiguities of these investigations themselves. The reliance on hypothetical scenarios and the absence of even hypothetical measures of compliance, we suggest, is the source of the difficulty.

We suggest that hypothetical strategy selection studies are part of borderline persuasion rather than pure persuasion, since they involve intentional, but not necessarily successful, efforts to persuade. We would locate such investigations midway between the upper left and lower left quadrants (see figure 2.3). Such a classification acknowledges that in these investigations compliance is an open question; there is neither success nor failure, because the issue of success is never raised. Of course, compliance-gaining studies

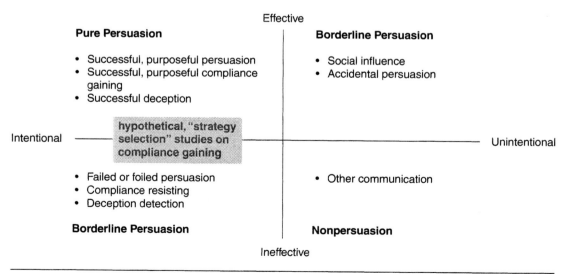

FIGURE 2.3 *Four Quadrants Model Differentiating Persuasion, Influence, Compliance Gaining, and Compliance Resisting*

that do measure tangible effects in the form of raffle tickets sold, tips left by restaurant patrons, willingness to relinquish a photocopy machine, compliance with physician recommendations, and so on would qualify as pure persuasion.

A final consideration, though not necessarily a limitation, is that our approach seems to suggest that any intentional communication that produces an effect must be regarded as persuasion. To the contrary, however, we suggest that communication can be both intentional and effective without necessarily being classified as persuasion. One could, for example, desire to have an enjoyable conversation with a friend and succeed in doing so. If the goal were simply to relay information, swap stories, or share experiences, and not to change the other's mind or behavior, one would be hard pressed to classify such an interaction as pure persuasion. Perhaps, then, it would be useful to distinguish between a *communicative* intent and a *persuasive* intent, the latter seeking the traditional goals of attitude, belief, or behavior change. We would suggest that when a communicator's primary goals entail attitude, belief, or behavior change, the interaction would best be characterized as pure persuasion, but when these constitute a communicator's secondary or tertiary goals, then the interaction would best be characterized as borderline persuasion, or nonpersuasion. In any case, we're not terribly bothered by this concern, because it seems to us that the ingredients for persuasion are present in most forms of human interaction. Most communication is, at least in part, instrumental in nature. Most language usage is, as Richard Weaver (1970) has surmised, sermonic, that is, inherently normative or evaluative.

We believe that the approach offered here serves to clarify uncertainties and ambiguities involved in definitions of persuasion, influence, and compliance gaining. The two limiting criteria we have identified can assist in framing a discussion of how each of these terms should be conceptualized. Regardless of whether one agrees with our conceptualization, the discussion provided should serve to clarify some of the central issues involved in any attempt to define persuasion and closely related terms.

Definitions shape fields of inquiry. They direct attention toward some research foci and deflect attention away from others. As Shepherd (1992) observes, "definitions are consequential" (p. 203). They affirm or deny, encourage or discourage, permit or omit. Definitions contain assumptions, they embody values, and they espouse points of view. "These perspectives," writes Andersen (1990), "launch scholars down different theoretical trajectories, predispose them to ask distinct questions, and set them up to conduct different kinds of communication studies" (p. 309). We believe that our approach to conceptualizing persuasion is both meaningful and practical because it is inclusive. It encompasses and affirms both traditional and nontraditional approaches to understanding persuasion. Such inclusiveness is desirable to ensure that nontraditional studies, such as those focusing on compliance gaining and deception detection, are recognized as instances of persuasion research, and to ensure that the term "persuasion" is not equated solely with traditional topics and variables, such as fear appeals, source credibility, and the like.

We hope the viewpoint we have offered prompts greater interest in conceptualizing about persuasion. Conceptual discussions perform a heuristic function insofar as theory building is concerned. Conceptualizations not only influence what theories are formed, but *how* the process of theorizing takes place. Conceptualizations also influence the kinds of research questions that are asked, as well as the methods used in trying to answer them.

Notes

1. The degree of fuzziness or distinctiveness in the threshold between pure persuasion and borderline persuasion depends largely on which limiting criterion one is employing. Intentionality offers a clear demarcation between pure and borderline persuasion, but only if there is agreement on how persuasive intent is established. (Is it a persuader's stated intent that counts, or a receiver's perception of an intent to persuade, or a third party's inference of an intent to persuade?) An effects criterion is more continuous; successful persuasion is typically a matter of degree.

2. We see little difference between the terms "influence" and "social influence," other than the obvious implication that the latter entails social factors of some kind. One could easily argue that all influence entails social factors in one form or another. Even self-persuasion would entail certain socialization processes.

3. Ironically, O'Keefe, who highlighted the distinction between argument as a product and argument as a process, himself subscribes to an effects criterion for defining persuasion (O'Keefe, 1990). "The notion of *success*," he wrote, "is embedded in the concept of persuasion. Notice, for instance, that it doesn't make sense to say, 'I persuaded him, but failed.' One can say, 'I *tried* to persuade him, but failed,' but to say simply, 'I persuaded him' is to imply a successful attempt to influence" (1990, p. 15). In our view, O'Keefe begged the question in the above examples by using the term "persuaded." If one uses the term "persuasion" instead, one could easily say "I used every tactic of persuasion I could think of, but I still couldn't get the client to budge," or, "That was one of the best efforts at persuasion I've ever seen, but the jury wasn't swayed."

References

Andersen, P. A. (1991). When one cannot not communicate: A challenge to Motley's traditional communication postulates. *Communication Studies, 42*(4), 309–325.

Bandura, A. (1977). *Social learning theory*. Englewood Cliffs, NJ: Prentice Hall.

Bavelas, J.B. (1990). Behaving and communicating: A reply to Motley. *Western Journal of Speech Communication, 54*(4), 593–602.

Beach, W.A. (1990). On (not) observing behavior interactionally. *Western Journal of Speech Communication, 54*(4), 603–612.

Berger, C. R., & Burgoon, M. (1995). Preface. In C. R. Berger & M. Burgoon (Eds.), *Communication and social influence processes* (pp. ix–xi). East Lansing, MI: Michigan State University Press.

Bettinghaus, E. P., and Cody, M. J. (1994). *Persuasive communication* (6th ed.). Fort Worth, TX: Harcourt Brace.

Boster, F. (1995). A commentary on compliance-gaining message behavior research. In C. R. Berger & M. Burgoon (Eds.), *Communication and social influence processes* (pp. 91–113). East Lansing, MI: Michigan State University Press.

Buller, D. B., & Burgoon, J. K. (1996). Interpersonal deception theory. *Communication Theory, 6*(3), 203–242.

Burgoon, M., & Dillard, J. P. (1995). Communication and social influence: A prolegomenon. *Communication Research, 22*(4), 397–401.

Burgoon, M., Hunsacker, F. G., & Dawson, E. J. (1994). *Human communication* (3rd ed.). Thousand Oaks, CA: Sage.

Burke, K. (1966). *Language as symbolic action*. Los Angeles, CA: University of California, Berkeley Press.

Cegala, D. J. (1987). *Persuasive communication: Theory and practice* (3rd ed.). Edina, MN: Burgess International.

Clevenger, T. (1991). One cannot not communicate? A conflict of models. *Communication Studies, 42*(4), 340–353.

Cooper, M., & Nothstine, W. L. (1992). *Power persuasion: Moving an ancient art into the media age*. Greenwood, IN: Educational Video Group.

Cronkhite, G. (1986). On the focus, scope, and coherence of the study of human symbolic activity. *Quarterly Journal of Speech, 72*, 231–248.

Dance, F. E. X. (1970). The concept of communication. *Journal of Communication, 20,* 201–210.

Dance, F. E. X., & Larson, C. E. (1976). *The functions of human communication.* New York: Holt, Rinehart, and Winston.

Dillard, J. P. (1988). Compliance-gaining message selection: What is our dependent variable? *Communication Monographs, 55,* 162–183.

Dillard, J. P. (1989). Types of influence goals in personal relationships. *Journal of Social and Personal Relationships, 6,* 293–308.

Dillard, J. P. (1990). A goal-driven model of interpersonal influence. In J. P. Dillard (Ed.), *Seeking compliance: The product of interpersonal influence messages* (pp. 41–56). Scottsdale, AZ: Gorsuch Scarisbrick.

Dillard, J. P., Segrin, C., & Harden, J. (1989). Primary and secondary goals in the interpersonal influence process. *Communication Monographs, 56,* 19–39.

Feeley, T. H., & Young, M. J. (1998). Humans as lie detectors: Some more second thoughts. *Communication Quarterly, 46,* 109–126.

Gass, R.H., & Seiter, J. S. (2003). *Persuasion, social influence, and compliance gaining* (2nd ed.). Boston: Allyn & Bacon/Longman.

Gass, R. H., & Seiter, J. S. (1997, November). On defining persuasion: Toward a contemporary perspective, "top three" paper presented at the annual convention of the Western Communication Association, Monterey, CA.

Gerbner, G. (1966). On defining communication: Still another view. *Journal of Communication, 16,* 99–103.

Greenberg, J., & Pyszczynski, T. (1985). The effect of an overheard ethnic slur on evaluations of the target: How to spread a social disease. *Journal of Experimental Social Psychology, 21,* 61–72.

Hale, J. S., & Stiff, J. B. (1990). Nonverbal primacy in veracity judgments. *Communication Reports, 3,* 75–83.

Ifert D. E., & Bearden, L. (1998). The influence of argumentativeness and verbal aggressiveness on responses to refused requests. *Communication Reports, 11*(2), 145–154.

Ifert, D. E., & Roloff, M. E. (1996). Responding to rejected requests: Persistence and response type as function of obstacles to compliance. *Journal of Language and Social Psychology, 15,* 40–58.

Johnston, D. D. (1994). *The art and science of persuasion.* Madison, WI: William C. Brown.

Kazeolas, D. (1993). The impact of argumentativeness on resistance to persuasion. *Human Communication Research, 20,* 118–137.

Kearney, P., Plax, T. G., & Burroughs, N. F. (1991). An attributional analysis of college students' resistance decisions. *Communication Education, 40,* 325–342.

Kirkland, S. L., Greenberg, J., & Pyszczynski, T. (1987). Further evidence of the deleterious effects of overheard derogatory ethnic labels: Derogation beyond the target. *Personality and Social Psychology Bulletin, 13*(2), 216–227.

Langer, E. J. (1989a). *Mindfulness.* Reading, MA: Addison-Wesley.

Langer, E. J. (1989b). Minding matters. In L. Berkowitz (Ed.), *Advances in experimental social psychology* (vol. 22, pp. 137–173). New York: Addison-Wesley.

Larson, C. U. (1995). *Persuasion: Reception and responsibility* (7th ed.). Belmont, CA: Wadsworth.

Lim (1990). The influence of receivers' resistance on persuaders' verbal aggressiveness. *Communication Quarterly, 38,* 170–188.

Miller, G. R. (1980). On being persuaded: Some basic distinctions. In M. E. Roloff & G. R. Miller (Eds.), *Persuasion: New directions in theory and research* (pp. 11–28). Beverly Hills, CA: Sage.

Miller, G. R., & Stiff, J. B. (1993). *Deceptive communication.* Newbury Park, NJ: Sage.

Motley, M. T. (1990a). Communications interaction: A reply to Beach and Bavelas. *Western Journal of Speech Communication, 54*(4), 613–623.

Motley, M. T. (1990b). On whether one can(not) not communicate: An examination via traditional communication postulates. *Western Journal of Speech Communication, 54*(1), 1–20.

Motley, M. T. (1991) How one may not communicate: A reply to Andersen. *Communication Studies, 42*(4), 326–339.

Neer, M. R. (1994). Argumentative flexibility as a factor influencing message response style to argumentative and aggressive arguers. *Argumentation and Advocacy, 31,* 17–33.

O'Donnell, V., & Kable, J. (1982). *Persuasion: An interactive-dependency approach.* New York: Random House.

O'Hair, M. J., Cody, M. J., & O'Hair, D. (1991). The impact of situational dimensions on compliance-resisting strategies: A comparison of methods. *Communication Quarterly, 39*(3), 226–240.

O'Keefe, D. J. (1976). Two concepts of argument. *Journal of the American Forensic Association* [renamed *Argumentation and Advocacy*], *13*, 121–128.

O'Keefe, D. J. (1990). *Persuasion: Theory and research.* Newbury Park, CA: Sage.

Perloff, R. M. (1993). *The dynamics of persuasion.* Hillsdale, NJ: Erlbaum.

Petty, R. E., & Cacioppo, J. (1981). *Attitudes and persuasion: Classic and contemporary approaches.* Dubuque, IA: Wm. C. Brown.

Pfau, M., Kenski, H. C., Nitz, M., & Sorenson, J. (1990). Efficacy of inoculation strategies in promoting resistance to political attack messages: Application to direct mail. *Communication Monographs, 57*, 25–43.

Pfau, M., & Perot, R. (1993). *Persuasive communication campaigns.* Boston: Allyn & Bacon.

Pfau, M., & Van Bockern, S. (1994). The persistence of inoculation in confirming resistance to smoking initiation among adolescents: The second year. *Human Communication Research, 20*, 413–430.

Pfau, M., Van Bockern, S., & Kang, G. J. (1992). Use of inoculation to promote resistance to smoking initiation among adolescents. *Communication Monographs, 59*, 213–230.

Reardon, K. K. (1981). *Persuasion: Theory and context.* Beverly Hills, CA: Sage.

Roloff, M. E. (1980). Self-awareness and the persuasion process: Do we really know what we're doing? In M. E. Roloff & G. R. Miller (Eds.), *Persuasion: New directions in theory and research* (pp. 29–66). Beverly Hills, CA: Sage.

Roloff, M. E., and Miller, G. R. (Eds.) (1980). *Persuasion: New directions in theory and research.* Beverly Hills, CA: Sage.

Seiter, J. S. (1997). Honest or deceitful? A study of persons' mental models for judging veracity. *Human Communication Research, 24*(2), 216–259.

Shepherd, G. J. (1992). Communication as influence: Definitional exclusion. *Communication Studies, 43*, 203–219.

Simons, H. W. (1986). *Persuasion: Understanding, practice, and analysis* (2nd ed.). New York: McGraw-Hill.

Stiff, J. B. (1995). Conceptualizing deception as a persuasive activity. In C. R. Berger & M. Burgoon (Eds.), *Communication and social influence processes* (pp. 73–90). East Lansing, MI: Michigan State University Press.

Stiff, J. B. (1994). *Persuasive Communication.* New York: Guilford Press.

Trenholm, S. (1989). *Persuasion and social influence.* Englewood Cliffs, NJ: Prentice-Hall.

Vrij, A. (2000). *Detecting lies and deceit: The psychology of lying and the implications for professional practice.* Chichester, England: John Wiley & Sons.

Weaver, R. M. (1970) Language is sermonic. In R. L. Johannesen, R. Strickland, & R. Eubanks (Eds.), *Language is sermonic: Richard M. Weaver on the nature of rhetoric* (pp. 179–211). Baton Rouge, LA: Louisiana State University Press.

Wilson, S. R. (1998). Introduction to the special issue on seeking and resisting compliance: The vitality of compliance-gaining research. *Communication Studies, 49*, 273–275.

Wiseman, R. L., Sanders, J. A., Congalton, K. J., Gass, R. H., Sueda, K., & Ruiqing, D. (1995). A cross-cultural analysis of compliance gaining: China, Japan, and the United States. *Intercultural Communication Studies, 5*(1), 1–17.

Witte, K. (1994). Fear control and danger control: A test of the extended parallel process model. *Communication Monographs, 61*(2), 113–134.

Witte, K. (1995). Using scare tactics to promote safe sex among juvenile detention and high school youth. *Journal of Applied Communication Research, 23*(2), 128–142.

Woodward, G. C., and Denton, R. E. (1992). *Persuasion and influence in American life* (2nd ed.). Prospect Heights, IL: Waveland.

3

Trends and Prospects in Persuasion Theory and Research

Daniel J. O'Keefe

Systematic thinking about persuasion dates at least as far back as the fifth century B.C.E., to Greek scholars such as Protagoras, Gorgias, Plato, Isocrates, and (especially) Aristotle. And in subsequent years persuasion received continuing attention from a variety of scholars within a broadly humanistic tradition (for a review, see Conley, 1990). But in the first part of the twentieth century, the development of social scientific methods provided new avenues to the illumination of persuasion. The social scientific study of persuasion is often traced to Carl Hovland, a Yale University psychologist who, following World War II, initiated a systematic program of persuasion research (see, e.g., Hovland, Janis, & Kelley, 1953). On a great many topics in persuasion research, the first work was done by Hovland or his associates (though historical accuracy compels some notice of the persuasion research that considerably predated Hovland's, e.g., Knower, 1936; Lund, 1925; Schanck & Goodman, 1939).

Over the last 50 years, social scientific persuasion research has flowered. Indeed, relevant research has been conducted in a great many academic fields. Nearly all the social sciences (including communication, psychology, sociology, political science, and anthropology) and related applied endeavors in which social scientific questions and methods appear (such as advertising, marketing, public health, medicine, law, business, education, environmental studies, and so on) contain research focused on persuasion. This surely reflects the pervasiveness of persuasion in human affairs. The marketplace, the courtroom, the campaign trail, the boardroom, the family—in all these settings (and more) human decision making is shaped by persuasive communication.

This chapter discusses three broad recent developments in the social scientific study of persuasion and social influence. Some aspects of these developments are already rather well along and have begun to bear significant fruit; others are on the horizon and offer substantial promise. But all testify to the continuing vitality of persuasion theory and research.

Beyond Attitude Change

In its most basic form, persuasion involves changing persons' mental states, usually as precursors to behavioral change. Of the various mental states that might be implicated in persuasion, attitude (understood as a person's general evaluation of an object) has been the center of research attention. Correspondingly, persuasion has often been conceived of as fundamentally involving attitude change. This might involve a change in the valence (positive or negative) of the evaluation or a change in the extremity of the evaluation (as when an attitude changes from extremely negative to only slightly negative).

Thus understood, attitude change is obviously an important aspect of persuasion. All sorts of decisions, from what products to buy to which candidate to support, are plainly subject to changes in attitudes. But in various ways persuasion research has seen a broadening of interest beyond this usual focus, as reflected specifically in interests in three other sorts of outcome variables.

Other Attitude Properties

First, properties of attitude other than valence and extremity have come to be recognized as potentially important foci for persuasive efforts. That is, rather than influencing the direction or extremity of an attitude, a persuader might want to influence some other attribute of the attitude, such as its salience (prominence, accessibility), the confidence with which it is held, the degree to which it is linked to other attitudes, and so forth (for discussions of some such attitudinal properties, see Bromer, 1998; Eagly & Chaiken, 1998; Petty & Krosnick, 1995; Roskos-Ewoldsen, 1997). For instance, where receivers already have positive attitudes toward one's product, the persuasive task may be to ensure that those attitudes are salient (activated) at the right time, perhaps by somehow reminding receivers of their attitudes. So, for example, a manufacturer of food products may not particularly care whether people are thinking of its products while driving, but it does care what attitudes are activated when people are shopping for groceries—so it places advertising displays in supermarkets precisely in order to engage existing positive attitudes at the point of purchase.

A number of such attitudinal properties have been grouped together under the general heading of "attitude strength" (for some discussions, see Bassili, 1996; Eagly & Chaiken, 1998, pp. 290–292; Petty & Krosnick, 1995; Raden, 1985). Conceptualizations of attitude strength vary, but a useful illustration is provided by Krosnick and Petty's (1995) proposal that attitude strength is best understood as an amalgam of persistence (stronger attitudes are more persistent than are weaker ones), resistance (stronger attitudes are more resistant to change than are weaker ones), impact on information processing and judgments (stronger attitudes are more likely to affect such processes than are weaker attitudes), and impact on behavior (stronger attitudes will have more effect on behavior than will weaker ones). Consider, for instance, that two persons might have attitudes toward a particular political candidate that were equally positive (say, with a rating of 6 on a scale of 1 to 7) but differed in strength: Pat's positive attitude is weakly held, liable to fluctuate from moment to moment, not very resistant to persuasion, and not very strongly connected to behavior, whereas Chris's (equally positive) attitude is more strongly held, more stable over time, less likely to be altered by counterpersuasion, and more likely to be expressed in corresponding behavior (such as voting for the candidate, working in the candidate's campaign, and so on). Therefore, even though Pat and Chris have identical attitudes in one sense (they have the same overall evaluation), their attitudes are rather different in other ways (Chris's is stronger than Pat's). In such a circumstance, obviously, the candidate would like to strengthen Pat's attitude—not necessarily to make the evaluation more extreme, but to make the attitude better anchored, more stable, more connected to behavior, more resistant to counterpersuasion (in short, to make it more like Chris's attitude). To put the matter more generally, persuaders sometimes will have an interest in influencing not merely the valence and extremity of an attitude but also its strength.

Other Mental States

Second, mental states other than attitude have been recognized as potential persuasion targets. Two examples of such states are normative considerations and self-efficacy.

Normative Considerations.   Various kinds of beliefs about norms can be relevant targets for persuaders. For instance, people's beliefs about "descriptive norms"—perceptions of what most people do—may influence actions and thus be a focus for persuasive efforts (Cialdini, Kallgren, & Reno, 1991). For instance, college students appear commonly to overestimate the frequency of drug and alcohol use on their campuses (Perkins, Meilman, Leichliter, Cashin, & Presley, 1999). Such overestimation can in turn lead students themselves to engage in excessive drug and alcohol use (because of a belief that "everybody is doing it, so it must be okay"). Obviously, then, persuasive interventions aimed at correcting such misperceptions of descriptive norms might be helpful in reducing drug and alcohol abuse (Haines & Spear, 1996; Miller, Monin, & Prentice, 2000; Steffian, 1999).

   Similarly, what the Theory of Reasoned Action (Fishbein & Ajzen, 1975) terms the "subjective norm"—the person's perception that significant others desire the performance (or nonperformance) of the behavior—may be a persuasion target. For instance, one way of persuading a smoker to quit may be to convince him that others who are important to him (his spouse, his children, his best friend) think that he should quit. That is, by altering the receiver's conception of what significant other people think the receiver should do, the receiver's conduct may be influenced.

Self-Efficacy.   Self-efficacy (or perceived behavioral control), the person's perception of his or her ability to perform the behavior, is another mental state that has come to be seen as an important potential focus for persuasive efforts (see Ajzen, 1991; Bandura, 1986). Sometimes the barrier to a receiver's compliance seems not to be a negative attitude or negative norms, but rather a perceived inability to perform the action successfully. For instance, a person might have a positive attitude toward engaging in regular exercise and have positive normative beliefs about that activity, but might nevertheless not even try to exercise regularly because she believes that she is incapable of exercising regularly (because exercise is too time-consuming, doesn't fit her schedule, requires too much specialized equipment, and so forth). It is easy to imagine how a perceived inability to perform the behavior might underlie failures to exercise, use condoms, quit smoking, and so forth.

Research is only beginning to accumulate concerning how persuaders might address such self-efficacy concerns; there is some indication, for example, that modeling (showing someone successfully performing the behavior) and rehearsal (giving persons an opportunity to practice the behavior) can be useful avenues to influencing self-efficacy (Anderson, 1995, 2000; Hagen, Gutkin, Wilson, & Oats, 1998; Maibach & Flora, 1993; Weisse, Turbiasz, & Whitney, 1995).

Behavioral Outcomes

Third, some lines of research have focused directly on behavioral outcomes, as in studies of the foot-in-the-door and door-in-the-face strategies. (For a general discussion of such strategies, see chapter 12.) Research that is focused on behavioral outcomes serves as a reminder that even when persuaders seek to change mental states (such as attitudes, normative beliefs, or self-efficacy perceptions), influencing mental states is only a means to an end. Behavioral change is commonly the ultimate goal. In a sense, studies emphasizing behavioral outcomes approach persuasion effects from a direction exactly opposite to that taken by research emphasizing mental states: Instead of first centering on attitude change and subsequently taking up the question of how attitudes are related to actions, these lines of research center on behavioral effects and then take up the question of what mental-state mechanisms might account for the observed behavioral effects.

Summary

In sum, persuasion research has come to recognize that attitude change is not the only outcome variable of interest. Although persuasion research has typically focused on attitude change, increasing attention is being given to other outcomes—and, correspondingly, to new mechanisms of persuasion. After all, the means by which one might influence attitudes are not necessarily the same as the means by which one might influence other outcomes. One may hope that the continuing attention of researchers to these additional outcome variables will lead to new understandings about means of social influence.

Context-Specific Research

Persuasion research has generally been aimed at developing concepts, findings, principles, and theories that are useful across a wide range of persuasion settings. Of course, any particular persuasion study commonly involves some particular context of persuasion: The study examines consumer advertisements, or appeals on some public policy question, or arguments about a legal case, and so on. Still, the research aim has typically been the development of findings not bound to any particular persuasive circumstance. However, an increasing amount of persuasion research has been appearing in studies addressed at specific contexts of application, with corresponding development of context-specific concepts and models. (For some discussions of such contexts, see chapter 16 by Klingle, chapter 17 by Baxter and Bylund, chapter 18 by Hirokawa and Wagner, and chapter 19 by Seiter and Cody.)

A useful example is provided by the articulation of various "stage" models of health related behavior, exemplified by the transtheoretical model of health behavior (so named because putatively it integrates a number of different theoretical perspectives). The transtheoretical model (sometimes called the "stages of change" model) identifies a number of distinct stages in a person's adoption of a given health-related behavior such as engaging in an exercise program (see Prochaska & DiClemente, 1984; Weinstein, Rothman, & Sutton, 1998). In the precontemplation stage, a person is not even thinking about undertaking an exercise program anytime soon; in the contemplation stage, she is at least seriously thinking about doing so; a person in the preparation stage is ready to change and may have undertaken planning or other preparatory action (such as signing up for a health club); in the action stage, she is undertaking the exercise program; finally, a person who continues to engage in exercise for some time is said to be in the maintenance stage.

Stage models offer the prospect of shedding light on persuasion, because of their potential usefulness in suggesting how best to tailor persuasive efforts to a particular audience. For example, for persons in the precontemplation stage, the persuader's challenge will presumably be to get receivers thinking about the target behavior (i.e., moving persons from precontemplation to contemplation). By contrast, for people in the preparation stage, the persuader will want to help people translate their plans and intentions into actions. (For some examples of investigations of the effectiveness of stage-matched health interventions, see Jamner, Wolitski, & Corby, 1997; Naylor, Simmonds, Riddoch, Velleman, & Turton, 1999; Quinlan & McCaul, 2000.)

As another example of context-specific research, consider investigations of the persuasive effects of negative political campaign advertisements that attack a political candidate without necessarily even mentioning the preferred candidate. Studies of the effects of negative political advertising are commonly not especially concerned with contributing to general cross-context understandings of persuasion processes, but rather reflect a specific interest in illuminating this one facet of political campaigns (see, e.g., Basil, Schooler, & Reeves, 1991; Garramone, 1985; Haddock & Zanna, 1997; for a review, see Lau, Sigelman, Heldman, & Babbitt, 1999). Indeed, quite independent of whatever light such studies might shed on persuasion processes generally, they are valuable contributions to an understanding of how persuasion works in this particular setting.

One may detect in these developments an implicit recognition of the potential limits of general models of persuasion. No single theoretical view of persuasion is likely to provide a complete, wholly detailed account of every single possible persuasion circumstance—and such should not be asked of a persuasion theory. It's enough that a general theory of persuasion offers broadly useful concepts and principles that are helpful in a variety of circumstances, even if insufficient to answer every possible question about any given persuasion setting. But this in turn suggests that particular persuasion contexts may demand correspondingly particular treatment—context-specific concepts, context-specific principles.

Of course, the study of a specific persuasion context may both feed and be fed by general theorizing about persuasion. A nice example is provided by research on inoculation mechanisms, that is, mechanisms for making receivers resistant to counterpersuasion. Several studies have examined how general understandings of inoculation might be applied to the specific problem of creating resistance to negative political advertising; the research suggests that the effects of such ads can be blunted if, before they appear, the candidate "inoculates" voters by engaging in appropriate rebuttal of the attacks (see, e.g., Pfau & Burgoon, 1988; Pfau, Kenski, Nitz, & Sorenson, 1990). Previous general research on inoculation guided the context-specific work concerning inoculation against negative campaign ads—and the context-specific work in turn has provided additional general information about inoculation processes. (For more on inoculation, see chapter 15.)

The Complexity of Persuasion Effects

Persuasion phenomena are complicated, making the development of dependable generalizations rather difficult. For example, it is difficult to identify any particular persuasion tactic that is effective in all situations. Indeed, the research literature on persuasive effects contains many examples of apparently inconsistent findings. One researcher's study finds that better liked communicators are significantly more persuasive than less well liked ones, whereas another study finds no such effect; one investigation reports that stating the message's conclusions explicitly significantly enhances persuasion, whereas a subsequent study fails to obtain a significant effect, and so on. But several recent developments in the study of persuasion have helped to identify some of the sources of such complexities, thus providing a basis for better understanding how and why such diverse effects might arise. These developments are expressed briefly in the following three subsections.

Moderating Factors

First, a given persuasion variable can produce different effects under different conditions; a variable might significantly influence persuasive outcomes in one circumstance, but have relatively little effect in another. For instance, acknowledging potential counterarguments (arguments against the advocated view) has different effects depending on the message's topic: It reduces the persuasiveness of messages concerning public policy questions, but not the persuasiveness of consumer product advertisements (O'Keefe, 1999a). Many studies of persuasive effects can be described as a search for possible moderating factors, that is, factors that alter the impact that one variable has on another.

This general idea is particularly prominent in dual-process models of persuasion such as the Elaboration Likelihood Model (ELM) (Petty & Cacioppo, 1986; see also chapter 5). The ELM sketches two broad avenues to persuasion: (1) a "central route" in which receivers carefully process message arguments and (2) a "peripheral route" in which receivers rely on mental shortcuts ("heuristics") as a means of reaching a conclusion. One important moderating variable that affects which route is activated is the receiver's degree of involvement with the topic. As involvement increases, reliance on heuristics decreases and close message processing increases. From the point of view of the ELM, it makes perfectly good sense that, for example, the communicator's likability will sometimes have a substantial influence on persuasiveness but on other occasions will play a very small role. When involvement is relatively low, communicator likability may have considerable impact (because receivers decide whether to agree with the message by using the shortcut of whether they like the communicator). When involvement is high, however, the persuasive effect of likability will presumably be muted (because receivers will be paying more attention to the details of the message's arguments). One of the signal contributions of the ELM is to have systematized a number of apparently inconsistent findings by distinguishing central-route and peripheral-route persuasion processes.

Multiple Roles for Variables

Second—and also closely connected with the ELM—it has become clear that a given variable might play different roles in persuasion in different circumstances (for general discussion of this point, see Petty, 1997; Petty & Wegener, 1998). As a simple example, consider the impact of variations on the sheer length of a written message. Message length might play a role in persuasion by serving as a cue for a heuristic such as "longer messages probably have more good arguments." That is, receivers might rely on message length as a shortcut for deciding whether the advocated view has merit (see, e.g., Wood, Kallgren, & Preisler, 1985). Alternatively, message length might influence how much attention the receiver pays to the message (more specifically, might influence the audience's motivation to process the message's arguments closely). For example, on a complex technical subject, receivers might decide not to pay much attention to a short message (reasoning that it wouldn't be likely to provide the necessary detail), whereas a longer message would engage their attention (see, e.g., Soley, 1986).

Again, notice that such variations in the role played by a given variable can lead to apparently inconsistent results across studies. Longer messages might produce enhanced persuasion when receivers rely on message length as a shortcut to reaching a conclusion about the advocated position, but length might have little systematic effect on persuasive outcomes when it influences the audience's motivation to process the message (because closer processing of the message does not necessarily guarantee greater persuasiveness of the message, and the audience's close scrutiny might uncover weaknesses in the advocate's argumentation).

Message-to-Message Variability

Third, above and beyond the first two complexities, accumulating empirical evidence suggests that there is message-to-message variation in the persuasive effects of message variables. That is, even taking into account known moderating factors, a given message variable (for example, high versus low fear appeals, as discussed in chapter 13 by Cho and Witte) will not necessarily have identical effects in every message; rather, the effect is likely to vary from message to message (see Jackson & Jacobs, 1983; O'Keefe, 1999b).

The existence of such variability points to a potential weakness in the kind of research design that has commonly been used in experimental persuasion studies. In the most common sort of design, an abstract message category is represented by only one concrete message. So, for instance, in studies of the relative persuasiveness of high and low fear-appeal messages, researchers have usually compared one particular low fear-appeal message against one particular high fear-appeal message (the experimental counterpart of the low fear-appeal message, identical in every way except for the fear-appeal variation).

In this "single message" research design, each message category (such as "high fear appeal") is represented by only one sample message. But the effect of variations in fear-appeal level is likely to be different from one case to another and from one message to another. To put the point more generally, the effect of a given experimental message manipulation (such as fear-appeal level) in the one particular message being studied is likely to be different from the effect of that same variation in other messages. Thus a single-message research design leaves something to be desired insofar as generalization is concerned; gauging the overall effect of a message variation requires examining its effect in multiple messages, not just a single one. In other words, dependable generalization across messages requires multiple instances.

One way to obtain multiple-message research evidence is through the inclusion of multiple messages in a single study. For example, suppose a researcher wanted to investigate the relative effectiveness of two different kinds of political attack ads: those focused on the opponent's issue positions and those focused on the opponent's image or character. Rather than comparing just one particular issue-attack ad with just one particular image-attack ad (where the results might reflect peculiarities of the ads in question), the researcher could gather a large number of examples of each kind of ad and compare the average persuasiveness across the two sets of ads. Such multiple-message evidence would obviously provide a better basis for generalization than would a single-message design.

A second way to obtain multiple-message research evidence is through collating results across a large number of existing single-message studies. The most systematic procedures for such collation are to be found in meta-analytic statistical procedures. Meta-analysis is a family of procedures for producing a quantitative summary of a set of existing research studies (for a general introduction, see Rosenthal, 1991). In a sense, a meta-analysis is a "superstudy" that combines the results of earlier separate investigations.

A meta-analysis can provide information not only about the overall average result (across all the studies) but also about the results within subsets of studies. In particular, the existing studies can be subdivided based on levels of a suspected moderator variable, and the results within these subgroups can then be compared. For example, consider the question of whether the effectiveness of the door-in-the-face (DITF) strategy depends on whether the two requests were made by the same person or by two different people. In some DITF studies, the same person made the two requests, whereas in other DITF studies different people made these requests. Thus, some indication of the role of this variation as a potential moderator of the effect of the DITF strategy can be obtained by subdividing the studies, assessing the results within each subset, and then comparing the results. (As it happens, this moderator variable does make a difference: The DITF strategy is more successful when the same person makes the two requests than when different persons make them; O'Keefe & Hale, 1998.)

Meta-analyses are not easy to do, and analyzing multiple-message evidence—whether obtained across studies, that is, meta-analytically, or within a single study—raises some complicated issues concerning the appropriate statistical analysis to be employed (for some discussion, see Brashers & Jackson, 1999; Hedges & Vevea, 1998; Jackson, 1992; Jackson & Brashers, 1994; Jackson, Brashers, & Massey, 1992). Obviously, however, meta-analysis offers an appealing way of synthesizing the results from many individual persuasion studies (for some examples, see Allen & Preiss, 1998).

Summary

Taken together, the three complexities mentioned here—the importance of moderator factors in persuasion, the multiple roles that a persuasion variable can play, and the existence of message-to-message variability in persuasive effects—quite naturally underscore the problems of generalizing about persuasion processes and effects. Each of these complexities suggests that the results of any single persuasion study may need to be held rather tentatively, while the development of increasingly deep understandings of persuasion phenomena will require continuing systematic research attention.

The Future

To some extent, the near-term future in persuasion research will likely involve further articulation of some of the developments discussed here: increasing attention to outcomes other than attitude change, encouraging more context-specific studies, and developing greater sensitivity to matters of generalization (multiple-message studies, meta-analyses, and so forth). As in any research endeavor, there will undoubtedly be developments that cannot be foreseen, but two specific research subjects bear watching: (1) visual aspects of persuasion and (2) computer-mediated persuasion.

Persuasion research has typically focused on linguistic aspects of messages, such as whether the message discusses counterarguments or explicitly states the advocate's conclusion. By comparison, relatively little attention has been given to nonlinguistic features such as visual images; yet visual message elements might substantially influence persuasive effects (for some general treatments, see Messaris, 1997; Scott, 1994).

This is a particularly complex subject, especially as printed linguistic messages are also visual images. That is, printed text is itself a visual object (even if there are no accompanying pictures); there appears to have been little systematic persuasion-related research addressing these visual aspects of text. (The idea that printed text is a visual object is certainly familiar to any student who has fiddled with a term paper's margins so as to affect the apparent length of the paper, or to any job applicant who has chosen a particular font so as to make a resume look more professional.)

Additionally, of course, a printed message might contain nontextual (that is, nonlinguistic) visual material, such as pictures or drawings. Analyzing such images for argumentative content is notoriously difficult (for some discussion and examples, see Birdsell & Groarke, 1996; Blair, 1996; Fleming, 1996; Lake & Pickering, 1998; Nelson & Boynton, 1997; Oestermeier & Hesse, 2000). Moreover, when a message contains both linguistic and (nontextual) visual material, the relationship between the two may be important. Within a print advertisement, for example, the relationship between the linguistic and nonlinguistic visual aspects of the ad may play an important role in influencing persuasive effects. Within a television commercial, the relationship between visual images, voice-over linguistic content, and printed linguistic content may play a similar role.

The persuasive contributions of visual message elements (or of different relationships of visual and verbal elements in a message) are only beginning to be explored, and confident conclusions are some way off. For some examples of relevant studies, see Areni

& Cox, 1994; Figueiras, Price, & Marteau, 1999; Miniard, Bhatla, Lord, Dickson, & Unnava, 1991; Morrison & Vogel, 1998. Plainly, though, the study of visual aspects of persuasion will be an important focus for future research.

A second, and not unrelated, potential focus for future research is persuasion and computer-mediated communication. Widespread access to computing is a relatively recent phenomenon. The personal computer was introduced in the 1980s, and the first Web browser appeared in 1993. Correspondingly, there is as yet relatively little empirical evidence concerning aspects of computer-mediated persuasion. But obviously, a variety of relevant questions can arise. For example, what makes expert systems (computer-based reasoning systems that model human expert problem-solving) persuasive to users? (See Dijkstra, Liebrand, & Timminga, 1998; Jiang, Klein, & Vedder, 2000.) What elements make interactive or Web-based advertisements effective? (See Bezjian-Avery, Calder, & Iacobucci, 1998; Li & Bukovac, 1999.) How might the physical properties of computer-mediated communication systems influence persuasion processes? (See Moon, 1999.) Though relatively little can yet be said with much certainty about such matters, computer-mediated persuasion is likely to receive increasing research attention in the future.

Conclusion

The developments surveyed here suggest that persuasion research is at once becoming broader (in expanding beyond attitude change as an outcome of interest), deeper (by developing context-specific concepts and principles), and more complex (in recognizing the complexities of persuasion processes and the attendant challenges to generalization). Systematic thought about processes of persuasion can be traced back to the ancient Greeks, but as these developments attest, the study of persuasion continues to be a locus of exciting theoretical, empirical, and methodological developments.

References

Ajzen, I. (1991). The theory of planned behavior. *Organizational Behavior and Human Decision Processes, 50*, 179–211.

Allen, M., & Preiss, R. W. (Eds.). (1998). *Persuasion: Advances through meta-analysis.* Cresskill, NJ: Hampton Press.

Anderson, R. B. (1995). Cognitive appraisal of performance capability in the prevention of drunken driving: A test of self-efficacy theory. *Journal of Public Relations Research, 7*, 205–229.

Anderson, R. B. (2000). Vicarious and persuasive influences on efficacy expectations and intentions to perform breast self-examination. *Public Relations Review, 26*, 97–114.

Areni, C. S., & Cox, K. C. (1994). The persuasive effects of evaluation, expectancy and relevancy dimensions of incongruent visual and verbal information. *Advances in Consumer Research, 21*, 337–342.

Bandura, A. (1986). *Social foundations of thought and action: A social cognitive theory.* Englewood Cliffs, NJ: Prentice-Hall.

Basil, M., Schooler, C., & Reeves, B. (1991). Positive and negative political advertising: Effectiveness of ads and perceptions of candidates. In F. Biocca (Ed.), *Television and political advertising, vol. 1: Psychological processes* (pp. 245–262). Hillsdale, NJ: Erlbaum.

Bassili, J. N. (1996). Meta-judgmental versus operative indexes of psychological attributes: The case of measures of attitude strength. *Journal of Personality and Social Psychology, 71*, 637–653.

Bezjian-Avery, A., Calder, B., & Iacobucci, D. (1998). New media interactive advertising versus traditional advertising. *Journal of Advertising Research, 38*(4), 23–32.

Birdsell, D. S., & Groarke, L. (1996). Toward a theory of visual argument. *Argumentation and Advocacy, 33*, 1–10.

Blair, J. A. (1996). The possibility and actuality of visual arguments. *Argumentation and Advocacy, 33*, 23–39.

Brashers, D. E., & Jackson, S. (1999). Changing conceptions of "message effects": A 24-year overview. *Human Communication Research, 25*, 457–477.

Bromer, P. (1998). Ambivalent attitudes and information processing. *Swiss Journal of Psychology, 57*, 225–234.

Cialdini, R. B., Kallgren, C. A., & Reno, R. R. (1991). A focus theory of normative conduct: A theoretical refinement and reevaluation of the role of norms in human behavior. In M. P. Zanna (Ed.), *Advances in experimental social psychology* (vol. 24, pp. 201–234). New York: Academic Press.

Conley, T. M. (1990). *Rhetoric in the European tradition.* New York: Longman.

Dijkstra, J. J., Liebrand, W. B. G., & Timminga, E. (1998). Persuasiveness of expert systems. *Behaviour and Information Technology, 17*, 155–163.

Eagly, A. H., & Chaiken, S. (1998). Attitude structure and function. In D. T. Gilbert, S. T. Fiske, & G. Lindzey (Eds.), *Handbook of social psychology* (4th ed., vol. 1, pp. 269–322). Boston: McGraw-Hill.

Figueiras, M., Price, H., & Marteau, T. M. (1999). Effects of textual and pictorial information upon perceptions of Down syndrome: An analogue study. *Psychology and Health, 14*, 761–771.

Fishbein, M., & Ajzen, I. (1975). *Belief, attitude, intention, and behavior.* Reading, MA: Addison-Wesley.

Fleming, D. (1996). Can pictures be arguments? *Argumentation and Advocacy, 33*, 11–22.

Garramone, G. M. (1985). Effects of negative political advertising: The roles of sponsor and rebuttal. *Journal of Broadcasting and Electronic Media, 29*, 147–159.

Haddock, G., & Zanna, M. P. (1997). Impact of negative advertising on evaluations of political candidates: The 1993 Canadian federal election. *Basic and Applied Social Psychology, 19*, 205–223.

Hagen, K. M., Gutkin, T. B., Wilson, C. P., & Oats, R. G. (1998). Using vicarious experience and verbal persuasion to enhance self-efficacy in pre-service teachers: "Priming the pump" for consultation. *School Psychology Quarterly, 13*, 169–178.

Haines, M., & Spear, S. F. (1996). Changing the perception of the norm: A strategy to decrease binge drinking among college students. *Journal of American College Health, 45*, 134–140.

Hedges, L. V., & Vevea, J. L. (1998). Fixed- and random-effects models in meta-analysis. *Psychological Methods, 3*, 486–504.

Hovland, C. I., Janis, I. L., & Kelley, H. H. (1953). *Communication and persuasion: Psychological studies of opinion change.* New Haven, CT: Yale University Press.

Jackson, S. (1992). *Message effects research: Principles of design and analysis.* New York: Guilford Press.

Jackson, S., & Brashers, D. E. (1994). M > 1: Analysis of treatment x replication designs. *Human Communication Research, 20*, 356–389.

Jackson, S., Brashers, D. E., & Massey, J. E. (1992). Statistical testing in treatment by replication designs: Three options reconsidered. *Communication Quarterly, 40*, 211–227.

Jackson, S., & Jacobs, S. (1983). Generalizing about messages: Suggestions for design and analysis of experiments. *Human Communication Research, 9*, 169–181.

Jamner, M. S., Wolitski, R. J., & Corby, N. H. (1997). Impact of a longitudinal community HIV intervention targeting injecting drug users' stage of change for condom and bleach use. *American Journal of Health Promotion, 12*, 15–24.

Jiang, J. J., Klein, G., & Vedder, R. G. (2000). Persuasive expert systems: The influence of confidence and discrepancy. *Computers in Human Behavior, 16*, 99–109.

Knower, F. H. (1936). Experimental studies of changes in attitudes: II. A study of the effect of printed argument on changes in attitude. *Journal of Abnormal and Social Psychology, 30*, 522–532.

Krosnick, J. A., & Petty, R. E. (1995). Attitude strength: An overview. In R. E. Petty & J. A. Krosnick (Eds.), *Attitude strength: Antecedents and consequences* (pp. 1–24). Mahwah, NJ: Erlbaum.

Lake, R. A., & Pickering, B. A. (1998). Argumentation, the visual, and the possibility of refutation: An exploration. *Argumentation, 12,* 79–93.

Lau, R. R., Sigelman, L., Heldman, C., & Babbitt, P. (1999). The effects of negative political advertisements: A meta-analytic assessment. *American Political Science Review, 93,* 851–875.

Li, H., & Bukovac, J. L. (1999). Cognitive impact of banner ad characteristics: An experimental study. *Journalism and Mass Communication Quarterly, 76,* 341–353.

Lund, F. H. (1925). The psychology of belief: A study of its emotional and volitional determinants. *Journal of Abnormal and Social Psychology, 20,* 174–196.

Maibach, E., & Flora, J. A. (1993). Symbolic modeling and cognitive rehearsal: Using video to promote AIDS prevention self-efficacy. *Communication Research, 20,* 517–545.

Messaris, P. (1997). *Visual persuasion: The role of images in advertising.* Thousand Oaks, CA: Sage.

Miller, D. T., Monin, B., & Prentice, D. A. (2000). Pluralistic ignorance and inconsistency between private attitudes and public behaviors. In D. J. Terry & M. A. Hogg (Eds.), *Attitudes, behavior, and social context: The role of norms and group membership* (pp. 95–113). Mahwah, NJ: Erlbaum.

Miniard, P. W., Bhatla, S., Lord, K. R., Dickson, P. R., & Unnava, H. R. (1991). Picture-based persuasion processes and the moderating role of involvement. *Journal of Consumer Research, 18,* 92–107.

Moon, Y. (1999). The effects of physical distance and response latency on persuasion in computer-mediated communication and human-computer communication. *Journal of Experimental Psychology: Applied, 5,* 379–392.

Morrison, J., & Vogel, D. (1998). The impacts of presentation visuals on persuasion. *Information and Management, 33,* 125–135.

Naylor, P. J., Simmonds, G., Riddoch, C., Velleman, G., & Turton, P. (1999). Comparison of stage-matched and unmatched interventions to promote exercise behaviour in the primary care setting. *Health Education Research, 14,* 653–666.

Nelson, J. S., & Boynton, G. R. (1997). *Video rhetorics: Televised advertising in American politics.* Urbana, IL: University of Illinois Press.

Oestermeier, U., & Hesse, F. W. (2000). Verbal and visual causal arguments. *Cognition, 75,* 65–104.

O'Keefe, D. J. (1999a). How to handle opposing arguments in persuasive messages: A meta-analytic review of the effects of one-sided and two-sided messages. In M. E. Roloff (Ed.), *Communication yearbook, 22,* 209–249. Thousand Oaks, CA: Sage.

O'Keefe, D. J. (1999b). Variability of persuasive message effects: Meta-analytic evidence and implications. *Document Design, 1,* 87–97.

O'Keefe, D. J., & Hale, S. L. (1998). The door-in-the-face influence strategy: A random-effects meta-analytic review. In M. E. Roloff (Ed.), *Communication yearbook, 21,* 1–33. Thousand Oaks, CA: Sage.

Perkins, H. W., Meilman, P. W., Leichliter, J. S., Cashin, J. R., & Presley, C. A. (1999). Misperceptions of the norms for the frequency of alcohol and other drug use on college campuses. *Journal of American College Health, 47,* 253–258.

Petty, R. E. (1997). The evolution of theory and research in social psychology: From single to multiple effect and process models of persuasion. In C. McGarty & S. A. Haslam (Eds.), *The message of social psychology: Perspectives on mind in society* (pp. 268–290). Oxford, England: Blackwell.

Petty, R. E., & Cacioppo, J. T. (1986). *Communication and persuasion: Central and peripheral routes to attitude change.* New York: Springer-Verlag.

Petty, R. E., & Krosnick, J. A. (Eds.). (1995). *Attitude strength: Antecedents and consequences.* Mahwah, NJ: Erlbaum.

Petty, R. E., & Wegener, D. T. (1998). Attitude change: Multiple roles for persuasion variables. In D. T. Gilbert, S. T. Fiske, & G. Lindzey (Eds.), *Handbook of social psychology* (4th ed., vol. 1, pp. 323–390). Boston: McGraw-Hill.

Pfau, M. & Burgoon, M. (1988). Inoculation in political campaign communication. *Human Communication Research, 15,* 91–111.

Pfau, M., Kenski, H. C., Nitz, M., & Sorenson, J. (1990). Efficacy of inoculation strategies in promoting resistance to political attack messages: Application to direct mail. *Communication Monographs, 57,* 25–43.

Prochaska, J. O., & DiClemente, C. C. (1984). *The transtheoretical approach: Crossing the traditional boundaries of therapy.* Homewood, IL: Dow Jones Irvin.

Quinlan, K. B., & McCaul, K. D. (2000). Matched and mismatched interventions with young adult smokers: Testing a stage theory. *Health Psychology, 19,* 165–171.

Raden, D. (1985). Strength-related attitude dimensions. *Social Psychology Quarterly, 48,* 312–330.

Rosenthal, R. (1991). *Meta-analytic procedures for social research* (rev. ed.). Newbury Park, CA: Sage.

Roskos-Ewoldsen, D. R. (1997). Attitude accessibility and persuasion: Review and a transactive model. In B. R. Burleson (Ed.), *Communication yearbook, 20* (185–225). Thousand Oaks, CA: Sage.

Schanck, R. C., & Goodman, C. (1939). Reactions to propaganda on both sides of a controversial issue. *Public Opinion Quarterly, 3,* 107–112.

Scott, L. M. (1994). Images in advertising: The need for a theory of visual rhetoric. *Journal of Consumer Research, 21,* 252–273.

Soley, L. C. (1986). Copy length and industrial advertising readership. *Industrial Marketing Management, 15,* 245–251.

Steffian, G. (1999). Correction of normative misperceptions: An alcohol abuse prevention program. *Journal of Drug Education, 29,* 115–138.

Weinstein, N. D., Rothman, A. J., & Sutton, S. R. (1998). Stage theories of health behavior: Conceptual and methodological issues. *Health Psychology, 17,* 290–299.

Weisse, C. S., Turbiasz, A. A., & Whitney, D. J. (1995). Behavioral training and AIDS risk reduction: Overcoming barriers to condom use. *AIDS Education and Prevention, 7,* 50–59.

Wood, W., Kallgren, C. A., & Preisler, R. M. (1985). Access to attitude-relevant information in memory as a determinant of persuasion: The role of message attributes. *Journal of Experimental Social Psychology, 21,* 73–85.

4

Theorizing about Persuasion

Cornerstones of Persuasion Research

Robert H. Gass and John S. Seiter

Persuasion theories are a lot like noses; everybody has one, some big, some small, and no two exactly alike. This chapter reviews and evaluates some of the better-known theories and models of persuasion, social influence, and compliance gaining. The goal is to provide you with a general framework for understanding these theories and models as they relate to the chapters that follow.

That said, not all theories or models are represented here. This review is, of necessity, selective rather than exhaustive. There are simply too many theories, especially smaller, specialized theories related to specific contexts or strategies to address them all. This does not mean we regard such theories as unimportant. We consider the theories covered here to be staples of persuasion research. They have been studied extensively and are widely cited in the scholarly literature. They have heuristic value in that they've sparked further theorizing and research on persuasion. We would therefore include them in any "must know" list for students of persuasion.

We should also note that the emphasis here is on "social scientific" theories and models of persuasion, rather than "rhetorical" theories of persuasion or other symbolic perspectives of how people influence each other. Our aim is not to devalue such theories by excluding them, but simply to acknowledge that practical constraints must govern any effort of this sort.

With the foregoing caveats in mind, perhaps the best place to begin is by stating that there is not so much *a* theory of persuasion, as there are *theories* of persuasion. Persuasion research is based upon a patchwork quilt of perspectives, some that can be characterized as "umbrella" theories accounting for a wide variety of persuasive phenomena and some representing "micro" theories that explain specific forms of influence in very limited circumstances. Berger and Burgoon's observation that "By the late 1960s Ostrum (1968) counted some 34 different persuasion theories, none of which could provide a plausible explanation for the broad range of observed communication-persuasion relationships"

(1995, p. x) is telling in this regard. This situation has changed little. If anything, the expansion of traditional, one-to-many persuasion studies to encompass interpersonal or one-on-one influence attempts has served to increase the number of theories under consideration. While some theories have generated more research interest or found more favor within certain camps, at present no single, unifying perspective can be identified in the literature, at least not one upon which all scholars and researchers agree.

What's more, at least some persuasion research, including some studies in the area of nonverbal influence and some in the area of compliance gaining, appears to be largely atheoretical in nature. That is, either there is no clearly defined theoretical framework that guides the research, or a guiding theory, such as it may be, is implicit at best.

One should not be overly bothered by this state of affairs, however. A certain amount of overlap among theories is to be expected, along with gaps and occasional contradictions. Human communication is complex. There are a lot of variables to consider in the persuasion equation. It should come as no surprise, then, that researchers have found it difficult to explain how people come to be persuaded all in one go. Theories are always provisional. They are subject to revision, modification, refinement, and extension. Empirical findings may increase social scientists' confidence in a given theory, but it remains just that, a theory. And even if one could embrace a single theory of persuasion today, it wouldn't be the same theory 10 years from now. In short, we are a long way from proclaiming anything like a "unified" theory of persuasion.

All told, eight theories and/or models are examined in this chapter. They include attitude change processes, Mere Exposure Theory (ME), and a variety of related theories grouped under the heading "Consistency Theories," such as Cognitive Dissonance Theory (CDT). We also examine the Theory of Reasoned Action (TRA), Social Judgment Theory, Expectancy Violations Theory, the Elaboration Likelihood Model (ELM), and the Heuristic-Systematic Model (HSM). We begin by examining what is not so much a specific theory as it is a mosaic of theories and research on attitudes and attitude change.

Attitudes and Attitude Change Processes

Attitudes are to persuasion research what Elvis Presley is to rock-and-roll. Modern persuasion research is rooted in the study of attitudes, work that originated in the 1940s under the stewardship of Carl Hovland, founder of the Yale Attitude Research Program. Attitude research continues to flourish today. A more thorough discussion of recent literature on attitude change processes can be found in several excellent reviews (Eagly & Chaiken, 1998; Petty, Wegener, & Fabrigar, 1997; Wood, 2000).

There is now general agreement that an attitude is "a learned predisposition to respond in a consistently favorable or unfavorable manner with respect to a given object" (Fishbein & Ajzen, 1975, p. 6). That is, attitudes are learned rather than innate, they reflect tendencies to respond or react in predictable ways, and they represent favorable or unfavorable evaluations of things. It is this last feature of attitudes, their evaluative nature (that is, appraisals of things as good or bad, right or wrong), that represents the hallmark of attitude research (see Dillard, 1993).

From the standpoint of persuasion, attitudes are important because they are thought to correlate with and predict behavior. Just how well attitudes correlate with behavior, known as the "A–B relationship," has been the subject of intense investigation. Earlier studies were pessimistic about the extent to which attitudes predicted behavior (Dillehay, 1973; Wicker, 1969). At least some of the inconsistencies, however, were due to methodological shortcomings in researchers' measurements of attitudes and behaviors (Ajzen & Fishbein, 1977; Kelman, 1974). Recent meta-analyses suggest that the correlation between attitudes and behavior ranges from moderate (r = .30) (Krauss, 1995) to strong (r = .79), if methodological artifacts are excluded (Kim & Hunter, 1993a), to stronger still (r = .87), once the moderating role of receiver involvement is taken into account (Kim & Hunter, 1993b).

Regardless of the exact correlation involved, the important point is that attitudes do seem to predict behavior reasonably well. Another important point is that because attitudes and behavior are related, changing an individual's attitude(s) should lead to changes in her/his behavior(s). Thus, attitude change research, in a nutshell, attempts to identify ways of modifying receivers' attitudes in order to bring about corresponding changes in their behavior.

A good deal of research on attitude change has focused on the role of moderating variables that mediate the strength of the A-B relationship. A number of such moderating variables have been identified to date. While we do not have sufficient space to devote to all of them here, we highlight some of the key moderators in table 4.1.

Attitudes remain central to the study of persuasion, although, as Daniel O'Keefe noted in chapter 3, researchers have moved beyond the attitude construct to explain a variety of other persuasive phenomena. Studies focusing on compliance gaining, for example, are primarily concerned with behavioral conformity, with or without any accompanying change in attitudes. Because attitude change research has occupied researchers' attention for more than 50 years, there isn't sufficient space here to examine all the ways in which attitudes can be modified. However, one well-known way is through what is called Mere Exposure Theory, which we discuss next.

Mere Exposure Theory

Mere Exposure Theory, also known as the Mere Exposure Effect, states that repeated exposure to an unfamiliar stimulus can in and of itself increase positive affect toward the stimulus (Zajonc, 1968). Stated simply, some messages "grow on us." Thus, a consumer who encountered a product logo on several different occasions would tend to evaluate that logo more favorably than he or she would other, unfamiliar logos. It wouldn't matter whether the consumer knew what the familiar logo represented.

The reason the theory is called "mere" exposure is that, unlike Classical Conditioning, repeated exposure to a stimulus produces increased liking in the absence of any reinforcement. You may recall that, according to Classical Conditioning (think Pavlov's dog here), an unconditioned stimulus (food) will produce an unconditioned response (salivation). That is, Pavlov's dog naturally drools at the sight of food. When an unconditioned

TABLE 4.1   *Moderating Variables Affecting the A–B Relationship*

- *Attitude salience or centrality:* Attitudes that are central to one's core beliefs and values are more likely to square with behavior than attitudes that are more marginal or tangential.
- *Specificity of the attitude(s) and behavior(s):* Attitudes are more likely to correspond with behavior when specific attitudes and specific behaviors are involved.
- *Attitudes based on direct experience:* Attitudes formed via personal experience correspond more closely to behavior than attitudes that are formed secondhand (Fazio, 1986; Fazio & Zanna, 1981).
- *Social desirability bias:* People tend to behave in ways they consider to be socially polite or correct, especially in public settings (Furnham, 1986). For this reason, some researchers have advocated the use of unobtrusive measures (Andersen, 1989) and indirect questioning (Fisher, 1993) as a means of reducing social desirability bias.
- *Self-monitoring:* The A–B relationship is stronger for low self-monitors than high self-monitors, because the latter are more "chameleonlike" and more inclined to tailor their behavior to specific situations (Snyder, 1974, 1979).
- *Activation of relevant attitudes:* Attitudes tend to predict behavior more accurately when they are activated, that is, brought to the forefront of an individual's conscious awareness. Sometimes people need to be reminded what their attitudes are in order for them to adjust their behavior accordingly.
- Lastly, the A–B relationship is likely to be strengthened when "multiple act criteria" are employed. Giving people more than one opportunity to manifest their attitudes through their behavior improves the fit between the two.

stimulus (food) is repeatedly paired with a conditioned stimulus (bell), the conditioned stimulus (bell) will eventually elicit the conditioned response (salivation) all by itself. Thus, by ringing a bell every time the dog sees food, Pavlov eventually gets his dog to drool at the sound of the bell alone. The difference between Mere Exposure Theory and Classical Conditioning, then, is that mere exposure doesn't require the presence of any additional reinforcement to work its magic. Mere Exposure Theory (ME) postulates that repeated exposure to a stimulus (bell) will result in more favorable evaluations of that stimulus than of other unfamiliar stimuli (whistle, buzzer, chime, etc.).

As an illustration of ME in a laboratory setting, Smith and Zarate (1992) found that research participants who were exposed to general knowledge statements tended to regard those statements as more valid or true than other, unfamiliar knowledge statements. As an example of ME in action, when the large insurance corporation Aetna changed its name to Ing, the company launched a marketing campaign in which the new name was advertised repeatedly, without explaining what the company did. A series of commercials showed people on the street scratching their heads and wondering what the new name meant. Frequent exposure to the new name was designed to "soften up" consumers. By familiarizing consumers with the corporation's name, Ing was making consumers more receptive to that name and, indirectly, to the company itself.

More than 200 studies conducted in both controlled laboratory and more naturalistic settings have demonstrated that ME is a fairly robust phenomenon (Bornstein, 1989;

Moreland & Zajonc, 1977; Zajonc, 2001; Zajonc & Rajecki, 1969). Moreover, the phenomenon has been demonstrated using a wide variety of stimuli, including general knowledge statements, works of art, yearbook photos, musical compositions, product names, nonsense words, and geometric figures (see Bornstein, 1989; Harrison, 1977). ME has also been demonstrated to work across different cultures.

There are differing explanations as to why or how ME works. Some scholars believe that cognitive processing, or mediation, is involved. Others assume that ME is a more automatic, unconscious process. One of the most common cognitive explanations involves learning. With each additional exposure, a person acquires additional information about a stimulus. The additional information enhances the person's appraisal of the stimulus. However, the assumption that the more you learn about something, the more you'll like it is not without limitations. Some studies have shown that ME *decreases* liking if the initial stimulus is evaluated negatively (Amir, 1969; Brickman, Redfield, Harrison, & Crandall, 1972; Perlman & Oskamp, 1971).

Another common explanation is based on a misattribution involving "fluency." According to this view, individuals mistake "fluency," or the proficiency with which they process a stimulus, with positive affect or liking (Jacoby & Kelley, 1990). The fluency is a result of their previous exposure to the stimulus, but observers don't realize this. This explanation accounts for the fact that in studies in which participants are aware of their previous exposure, reduced ME effects are observed (Bornstein, 1989). There is also some evidence that fluency has a greater effect on cognitive judgments compared with affective judgments (Lee, 2001).

Other explanations suggest that ME takes place at a low level of awareness or even unconsciously (Moreland & Zajonc, 1977). One such explanation involves familiarity. According to this view, familiarity tends to enhance liking. A familiar stimulus is perceived as more inviting or attractive than a novel or unfamiliar stimulus. Based on this explanation, if a voter saw a candidate's name repeatedly on bumper stickers and lawn placards, that candidate would enjoy an advantage over unfamiliar opponents in that voter's mind on election day. In support of the unconscious-processing explanation, Bornstein's (1989) meta-analysis revealed that when ME takes place without conscious awareness, it tends to be more effective than when it takes place with conscious awareness.

A recent study offers some intriguing evidence that different types of ME can take place through different brain hemispheres (Compton, Williamson, Murphy, & Heller, 2002). Words or text may be processed in one hemisphere, images in the other. This finding may explain some of the inconsistencies in previous studies. In addition, complex stimuli appear to be evaluated more favorably with increasing exposures than are simple stimuli (Bornstein, Kale, & Cornell, 1990; Heyduk, 1975; Zajonc et al., 1972). Research also indicates that ME may facilitate a preference for familiar over unfamiliar brands, but not over equally familiar, or more familiar, brands (Baker, 1999). Other studies suggest that ME works best if the exposures are brief in duration (Hamid, 1973). Finally, some research indicates that there are diminishing returns to increasing exposure, with a leveling off or drop-off in effectiveness after 10 to 20 exposures (Stang & O'Connell, 1974; Zajonc et al., 1972). In the real world, it is difficult for persuaders, such as advertisers, to control the number of times consumers are exposed to a message. A commercial might air

100 times, but some viewers may see the commercial only a few times or not at all, whereas other viewers may see it dozens of times.

At present, it is unclear whether ME operates via conscious or unconscious processing, or both. The literature seems to indicate that ME is more effective when it takes place at a low level of awareness or unconsciously. Whatever the underlying mechanism, however, the literature suggests that ME works and works well. Although questions remain as to exactly how and why ME works, it is a relatively simple theory of persuasion: Repeated, unreinforced exposure to a stimulus facilitates liking for the stimulus, even in the absence of awareness.

Psychological Consistency Theories

A variety of theories fall under the rubric of what have come to be known as "consistency theories." These include Heider's Balance Theory (1958), Newcomb's Symmetry Theory (1953), and Osgood and Tannenbaum's Congruity Theory (1955; Osgood, Tannenbaum, & Suci, 1957), among others. These theories share the common assumption that individuals have an innate desire to hold consistent beliefs, attitudes, and behaviors. Holding disparate beliefs, attitudes, or behaviors is thought to be psychologically uncomfortable. A person who had trouble "looking himself in the mirror" would be experiencing psychological inconsistency, as would a person who felt she was "between a rock and a hard place" insofar as an important decision was concerned. This psychological tension motivates individuals to adjust their thoughts, feelings, or actions accordingly. As an example, a health-oriented person might be bothered by the fact that he or she eats red meat because red meat is associated with increased cholesterol levels. Persuasive messages can be designed either to create or restore consistency by bringing such inconsistent cognitions into line. Using the same example, a persuasive message could differentiate between eating red meat occasionally, as opposed to frequently, and eating lean red meat rather than meat that is high in fat. Such *differentiation* is one of the psychological mechanisms for bringing about consistency. Other common mechanisms for preserving or restoring consistency include *denial* ("I don't believe there is a well-established link between red meat and cholesterol or cholesterol and heart disease"), *bolstering* ("I don't eat that much meat anyway; red meat is a good source of protein"), *attitude or belief modification* ("I think eating red meat is okay as long as I have small portions"), and *transcendence* (Hey, we've all got to die of something").

Consistency was originally viewed as a drive-reduction theory. That is, inconsistency creates a psychological drive to maintain or restore consistency. More recent thinking, however, suggests that consistency is as much an effort to manage one's self image or maintain face in the eyes of others as it is an internal drive state (Aronson, Cohen, & Nail, 1999; Greenwald & Ronis, 1978; Scher & Cooper, 1989). *We* may know we are not being consistent, but we want *others* to think we are. How much inconsistency an individual can tolerate is related in large part to the *centrality* of the beliefs, attitudes, or behaviors in question. Inconsistencies involving core beliefs are more troubling than those involving tangential beliefs. Thus, the notion of cheating on a diet would bother most people far less than the notion of cheating on a spouse. Current research also suggests that there are individual differences in people's tolerance for inconsistency. An inconsistency that "bugs" one person might not faze another. Research further suggests that there is a cultural component involved in the degree to which people strive for consistency (Cialdini, Wosinska, Barret, Butner, & Gornik-Durose, 1999).

All of the consistency theories suffer from the drawback of being unable to accommodate more than three cognitive relations at one time. If we know, for example, that Timmy likes Popeye, the cartoon character (favorable attitude), and Popeye is positively associated with eating spinach (favorable attitude), then Timmy's attitudes will be psychologically consistent if he too likes spinach. Yet such a model tends to oversimplify the complex associative networks in which beliefs, attitudes, and other cognitions exist. Timmy might like Popeye and, therefore, spinach, but his best friend, Emile, might hate spinach; or Timmy might not like the way his mother serves spinach (Popeye, after all, gulps it straight from the can); or he might like other vegetables more than spinach; or he might identify with Wimpy, the character who loves hamburgers, more than he identifies with Popeye. Attitudes don't exist in isolation, but rather in clusters of beliefs, attitudes, and values. These clusters are in turn interrelated with other clusters. Even consistency theories that take into account degrees of attitude and not just their valences, such as Congruity Theory, suffer from this limitation. Consistency theories are useful as far as they go, but their explanatory and predictive power is typically confined to one triad at a time.

Cognitive Dissonance Theory

A specialized version of consistency, known as Cognitive Dissonance Theory (CDT), was developed by Leon Festinger (1957, 1964; Festinger & Carlsmith, 1959). The theory, which fell out of favor in the 1970s and 1980s, has come roaring back since the 1990s. Nearly 100 articles have been published on cognitive dissonance in the last decade. While Festinger's original theory has been modified and extended by others (see Cooper & Fazio, 1984; Scher & Cooper, 1989), many scholars argue that the original theory remains viable today (Beauvois & Joule, 1999; Harmon-Jones, 1999; Mills, 1999). Similar to other consistency theories, CDT postulates that holding dissonant cognitions (beliefs, attitudes, perceptions, etc.) is an aversive psychological state. Cognitive dissonance isn't an all-or-nothing phenomenon—it occurs in varying degrees. An important decision evokes more dissonance than an unimportant one.

Persuasive messages can be aimed at either increasing or decreasing dissonance. On the one hand, a persuader might want to increase dissonance in order to get another person to rethink his or her position on an issue. A parent might tell a college-age son, for example, "Are you sure you want to get a new car, rather than a used one? Your car payments will be higher and you'll have to pay more for insurance too." On the other hand, a persuader might want to minimize dissonance by reassuring another person that the decision she or he made was the right one. A parent might tell a college-age daughter, for instance, "You made the right choice in buying a car, rather than leasing one. If you take care of it, you'll have reliable transportation long after it is paid off."

Four common research paradigms have been used to study cognitive dissonance; the free-choice paradigm, the belief-disconfirmation paradigm, the effort-justification paradigm, and the induced-compliance paradigm (Harmon-Jones & Mills, 1999). The *free-*

choice paradigm focuses on the psychological angst a person experiences following a freely made decision. For this reason, CDT is often referred to as a "post-decision theory." Once a person makes a decision, the person worries about whether she or he made the right choice. This phenomenon is commonly referred to in sales as "buyer's remorse." The person seeks to reduce her or his dissonance by justifying the decision that was made. Attempts to justify or reinforce the decision can take place through the individual's thought processes, words, or actions. For a more detailed discussion of some of the modes of dissonance reduction, see Steele (1988), Stone, Wygand, Cooper, and Aronson (1997), and Burris, Harmon-Jones, and Tarpley (1997).

A second paradigm for research on CDT involves *belief disconfirmation.* Dissonance is aroused when an individual is exposed to information that is inconsistent with her or his beliefs. The theory predicts that a person will reject, distort, or avoid information that arouses dissonance. When there is a bear market, for instance, some investors can't stand opening their quarterly statements, much less reading them, because they don't want to know how much money they've lost. When there is a bull market, the same investors can't wait to tear open the mail to see how much money they've made. CDT also predicts that, having made a decision, individuals will engage in *selective exposure* by seeking out information that is consonant with their choice and avoiding information that is dissonant with their choice. Before buying a car, for example, a consumer might look at ads for a variety of makes and models. After purchasing a car, however, the same consumer will tend to look for ads or favorable reviews of the specific car purchased. Nevertheless, people don't always stick their heads in the sand when confronted with dissonant information. Empirical studies suggest that people can and do tolerate a certain amount of dissonant information (see Cotton, 1985; Cotton & Heiser, 1980).

A third avenue of research for studying CDT is known as the *induced compliance paradigm* (originally called the forced-choice paradigm). This is perhaps the most widely studied of all the dissonance paradigms (Devine, Tauer, Barron, Elliot, & Vance, 1999). When a person is induced to engage in behavior that is contrary to his or her attitudes or self-image, the magnitude of dissonance is less. When a person performs a counter-attitudinal action of his or her own volition, however, the magnitude of dissonance is greater. By way of illustration, an attorney who was paid handsomely for defending an unsavory client would find his or her actions easier to justify than if he or she took on the case pro bono. The greater the external incentives, whether positive (promises of reward) or negative (threats of punishment), the easier it is for an individual to ascribe his or her behavior to the external inducement. Research based on this paradigm has also revealed a *negative incentive effect* (Festinger & Carlsmith, 1959; Harmon-Jones & Mills, 1999). The larger the external incentive for engaging in counterattitudinal behavior, the less attitude change there will be in the direction of the behavior in question. The smaller the external incentive, the greater the change in attitude. Thus, people who volunteered to go door to door to raise money for a charity would tend to have more favorable attitudes toward the charity than people who were paid to do the same type of fund-raising.

The fourth paradigm that has prompted CDT research is the *effort justification paradigm* (see Beauvois & Joule, 1999). The basic notion here is that when a person has to earn something, he or she appreciates it all the more. The greater the sacrifice that is required to achieve an outcome, the more an individual will value the outcome. Conversely, the less sacrifice involved, the less value the individual will attach to the outcome. By way of illustration, a college student who pledged a fraternity or sorority and was required to perform embarrassing or humiliating acts during "hell week" would tend to rationalize the behavior by valuing the outcome of membership in the fraternity or sorority even more. Why? Because performing unpleasant acts would arouse dissonance, but the dissonance could be reduced by enhancing the perceived value of the outcome. A college student who did not have to undergo embarrassing or humiliating initiation rituals, however, would not experience as much dissonance and, according to the effort justification paradigm, would not value his or her membership as highly.

CDT has generated a number of useful insights regarding persuasion, especially the process of self-persuasion. While there is disagreement on the underlying motivation for dissonance, scholars agree that "genuine cognitive changes occur," that "these cognitive changes are motivated in nature and that the source of this motivation is a form of psychological discomfort" (Harmon-Jones & Mills, 1999, p. 15).

Theory of Reasoned Action

The Theory of Reasoned Action (TRA) was developed by Martin Fishbein and Isaac Ajzen in the late 1970s (Ajzen & Fishbein, 1977, 1980; Fishbein & Ajzen, 1975) and was followed by Ajzen's Theory of Planned Behavior (1991). The TRA is often referred to as a "rational" theory of persuasion, because it focuses on the deliberative process an individual engages in when she or he is presented with a persuasive message. The operating assumption is that individuals systematically analyze messages, evaluate all available information, and actively weigh the benefits and risks associated with compliance before making a decision.

The linchpin of the TRA is an individual's *behavioral intention*. That is, the most reliable indicator of what a person *will* do is what he or she *intends* to do. Although behavioral intentions don't always correspond to behavior—for example, the time a person intends to wake up when she or he sets an alarm clock at night is not necessarily the actual time the person gets up in the morning—a number of studies have confirmed that behavioral intentions are, by and large, predictive of behavior (Ajzen & Fishbein, 1973; Kim & Hunter, 1993a, 1993b; Sheppard, Hartwick, & Warshaw, 1988). Behavioral intentions are in turn guided by two major factors: a person's attitude toward the behavior and subjective norms.

The first major factor, *attitude toward the behavior*, refers to a person's evaluation of the benefits and risks associated with performing the action requested in a persuasive message. Favorable attitudes lead to approach behavior, and unfavorable attitudes lead to avoidance behavior. For example, the likelihood that Naomi would join a carpool to commute to work would be based on her intention to join a carpool. Her intention would in turn be based on her attitudes toward carpooling. If Naomi held favorable attitudes toward carpooling ("I get to work faster," "I'm helping the environment") then her intention to join a carpool would be stronger. If she held unfavorable attitudes toward carpooling ("I can't come and go as I please," "I don't enjoy talking to people on the way to and from work"), her intention to join a carpool would be weaker. The combination of positive and negative attitudes toward the behavior is one factor that determines a person's behavioral intent.

The TRA also states that an individual's attitude toward the behavior, in this case carpooling, will be based on his or her *beliefs about the outcome* of performing the behavior and his or her *evaluation of the outcome*. The more a person believes that performing an action will produce a favorable outcome, and the more favorably the person evaluates that outcome, the stronger the person's attitudes toward the behavior will be. Continuing with the same example, Naomi might believe that one outcome of carpooling is that she would save money on gasoline. Her evaluation of that outcome would be positive. But she might also believe that another outcome of carpooling is that she would be unable to leave work on lunch breaks to run errands. Her evaluation of that outcome would be negative. According to the TRA, the totality of Naomi's beliefs about these outcomes and her evaluation of them would guide her attitude toward joining a carpool.

A second major factor that determines a person's behavioral intent is *subjective norms*. Subjective norms are made up of a person's *normative beliefs* about what significant others think, along with the person's *motivation to comply* with significant others' opinions. Thus, if Naomi's friends were environmentalists, she would tend to have favorable beliefs toward carpooling. If Naomi also had a strong desire to live up to her friends' normative expectations, she would be even more inclined to join a carpool. The various components of the TRA—beliefs about the outcome, evaluation of the outcome, normative beliefs, and motivation to comply—are typically measured using self-report rating scales.

The TRA has been tested on a wide variety of topics and issues, including AIDS risk reduction (Cochran, Mays, Ciaretta, Caruso, & Mallon, 1992), belief in extraterrestrials (Patry & Pelletier, 2001), condom use (Albarracin, Johnson, Fishbein, & Muellerleile, 2001; Greene, Hale, & Rubin, 1997), dental hygiene (Toneatto & Binik, 1987), drinking and driving (Gastil, 2000), exposure to the sun (Steen, Peay, & Owen, 2000), mental practice (Trafimow & Miller, 1996), moral behavior in sports (Vallerand, Deshaies, Currier, Pelletier, & Mongeau, 1992), recycling (Park, Levine, & Sharkey, 1998), and voting behavior (Granberg & Holmberg, 1990). The TRA has been especially useful in predicting the role of intentions on health-related behavior. In addition, studies have shown that there are individual differences, gender differences, and cultural differences in the weight or importance people attach to the various components of the TRA (Greene, Hale, & Rubin, 1997; Godin et al., 1996; Lee & Green, 1991).

Social Judgment Theory

Social Judgment Theory, presented by Muzafer Sherif, Carolyn Sherif, and Robert Nebergall (Sherif & Sherif, 1967; Sherif, Sherif, & Nebergall, 1965), focuses on how people evaluate persuasive messages and how such evaluations affect whether or not persuasion occurs. According to the theory, on any given topic a person might hold a range of possible positions. By way of example, consider the debate among vegetarians, meat eaters, and some of those who are "in between." Here are several positions, some extreme, some moderate, that a person might embrace on this issue (see Corliss, 2002):

1. Sproutarianism—You should build your diet around beans, wheat, and other sprouts.
2. Fruitarianism—You should eat plant parts that the plant can easily replace (e.g., berries, apples, tomatoes, grains, seeds).
3. Veganism—You should eat plants and avoid meat, dairy, eggs, honey, or any other animal product.
4. Ovo-vegetarianism—You may eat plants and eggs, since hens would lay the eggs even if we didn't eat them.
5. Ovo-lacto-vegetarianism—You may eat vegetables, eggs, and dairy products, since doing so kills no animals.
6. Pesco-vegetarianism—You may eat fish because fish don't have sophisticated nervous systems.
7. Pollo-vegetarianism—You may eat chicken, but not red meat.
8. Meat eaters—You may put just about anything in your mouth.

Social Judgment Theory argues that on this, or any continuum, a person has a most preferred position, called an *anchor point*. This anchor point functions as a reference point or "psychological benchmark" against which other positions and viewpoints are evaluated. If, for example, Dean agrees most with position 2—that you should eat replaceable plant parts—position 2 is Dean's anchor point, but that doesn't mean that it is the only position he may find acceptable. For instance, though preferring to stick to position 2, he may think it is all right to eat honey, eggs, and ice cream (positions 3, 4, and 5). Such positions, together with his anchor point, represent Dean's *latitude of acceptance,* that is, the range of positions he finds acceptable. But what about the remaining positions on the continuum, which fall outside a person's latitude of acceptance? According to Social Judgment Theory, a person may feel ambivalent about some of these positions and strongly opposed to others. Those positions in the first category (ambivalent) are said to fall within a person's *latitude of noncommitment.* Those in the second category (strongly opposed) are said to fall within a person's latitude of rejection. Thus, if Dean feels neutral about eating fish, position 6 falls within his latitude of noncommitment. If he is adamantly against eating chicken and beef, positions 7 and 8 fall within his *latitude of rejection.*

How is this important to persuasion? First, Social Judgment Theory suggests that a person's anchor position is used as a standard to evaluate all other positions. As such, it may be difficult, if not impossible, to persuade a person to accept a position that is too disparate from his or her anchor point. In fact, when a persuasive message advocates a position that is highly discrepant from a person's anchor position, Social Judgment Theory predicts that the persuadee will perceive the position advocated in the persuasive message to be farther away from the anchor than it really is. This outcome, known as the *contrast effect*, makes rejection of a persuasive message more likely. In contrast, a persuasive message advocating a position that is not too far away from a person's anchor position, that is, one that falls within the person's latitude of noncommitment, may be deemed tolerable. In this case, Social Judgment Theory suggests that the persuadee may end up perceiving the advocated position to be closer to the anchor than it really is. This phenomenon, known as the *assimilation effect,* makes acceptance of a persuasive message more likely.

Not surprisingly, the breadth of any particular person's latitudes of acceptance, noncommitment, and rejection influences how difficult it may be to persuade that person. For instance, Social Judgment Theory conceptualizes an ego-involved person as someone with a narrow latitude of acceptance and a wide latitude of rejection. In our example, a person who makes a living selling cattle and who loves to eat beef with every meal would be such an ego-involved person. Social Judgment Theory suggests that trying to persuade such a person to become a sproutarian would probably be a waste of time. On the other hand, just because a person is ego-involved in one issue does not mean he or she will be that way on all issues. The cattle rancher, for example, may have a narrow latitude of rejection on issues such as gun control or capital punishment.

Expectancy Violations Theory

A number of persuasion theories focus on expectations, or, more precisely, what occurs when people's expectations are violated. Three such theories—Language Expectancy Theory (M. Burgoon, 1995), the Nonverbal Expectancy Violations Model (J. Burgoon, 1994), and Reinforcement Expectancy Theory (Klingle, 1996)—are discussed later in this volume (see chapters 9, 10, and 16) and will therefore be highlighted only briefly here.

Although there are some unique differences among these theories, all share the common assumption that people have expectations about what constitutes normal behavior. When such expectations are violated, it catches receivers off guard. Someone standing too close or using extremely intense language, for example, might violate a person's expectations for normal behavior. According to these theories, such violations cause receivers to shift their attention from the message to the source of the message. Whether such violations hinder or facilitate persuasion, then, depends on the receivers' perceptions of the person violating the expectations. For example, when perceptions are positive, that is, when sources are perceived as credible, attractive, or likable, sources may be more persuasive when violating expectations than when behaving in accordance with expectations. On the other hand, when perceptions are less positive, sources who violate expectations for normal behavior are probably less persuasive than they would be without such violations.

These related theories also suggest that some sources have a relatively wide bandwidth of acceptable behaviors, whereas others are permitted a relatively narrow bandwidth. By way of example, Reinforcement Expectancy Theory argues that because of social norms, female physicians can't get away with using aversive strategies in the same way that male physicians can. When female doctors use such strategies, they violate patients' expectations about what is appropriate, and as a result, patients are less likely to comply. According to the theory, then, male physicians can increase compliance by using either positive (e.g., "Regular eating will make you feel so much better") or negative ("You have two choices: change your diet or spend the rest of your life wishing you had") influence strategies, but female physicians can increase compliance only by using positive strategies.

Dual-Process Theories of Persuasion

Two of the most recent theories of persuasion are known as *dual-process* theories (Chaiken & Trope, 1999) because they postulate that persuasion operates via two basic paths. Both Petty and Cacioppo's Elaboration Likelihood Model and Chaiken and Eagly's Heuristic-Systematic Model maintain that people employ two qualitatively different modes of information processing when they are exposed to a persuasive message. Though the two theories differ in their particulars, both assume that one mode or route is more cognitive, deliberate, reflective, effortful, and generally slower than the other, which is more automatic, reflexive, habitual, affective, and generally faster. People rely on one mode when they need to think through a decision and rely on the other when they need to expedite their decision making. Other dual-process theories of persuasion also exist. For example, Kim Witte's Extended Parallel Processing Model, which is the subject of chapter 13, presumes that fear appeals are processed along one of two basic routes.

The Elaboration Likelihood Model

Richard Petty and John Cacioppo's (1986a, 1986b) Elaboration Likelihood Model of Persuasion (ELM) is one of the most widely cited models in the persuasion literature. Because the ELM is the focus of chapter 5, our discussion of it is truncated here. The ELM postulates that there are two basic routes to persuasion that operate in tandem. The first of these, known as the *central route,* involves cognitive elaboration, that is, effortful thought and deliberation about the content of a message. The second route, known as the *peripheral route*, emphasizes mental shortcuts, such as a reliance on source attractiveness or argument quantity in evaluating a persuasive message. According to the ELM, the predominant form of processing on which an individual relies depends on a number of factors, including the individual's involvement with the topic or issue, ability to process the message, motivation to process the message, and need for cognition.

As an illustration of the ELM in action, suppose that Alex is interested in joining a health club. If his determination to get in shape is high, meaning that he has high personal involvement in the issue, he will tend to rely on central processing. That is, he'll tend to read different ads for health clubs, compare their features and prices, ask questions to clarify points of information, and mull over the advantages and disadvantages of different plans in his mind. If, however, his motivation to get fit is low, that is, his doctor encouraged him to exercise more regularly but Alex isn't particularly eager to do so, he will tend to rely on peripheral processing. He might join a health club on the recommendation of a friend, or simply join the gym with the catchiest ad. He would tend to use central processing if he wanted to make a thoughtful decision and peripheral processing if he wanted to make an expedient decision.

A source of controversy surrounding the ELM has been the issue of *parallel or simultaneous processing*. Although Petty and Cacioppo acknowledged the possibility of parallel processing, that is, using both routes at once (Petty, Kasmer, Haugtvedt, & Cacioppo, 1987), the ELM has been criticized for not making this assumption more explicit (see Hamilton, Hunter, & Boster, 1993; Mongeau & Stiff, 1993; Stiff, 1986; Stiff & Boster, 1987). While Petty and Cacioppo argued that the ELM does not preclude the possibility of parallel processing, they suggested that there is usually a trade-off, in that a person tends to favor one route over the other. The controversy over parallel versus exclusive processing may involve a "difference that makes no difference," however, because to date there is limited empirical evidence from laboratory studies that simultaneous processing ever occurs (Booth-Butterfield et al., 1994; Chaiken, Liberman, & Eagly, 1989). Petty & Cacioppo address this and other criticisms of the ELM in chapter 5.

The Heuristic-Systematic Model of Persuasion

Another model of persuasion that bears many similarities to the ELM is Shelley Chaiken and Alice Eagly's Heuristic-Systematic Model (HSM) (Chaiken, 1980, 1987; Chaiken, Lieberman, & Eagly, 1989; Chen & Chaiken, 1999; Eagly & Chaiken, 1993). As with the ELM, the HSM operates on the assumption that individuals rely on two different modes of information processing. One mode, called *systematic processing*, is more thoughtful, deliberate, and analytical. This mode focuses on the content of the message and is roughly analogous to central processing in the ELM. The other mode, called *heuristic processing*, is more reflexive or automatic and is analogous to peripheral processing in the ELM. Heuristic processing is based on the application of what Chaiken and Eagly call *decision rules* or *heuristic cues,* such as mental shortcuts, which simplify information processing and decision making. A person who always tips 15 percent when dining out, regardless of the quality of the food service, would be employing a decision rule. Other examples of decision rules would be "size matters" when buying an SUV, "experts can be trusted" when evaluating a scientific study, or "never pay retail" when shopping for jewelry. According to the HSM, decision rules are stored in memory and activated under the appropriate circumstances. Heuristic cues operate similarly but tend to be based on appearance cues and subjective preferences. A consumer who selected one product or service over another because a celebrity endorser was more attractive, an advertising jingle was more catchy, or a commercial was more vivid than its competitors would be relying on heuristic cues. The activation of systematic processing via decision rules and heuristic cues places fewer cognitive demands on the individual.

Consistent with the ELM, the HSM states that a person's *motivation* and *ability* to process a message are both key determinants of whether a person will rely on systematic or heuristic processing, or both. Chaiken and Eagly also maintained that individuals are "economy-minded" when deciding which mode of processing to use (Chaiken, 1980). Thus, the theory postulates the operation of a *sufficiency principle*, which states that people seek to strike a balance between not thinking enough about a decision and thinking too much about it. According to the HSM, people attempt to expend as much mental energy as they need to, but no more (Chen & Chaiken, 1999).

A difference between the ELM and HSM is that Chaiken and Eagly's HSM explicitly acknowledges the prospect of *simultaneous processing* of messages. That is, messages travel the heuristic and systematic routes concurrently. While the ELM doesn't rule this out, neither does it incorporate simultaneous processing as an explicit assumption of the theory. The HSM assumes that the two routes can operate separately, in combination, or in opposition to one another. The *additivity hypothesis* (Maheswaran, Mackie, & Chaiken, 1992) states that systematic and heuristic processing can complement one another. For example, if a consumer preferred to buy name brand products (heuristic cue) and then read an article in a computer magazine (systematic processing) arguing that name-brand computers were superior to generic "clones," the two forms of processing would reinforce each other. The *bias hypothesis* (Chaiken & Maheswaran, 1994; Chen, Shechter, & Chaiken, 1996) states that initial heuristic processing of a message may bias subsequent systematic processing of the message. As an example, a receiver who thought a source was attractive (heuristic cue) might be more motivated than otherwise to pay attention to a message from that source (systematic processing) and to process ambiguous information contained in the message more favorably. The *attenuation hypothesis* (Chaiken & Maheswaran, 1994; Maheswaren & Chaiken, 1991; Maheswaran, Mackie, & Chaiken, 1992) states that one form of processing can offset or counteract the other. For example, a person who read a novel and admired the author's ideas and use of language (systematic processing) might not care what the author looked like (heuristic cue) if she or he later saw the author on a television talk show.

The ELM and HSM have been shown to have both practical and heuristic value insofar as their ability to explain and predict people's reactions to persuasive messages is concerned. Dozens upon dozens of studies based on these dual-process theories have been carried out on a variety of topics, receivers, and settings. The results to date have generally upheld both theories' utility as comprehensive, integrative explanations of how persuasion functions. While the theories are not without their critics (see Kruglanski, Thompson, & Spiegel, 1999; Mongeau & Stiff, 1993; Stiff & Boster, 1987 for criticisms), it is safe to say that they enjoy considerable support in the literature.

Conclusion

In this chapter we have examined eight different theories of persuasion, social influence, and compliance gaining. Although absorbing eight theories in one fell swoop is enough to make anyone "theory weary," we want to stress the importance of acquiring a solid grasp of basic theoretical frameworks when studying persuasion. Good research, we believe, is or should be theory driven. Theories inform research, and the results of empirical research in turn aid in extending, modifying, refining, and in some cases refuting theories. It is not enough to know that a particular study found a particular result. Theories and models help us to understand not only *what* the results of a study were but also *why* those results were obtained. Thus, to fully understand persuasion, social influence, and compliance gaining, we believe it is important that you learn not only about research findings but also about their theoretical underpinnings.

Even at eight theories, we have only scratched the surface when it comes to the multitude of theoretical explanations of persuasive phenomena. Anyone's list of "greatest baseball players" or "most important films" will likely vary from another person's list, so we apologize in advance if we "stiffed" your favorite theory in our list. Some theories that are specific to particular persuasive strategies (such as a "guilt-based" explanation for the door-in-the-face strategy, or Interpersonal Deception Theory as an explanation of deception detection) are covered in later chapters in this volume.

Hopefully, this review of persuasion theories has provided you with a basic foundation from which to understand various terms, concepts, principles, processes, strategies, and phenomena you will read about as you study persuasion, social influence, and compliance gaining. There are those who would argue that "all a theory and a dollar will get you is a cup of coffee," meaning that theories aren't worth much. We consider theories to be valuable, however, because it is not the findings of studies that tell us how persuasion works, but rather what the findings mean or how they are interpreted in light of prevailing theories of persuasion.

References

Ajzen, I. (1991). The theory of planned behavior. *Organizational Behavior and Human Decision Processes, 50,* 179–211.

Ajzen, I., & Fishbein, M. (1980). *Understanding attitudes and predicting social behavior: Attitudes, intentions and perceived behavioral control.* Englewood Cliffs, NJ: Prentice-Hall.

Ajzen, I., & Fishbein, M. (1977). Attitude-behavior relations: A theoretical analysis and review of empirical research. *Psychological Bulletin, 84,* 88–918.

Ajzen, I., & Fishbein, M. (1973). Attitudinal and normative variables as predictors of specific behaviors. *Journal of Personality and Psychology, 27,* 41–57.

Albarracin, D., Johnson, B. T., Fishbein, M., & Muellerleile, P. A. (2001). Theories of reasoned action and condom usage: A meta-analysis. *Psychological Bulletin, 127*(1), 142–161.

Amir, Y. (1969). Contact hypothesis in ethnic relations. *Psychological Bulletin, 71,* 319–342.

Andersen, J. W. (1989). Unobtrusive measures. In P. Emmert & L. L. Barker (Eds.), *Measurement of communication behavior* (pp. 249–266). White Plains, NY: Longman.

Aronson, J., Cohen, G., & Nail, P. R. (1999). Self-affirmation theory: An update and an appraisal. In E. Harmon-Jones & J. Mills (Eds.), *Cognitive dissonance: Progress on a pivotal theory in social psychology* (pp. 127–147). Washington, DC: American Psychological Association.

Baker, W. E. (1999). When can affective conditioning and mere exposure directly influence brand choice? *Journal of Advertising, 28*(4), 31–47.

Beauvois, J. L., & Joule, R. V. (1999). A radical point of view on dissonance theory. In E. Harmon-Jones & J. Mills (Eds.), *Cognitive dissonance: Progress on a pivotal theory in social psychology* (pp. 43–70). Washington, DC: American Psychological Association.

Berger, C. R., & Burgoon, M. (1995). *Communication and social influence processes.* East Lansing, MI: Michigan State University Press.

Bornstein, R. F. (1989). Exposure and affect: Overview and meta-analysis of research, 1968–1987. *Psychological Bulletin, 106,* 265–289.

Bornstein, R. F., Kale, A. R., & Cornell, K. R. (1990). Boredom as a limiting condition on the mere exposure effect. *Journal of Personality and Social Psychology, 58,* 791–800.

Booth-Butterfield, S., Cooke, P., Andrighetti, A., Casteel, B., Lang, T., Pearson, D., & Rodriguez, B. (1994). Simultaneous versus exclusive processing of persuasive arguments and cues. *Communication Quarterly, 42,* 21–35.

Brickman, P., Redfield, J. Harrison, A. A., & Crandall, R. (1972). Drive and predispositions as factors in the attitudinal effects of mere exposure. *Journal of Experimental Social Psychology, 8,* 31–44.

Burgoon, J. K. (1994). Nonverbal signals. In M. L. Knapp & G. R. Miller (Eds.), *Handbook of interpersonal communication* (2nd ed., pp. 229–285). Thousand Oaks, CA: Sage Publications.

Burgoon, M. (1995). Language Expectancy Theory: Elaboration, explication, and extension. In C. R. Berger & M. Burgoon (Eds.), *Communication and social influence processes* (pp. 29–51). East Lansing, MI: Michigan State University Press.

Burris, C. T., Harmon-Jones, E., & Tarpley, W. R. (1997). "By faith alone": Religious agitation and cognitive dissonance. *Basic Applications of Social Psychology, 19,* 17–31.

Chaiken, S. (1980). Heuristic versus systematic information processing and the use of source versus message cues in persuasion. *Journal of Personality and Social Psychology, 39*, 752–766.

Chaiken, S. (1987). The heuristic model of persuasion. In M. P. Zanna, J. M. Olson, & C. P. Herman (Eds.), *Social influence: The Ontario Symposium* (vol. 5, pp. 3–39). Hillsdale, NJ: Erlbaum.

Chaiken, S., Liberman, A., & Eagly, A. H. (1989). Heuristic and systematic information processing within and beyond the persuasion context. In J. S. Uleman & J. A. Bargh (Eds.), *Unintended thought* (pp. 212–252). New York: Guilford Press.

Chaiken, S., & Maheswaran, D., (1994). Heuristic processing can bias systematic processing: Effects of source credibility, argument ambiguity, and task importance on attitude judgment. *Journal of Personality and Social Psychology, 66*, 460–473.

Chaiken, S., & Trope, Y. (Eds.). (1999). *Dual process theories in social psychology*. New York: Guilford Press.

Chen, S., & Chaiken, S. (1999). The heuristic-systematic model in its broader context. In S. Chaiken & Y. Trope (Eds.), *Dual process theories in social psychology* (pp. 73–96). New York: Guilford Press.

Chen, S., Shechter, D., & Chaiken, S. (1996). Getting at the truth or getting along: Accuracy versus impression motivated heuristic and systematic information processing. *Journal of Personality and Social Psychology, 71*, 262–275.

Cialdini, R. B., Wosinska, W., Barrett, D. W., Butner, J., & Gornik-Durose, M. (1999). Compliance with a request in two cultures: The differential influence of social proof, commitment/consistency on collectivists and individualists. *Personality and Social Psychology Bulletin, 25*(10), 1242–1253.

Cochran, S. D., Mays, V. M., Ciaretta, J., Caruso, C., & Mallon, D. (1992). Efficacy of the theory of reasoned action in predicting AIDS related risk reduction among gay men. *Journal of Applied Social Psychology, 22*, 1481–1501.

Compton, R. J., Williamson, S., Murphy, S. G., & Heller, W. (2002). Hemispheric differences in affective response: Effects of mere exposure. *Social Cognition, 20*(1), 1–16.

Cooper, J., & Fazio, R. H. (1984). A new look at dissonance theory. *Advances in Experimental Social Psychology, 17*, 229–266.

Corliss, R. (2002, July 15). Should we all be vegetarians? *Time, 160* (3), 48–56.

Cotton, J. L. (1985). Cognitive dissonance in selective exposure. In D. Zillman & J. Bryant (Eds.), *Selective exposure to communication* (pp. 11–33). Hillsdale, NJ: Erlbaum.

Cotton, J. L., & Heiser, R. A. (1980). Selective exposure to information and cognitive dissonance. *Journal of Research in Personality, 14*, 518–527.

Devine, P. G., Tauer, J. M., Barron, K. E., Elliot, A. J., & Vance, K. M. (1999). Moving beyond attitude change in the study of dissonance-related processes. In E. Harmon-Jones & J. Mills (Eds.), *Cognitive dissonance: Progress on a pivotal theory in social psychology* (pp. 297–323). Washington, DC: American Psychological Association.

Dillard, P. (1993). Persuasion past and present: Attitudes aren't what they used to be. *Communication Monographs, 60*(1), 90–97.

Dillehay, R. C. (1973). On the irrelevance of the classical negative evidence concerning the effects of attitudes on behavior. *American Psychologist, 28*, 887–891.

Eagly, A. H., & Chaiken, S. (1993). *The psychology of attitudes*. New York: Harcourt, Brace, Jovanovich.

Eagly, A. H., & Chaiken, S. (1998). Attitude structure and function. In D. T. Gilbert, S. T. Fiske, & G. Lindzey (Eds.), *The handbook of social psychology* (4th ed., vol. 1, pp. 269–322). Boston: McGraw-Hill.

Fazio, R. H. (1986). How do attitudes guide behavior? In R. M. Sorrentino, & E. T. Higgins (Eds.), *The handbook of motivation and cognition: Foundations of social behavior* (pp. 204–243). New York: Guilford Press.

Fazio, R. H., & Zanna, M. P. (1981). Direct experience and attitude-behavior consistency. In L. Berkowitz (Ed.), *Advances in experimental social psychology* (vol. 14, pp. 161–202). New York: Academic Press.

Festinger, L. (1957). *A theory of cognitive dissonance*. Stanford, CA: Stanford University Press.

Festinger, L., & Carlsmith, J. M. (1959). Cognitive consequences of forced-compliance. *Journal of Abnormal and Social Psychology, 58*, 203–210.

Festinger, L. (Ed.). (1964). *Conflict, decision, and dissonance*. Stanford, CA: Stanford University Press.

Fishbein, M., & Ajzen, I. (1975). *Belief, attitude, intention, and behavior: An introduction to theory and research*. Reading, MA: Addison-Wesley.

Fisher, R. J. (1993). Social desirability bias and the validity of indirect questioning. *Journal of Consumer Research, 20*, 1993.

Furnham, A. (1986). Response bias, social desirability, and assimilation. *Personality and Individual Difference, 7*, 385–400.

Gastil, J. (2000). Thinking, drinking, and driving: An application of the theory of reasoned action to DWI prevention. *Journal of Applied Social Psychology, 30*(11), 2217–2232.

Godin, G., Maticka-Tynadale, E., Adrien, A., Manson-Singer, S., Williams, D., & Cappon, P. (1996). Cross-cultural testing of three social cognitive theories: An application to condom use. *Journal of Applied Social Psychology, 26*, 1556–1586.

Granberg, D., & Holmberg, S. (1990). Intention-behavior relationship among U.S. and Swedish voters. *Social Psychology Quarterly, 53*, 44–54.

Greene, K., Hale, J. L., & Rubin, D. L. (1997). A test of the Theory of Reasoned Action in the context of condom use and AIDS. *Communication Reports, 10*(1), 21–33.

Greenwald, A. G., & Ronis, D. L. (1978). Twenty years of cognitive dissonance: Case study of the evolution of a theory. *Psychological Review, 85*(1), 53–57.

Hamid, P. N. (1973). Exposure frequency and stimulus preference. *British Journal of Psychology, 64*, 569–577.

Hamilton, M. A., Hunter, J. E., & Boster, F. J. (1993). The elaboration likelihood model as a theory of attitude formation: A mathematical analysis. *Communication Theory, 3*, 50–65.

Harmon-Jones, E. (1999). Toward an understanding of the motivation underlying dissonance effects: Is the production of aversive consequences necessary? In E. Harmon-Jones & J. Mills (Eds.), *Cognitive dissonance: Progress on a pivotal theory in social psychology* (pp. 71–99). Washington, DC: American Psychological Association.

Harrison, A. A. (1977). Mere exposure. In L. Berkowitz (Ed.), *Advances in experimental social psychology* (vol. 10, pp. 39–83). New York: Academic Press.

Heider, F. (1958). *The psychology of interpersonal relations*. New York: John Wiley.

Heyduk, R. G. (1975). Rated preference for musical compositions as it relates to complexity and exposure frequency. *Perception and Psychophysics, 17*, 84–91.

Jacoby, L. L., & Kelley, C. M. (1990). An episodic view of motivation: Unconscious influences on memory. In E. T. Higgins & R. M. Sorrentino (Eds.), *The handbook of motivation and cognition* (vol. 2, pp. 451–581). New York: Guilford Press.

Kelman, H. C. (1974). Attitudes are alive and well and gainfully employed in the sphere of action. *American Psychologist, 29*, 310–324.

Kim, M-S., & Hunter, J. E. (1993a). Attitude-behavior relations: A meta-analysis of attitudinal relevance and topic. *Journal of Communication, 43*, 101–142.

Kim, M-S., & Hunter, J. E. (1993b). Relationships among attitudes, behavioral intentions, and behavior: A meta-analysis of past research, part 2. *Communication Research, 20*, 331–364.

Klingle, R. S. (1996). Physician communication as a motivational tool for long-term patient compliance: Reinforcement expectancy theory. *Communication Studies, 47*, 206–217.

Krauss, S. J. (1995). Attitudes and the prediction of behavior: A meta-analysis of the empirical literature. *Personality and Social Psychology Bulletin, 21*, 58–75.

Kruglanski, A. W., Thompson, E. P., & Spiegel, S. (1999). Separate or equal?: Bimodal notions of persuasion and a single process "unimodel." In S. Chaiken, & Y. Trope (Eds.), *Dual process theories in social psychology* (293–313). New York: Guilford Press.

Lee, A. Y. (2001). The mere exposure effect: An uncertainty reduction explanation revisited. *Personality and Social Psychology Bulletin, 27*(10), 1255–1266.

Lee, C., & Greene, R. T. (1991). Cross-cultural examination of the Fishbein behavioral intention model. *Journal of International Business Studies, second quarter*, 289–305.

Maheswaran, D., & Chaiken, S. (1991). Promoting systematic processing in low-motivation settings:

Effect of incongruent information on processing and judgment. *Journal of Personality and Social Psychology, 61,* 13–25.

Maheswaran, D., Mackie, D. M., & Chaiken, S. (1992). Brand name as a heuristic cue: The effects of task importance and expectancy conformation on consumer judgments. *Journal of Consumer Psychology, 1,* 317–336.

Mills, J. (1999). Improving the 1957 version of cognitive dissonance theory. In E. Harmon-Jones & J. Mills (Eds.), *Cognitive dissonance: Progress on a pivotal theory in social psychology* (pp. 25–42). Washington, DC: American Psychological Association.

Mongeau, P. A., & Stiff, J. B. (1993). Specifying causal relationships in the Elaboration Likelihood Model. *Communication Theory, 3,* 65–72.

Moreland, R. L., & Zajonc, R. B. (1977). Is stimulus recognition a necessary condition for the occurrence of exposure effects? *Journal of Personality and Social Psychology, 35,* 191–199.

Newcomb, T. M. (1953). An approach to the study of communicative acts. *Psychological Review, 60,* 393–404.

Osgood, C. E., & Tannenbaum, P. H. (1955). The principle of congruity in the prediction of attitude change. *Psychological Review, 62,* 42–55.

Osgood, C. E., Tannenbaum, P. H., & Suci, G. J. (1957). *The measurement of meaning.* Urbana, IL: University of Illinois Press.

Park, H. S., Levine, T. R., & Sharkey, W. F. (1998). The theory of reasoned action and self-construals: Understanding recycling in Hawaii. *Communication Studies, 49*(3), 196–208.

Patry, A. L., & Pelletier, L. G. (2001). Extraterrestrial beliefs and experiences: An application of the theory of reasoned action. *The Journal of Social Psychology, 141*(2), 199–217.

Perlman, D., & Oskamp, S. (1971). The effects of picture content and exposure frequency on evaluations of Negroes and Whites. *Journal of Personality and Social Psychology, 7,* 503–514.

Petty, R. E., & Cacioppo, J. T. (1986a). The Elaboration Likelihood Model of persuasion. In L. Berkowitz (Ed.), *Advances in experimental social psychology* (vol. 19, pp. 123–205). New York: Academic Press.

Petty, R. E., & Cacioppo, J. T. (1986b). *Communication and persuasion: Central and peripheral routes to attitude change.* New York: Springer-Verlag.

Petty, J. T., Kasmer, J. E., Haugtvedt, C. P., & Cacioppo, J. T. (1987). Source and message factors in persuasion: A reply to Stiff's critique of the Elaboration Likelihood Model. *Communication Monographs, 54,* 233–249.

Petty, R. E., Wegener, D. T., & Fabrigar, L. R. (1997). Attitudes and attitude change. *Annual Review of Psychology, 48,* 609–647.

Scher, S. J., & Cooper, J. (1989) The motivational basis of dissonance: The singular role of behavioral consequences. *Journal of Personality and Social Psychology, 56,* 899–906.

Sheppard, B. H., Hartwick, J., & Warshaw, P. R. (1988). The theory of reasoned action: A meta-analysis of past research with recommendations for modifications and future research. *Journal of Consumer Research, 15,* 325–343.

Sherif, M., & Sherif, C. W. (1967). Attitudes as the individual's own categories: the social-judgment approach to attitude and attitude change. In C. W. Sherif & M. Sherif (Eds.), *Attitude, ego-involvement, and change* (pp. 105–139). New York: Wiley.

Sherif, C. W., Sherif, M., & Nebergall, R. E. (1965). *Attitude and attitude change: The social judgment-involvement approach.* Philadelphia: W. B. Saunders.

Smith, E. R., & Zarate, M. A. (1992). Exemplar-based model of social judgment. *Psychological Review, 99,* 3–21.

Snyder, M. (1974). Self-monitoring of expressive behavior. *Journal of Personality and Social Psychology, 30,* 526–537.

Snyder, M. (1979). Self-monitoring processes. In L. Berkowitz (Ed.), *Advances in experimental and social psychology* (vol. 12, pp. 85–128). New York: Academic Press.

Stang, D. J., & O'Connell, E. J. (1974). The computer as experiment in social psychology research. *Behavior Research Methods and Instrumentation, 6,* 223–231.

Steele, C. M. (1988). The psychology of self-affirmation: Sustaining the Integrity of the Self. In L. Berkowitz (Ed.), *Advances in Experimental Social Psychology* (pp. 261–302). San Diego, CA: Academic Press.

Steen, D. M., Peay, M. Y., & Owen, N. (2000). Predicting Australian adolescents' intentions to minimize sun exposure. *Psychology and Health, 13*(1), 111–119.

Stiff, J. B. (1986). Cognitive processing of persuasion message cues: A meta-analytic review of supporting information on attitudes. *Communication Monographs, 53*, 75–89.

Stiff, J. B. ,& Boster, F. J. (1987). Cognitive processing: Additional thoughts and a reply to Petty, Kasmer, Haugtveldt, and Cacioppo. *Communication Monographs, 54*, 250–256.

Stone, J., Wygand, A. W., Cooper, J., & Aronson, E. (1997). When exemplification fails: Hypocrisy and the motive for self-integrity. *Journal of Personality and Social Psychology, 72*, 54–65.

Toneatto, T., & Binik, Y. (1987). The role of intentions, social norms, and attitudes in the performance of dental flossing: A test of the theory of reasoned action. *Journal of Applied Social Psychology, 17*, 593–603.

Trafimow, D., & Miller, A. (1996). Predicting and understanding mental practice. *Journal of Social Psychology, 136*, 173–180.

Vallerand, R. J., Deshaies, P., Cuerrier, J. P., Pelletier, L. G., & Mongeau, C. (1992). Ajzen and Fishbein's theory of reasoned action as applied to moral behavior: A confirmatory analysis. *Journal of Personality and Social Psychology, 62*, 98–109.

Wicker, A. W. (1969). Attitudes versus actions: The relationship of verbal and overt behavioral responses to attitude objects. *Journal of Social Issues, 25*, 41–78.

Wood, W. (2000). Attitude change: Persuasion and social influence. *Annual Review of Psychology, 51*, 539–570.

Zajonc, R. B. (2001). Mere exposure: A gateway to the subliminal. *Current Directions in Psychological Science, 10*(6), 224–228.

Zajonc, R. B. (1968). Attitude effects of mere exposure. *Journal of Personality and Social Psychology Monograph Supplement, 9*, (2, Pt. 2), 1–28.

Zajonc, R. B., & Rajecki, D. W. (1969). Exposure and affect: A field experiment. *Psychonomic Science, 17*, 216–217.

Zajonc, R. B., Shaver, P., Tavris, C., & Van Kraveld, D. (1972). Exposure, satiation, and stimulus discriminability. *Journal of Personality and Social Psychology, 21*, 270–280.

5

The Elaboration Likelihood Model of Persuasion

Richard E. Petty, Derek D. Rucker,
George Y. Bizer, and John T. Cacioppo

The Art of Persuasion: The Early Years

The study of persuasion and rhetoric dates back to the time of the ancient Greeks. In those times, persuasion was seen as the instrument by which debates could be resolved, individuals could be educated, and ideas could be communicated to an audience. Given that persuasion was such a vital aspect of Greek society, understanding the factors responsible for social influence was crucial. Recognizing this, Aristotle, one of the great thinkers of the time, provided a theory that specified what a speaker needed to know in order to understand how to persuade others. Aristotle reasoned that to be successful at persuasion, one had to understand characteristics of the source (*ethos*), the message (*logos*), and the emotions of the audience (*pathos;* Aristotle, 1954). For example, Aristotle remarked that if a source were well respected, it would be easier to persuade others of his views than if he was not well respected.

In the 2,400 years that have passed since the time of the ancient Greeks, the art of persuasion has become an even more integral part of society. Persuasion has become the chief tool by which important legislation gets passed, products get sold, and parents influence their children. Furthermore, it is Aristotle's ideas that provided the foundation for much of the early work on persuasion in the twentieth century. Nowhere is this more evident than in the work and theorizing of Carl Hovland and his colleagues who began assessing the effects of variables related to the source, the message, and the audience on the impact of persuasive attempts (Hovland, Janis, & Kelley, 1953; Hovland, Lumsdaine, & Sheffield, 1949; Hovland & Weiss, 1951). Early research in persuasion was guided by the belief that any given variable, for example, source credibility, had a single and unitary effect on persuasion: A variable was thought either to enhance the success of a persuasive attempt or reduce it. Furthermore, there was an assumption that there was one mechanism by which the effect was produced, for example, source credibility enhanced persuasion by increasing learning of the message. In essence, this research followed a "single effect" and "single process" approach to understanding the impact of variables on persuasion (see Petty, 1997). Thus, the goal of this research was to determine what the single effect of a variable was and what the process was by which this variable worked.

Initial endeavors following this approach appeared promising. For example, following Aristotle's notion of ethos, researchers found that credible sources increased persuasion (Hovland & Weiss, 1951). Following Aristotle's concept of logos, researchers found that increasing the number of arguments in favor of a position increased the overall amount of persuasion (Calder, Insko, Yandell, 1974). Finally, researchers following Aristotle's concept of pathos found that placing the audience in a negative emotional state reduced persuasion (Zanna, Kiesler, & Pilkonis, 1970). Furthermore, the researchers tied the effects of these variables to single processes. For example, negative emotion was said to reduce persuasion because of classical conditioning (Staats & Staats, 1958).

Although some early research was consistent with the idea that a variable had a single effect on persuasion via one mechanism, the single-effect and single-process approach soon became untenable. Research on persuasion began to experience a period of chaos and turmoil because subsequent research findings contradicting early results began to appear in the literature. For example, subsequent research on increasing the number of arguments in a message found that more arguments did not always lead to greater attitude change (Norman, 1976). Subsequent research on source credibility and negative emotions found that sometimes highly credible sources could be associated with reduced persuasion (e.g., Sternthal, Dholakia, & Leavitt, 1978) and that negative emotions could be used to increase persuasion (Rogers, 1983). Uncovering different findings led researchers to postulate different processes by which the variables worked. Even when researchers could agree on the single effect that was to be observed, they often disagreed on the process by which the effect came about (e.g., was it dissonance or self-perception?; Greenwald & Ronis, 1978). This state of affairs crippled the approach of searching for the single effect of a given variable and its single process. However, conflicting findings did more than simply destroy this approach: They placed the entire field of attitude change in a state of confusion (e.g., Himmelfarb & Eagly, 1974). This left the state of attitude research in need of a resolution of these apparent contradictions.

The Elaboration Likelihood Model (ELM) (Petty & Cacioppo, 1981, 1986b) was developed to explain and organize past conflicts in the persuasion literature as well as to guide new research. The goal of this chapter is to provide an understanding of the basic tenets of the ELM as a framework for understanding and investigating the effects of persuasive communications. To this end, the key postulates of the ELM are reviewed, and the utility of the model for resolving conflicting findings in the literature and guiding research is highlighted. Furthermore, misconceptions, misinterpretations, and challenges to the model are considered and addressed.

Overview of the Elaboration Likelihood Model.[1]

As articulated in more detail shortly, the ELM outlines a finite number of ways in which variables can impact judgments, and it specifies when variables take on these roles, as well as the consequences resulting from these different roles. That is, the ELM is a theory about the processes underlying changes in attitudes, the variables that induce these processes, and the strength of the judgments resulting from these processes. Unlike the single-process and single-effect approaches described earlier, the ELM does not hold that a given variable has only a single effect on persuasion or influences persuasion by only one process. Instead, the ELM posits that any one variable can influence attitudes in a number of different ways. The same variable, depending on the role it plays, can act either to increase or decrease persuasion. Furthermore, whether the variable serves to increase or decrease persuasion, it can do so through several different mechanisms.

At the core of the ELM is the elaboration continuum. The elaboration continuum is based on a person's *motivation* and *ability* to think about and assess the qualities of the issue-relevant information available in the persuasion context. When both motivation and ability to think are high, individuals are inclined to scrutinize carefully all issue-relevant information stemming from the source, message, context, and themselves (e.g., their emotions) in an attempt to make an accurate judgment about the merits of the issue (called the *central route* to persuasion). However, when either motivation to process is low (e.g., if personal relevance is low) or ability to process is hindered (e.g., if a person is distracted) attitudes can be changed by one or more of a family of relatively low-effort processes (called the *peripheral route* to persuasion).

Thus, the ELM posits that for the sake of simplicity, persuasion can be thought of as following one of two routes to persuasion: central and peripheral. More specifically, in their pure form the two routes to attitude change correspond to anchoring points on an elaboration continuum. The central route entails attitude change that requires much effort and thought to reach a decision. For example, carefully scrutinizing the merits of the substantive information in a message and integrating one's thoughts into a coherent position are prototypical actions based on the central route to persuasion. The second route, the peripheral route, entails attitude change that occurs primarily when elaboration is low, and it can involve thought processes that are quantitatively or qualitatively different from the high-elaboration central route. For example, a low-elaboration processor might carefully scrutinize only the first argument or two rather than all of them (quantitative difference in processing) or might process all of the arguments by counting them rather than scrutinizing them for merit (qualitative difference; see Petty, Wheeler, & Bizer, 1999). What these two processors have in common is the relatively low amount of thought involved in attitude change. The ELM specifies that whether attitude change occurs by the central or the peripheral route has important implications for the strength of the resulting attitude. That is, attitude changes brought about through high-elaboration processes tend to be more persistent, resistant, and predictive of behavior than changes brought about because of low elaboration processes (Petty, Haugtvedt, & Smith, 1995). This issue is discussed further later in this chapter. Of course, since elaboration is a continuum, attitude change is sometimes brought about by a medium amount of thought (rather than very high or low amounts) and can be determined by some combination of central and peripheral route processes.

A key idea of the ELM is that multiple persuasion processes operate along the elaboration continuum, and different persuasion processes require different amounts of thought. That is, the ELM recognizes that attitude change is influenced by a variety of specific processes such as cognitive responses (Greenwald, 1968; Petty, Ostrom, & Brock,

1981), integration of beliefs (Fishbein & Ajzen, 1981), self-perception (e.g., Bem, 1972), classical conditioning (e.g., Staats & Staats, 1958), reliance on heuristics (e.g., Chaiken, 1987), and cognitive dissonance (e.g., Festinger & Carlsmith, 1959). Some of these processes are more likely to influence attitudes at low levels of elaboration (e.g., classical conditioning), others require some minimal amount of thinking (e.g., self-perception), and still others are more likely to influence attitudes at high levels of elaboration (e.g., cognitive responses).

In short, the ELM is a multiprocess theory of persuasion that views persuasion processes as falling along an elaboration continuum. When attitudes change as a result of relatively high amounts of issue-relevant elaboration, people are said to follow the central route, but when attitudes change as a result of relatively low amounts of issue-relevant elaboration, they are said to follow the peripheral route. Whether persuasion occurs through the central or peripheral route is determined by a person's motivation and ability to think about the issue-relevant information available. A schematic representation of the ELM is depicted in figure 5.1. Having provided the basic outline of the model, we now discuss its specific postulates.

Postulates of the Elaboration Likelihood Model

Petty and Cacioppo (1986b) presented the ELM in seven postulates (see also Petty & Wegener, 1999). We do not present the full formal postulates here, only the gist. That is, we explain the essence of the postulates, along with a sampling of research relevant to each.

Postulate 1: The Correctness Postulate

The first postulate of the ELM states that people are motivated to hold what they believe to be "correct" attitudes. Correct attitudes need to be correct, not necessarily logically but in the sense of an individual's subjective appraisal. Correct attitudes are helpful because they often allow people to gain rewards and avoid punishments by approaching helpful objects and avoiding dangerous ones. Holding correct attitudes is important if people want to act on their attitudes.

People can determine which attitude is most correct in a number of ways. When motivation and ability to think are high (such as when the issue is an important one), perhaps the most obvious way for a person to gain confidence in the correctness of one's view is to consider carefully all of the issue-relevant information available. However, if either motivation or ability to think is low, one might attain sufficient confidence, for example, by simply relying on an expert source. If the issue is important but there is insufficient time for processing right now, the person might tag the issue for later scrutiny (see Petty, Jarvis, & Evans, 1996).

The assumption that people want to be correct does not imply that people cannot be biased in their assessment of evidence, however. In fact, being certain that one is correct and wanting to maintain one's correct attitude can lead to defensive processing of contrary information (Petty & Wegener, 1998). The first postulate of the ELM merely assumes that people are rarely explicitly motivated to be biased. Rather than explicitly being motivated

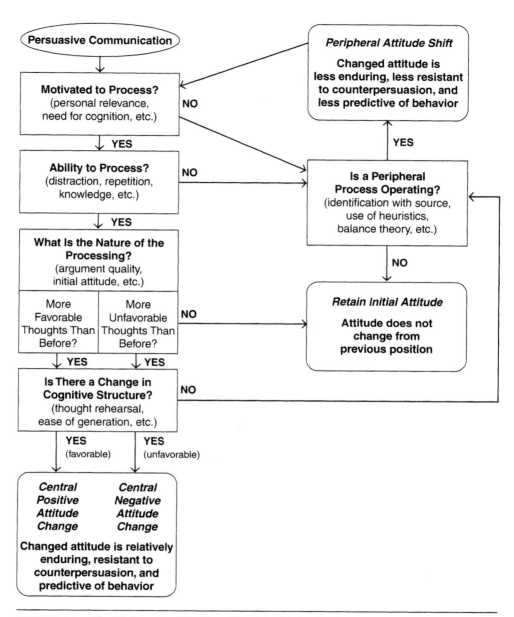

FIGURE 5.1 *The Elaboration Likelihood Model of Attitude Change*

Adapted from Petty & Cacioppo, 1986b.

to be biased, individuals may possess various goals or motivations that will promote bias. For example, people are sometimes motivated to be consistent over time (which can cause them to defend their attitudes), or they can be motivated to impress others, which might lead them to try to see the merits in whatever position a liked individual has (Kelman, 1961).

Postulate 2: The Elaboration Continuum Postulate

The second postulate states that the amount of mental processing (i.e., elaboration) in which a person engages regarding a message varies along a continuum. As stated earlier, at one end of the continuum, the person engages in no thought whatsoever about the issue-relevant information available in the persuasion context. Conversely, at the other end of the continuum, the person engages in extensive elaboration of all information available. Because a continuum exists between extreme and zero elaboration, people can engage in any middling degree of thinking about a persuasive communication.

The elaboration continuum is a *quantitative* dimension. For example, two different people may be elaborating on an advertisement for a mutual fund. One person may be evaluating the message because he is considering where to invest his entire life's savings; the other may be evaluating the message because she is considering where to invest a $50 check. The two people may both be using the arguments in the message to determine if the fund is a wise investment, but one may be evaluating the message more carefully or evaluating more information than the other. In such a case, although both people are engaging in the same *qualitative* process (i.e., thinking about issue-relevant information), they may be exhibiting *quantitative* differences in the extent of processing (cf. Friedrich, Fetherstonhaugh, Casey, & Gallagher, 1996). These quantitative differences in the amount of thought can lead to differences in the strength of the attitudes formed.

It is also possible that people may engage in different *qualitative* processes along the elaboration continuum. Returning to the above example, the individual who is carefully evaluating the message may use the quality of the arguments as the primary determinant of whether to invest in a particular fund. However, the individual who is not carefully evaluating the message may use the mere number of arguments rather than their quality to decide whether or not to invest her money in the fund. For example, if there are nine arguments in favor of the fund, the individual may conclude that since there are so many arguments, the fund must be good. Here, the two potential investors are processing the information in a different way both qualitatively and quantitatively. One person is effortfully assessing the merit of the arguments, whereas the other is using the less cognitively demanding strategy of counting the arguments. This might lead the potential investors to reach very different conclusions. For instance, if the nine arguments are all specious, the person processing the information by the counting mechanism should be more persuaded by nine weak arguments than by three strong arguments for the fund. Conversely, the person who is evaluating the merits of the arguments should be less persuaded by nine weak rather than by three strong arguments (see Petty & Cacioppo, 1984b). Thus, at different levels of elaboration, the same processes may be operating in varying degrees (a quantitative difference), or entirely different processes may be operating (qualitative difference).

Returning to the elaboration continuum, what determines where on the continuum the message recipient will fall? As noted earlier, when a person has a high degree of *motivation* and *ability* to elaborate carefully on the message arguments, processing will be further toward the central end of the continuum. When the person lacks either motivation or ability, the processing will be closer to the peripheral end. Consider an advertisement with a long list of arguments detailing the merits of a particular type of car. Whether people pay close attention to and elaborate on those arguments has much to do with the degree of *motivation* they have to do so. For example, if a person is in the market for a new car, he or she may be highly motivated to scrutinize carefully and think about the relevant information presented. If, however, a person has no interest in purchasing a car in the near future, he or she will lack the motivation to engage in effortful processing. This person is more likely to follow the peripheral route to persuasion (Petty, Cacioppo, & Schumann, 1983).

Next, consider an article about a new antihistamine in a medical journal. If a doctor has spent years in medical school and understands medical jargon, he or she has the *ability* to process the arguments in the article carefully. However, regardless of motivation, a first-year undergraduate student likely lacks the ability to understand and process the medical jargon. This undergraduate will therefore be more likely to resort to the peripheral route to persuasion. Whereas personal relevance serves as a motivational variable in the example involving the new car, knowledge of medical jargon serves as an ability variable in the example involving the antihistamine. A lack of either motivation or ability will move people toward the low end of the elaboration continuum.

It is important to point out that the distinction between high and low elaboration should not be viewed as a distinction between "good" versus "bad" persuasion. For example, the use of the peripheral route can be an adaptive, necessary tool in people's everyday lives. When motivation or capacity is low, one might forgo decision making—which is not always possible—or postpone it until conditions foster it (Petty et al., 1996). It is also important to note that thinking does not ensure an optimal outcome, as one's thoughts can be biased by various contextual factors. For example, when people are spending a lot of time on active thought, their assessment of arguments is biased by their mood states (e.g., DeSteno, Petty, Wegener, & Rucker, 2000; Wegener, Petty, & Klein, 1994).

Postulate 3: The Multiple-Roles Postulate

The third postulate of the ELM states that variables can play multiple roles in persuasion contexts. The role in which a variable is most likely to serve depends on the situation. First, when elaboration is not constrained by other variables to be high or low, variables tend to serve as determinants of the amount of thinking that takes place. Second, when elaboration is low variables tend to serve as cues or input to low-elaboration processes such as classical conditioning and use of decision heuristics (Chaiken, 1980).

Finally, if the elaboration likelihood is set at a high level by other variables in the persuasion context (e.g., high personal relevance, high knowledge, few distractions), variables tend to serve in yet additional roles and lead to persuasion through high-elaboration processes. For example, when people are actively thinking, the variable can be processed as an argument or can bias the ongoing information-processing activity. Thus, depending on the likelihood of elaboration in any context, variables can influence attitudes in a multitude of ways.

As an example of a variable serving in multiple roles depending on context, consider a person's mood state. Depending on the situation, mood can serve in a variety of roles specified by the ELM. First, a person's mood can serve as a determinant of the extent of elaboration when thinking is not already constrained to be high or low by other variables. Based on the Hedonic Contingency Model (Wegener & Petty, 1994) which holds that people in a positive mood are especially motivated to maintain this state, Wegener, Petty, and Smith (1995) hypothesized that being in a positive mood should enhance message elaboration relative to a sad mood if the message recipient believed that processing the message was likely to make people feel happy. Conversely, being in a positive mood should lead to less elaboration than a sad mood if an individual believed that processing the message would be likely to make people feel negative. To test this idea, Wegener and colleagues (1995) told some individuals that processing an upcoming message would be a generally positive or a negative experience. In actuality, everyone received the same message. When happy people expected processing the message to be uplifting, they processed the message more carefully than did people in a sad mood. However, when people expected processing the message to be unpleasant, happy individuals did not process the message as carefully as did individuals in a sad mood (see also Schwarz, Bless, & Bohner, 1991).

According to the ELM, when the likelihood of elaboration is low, mood can serve as a simple cue to decide whether or not to accept a message. This could be the result of a number of processes such as classical conditioning (Razran, 1940) or mood misattribution (Schwarz & Clore, 1983). In the case of mood misattribution, people mistakenly infer their attitude from their mood (e.g., "If I feel good, I must like it"). When the likelihood of elaboration is high, however, mood can serve as an argument (Martin, Abend, Sedikides, & Green, 1997) or bias the ongoing thoughts (Petty et al., 1993).

Research by Petty, Schumann, Richman, and Strathman (1993) provided an illustration of the multiple roles for mood under high- and low-thought conditions. In one study, Petty and colleagues had participants view a series of commercials, one of which contained an advertisement for a pen. Some participants were led to believe that they would get to select a pen as a gift at the end of the study (high-elaboration likelihood), whereas others were led to expect they would select an alternative gift (low-elaboration likelihood). The critical ad for the pen as well as other commercials was placed within a television program that invoked either a positive mood in the participants or invoked no mood. In both high- and low-elaboration conditions, participants rated the advertised pen more favorably when placed in the context of the television program that had invoked a positive mood.

Although the attitudinal effects of mood were the same in the high- and low-elaboration condition, the underlying processes were quite different. Using path analyses, Petty and his colleagues (1993) showed that, whereas mood had a direct effect on attitudes in the low-elaboration condition, the effect of mood on attitudes in the high-elaboration condition was mediated by the valence of thoughts generated. That is, being in a positive mood biased the type of thoughts people generated under high elaboration. Here, mood was not used as a simple cue; instead, mood influenced the valence of thoughts that were generated, and these thoughts in turn influenced attitudes (see Petty, Desteno, & Rucker, 2001, and Petty, Fabrigar, & Wegener, in press, for further discussion of the role of mood at different levels of elaboration). In addition to the work on emotions noted above, a variety of source, message, and recipient factors have also been shown to work in multiple ways in different situations (see Petty, Priester, & Briñol, 2002; Petty & Wegener, 1998, for reviews).

Postulate 4: The Objective-Processing Postulate

The fourth postulate of the ELM addresses situations in which people are engaged in objective processing, that is, they are interested in achieving the "truth" from a message rather than achieving a particular attitude toward a target. In such situations, the fourth postulate states that variables impact a person's motivation and/or ability to process a message by either enhancing or reducing the scrutiny of message arguments. Some variables affect a person's overall motivation to think about the message, whereas others affect his or her overall ability to think about the message. The processing is considered to be "objective" if people follow the evidence wherever it leads. That is, the information processing does not favor one particular outcome over another.

To demonstrate this notion, consider a person who wants to know whether an insurance policy is good or bad. Prior to processing, the person has no stake in the outcome. She may simply hope to learn whether the policy is a sensible one. If motivation and ability in this scenario are high, attitudes will be impacted by how compelling the *issue-relevant arguments* within the message are. Thus, if the arguments within the message are compelling, the recipient will generate favorable thoughts and develop a positive attitude toward the policy. If the arguments within the message are weak, however, she will generate unfavorable thoughts, leading to a relatively unfavorable attitude toward the policy. If, however, motivation or ability is low, her attitude likely will not be affected by scrutiny of the arguments. Rather, attitudes may change because of a peripheral process.

Research on the ELM has identified a large number of variables that influence the amount of thinking people do when confronted with a persuasive message. For example, Petty, Wells, & Brock (1976) demonstrated that distraction can either enhance or diminish attitude change depending on what kinds of thoughts the distraction disrupts. When a message contained compelling arguments, distraction disrupted the favorable thoughts that normally would have been elicited, thereby decreasing persuasion. However, when a message contained specious arguments, distraction disrupted the unfavorable thoughts that normally would have been elicited and thereby increased persuasion. Thus, distraction itself did not impact persuasion directly. Rather, it impacted the extent to which the arguments within the message were processed and thereby influenced the extent of attitude change.

In addition to distraction, other variables that have been shown to influence a person's ability to process a message include the message's complexity (Hafer, Reynolds, & Obertynski, 1996), the time a person has to process the message (Kruglanski & Freund, 1983), the number of opportunities a person has to scrutinize the arguments (e.g., Cacioppo & Petty, 1979), and a person's knowledge of the message topic (e.g., Wood, Kallgren, & Preisler, 1985). Variables that have been shown to affect a person's overall motivation to think about a message include the personal relevance of the communication (e.g., Petty & Cacioppo, 1979, 1990), an individual's need for cognition (Cacioppo, Petty, & Morris, 1983), one's personal responsibility for evaluating the message (Petty, Harkins,

& Williams, 1980), the expectation of having to discuss the message with someone else (Chaiken, 1980), presentation of the message in an unexpected format (Smith & Petty, 1996), and presentation of a message on a topic about which people feel ambivalent (Maio, Bell, & Esses, 1996).

Postulate 5: The Biased-Processing Postulate

Variables not only affect the amount of thinking that takes place but can also influence the nature of the thought process. Thus, the fifth postulate of the ELM deals with biased processing. Some variables affect a person's motivation to generate certain kinds of thoughts, whereas other variables affect a person's ability to generate certain kinds of thoughts.

Consider, for example, a situation in which a person has just purchased a new computer. She likely holds a positive attitude toward that computer and probably wants to maintain that positive attitude because it would be dissonance-arousing to believe that one's choice was incorrect (see Harmon-Jones & Mills, 1999, for a recent review of dissonance work). If she reads a *Consumer Reports* article shortly after purchasing her new computer, it is not likely that she will process the article in an objective manner. Because the person *wants* to hold a positive attitude, she will be motivated to think positive thoughts about the message. She will try to see any arguments presented in regard to the computer she purchased in the most favorable light possible.

Other variables can induce a desire to reject the message. For example, forewarning people of a speaker's persuasive intent can motivate counterarguing and resistance to the message (Petty & Cacioppo, 1979). Ability factors can also be important in producing resistance. For example, negative emotional states might make negative thoughts and ideas more readily accessible (Bower, 1981; Forgas, 1995). On the other hand, having a great deal of knowledge in support of one's attitude might make it easier to counterargue messages against one's viewpoint (Wood et al., 1985).

Often, people are not aware of the biases that influence their information processing. However, in some cases people may become aware of a bias that they consider inappropriate and attempt to correct for it (see Petty & Wegener, 1993; Wilson & Brekke, 1994). For example, in one study Petty, Wegener, and White (1998) gave students a persuasive message in favor of a policy requiring senior comprehensive exams that came from a source that either praised the students' school (likable source) or disparaged the students' school (unlikable source). In addition, half of the participants were told that the exam policy was for their own university (high relevance) and half were told the exam was for another university (low relevance). Finally, half of the participants were told not to let their personal opinion of the speaker influence their evaluation of the message. Petty et al. (1998) found that when participants were not cautioned about using their personal opinion of the speaker to evaluate the message, and the issue was low in personal relevance, they were significantly more persuaded by the likable source than by the unlikable source. However, low-involvement participants who were cautioned about using their opinion of the source to form their evaluation were equally persuaded by both the likable and unlikable source. That is, they corrected for the source bias. When the issue was high in personal relevance and participants were not cautioned about the possible source bias, attitudes were not influenced by the source (since, as expected by the ELM, under high-relevance conditions people focused on evaluating the substantive issue-relevant arguments). However, when issue relevance was high and people were forewarned of a possible source bias, people still corrected for a presumed bias, leading them to be more persuaded by the unlikable than by the likable source. This and other research (e.g., Wegener & Petty, 1995; Schwarz & Clore, 1983) has demonstrated that in some circumstances, people will attempt to bias their judgments. If a potential bias is made salient, people can and do correct their attitudes. This can lead them to remove the bias, though if overcorrection occurs, a reverse bias can become apparent.

Postulate 6: The Trade-off Postulate

The sixth postulate predicts a trade-off between the impact of argument elaboration and peripheral route processes on attitudes. That is, as the likelihood of issue-relevant thinking is increased, the impact of central route processes (e.g., examining information for merit) on attitudes increases, and the impact of peripheral route processes (e.g., counting arguments) on attitudes decreases. Conversely, as the likelihood of issue-relevant thinking decreases, the impact of peripheral route processes on attitudes increases, and the impact of central route processes decreases. It is important not to interpret the trade-off postulate as suggesting that certain variables (e.g., sources) are processed only when elaboration is low and others (e.g., message factors) only when elaboration is high. Rather, this postulate holds that variables are more likely to have their impact as a result of a low-effort process when the elaboration likelihood is low but by a higher effort process when the likelihood of elaboration is high. For example, a source variable can be processed under high-elaboration conditions, but it is evaluated for its evidentiary value rather than working by invoking a simple decision heuristic or other means. Likewise, message arguments can be processed under low-elaboration conditions, but the processing is either not as thorough as it is under high elaboration or represents a qualitatively different low-effort mechanism (e.g., counting the arguments rather than evaluating them for merit). It is also important to note that at most points along the elaboration continuum, both central and peripheral processes influence attitudes.

Postulate 7: The Attitude Strength Postulate

The final postulate of the Elaboration Likelihood Model deals with the outcome of message processing. Specifically, this postulate states that attitudes created or changed by the central route will be more persistent over time, will remain more resistant to persuasion, and will exert a greater impact on cognition and behavior than will attitudes changed or created through the peripheral route. That is, although attitudes can be changed to the same degree under the central and peripheral routes, the central route produces "stronger" attitudes. When attitudes are based on high levels of elaboration, people have the necessary "backing" to defend their attitudes against later counterattitudinal persuasion attempts and to maintain the attitude over time. These attitudes will also tend to be more accessible and held with greater confidence. Because of this higher accessibility and confidence, people will be more likely to act on central route attitudes. Attitudes based on peripheral processes and simple cues, however, are less likely to demonstrate these characteristics. Evidence that attitudes formed under high elaboration are stronger than those formed under low elaboration has been found in several studies (e.g., Cacioppo, Petty, Kao, & Rodriguez, 1986; Chaiken, 1980; Haugtvedt & Petty, 1992; see Petty, Haugtvedt, & Smith, 1995, for review and analysis).

Putting It All Together: Resolving Conflicting Findings with the ELM

As stated at the outset of this chapter, the ELM was developed in part to organize and explain apparent contradictions in the persuasion literature. Having reviewed the elaboration continuum and the multiple roles postulates, readers may already have a good grasp of how this is accomplished. Still, an illustration is worthwhile. Consider the effects of source credibility. Recall that early research found that credible sources typically increased persuasion (Hovland & Weiss, 1951), whereas later research found that this was not always the case (Sternthal et al., 1978). Using the ELM as a framework, one can derive specific predictions regarding when a credible source is likely to lead to more, less, or equal persuasion relative to a source of questionable credibility. Consider a situation in which a person is given a message containing either weak or strong arguments and presented either by a source with high credibility or by one with low credibility. How might the credibility of the source impact persuasion? This depends on the amount of elaboration involved.

First, consider the situation in which elaboration is low due to lack of effort or ability. In this case, the individual will not devote much effort to processing issue-relevant information and will instead rely on simple cues to decide whether to accept the message or not. In particular, a high-credibility source may be used as a cue to trust and accept the message, whereas a low-credibility source may be used as a cue to mistrust the message and reject it. Thus, when elaboration is low, the credibility of the source may serve as a peripheral cue invoking a persuasion heuristic (i.e., "experts can be trusted"), leading to more or less persuasion in the absence of much issue-relevant thinking. As a result, regardless of argument quality, people may have less favorable attitudes when the message is presented by a low-credibility source than by a high-credibility source (e.g., Petty, Cacioppo, & Goldman, 1981).

Now consider a situation in which elaboration is high and, as a result, people are motivated to process the arguments of a message. In this example, the credibility of the source may be relatively unimportant as a cue for deciding whether to accept or reject the message. Instead, if the quality of the arguments is unambiguous, only the substance should matter and source expertise is likely to have little impact (Petty, Cacioppo, & Goldman, 1981). However, if the arguments are ambiguous and open to multiple interpretations, expertise might bias the interpretation of the arguments, leading to more favorable interpretations of the arguments when expertise is high (e.g., he must have meant this) rather than low (Chaiken & Maheswaran, 1994).

Finally, consider a situation in which elaboration is moderate. In this situation, learning that the source is credible may cause people to decide the message is worth paying close attention to, leading to an increase in the amount of elaboration given to the message. If the message arguments are strong, those carefully attending to the message should be more persuaded than those who are paying little attention to it. If, however, the message arguments are weak, those carefully attending to the message should actually be less persuaded than those not paying close attention to it. As a result, relative to low-credibility sources, high-credibility sources would be less persuasive when the arguments are weak but more persuasive when the arguments are strong (Heesacker, Petty, & Cacioppo, 1983).

In sum, like the effects of a person's mood state described earlier, an expert source can influence attitudes as a simple persuasion cue when the likelihood of thinking is low, can bias the processing of message arguments when the likelihood of thinking is high, and can determine the extent of thinking when the likelihood of thinking is not constrained. The ELM allows specific predictions regarding when credible sources will lead to more, equal, or less persuasion than sources of questionable credibility. It is also significant that the ELM specifies the underlying processes by which these outcomes occur (see Moore, Hausknecht, & Thamordaran, 1986, for a study documenting multiple roles for source credibility under different elaboration conditions). Similar logic can be applied to resolve other contradictions in the persuasion literature with respect to both outcome and process.

In addition to resolving conflicting findings regarding the outcomes produced and the mechanisms of change of particular variables such as source credibility and mood, the ELM also helped to resolve other conflicting results regarding attitudes. Most notably, postulate 7 regarding attitude strength helped to explain a long-standing puzzle of why some attitudes lasted over time, resisted change, and predicted behavior, whereas other attitudes of the same valence did not. Thus, the ELM is a useful framework for reconciling apparent inconsistencies in the literature and for exploring novel hypotheses.

Confusions and Misinterpretations of the ELM

Although the ELM has proved useful in resolving contradictory findings in the persuasion literature and continues to serve as a useful framework for guiding research, it has not escaped some criticism. On the one hand, criticism that points to logical flaws in a theory or a mismatch between theory and data can be useful in fixing or advancing a theory or, in some cases, for putting a theory to rest. On the other hand, criticism that arises from misunderstandings can lead researchers to reject or modify a satisfactory theory unnecessarily. Several criticisms of the ELM based on misunderstanding of the theory have been made. Below, we address some of the more salient areas of confusion or misinterpretation.

Single- versus Multichannel Information Processing

In one of the earliest questionings of the theory, Stiff (Stiff, 1986; Stiff, 1994; Stiff & Boster, 1987) suggested that the ELM does not accurately reflect the way in which people process information. Stiff argued that the ELM depicts humans as single-channel information processors, capable of processing only peripheral cues *or* message arguments, even though prior research seemed to indicate that humans are capable of parallel information processing (e.g., Kahneman, 1973).

The assumption that the ELM does not allow for dual-channel (or parallel) information processing is simply wrong. Although early presentations of the ELM (Petty & Cacioppo, 1981, 1986a, 1986b) did not comment explicitly on the distinction between single versus parallel processing, the ELM never portrayed information processing as prohibiting parallel processing. This misunderstanding arose from Stiff's (1986) apparent view that because some ELM research has shown that argument quality had an impact on attitudes under high-processing conditions whereas source attractiveness did not (e.g., Petty, Cacioppo, & Schumann, 1983), people could process only arguments, but not sources, under high-elaboration conditions. In stark contrast to this assumption, the ELM holds that people process as much information as possible (including source and message factors) under high-elaboration conditions. This information can be processed either serially or in parallel. Just because information is processed, however, does not mean that it will affect attitudes. Thus, people might be cognizant of the mere number of arguments or the attractiveness of the message source under high-processing conditions but still might not view this information as a valid basis for attitude inference (Petty, Kasmer, Haugtvedt, & Cacippo, 1987; Petty & Wegener, 1999).

Thus, as articulated in our discussion of the trade-off postulate of the ELM, it is not the case that people process only peripheral cues when elaboration likelihood is low and only central arguments when elaboration likelihood is high. Rather, both types of information may be processed. The trade-off postulate addresses the *impact* of central and peripheral processes on attitudes (see Petty et al., 1987, for further commentary on this criticism).

Confusion over Source Versus Message Factors

Perhaps the most common misunderstanding of the ELM can be traced to the multiple-roles postulate—the idea that any one variable is capable of influencing attitudes by different means in different situations. Several researchers (e.g., Stiff, 1986; Kruglanski & Thompson, 1999) have mistakenly viewed the ELM as classifying all message variables (e.g., number of arguments, argument quality) as *arguments* influencing attitudes under the central route and all nonmessage variables (e.g., source credibility, a person's mood) as peripheral *cues* influencing attitudes only under the peripheral route. This has led researchers to claim that the theory cannot explain results of studies in which nonmessage factors (such as source credibility) influenced attitudes under high-elaboration conditions, or where message factors influence attitudes under low elaboration conditions (Kruglanski & Thompson, 1999).

However, as explained in the multiple-roles postulate, the ELM holds that the same variable can serve in different roles, depending on the extent of thinking. For example, early ELM research showed that the attractiveness of the message source could serve as a simple cue and influence attitudes by a heuristic process when thinking is low, but the same manipulation could influence attitudes under high-elaboration conditions if analysis of the variable as an argument provided cogent evidence for the merits of the attitude object (e.g., an attractive spokesperson for a shampoo might provide cogent visual testimony for the effectiveness of the product; Petty & Cacioppo, 1984a). Furthermore, just as early research showed that source variables could serve in multiple roles, so too did early research show that message variables could be processed in a heuristic manner (counting) or a more central manner (evaluating quality; Petty & Cacioppo, 1984b). Thus, source, message, recipient, and contextual variables can influence attitudes under high, low, and moderate levels of elaboration, but the underlying mechanism will vary (see Petty & Wegener, 1999; Petty et al., 1999, for further discussion).

Misunderstandings of the Use of Argument Quality as a Methodological Tool

There are several confusions regarding the use of argument quality (i.e., strong versus weak messages) in research-testing predictions made by the ELM. Some researchers (Mongeau & Stiff, 1993; O'Keefe, 1990) have criticized the ELM for manipulating so-called strong versus weak arguments without specifying the underlying factors that make an argument strong or weak. These criticisms fail to recognize that ELM studies use argument quality primarily as a methodological tool to help differentiate the different roles for variables. For example, if a variable (e.g., source expertise) produces the pattern in the top panel of figure 5.2, it suggests that the variable is serving as a simple cue as the variable increases persuasion regardless of argument quality. On the other hand, if a variable produces the pattern in the bottom panel of figure 5.2, it suggests that the variable is serving to influence the extent of information processing activity (see Petty, Wegener, Fabrigar, Priester, & Cacioppo, 1993).

Other researchers have assumed that argument quality is defined strictly in terms of logical quality or in terms of how likely an attitude object is to possess some attribute (Areni & Lutz, 1988). However, as a methodological tool, manipulations of argument quality refer to any features of the arguments that get people to think favorable thoughts (strong arguments) or unfavorable thoughts (weak arguments) to the advocacy. Petty and Wegener (1991) suggested that strong arguments were those that pointed to highly desirable consequences that would most certainly occur if some advocacy was accepted. These arguments could be made weaker either by pointing to less desirable consequences that would occur if the advocacy was adopted or to desirable consequences that were less likely to occur. That is, arguments could be weakened by reducing either the desirability or the likelihood of the consequences proposed in the argument (see also Fishbein & Ajzen, 1981).

Assertions That the ELM Is Not Falsifiable

Some researchers have argued that the ELM's multiple-roles hypothesis "allows the ELM to explain all possible outcomes of an experimental study" (Stiff & Boster, 1987, p. 251). More recently, Stiff (1994) remarked: "Until the ELM specifies a priori the conditions under which important stimulus variables reflect central processing, a peripheral cue, or both, it will remain impossible to falsify" (p. 188). As discussed earlier, the multiple-roles

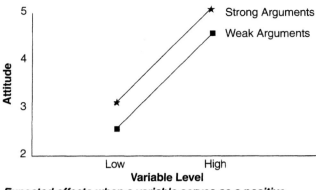

Expected effects when a variable serves as a positive peripheral cue

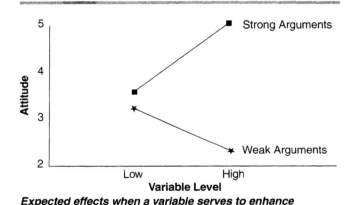

Expected effects when a variable serves to enhance information

FIGURE 5.2   *Argument Quality Versus Quantity with High or Low Involvement*

hypothesis is necessary to understand fully the dynamics of persuasion. However, this postulate does not make the ELM devoid of *a priori* predictions. In fact, the ELM clearly specifies when variables take on the different roles. For example, the predictions for a person's mood and source credibility at different levels of elaboration were discussed earlier, and available research supports these predictions (see also Petty et al., 2002).

Although the ELM postulates multiple roles for variables, it does not say that any role can be assumed at any time. Thus, contrary to Stiff's claim, the ELM does make *a priori* predictions regarding when a given variable (e.g., source attractiveness, mood) has an impact on attitudes by different processes. For example, the ELM holds that variables are more likely to influence attitudes by biasing processing when the elaboration is high and invoking a heuristic when elaboration is low, and that they are more likely to affect the extent of thinking when it is not already constrained to be high or low (moderate elaboration). Therefore, the ELM could be falsified, for example, if a variable produced a greater bias to the ongoing information processing under low- than under high-elaboration conditions, or if simple heuristics (e.g., "more is better") had a larger impact under high than low elaboration conditions.

Restricted Range of Topics

Some researchers (O'Keefe, 1990; Stiff, 1994) have criticized the ELM for relying on a limited number of message topics and message arguments. Specifically, they assert that research on the ELM is confined to message topics involving comprehensive exams and tuition increases. They further contend that a reliance on such a small number of topics challenges the generalizability of the ELM. We agree that confining message topics to comprehensive exams and tuition increases, while not damaging the validity of the theory, could limit its generalizability. However, this criticism reflects a lack of appreciation of the broader literature on the ELM rather than the topics used in some of the most widely cited studies.

While it is true that initial research on the ELM involved studies using the topics of comprehensive exams (e.g., Petty & Cacioppo, 1984a, 1984b; Petty, Cacioppo, & Goldman, 1981; Puckett, Petty, Cacioppo, & Fisher, 1983) and tuition increases (e.g., Cacioppo, Petty, & Morris, 1983), subsequent research has used a variety of diverse topics. A cursory review of the literature reveals experiments testing and confirming hypotheses of the ELM using topics such as condom use (Helweg-Larsen & Howell, 2000), the city sales tax (Desteno et al., 2001), the foster care system (Petty et al., 1993, experiment 2; Wegener, Petty, & Smith, experiment 1), nuclear power (Fabrigar, Priester, Petty, & Wegener, 1998, exp. 1; Haugtvedt & Wegener, 1994), vegetarianism (Fabrigar et al., 1998, exp. 2), and environmental conservation (Wood, Kallgren, & Priesler, 1985).

In addition to these social issues, research using the ELM framework has also been conducted with a variety of advertising messages for goods and services such as answering machines (Haugtvedt & Petty, 1992), bicycles (Haugtvedt & Strathman, 1990), cameras (Laczniak & Carlson, 1989), detergent (Shavitt & Brock, 1986), low-alcohol beer (Andrews & Shimp, 1990), food additives (Haugtvedt & Petty, 1992), pens (Petty et al., 1993, experiment 1), restaurants (Shavitt, Swan, Lowery, & Wanke, 1994), shampoo (Petty & Wegener, 1998), and vitamins (Smith & Petty, 1996).

The above research represents only a scant number of the diverse topics that have been studied under the framework of the ELM. Consequently, upon examination of the breadth of the literature on the ELM, it is clear that the ELM generalizes to multiple topics beyond senior comprehensive exams and tuition increases.

Replacing the ELM with a Single-Process Model of Persuasion

Perhaps the most ambitious critique of the ELM—and other multiprocess models of social judgment—comes from Kruglanski and Thompson (1999), who argued that a single route to persuasion was a more parsimonious way to account for the various persuasion findings generated by the ELM (and the related Heuristic-Systematic Model; Chaiken, Liberman, & Eagly, 1989). In proposing their unimodel, Kruglanski and Thompson (1999) argued that there are no *qualitative* differences between the two routes to persuasion. Instead, all that is necessary to account for persuasion is the elaboration continuum that ranges from minimal processing on one end to maximal processing on the other. The central and peripheral routes to persuasion are then solely a function of depth or extent of processing, and no qualitatively different processes operate along this continuum as specified by the ELM.

To make this point, Kruglanski and Thompson (1999) proposed that both cues and arguments could be conceptualized as types of "evidence." In this conceptualization, all forms of evidence can fit into Kruglanski's Lay Epistemic Theory (LET; Kruglanksi, 1989) in which evidence, when considered with its paired relevance, leads to attitude change. According to Kruglanski and Thompson, because both arguments and cues can be considered as "evidence," there is no need or theoretical rationale to differentiate them.

At first glance, the unimodel may seem attractive due to its parsimony. On the other hand, if it is useful to distinguish two or more qualitatively different processes of persuasion, the unimodel, though parsimonious, would not be accurate. As should be clear from our presentation earlier, the ELM highlights a continuum based on the extent of careful examination of the relevant evidence (the elaboration continuum). In fact, a considerable amount of persuasion results can be accounted for with just this continuum. However, in contrast to the unimodel, the ELM holds that different persuasion *processes* operate along this continuum and that some of these processes are qualitatively different from each other. Many variables can be viewed as "evidence," but how a person processes this evidence is what determines the effect that the variable has on persuasion. For example, an attractive source can be input to the heuristic "if she likes it, so do I," in which case anything that the attractive source endorses will be more persuasive (peripheral route). Alternatively, the attractive source can be evaluated as an argument so that the attractive source is persuasive when attractiveness is relevant and cogent (e.g., "if his hair looks great from using that shampoo, it must be a good product, so I'll buy it too") but is unpersuasive when irrelevant (e.g., "her hair is nice but what does that have to do with this refrigerator?"). Or to return to an example we used earlier, evaluating the arguments in a message by simply counting them (i.e., using the arguments as a numerical heuristic) versus carefully scrutinizing those arguments for merit can lead to different persuasion outcomes (Petty & Cacioppo, 1984b). Though Kruglanski and Thompson (1999) may contend that there is no interesting qualitative difference between counting and scrutinizing messages, proponents of the ELM argue that counting and elaborating are more than simple opposite ends of a quantitative continuum; they are two distinct, qualitatively different processes that can produce fundamentally different outcomes when applied to the *same* evidence. Furthermore, the ELM holds that there are other qualitatively different psychological processes (e.g., dissonance versus self-perception) that are of interest in understanding persuasion (Petty & Cacioppo, 1986a). The ELM specifically postulates that many of these processes operate at different points along the elaboration continuum and require different amounts of cognitive effort (i.e., a quantitative difference). But the difference in cognitive effort is not the only difference among these processes. Because of their qualitative differences, these processes often specify different mediators and moderators of persuasion effects (e.g., dissonance focuses on the presence of aversive arousal, whereas self-perception does not). This richness and predictive power is lost by focusing solely on quantitative differences in amount of thought. In sum, because of its accommodation of both qualitative and quantitative differences in persuasion processes, we believe that the ELM remains a more satisfactory model for accounting for persuasion effects than the unimodel.

Directions for Future Research

So far we have explained the ELM and addressed various controversies that have arisen regarding the model. Before concluding this chapter, we turn to a discussion of some current directions in persuasion research that have stemmed from an appreciation of the ELM.

Self-Validation Processes

The postulate of the ELM that has received the least research attention to date is the first one, that people seek correct attitudes. This postulate has been used in two ways. First, it helps to explain why people engage in greater information processing in certain circumstances than they do in others. That is, because careful scrutiny is often a good way to determine correctness, people will engage in more effortful scrutiny when it is important to be correct, such as when a message has high consequences for the self (Petty, Cacioppo, & Haugtvedt, 1992; Petty, Wheeler, & Bizer, 2000). Second, this postulate implies that in the absence of competing motives (e.g., consistency, reactance, impression management), the default goal is to be correct and to attempt to process messages in a relatively objective way.

Recent research has suggested another consequence of the correctness motive. Specifically, in some circumstances people will reflect on the validity of their thoughts and attitudes (referred to as *self-validation* processes; Petty, Briñol, & Tormala, 2002). For example, with respect to *attitude validation,* consider a person who has just processed a message and rejected it. Because the attitude survived an attack, the person might gain confidence in this attitude. In fact, in a series of studies, Tormala and Petty (in press) showed that the stronger the attack people believe their attitude resisted, the more confidence they gain in it. Furthermore, this enhanced confidence led people to be more willing to act on their attitudes. Thus, attitude validation processes can increase attitude strength.

People may also sometimes reflect on the validity of the individual thoughts that they have in response to a persuasive message. For example, in a series of studies on *thought validation,* Tormala, Petty, and Briñol (in press), showed that the easier it was for people to generate thoughts on a message, the more confidence they had in them, and the more they relied on them in forming their attitudes. In particular, these investigators made some people feel that generating favorable thoughts to a message was easy, because their task was to generate only two favorable thoughts to the arguments. Others were made to feel that generating favorable thoughts was difficult because eight were requested (see also Schwarz et al., 1991). When it was easy to generate favorable thoughts, people had more confidence in these thoughts and were more persuaded by the message than when it felt more difficult to generate the thoughts. Conversely, when people felt it was easy to generate counterarguments to the message because only two were requested, they were less persuaded than when they felt it was hard to generate counterarguments. Thus, research on self-validation processes suggests that another role for variables in persuasion settings is that they can help people assess the validity of their thoughts and attitudes. Numerous variables may influence attitudes and attitude strength in this way (e.g., people may be more confident in their favorable thoughts if they were generated in response to a source of high rather than low credibility).

Consequences of Objective Versus Biased Thinking

The ELM makes an important distinction between processing that is relatively objective versus that which is biased. Understanding whether a variable (e.g., source credibility, mood) is enhancing objective processing or imparting a bias to the processing is important for understanding both the valence of thoughts produced and the ultimate persuasion outcome. Recently, Rucker and Petty (2002) have discussed some implications of biased versus objective processing for the strength of the attitudes resulting from persuasion.

In an initial series of studies on this issue, Rucker and Petty (2002) compared situations in which individuals were instructed to process a message in a relatively objective manner (try to generate thoughts) or in a biased manner (try to generate negative thoughts). These participants were exposed to a message favoring a brand of aspirin that contained very strong arguments. Although both the objective and biased groups showed equivalent attitude change to these strong arguments, and equivalent amounts of cognitive effort in processing the message, individuals who had focused on finding fault with the message reported more certainty in their changed attitudes. Furthermore, the attitudes of individuals who had tried but failed to find fault were more predictive of subsequent behavioral intentions toward the aspirin. Rucker and Petty (2002) argued that people who tried to find fault but failed were more cognizant of the fact that the aspirin had no faults than were people who simply processed the message objectively. The latter group was cognizant mostly of the favorable aspects of the aspirin. Subsequent analyses confirmed that perceptions about the lack of negative features of the aspirin mediated the increased certainty in the changed attitudes. This research shows that qualitatively different approaches to processing the message can lead to differences in attitude strength even when the extent of message elaboration appears to be constant.

Conclusion

This chapter began by noting the chaos in attitude and persuasion research reflected by numerous conflicting findings in the literature and then focused on explaining how the ELM can organize past inconsistent findings in a manner that allows researchers to predict when a variable might have a given effect, and when a particular process responsible for that effect might occur. Furthermore, the chapter has provided representative examples of research based on the ELM framework throughout. Finally, in addition to stressing the utility of the model in explaining past conundrums in the literature, this chapter has focused on clarifying misconceptions about the ELM and pointing to directions for future research. In particular, recent work on people's assessment of the validity of their thoughts and attitudes has provided new means by which variables can affect persuasion (by affecting thought confidence) and attitude strength (by affecting attitude confidence).

Notes

1. Although not discussed in this chapter, other models of persuasion and social judgment have been developed that share a number of the features of the ELM. A discussion of these models is beyond the scope of this chapter, but the interested reader is referred to a compendium of dual-process models of social judgment in Chaiken and Trope (1999) and a comparison of the ELM with some of these models by Petty and Wegener (1998, 1999) and Petty, Fabrigar, and Wegener (in press).

References

Andrews, J. C., & Shimp, T. A. (1990). Effects of involvement, argument strength, and source characteristics on central and peripheral processing. *Psychology and Marketing, 7,* 195–214.

Areni, C. S., & Lutz, R. J. (1988). The role of argument quality in the Elaboration Likelihood Model. *Advances in Consumer Research, 15,* 197–203.

Aristotle, (1954). *Rhetoric.* In W. Roberts (trans.), *Aristotle, rhetoric and poetics.* New York: Modern Library.

Bem, D. J. (1972). Self-perception theory. In L. Berkowitz (Ed.), *Advances in experimental social psychology* (vol. 6, pp. 1–62). New York: Academic Press.

Bower, G. (1981). Mood and memory. *American Psychologist, 36,* 129–148.

Cacioppo, J. T., & Petty, R. E. (1979). Effects of message repetition and position on cognitive responses, recall, and persuasion. *Journal of Personality and Social Psychology, 37,* 97–109.

Cacioppo, J. T., Petty, R. E., Kao, C., & Rodriguez, R. (1986). Central and peripheral routes to persuasion: An individual difference perspective. *Journal of Personality and Social Psychology, 51,* 1032–1043.

Cacioppo, J. T., Petty, R. E., & Morris, K. J. (1983). Effects of need for cognition on message evaluation, recall, and persuasion. *Journal of Personality and Social Psychology, 45,* 805–818.

Calder, B. J., Insko, C. A., & Yandell, B. (1974). The relation of cognition and memorial processes to persuasion in a simulated jury trial. *Journal of Applied Social Psychology, 4,* 62–93.

Chaiken, S. (1980). Heuristic versus systematic information processing in the use of source versus message cues in persuasion. *Journal of Personality and Social Psychology, 39,* 752–766.

Chaiken, S. (1987). The heuristic model of persuasion. In M. P. Zanna, J. M. Olson, & C. P. Herman (Eds.), *Social influence: The Ontario symposium* (vol. 5, pp. 3–39). Hillsdale, NJ: Erlbaum.

Chaiken, S., Liberman, A., & Eagly, A. H. (1989). Heuristic and systematic information processing within and beyond the persuasion context. In J. S. Uleman & J. A. Bargh (Eds.), *Unintended thought* (pp. 212–252). New York: Guilford.

Chaiken, S., & Maheswaran, D. (1994). Heuristic processing can bias systematic processing: Effects of source credibility, argument ambiguity, and task importance on attitude judgment. *Journal of Personality and Social Psychology, 66,* 460–473.

Chaiken, S., & Trope, Y. (Eds.). (1999). *Dual-process theories in social psychology.* New York: Guilford Press.

DeSteno, D., Petty, R. E., Wegener, D. T., & Rucker, D. D. (2000). Beyond valence in the perception of likelihood: The role of emotion specificity. *Journal of Personality and Social Psychology, 78,* 397–416.

Fabrigar, L. R., Priester, J. R., Petty, R. E., & Wegener, D. T. (1998). The impact of attitude accessibility on elaboration of persuasive messages. *Personality and Social Psychology Bulletin, 24,* 339–352.

Festinger, L., & Carlsmith, J. M. (1959). Cognitive consequences of forced compliance. *Journal of Abnormal and Social Psychology, 58,* 203–210.

Fishbein, M., & Ajzen, I. (1981). Acceptance, yielding and impact: Cognitive processes in persuasion. In

R. E. Petty, T. M. Ostrom, & T. C. Brock (Eds.), *Cognitive responses in persuasion* (pp. 339–359). Hillsdale, NJ: Erlbaum.

Forgas, J. P. (1995). Mood and judgment: The affect infusion model (AIM). *Psychological Bulletin, 117,* 39–66.

Friedrich, J., Fetherstonhaugh, D., Casey, S., & Gallaher, D. (1996). Argument integration and attitude change: Suppression effects in the integration of one-sided arguments that vary in persuasiveness. *Psychological Bulletin, 22,* 179–191.

Greenwald, A. G. (1968). Cognitive learning, cognitive response to persuasion, and attitude change. In A. G. Greenwald, T. C. Brock, & T. M. Ostrom (Eds.), *Psychological foundations of attitudes* (pp. 147–170). New York: Academic Press.

Greenwald, A. G., & Ronis, D. L. (1979). Twenty years of cognitive dissonance: Case study of the evolution of a theory. *Psychological Review, 85,* 53–57.

Hafer, C. L., Reynolds, K., & Obertynski, M. A. (1996). Message comprehensibility and persuasion: Effects of complex language in counterattitudinal appeals to laypeople. *Social Cognition, 14,* 317–337.

Harmon-Jones, E., & Mills, J. (Eds.). (1999). Cognitive dissonance: Progress on a pivotal theory in social psychology. Washington, DC: American Psychological Association.

Haugtvedt, C. P., & Petty, R. E. (1992) Personality and persuasion: Need for cognition moderates the persistence and resistance of attitude changes. *Journal of Personality and Social Psychology, 63,* 308–319.

Heesacker, M. H., Petty, R. E., & Cacioppo, J. T. (1983). Field dependence and attitude change: Source credibility can alter persuasion by affecting message-relevant thinking. *Journal of Personality, 51,* 653–666.

Helweg-Larsen, M., & Howell, C. (2000). Effects of erotophobia on the persuasiveness of condom advertisements containing strong or weak arguments. *Basic and Applied Social Psychology, 22,* 111–117.

Himmelfarb, S., & Eagly, A. H. (Eds.). (1974). *Readings in attitude change.* New York: Wiley.

Hovland, C. I., Janis, I. L., & Kelley, H. H. (1953). *Communication and persuasion: Psychological studies of opinion change.* New Haven, CT: Yale University Press.

Hovland, C. I., Lumsdaine, A. A., & Sheffield, F. D. (1949). *Experiments on mass communication.* Princeton, NJ: Princeton University Press.

Hovland, C. I., & Weiss, W. (1951). The influence of source credibility on communication effectiveness. *Public Opinion Quarterly, 15,* 635–650.

Kahneman, D. (1973). *Attention and effort.* Englewood Cliffs, NJ: Prentice-Hall.

Kelman (1961). Processes of opinion change. *Public Opinion Quarterly, 25,* 57–78.

Kruglanski, A. W., & Freund, T. (1983). The freezing and unfreezing of lay-inferences: Effects of impressional primacy, ethnic stereotyping, and numerical anchoring. *Journal of Experimental Social Psychology, 19,* 448–468.

Kruglanski, A. W. (1989). *Lay epistemics and human knowledge: Cognitive and motivational bases.* New York: Plenum Press.

Kruglanski, A. W., & Thompson, E. P. (1999). Persuasion by a single route: A view from the unimodel. *Psychological Inquiry, 10,* 83–109.

Laczniak, R. N., & Carlson, L. (1989). Examining the influence of attitude-toward-the-ad on brand attitudes. *Journal of Business Research, 19,* 303–311.

Maio, G. R., Bell, D. W., & Esses, V. M. (1996). Ambivalence and persuasion: The processing of messages about immigrant groups. *Journal of Experimental Social Psychology, 32,* 513–536.

Martin, L. L., Abend, T. A., Sedikides, C., & Green, J. (1997). How would I feel if . . . ? Mood as input to a role fulfillment evaluation process. *Journal of Personality and Social Psychology, 73,* 242–253.

Mongeau, P. A., & Stiff, J. B. (1993). Specifying causal relationships in the elaboration likelihood model. *Communication Theory, 3,* 65–72.

Moore, D. L., Hausknecht, D., & Thamodaran, K. (1986). Time compression, response opportunity, and persuasion. *Journal of Consumer Research, 13,* 85–99.

Norman, R. (1976). When what is said is important. A comparison of expert and attractive sources. *Journal of Experimental Social Psychology, 12,* 295–300.

O'Keefe, D. J. (1990). *Persuasion: Theory and research.* Newbury Park, CA: Sage.

Petty, R. E. (1997). The evolution of theory and research in social psychology. From single to multiple effect and process models of persuasion. In C. McGarty & S. A. Haslam (Eds.), *The message of social psychology: Perspectives on mind in society* (pp. 268–290). Oxford, England: Basil Blackwell.

Petty, R. E., Briñol, P., & Tormala, Z. L. (2002). Thought confidence as a determinant of persuasion: The self-validation hypothesis. *Journal of Personality and Social Psychology, 82,* 722–741.

Petty, R. E., & Cacioppo, J. T. (1979). Issue-involvement can increase or decrease persuasion by enhancing message-relevant cognitive responses. *Journal of Personality and Social Psychology, 37,* 1915–1926.

Petty, R. E., & Cacioppo, J. T. (1984a). Source factors and the elaboration likelihood model of persuasion. *Advances in Consumer Research, 11,* 668–672.

Petty, R. E., & Cacioppo, J. T. (1984b). The effects of involvement on response to argument quantity and quality: Central and peripheral routes to persuasion. *Journal of Personality and Social Psychology, 46,* 69–81.

Petty, R. E., & Cacioppo, J. T. (1986a). *Communication and persuasion: Central and peripheral routes to attitude change.* New York: Springer-Verlag.

Petty, R. E., & Cacioppo, J. T. (1986b). The elaboration likelihood model of persuasion. In L. Berkowitz (Ed.), *Advances in experimental social psychology* (vol. 19, pp. 123–205). New York: Academic Press.

Petty, R. E., & Cacioppo, J. T. (1990). Involvement and persuasion: Tradition versus integration. *Psychological Bulletin, 107,* 367–374.

Petty, R. E., Cacioppo, J. T., & Goldman, R. (1981). Personal involvement as a determinant of argument-based persuasion. *Journal of Personality and Social Psychology, 41,* 847–855.

Petty, R. E., Cacioppo, J. T., & Haugtvedt, C. (1992). Involvement and persuasion: An appreciative look at the Sherifs' contribution to the study of self-relevance and attitude change. In D. Granberg & G. Sarup (Eds.), *Social judgment and intergroup relations: Essays in honor of Muzafer Sherif* (pp. 147–174). New York: Springer-Verlag.

Petty, R. E., Cacioppo, J. T., & Schumann, D. W. (1983). Central and peripheral routes to advertising effectiveness: The moderating role of involvement. *Journal of Consumer Research, 10,* 135–146.

Petty, R. E., DeSteno, D., & Rucker, D. (2001). The role of affect in persuasion and attitude change. In J. Forgas (Ed.), *Handbook of affect and social cognition* (pp. 212–233). Mahwah, NJ: Erlbaum.

Petty, R. E., Fabrigar, L. R., & Wegener, D. T. (in press). Emotional factors in attitudes and persuasion. In R. J. Davidson, H. H. Goldsmith, & K. R. Scherer (Eds.), *Handbook of affective sciences.* Cambridge: Cambridge University Press.

Petty, R. E., Harkins, S. G., & Williams, K. D. (1980). The effects of group diffusion of cognitive effort on attitudes. An information processing view. *Journal of Personality and Social Psychology, 38,* 81–92.

Petty, R. E., Haugtvedt, C., & Smith, S. M. (1995). Elaboration as a determinant of attitude strength: Creating attitudes that are persistent, resistant, and predictive of behavior. In R. E. Petty & J. A. Krosnick (Eds.), *Attitude strength: Antecedents and consequences* (pp. 93–130). Mahwah, NJ: Erlbaum.

Petty, R. E., Jarvis, W. B. G., & Evans, L. M. (1996). Recurrent thought: Implications for attitudes and persuasion. In R. S. Wyer (Ed.), *Advances in social cognition* (vol. 9, pp. 145–164). Mahwah, NJ: Erlbaum.

Petty, R. E., Kasmer, J. A., Haugtvedt, C. P., & Cacioppo, J. T. (1987). Source and message factors in persuasion: A reply to Stiff's critique of the elaboration likelihood model. *Communication Monographs, 54,* 232–249.

Petty, R. E., Ostrom, T. M., & Brock, T. C. (Eds.). (1981). *Cognitive responses in persuasion.* Hillsdale, NJ: Erlbaum.

Petty, R. E., Priester, J. R., & Briñol, P. (2002). Mass media and attitude change: Advances in the ELM. In J. Bryant & D. Zillmann (Eds.), *Media effects: Advances in theory and research* (2nd ed., pp. 155–198). Hillsdale, NJ: Erlbaum.

Petty, R. E., Schumann, D. W., Richman, S. A., & Strathman, A. J. (1993). Positive mood and persuasion:

Different roles for affect under high- and low-elaboration conditions. *Journal of Personality and Social Psychology, 64*, 5–20.

Petty, R. E., Tormala, Z., & Rucker (in press). Resistance to persuasion: An attitude strength perspective. In M. R. Banaji, J. T. Jost, & D. Prentice (Eds.), *The yin and yang of social cognition: Festchrift for William J. McGuire*. Washington, DC: American Psychological Association.

Petty, R. E., Wells, G. L., & Brock, T. C. (1976). Distraction can enhance or reduce yielding to propaganda: Thought disruption versus effort justification. *Journal of Personality and Social Psychology, 34*, 874–884.

Petty, R. E., & Wegener, D. T. (1991). Thought systems, argument quality, and persuasion. In R. S. Wyer & T. K. Srull (Eds.), *Advances in social cognition* (vol. 4, pp. 147–161). Hillsdale, NJ: Erlbaum.

Petty, R. E., & Wegener, D. T. (1993). Flexible correction processes in social judgment: Correcting for context-induced contrast. *Journal of Experimental Social Psychology, 29*, 137–165.

Petty, R. E., & Wegener, D. T. (1998). Attitude change: Multiple roles for persuasion variables. In D. T. Gilbert, S. T. Fiske, & G. Lindzey (Eds.), *The handbook of social psychology* (4th ed., vol. 1, pp. 323–390). New York: McGraw-Hill.

Petty, R. E., & Wegener, D. T. (1999). The elaboration likelihood model: current status and controversies. In S. Chaiken, & Y. Trope (Eds.), *Dual-process theories in social psychology* (pp. 41–72). New York: Guilford Press.

Petty, R. E., Wegener, D. T., Fabrigar, L. R., Priester, J. R., & Cacioppo, J. T. (1993). Conceptual and methodological issues in the Elaboration Likelihood Model of persuasion: A reply to the Michigan State critics. *Communication Theory, 3*, 336–362.

Petty, R. E., Wegener, D. T., & White, P. (1998). Flexible correction processes in social judgment: Implications for persuasion. *Social Cognition, 16*, 93–113.

Petty, R. E., Wheeler, S. C., & Bizer, G. Y. (1999). Is there one persuasion process or more? Lumping versus splitting in attitude change theories. *Psychological Inquiry, 10*(2), 156–163.

Petty, R. E., Wheeler, S. C., & Bizer, G. (2000). Matching effects in persuasion: An elaboration likelihood analysis (pp. 133–162). In G. Maio & J. Olson (Eds.), *Why we evaluate: Functions of attitudes*. Mahwah, NJ: Erlbaum.

Puckett, J., Petty, R. E., Cacioppo, J. T., & Fisher, D. (1983). The relative impact of age and attractiveness stereotypes on persuasion. *Journal of Gerontology, 38*, 340–343.

Razran, G. H. S. (1940). Conditioned response changes in rating and appraising sociopolitical slogans. *Psychological Bulletin, 37*, 481.

Rucker, D. D., & Petty, R. E. (2002). When resistance is futile: Implications for attitude strength. Unpublished manuscript, Ohio State University, Columbus, Ohio.

Rogers, R. W. (1983). Cognitive and physiological processes in fear appeals and attitude change: A revised theory of protection motivation. In J. T. Cacioppo & R. E. Petty (Eds.), *Social psychophysiology: A sourcebook* (pp. 153–176). New York: Guilford Press.

Schwarz, N., Bless, H., & Bohner, G. (1991). Mood and persuasion: Affective states influence the processing of persuasive communications. In M. P. Zanna (Ed.), *Advances in experimental social psychology* (vol. 24, pp. 161–201). San Diego: Academic Press.

Schwarz, N., Bless, H., Strack, F., Klumpp, G., Rittenauer-Schatka, H., & Simons, A. (1991). Ease of retrieval as information: Another look at the availability heuristic. *Journal of Personality and Social Psychology, 61*, 195–202.

Schwarz, N., & Clore, G. L. (1983). Mood, misattribution, and judgments of well-being: Informative and directive functions of affective states. *Journal of Personality and Social Psychology, 45*, 512–523.

Shavitt, S., Swan, S., Lowrey, T. M., & Wänke, M. (1994). The interaction of endorser attractiveness and involvement in persuasion depends on the goal that guides message processing. *Journal of Consumer Psychology, 3*, 137–162.

Smith, S. M., & Petty, R. E. (1996). Message framing and persuasion: A message processing analysis. *Personality and Social Psychology Bulletin, 22*, 257–268.

Staats, A. W., & Staats, C. K. (1958). Attitudes established by classical conditioning. *Journal of Abnormal and Social Psychology, 57*, 37–40.

Sternthal, B., Dholakia, R., & Leavitt, C. (1978). The persuasive effect of source credibility: A test of cognitive response analysis. *Journal of Personality and Social Psychology, 64*, 885–896.

Stiff, J. B. (1986). Cognitive processing of persuasive message cues: A meta-analytic review of the effects of supporting information on attitudes. *Communication Monographs, 53,* 75–89.

Stiff, J. B. (1994). *Persuasive Communication.* New York: Guilford Press.

Stiff, J. B., & Boster, F. J. (1987). Cognitive processing: Additional thoughts, and a reply to Petty, Kasmer, Haugtvedt, and Cacioppo. *Communication Monographs, 54,* 250–256.

Tormala, Z. L., & Petty, R. E. (in press). What doesn't kill me makes me stronger: The effects of resisting persuasion on attitude certainty. *Journal of Personality and Social Psychology.*

Tormala, Z. L., Petty, R. E., & Briñol, P. (in press). Ease of retrieval effects in persuasion: A self-validation analysis. *Personality and Social Psychology Bulletin.*

Wegener, D. T., & Petty, R. E. (1994). Mood-management across affective states: The hedonic contingency hypothesis. *Journal of Personality and Social Psychology, 66,* 1034–1048.

Wegener, D. T., & Petty, R. E. (1995). Flexible correction processes in social judgment: The role of naïve theories in corrections for perceived bias. *Journal of Personality & Social Psychology, 68,* 36–51.

Wegener, D. T., Petty, R. E., & Klein, D. J. (1994). Effects of mood on high elaboration attitude change: The mediating role of likelihood judgments. *European Journal of Social Psychology, 24,* 25–43.

Wegener, D. T., Petty, R. E., & Smith, S. M. (1995). Positive mood can increase or decrease message scrutiny: The hedonic contingency view of mood and message processing. *Journal of Personality and Social Psychology, 69,* 5–15.

Wilson, T. D., & Brekke, N. (1994). Mental contamination and mental correction: Unwanted influences on judgments and evaluations. *Psychological Bulletin, 116,* 117–142.

Wood, W., Kallgren, C. A., & Preisler, R. M. (1985). Access to attitude-relevant information in memory as a determinant of persuasion: The role of message attributes. *Journal of Experimental Social Psychology, 21,* 73–85.

Zanna, M. P., Kiesler, C. A., & Pilkonis, P. A. (1970). Positive and negative attitudinal affect established by classical conditioning. *Journal of Personality and Social Psychology, 14,* 321–328.

Part II

Persuasion Variables

Perspectives on Sources, Receivers, Channels, and Messages

Chapters 3 and 5 of this volume mentioned Carl Hovland, a psychologist from Yale University who is often credited with initiating the systematic, social scientific study of persuasion during World War II. After the war, Hovland and his colleagues (Hovland, Janis, & Kelley, 1953) continued to develop and investigate their "message learning approach," which among other things made it clear that persuasion is no simple process. Their approach suggested that in order to be effective, a persuasive message had to capture the audience's attention, be comprehended, be yielded to, and be remembered. It also suggested that this process could be facilitated with incentives for agreeing with the persuasive message.

More pertinent to this part of the book, however, are the moderating variables examined by Hovland and his group. Moderating variables can be thought of as the "it depends" of persuasion. In other words, whether persuasion is effective or not often *depends* on several factors. As just one example, whether the use of touch tends to facilitate or inhibit persuasion depends, in part, on whether the touch is perceived as a positive or negative violation of the recipient's perceptions. Hovland and his colleagues focused their attention primarily on four variables that might moderate the process of persuasion: the characteristics of the person sending the persuasive message (the source), the nature of the message itself, the channel or medium by which the message is sent, and the characteristics of the person receiving the persuasive message. Likewise, the chapters in this section discuss the role of communicator characteristics, messages, and channels in the process of persuasion. The chapters not only examine the role these variables play in effective persuasion, as Hovland and his colleagues did, they also discuss the ways in which such variables influence the production of persuasive messages.

There are, of course, several source characteristics that might affect persuasion, such as how likable, attractive, or similar to the audience a source is perceived to be. As important as such characteristics are, however, they have not received nearly as much research attention as the topic of credibility, which is without doubt one of the most thoroughly studied topics in the field of persuasion. Some of this research has attempted to discover the underlying dimensions that make up credibility (e.g., trustworthiness, competence, charisma, etc.). The first chapter in this section, chapter 6, by William Benoit and Alan Strathman, examines such research and expands it to broaden our understanding of how and when credibility works persuasively. The chapter does an excellent job of showing how theory (e.g., the Elaboration Likelihood Model) helps us predict the conditions under which credibility mediates persuasion. It is also important to note that this chapter discusses the ways in which a tarnished image may be repaired.

In addition to source credibility, other communicator characteristics mediate the process of persuasion. An enormous body of research, for example, has examined the ways in which demographic variables (e.g., age, ethnicity, intelligence) and personality traits (e.g., self-monitoring, ego-involvement, dogmatism) influence both the sending and receiving of messages. Given space considerations, however, this part of the book focuses on just three such characteristics. First, chapter 7, by Andrew Rancer, discusses two communication traits, argumentativeness and verbal aggressiveness, that affect people's orientations toward argumentative encounters. As you will see, individuals who possess one trait or the other have vastly different approaches when trying to persuade others or when being confronted with the influence attempts of others (e.g., others' attempts to resist persuasion). Similarly, chapter 8, by Linda Carli, examines the ways in which gender affects persuasion. While the lion's share of previous research on this topic has concentrated on gender and persuasibility, chapter 8 asks whether one gender is more influential than the other, and if so, why.

The last two chapters in this section examine whether messages and channels affect persuasion. A channel, of course, is a medium for communication. Two channels for persuasive messages are language and nonverbal communication.

The persuasive potential of language is well known. Most of us, for example, are probably aware of situations in which euphemisms and politically correct language are necessary. Moreover, research tells us that using profanity or "powerless language" (e.g., "uh," "you know") can have damaging effects on credibility (Bostrom, Baseheart, & Rossiter, 1973; Haleta, 1996). While such issues are important, we believe that when trying to understand the role of language in persuasion, perhaps the most significant factor to keep in mind is the old maxim, "Meanings are in people, not in words." This principle is one of the key tenets of Language Expectancy Theory, which is the subject of chapter 9, by Michael Burgoon and Jason Siegel. Indeed, the specific words a speaker uses when attempting to persuade an audience may be important, but not nearly so much as the way in which the speaker's audience *perceives* those words. This chapter, as you will see, suggests that understanding audiences' expectations about language usage is crucial to predicting how persuasive language will be.

Finally, chapter 10, by Peter Andersen, examines nonverbal influence. Interestingly, some definitions of persuasion suggest that a chapter on this topic might not belong in a book such as this. A number of authors (Larson, 2001; Miller, 1980; Reardon, 1981;

Roloff & Miller, 1980) have argued that persuasion involves only symbolic expression, including language and other meaning-laden acts such as civil disobedience and protest marches. Gerald Miller (1980), for example, asserted that "persuasion relies upon symbolic transactions . . . the scholarly endeavors of persuasion researchers—and for that matter, the ordinary language usages of the term 'persuasion'—have consistently centered on the manipulation of symbols" (pp. 14–15). Similary, Cooper and Nothstine (1992) argued, "Persuasion is the process by which language and symbolic actions influence choice-making by others" (p. 2). Finally, according to Larson (2001), "Persuasion is the co-creation of a state of identification or alignment between a source and a receiver that results from the use of symbols" (p. 10).

Though we understand the point of such definitions, we do not agree with them. In fact, we have argued elsewhere that limiting the study of persuasion to words or symbols leaves out too much (see Gass & Seiter, 2003). We hope that after reading chapter 9, you will agree. In our opinion this chapter demonstrates that some of the most intriguing aspects of persuasion can be found in nonverbal behavior, which lies on the periphery of symbolic action. While some texts' discussions of nonverbal persuasion are largely atheoretical in nature, we believe that this chapter does an excellent job of examining models and theories that explain why nonverbal behavior can be so influential.

References

Bostrom, R. N., Baseheart, J. R., & Rossiter, C. M. (1973). The effects of three types of profane language in persuasive messages. *Journal of Communication, 50,* 415–420.

Cooper, M., and Nothstine, W. L. (1992). *Power persuasion: Moving an ancient art into the media age.* Greenwood, IN: Educational Video Group.

Gass, R. H., & Seiter, J. S. (2003). *Persuasion, social influence, and compliance gaining* (2nd ed.). Boston: Allyn & Bacon.

Haleta, L. L. (1996). Student perceptions of teachers' use of language: The effects of powerful and powerless language on impression formation and uncertainty. *Communication Education, 45*(1), 16–28.

Hovland, C. I., Janis, I. L., & Kelley, J. J. (1953). *Communication and persuasion.* New Haven, CT: Yale University Press.

Larson, C. U. (2001). *Persuasion: Reception and responsibility* (9th ed.). Belmont, CA: Wadsworth.

Miller, G. R. (1980). On being persuaded: Some basic distinctions. In M. E. Roloff & G. R. Miller (Eds.), *Persuasion: New directions in theory and research* (pp. 11–28). Beverly Hills, CA: Sage.

Reardon, K. K. (1981). *Persuasion: Theory and context.* Beverly Hills, CA: Sage.

Roloff, M. E., & Miller, G. R. (1980). *Persuasion: New directions in theory and research.* Beverly Hills, CA: Sage.

6

Source Credibility and the Elaboration Likelihood Model

William L. Benoit and Alan Strathman

For thousands of years scholars who study persuasion have recognized that some message sources are more persuasive than others. The ancient Greek philosopher Aristotle, for example, explained in the fourth century B.C.: "We believe good men more fully and more readily than others; this is true generally whatever the question is, and absolutely where exact certainty is impossible and opinions divided" (1954, 1356a6-8). Isocrates, a contemporary of Aristotle, was known more as an educator than a philosopher, and Cicero declared that from Isocrates' "school, as from the Horse of Troy, none but leaders emerged" (1942, II.94). Isocrates indicated his belief in the importance of credible sources when he asked, "Who does not know that words carry a greater conviction when spoken by men of good repute than when spoken by men who live under a cloud, and that the argument which is made by a man's life is of more weight than that which is furnished by words?" (1976, p. 278). In the twentieth century several literature reviews have concluded that source credibility is an important element in persuasion (Anderson & Clevenger, 1963; Benoit, 1998; Hass, 1991; Littlejohn, 1971). Petty and Cacioppo (1981a) wrote, "The expertise of the source of a message is one of the most important features of the persuasion situation and one of the earliest variables to be investigated. It remains, however, one of the least understood manipulations" (p. 235). This chapter is devoted to explaining how and when source credibility influences persuasion.

Message sources have multiple dimensions, including the source's physical attractiveness (see, e.g., Bersheid & Walster, 1974; Chaiken, 1979; DeBono & Harnish, 1988; Kahle & Homer, 1985), similarity to the audience (see, e.g., Berscheid, 1985; Simons, Berkowitz, & Moyer, 1970), and other demographic factors. The two principal elements of *source credibility* are traditionally considered to be *expertise* (the level of the source's knowledge of the topic of the message, typically established by education, training, or experience in the field) and *trustworthiness* (whether the source can be expected to provide an objective or unbiased perspective on the topic). Wilson and Sherrell's (1993) meta-analysis found that the effect of expertise on persuasion is greater than the effect of trustworthiness, attractiveness, or similarity. Fewer of the studies they reviewed manipulated trustworthiness, but the effect of trustworthiness also appeared to be stronger than that of attractiveness or similarity. McCroskey and Teven (1999) argued that there are three dimensions of credibility: expertise, trustworthiness, and goodwill. However, most research has focused on the first two dimensions. Accordingly, this chapter will focus on expertise and trustworthiness.

The Elaboration Likelihood Model (ELM) will be employed as a theoretical framework for understanding the nature of source credibility effects in persuasion. After elucidating the ELM, we use it to explain how the nature of a message's source influences the process of persuasion. We then take up several topics explaining how (and when) source credibility affects attitude change. Next, we evaluate the research on source credibility, and finally, we discuss options for repairing damaged credibility.

The Nature of the Elaboration Likelihood Model

The cognitive response model (Greenwald, 1968; Perloff & Brock, 1980) and the ELM specifically (Petty & Cacioppo, 1981a, 1986a, 1986b) portray auditors as active participants in persuasion (see also Chaiken, 1980). Receivers produce cognitions (thoughts, elaborations) in response to the stimulus of persuasive discourse; attitude change does not result directly from persuasive messages but arises from the thoughts of audience members when they are exposed to persuasive messages. Petty and Cacioppo (1986a, 1986b) posit two "routes" to persuasion: central and peripheral. The *central route* consists of thoughtful consideration of the arguments (ideas, content) in the message and is adopted when a receiver has both *motivation* and *ability* to think about the message and its topic. The *peripheral route* is used when the listener bases reaction to the message on cues other than message content, such as attractiveness of the source, the number of arguments in the message, or the length of the message. This route is adapted when the auditor is unable and/or unwilling to engage in much thought on the message.

The ELM is important in part because it enjoys considerable empirical support:

> The assumption that systematic or central route processing requires motivation and ability has been documented in many studies, using a variety of motivational and ability variables: Persuasive argumentation is a more important determinant of persuasion when recipients are motivated and able to process attitude-relevant information than when they are not. There is also substantial empirical support for the hypothesis of these models that heuristic or peripheral cues exert a sizable persuasive impact when motivation or ability for argument processing is low, but little impact when motivation and ability are high. (Eagly & Chaiken, 1993, p. 333)

This distinction between central and peripheral processing is important because these two routes are asserted to have different effects on receivers: "Attitude changes that result mostly from processing issue-relevant arguments (central route) will show greater temporal persistence, greater prediction of behavior, and greater resistance to counterpersuasion than attitude changes that result mostly from peripheral cues" (Petty & Cacioppo, 1986a, p. 21). Attitude change can occur via either process, but the route (central or peripheral) makes a difference.

Petty and Cacioppo selected a nettlesome metaphor in describing these as "routes" to persuasion. Ordinarily, when there are two routes to a destination, only one is taken. A person traveling from St. Louis to Detroit could take two routes (via Chicago or Indianapolis) but would not take both routes on the same trip. However, "central" and "peripheral" processing are not two dichotomous choices but two endpoints of a continuum of message processing. Different people listening to the same persuasive message might engage in varying amounts of central and peripheral processing (depending upon each receiver's motivation and ability). So the metaphor of two "routes" is in some respects unfortunate, because it implies that auditors will take one route or the other, whereas cognitive processing can actually occur at any point on the elaboration continuum. Petty and Cacioppo (1986a) do acknowledge that elaboration is a continuum: "We view the extent of elaboration received by a message as a continuum going from no thought about the issue-relevant information presented, to complete elaboration of every argument" (p. 8).

According to the ELM, the key to persuasion is understanding the thoughts about, responses to, or elaborations of a message. Cognitions vary on many dimensions, but two are particularly important: valence and amount. First, thoughts can agree or disagree with the message (or be irrelevant to the message). Agreeing, positive, or favorable thoughts facilitate persuasion; disagreeing, negative, or unfavorable thoughts inhibit persuasion and can cause a backlash. Persuaders who elicit favorable thoughts are therefore more likely to create the desired attitude change. Receivers can experience a mix of favorable and unfavorable cognitive responses to a message.

Second, receivers can generate many or few thoughts in response to a persuasive message. The number of thoughts also shapes the kind of influence that is likely to occur. Attitude change is more likely to ensue from many than from a few favorable thoughts. On the other hand, large numbers of unfavorable thoughts reduce the likelihood that a message will be persuasive.

As noted above, a receiver's cognitive responses can be a mixture of favorable and unfavorable thoughts. All things being equal, when the "net" favorable cognitive response is larger (more favorable than unfavorable thoughts), persuasion is more likely to occur in response to a message. As the margin of favorable to unfavorable thoughts increases, the likelihood (and amount) of persuasion should increase. When the "net" favorable cognitive response is smaller (or a negative number, with unfavorable thoughts outnumbering favorable ones), persuasion is less likely. If the unfavorable thoughts outnumber favorable ones, a "boomerang" effect of attitude change in the opposite direction of that advocated by the message becomes more likely. This explains why both the *number* and *valence* of cognitive responses are so important to persuasion.

Number of Cognitive Responses

The number of cognitive responses is determined by two factors: the receiver's *motivation* and *ability* to process a message cognitively. Motivation is directly related to involvement in the message: The more important a message topic is to a receiver (the greater the involvement), the more motivated that person is to think about the message (and produce thoughts). The less a topic matters to a listener, the less motivated that person is to think about the message (and fewer thoughts should occur). Research confirms that auditors are more likely to scrutinize a message—or use the central route to persuasion, or produce more cognitive responses—on an involving (salient, relevant, important) than a noninvolving topic (see, e.g., Johnson & Eagly, 1989; Petty & Cacioppo, 1979a, 1979b, 1981b, 1984; Petty, Cacioppo, & Goldman, 1981; Petty, Cacioppo, & Schumann, 1983; Roser & Thompson, 1995). Thus, topic involvement increases receivers' *motivation* to process a message and increases the number of cognitive responses they are likely to produce in response to that message.

However, the audience must also have the *ability* to process centrally. One variable that has frequently been employed to study processing ability is distraction: Receivers who are distracted produce fewer thoughts in response to a persuasive message than those who are not (Osterhouse & Brock, 1970; Petty, Wells, & Brock, 1976). Other factors also influence the receiver's ability to process a message. Messages that are more difficult to understand should produce fewer thoughts. Message repetition can increase the audience's ability to process a message, although too much repetition could create boredom or tedium, reducing that message's effectiveness (Cacioppo & Petty, 1985; Petty & Cacioppo, 1979b). If the audience knows little about a topic, it should be difficult to produce many thoughts about that message. Thus, many variables can influence the extent of people's ability to process a message and, therefore, the number of cognitive responses produced when processing a message.

Distraction, for example, can either hinder or help persuasion depending upon the valence of the thoughts it suppresses. If a receiver is likely to *disagree* with a persuasive message, distraction means that this auditor would probably have *fewer unfavorable* cognitive responses (compared with undistracted listening). In this case, the auditor who is distracted is likely to experience more persuasion with distraction than without it. On the other hand, if a receiver is likely to *agree* with a message, distraction would mean *fewer favorable* thoughts and thus less persuasion (compared, of course, with undistracted reception). Distraction thus interferes with the listener's ability to process a message and reduces the number of cognitive responses. When fewer unfavorable thoughts are "suppressed" by distraction, the listener should be more persuaded; when fewer favorable thoughts occur, the listener should be less persuaded.

Valence of Cognitive Responses

Several factors influence the valence of cognitive responses. First, the valence of thoughts is influenced by the position advocated by the persuader. Listeners are likely to produce favorable thoughts when they agree with the messages they receive. Conversely, receivers are likely to produce unfavorable thoughts in response to messages they do not accept. The position of the message relative to the audience's attitudes therefore influences the valence of thoughts.

Second, forewarning auditors about a persuasive message can influence the thoughts they are likely to produce in response to that message. When people are warned that they will disagree with a message (counterattitudinal message), they are likely to produce negative thoughts in anticipation of that message (Brock, 1967; Petty & Cacioppo, 1977).

Third, argument quality influences the valence of cognitive responses. Stronger arguments are more likely to elicit favorable thoughts than weaker messages, whereas weak arguments are more likely to evoke negative thoughts than stronger or high-quality messages. Petty and Cacioppo (1984) found that auditors produce more favorable cognitive responses to messages with strong arguments than those with weak arguments and generate more unfavorable thoughts in regard to messages comprising weak rather than strong arguments. Benoit (1987) found that messages with strong arguments produced more favorable thoughts, fewer unfavorable thoughts, and more attitude change than messages with weak arguments. These effects are more pronounced on involving than uninvolving topics (Andrews & Shimp, 1990; Petty & Cacioppo, 1984).

Thus, several factors can influence the valence of cognitive responses. Messages that disagree with the audience are more likely to produce unfavorable thoughts, whereas agreeing messages are more likely to encourage favorable thoughts. Strong messages are more likely to produce favorable thoughts, whereas weak messages are prone to elicit unfavorable thoughts.

Peripheral Processing

Most of the discussion thus far has focused on central processing, although the amount of central processing employed depends on the motivation and ability of the receiver. Peripheral processing is associated with fewer thoughts. However, peripheral processing is thought to be qualitatively different from central processing. The receiver who engages in peripheral processing uses a cue or a decision rule to decide whether to agree with the message (instead of thinking about the arguments in the message). Peripheral processing occurs when receivers lack the ability and/or motivation to think about the arguments in the message; however, they may find other bases for deciding whether to accept the message.

Several peripheral cues (which may be thought of as mental shortcuts) have been identified. For example, when receivers perceive the source as physically attractive, they may use attractiveness as a peripheral cue (Petty & Cacioppo, 1981a). An audience member might think, "This is a very attractive source. I think I should agree with him (or her)." Remember that peripheral processing is more likely to occur when the topic is less important or less involving, so deferring to an attractive source (instead of expending the effort to think about the ideas and arguments in the message) may not be problematic for the listener.

Second, if a message contains a large number of arguments, a receiver may decide to accept the message on the basis that any message with so many arguments is probably correct (Petty & Cacioppo, 1984a). We may have a decision rule that, all things being equal, a message with many arguments is more likely to be true than one with few arguments.

Third, when a listener believes that several sources collectively endorse a message position, the listener may be more likely to accept that message. Harkins and Petty (1981) found that more arguments and more sources each generate more favorable cognitive responses and more attitude change than messages with fewer arguments and sources. All things being equal, an idea that many people accept is more likely to be true than one that few people believe.

Source Credibility

With this understanding of how persuasive messages are processed, we can turn to an analysis of source credibility, which can influence persuasion by influencing *how receivers process messages*—the number of cognitive responses, the valence of cognitive responses, and the object of their thoughts: message versus source. The claim that source credibility influences persuasion by affecting message processing is supported by research suggesting that source credibility affects persuasion only if the source is identified *before* the message has been processed (Husek, 1965; Mills & Harvey, 1972). Ward and McGinnies (1974; see also Greenberg & Tannenbaum, 1961; Sternthal, Dholakia, & Leavitt, 1978) found that there was no difference in attitude change between high- and low-credibility sources when those sources were identified *after* the message (see also O'Keefe's meta-analysis, 1987). In addition, Greenberg and Miller (1966) reported that low-credibility sources hindered persuasion only when they were identified as disreputable before the message. These findings all suggest that source credibility influences persuasion by altering how people process (or elaborate) messages. When the source is identified *after* the message, that message has already been processed. Any thoughts the audience may have about the message have already occurred, so it is too late for identification of the source to have any effect. Similarly, Rhine and Kaplan (1972) found that when there is no message to process (merely an assertion or claim), there is no persuasive effect from variations in source credibility. Thus, research indicates that credibility cues mediate persuasion by influencing *how messages attributed to that source are processed.*

Second, the persuasive effects of source credibility are more likely to manifest themselves on less involving topics, suggesting that credibility can also serve as a peripheral cue. Petty, Cacioppo, and Goldman (1981) found that on highly involving topics, message arguments produce attitude change but source credibility does not. On uninvolving topics, both arguments and credibility mediate persuasion, but credibility has more influence (see also Benoit, 1987; Chaiken, 1980; Johnson & Scileppi, 1969; Petty, Cacioppo, & Goldman, 1981; Petty, Cacioppo, & Schumann, 1983).

The authors of the ELM have specifically addressed the relationship between source factors and persuasion. Petty and Cacioppo explain how characteristics of message sources can influence attitude change: "In the ELM, source factors can influence attitude change in three ways: They can serve as arguments [an attractive model is evidence for a beauty product], they can serve as [peripheral] cues, and they can affect argument processing" (1986a, p. 205). It is possible that these factors could come into play in situations involving expertise as well as attractiveness. For example, the cigarette smoker who is dying from cancer could be seen as the embodiment of the argument to quit (or never to start) smoking. However, we were unable to locate any research on the first method of influence, in which the nature of the source actually functions as an argument to support the claims advanced in the message. Our review will discuss how expertise and trustworthiness can influence argument processing and serve as peripheral cues.

Number of Cognitive Responses

Source credibility can influence persuasion by influencing both important components of cognitive responses. First, source credibility may influence the *number of thoughts* produced in response to a message. Here, belief that the source is an expert on the topic of the message could encourage receivers to "relax their guards," or feel less motivation to scrutinize the message (produce fewer cognitive responses). In contrast, if the source is thought to be disreputable, that belief may lead receivers to be more wary, subjecting the message to greater scrutiny (produce more cognitive responses). Gillig and Greenwald (1974) found that fewer unfavorable thoughts are produced in response to a message attributed to a high-credibility source, whereas more unfavorable thoughts are elicited by a low-credibility source. Conversely, auditors are more motivated to think critically, and tend to produce more counterarguments, in regard to messages from apparently nonexpert sources, reducing persuasion from such sources (see Benoit, 1991; Cook, 1969; Gillig & Greenwald, 1974; Hass, 1981; Perloff & Brock, 1980).

Valence of Cognitive Responses

Source credibility also can influence the *valence of cognitive responses*. Benoit and Kennedy (1999) found that trusted sources produced more favorable and fewer unfavorable thoughts (and more attitude change) than untrusted sources. However, there was no difference in the total number of thoughts produced from these sources. That is, source trustworthiness influenced the distribution (valence) of thoughts in this study, but not the number of thoughts. The more favorable thoughts, and the fewer unfavorable thoughts, the more persuasion should occur. Conversely, cognitive responses that are more unfavorable than favorable should inhibit attitude change.

Source Credibility Effects

In this section we will describe and explain three specific topics: involvement, moderately credible sources, and discrepancy. These are important areas in which the ELM helps to explain source credibility effects.

Involvement. Several studies suggest that credibility is most important on uninvolving topics, which suggests again that it often functions as a peripheral cue. Johnson and Scileppi (1969) report that high-credibility sources were more persuasive on uninvolving than involving topics. Petty, Cacioppo, and Goldman (1981) found that argument quality but not credibility influences persuasion on involving topics, while on uninvolving topics credibility was more influential than argument quality (see also Chaiken, 1980). Benoit (1987) found that experts were no more persuasive than nonexperts on an involving topic (cf. Stiff, 1986). Neimeyer, Guy, and Metzler (1989) found that a credible source elicited more favorable and fewer unfavorable thoughts, but only in a low-involvement condition.

The meta-analysis by Wilson and Sherrell (1993) found that in two-thirds of the studies examined, source factors had a significant effect on attitude change only in a low-involvement condition.

On involving topics, audience members are motivated to scrutinize the message, engaging in central processing of the ideas and arguments in the message. Thus, source credibility should have a minimal impact on such topics. As noted above, Wilson and Sherrell's (1993) study identified a number of studies in which source credibility had effects in high-involvement conditions, but these effects were in the minority.

Moderately Credible Sources.   Ordinarily, highly credible sources are more persuasive than sources who appear less credible. However, there are circumstances in which a moderately credible source is more persuasive than a highly credible source. Several studies have found that when a message is *proattitudinal* (attempting to reinforce or strengthen rather than change attitudes), moderately credible sources are more persuasive than highly credible ones (Bochner & Insko, 1966; Bock & Saine, 1975; Dean, Austin, & Watts, 1971). Sternthal, Dholakia, and Leavitt (1978) reported that in such situations, the moderately credible source elicits more favorable cognitive responses than the highly credible source. Here, the high-credibility source reduces motivation to scrutinize the message (to engage in central processing). However, because a proattitudinal message *agrees* with the audience, the kind of cognitive responses that are suppressed are favorable, resulting in less attitude change. This is, of course, because valence of cognitive responses is so important.

This effect of source credibility is analogous to the effect of distraction discussed earlier. Receivers who are distracted produce fewer thoughts. If undistracted they would have produced primarily *favorable* thoughts, when they are distracted they produce fewer favorable thoughts and are less persuaded (than if they were not distracted). If they would have produced primarily *unfavorable* thoughts when undistracted, distraction would reduce the number of unfavorable thoughts and they will be more persuaded (than those who are undistracted). Similarly, high-credibility sources decrease the audience's motivation to think about a message, reducing the number of thoughts on proattitudinal topics and producing less persuasion than a moderately credible source (a disreputable source is likely to provoke unfavorable thoughts, by the way).

Discrepancy and Attitude Change.   If persuaders wish to change an audience's attitude, they must disagree with the audience. If the persuader parrots their own attitudes back to them, there will be no reason for the audience to change those attitudes. Of course, if persuaders disagree too much, the audience may consider their message to be unreasonable, and it may produce unfavorable cognitive responses and no attitude change. Thus, the degree of discrepancy between the message position and the audience's attitude is an important variable in persuasion. Considerable research has documented a curvilinear relationship between discrepancy and persuasion. Disagreeing with the audience a little produces little attitude change, disagreeing moderately produces more persuasion, and disagreeing a great deal produces little or no persuasion (Bochner & Insko, 1966; Insko, Murashima, & Saiyadain, 1966; Johnson, 1966; Osgood & Tannenbaum, 1955; Peterson & Koulack, 1969; Tannenbaum, 1967). Note that Stiff (1994) claimed support for a linear relationship between discrepancy and attitude change, but he then provided three reasons why high levels of discrepancy would be unpersuasive, undercutting his own argument.

However, some research has found a different pattern of results for highly and moderately credible sources. Aronson, Turner, and Carlsmith (1963; see also Bochner & Insko, 1966) reported that for moderately credible sources, the relationship between discrepancy and attitude change was indeed curvilinear (little attitude change for low and high discrepancy; more attitude change for moderate discrepancy). However, for highly credible sources there was a direct relationship between highly credible sources and discrepancy: the greater the discrepancy, the more attitude change. Although these researchers did not measure cognitive responses, the likely explanation is that highly credible sources reduced the receivers' motivation, so the audience produced fewer unfavorable thoughts to high levels of discrepancy. Thus, without the inhibition of counterarguments, the more discrepancy advocated by highly credible sources, the more persuasion results. Moderately credible sources, on the other hand, do not reduce motivation to think about messages, and highly discrepant messages are thus likely to evoke more unfavorable thoughts than less discrepant messages, resulting in less persuasion.

Rhine and Severance (1970) presented data suggesting that these results are likely to occur for uninvolving, but not for involving topics. This finding is consistent with the ELM, which would suggest that receivers who are highly involved in the topic are likely to engage in central processing regardless of the credibility of the message source. Furthermore, Choo (1964) failed to replicate the finding that for moderately credible sources there is a curvilinear relationship between discrepancy and persuasion but found that highly credible sources have a direct relationship. However, this study operationalized credibility as trustworthiness rather than expertise, and trustworthiness may not influence the number of thoughts. It is clear that we would benefit from studies that replicated this research, clearly distinguishing between expertise and trustworthiness, and measuring cognitive responses.

Evaluation of Work on Credibility

There can be no doubt that source characteristics are capable of influencing persuasion.

Probably the most basic question here is, what is source credibility? Research manipulates and measures credibility in troubling ways. Research does not always distinguish between different source manipulations. Some research employs celebrity sources (Petty, Cacioppo, & Schumann, 1983), but it is not clear in all cases whether such source manipulations concern expertise or trustworthiness (or attractiveness).

Furthermore, expertise, trustworthiness, liking, and attractiveness are often confounded. For example, Johnson & Scileppi (1969) manipulated credibility by telling message recipients that the source of the communication was either a medical authority described as an expert on the topic or a "medical quack" who had served a prison term and who had written the article for a sensationalist publication. In contrast, Ward and McGinnies (1974) described their high credibility source as an expert on the issue and someone who was considered trustworthy. Their low-credibility source was presented as having no expertise and as being devious and calculating. In both studies the high-credibility source was associated with greater attitude change. However, given that expertise and trustworthiness were confounded in these manipulations, it is impossible to ascertain whether the effects are due mainly to expertise or to trustworthiness. Similarly, Chaiken and Maheswaran (1994) attributed a message either to *Consumer Reports* or to a K-Mart circular. Subjects perceived *Consumer Reports* to be the more credible source, but it isn't clear whether this was due to greater perceived expertise or greater perceived trustworthiness.

Some research contains other potential confounds. For example, Chebat, Filiatrault, Larouche, and Watson (1988) employed a fairly common method of manipulating expertise: The expert was described as a professor (in a discipline relevant to the topic of the message), the nonexpert as a student. However, this could confound expertise with similarity, because the low-expert source, a student, is probably seen as more similar to the subjects than the high-expert professor. Future research must be clear about which source characteristics are being studied and how they are manipulated.

Concerns can also be raised about how credibility is measured. Some studies do not report the items used in manipulation checks (Chebat, Filiatrault, Laroche, & Watson, 1988). Others combine arguably dissimilar traits. Chebat, Filiatrault, and Perrien (1990), for example, operationalized credibility as four questions (expertise, trustworthiness, attractiveness, and prestige) that were averaged into a single credibility score. It is not clear exactly what construct is being measured here.

The role of cognitive responses in attitude change is not always investigated (or reported). For example, Petty, Cacioppo, and Goldman (1981) did not report measures of cognitive responses. Other studies failed to report effects of manipulations of the independent variable on cognitive responses. Petty, Cacioppo, and Schumann (1983) found no effects of the manipulations on cognitive responses, possibly because the thought-listing measure was administered after a series of other messages. Given the importance of cognitive responses in the ELM, and the fact that the ELM is clearly a process model of persuasion, this is not a trivial concern. We speculate that the common method of measuring cognitive responses—thought listing—may not be a reliable indicator. Other approaches, like concurrent verbalization, might yield better results.

Repairing Damaged Credibility

The discussion so far has not addressed the question of whether a persuader's credibility is static. Politicians like President Bill Clinton and Representative Gary Condit, public figures like Tonya Harding or Martha Stewart, and corporations like Firestone and Enron have learned the hard way that public perceptions of a person or organization can change—and change precipitously—for the worse. Research reviewed earlier (e.g., Benoit & Kennedy, 1999) makes plain that influence attempts from persuaders with low credibility are likely to produce more unfavorable thoughts, fewer favorable thoughts, and less attitude change than attempts from persuaders with positive reputations. This raises the question of whether persuaders who have suffered damage to their reputations (and who can thus expect to be less effective persuaders) can do anything to remedy this situation.

Typology of Image Repair Options

Benoit (1995a, 1997c, 2000a) has developed a theory of image repair discourse that discusses the options available to people or organizations who need to recover from a damaged reputation. He begins with the assumption that a threat to an image has two components: *offensiveness* and *responsibility*. First, there must be a problem or breach of expected conduct. If nothing bad happened, there is no blame to apportion. Second, a person (or organization) accused or suspected of wrongdoing must have caused (or encouraged, permitted, or failed to prevent) the problem. If a bad thing has occurred but I had nothing to do with it, I cannot reasonably be blamed for that problem. Benoit and his associates (Benoit & Dornes, 1996; Benoit & Harthcock, 1999; Benoit & Wells, 1996) have argued that the damage from an attack or criticism can be exacerbated by increasing the apparent offensiveness of the act or the accused's apparent responsibility for that act.

Furthermore, Benoit (1995, 1997) has explained that image repair efforts can proceed through three general approaches: Reduce or eliminate the apparent offensiveness of the act in question, reduce or eliminate the accused's responsibility for the act, or concede both offensiveness and responsibility with an apology and request for forgiveness (which, following Kenneth Burke, he calls "mortification"). Thus, the potential strategies or options for restoring a tarnished image grow out of the two components of an attack, criticism, or accusation.

Table 6.1 lists five general strategies and 14 specific tactics for image repair. The first two general categories, denial and evasion of responsibility, attempt to reduce (or eliminate) the accused's apparent responsibility for the offensive act. The next two general strategies, reducing effectiveness and corrective action, attempt to reduce the perceived offensiveness of the act in question. Finally, as indicated earlier, mortification admits performing an offensive act but apologizes and asks for forgiveness. All of these strategies have the potential to rehabilitate, at least in part, a damaged image or reputation.

Effectiveness of Image Repair Strategies

Some quantitative research has investigated the effectiveness of attempts to restore a damaged reputation. Benoit and Drew (1997) reported that offering corrective action and apologizing (mortification) are perceived to be the most effective and appropriate strategies. However, a good deal of this work has used rhetorical criticism or a case-study approach. Benoit (1997) summarized this work and offered several suggestions for repairing a damaged reputation. First, it is important to identify all of the key accusations; a message that ignores key allegations will not repair one's credibility. Second, it is vital to identify the key audience. The persuader need not necessarily restore lost credibility for everyone; the ones who matter the most are those he or she will try to persuade (the target audience for a persuasive message should be the target audience for repairing a tarnished image).

Benoit also offered suggestions for constructing a message to repair a damaged image. He begins by cautioning that the image repair message itself must be persuasive, using strong arguments, providing adequate support for claims, and so forth. He recommends that people who have committed wrongdoing confess and apologize; for example,

TABLE 6.1   *Image Restoration Strategies*

Strategy	Key Characteristic	Example
Denial		
Simple denial	did not perform act	Tylenol: did not poison capsule
Shift the blame	another performed act	Tylenol: a "madman" poisoned capsules
Evasion of Responsibility		
Provocation	responded to act of another	firm moved because of new taxes
Defeasibility	lack of information or ability	executive not told meeting changed
Accident	mishap	tree fell on tracks causing train wreck
Good intentions	meant well	Sears eager to provide good auto repair service
Reducing Offensiveness of Event		
Bolstering	stress good traits	Exxon's "swift and competent" cleanup of oil spill
Minimization	act not serious	Exxon: few animals killed in oil spill
Differentiation	act less offensive than similar acts	Sears: unnecessary repairs preventive maintenance, not fraud
Transcendence	more important values	helping humans justifies testing animals
Attack accuser	reduce credibility of accuser	Coke: Pepsi owns restaurants, competes directly with you for customers
Compensation	reimburse victim	disabled moviegoers given free passes after being denied admission to movie
Corrective Action		
	plan to solve/prevent recurrence of problem	AT&T long-distance upgrades; will spend billions more to improve service
Mortification		
	apologize	AT&T apologized for service interruption

Derived from Benoit, 1995, 1997.

President Clinton probably got into more trouble from deceiving people about his relationship with Monica Lewinsky than from the relationship itself. On the other hand, those who are truly innocent (e.g., Tylenol apparently was not responsible for tainted medication) should proclaim innocence and if possible identify the "true" culprit. However, blame should be shifted away from the persuader. Nixon blamed his closest, hand-picked subordinates for Watergate. Clearly, this did not clear him from blame. At times factors beyond one's control are to blame. Exxon could have blamed the slow oil spill cleanup on poor weather. However, they chose to blame the U.S. Coast Guard and the state of Alaska (implausible targets of blame). It is important to implement corrective action, either by fixing the problem or preventing its recurrence (or both). Even though Tylenol established its innocence, it introduced tamper-resistant packaging and then gradually replaced capsules with caplets to prevent future episodes of poisoning. Some strategies (e.g., minimization, provocation) have not been found to be effective.

It is also possible to combine some of these strategies, but not all combinations are equally effective. For example, mortification and corrective action seem to complement one another: "I am sorry for the damage I caused and I will fix the problem" is a plausible response. On the other hand, "I did nothing wrong and I apologize" seems to be an awkward combination: Why would you apologize if you (truly) did nothing wrong? It is therefore important to develop strategies that work in harmony.

Thus, while some reputations may be beyond repair (e.g., Jeffrey Dahmer), it *is* possible for persuaders to improve their credibility. Research has identified a number of options available to those who need to repair a tarnished reputation. We are beginning to develop an understanding of how and when to use these options. It is clear, however, that more empirical work would be helpful in this area.

Conclusion

In this chapter we took the ELM as a theoretical standpoint for understanding source effects in persuasion. Unlike attractive sources, expert and trustworthy sources influence persuasion only when they are identified as such before a message is processed. We hold that attitude change is a function of the number and valence of thoughts produced in response to persuasive messages. Because it often functions as a peripheral cue, credibility is more likely to influence persuasion on less involving topics. Credible sources may reduce motivation to process messages, which means that they are likely to facilitate persuasion when thoughts are likely to be unfavorable and may actually impede persuasion when thoughts are likely to be favorable. Disreputable sources are likely to encourage unfavorable cognitive responses and result in less persuasion. Highly credible sources may increase a message's persuasiveness by permitting higher levels of discrepancy (without an increase in unfavorable thoughts).

We also expressed several reservations about current research on source effects in persuasion. Some studies do not make it clear how credibility is manipulated or measured. Other studies clearly confound multiple constructs (expertise, trustworthiness, attractiveness, and prestige). Some research does not measure (or report) the effects of independent variables on cognitive responses, which are conceptualized as a mediating variable in the process of persuasion. It may be useful to employ alternative methods of measuring cognitive responses (concurrent verbalization). Despite literally centuries of inquiry into the effects of source variables on persuasion, this construct would benefit from more focused research.

Finally, we addressed the topic of changes in perceived credibility. Persuaders who suffer damage to credibility do have a chance of repairing their tarnished reputations, and thereby enhancing future attempts at persuasion. However, it is clear that more empirical investigation into this topic would greatly enhance our understanding.

References

Andersen, K., & Clevenger, T. (1963). A summary of experimental research in ethos. *Speech Monographs, 30,* 59–78.

Andrews, J. C., & Shimp, T. A. (1990). Effects of involvement, argument strength, and source characteristics on central and peripheral processing in advertising. *Psychology & Marketing, 7,* 195–214.

Aristotle. (1954). *The rhetoric* (W. R. Roberts, trans.). New York: Random House, Modern Library.

Aronson, E., Turner, J. A., & Carlsmith, J. M. (1963). Communicator credibility and communication discrepancy as determinants of opinion change. *Journal of Abnormal and Social Psychology, 67,* 31–36.

Benoit, W. L. (1987). Argument and credibility appeals in persuasion. *Southern Speech Communication Journal, 52,* 181–197.

Benoit, W. L. (1991). A cognitive response analysis of source credibility. In B. Dervin & M. J. Voigt (Eds.), *Progress in communication sciences* (vol. X, pp. 1–19). Norwood, NJ: Ablex.

Benoit, W. L. (1995). *Accounts, excuses, apologies: A theory of image restoration strategies.* Albany, NY: State University of New York Press.

Benoit, W. L. (1997). Image restoration discourse and crisis communication. *Public Relations Review, 23,* 177–186.

Benoit, W. L., & Dornes, B. (1996). *Dateline NBC*'s persuasive attack of WalMart. *Communication Quarterly, 44,* 463–477.

Benoit, W. L., & Drew, S. (1997). Appropriateness and effectiveness of image repair strategies. *Communication Reports, 10,* 153–163.

Benoit, W. L., & Harthcock, A. (1999). Functions of the Great Debates: Acclaims, attacks, and defenses in the 1960 presidential debates. *Communication Monographs, 66,* 341–357.

Benoit, W. L., & Kennedy, K. A. (1999). On reluctant testimony. *Communication Quarterly, 47,* 367–387.

Benoit, W. L., & Wells, W. T. (1996). *Candidates in conflict: Persuasive attack and defense in the 1992 presidential debates.* Tuscaloosa, AL: University of Alabama Press.

Berscheid, E. (1985). Interpersonal attraction. In G. Lindsey & E. Aronson (Eds.), *Handbook of social psychology* (3rd ed., vol. 2, pp. 413–484). New York: Random House.

Berscheid, E., & Walster, E. (1974). Physical attractiveness: In L. Berkowitz (Ed.), *Advances in experimental social psychology, 7,* 157–215. New York: Academic Press.

Bochner, S., & Insko, C. (1966). Communication discrepancy, source credibility, and opinion change. *Journal of Personality and Social Psychology, 4,* 614–621.

Bock, D., & Saine, T. (1975). The impact of source credibility, attitude valence, and task sensitivity on trait errors in speech evaluation. *Speech Monographs, 37,* 148–155.

Brock, T. C. (1967). Communication discrepancy and intent to persuade as determinants of counterargument production. *Journal of Experimental Social Psychology, 3,* 296–309.

Cacioppo, J. T., & Petty, R. E. (1985). Central and peripheral routes to persuasion: The role of message repetition. In L. F. Alwitt & A. A. Mitchell (Eds.), *Psychological processes and advertising effects: Theory, research, and application* (pp. 91–111). Hillsdale, NJ: Erlbaum.

Cacioppo, J. T., Petty, R. E., & Kao, C. F. (1984). The efficient assessment of need for cognition. *Journal of Personality Assessment, 48,* 306–307.

Cacioppo, J. T., Petty, R. E., & Morris, K. (1983). Effects of need for cognition on message evaluation, recall, and persuasion. *Journal of Personality and Social Psychology, 45*, 805–818.

Calder, B. J., Insko, C. A., & Yandell, B. (1974). The relation of cognitive and memorial processes to persuasion in a simulated jury trial. *Journal of Applied Social Psychology, 4*, 62–93.

Chaiken, S. (1979). Communicator physical attractiveness and persuasion. *Journal of Personality and Social Psychology, 37*, 1387–1397.

Chaiken, S. (1980). Heuristic versus systematic information processing and the use of source versus message cues in persuasion. *Journal of Personality and Social Psychology, 39*, 752–756.

Chaiken, S., & Maheswaran, D. (1994). Heuristic processing can bias systematic processing: Effects of source credibility, argument ambiguity, and task importance on attitude judgment. *Journal of Personality and Social Psychology, 66*, 460–473.

Chebat, J-C., Filiatrault, P., Larouche, M., & Watson, C. (1988). Compensatory effects of cognitive characteristics of the source, the message, and the receiver upon attitude change. *Journal of Psychology, 122*, 609–621.

Chebat, J-C., Filiatrault, P., & Perrien, J. (1990). Limits of credibility: The case of political persuasion. *Journal of Social Psychology, 130*, 157–167.

Choo, T. (1964). Communicator credibility and communication discrepancy as determinants of attitude change. *Journal of Social Psychology, 64*, 65–76.

Cicero. (1942). *De oratore* (E. W. Sutton & H. Rackham, trans.). Cambridge, MA: Harvard University Press.

Cook, T. D. (1969). Competence, counterarguing, and attitude change. *Journal of Personality, 37*, 342–358.

Dean, R., Austin, J., & Watts, W. (1971). Forewarning effects in persuasion: Field and classroom experiments. *Journal of Personality and Social Psychology, 18*, 210–221.

Debono, K. G., & Harnish, R. (1988). Source expertise, source attractiveness, and the processing of persuasive information: A functional approach. *Personality and Social Psychology Bulletin, 17*, 245–251.

Eagly, A. H., & Chaiken, S. (1975). An attribution analysis of the effect of communicator characteristics on opinion change: The case of communicator attractiveness. *Journal of Personality and Social Psychology, 32*, 136–44.

Eagly, A. H., & Chaiken, S. (1993). *The psychology of attitudes.* Fort Worth, TX: Harcourt Brace Jovanovich.

Gillig, P. M., & Greenwald, A. G. (1974). Is it time to lay the sleeper effect to rest? *Journal of Personality and Social Psychology, 29*, 132–139.

Greenberg, B. S., & Miller, G. R. (1966). The effects of low-credible sources on message acceptance. *Speech Monographs, 33*, 127–136.

Greenberg, B. S., & Tannenbaum, P. H. (1961). The effects of bylines on attitude change. *Journalism Quarterly, 38*, 535–537.

Greenwald, A. G. (1968). Cognitive learning, cognitive response to persuasion, and attitude change. In A. G. Greenwald, T. C. Brock, & T. M. Ostrom (Eds.), *Psychological foundations of attitudes* (pp. 147–170). New York: Academic Press.

Harkins, S. G., & Petty, R. E. (1981). Effects of source magnification of cognitive effort on attitudes: An information processing view. *Journal of Personality and Social Psychology, 40*, 401–413.

Hass, R. G. (1981). Effects of source characteristics on cognitive responses and persuasion. In R. E. Petty, T. M. Ostrom, & T. C. Brock (Eds.), *Cognitive responses in persuasion* (pp. 44–72). Hillsdale, NJ: Erlbaum.

Husek, T. R. (1965). Persuasive impacts of early, late, or no mention of the negative source. *Journal of Personality and Social Psychology, 2*, 125–128.

Insko, C. A., Murashima, F., & Saiyadain, M. (1966). Communicator discrepancy, stimulus ambiguity, and influence. *Journal of Personality, 34*, 262–274.

Isocrates. (1976). Antidosis. *Isocrates* (G. Norlin, trans.). Cambridge, MA: Harvard University Press, Loeb Classical Library, vol. 1.

Johnson, B. T., & Eagly, A. H. (1989). The effects of involvement on persuasion: A meta-analysis. *Psychological Bulletin, 106*, 290–314.

Johnson, H. H. (1966). Some effects of discrepancy level on responses to negative information about one's self. *Sociometry, 29,* 52–66.

Johnson, H. H., & Scileppi, J. A. (1969). Effects of ego-involvement conditions on attitude change to high and low communicators. *Journal of Personality and Social Psychology, 13,* 31–36.

Kahle, L. R., & Homer, P. M. (1985). Physical attractiveness of the celebrity endorser: A social adaptation perspective. *Journal of Consumer Research, 11,* 954–961.

Littlejohn, S. (1971). A bibliography of studies related to variables of source credibility. In N. A. Shearer (Ed.), *Bibliographic Annual in Speech Communication, 2,* 1–40.

McCroskey, J. C., & Teven, J. J. (1999). Goodwill: A reexamination of the construct and its measurement. *Communication Monographs, 66,* 90–103.

Mills, J., & Harvey, J. (1972). Opinion change as a function of when information about the communicator is received and whether he is attractive or expert. *Journal of Personality and Social Psychology, 21,* 52–55.

Neimeyer, G. J., Guy, J., & Metzler, A. (1989). Changing attitudes regarding the treatment of disordered eating: An application of the Elaboration Likelihood Model. *Journal of Social and Clinical Psychology, 8,* 70–86.

O'Keefe, D. J. (1987). The persuasive effects of delaying identification of high- and low-credibility communicators: A meta-analytic review. *Central States Speech Journal, 38,* 63–72.

Osgood, C. E., & Tannenbaum, P. H. (1955). The principle of congruity in the prediction of attitude change. *Psychological Review, 62,* 42–55.

Osterhouse, R. A., & Brock, T. C. (1970). Distraction increases yielding to propaganda by inhibiting counterarguing. *Journal of Personality and Social Psychology, 15,* 344–358.

Perloff, R. M., & Brock, T. C. (1980). . . . 'And thinking makes it so': Cognitive responses to persuasion. In M. E. Roloff & G. R. Miller (Eds.), *Persuasion: New directions in theory and research* (pp. 67–99). Beverly Hills, CA: Sage.

Peterson, P. D., & Koulack, D. (1969). Attitude change as a function of latitudes of acceptance and rejection. *Journal of Personality and Social Psychology, 11,* 309–311.

Petty, R. E., & Cacioppo, J. T. (1977). Forewarning, cognitive responding, and resistance to persuasion. *Journal of Personality and Social Psychology, 35,* 645–655.

Petty, R. E., & Cacioppo, J. T. (1979a). Effects of forewarning of persuasive intent and involvement on cognitive responses and persuasion. *Personality and Social Psychology Bulletin, 5,* 173–176.

Petty, R. E., & Cacioppo, J. T. (1979b). Issue involvement can increase or decrease persuasion by enhancing message-relevant cognitive processes. *Journal of Personality and Social Psychology, 37,* 1915–1926.

Petty, R. E., & Cacioppo, J. T. (1981a). *Attitudes and persuasion: Classic and contemporary approaches.* Dubuque, IA: William C. Brown.

Petty, R. E., & Cacioppo, J. T. (1981b). Issue involvement as a moderator of the effects on attitude of advertising content and context. In K. B. Monroe (Ed.), *Advances in Consumer Research* (vol. 8, pp. 20–24). Ann Arbor, MI: Association for Consumer Research.

Petty, R. E., & Cacioppo, J. T. (1984). The effects of involvement on responses to argument quantity and quality: Central and peripheral routes to persuasion. *Journal of Personality and Social Psychology, 46,* 69–81.

Petty, R. E., & Cacioppo, J. T. (1986a). *Communication and persuasion: Central and peripheral routes to attitude change.* New York: Springer-Verlag.

Petty, R. E., & Cacioppo, J. T. (1986b). The elaboration likelihood model of persuasion. In L. Berkowitz (Ed.), *Advances in experimental social psychology* (vol. 19, pp. 123–205). San Diego, CA: Academic Press.

Petty, R. E., Cacioppo, J. T., & Goldman, R. (1981). Personal involvement as a determinant of argument-based persuasion. *Journal of Personality and Social Psychology, 41,* 847–855.

Petty, R. E., Cacioppo, J. T., & Schumann, D. (1983). Central and peripheral routes to advertising effectiveness: The moderating role of involvement. *Journal of Consumer Research, 10,* 135–146.

Petty, R. E., Haugtvedt, C. P., & Smith, S. M. (1995). Elaboration as a determinant of attitude strength: Creating attitudes that are persistent, resistant, and predictive of behavior. In R. E. Petty & J. A.

Krosnick (Eds.), *Attitude strength: Antecedents and consequences* (pp. 93–130). Mahwah, NJ: Erlbaum.

Petty, R. E., Ostrom, T. M., & Brock, T. C. (Eds.) (1981). *Cognitive responses in persuasion.* Hillsdale, NJ: Erlbaum.

Petty, R. E., Ostrom, T. M., & Brock, T. C. (1981). Historical foundations of the cognitive response approach to attitudes and persuasion. In R. E. Petty, T. M. Ostrom, & T. C. Brock (Eds.), *Cognitive responses in persuasion* (pp. 5–29). Hillsdale, NJ: Erlbaum.

Petty, R. E., Schumann, D. W., Richman, S. A., & Strathman, A. J. (1993). Positive mood and persuasion: Different roles for affect under high- and low-elaboration conditions. *Journal of Personality and Social Psychology, 64,* 5–20.

Petty, R. E., Wells, G. L., & Brock, T. C. (1976). Distraction can enhance or reduce yielding to propaganda: Thought disruption versus effort justification. *Journal of Personality and Social Psychology, 34,* 874–884.

Rhine, R. J., & Kaplan, R. M. (1972). The effect of incredulity upon evaluation of the source of a communication. *Journal of Social Psychology, 88,* 255–266.

Rhine, R. J., & Severance, L. J. (1970). Ego-involvement, discrepancy, source credibility, and attitude change. *Journal of Personality and Social Psychology, 16,* 175–190.

Roser, C., & Thompson, M. (1995). Fear appeals and the formation of active publics. *Journal of Communication, 45,* 103–121.

Shavitt, S., Swan, S., Lowrey, T. M., & Wanke, M. (1994). The interaction of endorser attractiveness and involvement in persuasion depends on the goal that guides message processing. *Journal of Consumer Psychology, 3,* 137–162.

Simons, H. W., Berkowitz, N. N., & Moyer, R. J. (1970). Similarity, credibility, and attitude change: A review and a theory. *Psychological Bulletin, 42,* 285–314.

Sivacek, J., & Crano, W. D. (1982). Vested interest as a moderator of attitude-behavior consistency. *Journal of Personality and Social Psychology, 43,* 210–221.

Sternthal, B., Dholakia, R., & Leavitt, C. (1978). The persuasive effect of source credibility: A situational analysis. *Public Opinion Quarterly, 42,* 285–314.

Stiff, J. B. (1986). Cognitive processing of persuasive message cues: A meta-analytic review of the effects of supporting information on attitudes. *Communication Monographs, 53,* 75–89.

Stiff, J. B. (1994). *Persuasive communication.* New York: Guilford Press.

Tannenbaum, P. H. (1967). The congruity theory revisited: Studies in the reduction, induction, and generalization of persuasion. In L. Berkowitz (Ed.), *Advances in experimental social psychology* (vol. 3, pp. 271–320). New York: Academic Press.

Ward, C. D., & McGinnies, E. (1974). Persuasive effect of early and late mention of credible and noncredible sources. *Journal of Psychology, 86,* 17–23.

Wilson, E. J., & Sherrell, D. L. (1993). Source effects in communication and persuasion research: A meta-analysis of effect size. *Journal of the Academy of Marketing Science, 21,* 101–112.

7

Argumentativeness, Verbal Aggressiveness, and Persuasion

Andrew S. Rancer

Introduction

Over the last several decades, scholars in the communication discipline have advanced many models of persuasion. For several years, the "one to many" model prevailed. In that model, scholars were generally concerned with how source and message variables influence large groups of people. Since then, a new emphasis has emerged. The publication of a seminal study on compliance gaining by Miller, Boster, Roloff, & Seibold (1977) focused renewed interest and attention on *interpersonal persuasion*. This model concerned itself with issues such as how we persuade people to do something we want them to, how we resist attempts by others to influence us, and the role of aggressive communication in interpersonal relations (Infante, Rancer, & Womack, 1997).

Very often, such compliance-gaining attempts involve the use of *argumentative behavior*. That is, when attempting to persuade others, sometimes people present arguments supporting the position(s) they are advocating, while attempting to refute the position(s) of others. These compliance-gaining attempts can vary considerably. For example, they might involve arguing with a variety of people, including strangers or intimates. They can also involve arguing over both "major" issues, such as where you and your partner should take your annual vacation, and more "minor" ones, such as what flavor toothpaste you should buy. It should be noted, however, that a minor issue to one person may be seen as a major issue to another.

The manner in which partners communicate during these compliance-gaining efforts can help determine whether their relationship will be seen as satisfying or unsatisfying, or whether the compliance-gaining attempt will be successful or unsuccessful. For example, a person who communicates aggressively, attacking the self-esteem of his or her partner, might damage the relationship and be less persuasive as a result. Accordingly, an understanding of argumentativeness and verbal aggressiveness can facilitate a better understanding of persuasion in one-on-one settings. With this context in mind, the focus of this chapter is a discussion of interpersonal (or informal) persuasion as it is exhibited via aggressive communication.

A Conceptualization of Aggressive Communication

A communicative behavior is "aggressive if it applies force . . . symbolically in order, minimally, to dominate and perhaps damage, or maximally, to defeat and perhaps destroy the locus of the attack" (Infante, 1987a, p. 158). To pressure someone into behaving a particular way, for example, a persuader might attack that person's self-esteem by using profanity or by calling the other person names. Though many behaviors are aggressive in nature, not all are as "bad" as this example suggests. To be sure, some aggressive behaviors are "bad" while others are "good." Let us say, for example, that you hire an attorney to defend you. More than likely you would not want him or her to sit passively in the courtroom while the opposing attorney "trounces" you. Rather, you would want your own attorney to respond aggressively, offering a barrage of arguments and convincing legal points. In this example, aggressiveness on the part of your attorney would be considered "a good thing."

This duality in aggressive communication, that is, the fact that such communication can be "good" or "bad," can be clarified in a model that provides a framework for the research examined in this chapter. The model posits that a cluster of four traits controls aggressive communication. Each of these traits interacts with factors in the environment to energize message behavior (Infante, 1987a). Two of the traits are basically constructive and two are destructive. They are discussed in turn in the next sections.

Assertiveness and Argumentativeness:
The Constructive Traits

Assertiveness and argumentativeness are the constructive traits. *Assertiveness* is the more global of the two. If you are assertive, you tend to be interpersonally ascendant, dominant, and forceful, using this behavior to achieve personal goals while creating positive affect in people. If you are highly *argumentative,* you tend to advocate and defend positions on controversial issues while attempting to refute other people's positions on those issues (Infante & Rancer, 1982, 1996). Argumentativeness is a subset of assertiveness, because all argument is assertive, though not all assertiveness involves argument (e.g., a request).

Depending on their predisposition to argue, people can be considered either high or low argumentatives. In addition, there are at least two types of moderate argumentatives: those with conflicting feelings and those who are apathetic. In each case, the situation influences whether such people engage in argumentation. Moderate argumentatives who have "conflicting feelings" argue mainly when the probability of success is high and the importance of failure is low. This is because they wish to avoid feeling anxious about the possibility of losing an important argument. In contrast, moderate argumentatives who are "apathetic" generally argue when the incentive of success is high. They neither like nor dislike arguing and engage in it mainly for utilitarian reasons.

Hostility and Verbal Aggressiveness: The Destructive Traits

When people "argue," they can move from constructive, argumentative behavior to another form of aggressive communication behavior. That is, with conscious intent, interactants can get "mean" or "hurtful." This switch in interaction styles can occur when people believe that they are losing the argument and/or when they have trouble generating additional arguments to employ in support of their position on a controversial issue.

The two destructive traits in the model of aggressive communication are hostility and verbal aggressiveness. *Hostility* is more global. People with this trait use messages to express irritability, negativism, resentment, and suspicion. People high in *verbal aggressiveness* tend to attack the self-concepts of other people in order to inflict psychological pain such as humiliation, embarrassment, depression, and other negative feelings about self (Infante & Wigley, 1986). The model of verbal aggressiveness specifies that there are several types of verbally aggressive messages: character, competence, background, and physical appearance attacks; ridicule; threats; profanity; maledictions; teasing; and nonverbal emblems. Kinney (1994) suggested there are three broad domains of self-concept attack: group membership, personal failings, and relational failings.

Several causes of verbal aggression have been suggested, including psychopathology, disdain, social learning, and argumentative skill deficiencies (Infante & Rancer, 1996). More recently, it has been argued that verbal aggressiveness may be largely the result of genetics (Beatty & McCroskey, 1997, 1998; Valencic, Beatty, Rudd, Dobos, & Heisel, 1998). Under this framework, verbal aggressiveness may be considered an inherited predisposition.

High verbal aggressives seem desensitized to the hurt they cause others because they do not view verbally aggressive messages in the same way other people do. The main reasons they give for their use of verbal aggression are disdain for the target, desire to be mean, eagerness to appear tough, and involvement in discussions that degenerate into verbal fights (Infante et al., 1992).

According to Costa and McCrae's (1980) three-factor model of personality, argumentativeness and verbal aggressiveness are situated in different, independent dimensions of personality. Argumentativeness is a facet of the extroversion dimension of personality, while verbal aggressiveness is a facet of the neuroticism dimension of personality (Costa & McCrae, 1980). As such, researchers have traditionally viewed the two traits as unrelated. Thus, high, moderate, and low argumentatives were thought to be equally likely to be high verbal aggressives. Although this assumption was supported by several earlier studies (e.g., Infante & Rancer, 1982; Infante & Wigley, 1986), more recent empirical research has suggested that at least for some populations (e.g., adolescents), argumentativeness and verbal aggressiveness are moderately correlated (Rancer, Whitecap, Kosberg, & Avtgis, 1997; Rancer, Avtgis, Kosberg, & Whitecap, 2000; Roberto & Finucane, 1997).

Understanding Aggressive Communication in Persuasion: Situational Factors Also Matter

So far, we have seen that people's traits influence the degree to which their behavior is aggressive. In addition to the trait component, situational factors are assumed to influence aggressive communication behavior. In other words, aggressive communication can be understood as a joint product of situational factors *and* the characteristics of the person (Andersen, 1987; Atkinson, 1957; Epstein, 1979). This constitutes an *interactionist approach to personality* (e.g., Epstein, 1979; Magnusson & Endler, 1977).

Consistent with this approach, Infante's (1987b) model of argumentativeness included both trait and situational factors to predict more accurately how motivated a person will be to argue in any given situation. This model suggests that a person's motivation to argue in a given situation is determined by his or her trait argumentativeness (ARGgt), as well as perceptions of how likely he or she is to succeed or fail and how important it is to succeed in the given situation. An example of this interactionist approach would be the following: If Brandon thinks his argument will probably fail, and he doesn't mind failing, his motivation to argue may be low. On the other hand, if he thinks he will succeed, and success is important in the particular situation, his motivation to argue may be high. A high motivation to argue, coupled with high trait argumentativeness, should increase argumentativeness even further.

Several studies have supported the central contention of this interactionist model, that predictions based on traits or situations alone are not as accurate as predictions based on both traits and situations (Infante, 1987b; Infante & Rancer, 1982, 1993; Stewart & Roach, 1993). For example, one situational factor that might influence argumentative behavior is the nature of the topic itself. To be certain, Onyekwere, Rubin, and Infante (1991) found that ego-involvement in the topic of an argument influenced the behavior of high and low argumentatives. Specifically, when people were highly involved in an issue (e.g., a gun store owner arguing about gun control), they were not only more motivated to argue, their argumentative behavior was improved as well. Similarly, Infante and Rancer (1993) found that high argumentatives argued more about certain topics than did moderate and low argumentatives (e.g., social, political, personal behavior, others' behavior, and moral-ethical issues) but behaved no differently than low and moderate argumentatives on other topics (e.g., sports, entertainment, religious issues). Finally, based upon this interactionist perspective, Stewart and Roach (1993) investigated how a situational factor (e.g., the topic of an argument) and a characteristic of the communicator (e.g., religious orientation) influenced argumentative behavior. They found that in general, trait argumentativeness was the most important factor associated with a person's willingness to argue. However, extrinsically religious persons (those who view religion mainly as an instrumental social convention and are more utilitarian and irregular in their churchgoing behavior) were more argumentative than were either intrinsically religious persons (those who view religion as the source of meaning in life and are regular in their churchgoing behavior) or proreligious persons (those who have high levels of intrinsicness and high levels of extrinsicness) (Stewart & Roach, 1993, p. 28). Nonreligious persons were also more willing to argue than were proreligious persons.

In addition to the topic of argument, characteristics of the communicators can act as determinants of argumentative behavior (Wigley, 1998). One such factor is a person's gender. For example, Infante (1989) examined what types of messages males and females used when trying to persuade people. Male and female participants were asked to imagine themselves trying to persuade a friend. After each attempt, the friend responded with either argumentative or verbally aggressive messages. Moreover, after each of the friend's rejections, participants were asked to choose one of four follow-up strategies: rewarding, punishing, argumentative, or verbally aggressive messages. Results indicated that when the target was verbally aggressive, males were more likely than females to respond with verbal aggression, whereas females were more likely that males to respond argumentatively.

Another situational factor that may influence one's argumentativeness includes the nature or behavior of one's partner. For example, Rancer and Infante (1985) found that the argumentativeness of an individual and that of his or her adversary interact to determine motivation for arguing in a specific situation. Waggenspack and Hensley (1989) examined how the interpersonal situation (socially oriented or conflict oriented) and gender influence preference for having a partner who is argumentative. Lim (1990) found that situational factors, such as the friendliness and intensity of resistance by a target of persuasion, are important in identifying whether a persuader will exhibit verbal aggressiveness. Specifically, persuaders were more verbally aggressive when targets of the persuasive attempt were unfriendly than when they were friendly. In addition, persuaders resorted to higher levels of verbal aggressiveness more quickly when targets exhibited more intense resistance to the persuasive attempt. That is, when individuals felt that their efforts at persuasion were going to fail, they were quicker to resort to higher levels of verbally aggressive communication (Lim, 1990).

Along these same lines, Infante, Trebing, Shepherd, and Seeds (1984) found that verbal aggressiveness is dependent upon the individual's argumentativeness and the obstinacy (i.e., stubbornness) of his or her opponent. A study conducted from the perspective of the receiver of the message (Infante, Wall, Leap, & Danielson, 1984) found that the gender of the message source determined whether more argumentative people received verbal aggression.

In summary, these studies indicate that situational factors do indeed influence aggressive communication and as such should be considered along with trait predispositions when attempting to explain a person's behavior during social influence.

Argumentativeness, the Interactionist Perspective, and the Theory of Reasoned Action

Stewart and Roach (1998) tested two competing theoretical frameworks for determining a person's "intentions to argue": the interactionist perspective and the Theory of Reasoned Action (TRA) (Ajzen & Fishbein, 1980; Fishbein & Ajzen, 1975). Recall that the "interactionist perspective" maintains that people's motivation to argue is determined by the interaction of situational factors and traits (i.e., argumentativeness) as well as the perceived probability and importance of success and failure in a given situation. The TRA maintains that a person's decision to engage in a purposeful activity depends on several factors, some of which are situational and some of which are mediated by personal dispositions or traits (for a more detailed description of TRA, see chapter 4).

Stewart and Roach (1998) argued that the TRA might have "greater explanatory power" than the interactionist framework for understanding argumentative intentions, because the TRA takes into account a greater number of situational factors (Stewart & Roach, 1998, p. 182)—for example, people's beliefs about arguing (e.g., Rancer, Baukus, & Infante, 1985; Rancer, Kosberg, & Baukus, 1992), the importance (ego-involvement) placed on the issue of the argument (e.g., Infante & Rancer, 1993; Onyekwere, Rubin, & Infante, 1991), the effects of other dispositional factors (e.g., Stewart & Roach, 1993), and the influence of other people. It was reasoned that all of these factors might combine to influence a person's intentions to argue in a given situation. Since arguing is an intentional behavior under the control of the arguer, it can legitimately be called a form of "reasoned action" (Stewart & Roach, 1998).

The results of Stewart and Roach's (1998) study showed that the TRA was no better than the interactionist model at predicting argumentative intentions. Indeed, the TRA was less powerful than the interactionist model in predicting motivation to argue. This prompted the researchers to state, "As such, the interactionist model warrants further use as a framework for the study of trait versus situational determinants of argumentative intentions" (Stewart & Roach 1998, p. 191).

However, Stewart and Roach found that people's attitudes toward arguing in a particular situation, coupled with their beliefs about what people who are important to them think about arguing, are the primary determinants of intentions to argue. Their findings also revealed that whereas high argumentatives generally had a more positive attitude about arguing than did low argumentatives, the direct effect of those attitudes on intentions to argue came from sources other than trait argumentativeness (i.e., the normative component and the perceived behavioral control portions of the TRA—see chapter 4). This finding suggests that beliefs and motivations to argue may be more socially driven than individually determined. Stewart and Roach (1998) speculated that because high argumentatives are more competent communicators, they may be more open to normative pressures in deciding whether to engage in an argument, as well as experiencing strong social pressure to perform well in an argumentative situation.

Identifying Beliefs About Arguing

One way to understand aggressive communication is to study the beliefs people have about arguing and employing verbal aggression. For example, Rancer, Baukus, and Infante (1985) found that people maintain several belief structures about arguing. These include the following:

- *Hostility*—the belief that arguing is a combative encounter.
- *Activity/process*—the belief that arguing is a mode of interaction, like having a conversation.

- *Control/dominance*—the belief that arguing is a way of having one's opinions prevail.
- *Conflict/dissonance*—the belief that arguing is a source of conflict or dissonance between antagonists.
- *Self-image*—the belief that arguing is an encounter that impacts on a person's sense of self.
- *Learning*—the belief that arguing is a way to learn about self, others, or the environment.
- *Skill*—the belief that arguing is an indicator of one's verbal skills.

These belief structures were found to distinguish individuals who vary in argumentativeness. A greater proportion of high argumentatives had positive beliefs about activity/process, control/dominance, conflict/dissonance, self-image, learning, and skill. More low argumentatives held negative beliefs of hostility, control/dominance, and conflict/dissonance.

In addition, high, moderate, and low argumentatives were found to have different perceptions of two functions of arguing: *cultivation* and *antagonism*. High argumentatives view arguing as a source for cultivating information, whereas low argumentatives see it as a behavior that reveals their lack of argumentative and rhetorical competence. Moreover, while high argumentatives view arguments as a means of reducing conflict, low argumentatives see them as unfavorable and hostile acts to be avoided at all costs (Rancer, et al., 1985).

Understanding such beliefs about arguing is significant because it may help individuals function more effectively in compliance-gaining, persuasive, and conflict management situations. For example, some spouses have difficulty managing their communication when they are trying to influence each other. It may be that spouses' differing beliefs about arguing contribute to the tension they experience. The husband, for example, may possess a positive belief about arguing as learning (a way to gather information), and manifest this belief whenever he tries to understand his wife's position on an issue on which they disagree. His wife, however, may possess a negative learning belief that causes her to become agitated and uncomfortable when her husband begins "arguing" with her (i.e., when he asks her probing questions concerning the position she holds, or continues to probe her position beyond what she feels is a "reasonable" amount of time).

Following this same vein, Rancer, Kosberg, and Baukus (1992) examined which beliefs best predict argumentativeness and which best discriminate between high and low argumentatives. Results of their study indicated that high argumentatives believe that arguing has enjoyable, functional, and pragmatic outcomes, as well as having a positive impact on their self-concept. Low argumentatives' beliefs about arguing lay in the opposite direction. Using this "beliefs about arguing" framework, Rancer and Baukus (1987) concluded that males and females differ in belief structures about arguing, with females holding more negative beliefs than males.

A related line of research has investigated beliefs about engaging in verbal aggression. For instance, Infante, Riddle, Horvath, and Tumlin (1992) found differences in beliefs about verbal aggression between those who vary in the trait. Specifically, high verbal aggressives believed that competence attacks, physical appearance attacks, and threats were less hurtful to others than did individuals low in verbal aggressiveness.

A Transactional Approach to Argumentativeness and Persuasion

A "transactional approach" to personality suggests that an individual's personality may influence others' behavior as well as his or her own. This approach assumes that one person's message behavior affects the other's message behavior and vice versa. Levine and Boster (1996) expanded our understanding of argumentativeness and persuasion by incorporating a transactional approach to examining argumentative behavior. Their study involved observing persuasive interactions (i.e., five-minute arguments over controversial issues) between individuals who were matched and mismatched on argumentativeness (i.e., high argumentatives talking with high argumentatives, low argumentatives talking with low argumentatives, and high argumentatives talking with low argumentatives). The researchers studied the impact of each actor's argumentativeness on the number of arguments and the type of resolution generated in these arguments. The results revealed that *both* conversational partners' levels of argumentativeness interacted to influence both the number of arguments generated and the extent to which one person yielded to the position advocated by the other. In general, the "high argumentativeness–low-argumentative other" condition emerged as the one in which persons generated the greatest number of arguments and showed the most resistance to yielding to the other. More specifically, highly argumentative individuals were more argumentative when paired with a low-, rather than high-argumentative partner. The results also revealed that the argumentativeness of the adversary did not substantially affect the argumentative behavior of low argumentatives.

In order to explain these findings, Levine and Boster (1996) speculated that high argumentatives like winning and, when paired with a low argumentative partner, seize this opportunity to demonstrate their superior argumentative skill. They also suggested that when paired with an equally argumentative adversary, the high argumentative might experience some frustration in his or her inability to dominate his or her adversary, which would then be reflected in his or her less assertive behavior. These findings, however, are contrary to earlier research by Rancer and Infante (1985), who discovered that highly argumentative individuals reported more motivation to argue when paired with a similar adversary. While the Levine and Boster (1996) findings may have more limited generalizability (only males were included in the study), they do underscore the value of using a transactional approach to studying aggressive communication and persuasion.

Processing Persuasive Messages: The Influence of Aggressive Communication Predispositions

In addition to investigating how argumentativeness and verbal aggressiveness affect the manner in which people seek compliance, research has explored how these traits affect people's processing of persuasive messages. First, Hample and Dallinger (1987) examined how people "edit" their own arguments before they actually deliver them. According to tradition, there are two parts to the process of argumentation: people create or invent arguments, and then they select which ones to present during a compliance-gaining attempt. Hample and Dallinger's study sought to investigate the second part, that is, "why is one argument offered, and another suppressed?" (p. 124). In previous research, Hample and Dallinger (1985a, 1985b) identified four general categories of cognitive editing standards that most people use:

1. *Effectiveness*—people reject certain arguments because they feel the argument won't work or might backfire.
2. *Principled objections*—people reject arguments because they have disdain for the type of argument strategy (e.g., threats, bribes).
3. *Person-centered issues*—an argument may be rejected because it violates the arguer's self-image, might injure the adversary, or might do irreparable harm to the relationship.
4. *Discourse competence*—people might reject an argument because it is judged to be false, too easily refuted, or irrelevant to the conflict.

Hample & Dallinger's (1987) study examined how argumentativeness, verbal aggressiveness, interpersonal orientation, and gender influence cognitive editing. Their results demonstrated that people who vary in argumentativeness and verbal aggressiveness use different cognitive editing standards in suppressing arguments. More specifically, females, people high in interpersonal orientation (those who are more sensitive and attuned to the personal characteristics of a relationship and more responsive to a partner's behavior, Swap & Rubin, 1983), and people low in verbal aggressiveness are less likely to use the effectiveness category or to endorse arguments in general. Instead, they are likely to use principled objections and person-centeredness (e.g., harm to others) to suppress the use of persuasive appeals. Results of the study also demonstrated a tendency for people high in argumentativeness to endorse more compliance-gaining messages. In short, it seems clear from this research that the argumentativeness and verbal aggressiveness traits do influence the cognitive editing of arguments.

Second, Mongeau (1989) studied how argumentativeness and need for cognition impact persuasive message processing. *Need for cognition* has been defined as "enjoyment individuals derive from engaging in effortful information processing" (Cacioppo, Petty, Kao, & Rodriguez, 1986, p. 1033). In other words, people high in the need for cognition like to scrutinize messages more than those who are low in the need for cognition. An experiment was conducted to explore whether argument quality (i.e., high quality versus low quality), need for cognition (high, low), and argumentativeness (high, low) influenced participants' attitudes toward a proposal (e.g., comprehensive exams for undergraduate students) and their behavioral intentions (to work for or against the proposal) (Mongeau, 1989). Results of the study suggested that while low and high argumentatives did not differ in their perceptions of the higher-quality arguments, high argumentatives did perceive the lower-quality messages to be weaker than the low argumentatives did. In addition, high argumentatives exhibited significantly greater attitude–behavioral intention consistency than did low argumentatives. Finally, trait argumentativeness influenced persuasive message processing and the relationship between attitudes and behavior in a very similar fashion to the need for cognition. This finding further supports the notion that argumentativeness has a cognitive as well as behavioral component (Mongeau, 1989).

Third, Kinney and Segrin (1998) discovered that people's ability to process information, their sensitivity to feedback, and their beliefs about themselves can make them susceptible (or impervious) to the negative effects of verbally aggressive messages. Specifically, people who are less certain about themselves are more likely to experience negative emotions when friends who are usually supportive behave in verbally aggressive ways (Kinney & Segrin, 1998). This finding was explained by Expectancy Violations Theory (Burgoon & Hale, 1988) as follows: When supportive friends engage in verbal aggression, the emotional effects of this behavior are significant, because these friends have violated expectancies. Sensitivity to feedback may be a characteristic that can "protect" individuals from verbal aggression and as such may be another cognitive moderator of the effects of verbal aggression (Kinney & Segrin, 1998, p. 66).

Argumentativeness, Verbal Aggressiveness, and Compliance-Gaining Behavior

Research examining the types of compliance-gaining messages that people tend to select has been based on the assumption that persuaders are generally aware of the choices they make. Such choices might be affected by situational factors. For example, Hunter and Boster (1987) argued that a persuader's choice of compliance-gaining messages depends in part on the expected emotional impact on the target. They presented a model arguing that "the more negative the emotional impact of a compliance-gaining message on the listener, the less any given persuader will want to use the message" (p. 65). Although this model might describe most people's selection of compliance-gaining strategies, what if the person selecting a strategy is argumentative or verbally aggressive? The amount and type of strategy preferences a person uses may depend on whether he or she is high or low in these traits (Hunter & Boster, p. 82). Indeed, Hunter and Boster (1987) advanced several hypotheses examining the relationship between aggressive communication traits and compliance-gaining behavior. These suggested the following conclusions:

1. Individuals high in argumentativeness and verbal aggressiveness would be likely to transmit numerous compliance-gaining messages that vary widely in emotional impact.
2. Individuals high in argumentativeness but low in verbal aggressiveness would be likely to send numerous messages of relatively homogeneous emotional impact, that is, the messages would be predominantly positive.
3. Individuals low in argumentativeness and high in verbal aggression probably would send few messages, most of which would be relatively negative in emotional impact.
4. Individuals low in both traits would be likely to send few messages; they might simply request compliance and, if it were not forthcoming, cease the effort (Hunter & Boster, p. 82).

While these speculations await empirical examination, they did lead the way for an examination of aggressive communication traits and their impact on compliance-gaining behavior. One of the first efforts was conducted by Reynolds (1987), who studied the effects of argumentativeness, assertiveness, and need for cognition on the selection of compliance-gaining strategies. Among the major findings was that *proactive assertiveness* (being forceful and ascendant in support of self, e.g., "When standing in line and a person pushes in front of me, I tell them to go to the back of the line") and *argument avoidance* (the general tendency to avoid arguments) are associated with the use of *fewer* compliance-gaining strategies. This suggests that proactive assertiveness and the tendency to avoid arguing may be associated less with overt compliance-gaining strategies than with "subtle or nonverbal suasory message strategies" (Reynolds, 1987, p. 15).

Boster and Levine (1988) and Boster, Levine, and Kazoleas (1993) replicated as well as extended this line of research by examining how argumentativeness and verbal aggressiveness correlate with compliance-gaining message choices. In general, both studies found that, compared with low argumentatives, high argumentatives used a greater variety of strategies and were generally more persistent (Boster & Levine, 1988, p. 117). In addition, verbally aggressive individuals used more negatively oriented compliance-gaining messages (Boster, Levine, & Kazoleas, 1993), perhaps due to their lack of skill in arguing, which impedes their ability to create and use compliance-gaining strategies that are more "positive" in nature.

In an interesting twist on this line of research, Ifert and Bearden (1998) explored whether argumentativeness and verbal aggressiveness influenced the types of appeals individuals say they would use when responding to refusals of interpersonal requests. The researchers argued that in persuasive situations, individuals often respond to refusals with two types of messages: evidentiary and nonevidentiary. *Evidentiary appeals* are often referred to as rational appeals because they are arguments (claims) that contain information to support a claim (Cody, Canary, & Smith, 1994; Ifert & Bearden, 1998; Reardon, 1991). As such, evidentiary appeals are seen positively and judged more favorably and effectively. *Nonevidentiary appeals* are arguments (claims) that contain little or no supporting material but instead rely on simple assertions. These types of appeals tend to be more emotional in nature and are seen less favorably than evidentiary appeals (Ifert & Bearden, 1998).

In the study by Ifert and Bearden (1998), participants were asked to imagine themselves trying either to persuade a professor to change a low grade or to influence a meter enforcement officer to refrain from ticketing their car. Participants were then given a hypothetical statement that the professor or officer might give to reject their persuasive request. They responded to various refusal statements (e.g., "You didn't fulfill the assignment guidelines" or "The law says I have to ticket you") by writing out what they would say in response. Participants also completed both the argumentativeness and verbal aggressiveness scales.

The results of the study showed that both types of aggressive communication traits influenced participants' choices of appeals to the refused requests. People higher in trait argumentativeness reported constructing more evidentiary appeals in response to these refusals. In addition, people high in verbal aggressiveness reported constructing a greater number of nonevidentiary appeals than did those lower in verbal aggressiveness. Ifert and

Bearden (1998) suggested that these results support the notion that verbal aggressiveness may be the result of an argumentative skill deficiency (see Infante & Rancer, 1996).

Aggressive Communication and Resistance to Persuasion

Some research in persuasion suggests that high argumentatives may enjoy an advantage over low argumentatives in persuasion. For example, when compared with low argumentatives, highly argumentative individuals are more competent communicators in a variety of contexts (Rancer, Kosberg, & Silvestri, 1992; Richmond, McCroskey, & McCroskey, 1989), have internal loci of control (Avtgis & Rancer, 1997; Canary, Cunningham, & Cody, 1988), and have more solution-oriented conflict styles (Nicotera, Smilowitz, & Pearson, 1990). Besides that, argumentative people may have characteristics that make them more resistant to persuasion. With that in mind, a series of studies has investigated the influence of argumentativeness (and verbal aggressiveness) on resistance to persuasion.

One factor that may make an individual more resistant to persuasion is the ability to generate or construct counterarguments. A study by Kazoleas (1993) suggested that high and low argumentatives might differ in this ability. Specifically, Kazoleas found high argumentatives more resistant to persuasion because they generate more counterarguments when they think about a counterattitudinal message (i.e., a message inconsistent with one's existing attitude). This cognitive activity can be thought of as "another message" in the persuasion context. Thus, the results of Kazoleas's (1993) research may mean that high argumentatives tend to "persuade themselves" even if they should disagree with the position taken by an advocate (Infante, Step, & Horvath, 1997, p. 80).

This "cognitive response perspective" (Kazoleas, 1993) represented a shift toward *intrapersonal argumentation* (Infante et al., 1997) and formed the basis of another study. In it, Infante, Step, and Horvath (1997) suggested that arguing with oneself might be more enjoyable for high argumentatives than it is for low argumentatives. In the study, participants were asked to create either a proattitudinal or counterattitudinal message on a proposal (registration of all firearms in the United States). After encoding these messages, attitudes toward the proposal were measured. Infante and colleagues (1997) found that argumentatives who encoded a counterattitudinal message (a message inconsistent with their existing attitudes toward the proposal) were no less favorable toward the task than people who engaged in proattitudinal advocacy. Thus, for high argumentatives, enjoying an argument is possible even when one's opponent is oneself. This willingness to construct arguments that oppose one's currently held positions may help explain why argumentativeness has been associated with numerous positive outcomes (Infante et al., 1997; Johnson & Johnson, 1979). Moreover, these findings support the notion that high argumentatives differ from other people both cognitively and affectively during arguments.

These findings, however, were not replicated by Levine and Badger (1993). Using the Cognitive Response Model, they predicted that highly argumentative individuals would be more resistant to persuasion than low argumentatives. To test this assumption, Levine and Badger (1993) had high and low argumentatives listen to several persuasive presentations on a variety of topics (forest conservation, organ donation, prevention of heart attacks, abortion, voting, better eating habits, etc.). The results of the study surprisingly contradicted what was expected: High argumentatives demonstrated significantly greater attitude change in the direction of the message than low argumentatives. This finding was also true across the different message topics.

Several explanations for these surprising and contradictory findings were offered. First, since sources chose their own topics, they may have selected topics or positions that they already favored. Thus, they may have heard only proattitudinal persuasive messages. Second, high argumentatives may also have generated more "pro" messages when faced with an acceptable message. Thus, it was suggested that highly argumentative individuals may indeed be more open-minded (Levine & Badger, 1993, p. 76).

Finally, Lim (1990) investigated whether receivers' resistance to compliance-gaining efforts led persuaders to be more verbally aggressive in subsequent persuasive efforts. More specifically, the study examined whether friendliness (the extent of liking toward the receiver) and intensity of resistance affected persuaders' verbal aggressiveness. The results demonstrated that persuaders who encountered strong resistance to a persuasive attempt exhibited verbally aggressive behavior more quickly than those facing weaker resistance. In addition, persuaders engaged in more verbal aggression when encountering unfriendly targets. An outright rejection of a persuasive appeal by the target made persuaders the most verbally aggressive of all. This study further underscores the transactional nature of interpersonal persuasion by showing that persuaders decide on a persuasive course of action not only based on situational and personal preferences but also as a result of the responses that they receive from the targets of their persuasive attempts (Levine & Boster, 1996; Lim, 1990).

The Display of Aggressive Communication During Persuasion

The ways in which a person perceives constructive or destructive attacks can influence the outcomes of a compliance-gaining effort. For example, based on Norton's (1978, 1983) research, Infante and Gorden (1989) identified two communicator styles. The first, an *affirming communicator style*, is highly relaxed, friendly, and attentive, and is accompanied by relatively low levels of verbal aggressiveness. This style seems to mediate perceptions of aggressive communication so as to yield more positive than negative outcomes (Infante, Anderson, Martin, Herington, & Kim, 1993; Infante & Gorden, 1987, 1989). For instance, individuals who engage in argumentative behavior and do so with an affirming communicator style seem to make the argumentative behavior appear more "palatable." Conversely, if someone engages in argumentativeness according to the second, *non-affirming communicator style*, which is highly agitated, unfriendly, and inattentive, he or she may be mistakenly regarded as engaging in verbal aggression.

Empirical support for these assumptions was obtained in a study conducted by Infante, Rancer, and Jordan (1996). They suspected that observers would be less likely to overestimate verbally aggressive messages and more likely to perceive argumentative behavior when they read transcripts of a compliance-gaining effort marked by an affirming versus a nonaffirming communicator style. In the study, participants read a transcript of a conversation depicting a compliance-gaining effort between two roommates. The conversation described a conflict that arose, climaxed, and then ended in a resolution or solution. All statements in the transcripts pertained to the issue under controversy, except for several statements made by both parties that were in fact verbally aggressive. Results of the study found more argumentative behavior, along with less verbal aggression, when the messages were presented with an affirming communicator style (Infante, Rancer, & Jordan, 1996). In addition, fewer mistakes were made in identifying verbal aggression in that text. A similar study (Rancer, Jordan, & Infante, 2000) supported the earlier findings. Participants significantly overestimated the amount of verbal aggression when individuals communicated with a nonaffirming communicator style, regardless of whether conversations were presented on videotapes or on written transcripts. These findings have clear implications, underlining the important role of nonverbal behavior in mediating perceptions of constructive and destructive behavior during compliance-gaining attempts. That is, when involved in a persuasive effort, individuals should engage in argumentative behavior but make sure to do so in an affirming (i.e., highly relaxed, friendly, and attentive) way.

Aggressive Communication and Persuasion in the Organizational Context: What Makes for a Persuasive Supervisor?

The question of what makes a persuasive supervisor has been investigated in a number of studies (Gorden & Infante, 1987, 1991; Gorden, Infante, & Izzo, 1988; Infante & Gorden, 1987, 1989, 1991). Much of this research has been based on the Independent-Mindedness Theory of organizational communication. The basic tenet of this theory suggests that the values held by the general society should be affirmed in the workplace. As such, "American" corporations should encourage free speech and promote individualism and independent-mindedness.

This body of research has revealed that superiors who are high in argumentativeness and low in verbal aggressiveness (and who communicate with an affirming style) have a number of positive qualities. They are perceived as encouraging subordinates to express their views on controversial issues (Gorden et al., 1987); they are more effective in upward influence situations (Infante & Gorden, 1985a, 1985b, 1987); they are judged by their subordinates as having more constructive persuasion styles (Gorden, Infante, & Izzo, 1988); and they enjoy higher credibility perceptions (Infante & Gorden, 1987, 1989).

Conclusion

This chapter has suggested that argument is inherent in the process of persuasion. As such, an individual difference perspective regarding aggressive communication behavior and persuasion is illuminating. Research on argumentativeness and verbal aggressiveness has examined how the persuasion process is influenced by these traits. This research has studied both the source and receiver. As dyadic persuasion is a more common form of persuasion and one we need to understand better, incorporating an understanding of aggressive communication traits helps us understand the process more fully.

The research reviewed in this chapter suggests that argumentativeness and verbal aggressiveness are predispositions that warrant further research, since it has been demonstrated that these two traits have considerable bearing on interpersonal social influence. What should the future of this line of research be? What are some types of research that should be conducted?

First, this line of research should be extended from the laboratory into the field. That is, while a few studies cited in this review asked people to engage in "interactive" persuasive efforts, the majority did not. Much of the research also involved persuasive and compliance-gaining efforts conducted under traditional "laboratory" conditions and in nonspecified or "stranger only" contexts. This approach is beneficial to understanding how these aggressive communication traits function in persuasive contexts and helpful in building theoretical frameworks that attempt to explain the interaction of these constructs. However, the generalizability of these findings is limited. Thus, exploring the effect of argumentativeness and verbal aggressiveness in field settings and in specified persuasive contexts seems appropriate. For example, Infante et al. (1997) found that high argumentatives indicated the greatest self-persuasion under conditions involving counterattitudinal advocacy. This willingness to argue with one's own position might be observed in the dating/courtship contexts and in the organizational context (e.g., in employee interviews and job-related meetings). This speculation should be subject to empirical scrutiny.

A better understanding of the low-argumentative individual, especially during different advocacy situations, is also worthy of empirical examination (Infante et al., 1997). In one study, Infante and his colleagues found that a proattitudinal task was liked equally by slightly, moderately, and highly argumentative individuals. It was speculated that proattitudinal advocacy, especially if not engaged in via a face-to-face encounter with an adversary, may not be seen as distasteful by low-argumentative individuals (p. 85). Thus, alternative channels of communication, especially e-mail, might engender more favorable proattitudinal (and possibly even counterattitudinal) advocacy feelings for low-argumentative individuals. As such, research that varies the channel through which persuasive efforts are attempted (by those who vary in argumentativeness and verbal aggressiveness) is also worthy of study.

Along these lines, Levine and Badger (1993) observed an interesting yet counterintuitive finding: Low argumentatives were more resistant to persuasion than highly argumentative individuals. The researchers suggested that argumentativeness leads to less resistance to proattitudinal messages (p. 76) and proposed that the effect of argumentativeness in instilling resistance to persuasion is valid primarily for "positions that individuals would not readily endorse" (p. 76). Again, this speculation awaits empirical scrutiny. Further, the relationship between argumentativeness and dogmatism, as well as the relationship between the trait and initial attitudes, deserves increased attention.

In summary, this corpus of research underscores the importance of aggressive communication predispositions in understanding the persuasive and compliance-gaining processes. Additional research conducted in varied communication settings and contexts should be helpful in developing guidelines to enhance persuasive and compliance-gaining outcomes.

References

Ajzen, I., & Fishbein, M. (1980). *Understanding attitudes and predicting social behavior.* Englewood Cliffs, NJ: Prentice-Hall.

Andersen, P. A. (1987). The trait debate: A critical examination of the individual differences paradigm in interpersonal communication. In B. Dervin & M. J. Voigt (Eds.), *Progress in communication sciences* (vol. 7, pp. 47–52). Norwood, NJ: Ablex.

Atkinson, J. W. (1957). Motivational determinants of risk-taking behavior. *Psychological Review, 64,* 359–372.

Avtgis, T. A., & Rancer, A. S. (1997). Argumentativeness and verbal aggressiveness as a function of locus of control. *Communication Research Reports, 14,* 441–450.

Beatty, M. J., & McCroskey, J. C. (1997). It's in our nature: Verbal aggressiveness as temperamental expression. *Communication Quarterly, 45,* 446–460.

Beatty, M. J., & McCroskey, J. C. (1998). Interpersonal communication as temperamental expression: A communibiological paradigm. In J. C. McCroskey, J. A. Daly, M. M. Martin, & M. J. Beatty (Eds.), *Communication and personality: Trait perspectives* (pp. 41–67). Cresskill, NJ: Hampton Press.

Boster, F. J., & Levine, T. (1988). Individual differences and compliance-gaining message selection: The effects of verbal aggressiveness, argumentativeness, dogmatism, and negativism. *Communication Research Reports, 5,* 114–119.

Boster, F. J., Levine, T., & Kazoleas, D. (1993). The impact of argumentativeness and verbal aggressiveness on strategic diversity and persistence in compliance-gaining behavior. *Communication Quarterly, 41,* 405–414.

Burgoon, J. K., & Hale, J. L. (1988). Nonverbal expectancy violations: Model elaboration and application to immediacy behaviors. *Communication Monographs, 55,* 58–79.

Cacioppo, J. T., Petty, R. E., Kao, F. C., & Rodriguez, R. (1986). Central and peripheral routes to persuasion: An individual difference perspective. *Journal of Personality and Social Psychology, 51,* 1032–1043.

Canary, D., Cunningham, E. M., & Cody, M. J. (1988). Goal types, gender, and locus of control in managing interpersonal conflict. *Communication Research, 15,* 426–446.

Cody, M. J., Canary, D. J., & Smith, S. W. (1994). Compliance-gaining goals: An inductive analysis of actors' goal types, strategies, and successes. In J. A. Daly & J. M. Wiemann (Eds.), *Strategic interpersonal communication* (pp. 33–90). Hillsdale, NJ: Erlbaum.

Costa, P. T., & McCrae, R. R. (1980). Still stable after all these years: Personality as a key to some issues in adulthood and old age. In P. B. Baltes & O. G. Brim (Eds.), *Life-span development and behavior* (vol. 3, pp. 65–102). New York: Academic Press.

Epstein, S. (1979). The stability of behavior 1. On predicting most of the people much of the time. *Journal of Personality and Social Psychology, 37,* 1097–1126.

Fishbein, M., & Ajzen, I. (1975). *Belief, attitude, intention, and behavior: An introduction to theory and research.* Reading, MA: Addison-Wesley.

Gorden, W. I., & Infante, D. A. (1987). Employee rights: Context, argumentativeness, verbal aggressiveness, and career satisfaction. In C. A. B. Osigweh (Ed.), *Communicating employee responsibilities and rights* (pp. 149–163). Westport, CT: Quorum.

Gorden, W. I., Infante, D. A., & Izzo, J. (1988). Variations in voice pertaining to dissatisfaction/satisfaction with subordinates. *Management Communication Quarterly, 2,* 6–22.

Gorden, W. I., & Infante, D. A. (1991). Test of a communication model of organizational commitment. *Communication Quarterly, 39,* 144–155.

Hample, D., & Dallinger, J. M. (1985a). Unused compliance gaining strategies. In J. R. Cox, M. O. Sillars, & G. B. Walker (Eds.), *Argument and social practice: Proceedings of the fourth SCA/AFA conference on argumentation* (pp. 675–691). Annandale, VA: Speech Communication Association.

Hample, D., & Dallinger, J. M. (1985b, November). *Cognitive editing of argument strategies.* Paper presented at the annual meeting of the Speech Communication Association, Denver, CO.

Hample, D., & Dallinger, J. M. (1987). Individual differences in cognitive editing standards. *Human Communication Research, 14,* 123–144.

Hunter, J. E., & Boster, F. J. (1987). A model of compliance-gaining message selection. *Communication Monographs, 54,* 63–84.

Ifert, D. E., & Bearden, L. (1998). The influence of argumentativeness and verbal aggression on responses to refused requests. *Communication Reports, 11,* 145–154.

Infante, D. A. (1987a). Aggressiveness. In J. C. McCroskey & J. A. Daly (Eds.), *Personality and interpersonal communication* (pp. 157–192). Newbury Park, CA: Sage.

Infante, D. A. (1987b). Enhancing the prediction of response to a communication situation from communication traits. *Communication Quarterly, 35,* 308–316.

Infante, D. A. (1989). Response to high argumentatives: Message and sex differences. *Southern Communication Journal, 54,* 159–170.

Infante, D. A., Anderson, C. M., Martin, M. M., Herington, A. D., & Kim, J. K. (1993). Subordinates' satisfaction and perceptions of superiors' compliance-gaining tactics, argumentativeness, verbal aggressiveness, and style. *Management Communication Quarterly, 6,* 307–326.

Infante, D. A., Chandler Sabourin, T., Rudd, J. E., & Shannon, E. A. (1990). Verbal aggression in violent and nonviolent marital disputes. *Communication Quarterly, 38,* 361–371.

Infante, D. A., & Gorden, W. I. (1985a). Benefits versus bias: An investigation of argumentativeness, gender, and organizational communication outcomes. *Communication Research Reports, 2,* 196–201.

Infante, D. A., & Gorden, W. I. (1985b). Superiors' argumentativeness and verbal aggressiveness as predictors of subordinates' satisfaction. *Human Communication Research, 12,* 117–125.

Infante, D. A., & Gorden, W. I. (1987). Superior and subordinate communication profiles: Implications for independent-mindedness and upward effectiveness. *Central States Speech Journal, 38,* 73–80.

Infante, D. A., & Gorden, W. I. (1989). Argumentativeness and affirming communicator style as predictors of satisfaction/dissatisfaction with subordinates. *Communication Quarterly, 37,* 81–90.

Infante, D. A., & Gorden, W. I. (1991). How employees see the boss: Test of an argumentative and affirming model of superiors' communicative behavior. *Western Journal of Speech Communication, 55,* 294–304.

Infante, D. A., & Rancer, A. S. (1982). A conceptualization and measure of argumentativeness. *Journal of Personality Assessment, 46,* 72–80.

Infante, D. A., & Rancer, A. S. (1993). Relations between argumentative motivation, and advocacy and refutation on controversial issues. *Communication Quarterly, 41,* 415–426.

Infante, D. A., & Rancer, A. S. (1996). Argumentativeness and verbal aggressiveness: A review of recent theory and research. In B. R. Burleson (Ed.), *Communication yearbook 19,* (pp. 319–351). Beverly Hills, CA: Sage.

Infante, D. A., Rancer, A. S., & Jordan, F. F. (1996). Affirming and nonaffirming style, dyad sex, and the perception of argumentation and verbal aggression in an interpersonal dispute. *Human Communication Research, 22,* 315–334.

Infante, D. A., Rancer, A. S., & Womack, D. F. (1997). *Building communication theory* (3rd ed.). Prospect Heights, IL: Waveland Press.

Infante, D. A., Riddle, B. L., Horvath, C. L., & Tumlin, S. A. (1992). Verbal aggressiveness: Messages and reasons. *Communication Quarterly, 40,* 116–126.

Infante, D. A., Step, M. M., & Horvath, C. L. (1997). Counterattitudinal advocacy: When high argumentatives are more persuasible. *Communication Research Reports, 14,* 79–87.

Infante, D. A., Trebing, J. D., Shepherd, P. E., & Seeds, D. E. (1984). The relationship of argumentativeness to verbal aggression. *Southern Speech Communication Journal, 50,* 67–77.

Infante, D. A., Wall, C. H., Leap, C. J., & Danielson, K. (1984). Verbal aggression as a function of the receiver's argumentativeness. *Communication Research Reports, 1,* 33–37.

Infante, D. A., & Wigley, C. J. (1986). Verbal aggressiveness: An interpersonal model and measure. *Communication Monographs, 53,* 61–69.

Johnson, D. W., & Johnson, R. T. (1979). Conflict in the classroom: Controversy and learning. *Review of Educational Research, 49,* 51–70.

Kazoleas, D. (1993). The impact of argumentativeness on resistance to persuasion. *Human Communication Research, 20,* 118–137.

Kinney, T. A. (1994). An inductively derived typology of verbal aggression and its relationship to distress. *Human Communication Research, 21*, 183–222.

Kinney, T., & Segrin, C. (1998). Cognitive moderators of negative reactions to verbal aggression. *Communication Studies, 49*, 49–72.

Levine, T. R., & Badger, E. E. (1993). Argumentativeness and resistance to persuasion. *Communication Reports, 6*, 71–78.

Levine, T. R., & Boster, F. J. (1996). The impact of self and others' argumentativeness on talk about controversial issues. *Communication Quarterly, 44*, 345–358.

Lim, T. S. (1990). The influence of receivers' resistance on persuaders' verbal aggressiveness. *Communication Quarterly, 38*, 170–188.

Magnusson, D., & Endler, N. S. (1977). Interactional psychology: Present status and future prospects. In D. Magnusson & N. Endler (Eds.), *Personality at the crossroads: Current issues in interactional psychology* (3–35). Hillsdale, NJ: Erlbaum.

Miller, G. R., Boster, F. J., Roloff, M. E., & Seibold, D. R. (1977). Compliance-gaining message strategies: A typology and some findings concerning the effects of situational differences. *Communication Monographs, 44*, 37–51.

Mongeau, P. A. (1989). Individual differences as moderators of persuasive message processing and attitude-behavior relations. *Communication Research Reports, 6*, 1–6.

Nicotera, A. M., Smilowitz, M., & Pearson, J. C. (1990). Ambiguity tolerance, conflict management style and argumentativeness as predictors of innovativeness. *Communication Research Reports, 7*, 125–131.

Norton, R. W. (1978). Foundation of a communicator style construct. *Human Communication Research, 4*, 99–112.

Norton, R. W. (1983). *Communicator style: Theory, application, and measures.* Beverly Hills, CA: Sage.

Onyekwere, E. O., Rubin, R. B., & Infante, D. A. (1991). Interpersonal perception and communication satisfaction as a function of argumentativeness and ego-involvement. *Communication Quarterly, 39*, 35–47.

Rancer, A. S., Avtgis, T. A., Kosberg, R. L., & Whitecap, V. G. (2000). A longitudinal assessment of trait argumentativeness and verbal aggressiveness between seventh and eighth grades. *Communication Education, 49*, 114–119.

Rancer, A. S., & Baukus, R. A. (1987). Discriminating males and females on belief structures about arguing. In L. B. Nadler, M. K. Nadler, & W. R. Todd-Mancillas (Eds.), *Advances in gender and communication research* (pp. 155–173). Lanham, MD: University Press of America.

Rancer, A. S., Baukus, R. A., & Infante, D. A. (1985). Relations between argumentativeness and belief structures about arguing. *Communication Education, 34*, 37–47.

Rancer, A. S., & Infante, D. A. (1985). Relations between motivation to argue and the argumentativeness of adversaries. *Communication Quarterly, 33*, 209–218.

Rancer, A. S., Jordan, F. F., & Infante, D. A. (2000, November). *Observers' perceptions of an interpersonal dispute as a function of affirming style and mode of presentation.* Paper presented at the annual meeting of the National Communication Association, Seattle, WA.

Rancer, A. S., Kosberg, R. L., & Baukus, R. A. (1992). Beliefs about arguing as predictors of trait argumentativeness: Implications for training in argument and conflict management. *Communication Education, 41*, 375–387.

Rancer, A. S., Kosberg, R. L., & Silvestri, V. N. (1992). The relationship between self-esteem and aggressive communication predispositions. *Communication Research Reports, 9*, 23–32.

Rancer, A. S., Whitecap, V. G., Kosberg, R. L., & Avtgis, T. A. (1997). Testing the efficacy of a communication training program to increase argumentativeness and argumentative behavior in adolescents. *Communication Education, 46*, 273–286.

Reardon, K. K. (1991). *Persuasion in practice.* Newbury Park, CA: Sage.

Reynolds, R. A. (1987, May). *Argumentativeness, need for cognition, and assertiveness as predictors of compliance gaining message strategy selections.* Paper presented at the annual meeting of the International Communication Association, Montreal, Canada.

Richmond, V. P., McCroskey, J. C., & McCroskey, L. L. (1989). An investigation of self-perceived communication competence and personality orientations. *Communication Research Reports, 6*, 28–36.

Roberto, A. J., & Finucane, M. (1997). The assessment of argumentativeness and verbal aggressiveness in adolescent populations. *Communication Quarterly, 45*, 21–36.

Stewart, R. A., & Roach, K. D. (1993). Argumentativeness, religious orientation, and reactions to argument situations involving religious versus nonreligious issues. *Communication Quarterly, 41*, 26–39.

Stewart, R. A., Roach, K. D. (1998). Argumentativeness and the theory of reasoned action. *Communication Quarterly, 46*, 177–193.

Swap, W. C., & Rubin, J. Z. (1983). Measurement of interpersonal orientation. *Journal of Personality and Social Psychology, 44*, 208–219.

Valencic, K. M., Beatty, M. J., Rudd, J. E., Dobos, J. A., & Heisel, A. D. (1998). An empirical test of a communibiological model of trait verbal aggressiveness. *Communication Quarterly, 46*, 327–341.

Waggenspack, B. M., & Hensley, W. E. (1989). Perception of the argumentativeness trait in interpersonal relationship situations. *Social Behavior and Personality, 17*, 111–120.

Wigley, C. J. (1998). Verbal aggressiveness. In J. C. McCroskey, J. A. Daly, M. M. Martin, & M. J. Beatty (Eds.), *Communication and personality: Trait perspectives* (pp. 191–214). Cresskill, NJ: Hampton Press.

8

Gender Effects on Social Influence

Linda L. Carli

The status of women has improved in recent years. The presence of women such as National Security Adviser Condoleezza Rice, former attorney general Janet Reno, and producer and media mogul Oprah Winfrey in highly visible positions of power is emblematic of this improved status. In fact, currently about 47 percent of workers in the United States are women, up from 40 percent in 1976 (U.S. Bureau of Labor Statistics, 2001). Whereas 25 years ago 25 percent of managers were women, now women fill nearly half of all managerial and administrative positions (U.S. Bureau of Labor Statistics, 2001). The salary differential between men and women has also shrunk. Today, on average, women earn about 74 percent of what men earn, whereas in 1976 they earned only 58 percent of men's income (U.S. Bureau of the Census, 2000). Nevertheless, in spite of the advances that women have made and the presence of a small but highly visible number of women in positions of authority, women continue to be underrepresented in the upper echelons of power. In Fortune 500 companies, fewer than 1 percent of CEOs are women and women hold only 5 percent of the top executive positions (Catalyst, 2000). In the United States government, only 13 percent of senators, 14 percent of congressional representatives, and 10 percent of state governors are women (Center for the American Woman and Politics, 2001). Women are likewise absent from the highest positions of power in the legal profession (Rhode, 2001), higher education (Chronicle of Higher Education, 1998), medicine (Reed & Buddeberg-Fischer, 2001), broadcasting and telecommunications (Jamieson & Slass, 2001), and the U.S. military (U.S. Department of Defense, 1998). The persistence of women's exclusion from the most powerful positions underscores the continued resistance to women's influence and authority. Indeed, the literature on gender and social influence has typically reported that women are less influential than men.

This chapter will review research showing gender differences in social influence and will argue that these differences occur as the result of gender stereotypes. In particular, it will show that women and girls exert less influence than men and boys, because females more than males must establish themselves as competent and likable sources in order to be influential. Likable sources appeal to their audience because they are similar to them, are physically attractive, or possess other socially desirable characteristics. Competent sources appear knowledgeable, intelligent, and articulate, conveying competence and expertise. Influence agents who establish themselves as competent (Bradley, 1980; Driskell, Olmstead, & Salas, 1993; Erickson, Lind, Johnson, & O'Barr, 1978; Holtgraves & Lasky, 1999; Son & Schmitt, 1983) and likable (Carli, 1989; Chaiken, 1980; Chaiken & Eagly, 1983; Wood & Kallgren, 1988) exert greater influence than those who do not. People trust competent, likable influence agents and yield to their influence. The present analysis suggests that men exert greater influence than women because, according to gender stereotypes, males are more competent than females. Moreover, based on stereotypes, people expect females to be warmer, nicer, and more likable than males and consequently are more likely to resist the influence of females than that of males for not being likable enough.

Gender Stereotypes and Social Influence

The Stereotype of the Competent Male

Research examining people's gender stereotypes about the types of traits that men and women possess reveals that men are considered to possess more agentic qualities, which reflect greater competency and instrumentality, than women, who in turn are thought to possess more communal qualities than men. Specifically, men are considered more leaderlike, intellectual, analytical, capable of abstract thinking, and able to solve problems, whereas women are considered kinder, warmer, more expressive, more supportive, and gentler (Broverman, Vogel, Broverman, Clarkson, & Rosenkrantz, 1972; Deaux & Kite, 1993; Eagly & Mladinic, 1989; Fiske & Ruscher, 1993; Ruble, 1983; Williams & Best, 1990). Similar stereotypes have been reported in work settings; executives consider male managers to be more competent than female managers (Heilman, Block, & Martell, 1995), and management ability and competence is considered more characteristic of men than of women (Schein, in press).

Other research examining evaluation of men's and women's performances has likewise revealed this same stereotype. For example, a small bias favoring male expertise was reported in a meta-analytic review of studies using the "Goldberg paradigm," in which participants evaluated identical behaviors or products but were sometimes told that those behaviors or products were produced by men and sometimes that they were produced by women (Swim, Borgida, Maruyama, & Myers, 1989). The review revealed that male performance is rated more favorably when the stimulus materials are either gender neutral or in a stereotypically masculine domain, but that men and women receive equal evaluations when the domain is stereotypically feminine. These effects, although small, indicate that men are presumed to be more competent than women unless the task favors female expertise, but even then women are considered equal to, but not more competent than men.

Studies examining stereotypes usually provide subjects with little information about the target individuals whom they are evaluating and often simply ask participants to describe a typical man or a typical woman. Studies employing the Goldberg paradigm generally present brief descriptions of the target, such as a résumé, or something the target has written or created before being evaluated. Perhaps participants rely on stereotypes under these conditions because they have little objective information upon which to base their evaluations. If true, then the bias in evaluating male and female competence should disappear when participants are exposed to actual behaviors by men and women and can base their evaluations on their firsthand observations of male and female performances. Unfortunately, even in face-to-face interactions with men and women with no objective differences in performance, undergraduate subjects rated men as having performed more competently than women (Carli, 1991; Carli, 1997; Wood & Karten, 1986). Indeed, research has revealed a double standard in the evaluation of men and women. Women must display greater evidence of skill than men to be considered equally competent (Biernat & Kobrynowicz, 1997; Foschi, 1996). Moreover, in order for people to perceive a woman as more competent than a man, they must be given very clear and explicit evidence of the woman's substantial superiority relative to the man's (Shackelford, Wood, & Worchel, 1996; Wagner, Ford, & Ford, 1986; Wood & Karten, 1986). The double standard for competence has also been revealed in research with children. A study of fourth and fifth graders playing a cooperative game revealed that girls were perceived by other children to be less competent at it than boys were, even though objective analysis of the children's actual performance did not reveal a gender difference (Lockheed, Harris, & Nemceff, 1983).

Status, Social Roles, and Gender

Why do people perceive men to be generally more competent and agentic? According to Alice Eagly's (1987) Social Role Theory, men and women are distributed differently into social roles. First, based on the traditional division of labor in the family, men have more often had the role of financial provider and women the role of homemaker. Second, paid occupations are highly gender segregated, with men's positions conferring higher levels of status and power than women's. Typically, the higher-status occupational roles to which men have been assigned require agentic behaviors, such as task competence, leadership, and dominance. Conversely, women's domestic roles and lower-status occupational roles more often require communal behaviors, such as nurturance, kindness, and selflessness. Eagly argues that people have deduced the gender stereotypes through observation of men and women in these highly segregated roles and as a result have come to expect men to behave in a more agentic manner than women.

The association of men with powerful, high-status roles has resulted in their generally gaining higher status than women. According to Expectation States Theory (Berger, Fisek, Norman, & Zelditch, 1977), gender acts as a *diffuse status characteristic*, a general attribute that is associated with an individual's relative status in society. Diffuse status characteristics include gender, race, degree of physical attractiveness, and education. Characteristics that are valued or considered desirable, such as being male, white, physically attractive, and well educated, confer high status. Research indicates that a high-status individual is assumed to be more competent than someone of low status, and as a result, people seek the opinions of high-status people and yield to their influence more than to people of low status (Berger et al., 1977). This tendency to encourage high-status people to contribute their ideas and act as task leaders creates a self-fulfilling prophecy: the more individuals make task contributions, the more they enhance their status, increase their influence, and emerge as leaders (Hawkins, 1995; Ridgeway, 1978; Stein & Heller, 1979; Wood & Karten, 1986). Therefore, high-status individuals are not only expected to exhibit higher levels of competence and performance, but these expectations lead them actually to be more successful in influencing others.

In the same way that high-status individuals are given opportunities to exert influence, low-status individuals are denied these opportunities. Individuals' diffuse status affects not only their perceived competence and expectations about their future performance but also their expectations about what constitutes appropriate behavior in the group. People perceive low-status individuals, because of their presumed lower competence, as lacking in legitimacy as authorities; as a result, they are more likely to resist the influence of low-status than of high-status individuals (Meeker & Weitzel-O'Neill, 1985; Ridgeway & Berger, 1986). Instead, when low-status individuals behave in a status-asserting manner, overtly attempting to influence others or taking on leadership roles, they are ignored, penalized, or rejected, which drops their status further (Meeker & Weitzel-O'Neill, 1985).

This analysis suggests that because men generally possess higher status than women, more men than women would be given opportunities to make task contributions in groups and would be more likely than women to enhance their status, influence others, and emerge as leaders when doing so. In fact, a recent meta-analytic review of gender differences in group interactions revealed that men do make a higher proportion of task contributions than women do (Carli & Olm-Shipman, 2000). In addition, although men's task contributions in mixed-sex groups predict their ability to influence other group members, women's task contributions are unrelated to influence (Walker, Ilardi, McMahon, & Fennell, 1996). Further, women's task-related behavior is more likely than that of men to evoke negative reactions from others (Butler & Geis, 1990). Further support for this analysis can be found in Eagly and Karau's (1991) meta-analytic review of gender differences in leader emergence, which revealed that in initially leaderless groups, men emerge more often than women as leaders.

In summary, the presumption of greater male competence is based on the different distribution of men and women into social roles and the relatively high status of men's roles compared with women's roles. Because competent individuals exert greater influence than less competent individuals, women and girls would be expected to exert less influence than men and boys. The male advantage would be expected to occur except in contexts that favor female expertise and competence, either because a particular female has demonstrated clear superiority over her male counterpart or because the domain of the interaction is stereotypically female, such as child care.

The Stereotype of the Communal Female

Just as men are perceived to be more competent than women, women are perceived to be nicer and more communal than men (Broverman et al., 1972; Deaux & Kite, 1993; Eagly & Mladinic, 1989; Fiske & Ruscher, 1993; Ruble, 1983; Williams & Best, 1990). Research indicates that people value communal traits highly enough so that attitudes toward women tend to be more favorable overall than attitudes toward men, a finding that has been labeled the "women are wonderful" effect (Eagly & Mladinic, 1989, 1994; Eagly, Mladinic, & Otto, 1991). Yet even though women are held in esteem for possessing desirable communal traits, this esteem does not confer them with increased influence in task-oriented groups. On the contrary, people view communal traits as important in stereo-typical feminine contexts, so that communal individuals are seen as best suited for domestic roles and traditionally female-dominated professions (Cejka & Eagly, 1999; Eagly & Steffen, 1984). Consequently, women's greater communality should enhance their influence in stereotypical female contexts but should provide no particular advantage to them in gender-neutral or masculine domains.

Although the "women are wonderful" effect may be viewed as generally beneficial, this stereotype is not merely descriptive but also highly prescriptive. *Descriptive gender stereotypes* reflect beliefs about the way men and women are perceived to be, whereas *prescriptive gender stereotypes* delineate how men and women ought to be, that is, the behaviors considered appropriate for each gender. In the case of the stereotype of female communality, people not only believe that women are nicer than men, they require women to be so (Burgess & Borgida, 1999; Eagly, 1987). This prescription demands that women be warm, nurturing, and selfless or be perceived as violating gender-role norms. This finding suggests that observers may dislike and penalize a woman whom they consider lacking in communality and resist her influence as a result.

Notably, the prescription for women includes avoiding behavior that is too status-asserting, threatening, or directive. In essence, people do not consider it appropriate for women to seek leadership or status overtly or to attempt to influence others too directly or forcefully (Carli, 1999). This attitude is based on the lower diffuse status of women relative to men and on the domestic and lower-status occupational roles that women more often hold, which involve a greater amount of selflessness and other-directedness than men's roles do. Certainly, status theorists have argued that low-status individuals must show warmth and communality more than high-status individuals in order to be influential. This is because those of low status lack legitimacy and do not have the right to take charge, direct others, or act as leaders. Instead, low-status individuals must communicate that they have little desire to take charge or lead others and are motivated merely by a desire to help other members of their group (Meeker & Weitzel-O'Neill, 1985). As a result, people are generally more open to a man's than a woman's influence, regardless of the man's influence style, but would give greater scrutiny to the style of influence of a woman and penalize her for behavior that is too status-asserting or insufficiently communal. Indeed, research with children (Connor, Serbin, & Ender, 1978) and adults (Carli, LaFleur, & Loeber, 1995) has confirmed that people prefer females who are indirect, agreeable, and communal to those who are direct, threatening, and status-asserting, whereas they like males equally well regardless of communality or status assertion. Clearly, in most situations, women's ability to influence others, compared with that of men, would be more dependent on the use of an influence style that corresponds prescriptively to the stereotypical female role. Displays of warmth and communality should therefore be expected to enhance the influence of women and girls, whereas dominant or assertive behaviors should be expected to reduce their influence.

One of the unfortunate effects of gender stereotypes is that highly competent behavior in women may be viewed as too status-asserting and incompatible with the traditional female gender role. Therefore, unlike men, women experience a double bind. On the one hand their competence is more likely to be questioned than the competence of men, and on the other hand, behavior that clearly conveys competence may be considered inappropriate in women. Competent women are often not liked as much as competent men or less competent women (Carli, 1991; Falbo, Hazen, Linimon, 1982). Status theorists have argued that the problem of low-status individuals appearing too status-asserting is most pronounced in interactions with high-status individuals (Ridgeway & Berger, 1986). That is, women's lower status relative to men is particularly highlighted in interactions between men and women. As a result, more men than women should be expected to disapprove of high levels of competence and authority in women, and therefore more men than women should be expected to resist women's influence. Indeed, research indicates that men show greater resistance to women's leadership than do women (Eagly, Makhijani, & Klonsky, 1992; Schein, in press), and men are more likely than women to endorse traditional gender roles (Twenge, 1997).

In summary, the presumption of greater female communality is based on the different distribution of men and women into social roles, with women more often in domestic roles and lower-status occupational roles. In addition, women, like others of low status, have less legitimacy as leaders and consequently are penalized for status-asserting behavior. Because female communality has become prescriptive, women who do not behave in a warm communal manner are likewise penalized. As a result, women's influence is perceived to be more conditional than men's, with women exerting greater influence while displaying communal behavior and less influence in response to status-asserting behavior. Furthermore, it is men more than women who should resist the influence of competent females.

Gender Differences in Influence

As one would expect, given the greater perceived competence and legitimacy of male influence agents, research confirms that men exert greater influence than women do. Lockheed (1985) conducted a meta-analytic review of 29 studies examining gender differences in task-oriented mixed-gender groups. She reported that men exert greater influence and exhibit more leadership behaviors than do women. Moreover, research reveals that the gender difference in social influence is not merely due to higher-quality performances by men. For example, Propp (1995) reported that in group interactions members were more likely to attend to ideas contributed by men and to use them in solving group problems than to the identical ideas contributed by women. Similarly, research has shown that men remain more influential than women, even when the persuasive messages of the male and female agents are manipulated to be identical (Altemeyer & Jones, 1974; DiBerardinis, Ramage, & Levitt, 1984) or when the performances of the male and female agents are manipulated to be equally good (Schneider & Cook, 1995; Wagner, Ford, & Ford, 1986). The same pattern of results has been reported in research on children. In interactions with peers, boys are more influential than girls (Jacklin & Maccoby, 1978).

Competence, Gender, and Social Influence

Further research specifically links gender differences in perceived competence to gender differences in social influence. In one study, women and men attempted to influence others by speaking either in a competent manner (by supporting their arguments with evidence) or in a less competent manner (with no supporting arguments) (Bradley, 1981). Consistent with the double standard for competence, results revealed that men were perceived to be equally competent and were equally influential regardless of their communication style, whereas women were perceived to be more competent and exerted greater influence when using a competent style than when using the less competent style. Other research reveals that women exert less influence than men in stereotypically masculine and gender-neutral domains, in which men are expected to show higher competence than women, but are more influential than men in stereotypically feminine domains and contexts in which women are expected to be more competent. For example, men exert greater influence over the opinions of others for masculine topics such as sports, gun control, and military affairs, whereas women exert greater influence for feminine topics such as women's fear of crime and child care (Falbo, Hazen, & Linimon, 1982; Feldman-Summers, Montano, Kasprzyk, & Wagner, 1980; Javornisky, 1979; Gerrard, Breda, & Gibbons, 1990). Moreover, evidence of clear female superiority at a task increases women's influence and decreases men's (Pugh & Wahrman, 1983; Shackelford, Wood, & Worchel, 1996).

As already noted, although competence generally facilitates influence, this is not always the case for women, whose competent behavior may sometimes be perceived as too status-asserting. A number of studies have revealed that women can be disadvantaged by competence displays. For example, in one study, male and female influence agents attempted to persuade others using either a direct, competent style of communication or a more indirect style. Results showed that men were equally persuasive regardless of their communication style, whereas women exerted greater influence when communicating in a more indirect manner (Burgoon, Jones, & Stewart, 1975). In another study, corporate executives were asked to evaluate the competence of male and female job applicants and indicate whether they would hire a candidate after reading the applicant's résumé and a transcript of the job interview (Buttner & McEnally, 1996). Results revealed that the executives were most persuaded by and preferred to hire men who communicated in a highly competent manner, showing directness and initiative, rather than men using a less competent style. The reverse was found for women applicants; the executives reported being least persuaded by and least likely to hire a woman using the highly competent style compared with women using other, less competent styles.

Research shows that men are much more inclined to resist women's influence than men's (Ridgeway, 1981). Moreover, men also particularly resist the influence of competent women. A study examining the effectiveness of assertive versus tentative speech revealed that women who used tentative speech, which involved verbal qualifiers such as disclaimers (e.g., "I may be wrong" or "I'm no expert") and hedges (e.g., "sort of," "kind of"), were perceived to be less competent than those using assertive speech that did not contain such verbal qualifiers (Carli, 1991). In that study, males were perceived to be equally competent regardless of their speech style and, not surprisingly, equally influential using either type of speech. Of particular interest was the effect of perceived competence on women's influence. When speaking competently rather than tentatively, women exerted greater influence over a female audience but less influence over a male audience. In essence, men were more influenced by a woman they perceived to be lacking in competence than one who appeared highly competent, rating the competent woman as less trustworthy and less likable than her less competent counterparts.

Other research confirms the finding that men resist the influence of competent women. In one study, women were equally influenced by competent male and female influence agents and liked them equally well, whereas men were more influenced by a competent man than by a competent woman (Carli, LaFleur, & Loeber, 1995). In that study, men reported that they felt more threatened by a competent woman and liked her less than they liked a competent man. Similarly, a recent study revealed that a woman who presented herself as a feminine woman who preferred traditional gender roles was perceived to be less competent than a woman who presented herself as less traditionally feminine (Matschiner & Murnen, 1999). As expected, the traditional woman exerted more influence over men and less influence over women than the less traditional woman did. Again, men, but not women, judged the more competent, nontraditional woman to be less likable and were more resistant to her influence than a woman with lesser competence. In a similar study, participants listened to an audiotape of a male or female expert who presented a speech advocating nontraditional gender roles; results revealed that women were equally persuaded by male and female speakers, but men were less persuaded by women than by men (Rhoades, 1979). Male resistance to female competence has also been found cross-culturally. In this study, the researcher examined the responses of male and female officials working in Israeli bureaucratic organizations to the requests of male and female confederates (Weimann, 1985). In general, confederates were not particularly effective when their requests conveyed helplessness and dependence on the official, with one exception. Female confederates exerted greater influence over male officials when using this relatively incompetent style of communication than when using other, less helpless and more competent appeals.

The tendency of males to resist female influence has been found not only in research on adults but also in research on children, including toddlers and preschoolers. Jacklin and Maccoby (1978) examined the influence patterns among mixed- and same-sex pairs of 33-month-old toddlers. They found that boys and girls were equally likely to issue verbal prohibitions (e.g., "no" or "don't") when another child attempted to take their toys, but girls issuing prohibitions exerted less influence over their male playmates than over female playmates and less influence than boys exerted over either males or females. Indeed, the boys' behavior was completely unaffected by girls' prohibitions, which the boys simply ignored. Similar findings have been reported with a slightly older sample of children. In that study, researchers studying the influence of preschoolers when issuing direct requests reported that girls exerted less influence over boys than over girls, but that boys were equally influential with both male and female classmates (Serbin, Sprafkin, Elman, & Doyle, 1982). In a study of middle school children, boys and girls attempted to persuade their peers to eat bitter-tasting crackers (Dion & Stein, 1978). Although the authors reported that attractive children were generally more influential with the opposite sex than unattractive children, overall, boys were more inclined to eat the crackers after being persuaded by a male than female peer, whereas girls were equally influenced by both genders. Finally, research reveals that boys resist the influence of adult females, as well. A study assessing the effectiveness of parents' imperatives and requests to their two- to six-year-old children revealed that girls were equally likely to comply with their mothers and fathers, but boys complied less with their mothers' influence attempts than with those of their father (Power, McGrath, Hughes, & Manire, 1994).

Communality, Gender, and Social Influence

Women's influence depends not only on their apparent competence but also on the extent to which they display communal behavior, conveying a concern for others and a lack of interest in asserting their status. Men's influence does not. Instead, research indicates that men are often equally influential, regardless of how communally they behave. In one study, male and female confederates communicated either in a communal style, by agreeing with others, or in a dominant, status-asserting style, by overtly disagreeing with others. Results revealed that women exerted greater influence when communal than when dominant, while men were equally influential in both cases (Carli, 1998). Moreover, in this study people disliked the dominant woman and responded to her dominance with anger, irritation, and hostility, whereas they did not express hostility toward men who were equally dominant. Other research confirms that women using a self-asserting, dominant, or threatening style exert less influence than men using the same style (Burgoon, Dillard, & Doran, 1983; Perse, Nathanson, & McLeod, 1996) and less influence than women using a group-oriented, communal style (Burgoon, Birk, & Hall, 1991; Shackelford, Wood, & Worchel, 1996). Likewise, research reveals that asserting one's status through self-promotion is perceived more favorably in men than in women. For example, women who describe their achievements in a self-promoting manner are perceived as less deserving of recognition or support than less self-promoting women, whereas men are not penalized for self-promotion (Giacalone & Riordan, 1990; Wosinska, Dabul, Whetstone-Dion, & Cialdini, 1996). Research also reveals that women who self-promote generally exert less influence than more modest women and are less well liked, even though self-promoting women are considered more competent than their more modest counterparts (Rudman, 1998). In effect, women who appear to be too status-asserting, directive, or aggressive in their communications are penalized for their gender-role violations. People dislike such women and resist their influence.

Even nonverbal self-assertion has costs for women. For example, visual dominance, which involves maintaining a relatively higher level of eye gaze while speaking than while listening and which is associated with possessing status and authority, is more acceptable in men than in women. Women who show high amounts of visual dominance are less well liked and less influential than less visually dominant women (Copeland, Driskell, & Salas, 1995; Mehta, Dovidio, Gibbs, Miller, Huray, Ellyson, & Brown, 1989, cited in Ellyson, Dovidio, & Brown, 1992), although high amounts of visual dominance are acceptable in men and do not reduce men's influence (Mehta et al., 1989, cited in Ellyson, Dovidio, & Brown, 1992).

Similar findings have been reported in research on children. Killen and Naigles (1995) examined the effectiveness of dominant and communal influence attempts by boys and girls who were interacting with peers. They found that girls exerted greater influence when using communal behaviors—agreeing, collaborating, and compromising—than when using dominant behaviors—commanding others, issuing orders, or disagreeing. Two very recent studies examined preschoolers' reactions to female and male puppets exhibiting competent and communal behaviors (Carli, Olm-Shipman, & Kishore, 2001). The first study revealed that boys disliked girl puppets that displayed leaderlike and competent behavior more than boy puppets displaying the same behaviors, but girls liked competent boy and girl puppets equally; both boys and girls had equally favorable reactions to communal boy and girl puppets. The second study revealed that boys, but not girls, considered direct influence attempts by girl puppets to be less influential than indirect attempts when the girl puppet was attempting to influence a male puppet, whereas both boys and girls considered boy puppets to be equally influential in either direct or indirect mode, regardless of whom the puppet was influencing. In general, then, the research on children reveals that, just as with adults, males' influence is unaffected by whether they use communal or dominant behaviors. Moreover, these findings, along with those discussed earlier comparing the effectiveness of communal versus dominant communications by females, suggest that boys in particular resist the influence of dominant or competent females.

Finally, a study examining adult reactions to the communications of one-year-old infants revealed that adults were three to four times more likely to respond to girls who talked, babbled, or gestured than to girls who demanded attention, cried, or screamed (Fagot, Hagan, Leinbach, & Kronsberg, 1985). This same study revealed that adults responded to boys about the same amount, regardless of their behavior. Clearly, even in childhood, girls' ability to influence depends on their use of a communal style of interaction and avoidance of a dominant or self-asserting style, whereas boys' ability to influence is relatively unaffected by their style of communication.

The research reviewed so far indicates that the prescriptive gender stereotype requiring communal behavior in women and girls is endorsed by both males and females. Because being warm and likable is prescriptive for women but not for men, likability is associated with social influence for women more than it is for men (Carli, 1989). That is, people are more influential when they are likable, but the link between being likable and influence is stronger for women than for men. However, there is evidence that men, in particular, prescribe communality for women. Men respond unfavorably to women who communicate self-interest rather than friendliness, warmth, and other communal characteristics (Ridgeway, 1982) and like communal women more than women who are not communal (Carli, LaFleur, & Loeber, 1995). Similarly, a meta-analysis of research on evaluation of leaders indicates that women leaders are denigrated for using an autocratic rather than democratic leadership style, especially by men, whereas male leaders are perceived to be equally effective regardless of how they lead (Eagly, Makhijani, & Klonsky, 1992). As this research on women leaders suggests, men's resistance to the influence of competent women can be overcome when the women display communality as well as competence. One study specifically testing this revealed that men were less influenced by women who spoke in a highly competent manner, using rapid clear speech, than by men who spoke in the same manner (Carli, LaFleur, & Loeber, 1995). In this same study, with a male audience, women exerted as much influence as men when they combined competent speech with warmth, by smiling and nodding, and more influence than women who were merely competent. Warm and competent women were perceived as more likable and less threatening to men than women who were competent but not warm. These results clearly demonstrate that women who adhere to the prescription for female communality and combine competence with warmth reduce male resistance to their influence. Essentially, communal behavior reduces the threat of female competence.

Conclusion

The different distribution of men and women into social roles, according to which women are more often found in domestic and lower-status occupational roles and generally have lower overall status than men, has resulted in descriptive gender stereotypes that women are less competent and less legitimate than men as authorities and leaders. In addition, prescriptive stereotypes require females to exhibit greater communality than males. These descriptive and prescriptive stereotypes create an unfortunate double bind for women, who must both demonstrate exceptional competence to be seen as equal in ability to men and simultaneously avoid threatening others with their competent behavior. As this review has shown, although people who are perceived as competent and likable exert greater influence than those who are not, achieving this balance of competence and likability is more of a challenge for women. Behavior that increases a man's perceived competence may enhance, or at least not reduce, his likability, competence being consistent with stereotypes about men. In contrast, competent behavior can enhance a woman's influence by increasing her perceived competence, which may be in doubt as the result of gender stereotypes, while at the same time reducing her influence by lowering her likability. This twin phenomenon occurs because behavior that appears competent often also appears status-asserting and lacking in the communal qualities prescribed by stereotypes about women. Certainly, women who appear to be direct, competent, and assertive may also be penalized for being seen as illegitimately seeking status, leadership, or influence. As a result, in order to exert influence, women must somehow combine competence with behavior that conveys a lack of desire for self-gain. Communal behavior serves this purpose. Women who combine competence with communality can overcome resistance to their influence while still adhering to traditional gender-role expectations.

For women, influence depends more on being likable than it does for men (Carli, LaFleur, & Loeber, 1995). The greater importance of likability for women's than men's influence is underscored by research on gender differences in power. Compared with men, women typically possess lower levels of expert power, which is based on perceived competence, and legitimate power, which is based on status and legitimate authority; women do, however, possess relatively high levels of referent power, which is based on women's perceived warmth and communality (Carli, 1999). Clearly, women have relatively less access to sources of power that are more available to men. As a result, women must rely on their referent power, or likability, more than men do in order to be influential. Indeed, this may account in part for the greater communal behavior shown by women than men. This behavior includes higher levels of positive social behavior (Carli & Olm-Shipman, 2000), nonverbal warmth, (Hall, 1984) and democratic leadership (Eagly & Johnson, 1990).

Being likable is especially important when women interact with men. Resistance to female influence is particularly pronounced in men and boys, who are more likely to dislike and negatively sanction females who are seen as too competent and direct. It is primarily in interactions with men that women lack authority and legitimacy, and it is therefore not surprising that men respond less favorably than women do to status-asserting behavior in women.

Given the resistance to women's influence, particularly by men, how should women behave in order to be influential? First, women can increase their influence by communicating in a warm and other-directed manner and avoiding displays of highly dominant or self-asserting behavior. In addition, in order to overcome the double standard in evaluation, women can enhance their influence by combining a warm communication style with outstanding levels of competence. Clearly, the need to exhibit competence combined with warmth places an additional burden on women that is not shared by men.

In contrast to women, the manner in which men and boys communicate has little apparent effect on their likability or influence. Studies show that men are given the benefit of the doubt and are presumed to be competent, even when their behavior might be seen as incompetent if exhibited by women. Similarly, men who lack communality, self-promote, or behave in an overtly directive or dominant manner are perceived more favorably than their female counterparts. Indeed, much of the research in this review reveals that male influence is relatively unaffected by how much competence or communality they display. As influence agents, males seem to have greater behavioral latitude than females. Because stereotypes dictate that females lack competence and should be warm and communal, the behavior of female influence agents receives greater scrutiny than that of males, and their influence depends much more on their displaying a careful balance of competence and warmth. Unfortunately, the path to influence is less easily navigated for women than it is for men, as a result.

*References*_____

Altemeyer, R. A., & Jones, K. (1974). Sexual identity, physical attractiveness and seating position as determinants of influence in discussion groups. *Canadian Journal of Behavioral Science, 6,* 357–375.

Berger, J., Fisek, M. H., Norman, R. Z., & Zelditch, M., Jr. (1977). *Status characteristics and social interactions: An expectation states approach.* New York: Elsevier Science.

Biernat, M., & Kobrynowicz, D. (1997). Gender and race-based standards of competence: Lower minimum standards but higher ability standards for devalued groups. *Journal of Personality and Social Psychology, 72,* 544–557.

Bradley, P. H. (1980). Sex, competence and opinion deviation: An expectation states approach. *Communication Monographs, 47,* 101–110.

Bradley, P. H. (1981). The folk-linguistics of women's speech: An empirical examination. *Communication Monographs, 48,* 73–90.

Broverman, I. K., Vogel, S. R., Broverman, D. M., Clarkson, F. E., & Rosenkrantz, P. S. (1972). Sex role stereotypes: A current appraisal. *Journal of Social Issues, 28*(2), 59–78.

Burgess, D., & Borgida, E. (1999). Who women are, who women should be: Descriptive and prescriptive gender stereotyping in sex discrimination. *Psychology, Public Policy, and Law, 5,* 665–692.

Burgoon, M., Birk, T. S., & Hall, J. R. (1991). Compliance and satisfaction with physician-patient communication: An expectancy theory interpretation of gender differences. *Human Communication Research, 18,* 177–208.

Burgoon, M., Dillard, J. P., Doran, N. E. (1983). Friendly or unfriendly persuasion: The effects of violations by males and females. *Human Communication Research, 10*, 283–294.

Burgoon, M., Jones, S. B., & Stewart, D. (1975). Toward a message-centered theory of persuasion: Three empirical investigations of language intensity. *Human Communication Research, 1*, 240–256.

Butler, D., & Geis, F. L. (1990). Nonverbal affect responses to male and female leaders: Implications for leadership evaluations. *Journal of Personality and Social Psychology, 58*, 48–59.

Buttner, E. H., & McEnally, M. (1996). The interactive effect of influence tactic, applicant gender, and type of job on hiring recommendations. *Sex Roles, 34*, 581–591.

Carli, L. L. (1989). Gender differences in interaction style and influence. *Journal of Personality and Social Psychology, 56*, 565–576.

Carli, L. L. (1991). Gender, status, and influence. In E. J. Lawler, B. Markovsky, C. Ridgeway, & H. A. Walker (Eds.), *Advances in group processes: Theory and research* (vol. 8, pp. 89–113). Greenwich, CT: JAI Press.

Carli, L. L. (1997, October). *Effect of gender composition on self-evaluation.* Paper presented at the meeting of the New England Social Psychological Association, Williams College, Williamstown, MA.

Carli, L. L. (1998, June). *Gender effects in social influence.* Paper presented at meeting of the Society for the Psychological Study of Social Issues, Ann Arbor, MI.

Carli, L. L. (1999). Gender, interpersonal power, and social influence. *Journal of Social Issues, 55*, 81–99.

Carli, L. L., LaFleur, S. J., & Loeber, C. C. (1995). Nonverbal behavior, gender, and influence. *Journal of Personality and Social Psychology, 68*, 1030–1041.

Carli, L. L., & Olm-Shipman, C. (2000). Gender differences in task and social behavior: A meta-analytic review. Manuscript in preparation, Wellesley College, Wellesley, MA.

Carli, L. L., Olm-Shipman, C., & Kishore, S. (2001). Gender, interaction, and influence among preschool children. Manuscript in preparation, Wellesley College, Wellesley, MA.

Catalyst. (2000). *Census of women corporate officers and top earners.* New York: Catalyst.

Center for the American Woman and Politics. (2001). *Fact sheet.* New Brunswick, NJ: Eagleton Institute of Politics, Rutgers University. Available online: http://www.rci.rutgers.edu/~cawp/pdf/elective.pdf.

Cejka, M. A., & Eagly, A. H. (1999). Gender-stereotypic images of occupations correspond to the sex segregation of employment. *Personality and Social Psychology Bulletin, 25*, 413–423.

Chaiken, S. (1980). Heuristic versus systematic information processing and the use of source versus message cues in persuasion. *Journal of Personality and Social Psychology, 39*, 752–766.

Chaiken, S., & Eagly, A. H. (1983). Communication modality as a determinant of persuasion: The role of communicator salience. *Journal of Personality and Social Psychology, 45*, 241–256.

Chronicle of Higher Education. (1998). *Almanac* (vol. 45, no. 1). Washington, DC: Chronicle of Higher Education.

Connor, J. M., Serbin, L. A., & Ender, R. A. (1978). Responses of boys and girls to aggressive, assertive, and passive behaviors of male and female characters. *Journal of Genetic Psychology, 133*, 59–69.

Copeland, C. L., Driskell, J. E., & Salas, E. (1995). Gender and reactions to dominance. *Journal of Social Behavior and Personality, 10*, 53–68.

Deaux, K., & Kite, M. (1993). Gender stereotypes. In F. L. Denmark & M. A. Paludi (Eds.), *Psychology of women: A handbook of issues and theories* (pp. 107–139). Westport, CT: Greenwood Press.

DiBerardinis, J., Ramage, K., & Levitt, S. (1984). Risky shift and gender of the advocate: Information theory versus normative theory. *Group & Organization Studies, 9*, 189–200.

Dion & K. K., & Stein, S. (1978). Physical attractiveness and interpersonal influence. *Journal of Experimental Social Psychology, 14*, 97–108.

Driskell, J. E., Olmstead, B., & Salas, E. (1993). Task cues, dominance cues, and influence in task groups. *Journal of Applied Psychology, 78*, 51–60.

Eagly, A. H. (1987). *Sex differences in social behavior: A social-role interpretation.* Hillside, NJ: Erlbaum.

Eagly, A. H., & Johnson, B. T. (1990). Gender and leadership style: A meta-analysis. *Psychological Bulletin, 108*, 233–256.

Eagly, A. H., & Karau, S. J. (1991). Gender and the emergence of leaders: A meta-analysis. *Journal of Personality and Social Psychology, 60*, 685–710.

Eagly, A. H., Makhijani, M. G., & Klonsky, B. G. (1992). Gender and the evaluation of leaders: A meta-analysis. *Psychological Bulletin, 111*, 3–22.

Eagly, A. H., & Mladinic, A. (1989). Gender stereotypes and attitudes toward women and men. *Personality and Social Psychology Bulletin, 15*, 543–558.

Eagly, A. H., Mladinic, A., & Otto, S. (1991). Are women evaluated more favorably than men? *Psychology of Women Quarterly, 15*, 203–216.

Eagly, A. H., & Steffen, V. J. (1984). Gender stereotypes stem from the distribution of women and men into social roles. *Journal of Personality and Social Psychology, 46*, 735–754.

Ellyson, S. L., Dovidio, J. F., & Brown, C. E. (1992). The look of power: Gender differences in visual dominance behavior. In C. L. Ridgeway (Ed.), *Gender, interaction, and inequality* (pp. 50–80). New York: Springer-Verlag.

Erickson, B., Lind, E. A., Johnson, B. C., & O'Barr, W. M. (1978). Speech style and impression formation in a court setting: The effects of "powerful" and "powerless" speech. *Journal of Experimental Social Psychology, 14*, 266–279.

Fagot, B. I., Hagan, R., Leinbach, M. D., & Kronsberg, S. (1985). Differential reactions to assertive and communicative acts of toddler boys and girls. *Child Development, 56*, 1499–1505.

Falbo, T., Hazen, M. D., & Linimon, D. (1982). The costs of selecting power bases or messages associated with the opposite sex. *Sex Roles, 8*, 147–157.

Feldman-Summers, S., Montano, D. E., Kasprzyk, D., & Wagner, B. (1980). Influence attempts when competing views are gender-related: Sex as credibility. *Psychology of Women Quarterly, 5*, 311–320.

Fiske, S. T., & Ruscher, J. B. (1993). Negative interdependence and prejudice: Whence the affect? In D. M. Mackie & D. L. Hamilton (Eds.), *Affect, cognition, and stereotyping: Interactive processes in group perception* (pp. 239–268). New York: Academic Press.

Foschi, M. (1996). Double standards in the evaluation of men and women. *Social Psychology Quarterly, 59*, 237–254.

Gerrard, M., Breda, C., & Gibbons, F. X. (1990). Gender effects in couples' decision making and contraceptive use. *Journal of Applied Social Psychology, 20*, 449–464.

Giacalone, R. A., & Riordan, C. A. (1990). Effect of self-presentation on perceptions and recognition in an organization. *Journal of Psychology, 124*, 25–38.

Hall, J. A. (1984). *Nonverbal sex differences: Communication accuracy and expressive style.* Baltimore, MD: Johns Hopkins University.

Hawkins, K. W. (1995). Effects of gender and communication content on leadership emergence in small task-oriented groups. *Small Group Research, 46*, 234–249.

Heilman, M. E., Block, C. J., & Martell, R. (1995). Sex stereotypes: Do they influence perceptions of managers? In N.J. Struthers (Ed.), *Gender in the workplace* (special issue). *Journal of Social Behavior and Personality, 10*(6), 237–252.

Holtgraves, T., & Lasky, B. (1999). Linguistic power and persuasion. *Journal of Language and Social Psychology, 18*, 196–205.

Jacklin, C. N., & Maccoby, E. E. (1978). Social behavior at 33 months in same-sex and mixed-sex dyads. *Child Development, 49*, 557–569.

Jamieson, K. H., & Slass, L. (2001). *Progress or no room at the top? The role of women in telecommunications, media, and e-companies.* Philadelphia: Annenberg Public Policy Center of the University of Pennsylvania.

Javornisky, G. (1979). Task content and sex differences in conformity. *Journal of Psychology, 108*, 213–220.

Killen, M., & Naigles, L. R. (1995) Preschool children pay attention to their addressees: Effects of gender composition on peer disputes. *Discourse Processes, 19*, 329–346.

Lockheed, M. E. (1985). Sex and social influence: A meta-analysis guided by theory. In J. Berger & M. Zelditch, Jr. (Eds.), *Status, rewards, and influence: How expectations organize behavior* (pp. 406–429). San Francisco: Jossey-Bass.

Lockheed, M. E., Harris, A.M., & Nemceff, W. P. (1983). Sex and social influence: Does sex function as a status characteristic in mixed-sex groups of children? *Journal of Educational Psychology, 75*, 877–888.

Matschiner, M., & Murnen, S. K. (1999). Hyperfemininity and influence. *Psychology of Women Quarterly, 23*, 631–642.

Meeker, B. F., & Weitzel-O'Neil, P. A. (1985). Sex roles and interpersonal behavior in task-oriented groups. In J. Berger & M. Zelditch (Eds.), *Status, rewards, and influence* (pp. 379–405). Washington, DC: Jossey-Bass.

Perse, E. M., Nathanson, A. I., & McLeod, D. M. (1996). Effects of spokesperson sex, public announcement appeal, and involvement on evaluations of safe-sex PSAs. *Health Communication, 8*, 171–189.

Power, T. G., McGrath, M. P., Hughes, S. O., & Manire, S. H. (1994). Compliance and self-assertion: Young children's responses to mothers versus fathers. *Developmental Psychology, 6*, 980–989.

Propp, K. M. (1995). An experimental examination of biological sex as a status cue in decision-making groups and its influence on information use. *Small Group Research, 26*, 451–474.

Pugh, M. D., & Wahrman, R. (1983). Neutralizing sexism in mixed-sex groups: Do women have to be better than men? *American Journal of Sociology, 88*, 746–762.

Reed, V., & Buddeberg-Fischer, B. (2001). Career obstacles for women in medicine: An overview. *Medical Education, 35*, 139–147.

Rhoades, M. J. R. (1981). A social psychological investigation of the differential influence of male and female advocates of nontraditional sex roles (doctoral dissertation, Ball State University, 1979). *Dissertation Abstracts International, 41*, 4747.

Rhode, D. L. (2001). *The unfinished agenda: Women and the legal profession.* Chicago: American Bar Association, Commission on Women in the Profession.

Ridgeway, C. (1978). Conformity, group-oriented motivation, and status attainment in small groups. *Social Psychology Quarterly, 41*, 175–188.

Ridgeway, C. L. (1981). Nonconformity, competence and influence in groups: A test of two theories. *American Sociological Review, 46*, 333–347.

Ridgeway, C. L. (1982). Status in groups: The importance of motivation. *American Sociological Review, 47*, 76–88.

Ridgeway, C. L., & Berger, J. (1986). Expectations, legitimation, and dominance behavior in task groups. *American Sociological Review, 51*, 603–617.

Ruble, T. L. (1983). Sex stereotypes: Issues of change in the 1970s. *Sex Roles, 9*, 397–402.

Rudman, L. A. (1998). Self-promotion as a risk factor for women: The costs and benefits of counter-stereotypical impression management. *Journal of Personality and Social Psychology, 74*, 629–645.

Schein, V. E. (in press). A global look at psychological barriers to women's progress in management. *Journal of Social Issues.*

Schneider, J., & Cook, K. (1995). Status inconsistency and gender. *Small Group Research, 26*, 372–399.

Serbin, L., Sprafkin, C., Elman, M., & Doyle, A. (1982). The early development of sex-differentiated patterns of social influence. *Canadian Journal of Behavioral Science, 14*, 350–363.

Shackelford, S., Wood, W., & Worchel, S. (1996). Behavioral styles and the influence of women in mixed-sex groups. *Social Psychology Quarterly, 59*, 284–293.

Son, L., & Schmitt, N. (1983). The influence of sex bias upon compliance with expert power. *Sex Roles, 9*, 233–246.

Stein, R. T., & Heller, T. (1979). An empirical analysis of the correlations between leadership status and participation rates reported in the literature. *Journal of Personality and Social Psychology, 37*, 1993–2002.

Swim, J., Borgida, E., Maruyama, G., & Myers, D. G. (1989). Joan McKay versus John McKay: Do gender stereotypes bias evaluations? *Psychological Bulletin, 105*, 409–429.

Twenge, J. M. (1997). Attitudes toward women, 1970-1995. *Psychology of Women Quarterly, 21*, 35–51.

U.S. Bureau of Labor Statistics. (2001). *Labor force statistics from the current population survey: Annual averages—household data.* Table 2: Employment status of the civilian noninstitutional population 16 years and over by sex, 1969 to date. Available online: http://www.census.gov/hhes/income/histinc/p36.html.

U.S. Bureau of the Census. (2000). *Historical income tables: People.* Table P36: Full time, year-round workers (all races) by median income and sex: 1970 to 2000. Available online: Internet http://www.bls.gov/cps/home.htm#charemp.

U.S. Department of Defense (1998). *Active duty military personnel by service by rank/grade* (for September 30, 1997). Available online: http://web1.whs.osd.mil/mmid/military/miltop.htm.

Wagner, D. G., Ford, R. S., & Ford, T. W. (1986). Can gender inequalities be reduced? *American Sociological Review, 51*, 47–61.

Walker, H. A., Ilardi, B. C., McMahon, A. M., & Fennell, M. L. (1996). Gender, interaction, and leadership. *Social Psychology Quarterly, 59*, 255–272.

Weimann, G. (1985). Sex differences in dealing with bureaucracy. *Sex Roles, 12*, 777–790.

Williams, J. E., & Best, D. L. (1990). *Measuring sex stereotypes: A multinational study.* Newbury Park, CA: Sage.

Wood, W., & Kallgren, C. A. (1988). Communicator attributes and persuasion: Recipients' access to attitude relevant information in memory. *Personality and Social Psychology Bulletin, 14*, 172–182.

Wood, W., & Karten, S. J. (1986). Sex differences in interaction style as a product of perceived sex differences in competence. *Journal of Personality and Social Psychology, 50*, 341–347.

Wosinska, W., Dabul, A. J., Whetstone-Dion, R., & Cialdini, R. B. (1996). Self-presentational responses to success in the organization: The costs and benefits of modesty. *Basic and Applied Social Psychology, 18*, 229–242.

9

Language Expectancy Theory

Insight to Application

Michael Burgoon and Jason T. Siegel

Language Expectancy Theory: Explication

The book you presently have open is replete with a variety of theoretical frameworks designed to increase your understanding of persuasion and social influence. Unfortunately, too frequently students of social influence are presented with theories of the literature in a fashion that falsely suggests a rather simplistic journey from thought to insight to theories of human behavior. However, of obvious import to those studying persuasion, and of vital import to those who wish one day to be on the opposite side of the metaphoric textbook, is how theories of persuasion are spawned from what sometimes begins as little more than a seedling of thought. As Michael Burgoon stated in creating Language Expectancy Theory (LET): ". . . this theoretical formation has taken a few steps forward and some steps backward over the years in attempting to develop a sound basis for understanding how expectations and a host of message variables interact to enhance or inhibit persuasion effects" (Burgoon, Denning, Roberts, in press). In short, the goal of this chapter is not only to introduce you to LET's most useful propositions about attitude change but also to introduce the experiments and revelations that spawned the theory.

LET (Burgoon & Miller, 1985) is based on a relatively simple yet intuitively elegant assumption: Language is a rule-governed system whereby people develop expectations concerning how language and message strategies are used in persuasion attempts. Specifically, LET explicates three different paradigms: (1) the traditional passive message reception situation, in which a persuader presents a message to a target audience with a desire to change attitudes and/or behaviors; (2) the active participation paradigm, in which individuals are "self-persuaded" by actually producing messages, usually at odds with their own privately held attitudes that result in their changing their private attitude to conform more closely to their public communication behavior; and, (3) the resistance-to-persuasion paradigm, which centers on how the language and expectations can work in tandem to *decrease* or inhibit the persuasive strength of a future persuasive attempt, a message yet to come. However, rather than addressing all three paradigms, this chapter will just present a detailed explanation of the passive paradigm, the most studied and practical use of persuasion principles (for a detailed review of all three paradigms of LET see Burgoon, Denning, Roberts, in press).

Language Expectancy Theory: The Core Propositions

Two studies have been credited by M. Burgoon and Miller (1985) with being catalysts for the core propositions of LET: Brooks (1970) and McPeek and Edwards (1975). While the story of how Brooks's study came to the attention of Burgoon has been told elsewhere (Burgoon, 1995), due to its seminal importance to the development of this perspective, this story will be repeated one more time.

Burgoon sent off one of his articles investigating what would become part of LET's *active paradigm* (Burgoon 1970) to be considered for publication in a journal. In response, the editor of the journal, Robert Brooks, sent him a copy of another article, which had been accepted for publication but not yet published. While the study itself was of interest to Burgoon, it was the concluding paragraph of this piece that he credits with the insightful discussion that eventually led to the development of LET. This concluding paragraph reads as follows:

> . . . the possibility of contrast effects should be considered. This principle assumes that we carry stereotypes into such social situations as the public speech. There, the speaker's behavior may be discrepant with stereotyped expectations. If the discrepant expectations still cannot be assimilated or ignored, they are likely to be exaggerated in a listener's perception. So viewed, mere civil behavior on the part of Malcolm X may be perceived as extraordinarily genteel by an auditor who expects barbaric actions from a black [sic] nationalist. One explanation . . . is this: unfavorable (or favorable) speakers may be perceived more (or less) favorably not because their behavior is intrinsically persuasive (or dissuasive) but because it contrasts with stereotyped expectations which audiences hold for notorious (or popular) public figures. (p. 155)

This article by Brooks (1970) led Burgoon to begin thinking about the nature of stereotypes and also the ingredients that comprised and determined expectations. Burgoon began to ponder whether there are expectations that are specific not only to a person but also to a culture. Also, if expectations about behavior exist, are there also enduring expectations about the patterns of ordinary language? Lastly, do expectations of language use, if they do indeed exist, differ based on a speaker's gender, socioeconomic class, and/or credibility?

Burgoon and Chase (1973) took these skeletal notions of expectations violations and investigated what occurs when receivers' expectations of language intensity are intentionally violated. Specifically, Burgoon and Chase (1973) hypothesized that if participants in the study were presented with a pretreatment message (message 1) of high intensity, they would expect a follow-up message to be of at least equal intensity (see appendix A following this chapter for an example of a low- and high-intensity message). However, if the participants' expectations were violated with a message of moderate intensity, they would see the speaker as more "reasonable." As a result, the speaker would be more successful with a follow-up appeal (message 2). Moreover, Burgoon and Chase predicted that people who were initially exposed to a message of low intensity would similarly expect the follow-up message to be of equal intensity. It was reasoned, therefore, that if these people initially received a message that was either of moderate or high intensity, they would not expect a follow-up message of even greater intensity. Thus, they would be most persuaded by the moderate or high-intensity second message. Burgoon and Chase further predicted that if people expected a follow-up persuasive appeal of moderate intensity and received such a message, their expectations would not be violated. Thus, they would perceive the message as more reasonable. However, because they would expect this level of intensity, the persuasive strength of the message would be minimized.

To test their hypothesis, five weeks prior to an actual experiment, students were presented with a pretest questionnaire asking them their opinions on a variety of campus and national issues. Considering that the hypothesis was predicting the students' responses when presented with a (second) refutational message (a message they would unquestionably disagree with), it was crucial for the experimenters to find an issue to which students were unanimously opposed. The issue that was most offensive to the students was a proposed plan by the university to admit only seniors and juniors. Specifically, on the day of the actual experiment, all subjects who took part were unanimously opposed to such a plan.

In the experimental sessions, 114 participants were randomly assigned to seven different conditions: one control and six experimental. All subjects received a high-, moderate-, or low-intensity pretreatment message arguing for the policy disallowing freshman or sophomores from being admitted. As discussed, this pretreatment message was used to create expectations on the part of the receiver. For example, if a participant received a supportive message of low intensity, it was assumed that this would create an expectation on the part of the participant that the next message would be of similar intensity. Following the pretreatment message, all students received a message of moderate intensity.

As predicted, those students who had heard a message of high intensity and then heard one of moderate intensity were significantly more persuaded than those students who had heard a message of moderate intensity followed by another message of moderate intensity (positive violation). The reason the violation is considered positive is that the message was less intense than expected. Since the first message was highly intense, the audience prepared for a message of similar intensity. However, when the message was of only moderate intensity, the audience's expectations were positively violated. The change is considered a positive violation because the enacted behavior was better or more preferred than that expected in the situation. A positive violation can also occur when negatively evaluated sources conform more closely than expected to cultural values, societal norms, or situational exigencies. Returning to the experiment, those students who heard a message of low intensity followed by a message of moderate intensity were also significantly more persuaded (although the violation was negative) than those (unprepared) students who did not have their expectations violated (i.e., the students who heard a message of moderate intensity followed by another message of moderate intensity). The reason this result occurred is that the students who had originally heard a message of low intensity dropped their counterarguing defenses, expecting another message of low intensity. However, when the second message used language of greater intensity than they expected, the students were unprepared to counterargue it. The violation is considered negative, because the language being used fell outside the bandwidth of socially acceptable or expected behavior in a negative direction.

Two years later, McPeek and Edwards (1975) published a second major precursor to LET. While Burgoon and Chase (1973) investigated the effects of violating expectations that were created by the investigator, McPeek and Edwards (1975) investigated the outcome of speakers who argue for a position that is opposite of what would be expected, based not on expectations set by the investigator, but on expectations set by societal and cultural norms with the following claims and questions:

> Interpersonal perceptions and behaviors are partly guided by the prior expectations which the participants bring to social interactions. It has been suggested (Kelly, 1955) that everyone forms and tests expectancies about the characteristics and behavior of other people in a process similar to the scientific method. . . . These expectations are of special importance in studies of attitude change, where, in addition to the experimenter, the S [subject] often encounters a communicator of an attitudinal message. . . . These expectancies, although they may be deeply rooted in the S's personal biases and may even be irrelevant to the topic of the persuasive message (e.g., Aronson & Golden, 1962), nevertheless may strongly affect the degree to which the communicator can influence the S. . . . Both in and outside the laboratory, one's expectancies about the behavior and opinions of others are usually confirmed. But, what happens when one's predictions are violated, and a communicator fails to behave in an expected fashion? (pp. 193–194)

McPeek and Edwards (1975) made predictions concerning the effectiveness of antimarijuana messages based upon how "expected" the message source would be to make such an argument. It was posited that a hippie arguing against marijuana, the obviously unexpected position, would be seen as more credible than a seminarian making the same, albeit expected, anti-marijuana argument. Conversely, it was hypothesized that when a hippie took the expected pro-marijuana position, he would be less persuasive than a seminarian taking an unexpected, pro-marijuana, position.

When a study was conducted, the hypotheses gained only partial support. The hippie putting forth an anti-marijuana argument was more persuasive than the seminarian arguing the same position; however, the seminarian arguing for marijuana was no more persuasive than the hippie putting forth the same argument. However, it is important to note that the communicators taking unexpected positions, whether the hippie arguing against marijuana or the seminarian arguing for it, were perceived as being more honest and more sincere then the communicators who took the expected position.

At about the same time that the McPeek and Edwards' (1975) piece was published, a piece by Burgoon, Jones, and Stewart (1975) introduced what would become the initial roots of LET. This seminal article provided evidence that persuasive success can be moderated by the linguistic choices made by the communicator. Specifically, Burgoon, Jones, and Stewart put forth the following propositions in relation to LET's passive paradigm:

Proposition A: Attitude change is a function of the level of language intensity in a persuasive message, type of persuasive paradigm employed, and the receiver's expectations of the source's communication behavior.

Proposition B: Given the passive message reception condition, when a source uses a level of language intensity that violates the receiver's expectations in a positive manner, significant attitude change will occur in the direction advocated by the source.

Proposition C: Given the passive message reception condition, when a source takes an unexpectedly intense position, it will result in minimal or even negative attitude change.

At the time this piece was published, the investigation of language intensity was by no means novel, nor was the investigation into expectations, but this was the first piece to combine the role of societal expectations and language intensity in persuasion research on an a priori basis. As put forth by Burgoon and colleagues: ". . . all present evidence suggests that expectations develop in receivers about syntactic, linguistic, and pragmatic variables in persuasive messages. Most of the studies explained unexpected findings on a post hoc basis" (Burgoon, Jones, & Stewart, 1975, p. 243). In short, the realization that violating receivers' expectations could be a moderating variable in the equation of persuasion was stepping into the spotlight.

The experiment to test these propositions was similar to prior experimental designs. Two messages were created, this time concerning a required GPA of 3.25 to enter the university where the experiment took place. These messages were identical except for key verb phrases that were either highly intense or low in intensity. One of the key tests of this experiment focused on societal expectations of the communicators of persuasive messages based on gender. The hypotheses were as follows:

Hypothesis 1: Male receivers will demonstrate less attitude change than will female receivers.

Hypothesis 2: There will be an interaction between language intensity and sex of the source such that a female source will be most effective with low-intense language and a male will be least effective with low-intense language.

This was the first test in this line of research where expectations were not created by the experimenter but were expected due to societal norms. Explaining the logic behind their prediction, Burgoon, Jones, and Stewart stated:

Bem and Bem (1970) suggest that the socialization process, whether it be intentional or not, has programmed females to be complementary rather than independent of the male, submissive rather than dominant, domestic rather than business- or scientific-minded, and to generally consider themselves less knowledgeable than men. If the suggested stereotypes of submissiveness are correct, then certain communication behaviors would be expected to differ for men and women. Females are probably expected to be less intense than males. If highly intense encoding by a female occurs, a "boomerang effect" should occur because she will be taking an "unconventionally and unexpectedly strong position." A male who is expected to be strong will likely be less effective using low-intense language. (p. 245)

This hypothesis was supported. The female speaker was more successful when using a low-intensity message than when using a highly intense message; and the male speaker was more persuasive when using a highly intense message than when using a low-intensity message. This finding was crucial for two reasons. First, it gave support to the notion that there are societal expectations concerning language and language intensity; second, it showed that violating these expectations could impair the persuasive strength of a message.

Another area of interest was the arena of fear appeals. Fear appeals are any messages that use fear or anxiety arousal in the hope of scaring the audience into complying with the message. Obviously, knowing societal expectations in regard to the quantity of fear used in such messages is key to any speaker who wishes to scare his or her audience into compliance. Violating the expectations of the audience can either greatly increase or decrease the persuasive strength of the message. Unfortunately, early studies of fear appeals presented often conflicting, seemingly confounded results. For example, one of the first studies on fear appeals found that *mild* fear appeals were *more* successful than strong fear appeals (Janis & Feshbach, 1953); however, other studies (e.g., Leventhal & Niles, 1965) found the opposite result, while yet other investigations revealed no significant difference between level of fear and attitude change (Beach, 1966; Powell 1965). Fortunately, Hewgill and Miller (1965) attempted to clarify the influence of fear appeals by combining the influence of fear appeals with the influence of source credibility.

The study hypothesized the following:

1. If a source has high credibility with a listener, appeals that elicit strong fear for persons highly valued by the listener will affect greater attitude change than appeals that elicit mild fear.
2. If a source has low credibility with a listener, appeals that elicit mild fear for persons highly valued by the listener will affect greater attitude change than appeals that elicit strong fear.

Taken together, these two hypotheses predicted an interaction between level of fear and source credibility. To test these hypotheses, the investigators split up 90 subjects into four experimental groups and one control group: (1) high-fear message, high-credibility source; (2) high-fear message, low-credibility source; (3) low-fear message, high-credibility source; and (4) low-fear message, low-credibility source. Each group heard a message emphasizing the advantages of community shelters while stressing the disadvantages of family shelters. It's important to note that this study took place at the height of the cold war when people feared a nuclear attack. The four messages contained the same content, but the high-fear messages contained 13 statements concerning physical injury or death to spouse or children. Specifically, the high-fear message stated the following:

Unless proper shelter precautions are taken against fallout, the children of thousands of families would be killed in nuclear war. The most dangerous fallout is the early fallout that falls within 24 to 48 hours after the thermonuclear explosion, and this is the primary hazard from which we should be prepared to protect our husbands or wives, and our children, since many of them will perish if such protection is not available. Even minimal community shelter precautions would spare the lives of thousands of adults and children. Children would probably suffer severe radiation burns while going from school to home and then have to endure radiation sickness while confined in a small family shelter. (Hewgill & Miller, 1965, p. 96)

Credibility was manipulated by either attributing the message to a professor of nuclear research or to a high school sophomore. After each group heard their message, they immediately underwent a series of tests to assess their attitudes toward community and family shelters. As predicted, participants who heard a message containing a high-fear appeal attributed to a highly credible source were more persuaded than those participants who heard a message employing a mild-fear appeal attributed to a low-credibility source. Additionally, the participants who heard the message using high-fear appeals attributed to a highly credible source were significantly more persuaded than any of the three other groups; however, there were no differences in attitudes between the groups who heard messages attributed to a low-credibility source, regardless of the fear appeal used. Of import is that in a follow-up study, Miller and Hewgill (1966) hypothesized that a low-credibility source using strong language would reduce his or her credibility further, whereas a highly credible source would increase his or her credibility by using a strong fear-arousing message. Their hypotheses were generally supported. The reason low-credibility sources using highly intense language are problematic is that cultural expectations grant high-credibility sources a greater range of options in their language use. For example, a full professor giving a passionate, high-intensity speech about the need for stricter college standards would likely be accepted; however, imagine a young teacher's assistant giving the same passionate, high-intensity speech. The teaching assistant would be seen as unprofessional and possibly overemotional. Simply put, if someone of high credibility uses extremely intense language, his or her language use is perceived to be a necessary act. However, a low-credibility source using the same language may be perceived as "out of control" or immature.

By incorporating research in fear appeals, compliance gaining, language intensity, opinionated language, and a host of other message variables, amongst others, the following propositions of LET's passive paradigm were put forth (Burgoon, 1989; Burgoon, 1995; Burgoon, Denning, & Roberts, 2001; Burgoon & Miller, 1985):

Proposition 1: People develop cultural and sociological expectations about language behaviors that subsequently affect their acceptance or rejection of persuasive messages.

Proposition 2: Use of language that negatively violates societal expectations about appropriate persuasive communication behavior inhibits persuasive behavior and either results in no attitude change or changes in position opposite to that advocated by the communicator.

Proposition 3: Use of language that positively violates societal expectations about appropriate persuasive communication behavior facilitates persuasive effectiveness.

Proposition 4: Highly credible communicators have the freedom (wide bandwidth) to select varied language strategies and compliance-gaining techniques in developing persuasive messages, while low-credibility communicators must conform to more limited language options if they wish to be effective.

Proposition 5: Because of the normative impact of source credibility, highly credible sources can be more successful using low-intensity appeals and more aggressive compliance-gaining messages than low-credibility communicators using either strong or mild language or more prosocial compliance-gaining strategies.

Proposition 6: Communicators perceived as low in credibility or those unsure of their perceived credibility will usually be more persuasive if they employ appeals low in instrumental verbal aggression or elect to use more prosocial compliance-gaining message strategies.

Proposition 7: People in this society have normative expectations about appropriate persuasive communication behavior that are gender specific, for example: (a) males are usually more persuasive using highly intense persuasive appeals and compliance-gaining message attempts, while (b) females are usually more persuasive using low-intensity appeals and nonaggressive compliance-gaining messages.

Application of LET: The Family Sun Safety Campaign

Although the ability to explain past experiments shines positive light on a theory, the spotlight shines much brighter when the theory can be applied to a real-world context. Such is the case with the LET passive paradigm.

In 1999 alone, 44,200 people were diagnosed with life-threatening malignant melanoma; 7,300 of them died. This figure is even more staggering in light of the fact that 90 percent of skin cancers are preventable (America Cancer Society, 1999). While there is no shortage of ways to decrease these figures—sunscreens, use of shade, etc.—the difficulty lies in persuading individuals to comply with the aforementioned preventive measures. The goal of this Family Sun Safety Project, funded by the National Cancer Institute, was rather straightforward: create sun safety messages differing in language intensity and logical style while using LET's explanatory power to hypothesize which messages will be most effective.

Based on LET, it was predicted that a sun safety campaign containing more intense language would be more successful than a campaign using low-intensity language, since past empirical research suggested that schools and pediatricians, the sources to which sun safety messages were attributed, are highly credible (Buller, Callister, & Reichert, 1995). As discussed earlier, communicators of high credibility are granted a "wider bandwidth" of acceptable communication, whereas speakers of low credibility are relegated to a much narrower bandwidth. Practically speaking, a speaker of low credibility is excluded, under penalty of a potential boomerang effect, from using aggressive strategies such as threats, highly intense language, and fear appeals. A low-credibility speaker who chooses such aggressive strategies over nonaggressive strategies such as promises, less intense language, and reassurances will negatively violate the receivers' expectations. On the contrary, speakers of high credibility who decide to use the more aggressive language strategies just mentioned will be treated to an increase in the persuasive strength of their message (e.g., Burgoon, Dillard, & Doran, 1983).

Based on this theoretical rationale and empirical findings, it was predicted that a sun safety campaign containing more intense language would be more successful than a campaign using less intense language. The logic was rather straightforward: Since highly intense language is not the norm for most campaigns focusing on health promotion, such intense language would be a violation of expectations. Furthermore, since past research has put forth data suggesting that schools and pediatricians, the sources of the sun safety messages, are highly credible (Burgoon, Birk, & Hall, 1991), there exists a greater bandwidth of acceptable language for these sources. It was predicted that since there was a large bandwidth of acceptance, the intense language would be perceived as a positive violation and would therefore produce greater compliance with the sun safety advice than the message using low-intensity language. The low-intensity language messages do not negatively violate expectations, but rather conform. Therefore, while there will not be a boomerang effect, the messages using highly intense language were predicted to be more effective than the former. Statements with high-intensity language included the following: "Skin cancer is a grotesque growth of skin cells," "Treatment of skin cancer involves removing tumors from the skin," and "Tragically, about 7,200 Americans will die from melanoma, a very serious type of skin cancer, this year alone." Statements of low intensity included the following: "Skin cancer is an unusual growth of skin cells" and "Sadly about 7,200 Americans will die from melanoma, a very serious type of skin cancer, this year alone" (Buller, Borland, & Burgoon, 1998, p. 450).

Parents were recruited for the Family Sun Safety Project from elementary schools and a pediatric clinic. Participants received sun safety prevention messages in the form of newsletters, brochures, and tip cards. The project accrued over 800 families and lasted over a year. In short, as predicted by LET, messages using intense language produced more compliance than messages of low intensity. Specifically, as reported by Buller, Burgoon, Hall, and colleagues (2000):

> Compared to parents receiving low-intensity messages, parents in the high intensity message (a) decreased the frequency of their own midday sun exposure during the current summer, (b) were more likely to say that they in general planned to protect their children more next summer and planned to protect themselves and their children more in the upcoming winter, and (c) reported a larger increase in their planned frequency of applying sunscreen, using protective clothing, and limited midday sun exposure with their children in the upcoming winter. (p. 108)

In summary, by using the LET proposition framework, the experimenters were able to predict successfully which messages would be more effective purely on the basis of the intensity of the language used. Most important, multiple behaviors were changed and those changes persisted over a long period of time.

LET's Passive Paradigm: New Directions

To state that LET's passive paradigm is just beginning to hit its stride might be an understatement. In the past decade the theory has been successfully used to (1) explain the success of negative attack campaigns in politics (Pfau, Parrott, & Lindquist, 1992), (2) explain compliance and satisfaction with physicians' instructions (M. Burgoon, Birk, & Hall, 1991), (3) assess the effectiveness of communication strategies designed to improve *both* initial and long-term medical adherence (Klingle, 1993; Klingle & M. Burgoon, 1995), and (4) improve adherence to sun safety recommendations (Buller, Burgoon, Hall, Levine, Taylor, Beach, Melcher, Buller, Bowen, Hunsaker, & Bergen, 2000). However, the theory continues to be ripe with opportunities for refinement and expansion. To conclude, we shall present at least one venue where the theory's framework can be expanded and one realm where the theory could be fruitfully applied.

Ethnicity and Culture

Just as males have greater bandwidths of acceptable ordinary language use than females, it seems plausible that ethnicity might also be a variable that moderates expectations. Certain ethnic groups may be penalized, much as females are, for using language of high intensity. This scenario could depend on the dynamics of the culture or ethnicity of the presenter and the culture or ethnicity of the audience. For example, a high-credibility source who is part of one social minority presenting to members of a different social minority may well forfeit his/her wider bandwidth of communication in such a situation.

Public Service Announcements

Anyone who views a modicum of television has undoubtedly seen advertisements urging adolescents to avoid drug use. While some of these advertisements are unquestionably effective, LET can be used to explain why some ads (maybe most) may not be as successful as they could be (see Siegel & Burgoon, 2001 for a more detailed explanation). For example, one of the more popular ads highlights a teenager armed with a frying pan alerting the audience members to what their friends and family will go through if they use drugs. As the female teenager states in the commercial: "This is your brain. This is heroin. This is what happens to your brain after snorting heroin." The actress then smashes the egg with the pan and exposes the cracked egg sliding off the back of the pan to the audience. The rest of the actress's dialogue is spoken as she uses the pan as a weapon to break several kitchen appliances and dishes: "It's not over yet. This is what your family goes through. And your friends. And your money. And your job. And your self-respect. And your future. Any questions?"

Looking at this commercial from a LET standpoint it's rather clear that the commercial uses highly intense language and nonverbal behavior. However, as discussed earlier, females have a narrower bandwidth of acceptable communication than males. Is it possible that the commercial negatively violates expectations by having the female actress use such intense language, thereby reducing the persuasive strength of the message? Furthermore, it is unknown whether or not the creators of the message are considered to be highly credible by their target audience. If the audience does not perceive the creators of the commercial to be credible, the high-intensity fear appeal will at best be ineffective and at worst will cause a boomerang effect, persuading the audience in the direction opposite of that advocated by the commercial. It is also possible that the actress in the commercial will lose some of her credibility.

LET: The Most Recent Finding

Recent research supported by the National Institute of Drug Abuse through a multimillion dollar experiment using LET to explain adolescent reaction to antidrug inhalant and marijuana messages (Burgoon 2001, Grant #DA12578) obtained interesting results about expectations regarding media commercials and interpersonal communication. This experiment involved over 1,300 adolescent students exposed to antidrug/inhalant messages. While the participants all saw the *same* messages, students were exposed to footage of one of four different scripted focus groups discussing the advertisements. Specifically, after viewing each of three advertisements, the students either saw a focus group consisting of peers or adults using either implicit or explicit antidrug language. This resulted in four different experimental conditions (adult explicit, adult implicit, peer implicit, peer explicit) discussing both the advertisements and the topic of adolescents and drug/inhalant use. In the implicit condition, the individuals made statements such as, "When it comes right down to it . . . it's your own decision" or "Why would anyone want to do that stuff?" In the explicit condition the comments were more to the point and outspoken: "Don't do drugs . . . it's as simple as that" or "Only complete idiots do drugs" (see Burgoon, Alvaro, Broneck, Miller, Grandpre, Hall, & Frank, 2001).

The research literature, without much sound scientific support, has continually suggested that peers are *more* effective than authority figures in persuading adolescents about tobacco prevention/cessation, alcohol use, and drug uptake. Language expectancy theorists would question such an intuitively appealing, but simplistic assessment. Specifically, LET would posit that only those conditions that positively violated expectations would produce desired changes, and those would probably not be most likely in peer-to-peer situations. Rather, it was predicted that students would have their expectations positively violated by the adults who used implicit language, since the notion of adults offering adolescents a choice when it comes to drug use is certainly not the social norm. Furthermore, it was predicted that adults using explicit language when discussing adolescent drug use would conform to social norms, thereby confirming expectations. In short, it was hypothesized under the LET framework that the adolescents would react more favorably toward the adults who used implicit language than to the adults who used explicit language.

Preliminary results suggest that not only were students significantly more favorable toward the adults who used implicit language, but the adults' use of implicit language was such a positive violation of expectations that the students preferred the scenes of adults using implicit language even more than seeing their own peers discussing drugs or inhalants, regardless of the type of language used. Moreover, the students who viewed the adults using explicit language were less favorable toward the adults than were students who viewed any of the three other conditions (adult implicit, peer implicit, peer explicit).

The set of experimental questions focused on how participants hearing the focus groups discuss the advertisement would influence the students' perceptions of the ads themselves. Specifically, after viewing all the ads that were all followed by footage of one of the four aforementioned focus groups, the students were asked to evaluate the advertisements *without* taking the focus groups' comments into consideration.

The results indicate, as LET would suggest, that the students who had their expectations positively violated by witnessing the focus group of adults or peers using *implicit* language to discuss drug use also reconstructed their evaluation of the advertisements. Even though all four conditions viewed the same advertisements (remember only the video of the focus groups differed, not the ads themselves), the students who viewed the implicit focus groups were significantly more likely to evaluate the advertisements positively than were any of the three other groups. Additionally, the students who viewed the ads supplemented with the adult-explicit focus group found the ads themselves significantly more controlling than the students who viewed the ads in any of the three other conditions.

These findings suggest that not only can the violation of language expectations alter how we perceive the speaker, but the violation can also change our evaluation of what the speaker is speaking *about*. Once again, all four groups viewed the same advertisements; only the conversations heard after the ads were viewed differed. These results suggest that we construct or reconstruct our evaluation of a message based upon whether what is said *about* the messages confirms or violates our expectations.

Additional implications for this finding can also lead one to muse about the political arena. After televised political speeches or debates, almost all news networks provide some form of commentary. These recent findings suggest that when a political speech is followed by a newscast of pundits, talking heads and analysts can positively or negatively violate expectations with their own conversation, thereby changing our perception of the political figure and his or her message content. That such commentary influences public opinion is not new information. However, this interpretation from LET puts in high relief how important such analyses can be not only in shaping perception of public figures but also in actually changing the evaluation of message content already processed.

In sum, a theory must be judged not only by how well it fares under scientific scrutiny but also by the extent to which it informs us about how humans behave in everyday situations. It is certainly our contention that LET, in its main incarnations, has risen to these challenges in an admirable manner.

References

American Cancer Society (1999). *Cancer facts and figures.* Atlanta, GA: American Cancer Society.

Aronson, E., & Golden, B. (1962). The effect of relevant and irrelevant aspects of communicator credibility on opinion change. *Journal of Personality, 30,* 135–146.

Beach, R. I. (1966). The effect of a "fear-arousing" safety film on physiological, attitudinal and behavioural measures: A pilot study. *Traffic Safety Research Review, 10,* 53–57.

Bem, S. L., & Bem, D. J. (1970). Case study of a nonconscious ideology: Training the woman to know her place. In D. J. Bem, *Beliefs, attitudes and human affairs.* (pp. 89–99). Belmont, CA: Wadsworth.

Brooks, R. D. (1970). The generalizability of early reversals of attitudes toward communication sources. *Speech Monographs, 37,* 152–155.

Buller, D. B., Borland, R., & Burgoon, M. (1998). Impact of behavioral intention on effectiveness of message features. Evidence from the Family Sun Safety project. *Human Communication Research, 24,* 433–453.

Buller, D. B., Burgoon, M., Hall, J. R., Levine, N., Taylor, A. M., Beach, B., Buller, M. K., & Melcher, C. (2000). Long-term effects of language intensity in preventive messages on planned family solar protection. *Health communication, 12*(3), 261–275.

Buller, D. B., Burgoon, M., Hall, J. R., Levine, N., Taylor, A. M., Beach, B. H., Melcher, C., Buller, M. K., Bowen, S. L., Hunsaker, F. G., & Bergen, A. (2000). Using language intensity to increase the success of a family intervention to protect children from ultraviolet radiation: Predictions from language expectancy theory. *Preventive Medicine: An International Journal Devoted to Practice & Theory, 30*(2), 103–1147.

Buller, D. B., Callister, M. A., & Reichert, T. (1995). Skin cancer prevention by parents of young children: Health information sources, skin cancer knowledge, and sun-protection practices. *Oncology Nursing Forum, 22,* 1559–1566.

Burgoon, M. (1970). The effects of response set and race on message interpretation. *Speech Monographs, 37,* 264–268.

Burgoon, M. (1989). The effects of message variables on opinion and attitude change. In J. Bradac (Eds.), *Messages in communication science: Contemporary approaches to the study of effects* (pp. 129–164). Newbury Park, CA: Sage.

Burgoon, M. (1995). Language expectancy theory: Elaboration, explication, and extension. In C. R. Berger & M. Burgoon (Eds.), *Communication and social influence processes* (pp. 29–52). East Lansing, MI: Michigan State University Press.

Burgoon, M. (2001). Mass media drug prevention in a multicultural sample. National Institute of Drug Abuse, grant # DA12578.

Burgoon, M., Alvaro, E., Broneck, K., Miller, C., Grandpre, J., Hall, J., & Frank, C. (2001). Using multimedia tools to test mass media health promotion and prevention messages. In W. C. Crano & M. Burgoon (Eds.), *Mass Media and Drug Prevention: Classic and Contemporary Theories and Research* (pp. 69–87). Mahwah, NJ: Erlbaum.

Burgoon, M., Birk, T. S., & Hall, J. R. (1991). Compliance and satisfaction with physician-patient communication: An expectancy theory interpretation of gender differences. *Human Communication Research, 18,* 177–208.

Burgoon, M., & Chase, L. J. (1973). The effects of differential linguistic patterns in messages attempting to induce resistance to persuasion. *Speech Monographs, 40,* 1–7.

Burgoon, M., Denning, V., & Roberts, L. (2002). Language expectancy theory. In J. P. Dillard & M. Pfau (Eds.), *The persuasion handbook: Developments in theory and practice* (pp. 117–136). Thousand Oaks, CA: Sage.

Burgoon, M., Dillard, J. P., & Doran, N. (1983). Friendly or unfriendly persuasion: The effects of violations of expectations by males and females. *Human Communication Research, 10,* 283–294.

Burgoon, M., Jones, S. B., & Stewart, D. (1975). Toward a message-centered theory of persuasion: Three empirical investigations of language intensity. *Human Communication Research, 1,* 240–256.

Burgoon, M., & Miller, G. R. (1985). An expectancy interpretation of language and persuasion. In H. Giles & R. N. St. Clair (Eds.), *Recent advances in language communication and social psychology* (pp. 199–229). London, England: Lawrence Erlbaum.

Hamilton, M. A., Hunter, J. E., & Burgoon, M. (1990). An empirical test of an axiomatic model of the relationship between language intensity and persuasion. *Journal of Language and Social Psychology, 9,* 235–255.

Hewgill, M. A., & Miller, G. R. (1965). Source credibility and response to fear-arousing communications. *Speech Monographs, 32,* 95–101.

Janis, I. L., & Feshbach, S. (1953). Effects of fear-arousing communication *Journal of Abnormal and Social Psychology, 48,* 79–92.

Kelly, G. A. (1955). *The psychology of personal constructs.* New York: Norton.

Klingle, R. S. (1993). Bringing time into physician compliance gaining research: Toward a Reinforcement Expectancy Theory of strategy effectiveness. *Health Communication, 5,* 283–308.

Klingle, R. S., & Burgoon, M. (1995). Patient compliance and satisfaction with physician influence attempts: A reinforcement expectancy approach to compliance-gaining over time. *Communication Research, 22,* 148–187.

Leventhal, H., & Niles, P. (1965). Persistence of influence for varying durations of exposure to threat stimuli. *Psychological Reports, 16,* 223–233.

McPeek, R. W., & Edwards, J. D. (1975). Expectancy disconfirmation and attitude change. *Journal of Social Psychology, 96,* 193–208.

Miller, G. R., & Hewgill, M. (1966). Some recent research on fear-arousing message appeals. *Speech Monographs, 33,* 377–391.

Pfau, M., Parrott, R., & Lindquist, B. (1992). An expectancy theory explanation of the effectiveness of political attack television spots: A case study. *Journal of Applied Communication Research, 20,* 235–253.

Powell, F. A. (1965). The effects of anxiety-arousing messages when related to personal, familial, and interpersonal referents. *Speech Monographs, 32,* 102–106.

Siegel, J. T., & Burgoon, J. K. (2001). Expectancy theory approaches to prevention: Violating adolescent expectations to increase the effectiveness of public service announcements. In W. D. Crano & M. Burgoon (Eds.), *Mass Media and Drug Prevention: Classic and Contemporary Theories and Research* (163–186). Mahwah, NJ: Erlbaum.

Appendix A

High-Intensity Message (Hamilton, Hunter, & Burgoon, 1990, pp. 243–244)

The laws regulating the sale of heroin in this country have frequently done more harm than good, both to society and to the individual who must use heroin. The public is confronted with an astronomical number of crimes committed each year in every major city by addicts desperate for money to support their habit. The addict suffers not from heroin, but from painful secondary complications which are promoted by the drug's continued illegality.

In England, where the government controls the legal sale to addicts, heroin-related crimes are non-existent. Crime is not actually caused by the drug itself, but by completely outdated laws which prohibit its use. In the United States, addicts are driven to commit crimes against innocent citizens to obtain money to pay exorbitant black market prices charged by their underworld suppliers. As a result of these hugely expensive transactions, law enforcement agencies are constantly tempted by graft.

Many heroin addicts die needlessly from disease caused not by the drug, but from agonizing secondary complications. Medical authorities now strongly agree that heroin causes very little physical damage. Symptoms of heroin withdrawal are not nearly as dangerous as those associated with alcohol. Yet in New York City last year over 900 addicts died from tetanus and hepatitis caused by improper means of injection. Addicts almost always re-use and share filthy needles, or improvise with objects not designed for injecting drugs into the bloodstream, because hypodermic syringes are not legally available.

Low-Intensity Message (Hamilton, Hunter, & Burgoon, 1990, p. 244)

The laws regulating the sale of heroin in this country have sometimes done more harm than good, both to society and to the individual who must use heroin. The public is faced with a large number of crimes committed each year in most major cities by addicts searching for money to support their habit. The addict suffers not from heroin, but from unpleasant secondary complications which are promoted by the drug's continued illegality.

In England, where the government controls the legal sale to addicts, heroin-related crimes are almost non-existent. Crime is not caused by the drug itself, but by slightly outdated laws which prohibit its use. In the United States, addicts are forced to commit crimes against innocent citizens to obtain money to pay high black market prices charged by their underworld suppliers. As a result of these somewhat expensive transactions, all enforcement agencies are occasionally tempted by graft.

Some heroin addicts die needlessly from disease caused not by the drug, but from uncomfortable secondary complications. Medical authorities now tentatively agree that heroin causes very little physical damage. Symptoms of heroin withdrawal are not as dangerous as those associated with alcohol. Yet in New York City last year over 900 addicts died from tetanus and hepatitis caused by improper means of injection. Addicts from time to time re-use and share unsanitary needles, or improvise with objects not designed for injecting drugs into the bloodstream, because hypodermic syringes are not legally available.

10

Influential Actions

Nonverbal Communication and Persuasion

Peter A. Andersen

. . . the effects of nonverbal behaviors and various verbal message variables on persuasion and compliance were compared. This comparison revealed that nonverbal behaviors are as powerful, in some cases more powerful, than some of the message strategies that have been studied in producing compliance from others.

—Segrin, 1993, p. 183

. . . nonverbal communication is as important as, perhaps more important than, verbal communication in persuading others to change their attitudes and behavior.

—Andersen, 1999, p. 273

Perhaps the most common human enterprise is influencing other people. People are involved in thousands of persuasion attempts each week, from the mundane acts of getting your roommate to turn down the stereo or persuading your partner to arrive on time to more important issues such as getting your partner to marry you or persuading a troubled friend to seek counseling.

When people think of persuasion they think of talk; but there is more to persuasion than words. The unspoken, unwritten messages we send and receive have as much to do with the success of our influence attempts as the words we utter. Like most people, scholars have typically thought of persuasion as a verbal activity. From the rhetoric of Aristotle to contemporary social scientific studies, the vast majority of research, including most of the chapters in this book, has focused on verbal communication. Verbal communication is what we know the most about. This chapter is an exception, for it will focus on the multiple ways in which nonverbal communication influences attitudes and changes behavior.

This chapter will review the effects of nonverbal communication in the context of several communication theories.

The Direct Effects Model of Immediacy

Nonverbal immediacy behaviors are nonverbal acts that simultaneously signal warmth, decrease psychological or physical distance between communicators, are interpersonally stimulating, and signal availability for communication (Andersen, 1985). Behaviors like eye contact, touch, and close distances are prototypical examples of nonverbal immediacy behaviors. Overwhelmingly, persuasion research supports the Direct Effects Model of Immediacy, which suggests that warm, involving, immediate nonverbal behaviors significantly enhance the persuasive effects of a message (Andersen, 1985, 1999; Segrin, 1993). Dozens of studies support the model.

The Direct Effects Model of nonverbal persuasion has also been called the Social Meaning Model (Burgoon, Coker, & Coker, 1986; Burgoon, Manusov, Mineo, & Hale, 1985). Both models contend that warm, involving, immediate behavior results in increased compliance on the part of the receiver. Some scholars suggest that we may have an inborn predisposition to comply with someone we like (Cialdini, 1984). Complying with those whom we like may be the underlying basis of human cooperation that has evolved throughout the millennia. However, as Cialdini (1984) notes:

> Few people would be surprised to learn that, as a rule, we most prefer to say yes to requests of someone we know and like. What might be startling to note, however, is that this simple rule is used in hundreds of ways by total strangers to get us to comply with *their* requests. (p.163)

The fundamental impulse to trust and comply with people who engage in warm, friendly behavior has been used by persuaders of every stripe to persuade us to comply with their requests. Pretty, smiling actors on advertisements; friendly solicitors for charities; and warm, sincere political candidates are employing the Direct Effects Model of Nonverbal Immediacy. Research shows that increases in nonverbal immediacy, even by total strangers, substantially enhance a persuader's chance of influencing attitudes and changing behavior. Studies have shown that both single channeled immediacy increases, such as increased eye contact, and multichanneled immediacy behaviors result in increased persuasion. The sections that follow review research on each nonverbal immediacy behavior and document its impact on persuasion.

Eye Behavior

Studies of eye behavior have provided substantial support for the Direct Effects Model of Nonverbal Immediacy, particularly the persuasive effects of gaze (looking at another person) and eye contact (mutual gaze into one another's eyes).

In field studies research has shown that unacquainted persuaders are more effective if they use eye contact. Kleinke and Singer (1979) found that both male and female subjects took significantly more leaflets from campaigners who held their gaze than from those who did not, and the effect was stronger in the absence of any accompanying verbal communication. In a study by Bull and Gibson-Robinson (1981), poorly dressed solicitors for charity dramatically increased their effectiveness in obtaining contributions when using direct gaze. Additional field research by Valentine (1980) reported that bystanders were more likely to assist a disabled victim with a broken arm if the victim looked at them directly. This finding held true when the victim was accompanied by a friend as well as when the victim was alone. One study found that hitchhikers were more likely to obtain rides when they used direct eye contact than when they failed to use eye contact (Snyder, Grether, & Keller, 1974).

Laboratory studies likewise confirm the Direct Effects Model for gaze. Burgoon and colleagues (1986) provided additional empirical support for the Direct Effects Model (or Social Meaning Model) when they found that a person was judged more likely to be hired for a job when gazing than when not gazing. Specifically, they reported that gaze aversion carried very negative meanings and was very unpersuasive, whereas gaze was highly effective in interpersonal persuasion.

Gaze may be effective in gaining compliance because it is simultaneously powerful and immediate (Andersen, 1985; Segrin, 1990). Linkey and Firestone (1990), for example, examined a group discussion task and found that influence was primarily a function of the visual dominance ratio (the degree to which one person looked at his/her partner divided by the degree to which the partner looked at him/her). Research by Liss, Walker, Hazelton, and Cupach (1993) showed that compliance correlated strongly with mutual gaze, suggesting that eye contact by a persuader is a potent predictor of compliance. In a study of televised debates in Denmark, all of the eleven speakers who gazed intensely at their audience won their debates and lost none (Jorgensen, Kock, & Rorbeck, 1998) suggesting that the persuasive effects of eye gaze may be cross-cultural.

In a statistical summary of research called a meta-analysis, Segrin (1993) combined the results of 49 nonverbal studies, including 12 on gaze behavior. Gaze produced greater compliance than averted gaze in every one of the 12 studies. Though the persuasive effects of gaze were not huge, they were quite consistent: Gaze and eye contact increase compliance. This entire body of research, in study after study, shows that gaze, dominant gaze, and mutual gaze all seem to have persuasive effects.

Touch and Persuasion

Touch, like eye behavior, is generally perceived as a warm, friendly behavior except in situations where the touch is hostile or there is a preexisting negative relationship between the interactants. A large number of studies indicate that touch, even by a stranger, has positive effects on persuasion.

One study (Kleinke, 1977) tested whether strangers could be persuaded to return change left in an airport phone booth. When strangers who found the change were asked to return the change with a gentle touch, 96 percent of them complied. When no touch accompanied the request, only 63 percent complied. Similarly, in two field studies of compliance behavior, Willis and Hamm (1980) had experimenters ask strangers to comply by signing a petition or filling out a questionnaire. In both experiments half the strangers received touch, and half received no touch while other communication cues remained constant across the two groups. In the first experiment strangers signed the petition 81 percent of the time when touched but only 50 percent of the time when not touched. In the second experiment, strangers completed the questionnaire 70 percent of the time when touched but only 40 percent of the time when not touched. Results of both experiments showed significant, positive effects of touch on compliance.

Studies of service encounters have shown that waitresses' touch increases compliance behavior. In two studies, when waitresses touched the hand or arm of customers, they received bigger tips (Crusco & Wetzel, 1984; Stephen & Zweigenhaft, 1985). A recent study found that when waitresses asked bar patrons if they wanted something to drink, their touch resulted in significantly more alcohol consumption than when they did not touch the patron (Kaufman & Mahoney, 1999).

One common persuasive strategy is called the foot-in-the-door technique, where a small request is followed by a larger request (see chapter 12 of this text and Gass & Seiter, 2003 for a good summary). Several studies have shown that touch increases the foot-in-the-door effect. An investigation into the effects of touch on volunteering for charity, employing a foot-in-the-door appeal, showed that touch increased compliance in most experimental conditions (Goldman, Kiyohara, & Pfannensteil, 1985) and was effective even following an initially negative communication. Patterson, Powell, and Lenihan (1986) employed touch in an experiment in which students were asked to help score exams. After scoring some exams, students were asked to stay and score additional tests. Students who were touched stayed longer to score the exams than students who were not touched. The authors attributed the increased compliance to perceptions of greater liking and/or status of the experimenter who did the touching.

In a meta-analysis of 13 studies examining the influence of touch on compliance, Segrin (1993) reported that touch showed a positive, consistent effect on compliance across the 13 studies. In virtually all these studies experimenters touched a stranger on the arm while making a request and compared the response to that received when there was no touching.

Little is known about the effects of persuasive touch in close relationships, nor have we examined the effects of more intimate types of touch—such as strokes, caresses, or squeezes—or more intimate targets of touch such as the chest or face. Anecdotal evidence suggests that compliance requests in intimate relationships are often accompanied by a touch.

Kinesic Behavior and Persuasion

Kinesics is the study of communication via body movements. One kinesic behavior, the open body position, has been associated with greater immediacy and approachability (Andersen, 1985). Mehrabian (1969) reported that open arm and leg positions create positive attitudes in receivers. Morris (1977) has shown that kinesic "barrier signals" communicate defensiveness and avoidance, the opposite of the attitudes indicated by open body postures. In a study of opinion change, McGinley, LeFevre, and McGinley (1975) reported that open body positions result in more persuasion than when communicators keep their knees and feet together, arms folded and held close to the body. The study of 37 Danish televised political debates discussed earlier (Jorgensen et al., 1998) found that debaters with more open body postures did significantly better than those with closed body postures. The researchers also examined what they called "a dismissive attitude," conveyed by closed posture and an unfriendly facial expression. Five of the six debaters displaying this dismissive attitude lost.

The smile is particularly persuasive. Receivers of communication messages are disarmed by a smiling person and more likely to comply with his or her request. Burgoon, Birk, and Pfau (1990) examined the impact of several kinesic behaviors on persuasion and found that facial pleasantness was most predictive of persuasive success. Liss and colleagues (1993) examined the effect of smiling on compliance gaining and found that more smiling resulted in greater compliance.

Part of persuasive immediacy is bodily animation. Burgoon and colleagues (1990) also report that more overall bodily movement and animation correlated with persuasiveness. Similarly in the Danish debate study, winning debaters showed an animated and energetic kinesic style by a ratio of 11 to 1 and gesturally animated debaters won by a ratio of 12 to 2 (Jorgensen et al., 1998). Together these studies suggest that persuasion is facilitated by kinesic activity that includes open body positions, positive facial affect, and kinesic animation.

Vocal Cues and Persuasion

Studies tend to show a positive link between vocal immediacy and persuasion. A series of studies by Buller and his associates suggest that vocal immediacy cues, including a pleasant tone of voice and a fast delivery, are linked to greater compliance. Interestingly, these effects are particularly true for individuals who are skilled decoders of nonverbal communication (Buller & Aune, 1988, 1992; Buller & Burgoon, 1986; Buller, LePoire, Aune, & Eloy, 1992). Segrin's (1993) statistical summary of the research showed that both vocal rate and vocal pleasantness were associated with persuasion. A slightly different finding was reported by Burgoon and colleagues (1990), who found that persuasiveness increased with greater vocal fluency and pitch variety but not with greater vocal pleasantness.

In the Danish debate studies Jorgensen and colleagues (1998) found that speakers with modulated voices (e.g., greater pitch variation) were more likely to win than speakers with monotonous voices. Likewise, vocally energetic speakers were often debate winners and inarticulate debaters were often losers.

Other studies generally support the series of studies by Buller and his associates indicating that faster rates of vocal delivery are associated with greater persuasiveness (Apple, Streeter, & Krauss, 1979; MacLachlan, 1979; Miller, Maruyuma, Beaber, & Malone, 1976). These studies suggested that faster delivery is associated with competence and confidence and is unlikely to be used by an insecure or deceptive person.

While more research on vocalic influences on persuasion needs to be conducted, current research suggests that a fast, pleasant, vocally varied nonverbal communication style will make verbal communication more persuasive. This may be particularly true on the telephone, where vocalic information is the only available nonverbal cue.

Multidimensional Nonverbal Cues and Persuasion

So far the discussion has focused on the persuasive impact of single nonverbal cues like touching or smiling. But research has found that nonverbal immediacy is usually communicated though multidimensional displays that include several nonverbal immediacy cues simultaneously. Some nonverbal persuasion studies have examined the impact of several nonverbal cues in combination. The most common experimental manipulation has examined the simultaneous persuasive effects of touch and gaze.

Touch-Gaze Combinations and Persuasion.   A number of studies have examined the persuasive impact of both touch and gaze in combination. This approach permits an examination of whether one of these cues can substitute for the other, their relative persuasive impact, and whether they have additive or cumulative effects. Kleinke (1977) reported two such experiments that examined the effect of gaze and touch on compliance. In the first study, the experimenter left a dime in a phone booth, and when a subject found the dime the experimenter requested it back. The experimenter manipulated gaze and touch to generate four experimental combinations: (1) touch and gaze, (2) touch alone, (3) gaze alone, and (4) neither touch nor gaze. Combined touch and gaze resulted in the greatest number of dimes being returned, indicating that touch and gaze have additive effects on compliance. In the second study, experimenters asked strangers in a shopping mall if they would lend them a dime. As with the first experiment, four combinations of touch and gaze were employed and results again showed that combined touch and gaze produced increased compliance. The researcher's explanation is that touch and gaze increase both attention and involvement, making noncompliance more difficult. In another article, Kleinke (1980) reported two experiments, which replicated the 1977 study while also adding a legitimate request (dime for a phone call) and an illegitimate request (dime for a candy bar). Results replicated the 1977 study for the legitimate request, but for the illegitimate requests greater compliance was obtained through *absence* of touch or eye contact, since the experimenter may have appeared more tactful or humble. A replication of Kleinke's (1977) phone booth experiment by Brockner, Pressman, Cabitt, and Moran (1982) showed that both touch and eye contact independently increased compliance. The data from these five studies show cumulative effects of both touch and eye contact consistent with the Direct Effects, or Social Meaning, models. These findings have substantial practical importance for persuasion. When trying to promote positive health behaviors, soliciting for charity, or getting assistance from a stranger, the combination of touch and gaze considerably increases the chances of compliance with one's request.

Persuasion and Other Multidimensional Immediacy Behaviors.   Studies of the persuasive impact of multidimensional nonverbal immediacy cues show a pattern similar to single cues and combinations of gaze and touch; immediacy produces persuasion. One study of classroom compliance employing multiple indices of immediacy found that students were more likely to engage in communication practices suggested by immediate rather than nonimmediate teachers (J. Andersen, 1979). Burgoon, Birk, and Pfau (1990) reported a similar finding in a study of persuasive speakers. Specifically, they found that increased persuasive effects were associated with vocalic behaviors (such as longer pauses, vocal pleasantness, and pitch variety), increased eye gaze, more smiling, greater facial expressiveness, and more overall movement. Recently, research has also shown that individuals use nonverbal communication to resist persuasion. In a study of rejection strategies for flirtatious advances, Trost and Engstrom (1994) reported that rejecters avoid nonverbal contact, ignore the persuader, maintain larger personal space, act cold and uninterested, display alternative relational ties (e.g., engagement rings), and act nervous and uneasy.

Multichanneled, Mediated, Persuasive Cues.   Many of the persuasive messages we receive come through mediated channels such as radio, television, and the Internet. Immediacy cues also seem to produce persuasive effects in mediated as well as face-to-face communication. Studies of television newscasters, for example, have shown that nonverbal behaviors influence viewers in a variety of ways. We treat newscasters as virtual acquaintances who are nightly guests in our homes. For many years Walter Cronkite, the anchorman for CBS news, was considered the most credible man in America.

Studies show that the nonverbal behavior of television newscasters affects voting preferences. Friedman, Mertz, and DiMatteo (1980) reported that newscasters' facial expressions were consistently biased toward certain candidates at levels unlikely to occur by chance. In the 1976 election Walter Cronkite, David Brinkley, and Harry Reasoner showed more favorable facial expressions when reporting about Carter than about Ford. John Chancellor and Barbara Walters showed more facial positivity toward Ford than toward Carter. Verbal content showed no corresponding bias. Two studies replicated and extended these findings to the 1984 elections and showed that biased facial expressions were associated with voting behavior of viewers (Mullen, 1986). In the first study, these researchers found that Dan Rather of CBS and Tom Brokaw of NBC showed no facial bias during stories about Reagan or Mondale. However, Peter Jennings of ABC exhibited strong facial bias toward Reagan over Mondale. The second study examined voters in four cities in Ohio, Missouri, Massachusetts, and Pennsylvania and showed that in each city viewers of ABC had significantly more favorable attitudes toward Reagan than viewers of NBC or CBS. While pro-Reagan viewers might have tuned in more to ABC, Mullen and colleagues believed that their study actually demonstrated a subtle, peripheral route to persuasion, occurring without deliberate, conscious consideration of arguments. In either case this study suggested a strong association among nonverbal behavior, television viewing, and electoral decisions.

Recent studies of the Internet have suggested that perceived proxemic cues affect compliance. Moon (1999) reports that one proxemic variable, the perceived distance of one's partner during computer-mediated communication, correlated with the amount of persuasion. People who believed that they were communicating with someone several miles away complied more frequently than if they perceived that the person was thousands of miles away.

Appearance and Credibility: The Halo Effect

People use simple, obvious, nonverbal cues as shorthand indicators of status and credibility. While evidence has shown that good looks or nice clothes are not an indication of greater competence or credibility (Feingold, 1992), a large body of studies has suggested that we *believe* that well-dressed, good looking people are smarter, warmer, more honest and therefore more deserving of compliance than less well dressed, unattractive individuals. This is called the "halo effect," whereby one positive quality in a person causes us to assume that the individual has many positive qualities.

Our clothing does more than protect and conceal our bodies; it communicates our status and credibility. Studies have shown that apparel is not an immediacy behavior like touch, gaze, and smiling (Andersen, Andersen, & Jensen, 1979). Instead, research suggests that clothing is a status or credibility cue that has powerful persuasive effects (see Andersen, 1999).

People are more likely to comply with respectable and conventional persuaders than with those who appear to be weird and unreliable. Studies reveal that a conventional attire or appearance has more positive persuasive effects than does an unconventional appearance. In general, "dressing up" is recommended for most persuasive situations; people are more likely to comply with high-status people than with low-status ones. In one study (Bickman, 1971), a stimulus person left change in a public phone booth and waited until the next caller found it. When the stimulus person was well dressed, 77 percent of the subjects admitting finding the money and returned the change; when the stimulus person was poorly dressed, only 38 percent of callers returned the change. Similarly, Raymond and Unger (1972) found that passersby were more willing to make change for conventionally dressed individuals than for unconventionally dressed ones. Likewise, Kleinke (1977) found that more people "lent" a dime to a neatly rather than a sloppily dressed experimenter.

In a petition-signing study by MacNeill and Wilson (1972), experimenters obtained more signatures when dressed conventionally (suit and tie with short hair) than unconventionally (faded army jacket with long hair). Likewise, Keasey and Tomlinson-Keasey (1973) found that conventionally dressed male and female petitioners were able to obtain more signatures on petitions against the U.S. invasion of Cambodia than "hippie" petitioners. In a similar study, Darley and Cooper (1972) examined the impact of counter-cultural or "hippie" appearance on political campaign effectiveness. They found that voters were less likely to take a leaflet from a "hippie" than from a conventionally dressed campaigner—and were more likely to throw it away after having taken it. Moreover, voters attributed more radical, less acceptable views to candidates supported by hippies than to those supported by conventionally dressed campaigners. Similarly, people were found to be more likely to donate money to charity to a person with short hair dressed in a jacket and tie than to a person with long hair dressed in jeans and sandals (Chaikin, Derlega, Yoder, & Phillips, 1974). One study found that passersby were more likely to answer a survey administered by a conventionally dressed interviewer than by an unconventionally dressed one (Walker, Harriman, & Costello, 1980). However, another study that looked at the effects of five types of women's clothing on willingness to complete a questionnaire revealed no significant differences between women dressed in a formal skirt, formal pants, casual skirt, casual pants, and jeans (Harris et al., 1983).

Clothing also signifies authority. Hospital doctors, law enforcement officers, and soldiers wear uniforms to instantaneously communicate their authority; and people are exceedingly likely to comply with such authority figures. For example, medical profession-als, especially in hospitals, typically wear a white coat or dress to communicate authority. This enables them to make us wait, go to designated rooms, take off our clothes, and to submit to embarrassing or painful medical procedures. In Milgram's (1974) classic experiments, in which he successfully induced participants to provide shocks (that they believed were real) to students in laboratory learning studies, compliance was gained by an experimenter wearing a gray technician's coat over a white shirt and tie. Bushman (1988) conducted a study in which a female randomly stopped pedestrians and said, "This fellow is overparked at the meter and doesn't have any change. Give him a nickel." This female wore different clothing in three experimental conditions. When dressed in a uniform, she gained more compliance than when in business attire or casual dress. The nondescript blue uniform produced compliance 72 percent of the time, whereas only 48 percent compliance was gained in the business attire condition and 52 percent in the casual attire condition. Similarly, well-dressed men receive better and quicker service in department stores than less well-dressed men (Stead & Zinkhan, 1986). One study found that salespeople were more likely to comply with complaint-based requests in department stores from a well-dressed person than from a less well dressed one (Krapfel, 1988).

In his statistical summary of 19 studies, Segrin (1993) concluded that the more formal or high status the clothing, the greater the compliance rate obtained. Evidently, we are more likely to permit appropriately and well-dressed individuals to approach us and to gain our trust than we are to allow inappropriately or less conventionally dressed individuals to do so. Moreover, Segrin found that the greater the status manipulation in physical appearance studies, the greater the magnitude of the effect. Clearly, status persuades; and clothing acts as a highly salient surrogate for a person's status.

Expectancy Violations Theory

Expectancy Violations Theory emerged as an alternative explanation for the persuasive impact of immediacy behavior, particularly proxemic behavior (Burgoon & Jones, 1976). This theory claims that each person has cultural and personal expectations about the normal distances people maintain during interaction. Attractive or rewarding individuals are more persuasive if they stand closer or farther than the norm, whereas unattractive or unrewarding individuals will be more persuasive if they maintain normal distances. Highly rewarding individuals who violate norms draw attention to their positive characteristics and enhance their personal persuasiveness, perhaps through the halo effects discussed previously.

Several studies of proxemic behavior have provided support for the theory. Stacks and Burgoon (1979) found that rewarding communicators were more persuasive at either closer or farther distances than at normative distances. As predicted by the theory, unrewarding individuals produced no difference in persuasiveness at close, normal, or far distances. Two studies by Burgoon and Aho (1982) provided additional support for this theory. In both studies, distance had no significant effect on compliance for either low-reward or high-reward communicators, though reward itself produced significant effects. Albert and Dabbs (1970) reported that actual persuasion was greater at far distances (14 to 15 feet) than at either close or moderate distances (1 to 5 feet). Buller (1987) conducted a study in which experimenters assumed close, moderate, or far distances while attempting to get citizens to sign petitions. Findings showed that close distances resulted in the greatest compliance, while moderate and far distances resulted in lower levels of compliance. Neither Albert and Dabbs nor Buller manipulated the reward value, but their results suggest that non-normative distance can increase compliance.

In an extension of Expectancy Violations Theory to vocalic communication, Buller and Burgoon (1986) showed that pleasant voices (a positive norm violation) produced more compliance, but only for good decoders. Poor decoders complied more with hostile voices (a negative norm violation) than with neutral or pleasant ones. While reward value was not successfully manipulated, the study provided some support for the expectancy violation model.

Expectancy Violations Theory was expanded to eye behavior in two studies (Burgoon et al., 1985, 1986). Both studies employed either rewarding (well-qualified job interviewees) confederates or nonrewarding (unqualified job interviewees) confederates and differing levels of eye gaze. Results of these studies provided little support for the Expectancy Violations Theory, since the primary results showed direct persuasive effects for increased levels of gaze regardless of reward value. These results supported the Social Meaning or Direct Effects Model described previously.

Expectancy Violations Theory has received some general confirmation, but the support for its persuasive effects is mixed. Moreover, since few of the studies that have tested Expectancy Violations Theory have actually confirmed whether expectations were violated or not, a central tenet of the theory remains untested (Segrin, 1990). Proxemic behavior is best explained by Expectancy Violations Theory, which suggests that a rewarding individual should probably stand closer or farther than the normal interaction distance for maximal persuasive effects. Standing at a "normal" distance may be most persuasive for unrewarding communicators.

Distraction Models

Distraction models share some similarity with Expectancy Violations Theory. These models suggest that if a source's nonverbal behavior distracts, the receiver is more susceptible to persuasion. Stacks and Burgoon (1979) predicted that distance violations would produce more persuasion because of their distracting properties. Unfortunately, they found that distance violations had no effect on a self-reported distraction measure. However, close and far distance violations were more persuasive than a normal distance. Why did distance violations produce more persuasion? Perhaps distraction worked even though subjects were unaware of the distraction and were therefore unable to self-report it. Distance violations may also produce arousal effects. Another study by Stacks and Burgoon (1981) reported a significant effect of both distance violations and extremes of physical attraction on distraction. Small persuasive effects were found for physical attraction and none for distance violations, thus providing better support for distraction models. In a test of the distracting effects of rapidly spoken messages on persuasion, Woodall and Burgoon (1983) showed that fast messages were more distracting than messages delivered at a nomal pace, but no persuasive effects of faster messages were found.

Buller (1986) conducted a meta-analysis of 38 studies that examined the distraction-persuasion relationship. His study indicated that communication-irrelevant factors such as noise or visual distractions generally reduced persuasion and attitude change, because they impeded comprehension of the messages. However, communication-relevant distractions, such as highly attractive or credible sources, caused receivers to focus on these positive qualities and produced a positive effect on persuasion. If the source had low attractiveness or credibility, focusing on the speaker reduced attitude change because these negative distractions impeded believability and persuasion. In general, positively regarded sources may benefit by focusing the receiver's attention on that source's positive characteristics, a finding consistent with Expectancy Violations Theory. Petty and Cacioppo's (1986) work on persuasion and cognition may also help explain the process of distraction. Basically they have shown that distraction aids the persuasion process if the message is of low quality. In this circumstance a distracting appearance or proxemic behavior, for example, would distract a person so that the receiver might not be able to concentrate on the many flaws in the message. High-quality persuasive arguments, on the other hand, would be less effective when a receiver was distracted by conspicuous nonverbal cues, for much the same reason. The receiver cannot concentrate on the high-quality message, so its effectiveness is reduced.

Communication Accommodation Theory

Communication Accommodation Theory (CAT) deals primarily with the vocalic or paralinguistic effects of nonverbal communication. It posits that listeners perceive speech similar to their own as more attractive, pleasant, intelligible, and persuasive than unfamiliar speech (Street, 1982; Street & Brady, 1982; Street & Giles, 1982). Furthermore, speakers typically adjust or accommodate their speech to the style or rate of the other interactant, even though most speakers are unaware of this accommodation (Street, 1982). Based on this theory, speakers who adjust to the communication of their listeners should be more persuasive. Several recent studies provide support for the persuasive effects of communication accommodation. Buller and Aune (1988) reported that good decoders were most likely to comply with faster messages. This finding did not hold true for poor decoders. Why did good decoders prefer fast messages? The authors also found that good decoders spoke faster, so faster speakers seemed to prefer to listen to faster speech, a position consistent with CAT. A second study by Buller and Aune (1989) partially replicated the first study. Again, good decoders spoke faster than poor decoders, though no effect was found for actual or perceived similarity of speech rate on compliance. However, poor decoders, who generally speak slowly, complied most with the moderately slow voice, whereas good decoders (who generally speak fast) complied most with moderately fast and very fast voices. These findings suggest that people are influenced by those who speak at the same rate as they do.

Another study supportive of CAT, by Burgoon and colleagues (1987), examined the effects of a number of communication variables on patients' compliance with their physician's advice. Among the many communication variables tested, only perceived similarity correlated significantly with compliance, a finding consistent with CAT. A final study by Buller and Burgoon (1986) showed that good nonverbal decoders complied more with pleasant voices than with neutral or hostile voices, whereas poor decoders complied most in the hostile condition, moderately in the neutral condition, and least in the pleasant condition. Since good decoders are more affiliative, composed, and social than poor decoders, Buller and Burgoon suggested CAT as the explanation. People are more likely to comply with tones of voice that are similar to their own.

Several studies not based on CAT show that rapid speech enhances persuasion (Apple et al., 1979; Buller & Aune, 1988; MacLachlan, 1979; Miller et al., 1976). Rapid speech may enhance persuasion by increasing the effort it takes to perceive the message or by improving the perceived competence of the source. One study, however (Woodall & Burgoon, 1983), found that fast rates had the same persuasive effect as slow rates. One explanation for these results is the region in which the studies were conducted. As noted previously, both the Apple et al. study and the MacLachlan studies were conducted in New York, whereas the studies by both Buller and Aune and Miller and colleagues employed subjects from urban Southern California and Arizona, where fast speech is the norm. The Woodall and Burgoon study, in contrast, was conducted in the Southeast, where speech is considerably slower. Thus, it may be that slow speakers are more persuasive in the South whereas fast speakers are more persuasive in the North and Pacific West.

CAT, as applied to vocalic behaviors and persuasion, has received support. Communicators would probably be well advised to use vocalic cues similar to their persuasive targets to maximize compliance. Speech accommodation is a complex dyadic process in which both interactants adapt to the other's speaking style. Since no study of this dyadic type of social interaction has yet been conducted, the theory remains untested in its most complete form (Segrin, 1990). CAT could be applied to other areas of nonverbal communication. However, substantial support for the Direct Effects Model, according to which increased gaze, faster speech, or more touch is persuasive, presents a problem for CAT. Unless most receivers of persuasive messages were high gazers, fast speakers, and frequent touchers—a condition untrue by definition—the Direct Effects Model would be more predictive than CAT. The likelihood that more immediacy is more important than more accommodation also supports the Direct Effects Model rather than CAT. However, a combination of immediacy and accommodation may be highly effective, given that both forms of communication seek to enhance persuasion in prior research.

Elaboration Likelihood Model

In an attempt to create a comprehensive model of persuasion that subsumed all prior findings on persuasion, Petty and Cacioppo (1986) created the Elaboration Likelihood Model (ELM). As noted in previous chapters, the central concept of the ELM is that two types of persuasion exist. The first type of persuasion results from the careful and thoughtful consideration of the merits of the information presented in a message and is called the *central route*. The second type of persuasion results from cues in a persuasive context, such as an attractive source, without necessitating scrutiny of the actual merits of the information; this is called the *peripheral route*. Petty and Cacioppo (1986) asserted that persuasion processed through the central route appears to be more enduring than that which is processed "peripherally."

The ELM has been widely criticized in communication for weak and circular definitions of key components of the model and insufficient a priori specification of whether cues will be processed centrally or peripherally (see Stiff & Boster, 1987). Perhaps even more important, the ELM privileges the central route of verbal and logical persuasion and, by relegating most nonverbal communication to the peripheral route, fails to recognize both the power of nonverbal communication and the true intent of the persuasive message.

First, the very terms *central* and *peripheral* suggest that one type of communication (i.e., logical, thoughtful, verbal) has more validity than the other (intuitive, instinctual, nonverbal). Evidence suggests, however, that intuition about the character, expertise, or competence of a source is an equally valid type of persuasive assessment. Since Aristotle first introduced ethos as a central concept in rhetoric and persuasion, peripheral messages such as source characteristics have been considered a valid and rapid means of assessing the merits of an argument. Detection of deception and subtle incongruent cues may be more important than discerning the syllogistic and evidentiary structure of the arguments in human interaction. Indeed, the abundant literature on deception detection suggests that deception is often detected from subtle, incongruent cues.

Second, the available summaries of literature (see Andersen, 1999; Segrin, 1993) suggest that nonverbal communication is at least as powerful as the traditional central route message variables such as evidence that has relatively weak effects.

Third, central processing, the preferred or favored route according to the ELM, may still entail numerous errors of logic and reasoning (Kahneman, Slovic, & Tverksy, 1982). Indeed, the primary purpose of so-called logical communication in human beings may be more to rationalize and harmonize competing cognitions (Cialdini, 1984; Stacks & Andersen, 1989) than to search for truth with a capital *T*. Persuasion is as likely to be about harmonization of the relations among people and between disparate connections in the human brain as it is to be about the cold logic of "truth."

Finally, in their initial formulation Petty and Cacioppo insisted that the central and peripheral routes were separate paths and that receivers of persuasive messages chose between them. Communication researchers have criticized the ELM for this dichotomization of the central and peripheral route (Mongeau & Stiff, 1993). Though the founders of the ELM have recanted on this position (Petty et al., 1993) the best advice to receivers of a persuasive message is to use *both* verbal, logical processes and nonverbal, intuitive processes in making judgments about persuasive messages. Indeed, research on aspects of the ELM has suggested that so-called central and peripheral cues actually interact in good decision making (see Puckett, Petty, Cacioppo, & Fisher, 1983).

Conclusion

Research suggests that nonverbal communication has as much or more persuasive impact than verbal communication and overwhelmingly supports the Direct Effects Model of Immediacy. More immediate, involving communication produces more persuasive impact.

Whether nonverbal immediacy is increased in a single channel or in multiple channels, touch, gaze, smiling, and other nonverbal cues have a positive impact on persuasion.

*References*_____

Albert, S., & Dabbs, J. M. (1970). Physical distance and persuasion. *Journal of Personality and Social Psychology, 15,* 265–270.

Andersen, J. F. (1979). Teacher immediacy as a predictor of teaching effectiveness. In D. Nimmo (Ed.), *Communication yearbook 3* (pp. 543–559). New Brunswick, NJ: Transaction Books.

Andersen, J. F., Andersen, P. A., & Jensen, A. D. (1979). The measurement of nonverbal immediacy. *Journal of Applied Communication Research, 7,* 153–180.

Andersen, P. A. (1985). Nonverbal immediacy in interpersonal communication. In A. W. Seigman & S. Feldstein (Eds.), *Multichannel Integrations of Nonverbal Behavior* (pp. 1–29). Hillsdale, NJ: Erlbaum.

Andersen, P. A. (1999). *Nonverbal communication: Forms and functions.* Mountain View, CA: Mayfield.

Apple, W., Streeter, L. A., & Krauss, R. M. (1979). Effects of pitch and speech rate on personal attributions. *Journal of Personality and Social Psychology, 37,* 715–727.

Bickman, L. (1971). The effect of social status on the honesty of others. *Journal of Social Psychology, 85,* 87–92.

Brockner, J., Pressman, B., Cabitt, J., & Moran, P. (1982). Nonverbal intimacy, sex and compliance: A field study. *Journal of Nonverbal Behavior, 6,* 253–258.

Bull, R., & Gibson-Robinson, E. (1981). The influence of eye-gaze, style of dress, and locality on the amounts of money donated to charity. *Human Relations, 34,* 895–905.

Buller, D. B. (1986). Distraction during persuasive communication: A meta-analytic review. *Communication Monographs, 53,* 91–114.

Buller, D. B. (1987). Communication apprehension and reactions to proxemic violations. *Journal of Nonverbal Behavior, 11,* 13–25.

Buller, D. B., & Aune, R. K. (1988). The effects of vocalics and nonverbal sensitivity on compliance: A speech accommodation theory explanation. *Human Communication Research, 14,* 301–332.

Buller, D. B., & Aune, R. K. (1989, May). *The effects of vocalics and nonverbal sensitivity on compliance: Further tests of the speech accommodation explanation.* Paper presented at the annual meeting of the International Communication Association Convention, San Francisco.

Buller, D. B., & Aune, R .K. (1992). The effects of speech rate similarity on compliance: Application of communication accommodation theory. *Western Journal of Communication, 56,* 37–53.

Buller, D. B., & Burgoon, J. K. (1986). The effects of vocalics and nonverbal sensitivity on compliance. *Human Communication Research, 13,* 126–144.

Buller, D. B., Le Poire, B. A., Aune, R. K., & Eloy, S. V. (1992). Social perceptions as mediators of the effect of speech rate on compliance. *Human Communication Research, 19,* 286–311.

Burgoon, J. K., & Aho, L. (1982). Three field experiments on the effects of violations of conversational distance. *Communication Monographs, 49,* 71–88.

Burgoon, J. K., Birk, T., & Pfau, M. (1990). Nonverbal behaviors, persuasion, and credibility. *Human Communication Research, 17,* 140–169.

Burgoon, J. K., Coker, D. A., & Coker, R. A. (1986). Communicative effects of gaze behavior: A test of two contrasting explanations. *Human Communication Research, 12,* 495–524.

Burgoon, J. K., & Jones, S. B. (1976). Toward a theory of personal space expectations and their violations. *Human Communication Research, 2,* 131–146.

Burgoon, J. K., Manusov, V., Mineo, P., & Hale, J. L. (1985) Effects of gaze on hiring, credibility, attraction and relational message interpretation. *Journal of Nonverbal. Behavior, 9,* 133–146.

Burgoon, J. K., Pfau, M., Parrott, R., Birk, T., Coker, R., & Burgoon, M. (1987). Relational communication, satisfaction, compliance-gaining strategies, and compliance in communication between physicians and patients. *Communication Monographs, 54,* 307–324.

Bushman, B. J. (1988). The effects of apparel on compliance: A field experiment with a female authority figure. *Personality and Social Psychology Bulletin, 14,* 459–467.

Chaikin, A. L., Derlega, V. J., Yoder, J., & Phillips, D. (1974). The effects of appearance on compliance. *Journal of Social Psychology, 92*, 199–200.

Cialdini, R. B. (1984). *Influence, science and practice.* New York: William Morrow.

Crusco, A. H., & Wetzel, C. G. (1984). The Midas touch: The effect of interpersonal touch on restaurant tipping. *Personality and Social Psychology Bulletin, 10*, 512–517.

Darley, J. M., & Cooper, J. (1972). The "clean for gene" phenomenon: The effect of students' appearance on political campaigning. *Journal of Applied Social Psychology, 2*, 24–33.

Feingold, A. (1992). Good looking people are not what we think. *Psychological Bulletin, 111*, 304–341.

Friedman, H. S., Mertz, T . J., & DiMatteo, M. R. (1980). Perceived bias in the facial expressions of television news broadcasters. *Journal of Communication, 30*, 103–111.

Gass, R. H., & Seiter, J. S. (2003). *Persuasion, social influence and compliance-gaining* (2nd ed.). Boston: Allyn & Bacon.

Goldman, M., Kiyohara, O., & Pfannensteil, D. A. (1985). Interpersonal touch, social labeling, and the foot-in-the-door effect. *The Journal of Social Psychology, 125*, 143–147.

Harris, M. B., James, J., Chavez, J., Fuller, M. L., Kent, S., Massanari, C., Moore, C., & Walsh, F. (1983). Clothing: Communication, compliance, and choice. *Journal of Applied Social Psychology, 13*, 88–97.

Jorgensen, C., Kock, C., & Rorbeck, L. (1998). Rhetoric that shifts votes: An exploratory study of persuasion in issue-oriented debates. *Political Communication, 15*, 283–299.

Kahneman, D., Slovic, P., & Tversky, A. (1982). *Judgment under certainty: Heuristics and Biases.* New York: Cambridge University Press.

Kaufman, D., & Mahoney, J. M. (1999). The effect of waitress touch on alcohol consumption in dyads. *Journal of Social Psychology, 139*, 261–267.

Keasey, C. B., & Tomlinson-Keasey, C. (1973). Petition signing in a naturalistic setting. *Journal of Social Psychology, 89*, 313–314.

Kleinke, C. L. (1977). Effects of dress on compliance to requests in a field setting. *Journal of Social Psychology, 101*, 223–224.

Kleinke, C. L. (1980). Interaction between gaze and legitimacy of request on compliance in a field setting. *Journal of Nonverbal Behavior, 5*, 3–12.

Kleinke, C. L., & Singer, D. A. (1979). Influence of gaze on compliance with demanding and conciliatory requests in a field setting. *Personality and Social Psychology Bulletin, 5*, 386–390.

Krapfel, R. E. (1988) Customer complaint and salesperson response: The effect of the communication source. *Journal of Retailing, 64*, 181–198.

Linkey, H. E., & Firestone, I. J. (1990). Dyad dominance composition effects, nonverbal behaviors, and influence. *Journal of Research in Personality, 24*, 206–215.

Liss, B., Walker, M., Hazelton, V., & Cupach, W. D. (1993, February). *Mutual gaze and smiling as correlates of compliance-gaining success.* Paper presented at the annual meeting of the Western States Communication Association, Albuquerque, NM.

MacLachlan, J. (1979). What people really think of fast talkers. *Psychology Today, 13*(6), 112–117.

MacNeill, L., & Wilson, B. (1972). *A field study of the effects of conventional and unconventional dress on petition signing behavior.* Unpublished Manuscript, Illinois State University, Normal, IL.

McGinley, H., LeFevre, R., & McGinley, A. (1975). The influence of communicator's body position on opinion change in others. *Journal of Personality and Social Psychology, 31*, 686–690.

Mehrabian, A. (1969). Significance of posture and position in the communication, attitude and status relationships. *Psychological Bulletin, 71*, 359–372.

Milgram, S. (1974). *Obedience to authority.* New York: Harper & Row.

Miller, N., Maruyama, G., Beaber, R., & Malone, K. (1976). Speed of speech and persuasion. *Journal of Personality and Social Psychology, 34*, 615–624.

Mongeau, P. A., & Stiff, J. B. (1993) Specifying the ELM: Specifying casual relationships in the Elaboration Likelihood Model. *Communication Theory, 3*, 65–72.

Moon, Y. (1999). The effects of physical distance and response latency on persuasion in computer-mediated communication and in human-computer communication. *Journal of Experimental Psychology: Applied, 5*, 379–392.

Morris, D. (1977). *Manwatching: A field guide to human behavior.* New York: Abrams.

Mullen, B., Futrell, D., Stairs, D., Tice, D., Baumeister, R., Dawson, K., Riordan, C., Radioff, C., Goethals, G., Kennedy, J., & Rosenfeld, P. (1986). Newscasters' facial expressions and voting behavior of viewers: Can a smile elect a president? *Journal of Personality and Social Psychology, 51,* 291–295.

Patterson, M. L., Powell, J. L., & Lenihan, M. G. (1986). Touch, compliance, and interpersonal affect. *Journal of Nonverbal Behavior, 10,* 41–50.

Petty, R. E., & Cacioppo, J. (1986). The elaboration likelihood model of persuasion. In L. Berkowitz (Ed.), *Advances in Experimental Social Psychology* (vol. 19, pp. 123–205). New York: Academic Press.

Petty, R. E., Wegener, D. T., Fabrigar, L. R., Preister, J. R., & Cacioppo, J. T. (1993). Specifying the ELM: Conceptual and methodological issues in the Elaboration Likelihood Model of Persuasion: A reply to the Michigan State Critics. *Communication Theory, 3,* 336–362.

Puckett, J., Petty, R. E., Cacioppo, J. T., & Fisher, D. (1983). The relative impacts of age and attractiveness stereotypes on persuasion. *Journal of Gerontology, 38,* 340–343.

Raymond, B. J., & Unger, R. K. (1972). "The apparel oft proclaims the man": Cooperation with deviant and conventional youths. *Journal of Social Psychology, 87,* 75–82.

Segrin, C. (1990, November). *Nonverbal behavior and compliance: Affiliation, arousal or dominance.* Paper presented at the annual meeting of the Speech Communication Association, Chicago.

Segrin, C. (1993). The effects of nonverbal behavior on outcomes of compliance-gaining attempts. *Communication Studies, 44,* 169–187.

Snyder, M., Grether, J., & Keller, J. (1974). Staring and compliance: A field experiment on hitchhiking. *Journal of Applied Social Psychology, 4,* 165–170.

Stacks, D. W., & Andersen, P. A. (1989). The modular mind: Implications for intrapersonal communication. *Southern Communication Journal, 3,* 273–293.

Stacks, D. W., & Burgoon, J. K. (1979, April). *The persuasive effects of violating spacial distance expectations in small groups.* Paper presented at the annual meeting of the Southern Speech Communication Association Convention, Biloxi, MS.

Stacks, D. W., & Burgoon, J. K. (1981). The role of nonverbal behaviors as distractors in resistance to persuasion in interpersonal contexts. *Central States Speech Journal, 32,* 61–73.

Stead, B. A., & Zinkhan, G. M. (1986). Service priority in department stores: The effects of customer gender and dress. *Sex Roles, 15,* 601–611.

Stephen, R., & Zweigenhaft, R. L. (1985). The effect on tipping of a waitress touching male and female customers. *Journal of Social Psychology, 126,* 141–142.

Stiff, J. B., & Boster, F. J. (1987). Cognitive processing: Additional thoughts and a reply to Petty, Kasner, Haugtvedt, and Cacioppo. *Communication Monographs, 54,* 233–249.

Street, R. L. (1982). Evaluation of noncontent speech accommodation. *Language and Communication, 2,* 13–31.

Street, R. L., & Brady, R. M. (1982). Speech rate acceptance ranges as a function of evaluative domain, listener speech rate and communication context. *Communication Monographs, 49,* 290–308.

Street, R. L., & Giles, H. (1982). Speech accommodation theory: A social cognitive approach to language and speech behavior. In M. Roloff & C. Berger (Eds.), *Social cognition and communication* (pp. 193–226). Beverly Hills, CA: Sage.

Trost, M. R., & Engstrom, C. (1994, February). *"Hit the road Jack": Strategies for rejecting flirtatious advances.* Paper presented at the annual meeting of the Western States Communication Association, San Jose, CA.

Valentine, M. E. (1980). The attenuating influence of gaze upon the bystander intervention effect. *Journal of Social Psychology, 3,* 197–203.

Walker, M., Harriman, S., & Costello, S. (1980). The influence of appearance on compliance with a request. *Journal of Social Psychology, 112,* 159–160.

Willis, F., & Hamm, H. (1980). The use of interpersonal touch in security compliance. *Journal of Nonverbal Behavior, 5,* 49–55.

Woodall, W. G., & Burgoon, J. K. (1983). Talking fast and changing attitudes: A critique and clarification. *Journal of Nonverbal Behavior, 8,* 126–142.

Part III

Seeking and Resisting Compliance
Strategies and Tactics

The old phrase "There's more than one way to skin a cat" may not actually be referring to the process of persuasion, but it certainly applies. Indeed, there is no "one way" to persuade another person. The number of different approaches is endless. This fact, however, has not prevented researchers from trying to document the numerous strategies and tactics that people typically use when trying to influence others. An enormous amount of research has been devoted to identifying not only the different types of influence strategies available to would-be persuaders but also to examining how likely persuaders are to select such strategies and to describing the situational variables that influence their choices. For example, an early seminal effort by Marwell and Schmitt (1967) identified 16 such strategies, including making promises and threats, getting others to like you, rewarding others before asking a favor, and so on. Later attempts were even more ambitious. Kellerman and Cole (1994), for instance, integrated the typologies of other researchers into 64 distinct compliance-gaining strategies.

Although such efforts have shed a good deal of light on the topics of compliance gaining and compliance resisting, they have also generated considerable heat as well. They have little to say about three issues that we find both highly interesting and extremely relevant. First, a good deal of the compliance-gaining literature seems to be atheoretical in nature. Researchers often evaluate strategy preferences absent any theory or model to guide their research. Second, such efforts fail to consider the process by which influence messages are produced. That is, they focus on *what* strategies people select but not *why* they select them. Third, they often fail to examine the actual effectiveness of the influence strategies they identify. That is, they focus on which strategies people *prefer*, but not necessarily which ones enjoy the greatest chances of *success*. In fairness, some

181

compliance-gaining research has focused on outcome effectiveness, for example, studies on food server behaviors and restaurant patrons' tipping, or on sequential request strategies (e.g. foot-in-the-door and door-in-the-face techniques) in relation to charity contributions. Too many studies, however, have neglected to examine the actual effectiveness of strategies on message recipients, rendering the applicability of their results to the real world somewhat dubious. In contrast, the chapters in this part are designed to address these issues and others.

First, chapter 11, by James Price Dillard, presents the Goals-Plans-Action Model of interpersonal influence. The model is valuable because it helps us understand how and why persuasive messages are created. It suggests that people have different goals when engaging in persuasion and shows us how the configuration of such goals influences not only the persuasive plans and strategies that a person generates and selects but also how persuasion is enacted and reacted to.

In contrast, the following two chapters focus on the effectiveness of two particular types of persuasive strategies and tactics. Chapter 12, by Robert Cialdini and Rosanna Guadagno, examines the topic of sequential persuasion. Here you will read about a number of tactics aimed at getting people to behave in a particular way. Such tactics are labeled "sequential," because all of them involve increasing one's persuasiveness by saying or doing something before actually making a request. Similarly, chapter 13, by Hyunyi Cho and Kim Witte, focuses on the effects of persuasion by examining the use of fear appeals. This chapter presents the Extended Parallel Process Model, which integrates 40 years of research on fear appeals to explain the conditions under which fear succeeds or fails as an approach to persuasion. Both of these chapters do an outstanding job of examining the effectiveness of specific approaches to persuasion, but more significantly, they help us understand the underlying processes that explain *why* such tactics are often effective.

Chapter 14, by Judee Burgoon and David Buller, focuses on deception, a tactic that is frequently included in the compliance-gaining typologies we mentioned earlier. Although some might view deception as part of the "dark side of communication," this chapter shows that deception serves beneficial social functions and is a part of communication competence. And although some people might not consider deception a form of persuasion, in our view it clearly is. As Miller (cited in Miller & Stiff, 1993) argued:

> Deceptive communication strives for persuasive ends; or, stated more precisely, deceptive communication is a general persuasive strategy that aims at influencing the beliefs, attitudes, and behaviors of others by means of deliberate message distortion. (p. 28)

For this reason, then, we have included a chapter on this important form of influence in this book. As you will see, Burgoon and Buller's chapter underlines the interactional and interpersonal nature of deceptive communication. Their chapter contributes not only to understanding the process by which deception is enacted but also to the manner in which it is perceived and detected. As such, this chapter is as much about resisting persuasion as it is about how people attempt to persuade.

This last statement leads us to the final chapter in this part of the book. Specifically, the study of persuasion has focused not just on how persuasion occurs but also on how the persuasive attempts of others might be thwarted. Though there are many approaches to resisting persuasion, chapter 15, by Michael Pfau and Erin Szabo, is devoted to inoculation, which has received perhaps the most attention in this area. The chapter explains how inoculation works, and more important, it demonstrates the broad and socially significant applications of this approach to resisting persuasion.

References

Kellerman, K., & Cole, T. (1994). Classifying compliance gaining messages: Taxonomic disorder and strategic confusion. *Communication Theory, 4,* 3–60.

Marwell, G., & Schmitt, D. R. (1967). Dimensions of compliance-gaining behavior: An empirical analysis. *Sociometry, 30,* 350–364.

Miller, G. R., & Stiff, J. B. (1993). *Deceptive communication.* Newbury Park, NJ: Sage.

11

The Goals-Plans-Action Model of Interpersonal Influence

James Price Dillard

The Goals-Plans-Action Model

The *Goals-Plans-Action* (GPA) model is an attempt to shed light on the way in which messages are produced and on the effects that they have (Dillard, 1990a, 1990b). Because the structure of the model is quite general, it might be adapted to a variety of different communicative functions. For instance, it could be applied to self-disclosure, social support, or information seeking. Despite this versatility, it was developed specifically as part of an effort to better understand influence behavior. Accordingly, empirical research designed to test and inform the GPA model has tried to answer the question of how and why individuals influence one another.

Although the foundations of influence behavior are complex, the GPA model begins with a simple and well-accepted idea: That message production can be modeled as a sequence involving three components (Miller, Galanter, & Pribram, 1960). *Goals* are the first component. They are defined as future states of affairs that an individual is committed to achieving or maintaining (Dillard, 1997; Hobbs & Evans, 1980; Klinger, 1985). Goals motivate plans, the second component in the model. *Plans* are cognitive representations of the behaviors that are intended to enable goal attainment (Berger, 1997). Whereas goals and plans are cognitive entities, actions exist "in the world." *Actions* are the behaviors enacted in an effort to realize the goal. The behavioral response of the message target constitutes feedback to the message source that may produce changes in goals and plans.

These ideas provide the basis for the GPA model. Within this general framework, the model advances a number of specific claims regarding the nature of goals, plans, and actions as well as their relationship to one another. The aim of this chapter is to explicate those claims and to present some empirical tests of the tenets of the theory.

Goals

Types of Influence Goals

It might seem that people try to persuade others for an unlimited variety of reasons. However, research on interpersonal influence goals reveals that perceptions of infinite diversity are illusory (Cody, Canary, & Smith, 1994; Dillard, 1989; Rule, Bisanz, & Kohn, 1985). The most frequently identified reasons for influencing others are listed in table 11.1, along with a description and an example of each. Because this list is compiled from studies using a variety of methods (qualitative and quantitative) and data sources (e.g., recalled goals versus hypothetical goals), we can have some confidence that table 11.1 captures something of the psychological reality of natural social actors. In fact, the concept of psychological reality is important to this theory. Although there are certainly many mental and social processes that occur without awareness, the GPA model focuses on *volitional behavior*. This focus implies that individuals construct representations of situations that are meaningful to them and that they are capable of exercising a significant degree of conscious control over their actions. Hence, information concerning what an individual is trying to achieve constitutes a valid and meaningful explanation for his or her behavior.

Table 11.1 is not without certain limitations. First, these findings are inherently bound by the characteristics of the research procedures and the samples employed. All of

TABLE 11.1 *Influence Goals*

Type	Description	Examples
Gain assistance	Obtain material or nonmaterial resources.	Can I borrow your car?
Give advice	Provide counsel (typically about health & relationships).	I think that you should quit using so much Prozac.
Share activity	Promote joint endeavors between source and target.	Let's do something tonight. How about going to see that new band?
Change orientation	Alter target's stance toward a sociopolitical issue.	There is another, more realistic, way to look at the abortion laws.
Change relationship	Alter the nature of the source-target relationship.	I think that we ought to have a monogamous relationship.
Obtain permission	Secure the endorsement of the (more powerful) target.	Would it be OK if I handed in the assignment one day late?
Enforce rights and obligations	Compel target to fulfill commitment or role requirement.	You promised that you would keep the music down. So, how about it?

the data are grounded in the subjective experience of young adults living in North America and attending public universities. Studies of influence in organizations, for example, indicate that individuals hold goals that do not appear in table 11.1, such as initiating changes in work procedures and improving another's job performance (Kipnis, Wilkinson, & Schmidt, 1980). Thus, although the variety of influence goals is not infinite, it may be broader than is reflected in table 11.1.

Second, the goals described in table 11.1 exist at a particular level of abstraction that is subject to debate. One can easily imagine more general groupings of goals involving a smaller number of categories. For instance, we might distinguish between goals that substantially advance the interests of the individual versus those that remedy a problem, a distinction that yields only two goal types. Conversely, any one of the seven goals might be parsed more finely. The Change Relationship goal is a case in point. Even if one assumes that the communicative processes involved in relational escalation and deescalation bear some similarity, the experience of the two events is quite distinct and the utterances associated with each markedly different. Consequently, it may be desirable to consider several specific forms of the Change Relationship goal. Yet the studies that contribute to table 11.1 suggest that these seven goals reflect how individuals generally think about their influence attempts. In other words, whereas goals can be usefully conceptualized and researched at higher or lower levels of abstraction, the contents of table 11.1 are indicative of the level at which ordinary people typically conceive of their own and others' influence behavior (Cody et al., 1994; Dillard, 1989; Rule et al., 1985).

In sum, although individuals may have many different persuasive goals, research shows that this number is smaller than one might initially think. Although existing research is not without limitations, I believe that the seven goals described in table 11.1 represent common and recurring influence aims. They also possess particular properties that need to be explicated more fully. Those properties are discussed next.

Primary Goals

In the parlance of the GPA model, the goals listed in table 11.1 are *primary goals*. They are so named because the theory attributes several unique properties to them. For one, primary goals lie at the beginning of the GPA sequence. They are primary in the sense that they initiate the series of constructs that model message production. Hacker (1985, p. 278) made a similar point when she noted that goals "are reflections of a reality that does not yet exist, but has to be created, and they connect present with future" (p. 278). From this perspective, primary goals are potential realities that individuals strive to construct. Because primary goals energize cognition and behavior, it can be said that they serve a *motivational function*.

A second feature of primary goals derives from the previous point. That is, primary goals allow one to bracket the interaction, to identify its beginning and ending point. Knowledge of what is being attempted permits social actors to segment the stream of interaction into meaningful units (von Cranach, Machler, & Steiner, 1985). Such segmentation is surely valuable for making sense of what might otherwise be viewed as an undifferentiated outpouring of behavior. Meaningful segments of social interaction have been labeled "social episodes" by Newell and Stutman (1988). Bracketing is possible because the primary goal imbues the interaction with meaning (Dillard & Solomon, 2000). Knowledge of the primary goal allows the interactants to say what the exchange is about. Hence, as inspection of table 11.1 quickly reveals, primary goals are culturally viable explanations of the discourse produced by two or more interlocutors. This is the *social meaning function* of primary goals.

Finally, primary goals direct a number of mental operations. By providing an understanding of the intended purpose of an interaction, goals determine which aspects of a situation are perceived (Kanwisher, Driver, & Machado, 1995; Maruff, Danckert, Camplin, & Currie, 1999; Tipper, Weaver, & Houghton, 1994). They also influence which perceptions are encoded and retrieved (Cohen, 1981). In fact, primary goals set into motion an ensemble of lower-level cognitive processes that occur in parallel and align with the overall aim represented by the primary goal. In this fashion, primary goals serve a *guidance function* that promotes temporary reorientation and unification of various mental subsystems.[1]

Secondary Goals

In the course of pursuing or planning to pursue a primary goal, other concerns may arise. For example, one college student who hopes to initiate a relationship with another (goal #1) might recognize the risk of rejection and wish to avoid feeling hurt (goal #2). In a similar vein, the parent who wants to prevent his young child from inserting silverware into electrical sockets (goal #1) might also want to ensure that his warning does not create a generalized fear that extends beyond this specific problem (goal #2). Such concerns are called *secondary goals* because they follow from the adoption of a primary goal. In both examples above, the speaker holds a secondary goal only because he or she is considering trying to influence someone else. Thus, it is the desire to achieve the primary goal that brings into play one or more secondary goals. Primary and secondary goals can be distinguished in terms of their logical priority vis-à-vis one another.

Research on the GPA model supports the existence of five secondary goals (Dillard, Segrin, & Harden, 1989; Honeycutt, Cantrill, Kelly, & Lambkin, 1998; Schrader & Dillard, 1998; Wilson & Zigurs, 2001), though not every goal will be relevant to every situation. *Identity goals* focus on ethical, moral, and personal standards for behavior. They arise from individuals' principles and values and, at the broadest level, their self-concept. Although people generally desire to act in accordance with their principles, it is probably not the case that individuals actively consider their identity goals in every interaction. Many social episodes are routinized, and people have generally already made far-reaching decisions about what does and does not constitute ethical behavior. In such cases, it seems unlikely that an identity goal will be activated.

Conversation management goals involve concerns about impression management and face.[2] Though there are certainly exceptions (Tracy & Tracy, 1998), individuals usually prefer that interactions proceed smoothly rather than awkwardly and that neither interlocutor present a threat to his or her own or the other's face (Brown & Levinson, 1987). Thus, while conversation management goals may have implications that extend beyond the conversation, they also have a relatively short time frame (typically the duration of the conversation).

Relational resource goals focus on relationship management. They are manifestations of the value that individuals place on desired social and personal relationships.

Hence, it is most often the case that people try to maintain or improve their relationships with others. Of course, relational resource goals don't really come into play unless one has a preexisting relationship with the hearer or hopes to establish one. Relational resource goals focus on the benefits that flow to the source because of the relationship itself. As a consequence, relational resource goals have a longer time frame than conversation management goals.

Personal resource goals reflect the physical, temporal, and material concerns of the communicator. More specifically, they arise from the desire to maintain or enhance one's physical well-being, temporal resources, finances, and material possessions. The desire to behave efficiently is viewed as a personal resource goal (cf. Berger, 1997; Kellermann, 1988), although the GPA model does not suppose that individuals always prefer a high level of efficiency. Like some of the other secondary goals, personal resource goals will not be relevant to every interaction. But when they are relevant, they can be important in determining how messages are created and uttered.

By positing the existence of *affect management goals*, the model assumes that individuals strive to maintain preferred affective states. Significantly, affect management goals are not so simple as the wish to enjoy positive feeling and elude negative ones. For instance, individuals seek to increase their level of anxiety because it motivates vigilance or to enhance their level of anger so that they are emotionally aligned with a plan to take a hard interactional stance.[3]

The introduction of the concept of secondary goals has at least one broad implication for how we conceive of the task of interpersonal influence. Namely, it suggests that most, and possibly all, interactions involve multiple goals that individuals try to achieve more or less simultaneously. This premise is so broadly accepted among communication researchers as to be viewed as a truism (Berger, 1997, p. 23). Surprisingly, some writers in other fields claim that there is a paucity of data-based research underlying that truism: "Multiple goal striving appears to be the rule, *yet little empirical research addresses the topic*" [emphasis added] (Austin & Vancouver, 1996, p. 362). In reality, dozens of empirical studies have examined precisely that topic (e.g., Dillard et al., 1989; Meyer, 1997; O'Keefe & Shepherd, 1987; Saeki & O'Keefe, 1994; Tracy & Coupland, 1990; Waldron, 1990; Wilson, 1995). This solid and growing empirical base has helped to inform the GPA model and other theories of influence (e.g., Meyer, 1997; Wilson, 1995).

In sum, secondary goals are wants that arise in response to the consideration or adoption of a primary goal. Previous research supports the existence of five conceptually distinct secondary goals. However, the exact number is not so important as appreciation of the fact that individuals are almost always attempting to satisfy multiple goals. The primary goal defines the situation, while secondary goals are the entailments that follow in its wake. The GPA model holds that understanding the relationship between primary and secondary goals is crucial to explaining planning and action. Consequently, the next section begins an exploration of those issues.

The Relationships Between Primary Goals and Secondary Goals

Possibly the most fundamental communication decision is whether to engage another person in interaction or not. The interplay of primary and secondary goals can help to shed light on this choice point in the message production process. To simplify the illustration, it will be helpful to assume a primary goal and just one secondary goal and then to evaluate the compatibility between the two (cf. Kellermann, 1988; Samp & Solomon, 1999). Logically, just three possibilities exist. In the first case, the two goals may be *incompatible* with one another. In this vein, Brown and Levinson (1987) assert that influence attempts are by their very nature intrusive (but see Wilson, Kim, & Meischke, 1991/1992). If true, then any effort to produce behavioral change in another will necessarily run the risk of threatening that person's autonomy. A second logical possibility is that the secondary goals are *irrelevant* to the primary goal. For example, concern for a friend's physical well-being is not often an issue when asking the person if he or she would like to see a film with you.

In the third case, the primary and secondary goals align or are *compatible* with one another. Relational initiation offers one context in which this might occur. The norm of reciprocity demands that individuals repay favors provided to them by others. When one person asks another for help (e.g., a ride to the grocery store) that he or she cannot immediately repay, the message source is signaling a willingness to enter into a relationship in which reciprocity will occur over time. Such is a defining feature of friendships (Hatfield, Utne, & Traupmann, 1979). Thus, the speaker may obtain a ride and, in so doing, also solidify a nascent relationship.

Although the third case is clearly the most desirable of the three alternatives, I suspect that it is also the least common. Rather, most interactions can be characterized as a blend of cases one and two. Because there are multiple secondary goals, it is likely that some of them create opposition to the primary goal, while others will be irrelevant. Hence, in most instances the *set of relevant secondary goals* will constitute a counterdynamic to the primary goal. And, although I have drawn the possibilities in a categorical fashion, the degree to which primary and secondary goals are (in)compatible with one another is more accurately viewed as a matter of degree. To the extent that concern for the secondary goals outweighs the desire to achieve the primary goal (and any compatible secondary goals), the individual may view engaging the other as unduly risky and may therefore choose not to engage. Thus, knowledge of the relationship between primary and secondary goals can help explain why individuals make an influence attempt or not. However, to speak of *the* relationship between primary and secondary goals is something of an oversimplification. Actually, primary and secondary goals form *a set of* structured relationships. *Goal structure complexity* is the concept describing that set of relationships.

Goal Structure Complexity

Primary goals lend motion and meaning to social episodes. However, secondary goals also figure prominently in the message production process in that they reflect other psychologically significant, but logically subsidiary, concerns of the individual. In combination, the two goal types constitute the intrapersonal *goal structure* of the communication episode. Research reveals that influence episodes vary in goal structure complexity, in that various episodes comprise a greater or lesser number of active goals (Schrader & Dillard, 1998).

Participants in the Schrader and Dillard (1998) study were provided with one of 15 hypothetical scenarios, each of which represented a primary goal drawn from Cody and colleagues (1994). They were asked to recall an interaction from their own experience that was similar to the example and then to respond to a series of questions intended to assess retrospectively the importance of the primary goal and five secondary goals. The resulting data were submitted to a statistical routine called cluster analysis. In essence, the routine looks for patterns of similarity across variables and then creates groupings (i.e., clusters) on the basis of those similarities. In this application, the cluster program tried to create groups of social episodes that were similar with regard to the perceived importance of the primary and secondary goals.

Four such clusters emerged such that each possessed several notable features as a group. For one, the importance of the primary goal increased from cluster 1 to cluster 4. Generally, the secondary goals showed a pattern of increasing activation that corresponded to increases in the importance of the primary goal. In other words, as the importance of the primary goal increased, so did the importance of the secondary goals. The relational resource goal was the sole exception to this pattern. It declined in importance as the primary goal grew in importance. In addition to considering the goal clusters in these broad strokes, it is useful to examine each one individually.

The first cluster contained primary goals representing influence attempts that are common but not particularly important, focusing on issues concerning the close and collaborative nature of the source-target relationship. Secondary goals were of relatively little concern in these episodes, with the exception of the relational resource goal (cf. Wilson, Aleman, & Leatham, 1998). This grouping was called *maintenance episodes* to emphasize the habitual and relational aspects of the goals in the cluster.

Primary goals in the second cluster occurred mostly within close relationships. In this case the goals were not routine, but rather represented more important issues of a nonrecurring nature. Two primary goals, Change Orientation and Relational Escalation, were representative of the breadth of issues represented by this cluster, which was labeled *special issue episodes.* The goal structure of this cluster was more complex than that of *maintenance episodes,* but less complex than the remaining two clusters.

The third cluster, *problem-solving episodes,* consisted of goals that represented either high need or high rights to persuade. Such episodes tend to occur within more distant social relationships (e.g., strangers, neighbors, professors), a feature that was mirrored in the decreased importance of relational resource goals. However, overall goal structure complexity and the importance of the influence attempt were higher than in either of the two previous clusters.

The fourth cluster was called *high-stakes episodes* to reflect the fact that goals in this grouping showed a dramatic increase in the importance of personal resource and arousal management goals. Members of this cluster were not only rated highest in importance but also showed the greatest number of active secondary goals, that is, the highest goal structure complexity. This cluster included two highly risky activities: initiating a relationship and dealing with a bureaucrat.

It seems clear from the results of Schrader and Dillard's (1998) study that goal structure complexity is a useful concept for organizing our thinking about different types of primary goals. The findings also suggest that primary goals with complex goal structures are more difficult to achieve than those with simple structures. Furthermore, we might reasonably expect individuals to be more reluctant to engage another person in a highly complex episode because of the many potential risks of failure. Goal structure complexity might also shape our next topic, the planning process.

Plans

In this section, both the nature and content of plans are examined. Following that, attention is given to the manner in which plans come into being and how choices are made among them.

Features of Plans

Plans can be differentiated in terms of their hierarchy, complexity, and completeness (Dillard, 1990a). Hierarchy refers to the level of abstraction at which the plan is cast, whereas complexity captures the number of steps and contingencies it contains (cf. Berger, 1997). Plan completeness is a measure of the extent to which the plan is fleshed out. Because the behavior of others is sometimes difficult to predict, it is assumed that even when speakers engage in preconversational planning, the resulting plans are necessarily incomplete (Bratman, 1987). These three properties may be used to analyze plans of any sort, but it is the *content* of influence plans that sets them apart from plans more generally.

The Content of Compliance-Seeking and Resisting Plans

Influence plans contain guidelines for the production of verbal and nonverbal behaviors. Whereas *strategy level plans* are concerned with lines of action and sequences of behavior, *tactic plans* exist at a lower level of abstraction.[4] They are instructions for producing smaller units of behavior such as individual utterances. For example, though one might approach an influence attempt with the intention of implementing a liking strategy, there are many different ways to do this at the tactical level. The first move might consist of utterances such as, "You look great! Looks like you lost some weight" or, "That was a really smart thing that you said in our discussion group. I was impressed."

Research on the perception of message tactics suggests that four dimensions are particularly important to understanding influence plans (Dillard, Wilson, Tusing, & Kinney, 1997; Wiseman & Schenck-Hamlin, 1981). Any influence plan or behavior can be represented as a point (tactic) or a vector (strategy) in this four-dimensional space. The first of these dimensions, *explicitness*, is the degree to which the message source makes her or his intentions transparent in the message itself. Whereas implicit messages require little or no guesswork regarding the speaker's wants, inexplicit messages necessitate more interpretation (Blum-Kulka, 1987). Table 11.2 presents examples of both types of action.

Dominance references the relative power of the source vis-à-vis the target as that power is expressed in the message. An expression of dominance in any single utterance need not accurately reflect formal differences in status nor a consensual definition of the source-target relationship. Rather, message dominance simply expresses the source's perception of, or desire for, a particular source-target power relationship.

TABLE 11.2 *The Content of Compliance-Seeking Plans and Actions*

Dimension of Plan/Action	Example of One Roommate Urging Another to Exercise
Explicitness	High: "I would like you to come to the gym with me." Low: "Hey, I'm going to the gym."
Dominance	High: "You said that you wanted to work out. Now, let's do it." Low: "I would really, really appreciate it if you worked out with me."
Argument	High: "I sleep a lot better when I work out. I'll bet that you would too." Low: "We should go work out."
Source control	High: "If you want to get some exercise, I'll go to the gym with you." Low: "If you don't get some exercise, you are probably going to die."

Argument is defined as the extent to which the message presents a rationale for the sought-after action and refers to the degree to which the source provides explicit reasons for why s/he is seeking compliance, rather than simply making an unelaborated request. Of course, messages may be structured argumentatively even though the evidence is less than compelling (e.g., Langer, Blank, & Chanowitz, 1978). Argument refers to the perceived quantity rather than quality of reason giving (cf. Roloff, Janiszewski, McGrath, Burns, & Manrai, 1988; Samp & Solomon, 1999, on *embellishment*).

Control over outcomes is the fourth and final dimension that characterizes influence plans. The property indexes the extent to which the source can exercise control over the reasons for compliance. Among other things, this distinction makes clear the difference between a threat (e.g., I will hurt you, if . . .) and a warning (e.g., You could be harmed, if . . .).

As noted above, these four dimensions are central to characterizing the content of influence plans. However, they are also useful for understanding resistance. In fact, messages intended to refute compliance-seeking attempts can be analyzed in terms of the same four concepts. Table 11.3 provides an illustration of resistance messages that might be made in response to one or more of the influence messages in table 11.2.

Before turning to the question of how plans are generated and selected, it is important to ask what might be missing from the characterization of plans along these four dimensions. The answer is, "A great deal." There are many elements to plans and conversation that are *not* encompassed by explicitness, dominance, argument, and source control. For instance, persons who seek to influence often anticipate various forms of resistance and attempt to gain information about those obstacles prior to making a request (e.g., "Are you busy right now?" "No? Then you wouldn't mind helping me out with this, would

TABLE 11.3   *The Content of Compliance-Resisting Plans and Actions*

Dimension of Plan/Action	Responses to One Roommate Urging Another to Exercise
Explicitness	High: "I don't want to."
	Low: "I'm pretty busy right now."
Dominance	High: "I'll decide when I exercise, not you."
	Low: "I really appreciate you helping me out in this way, but now is not a good time for me."
Argument	High: "Can't do it now. I've got to study for an exam later today."
	Low: "Nope. I don't think so."
Source control	High: "I'm just going to take it easy right now, but I may go later."
	Low: "Can't do it. I have to wait for the telephone repair person to come."

you?") (Ifert & Roloff, 1994; Paulson & Roloff, 1997). Even after the target has complied, the source may revisit the request later in the episode and attempt to secure further commitment, such as when a source says "So, you did agree to pick me up at 6 P.M., right?" (Sanders & Fitch, 2001). Thus, the four dimensions should not be viewed as offering an exhaustive account of the content of influence/resistance plans. Nevertheless, because there is such strong evidence that social actors themselves view influence in these terms (Dillard, 1997), they must be considered essential aspects of any influence episode. Having now addressed the features and content of plans, we can turn our attention to where plans come from and how choices are made among them.

Generating and Selecting Plans

When the desire to influence another arises, individuals will initially search long-term memory for boilerplate plans that are likely to achieve the primary goal (Berger, 1997; Dillard, 1990a; Meyer, 1997; Waldron, 1997; Wilson, 1995). This search may yield plans that vary in abstraction, complexity, and completeness. If the available plan(s) meet or exceed some individually determined threshold of perceived plan adequacy, then the individual moves toward translating the cognitive representation of action into behavior. Of course, this involves a great many lower-level processes that must work in unison (and could fail to do so) if the plan is to be successfully instantiated as behavior.[5]

To the extent that the preexisting plans are judged to be less than satisfactory and the primary goal is viewed as important, individuals will devote additional cognitive effort to (1) making existing plans more complete or more complex and/or (2) creating new plans. This kind of top-down planning is constrained by the recognition that successful interaction partially depends on the behavior of the target. To the extent that the source views those responses as unpredictable, he or she will be less inclined to expend cognitive effort in the service of plan development. Moreover, it should be the case that the number of plans viewed as adequate should show a negative correspondence with goal structure complexity. Although there may be many different ways to achieve a primary goal if none of the secondary goals is activated, it should be more challenging to devise a plan that will satisfy the many competing desires that are present in an episode that is high in goal structure complexity.

When multiple plans or plan variations are available, the message source must select among them. The GPA model assumes that selection is made with regard to finding a satisfactory configuration of primary and secondary goals. This may be a drawn-out, contemplative process but very often is not because conversation moves so quickly. Indeed, an opportunity for influence may open up during the course of interaction that demands plan deployment in the next conversational turn. Berger (1997), Meyer (1990, 1997), and Wilson (1990, 1995) all provide more detailed accounts of the cognitive operations involved in plan generation and selection. Having now described the first two components of the GPA model—goals and plans—we can move to an examination of the third component: action.

Action and Interaction

GPA theory was designed to model the processes by which individuals produce actions intended to alter or maintain the behavior of others. The various subcomponents of the model and their relations to one another are depicted in figure 11.1. This segment of the chapter addresses theory and research regarding how individuals produce influence behaviors and how, together, two individuals create an interaction.

Message Production in the GPA Model

The model proposes two pathways to the production of influence behavior. In the first, individuals assess their goals, decide to engage the target, and then move to plan generation and selection. It is assumed that this sequence is likely to obtain when the importance of the primary goal substantially outweighs the counterdynamic represented by the set of relevant, incompatible secondary goals.[6] In the second sequence, the generation of one or more plans that are viewed as likely to succeed encourages the decision to engage, which is then followed by plan selection. This path is more likely when the approach and avoidance forces are fairly closely matched. It is worth emphasizing that although these two paths are logically distinct possibilities, they need not be approached in a deliberative manner. Rather, because real-time conversation takes place very quickly, we might expect travel time on these paths to be measured in milliseconds.

Movement from plan selection to tactic implementation is the translation of cognitive entities into empirical action. This process must necessarily involve a host of very rapid, elemental processes, many of which do not involve conscious awareness. The link from tactic implementation to target response assumes a target that processes the source's utterance and returns a more or less appropriate response. On the basis of that response,

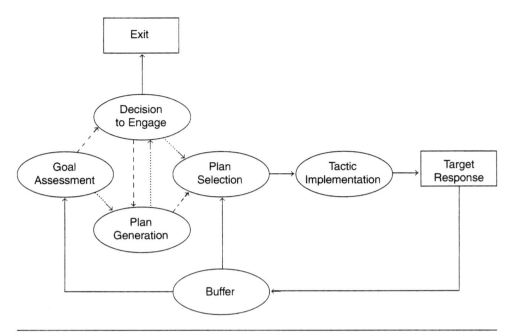

FIGURE 11.1   *The Goals-Plans-Action Model of Interpersonal Influence*

Note: The dashed lines show one of the two possible pathways to plan selection, while the dotted lines indicate the alternative. Solid lines show noncontingent, sequenced stages in the model.

the source may return to the goal awareness stage and move through the entire process again. In such a sequence, goals are reevaluated in light of the target's behavior. Alternatively, the source may store a number of tactic plans in a buffer and iterate only as far back as the tactic selection stage. When the source encounters noncompliant behavior from the target, the first tendency will be to change low level elements in the existing plan (Berger, 1997). But to the extent that the plan itself is seen as having failed, the source may discard it wholesale and move to other available options. In the event that no plan is available that can satisfy the primary-secondary goal array and that the perceived value of devising one is low, individuals may attempt to exit the episode. The most obvious means of accomplishing an exit is by changing the topic or physically leaving the interaction.

Research on Compliance-Seeking Message Production

Research on the message production process permits several empirical generalizations that are consistent with the logic of the GPA model. For example, there is evidence that individuals try harder to achieve influence goals that are important to them. As the importance of the primary goal increases, so does the amount of planning and cognitive effort that individuals expend in the service of that goal (Dillard et al., 1989; Wilson & Zigurs, 2001).

Primary goal importance also has implications for message construction. For instance, more important primary goals correspond with messages that use higher levels of argument (Dillard et al., 1989). In their study of computer-mediated communication, Wilson and Zigurs (2001) showed that primary goal importance is negatively associated with the use of images and emphatic text formatting (i.e., the use of bold, italics, underlines, font changes, or type size changes). Evidently, important primary goals promote a focus on message content and away from message style.

Of course, as predicted by the model, secondary goals shape message production as well. For example, in face-to-face interactions, increased importance of the identity goal is associated with increases in the use of argument and decreases in explicitness (Dillard et al., 1989). These findings suggest a desire to influence on principled grounds and to allow the target the option of refusal. In computer-mediated exchanges, heightened importance of the identity goal yields reductions in the use of images but increased use of emphatic text formatting (Wilson & Zigurs, 2001). The lowered use of images might be seen as a move away from form in the direction of function, but the growth in emphatic text is more difficult to understand. Certainly, additional research in both face-to-face and computer-mediated contexts is needed to paint a more complete picture of the operation of the identity goal.

The data also present a coherent pattern of results for the affect management goal. Greater efforts to manage one's arousal are associated with messages that are both more dominant (i.e., lower in positivity) and less dependent on argument (Dillard et al., 1989). In addition, as affect management becomes more important, individuals become less verbose and less concerned about conforming with rules of language use such as spelling, capitalization, and punctuation (Wilson & Zigurs, 2001). All of these findings suggest that strong concern with managing one's affect interferes with the ability to produce fluent, competent influence messages.

Various findings for other secondary goals are detailed in papers by Dillard et al. (1989) and by Wilson and Zigurs (2001). However, the results described above are sufficient to make two important points. First, they underscore the value of the distinction between primary and secondary goals. Second, they demonstrate that each of the two goal types contribute to message production in unique and predictable ways.

Interaction Processes and the Rebuff Phenomenon

The behavior of both the source and the target can be modeled as GPA processes. Thus, while the GPA model is essentially individualistic, it allows for the study of interaction as a pair of collaborating GPA processes. Examination of a stream of behavior as the output of two cooperating psychological systems reveals that top-down processes highlighted in the GPA sequence are receptive to many bottom-up influences, including the action of the other interactant. A brief analysis of one empirical regularity helps to make this point.

The *rebuff phenomenon* can be described as follows: ". . . when an initial persuasive effort is rebuffed, follow-up persuasive messages are ruder, more aggressive, and more forceful than the first one" (Hample & Dallinger, 1998, p. 305). Conceived in this way, the rebuff is clearly a pattern of interaction. Hample and Dallinger (1998) suggested that it may occur for two reasons: Individuals may become more aggressive because they exhaust their supply of prosocial appeals, or message sources may adjust their standards for behavior in such a way that more aggressive messages are seen as acceptable. Although their study did not address the first explanation, it did offer support for the second. People's concern for effectiveness increased as a positive function of number of rebuffs, while their concern for principles and desire to harm the hearer declined. In the terminology of the GPA model, it might be said that resistance (i.e., rebuffs) increased the importance of the primary goal and decreased the importance of the identity and conversational management goals.

Interaction Processes at Multiple Levels of Abstraction

The four variables that describe tactic and strategy plans and actions can also be conceived of as features of the interaction. In fact, the value of understanding the influence episode at the level of both utterance and episode can be seen in the following example. Consider that a single hint such as, "Do you think that it's a little breezy in here?" is low in explicitness. However, a series of such messages—"Do you think that it's a little breezy in here?"; "I'm kind of chilly"; "Do you suppose that someone meant to leave that window open?"—has the cumulative effect of conveying the source's intent very clearly. Given that the same variables are used to characterize both strategy and tactics, this example implies a surprising point: The impact of a series of utterances that occupy one location in the four-dimensional message space may produce an outcome opposite to that of a single utterance in the same location. Or, in this particular case, a series of inexplicit messages is explicit. The implication of this illustration is clear: If our understanding of influence interactions can vary so dramatically as a function of level of analysis, it may be important for future research to use both perspectives whenever possible.

Message Effects

Research on the GPA model has also stimulated research on message effects. The first portion of this segment considers the impact of influence messages on target emotions and relational judgments. The second portion addresses how the perceived competence of influence messages varies as a joint function of message form and goal structure.

The Relational and Emotional Implications of Influence Attempts

It seems self-evident that what individuals say to one another has implications for their feelings and the well-being of their relationship. Surely, this is as true of influence attempts as it is of communication more generally. Thus, it is not completely surprising that several studies have shown that influence attempts that are high in dominance have negative relational implications. Source dominance correlates negatively with perceptions of liking for the target (Dillard, Palmer, & Kinney, 1995) and with perceived politeness (Dillard & Kinney, 1994; Dillard et al., 1997). Conversely, highly dominant influence messages are viewed as illegitimate and as obstacles, two perceptions that typically result in anger (Dillard & Harkness, 1992; Dillard, Kinney, & Cruz, 1996).

Explicitness shows quite a different pattern. Whereas some theories of message production contend that explicit requests result in unfavorable relational inferences (e.g., Brown & Levinson, 1987; Leech, 1983), it appears that the reverse is true at least among interactants who are in friendly relationships with one another. In this relational context, highly explicit requests seem to signal solidarity between the interactants and correspondingly favorable emotions and interpretations of the influence attempt (Dillard et al., 1996; 1997). Although explicitness and dominance themselves tend to occur simultaneously (Dillard, Henwood, Giles, Coupland, & Coupland, 1990; Schrader, 1999), dominance is responsible for the negative relational judgments and for feelings of anger. The relational meaning of explicitness seems to be highly context-dependent (Dillard et al., 1996).

Finally, there is the argument dimension. Individuals generally report a preference for messages that provide reasons for complying versus those that do not (Kipnis et al., 1980). However, convincing evidence exists to show that reasons are not necessary for producing compliance in close relationships (Roloff et al., 1988). Roloff and colleagues contended that the obligations inherent in close relationships substitute for persuasion. Nonetheless, messages high in argument seem to indicate positive regard for the target (Dillard et al., 1997), and whether they are necessary or not, they may contribute to the long-term health of a close relationship. Research has yet to examine the relationship between argument and emotion, but on the basis of the research just reviewed, it seems quite likely that messages high in argument will engender favorable emotional responses.

Goal Structure Complexity and Perceived Communication Competence

The notion of communication competence hinges on the ability to comprehend the situation accurately and formulate messages appropriate to the circumstance. At the most general level, the Schrader and Dillard study (1998) on goal structure complexity suggested that some primary goals are much more difficult to achieve than others (because there are more secondary goals associated with them that speakers are trying to achieve simultaneously). Significantly, the study specified exactly which goals are more or less difficult and grouped them into four clusters. Knowledge of these clusters and their content provides individuals with advance knowledge about the difficulty of achieving various primary goals. In other words, a priori information concerning goal structure complexity can provide the basis for one aspect of communication competence, that is, accurate identification of the important aspects of the situation. This is the first step toward constructing effective and appropriate messages.

Schrader (1999) studied the relationship between message behavior and perceived competence as a function of goal structure complexity. His work provides several useful pieces of information concerning communication competence. First, higher levels of dominance are associated with higher levels of perceived *in*competence regardless of goal complexity. Second, whereas explicitness will not harm competence judgments in the low-complexity clusters, explicitness correlates negatively with competence in the high-complexity clusters.[7] Here we see evidence suggesting that one's ability to formulate inexplicit messages may substantially enhance effectiveness in complex situations (which, notably, contain highly important primary goals). Finally, the use of argument correlates positively with competence, except in the high stakes cluster (i.e., the most complex cluster). As Schrader noted, " In highly unpredictable circumstances wherein the target has the power to embarrass or humiliate the source, perceptions of argument use become decidedly negative" (pp. 196–197). As a group then, these conclusions present fairly specific guidelines for what qualifies as competent influence behavior across episodic variations in goal structure complexity. Knowledge of the way in which particular message forms will be perceived encourages planning aimed at developing competent messages.

Frequently Asked Questions About the GPA Model

Since the GPA model was first detailed in 1990, a number of questions have arisen in connection with it. Several of these are considered in the following section.

What Is the Role of Awareness in the GPA Model?

Some of the language used above, such as the "decision to engage" and "plan selection," might be taken to imply a high degree of conscious choice in the GPA process. In large measure however, these lexical choices are only matters of expository convenience. Many of the processes necessary to run the GPA model may take place with little or no conscious awareness. In this vein, people often find themselves embroiled in conversation without ever having made a reflective decision to enter that interaction. They expel air from their lungs to power their vocal apparatus, moving their tongue and lips in (usually) well-coordinated ways to produce sounds—all without awareness.

At the same time, the model does assume that primary and secondary goals are *in principle* accessible to conscious awareness. To make this assertion is, in many respects, equivalent to saying that people generally know what they are doing. When a college student ponders how to obtain permission to use her roommate's car to get to the grocery store, she is aware of her goal and, depending on its importance, aspects of the planning process. If the roommate in question unexpectedly mentions that she will be making a trip to the grocery store, the first student may quickly recall her own need for groceries and ask to accompany the car owner without any appreciable forethought. In this instance, it might appear that the first student acted on a goal without awareness. However, if she were queried about what she was doing with that request, she would very likely understand that portion of the interaction as attempting to gain compliance from her roommate. Put differently, she would be able to recover her goal consciously despite the fact that she might not have articulated it without being asked.

This example hints at another interesting property of goals: Once an individual begins to pursue a goal via interaction, that goal can be monitored without much conscious effort. Consequently, when a child attempts to persuade a parent to quit smoking (a Give Advice goal), he may not be acutely aware of that goal throughout the interaction. Rather, he is more likely to focus on the secondary goals that are at play on a turn-by-turn basis. Once a person becomes behaviorally committed to a primary goal, awareness shifts away from that overarching concern and toward the means of accomplishing it.

Do Goals Arise from Self-Interest?

It is surely the case that individuals often act out of self-interest, but it would be a mistake to conclude from that observation that they *always* seek to satisfy only their own needs (cf. Shepherd, 1998). Goals can be egotistic or altruistic, self-serving or philanthropic. As the existence of the Give Advice goal (table 11.1) implies, influence goals may arise for the purpose of benefiting others (Dillard & Schrader, 1998). Self-interest is not a defining feature of goals in the GPA model.

Can Goals Change During Conversation?

Much of the research conducted on the GPA model has relied on individuals' recollections of conversations in which they took part. Thus, they have been asked about their goals in the conversation as a whole and not asked to report on their aims before and after or on how their goals might have changed during the conversation. However, as should be clear from figure 11.1, interactants may conceivably change their goals at various times within an interaction. In principle, this could occur at every turn.[8]

Waldron (1997) described the results of a study that speaks to precisely this issue. In his investigation, interactants took part in an eight-minute conversation in which they attempted to acquire information about their partner's religious or political beliefs. Next, each interactant reviewed a videotape of the conversation and rated the importance of their primary and secondary goals every 30 seconds. Waldron reported that approximately 30 percent of the comparisons (from one time period to the next) showed a significant shift in goal importance, and over half of that 30 percent involved *multiple* changes in importance, such as an increase in the instrumental goal and a decrease in one or more of the secondary goals. Such results offer ready evidence of the fluidity of the GPA process.

Thinking about influence episodes in terms of distinct primary goals may offer a satisfactory account of an interaction after the fact. Moreover, characterizing interactions in terms of individual goals is an efficient means of explaining what took place and re-membering the relevant details. However, as Waldron's data indicate, when individuals are engaged in interaction, goals can shift quite rapidly, just as the GPA model suggests.

What Happens When a Secondary Goal Becomes More Important Than a Primary Goal?

One answer to this question might be that when a secondary goal eclipses a primary goal, the interaction is no longer about influence and is consequently beyond the purview of the model. However, as noted at the outset of this chapter, the GPA model can be applied to many different types of interaction. In fact, secondary goals can assume the status of primary goals. When they do, the interaction may not be defined in terms of influence, but it can be modeled as a GPA process nonetheless. Consider the following hypothetical exchange between a mother and her son:

01   Mother: "Did you remember to clean up your room?"

02   Son: "Yeah."

03   Mother: "And did it get done?"

04   Son: "I'll do it later, Mom."

05   Mother: "You know that part of your responsibilities as a member of this household includes cleaning your room. We're having guests for dinner, and I would like you to have it done before they arrive."

06   Son: "I know, Mom, and I'll get it done, but I've just got a lot to think about right now."

07   Mother: "What? Is something bothering you?"

08   Son: "Yeah, I did terrible on my geography exam yesterday, and I feel like dirt because of it. I guess I'm just dumb."

09   Mother: "Hmm. You know you said that you felt sick yesterday at breakfast. I wonder if you weren't just having a bad day."

Although it is not certain what the aims of these particular individuals might be, the interaction indicates that two primary goals might be in play. From conversational turns 01 to 05, it looks as if the mother is trying to get the son to clean his room. In fact, at turn 05, her explicit reference to his household responsibilities suggests that we might view the interaction up to this point as an instance of an Enforce Rights/Obligations primary goal. In turn 06, however, the son makes an explicit promise to comply but also shifts away from influence to something else (in the last clause). From that point on, it appears that the mother's primary goal has changed. In turn 07 she seeks information that would allow the conversation to be defined along some other line. By turn 09 it appears that she has adopted a primary goal of social support.

   This simple example is intended to illustrate two points about the GPA model. One is that it can be applied to a variety of different types of interaction. However, to move beyond influence episodes will require additional research aimed at uncovering the content of goals and plans in other communication domains. The second point bears on the utility of the notion of a primary goal. From the vantage point of the reader, one can easily view the sample interaction in terms of an influence goal and a social support goal. But breaking the conversation into two neat pieces may not be justified. Do we need to posit the existence of an information-acquisition goal to explain turn 07? Or, is turn 07 better understood as a point in the conversation that lacks a primary goal but represents a transition from one primary goal to another? In its current formulation, the GPA model does not provide a definitive answer to these questions. Indeed, rather than answer by theoretical decree, the best means of addressing this question may be through the interplay of theory and data.

Conclusion

This chapter presented a brief description of the workings of the GPA model, as well as answers to some questions that are sometimes raised about it. Like all current theories, the GPA model is an incomplete framework for understanding the complexities of human communication behavior. Nonetheless, it achieves many of the goals that a theory should accomplish. It provides traction on difficult conceptual issues, offers guidance for empirical research projects, and explains how and why individuals attempt to influence one another. By these standards, the GPA model has considerable utility.

Notes

1. Which is not to say that primary goals are invariably successful at reorienting and unifying these subsystems.

2. These were called "interaction goals" in Dillard (1990a, 1990b). Because that phrase has taken on a broader meaning in the current literature, it seemed advisable to choose an alternative label. "Interaction goals are states of affairs that individuals want to attain/maintain through talk" (Wilson, 1997, p. 22).

3. The 1990 version of the theory conceptualized these more narrowly as "arousal management goals." Affect management is now preferable insofar as it recognizes the multidimensional and multifunctional nature of feelings.

4. Certainly one can conceive of plans at many hierarchical levels different from the two offered here, and it may prove useful to do so depending on one's research question. Thus far, two levels have been sufficient for advancing research on interpersonal influence.

5. Although understanding these processes may be important, they are not the focus of the GPA model. Advancing our understanding of the role of these lower-level processes is left to those investigators who find them interesting (e.g., Greene, 1997).

6. Of course, any relevant secondary goals that were compatible with the primary goal would work against the set of relevant, incompatible secondary goals.

7. I have taken some small liberty with Schrader's (1999) data in this interpretation. The correlation between explicitness and competence is $-.10$ in the problem-solving cluster, which is not significant at $p < .05$. However, neither is it significantly different from the $-.18$ correlation in the high-stakes cluster. To my eye, it appears most meaningful to break the explicitness results into high- and low-complexity clusters. However, this move is not fully supported by the significance tests.

8. Of course, this is an oversimplification. In reality, individuals could change their goals or plans several times *within* a conversational turn. While there may be interesting possibilities to be explored in this regard, adopting this more rapid and more microscopic position is ill advised, because it turns attention away from what we seek to study: communication.

References

Austin, J. T., & Vancouver, J. B. (1996). Goal constructs in psychology: Structure, process, and content. *Psychological Bulletin, 120,* 338–375.

Berger, C. R. (1997). *Planning strategic interaction: Attaining goals through communicative action.* Mahwah, NJ: Erlbaum.

Blum-Kulka, S. (1987). Indirectness and politeness in requests: Same or different? *Journal of Pragmatics, 11,* 131–146.

Bratman, M. E. (1987). *Intentions, plans, and practical reason.* Cambridge, MA: Harvard University Press.

Brown, P., & Levinson, S. (1987). *Politeness: Some universals in language usage.* Cambridge: Cambridge University Press.

Cody, M. J., Canary, D. J., & Smith, S. W. (1994). Compliance-gaining goals: An inductive analysis of actor's goal types, strategies, and successes. In J. Wiemann & J. Daly (Eds.), *Communicating strategically.* Hillsdale, NJ: Erlbaum.

Cohen, C. E. (1981). Goals and schemata in person perception: Making sense from the stream of behavior. In N. Cantor & J. F. Kihlstrom (Eds.), *Personality, cognition, and social interaction* (pp. 45–68). Hillsdale, NJ: Erlbaum.

Dillard, J. P. (1989). Types of influence goals in close relationships. *Journal of Personal and Social Relationships, 6,* 293–308.

Dillard, J. P. (1990a). A goal-driven model of interpersonal influence. In J. P. Dillard (Ed.), *Seeking compliance: The production of interpersonal influence messages* (pp. 41–56). Scottsdale, AZ: Gorsuch Scarisbrick.

Dillard, J. P. (1990b). The nature and substance of goals in tactical communication. In M. Cody & M. McLaughlin (Eds.), *The psychology of tactical communication* (pp. 70–90). Clevedon, UK: Multilingual Matters.

Dillard, J. P. (1997). Explicating the goal construct: Tools for theorists. In J. O. Greene (Ed.), *Message production: Advances in communication theory* (pp. 47–69). Mahwah, NJ: Erlbaum.

Dillard, J. P., & Harkness, C. D. (1992). Exploring the affective impact of influence messages. *Journal of Language and Social Psychology, 11,* 179–191.

Dillard, J. P., Henwood, K., Giles, H., Coupland, N., & Coupland, J. (1990). Compliance gaining young and old: Beliefs about influence in different age groups. *Communication Reports, 3,* 84–91.

Dillard, J. P., & Kinney, T. A. (1994). Experiential and physiological responses to interpersonal influence. *Human Communication Research, 20,* 502–528.

Dillard, J. P., Kinney, T. A., & Cruz, M. G. (1996). Influence, appraisals, and emotions in close relationships. *Communication Monographs, 63,* 105–130.

Dillard, J. P., Palmer, M. T., & Kinney, T. A. (1995). Relational inference in an influence context. *Human Communication Research, 21,* 331–353.

Dillard, J. P., & Schrader, D. C. (1998). On the utility of the goals-plans-action sequence: Commentary reply. *Communication Studies, 49,* 300–304.

Dillard, J. P., Segrin, C., & Harden, J. M. (1989). Primary and secondary goals in the interpersonal influence process. *Communication Monographs, 56,* 19–38.

Dillard, J. P., & Solomon, D. H. (2000). Conceptualizing context in message-production research. *Communication Theory, 10,* 167–175.

Dillard, J. P., Wilson, S. R., Tusing, K. J., & Kinney, T. A. (1997). Politeness judgments in personal relationships. *Journal of Language and Social Psychology, 16,* 297–325.

Greene, J. O. (1997). A second generation action assembly theory. In J. O. Greene (Ed.), *Message production: Advances in communication theory* (pp. 151–170). Mahwah, NJ: Erlbaum.

Hacker, W. (1985). Activity: A fruitful concept in industrial psychology. In M. Frese & J. Sabini (Eds.), *Goal directed behavior: The concept of action in psychology* (pp. 262–284). Hillsdale, NJ: Erlbaum.

Hample, D., & Dallinger, J. M. (1998). On the etiology of the rebuff phenomenon: Why are persuasive messages less polite after rebuffs? *Communication Studies, 49,* 305–321.

Hatfield, E., Utne, M. K., & Traupmann, J. (1979). Equity theory and intimate relationships. In R. L. Burgess & T. L. Huston (Eds.), *Social exchange in developing relationships* (pp. 99–133). New York: Academic Press.

Hobbs, J. R., & Evans, D. A. (1980). Conversation as planned behavior. *Cognitive Science, 4,* 213–232.

Honeycutt, J. M., Cantrill, J. G., Kelly, P., & Lambkin, D. (1998). How do I love thee? Let me consider my options: Cognition, verbal strategies, and the escalation of intimacy. *Human Communication Research, 25,* 39–63.

Ifert, D. E., & Roloff, M. E. (1994). Anticipated obstacles to compliance: Predicting their presence and expression. *Communication Studies, 45,* 120–130.

Kanwisher, N., Driver, J., & Machado, L. (1995). Spatial repetition blindness is modulated by selective attention to color and shape. *Cognitive Psychology, 29,* 303–337.

Kellermann, K. (1988, March). *Understanding tactical choice: Metagoals in conversation.* Paper presented at the Temple University Discourse Conference, Philadelphia, PA.

Klinger, E. (1985). Missing links in action theory. In M. Frese & J. Sabini (Eds.), *Goal-directed behavior* (pp. 311–321). Hillsdale, NJ: Erlbaum.

Kipnis, D., Schmidt, S. M., & Wilkinson, I. (1980). Intraorganizational influence tactics: Explorations in getting one's way. *Journal of Applied Psychology, 65,* 440–452.

Langer, E. J., Blank, A., & Chanowitz, B. (1978). The mindlessness of ostensibly thoughtful action: The role of "placebic" information in interpersonal interaction. *Journal of Personality and Social Psychology, 36,* 635–642.

Leech, G. (1983). *Principles of pragmatics.* London: Longman.

Maruff, P., Danckert, J., Camplin, G., & Currie, J. (1999). Behavioral goals constrain the selection of visual information. *Psychological Science, 10,* 522–525.

Meyer, J. A. (1997). Cognitive influences on the ability to address interaction goals. In J. O. Greene (Ed.), *Message production: Advances in communication theory* (pp. 71–90). Mahwah, NJ: Erlbaum.

Miller, G. A., Galanter, E., & Pribram, K. H. (1960). *Plans and the structure of behavior.* New York: Holt.

Newell, S. E., & Stutman, R. K. (1988). The social confrontation episode. *Communication Monographs, 55,* 266–285.

O'Keefe, B. J., & Shepherd, G. J. (1987). The pursuit of multiple objectives in face-to-face persuasive interactions: Effects of construct differentiation on message organization. *Communication Monographs, 54,* 396–419.

Paulson, G. D., & Roloff, M. E. (1997). The effect of request form and content on constructing obstacles to compliance. *Communication Research, 24,* 261–290.

Roloff, M. E., Janiszewski, C. A., McGrath, M. A., Burns, C. S., & Manrai, L. A. (1988). Acquiring resources from intimates: When obligation substitutes for persuasion. *Human Communication Research, 14,* 364–396.

Rule, B. G., Bisanz, G. L., & Kohn, M. (1985). Anatomy of a persuasion schema: Targets, goals, and strategies. *Journal of Personality and Social Psychology, 48,* 1127–1140.

Saeki, M., & O'Keefe, B. J., (1994). Refusals and rejections: Designing messages to achieve multiple goals. *Human Communication Research, 21,* 67–102.

Samp, J. A., & Solomon, D. H. (1999). Communicative responses to problematic events in close relationships II: The influence of five facets of goals on message features. *Communication Research, 26,* 193–239.

Sanders, R. E., & Fitch, K. L. (2001). The actual practice of compliance-seeking. *Communication Theory, 11,* 263–289.

Schrader, D. C. (1999). Goal complexity and the perceived competence of interpersonal influence messages. *Communication Studies, 50,* 188–202.

Schrader, D. C., & Dillard, J. P. (1998). Goal structures and interpersonal influence. *Communication Studies, 49,* 276–293.

Shepherd, G. J. (1998). The trouble with goals. *Communication Studies, 49,* 294–299.

Tipper, S. P., Weaver, B., & Houghton, G. (1994). Behavioural goals determine inhibitory mechanisms in selective attention. *Quarterly Journal of Experimental Psychology, 47A,* 809–840.

Tracy, K., & Coupland, N. (1990). Multiple goals in discourse: An overview of issues. *Journal of Language and Social Psychology, 9,* 1–13.

Tracy, K., & Tracy, S. J. (1998). Rudeness at 911: Reconceptualizing face and face attack. *Human Communication Research, 25,* 225–251.

von Cranach, M., Machler, E., & Steiner, V. (1985). The organisation of goal-directed action: A research report. In Ginsburg, G. P., Brenner, M., & von Cranach, M. (Eds.), *Discovery strategies in the psychology of action* (pp. 19–61). London: Academic Press.

Waldron, V. R. (1990). Constrained rationality: Situational influences on information acquisition plans and tactics. *Communication Monographs, 57,* 184–201.

Waldron, V. R. (1997). Toward a theory of interactive planning. In J. O. Greene (Ed.), *Message production: Advances in communication theory* (pp. 195–220). Mahwah, NJ: Erlbaum.

Wilson, E. V., & Zigurs, I. (2001). Interpersonal influence goals and computer-mediated communication. *Journal of Organizational Computing and Electronic Commerce, 11,* 59–76.

Wilson, S. R. (1990). Development and test of a cognitive rules model of interaction goals. *Communication Monographs, 57,* 81–103.

Wilson, S. R. (1995). Elaborating the cognitive rules model of interaction goals: The problem of accounting for individual differences in goal formation. In B. R. Burleson (Ed.), *Communication yearbook 18* (pp. 3–26). Thousand Oaks, CA: Sage.

Wilson, S. R., Aleman, C., & Leatham, G. (1998). The identity implications of influence goals: A revised analysis of face-threatening acts and application to seeking compliance with same-sex friends. *Human Communication Research, 25,* 64–96.

Wilson, S. R., Kim, M.-S., & Meischke, H. (1991/1992). Evaluating Brown and Levinson's politeness theory: A revised analysis of directives and face. *Journal of Language and Social Interaction, 25,* 215–252.

Wiseman, R. L., & Schenck-Hamlin, W. J. (1981). A multidimensional scaling validation of an inductively-derived set of compliance-gaining strategies. *Communication Monographs, 48,* 251–270.

12

Sequential Request Compliance Tactics

Robert B. Cialdini and Rosanna E. Guadagno

Have you ever gone to a store or auto sales lot with the intent of purchasing the "bargain" item that was advertised in the Sunday paper? If your experiences are anything like ours, when you arrived, the salesperson may have told you that the bargain item was sold out, but that a similar item at a higher price was available for you to purchase instead. Many people in such a situation find themselves buying the more expensive item and, once they walk out of the store, end up wondering why. The reason most people buy the more expensive replacement item is that they have already committed themselves to the purchase. As you will read later in this chapter, commitment can be a very powerful motivating force. The above scenario is an example of a compliance tactic called *bait and switch,* wherein an individual commits to purchasing one item, only to have it replaced by another, more expensive one.

Often we find ourselves purchasing items or agreeing with requests made by friends, family, or salespersons when we may not have initially planned to do so. In these situations, the individuals around us may have used persuasive appeals to gain our *compliance.* Compliance occurs when an individual behaves or responds in a particular way because another individual is encouraging him or her to do so (Cialdini & Trost, 1998). For instance, individuals who end up purchasing the more expensive item as a result of the bait-and-switch procedure are complying with the salesperson's suggestion. At some point, they acquiesce. There are many types of compliance tactics that can be used to increase the likelihood that we will agree with another's request. The focus of this chapter will be on sequential compliance tactics, that is, tactics that require more than one step (usually two) to be effective. These types of tactics can be successful in gaining compliance.

However, before we move on to a discussion of why compliance tactics work, we need to introduce a few terms that we will use throughout the chapter. Because most sequential request compliance tactics are two-step maneuvers, there are common terms for each request or stage in the process. The first stage of a sequential request tactic is usually referred to as either *the initial* or *first request*. The next request or stage in the process is usually referred to as the *second* or *target request*, because it is the request on which the influence agent actually hopes to gain compliance. The first request is what helps to increase the likelihood of the target of influence acquiescing to the target request. This can occur for a number of reasons; the initial request may be too large or may be something that increases the target's commitment to the course of action.

Another set of terms that you will see throughout this chapter refers to the individuals involved in the attempt to gain compliance. First, the *target,* or target of influence, refers to the person at whom the attempt to gain compliance is directed. For instance, in the hypothetical example in the introduction, you would have been the target of influence. Next, the influence practitioner, or *agent* of influence, is the individual who makes the influence attempt—the one who wishes to induce compliance in others. In the example above, the salesperson was the influence practitioner. Now let us move on to answer the question of why influence tactics work.

Why Do Compliance Tactics Work?

Cialdini (2001) was interested in determining why influence practitioners such as salespersons are so successful in gaining compliance from their targets. To examine this question, he observed the methods used by sales practitioners in real situations such as advertising, fund-raising, recruiting, and sales. Based on his observations, Cialdini determined that six key principles of influence underlie most influence attempts: scarcity, reciprocity, consistency/commitment, authority, social proof, and similarity/liking.

When scarcity is used, an item or opportunity is presented as something that is not readily available, either due to low quantity or because the offer is only good for a short period of time. For example, when the Mazda Miata was first introduced, it was released in such low quantities that the cars usually sold for several thousand dollars over the manufacturer's suggested retail price. Because the Miata was both new and hard to get, its scarcity increased its desirability. The second principle, reciprocity, describes influence tactics that work because the influence practitioner has done a favor for or made a concession to the target of influence. Targets are more likely to agree with the request because they feel they "owe" the influence practitioner. Anyone who has received free address labels with a request for a charitable donation should be familiar with these types of tactics. Consistency-and-commitment tactics work because the influence practitioner is able to get the target to commit to the transaction before the practitioner alters the deal. The example of the bait-and-switch tactic mentioned at the beginning of this chapter illustrates this type of tactic. Next, experts can influence us because they are authorities on a topic. For instance, Senator Bob Dole is successful at selling Viagra because he has experienced prostate cancer. Social proof is most successful in situations where we look to others to guide our actions. We choose to engage in a behavior because we believe that others would do the same thing in that situation. Car salespeople take advantage of this when they emphasize how popular a particular car is. Internet service providers use this tactic when they emphasize the large number of subscribers to their service. Finally, similarity and liking tactics emphasize that the influence agent is likable or similar to us. For instance, a salesperson may state that he or she shares the same hobbies or drives the same car as a potential customer. The mention of this similarity is intended to make a customer more likely to purchase from the influence practitioner.

The majority of sequential request compliance tactics fit into one of two categories from the list above: commitment and consistency or reciprocity. We will start off with a discussion of commitment-and-consistency tactics and then move on to reciprocal tactics. In each section we will cover the basic mechanism of each tactic, factors that affect the likelihood of its success in gaining compliance, and defenses against each type of tactic.

Commitment-and-Consistency Tactics

Have you ever seen an advertisement encouraging you to enter a contest concerning a certain household product? In such contests, individuals are asked to write a short testimonial on the product to explain why they use a certain laundry detergent or toothpaste. The prize for the contest is frequently a one-year supply of the product. Well, that kind of contest sounds like a good deal for the winner, but the manufacturer of the product will have to give away a large quantity of its product. Why would the manufacturer want to give away money that way? In actuality the manufacturer has found a subtle way to increase sales: By asking consumers to extol the virtues of the product, the manufacturer is ensuring that many people will make a public commitment to the product. This written and public commitment will increase most individuals' loyalty to the brand. So while giving away a one-year supply to one winner, the company is actually gaining thousands of customers who will become more loyal and more likely to purchase the product consistently than before the contest. And, commitment can be a powerful motivating force.

A number of sequential request compliance tactics work by making the targets of influence feel committed to an action or a product. We will review three of these tactics in the sections below. Table 12.1 presents the basic mechanism of each tactic: the low-ball procedure, the foot-in-the-door technique, and the bait-and-switch tactic. Although each tactic is different in the way it is implemented, all rely on the same underlying mechanisms to make them successful: *commitment* and *consistency*.

The Low-Ball Procedure

The reason the second author of this chapter studies social influence has to do with the low-ball procedure. During her senior year of college, she bought a car. At the time it seemed like a good deal. Two weeks later, however, the salesperson from the dealership called to say there was an error in the loan paperwork and that she had to return the car or pay an additional $2,000 for it. Of course she chose to pay the money, because she was already committed to the car and had already shown it to her friends and family. It was only after this stressful predicament was over that she realized she had never received an updated loan statement and that the extra cash was never recorded on any of the paperwork. It was then that she realized she had been duped.

TABLE 12.1   *Commitment-Based Sequential Request Compliance Tactics*

Tactic	Initial Request		Second Request	
	How Initial Commitment Is Created	*Example*	*How the Initial Commitment Is Used to Trap the Target into a Less Desirable Outcome*	*Example*
Low-ball	Getting the target to agree to a specific desirable arrangement.	Negotiating a deal to purchase a car.	The terms of the agreement change to be less advantageous for the target.	Changing the deal due to an error in the financial paperwork so that it costs more.
Bait-and-Switch	Urging the target to commit to a certain behavior or action.	Getting the target to commit to purchasing a new stereo based on a low advertised price.	Making the behavior or action unadvisable or unavailable and proposing an alternative that is not as desirable an outcome for the target.	Informing the target that the desired stereo is sold out and offering an alternative, more expensive one.
Foot-in-the-Door	Asking the target to agree with a small request.	Getting the target to sign a petition advocating government aid to a group in need.	Following up with a request for more assistance on a (usually) related request.	Asking the target to volunteer time or donate money to help the same group.

This experience is one example of what social scientists refer to as the *low-ball technique*. This technique is used when an individual commits to one outcome, in this case purchasing the car for a specific price. Once the commitment has been made, the deal changes and becomes less desirable than the arrangement to which the target initially committed (i.e., the price on the car is raised). However, because of the existing commitment, many people will still agree to it. Thus, in the low-ball technique, an individual agrees to the first request because it is easy to agree to, or is advantageous to him or her. When the opportunity or deal changes to become less desirable, most individuals already feel committed and follow through on that commitment.

Cialdini, Cacioppo, Bassett, and Miller (1978) were first to demonstrate the low-ball technique. In their study, research participants were called and asked to participate in an experiment. Participants in the control group were told that the experiment was scheduled for a very undesirable time: 7:00 A.M. In contrast, participants in the low-ball group were first asked to participate in the experiment and then, once they agreed, were informed that it would take place at 7:00 A.M. As can be seen in figure 12.1, the initial commitment to the first request had the desired effect: Participants in the low-ball condition agreed to participate at a much higher rate than did control participants (56 percent to 24 percent respectively). In addition, the commitment made by the low-balled participants had a

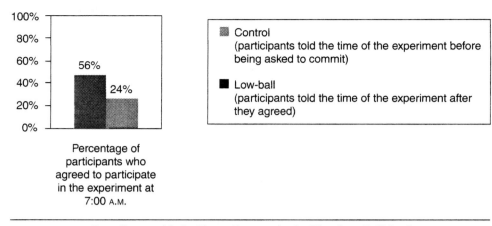

FIGURE 12.1   *Compliance with the Target Request in the First Low-Ball Study*

Source: Cialdini et al., 1978.

powerful impact on actual behavior: 95 percent of participants in the low-ball condition who agreed to participate actually showed up for the experiment.

Why is the low-ball technique so successful? It works because once someone agrees to a business deal or course of action, that individual feels committed and will stay committed to that course of action even when the details change. In addition, the initial request is usually perceived as a "good deal" by the target, and this perception helps enhance his or her commitment.

As the initial demonstration of the procedure presented above clearly illustrates, the low-ball approach is a powerful compliance tactic. However, a number of factors affect the likelihood of its success. For instance, additional research has indicated that the degree of commitment between the target and the influence agent plays an important role in the success of this technique. For example, Burger and Petty (1981) demonstrated that this tactic did not work when different people administered the first request and the target request. In addition, Burger and Cornelius (2001) demonstrated that both public and verbal commitment is necessary for this technique to work. In their study, participants who were interrupted before they had the opportunity to commit to the initial request were significantly less likely to agree to the less desirable target request than were participants in the low-ball condition. Additional research indicates that targets must also feel that they made the initial commitment freely in order to be successfully low-balled (Cialdini et al., 1978).

Bait and Switch

At the start of this chapter, we presented an example of the next consistency-based compliance tactic we will examine: *the bait-and-switch* technique. We are sure many people can remember instances when they have been drawn into a store after spotting the 40 percent off tag on a nice camera or pair of shoes. However, if your experiences have been anything like ours, you have probably been disappointed because the camera was out of stock or the bargain shoes were available only in extremely large or small sizes. In most situations like these, the typical sales associate is only too happy to recommend an alternative shoe or camera that is very similar in appearance or features but is pricier. And if you are anything like us, you may have purchased the alternative item even though it was not what you went into the store for in the first place. If so, you have experienced the bait-and-switch procedure.

The tactic works by getting a target to commit to an item or a course of action. Then, once the commitment has been made or the "bait" taken, the influence practitioner alters the situation so that the item or action that the target has committed to is no longer available. The influence practitioner then offers an alternative option or course of action that is not nearly as good a deal for the target. Many targets in this situation will accept the alternative item or action even though they would not have done so if that had been the initial option.

Although this tactic has been around in the sales industry for quite a while, the initial published experimental demonstration of the bait-and-switch tactic was authored by the French social psychologists Joule, Gouilloux, and Weber (1989). They referred to it as the *lure* procedure. In their study, they recruited participants to take part in a study on film clips—a very interesting experiment in the eyes of the typical research participant. This was the bait. Once willing participants arrived to take part in the experiment, participants in the lure condition were told that the experiment had been canceled. Then they were switched: They were offered an alternative experiment in which their task would be to memorize lists of numbers—a very boring task in comparison to the original experiment. The results attested to the success of this compliance tactic. Among a control group of participants who were just asked to do the number-matching task, only 15 percent agreed, whereas 47 percent in the bait-and-switch condition agreed to be in the memory study.

Why does it work? Much like the low-ball procedure, the bait-and-switch technique works by getting an initial commitment to comply, which makes people more likely to accept a less attractive arrangement than they ordinarily would have accepted. It is different from the low-ball tactic in that the outcome the target commits to is not altered to become something less desirable; rather, it is replaced by a *different* outcome that is less desirable than the one initially committed to. For example, a victim of the low-ball procedure would agree to buy the same car for a higher price, while a victim of the bait-and-switch procedure would agree to buy a different, more expensive, car.

Foot-in-the-Door Technique

A few years ago, while walking through a shopping mall, the second author was stopped by a clean-cut young man who asked her a few short questions about her household demographics. Once she answered his questions, he thanked her for her time. Then, before she could walk away, he asked her to provide more information about her family demographics and consumption habits in a longer interview. An hour later, she walked out of this young man's office carrying with her a box of "fire-roasted grill snaps" that she had agreed to taste-test for a week and wondered what had hit her. Her family tried the crackers, and a week later she participated in a 20-minute telephone interview to provide feedback on the taste test. She was amazed that agreeing to answer a few short questions had led her to commit to a course of action that she would have initially refused if she had been informed of what the clean-cut young man really wanted from her in the first place. This is an example of the next consistency-based compliance tactic, the foot-in-the-door (FITD) technique.

Essentially, the FITD technique works by asking for something small—usually a minor commitment—and building upon that commitment to gain compliance with a larger, usually related request. When two social psychologists, Jonathan Freedman and Scott Fraser (1966), initially investigated the FITD technique, they found that once an individual agrees to the small request, he or she is more likely to agree to a related, larger request. They labeled this effect the foot-in-the-door technique because the small request is like the proverbial foot in the doorway that makes it hard for a potential customer to close the door on a salesperson.

In their initial demonstration of the FITD effect, Freedman and Fraser (1966, study 2) asked participants either to sign a petition or to place a small card in a window in their home or car. The petition and the card advocated one of two prosocial messages: to keep California beautiful or to support safe driving. Both requests were easy to agree to. After all, most people living in California believe in safe driving, and most Californians want to keep California beautiful. Approximately two weeks after complying with the initial request, participants were contacted by a second experimenter and asked to place a large sign advocating safe driving in their front yard. Although initial acceptance of the small card that advocated safe driving led to the greatest amount of compliance with the large request, all experimental conditions generated more compliance than the control group.

Why Is the FITD Technique Effective in Gaining Compliance? Freedman and Fraser explained their results in terms of self-perception. They concluded that compliance with a small initial request for a public service action causes a change in the individual's self-perception. This small act of compliance produces a change in self-concept in which the person "becomes in his own eyes, the kind of person who does this sort of thing" (p. 201). Thus, the initial act of compliance with a small request, a request virtually no one would refuse, makes an individual more likely to agree to a later, larger request—particularly if it is similar to the initial request.

Other researchers have challenged this explanation of the FITD technique both because they suggest alternative explanations seem more likely and because the FITD technique has been notoriously difficult to replicate. In a literature review on the FITD effect, DeJong (1979) concluded that support for the self-perception theory is weak. Similarly, in a meta-analysis of 120 FITD studies, Beaman, Cole, Preston, Klentz, and Steblay (1983) concluded that the FITD is an effective compliance technique, but that the size of the effect is smaller than was suggested by the results of the Freedman and Fraser study. The results of the meta-analysis by Beaman and colleagues also suggest that support for the self-perception theory to explain the FITD effect is inconsistent. In addition, in another FITD study, Gorassini and Olson (1995) measured participants' self-perceived helpfulness between the first and second requests. Although participants in the FITD condition perceived themselves as more helpful than participants in the control condition, this greater perception of helpfulness did not predict compliance with the second request. In sum, much research on the FITD has indicated that other factors beyond self-perception may well influence susceptibility to it.

Factors That Affect the Likelihood of an FITD Effect. More recently, Burger (1999) conducted a meta-analysis on FITD tactics and found support for a number of factors that influence whether an attempted FITD tactic will be effective in increasing compliance. A detailed listing of many of the factors appears in table 12.2. The first, as we have already mentioned, is self-perception. Individuals who see the act of complying with the first request as indicative of the type of person they are will be more likely to comply with the target request than will individuals who do not experience this self-perception. For instance, Burger and Caldwell (2001) reported that a monetary reward for compliance with the first request reduces compliance with the second request. They explained this finding as indicating that a monetary reward leads people to believe that they agreed to the first request for the money, not because of the kind of people they were. In addition, Burger and Guadagno (in press) reported that individuals who have a clear or high self-concept are more susceptible to the FITD than are individuals who have a less clear sense

TABLE 12.2 *Factors That Impact the Likelihood of a Successful FITD Attempt*

Psychological Process	Potential Effect on the FITD	Example
Self-perception	Enhances the effect	If an individual sees him- or herself as the type of person who engages in actions such as the initial request, he or she will be more likely to agree with the target request because of that self-perception.
Reciprocity	Reduces the effect	Individuals who comply with the initial request because the requestor has done them a favor are unlikely to comply with the target request because they perceive the favor as already having been returned.
Consistency needs	May reduce or enhance the effect	Individuals for whom consistency is not a core need are unlikely to be susceptible to the FITD. However, when consistency is a core need, the opposite is true.
Attributions	May reduce or enhance the effect	If individuals attribute their compliance to an external factor (e.g., payment for complying), an FITD effect is unlikely to occur. However, if individuals attribute their compliance to an internal factor (they are helpful by nature), they are more likely to comply.
Involvement	Enhances the effect	The greater the involvement required to complete the initial request, the more likely individuals are to comply with the target request.

Source: Adapted in part from Burger, 1999.

of self, because such individuals are more likely to alter their self-concepts when reacting to new information than are individuals with less clear self-concepts. Thus, after complying with the first request in the FITD manipulation, individuals with high self-concepts are more likely than those with low self-concepts to experience the resulting change in self-perception that will incline them to agree with the second request.

Self-perception, however, is only one factor affecting the likelihood of a successful FITD. For instance, according to Burger's (1999) meta-analysis, if targets comply with the initial request because of reciprocity norms, that is, because they think they owe the influence agent something, they are less likely to agree with the target request. The perceived reciprocity produces a boomerang effect, because the targets come to believe that they agreed with the initial request only to return a favor. For instance, if an individual received a free gift for signing a petition to change the speed limit (first request), he or she would be less likely to agree to attend a demonstration on the topic (target request) than if he or she had not received the free gift.

Individual differences in consistency needs also have an impact on the likelihood of success of the FITD effect. Cialdini, Trost, and Newsom (1995) suggested that individuals might actually differ in the amount of consistency they prefer. In their study, Cialdini and colleagues introduced a personality scale that measured individuals' *preference for consistency* (PFC). The PFC scale measures individual differences in the desire to be both internally and externally consistent on three separate but highly interrelated subscales: the preference for consistency within oneself, the preference to appear consistent to others, and the preference for others to be consistent. Individuals who score low on this scale may actually prefer to behave in an inconsistent manner. Conversely, individuals who score high on this scale consider consistency very important.

Cialdini and colleagues (1995, Study 1) conducted an FITD study, examining whether PFC level would have an impact on the success of an FITD manipulation. Specifically, they predicted that high-PFC individuals would be susceptible to the FITD and show the traditional increase in compliance after first agreeing to a small, related request. For low-PFC participants, they predicted no difference between the FITD and the control conditions because consistency was not important to them. To test this hypothesis, the researchers contacted experimental participants by telephone and asked them to answer three short questions about their television viewing habits (the first request). Next, all participants received the target request: to fill out a 50-item questionnaire on their television viewing habits and return it in two weeks. The results showed, as predicted, that high-PFC individuals (people for whom consistency is important) were more susceptible than the low-PFC participants to the FITD effect. Figure 12.2 presents a graphic representation of the results. Thus, high-PFC participants who agreed to a small request were more likely to agree to a second, larger request. Conversely, low-PFC participants were just as likely to agree to the second request whether or not they had agreed to the small request first. These results were interpreted to support the hypothesis that individual differences in PFC are one reason the FITD effect is difficult to replicate reliably. Additional data analyses revealed that the low-PFC participants displayed a relatively strong tendency to say yes regardless of condition. This finding suggests that low-PFC individuals tend to be interested in novel opportunities and experiences such as the chance to participate in an unknown survey about television viewing habits.

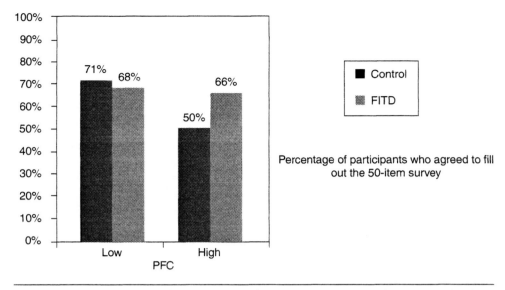

FIGURE 12.2   *Individual Differences in Compliance with the FITD Technique.* People with a low PFC are not susceptible to the tactic, whereas people with a high PFC show the traditional increase in compliance after first agreeing to a small initial request.

Source: Cialdini et al., 1995.

In a replication and expansion of the study by Cialdini and colleagues, Guadagno, Asher, Demaine, and Cialdini (2001, study 2) used the same method as in the previous study, with slightly modified FITD conditions. They found that for high-PFC individuals, reminding them of the concept of consistency between the first and second requests increased the extent of the FITD effect. For low-PFC individuals, however, reminding them of the concept of consistency had the opposite result, actually decreasing the FITD effect.

In addition to consistency needs, several other processes influence the likelihood of the FITD effect (Burger, 1999). For instance, the greater the action or involvement required to comply with the initial request, the greater the effectiveness of the FITD. Hansen and Robinson (1980), for example, reported a stronger effect when participants elaborated on their answers to questions than when they simply provided responses. Labeling the behavior as helpful also increases the likelihood of an FITD effect unless the target is low in PFC (Guadagno et al., 2001). Making the target request a continuation of the initial request also increases the effect. The many factors that affect the likelihood of a successful FITD make it one of the most difficult sequential compliance tactics to replicate reliably. Table 12.2 lists all of the factors that affect the likelihood of a successful FITD attempt.

Defense Against Commitment and Consistency Tactics

What can individuals do if they find themselves trapped by their own consistency and about to become a victim of the low-ball procedure, the bait-and-switch tactic, or the

FITD technique? Cialdini (2001) recommended two options, both based on the premise that consistency generally is a good thing unless it is foolish and rigid. Prospective targets of influence (e.g., most people) should learn to recognize both when a commitment and consistency tactic is being used on them and when they are engaging in such foolishly and rigidly consistent responses.

How can we tell the difference between healthy consistency and this perilous second variety? Sometimes when we are in a situation in which an influence agent is eliciting a foolishly consistent response from us, our instincts tell us that something is wrong and that we are being pressured to agree to a request with which we do not really want to comply. If this happens to you, we recommend that you inform the influence agent that complying with his or her request would be a foolish type of consistency that represents behavior in which you choose not to engage. A good way to judge the situation is to ask yourself whether you would make the same commitment if you could go back in time and make the initial choice knowing what you now know. If the answer is no, we suggest you refuse to comply with the influence agent's request.

Reciprocity-Based Sequential Request Compliance Tactics

While walking to class, have you ever been stopped by a friendly individual who offered you a free T-shirt or teddy bear if you would take the time to fill out a credit card application? Or, have you ever received free chocolate to entice you into a candy store? In either situation most of us have at some point in our lives found ourselves successfully influenced. We are influenced because we feel the need to "repay" the individual who has given us a "free" gift. This feeling stems from the *norm of reciprocity,* which states that it is appropriate for individuals to return favors (Gouldner, 1960). Although reciprocity is a prosocial behavior, influence practitioners can easily take advantage of this norm to induce compliance. The next two sequential request compliance tactics, the door-in-the-face and the that's-not-all-technique, work by using the norm of reciprocity against us. Each of these tactics is reviewed in the next section, while table 12.3 presents the basic mechanism of each.

The Door-in-the-Face Technique

Have you ever answered a knock on the door to find a salesperson asking you to buy 10 two-year magazine subscriptions for a total of over $350? For most of us, that is far too much money. Imagine you refused the request to buy the magazine subscriptions and the salesperson followed up by asking you to purchase a single two-year magazine subscription. This modified request seems so much more reasonable by comparison that you agree. As you shut your door, you immediately ask yourself why you just purchased a two-year subscription to *Modern Fishing* when you do not even fish. If you have ever had an encounter like this, you have experienced the door-in-the-face (DITF) technique.

In order for the DITF tactic to be successful, the influence practitioner has to come up with a request that is so large that most people would not even consider agreeing with

TABLE 12.3   *Reciprocity-Based Sequential Request Compliance Tactics*

Tactic	Initial Request		Second Request	
	How Reciprocity Is Initially Created	Example	How Reciprocity Is Used to Trap the Target into a Less Desirable Outcome	Example
Door-in-the-face	The target rejects an unreasonably large request from the influence agent.	Asking the target to spend five hours a week for the next two years doing volunteer work.	The influence agent concedes by making a second, smaller request, and the target feels normative pressure to reciprocate and agree to the concession.	Asking the target to spend one afternoon doing volunteer work.
That's-not-all	The influence agent offers to make a deal with the target.	Offering to sell someone a car for a certain price.	Before the target has a chance to respond, the influence agent sweetens the deal by offering more for the same price.	Adding a new CD changer to the offer without changing the price.

it. Once the target rejects the inordinately large request, the influence practitioner concedes and asks the target to agree to a smaller request. In this case, more people will agree with the second request than if they had been presented with that request initially. Most researchers believe that the concession on the part of the influence agent is essential for the DITF tactic to work. That is because the target feels normative pressure to reciprocate the concession of the target.

Cialdini, Cacioppo, Bassett, and Miller published the initial demonstration of the DITF technique in 1975. To examine the effectiveness of the technique, these experimenters approached students on a college campus and asked them to volunteer to chaperone juvenile delinquents on a daylong trip to the zoo on an upcoming Saturday. All participants received this request. For participants in the DITF condition, this seemingly large request followed an even larger one. Participants in the DITF condition were first asked to volunteer to counsel juvenile delinquents for two hours a week for two years. Once they refused to comply with this initial request, targets were then asked to volunteer for the trip to the zoo. As figure 12.3 shows, the results supported the effectiveness of the DITF: 50 percent of participants who received the request as part of the DITF technique agreed to chaperone the trip to the zoo, compared to 17 percent of participants who received only the target request.

In another DITF study, Cialdini and Ascanti (1976) demonstrated that this technique was more successful at getting individuals both to agree to donate and actually donate a pint of blood. That is, after refusing a request to donate a unit of blood every six weeks for two years, participants who then received a request to donate just one pint of blood were

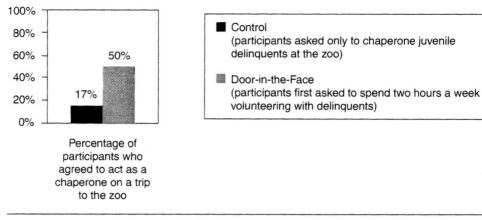

FIGURE 12.3 *Compliance with the Target Request in the First Door-in-the-Face Study*

Source: Cialdini et al., 1975.

more likely to agree than were those who had received only the request for one pint of blood. In addition, of those participants who agreed to donate blood, those in the DITF condition were more likely to follow through on their agreement and actually donate the blood. Thus, the DITF tactic has been shown to produce both verbal and behavioral compliance.

Another DITF study is of particular interest to students (Harai, Mohr, & Hosey, 1980). In it professors were the research participants. Initially, the professors were asked to spend two hours a week all term tutoring a student. The target request was to spend 15 to 20 minutes with the student. As predicted, compliance was much greater after the professors heard and refused the initial request: 79 percent agreed to spend 15 to 20 minutes with the student, compared with 59 percent of the control participants. Thus, one tip for students is that if you want some extra help or attention from your professor, ask for more time or help than you think you need. If your professor refuses, retreat to requesting a just adequate amount of help.

The That's-Not-All Technique

While flipping through the channels watching late-night television, have you ever stumbled across a commercial for a knife that slices wood and soda cans and is still sharp enough to slice a tomato? After demonstrating the knife's prowess, the announcer mentions that it is available for an all-time low price of $19.99. Then, after a short pause, the announcer says: "But wait, that's not all. For the same low price you'll also get a paring knife, a set of steak knives, and a knife sharpener." Getting additional items for the same price makes this seem like quite a bargain. At the end of the commercial, you may feel compelled to pick up the phone and order now. This is a classic example of the *that's-not-all* technique.

This technique works as follows: The influence practitioner offers the target a product for a specific price and then sweetens the deal by throwing in a "free" gift or lowering the price. It works because the anchor point is adjusted. An *anchor point* is an initial value that establishes the standard price of an item, telling us what the item is worth. Once the initial price point sets the value of an item, the free extra items or the lowered price make the second offer seem like a bargain in contrast to the first. Reciprocity is also a factor here. By lowering the price or providing additional items for the same price, the influence practitioner appears to be doing the target a favor, increasing the normative pressure on the target to reciprocate by making the purchase.

In the initial demonstration of this tactic, Burger (1986) gave research participants the opportunity to buy cupcakes at a university campus bake sale. They were offered a cupcake for a specific price, asked to "wait a second," and then told that the price also included a small bag of cookies. These participants turned out to be significantly more likely to buy the cupcake and cookies package than participants who were told at the outset that the price was for the cupcake and cookies package.

However, Burger, Reed, DeCesare, Rauner, and Rozilis (1999) demonstrated that the that's-not-all technique can boomerang if the initial request is too large. Participants in their study were offered free coffee mugs for a charitable donation of a specific amount. After a short pause, participants were told that the minimum donation to receive a mug had been reduced. Some of these participants heard that the minimum donation had been dropped from $10 to $3; others were told that it had been reduced from $5 to $3. Compared to a condition in which participants heard only about a $3 donation, the manipulation from $5 to $3 produced a significant increase in donations. However, the switch from $10 to $3 caused participants to give significantly less money than those in the control condition. The researchers reasoned that because the initial request was so large, it led to an immediate rejection of the request. The experimenters were therefore unable to alter the participants' anchor point, and the effectiveness of the that's-not-all manipulation was lost.

Defense Against Reciprocity Tactics

What can we do when a favor or concession turns out not to be the boon it was initially perceived to be, but instead merely the initial step in the DITF or the that's-not-all technique? The most extreme response would be to reject all favors and concessions that come our way to protect ourselves from the potential misuse of the norm of reciprocity. While that approach may successfully protect against this type of compliance tactic, it may also end up hurting the feelings of people who honestly meant to do us a favor or make a concession. We therefore recommend a more moderate response: to reframe the favor or concession as the trick that it actually is rather than see it as a true act of generosity. Once people recognize the trick for what it is, the normative pressure to comply by reciprocating with a concession or favor from their own end will dissipate (Cialdini, 2001). The authors use this defense every time they get "free" address labels in the mail along with a request for a charitable donation. They recognize that the labels are actually not a gift at all but merely a sales tool. While they may or may not choose to donate money to the charity, this choice is based on their opinion of the charitable cause, not the result of any pressure to comply and reciprocate because they received labels at no cost. Although this example is not a sequential request tactic, the same defense technique can be applied to situations in which the influence practitioner is using the DITF or the that's-not-all technique.

Conclusion

Sequential request compliance tactics require two steps to produce a successful influence attempt. The majority of influence tactics can be categorized into one of the six principles of influence: scarcity, reciprocity, consistency and commitment, authority, social proof, and similarity or liking. Most sequential request compliance procedures fall into one of two categories of influence: commitment and consistency or reciprocity. There are three main commitment-based procedures—the low-ball approach, the bait-and-switch technique, and the foot-in-the-door effect—and two reciprocity procedures—the door-in-the-face tactic and the that's-not-all technique. Although more research in this area is needed, social scientists are slowly learning more and more about the factors that compel us to say yes to a request when our initial inclination is to say no.

References

Beaman, A. L., Cole, C. M., Preston, M., Klentz, B., & Steblay, N. M. (1983). Fifteen years of the foot-in-the-door research: A meta-analysis. *Personality and Social Psychology Bulletin, 9,*181–196.

Burger, J. M. (1986). Increasing compliance by improving the deal: The that's-not-all technique. *Journal of Personality and Social Psychology, 51,* 277–283.

Burger, J. M. (1999). The foot-in-the-door compliance procedure: A multiple-process analysis and review. *Personality and Social Psychology Review, 3,* 303–325.

Burger, J. M., & Caldwell, D. F. (2001). *The effects of monetary incentives and labeling on the foot-in-the-door effect: Evidence for a self-perception process.* Manuscript submitted for publication.

Burger, J. M., & Cornelius, T. (2001). *Raising the price of agreement: Comparing the interruption and low-ball compliance procedures.* Manuscript submitted for publication.

Burger, J. M., & Guadagno, R. E. (in press). Self-concept clarity and the foot-in-the-door procedure. *Basic and Applied Social Psychology.*

Burger, J. M., & Petty, R. E., (1981). The low-ball compliance technique: Task or person commitment? *Journal of Personality and Social Psychology, 40,* 492–500.

Burger, J. M., Reed, M., DeCesare, K., Rauner, S., & Rozilis, J. (1999). The effects of initial request size on compliance: More about the that's not all technique. *Basic and Applied Social Psychology, 21* (3), 243–249.

Cialdini, R. B. (2001). *Influence: Science and practice* (4th ed.). New York: HarperCollins.

Cialdini, R. B., & Ascanti, K. (1976). Test of a concession procedure for inducing verbal, behavioral, and further compliance with a request to give blood. *Journal of Applied Psychology, 61,* 295–300.

Cialdini, R. B., Caccioppo, J. T., Bassett, R., & Miller, J. A. (1978). Low-ball procedure for producing compliance: Commitment then cost. *Journal of Personality and Social Psychology, 36,* 463–476.

Cialdini, R. B., & Trost, M. R., (1998) Social influence: Social norms, conformity, and compliance. In D. T. Gilbert and S. T. Fiske (Eds.), *The handbook of social psychology, vol. 2* (4th ed., pp. 151–192). Boston: McGraw-Hill.

Cialdini, R. B., Trost, M. R., & Newsom, J. T. (1995). Preference for consistency: The development of a valid measure and the discovery of surprising behavioral implications. *Journal of Personality and Social Psychology, 69,* 318–328.

Davis, B. P., & Knowles, E. S. (1999). A disrupt-then-reframe technique of social influence. *Journal of Personality and Social Psychology, 76,* 192–199.

DeJong, W. (1979). An examination of self-perception mediation of the foot-in-the-door effect. *Journal of Personality and Social Psychology, 37,* 2221–2239.

Freedman, J. L., & Fraser, S. C. (1966). Compliance without pressure: The foot-in-the-door technique. *Journal of Personality and Social Psychology, 4,* 195–202.

Gorassini, D. R., & Olson, J. M. (1995). Does self-perception change explain the foot-in-the-door effect? *Journal of Personality and Social Psychology, 69,* 91–105.

Gouldner, A. W. (1960). The norm of reciprocity: A preliminary statement. *American Sociological Review, 25,* 161–178.

Guadagno, R. E., Asher, T., Demaine, L. J., & Cialdini, R. B. (2001). When saying yes leads to saying no: Preference for consistency and the reverse foot-in-the-door effect. *Personality and Social Psychology Bulletin, 27,* 859–867.

Hansen, R. A., & Robinson, L. M. (1980). Testing the effectiveness of alternative foot-in-the-door manipulations. *Journal of Marketing Research, 17,* 359–364.

Harai, H., Mohr, D., & Hosey, K. (1980). Faculty helpfulness to students: A comparison of compliance techniques. *Personality and Social Psychology Bulletin, 6,* 373–377.

Joule, R. V., Gouilloux, F., & Weber, F. (1989). The lure: A new compliance procedure. *Journal of Social Psychology, 129,* 741–749.

13

A Review of Fear-Appeal Effects

Hyunyi Cho and Kim Witte

Since the beginning of recorded time and before, fear has been a powerful motivator. For example, the Bible abounds with fear appeals: ". . . but you must not eat from the tree of the knowledge of good and evil, for when you eat of it you will surely die" (Genesis 2: 17). Death in this passage is a key construct of the fear appeal, representing what researchers have termed "unfavorable consequences" (Hovland, Janis, & Kelley, 1953), "magnitude of noxiousness" (Rogers, 1975), or "severity" (Witte, 1992b). By describing the terrible consequences that may happen unless people do what the message recommends, fear appeals attempt to persuade them to change their attitudes and behaviors (Witte, 1992b).

The use of fear in persuasive appeals, however, is fraught with accounts of unsuccessful results and even adverse effects if used incorrectly (see Hale & Dillard, 1995). For example, despite the evocation of death, Eve ate the fruit from the tree, marking perhaps the earliest incidence of an unsuccessful fear appeal. Failed fear-appeal attempts can be unfortunate when you consider the consequences. Fortunately, current theories show how to develop fear appeals that work as well as how to avoid developing fear appeals that fail or even backfire (Rogers, 1983; Witte, 1992b, 1998; Witte, Meyer, & Martell, 2001).

For example, the Extended Parallel Process Model (EPPM), a fear appeal theory that integrates 40 years of research, clearly distinguishes the conditions under which fear appeals are likely to succeed from those under which fear appeals are prone to fail (Witte, 1992b, 1998; Witte et al., 2001). This theory will serve as the guiding framework for this chapter. In addition, this chapter acknowledges that despite the best theoretical advice, no messages produce uniform effects across a spectrum of audiences (McLeod & Becker, 1974). Because communication is a social process by definition (Berlo, 1960; Shepherd, 1999), the effects of fear appeals may differ from one audience to another as each processes messages differently. Fear is a universal emotion, but different audiences may hold different perceptions about what is scary and how scary a message is. The understanding of such audience differences is pivotal to the development of effective fear appeals. Therefore, the purpose of this chapter is to review the research on the effects of fear appeals on diverse audiences.

The Extended Parallel Process Model

Definitions

The two key constructs of the EPPM (Witte, 1992b, 1998; Witte et al., 2001) are perceived threat and perceived efficacy. First, imagine that you smoke two packs of cigarettes a day and have just heard an advertisement telling you that cigarettes cause cancer and that chewing nicotine gum can help you break your habit.

Perceived threat, the first construct of the EPPM, refers to whether you perceive you are in danger. It suggests that you perceive danger if you believe that (1) you are vulnerable to a threat and (2) that the threat is serious. In this case, if you consider that your chances of getting cancer from smoking are high (i.e., *perceived susceptibility*) and that cancer is a severe disease (i.e., *perceived severity*), the perceived threat is high.

Perceived efficacy, the second construct in the EPPM, refers to a person's perceptions about the response that is recommended in the fear appeal. In other words, what are your perceptions regarding the nicotine gum recommendation? Perceived efficacy comprises two elements; self-efficacy and response efficacy. *Perceived self-efficacy* refers to beliefs about whether or not you believe you can perform the recommended response, whereas *perceived response efficacy* refers to your beliefs about whether or not the recommended response works. For example, are you capable of chewing nicotine gum? If so, self-efficacy is high. Do you believe that the gum will break your habit? If so, response efficacy is high.

Appraisals and Processes

The EPPM suggests that upon exposure to a fear appeal, audiences will appraise it in one of the two ways and then respond in one of the three ways as a result of the appraisal (see figure 13.1). First, individuals appraise the threat. Is it severe? Are they susceptible to it? The greater the perceived threat, the greater the motivation to act. If no threat is perceived, *no action* is taken; the fear appeal is completely ignored, and the recommended response is not even evaluated. On the other hand, if the perceived severity of a threat is high and individuals feel susceptible to the serious threat, they are motivated to take action in any way possible. This leads to a second appraisal, in which individuals evaluate self-efficacy and response efficacy. It is this second appraisal that determines what type of action they will take.

If individuals believe that they are able to take some action that will effectively avert the threat—that is, if they have strong self-efficacy and response efficacy perceptions toward the recommended response—then they are motivated to *control the danger*. Danger control is a constructive response to fear. In the *danger control process*, individuals adopt the responses recommended in a fear appeal and make appropriate attitude, intention, or behavior changes. In the example above, they choose to chew nicotine gum.

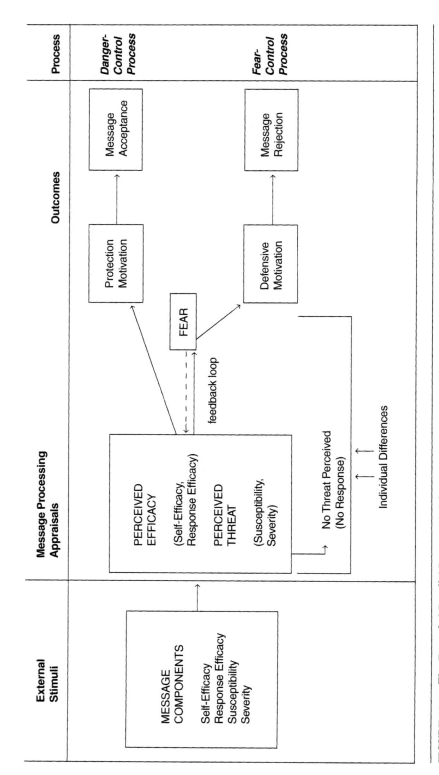

FIGURE 13.1 *The Extended Parallel Process Model*

If, on the other hand, individuals doubt their ability to carry out the recommended response effectively, or don't believe that the recommended response works, then they give up on trying to control the danger and instead attempt only to *control their fear*. Fear control is a nonconstructive or maladaptive response. In the *fear control process*, individuals engage in psychological defense mechanisms like defensive avoidance (avoiding thoughts about the threat), denial, or reactance. In this condition, the audience's responses to fear appeals are focused on controlling the unpleasant arousal of fear (hence the name "fear control process").

It is important to distinguish between *no effect*, which occurs when no threat is perceived, and *fear control effects*, which occur when perceived threat is high and perceived efficacy is low. Both result in rejection of the fear appeals' recommended responses; but the former calls for stronger fear appeals whereas the latter calls for the avoidance of fear appeals, that is, efficacy messages only.

The Role of Individual Differences

As shown above, the EPPM elucidates how audiences with different levels of perceived threat and efficacy may process a fear-appeal message differently and subsequently engage in either danger-control or fear-control processes. The EPPM delineates the role of individual differences in fear-appeal message processing, suggesting that individual differences affect one's perceptions of the message. For example, individual differences influence how a threat and a recommended response are perceived. A naturally anxious person may perceive a threat to be greater than it really is, whereas a naturally pessimistic person may perceive the recommended response to be less efficacious than it really is.

Once threat and efficacy are appraised, however, the same theoretical tenets apply. Specifically, threat motivates action, any kind of action, and perceived efficacy determines whether or not individuals engage in danger control or fear control.

In summary, individual differences can and do affect how a message is processed. Therefore, fear appeals must be designed with the nature and perceptions of the audience in mind, as the same fear appeal may have different levels of effectiveness and different kinds of effects among different audiences.

Fear-Appeal Effects: Message Topics

The EPPM has been tested in a variety of persuasion contexts, including fear appeal messages advocating preventive behavior against AIDS (Witte, 1992a), genital warts (Witte, Berkowitz, Cameron, & McKeon, 1998), tooth decay (Berkowitz, 1998), bulimia (Smalec, 1996), skin cancer (Stephenson & Witte, 1998), electromagnetic fields (McMahan, Witte, & Meyer, 1998), tractor-related injuries (Witte, Peterson, Vallabhan, Stephenson, Plugge, Givens, Todd, Becktold, Hyde, & Jarrett, 1993), and others.

Regardless of the study topic, messages that made individuals feel seriously at risk *and* made them believe that they could do something that would effectively avert the threat promoted the most attitude, intention, or behavior change (Witte & Allen, 2000). These results suggest that the most persuasive messages are those that promote perceptions of both high threat and high efficacy.

Fear-Appeal Effects: Audience Characteristics

Age

One demographic factor that has been shown to influence the effectiveness of fear appeals is the age of the audience. A number of meta-analyses of fear appeals have been conducted (Boster & Mongeau, 1984; Mongeau, 1998; Sutton, 1982; Witte & Allen, 2000). These meta-analyses have consistently reported that such appeals are more effective for older audiences than for younger audiences, suggesting that the interaction of age with the perceived fear influences the attitude change. That younger audiences tend to believe they are invulnerable to possibly serious consequences of their behavior and environmental events is well documented (e.g., Weinstein, 1980, 1982). Researchers attribute this tendency to younger audiences' lack of experience and exposure to unfavorable life events relative to older audiences (e.g., Mongeau, 1998).

Witte and colleagues (2000) suggested that the key to effective fear appeals in young audiences is finding out what they truly find threatening or scary. Death or terminal illnesses may not be scary to a teenager, but losing one's friends or facing changes in physical appearance could be. To create effective fear appeals for young audiences, message designers need to identify the kind of threats that the young can relate to.

For example, adolescents may view the prospect of developing lung cancer as a result of smoking as quite remote. A more immediate or pertinent threat may be a better vehicle to persuade them. Hansen and Malotte (1986) noted that although adolescent smokers tended to deny the ultimate severity of the danger of smoking, they readily acknowledged that as smokers they were at risk of being out of breath during exercise, presumably because of their own experience.

Schoenbachler and Whittler (1996) found that for adolescents, the social threat of rejection by peers was more effective than physical threats in a fear appeal, persuading them to change their attitudes and intentions toward drug use. Therefore, it is critical to find out exactly what is threatening to a target audience about a given topic. The perceived harm may be physical, social, economic, spiritual, and so on.

Anxiety

Some people are more chronically anxious than others. Trait anxiety refers to "one's characteristic level of anxiousness in response to a threat that leads one to react in either an avoidant or coping/sensitizing manner" (Witte & Morrison, 2000, p. 6). The very nature of the trait, characteristic anxiousness, has invited fear-appeal researchers' attention, because individuals with high levels of the trait may be particularly likely to be adversely affected by fear appeals (e.g., Boster & Mongeau, 1984; Dabbs & Leventhal, 1966; Dziokonsk & Weber, 1977; Goldstein, 1959; Hill & Gardner, 1980; Jepson & Chaiken, 1990; Witte & Morrison, 2000). Research to date reports that audiences with different levels of trait anxiety respond differently to fear appeals. However, the pattern of results remains inconsistent: Some studies have found that people with high rather than low levels of trait anxiety are persuaded by strong fear appeals. However, other research has shown that it is low- rather than high-anxiety persons who change their attitudes when exposed to strong fear appeals (Witte & Morrison, 2000).

One notable factor explains the inconsistency. Specifically, the terms used to describe individuals with high versus low trait anxiety have been mislabeled (Witte & Morrison, 2000). For instance, the terms that have been used to label the construct have included individuals high and low in trait anxiety, repressors/sensitizers, and copers/avoiders.[1] According to Witte and Morrison, researchers have long mistakenly grouped individuals high in trait anxiety with repressors/avoiders and individuals low in trait anxiety with sensitizers/copers (see Witte & Morrison, 2000, p. 8 for a full review). As a result, with this categorization, the pattern of results appears consistent: individuals high in trait anxiety and repressors/avoiders are less persuaded, whereas individuals low in anxiety individuals or sensitizers/copers are more persuaded as perceived fear increases.

However, Witte and Morrison (2000) pointed out that according to the scales used to measure these constructs, high-anxiety individuals are in fact sensitizers/copers and that low-anxiety individuals are repressors/avoiders. With this clarification, it became clear that there is no consistent pattern regarding trait anxiety and fear appeals' effects.

Overall, two major hypotheses have been tested as explanations for the influence of fear appeals on high- versus low-anxiety individuals. First, meta-analyses of fear-appeal studies (Boster & Mongeau, 1984; Mongeau, 1994) suggested that an interaction between fear and trait anxiety influences attitude, intentions, and behavior, to the extent that high-anxiety individuals were not influenced by strong fear appeals, whereas low-anxiety individuals were. Second, Witte and Morrison (2000), using the EPPM, hypothesized that trait anxiety (1) directly influences threat and efficacy perceptions and (2) indirectly influences fear-appeal outcomes as mediated by perceptions of threat and efficacy. Studies have been relatively unsupportive of any of these explanations.

For example, the results of Witte and Morrison's (2000) study indicated that trait anxiety is positively associated with perceived threat and efficacy. However, the fact that trait anxiety did not correlate with attitude, intentions, or behavior was consistent with the results of earlier research (e.g., Dziokonski & Weber, 1977; Goldstein, 1959; Wheatley & Oshikawa, 1970). Nor did trait anxiety influence fear-control responses of message derogation and perceived manipulation. Witte and Morrison (2000) also tested the other two proposed relationships described above (direct effects and interaction effects) and found no support for either of these hypotheses. Overall, it appears that the designers of fear-appeal messages do not have to worry about particularly anxious or particularly repressive audiences, as these variables appear to have little influence on how fear appeals affect people.

Fatalism

The possible role of fatalism in processing and responding to fear-appeal messages was first noted by Casey (1995). According to Casey, fatalism refers to "the belief that death is imminent and unavoidable, a fulfillment of a socially-constructed reality" (p. 20). In other words, we're all going to die someday and we can't do much about it. Although the effects of fear appeals on audiences with a fatalistic perspective have not been specifically investigated, other evidence suggests that this trait may well be a limiting factor.

For example, fatalism has been positively associated with attitudes and behaviors that increased the risk of occupational hazards (e.g., Suchman, 1967), traffic accidents (e.g., Kouabenan, 1998), and contraction of HIV/AIDS (e.g., Hardeman, Pierro, & Mannetti, 1997; Kalichman, Kelly, Morgan, & Rompa, 1997). Some research has shown that certain ethnic groups may hold greater fatalistic tendencies than others and thus may be less likely to engage in danger control processes for threats such as cancer (e.g., Domino, Fragoso, & Moreno, 1991; Straughan & Seow, 1995). Indeed, if a person considers such dangers are imminent and unavoidable, why bother trying to control them?

Research is needed to assess whether fatalism moderates responses to fear appeals. Studies to date suggest that understanding the role of perceived response efficacy may be important in persuading fatalistic audiences with fear appeals. For example, in focus groups of Chinese women regarding their attitudes toward mammography, the results revealed that "faith in medicine" may motivate them to adopt mammography, while fatalism works as a barrier to such adoption (Straughan & Seow, 1995). Special messages that provide hope and strong self-efficacy perceptions may also be needed to counteract the fatalistic perspective.

Finally, societal and structural inequities must be addressed to prevent fatalistic responses. For example, if condoms are promoted in rural Africa, they must be readily available at a reasonable cost. Similarly, if immunizations are promoted in poor, crime-ridden areas, low-cost clinics must be made safely available to clients.

Reactance

Psychological reactance (Brehm, 1966; Brehm & Brehm, 1981), a process that occurs when individuals perceive threats to freedom and freedom of choice, typically results in a boomerang effect whereby people react in a manner opposite to the message's recommendations. For example, a parent might try to scare a child into riding more slowly on her/his bicycle by saying, "You're going to knock your teeth out." This might, however, cause the child to ride even faster. Reactance was originally conceptualized as a state, but in recent research it is treated both as a trait and a state (Brehm & Brehm, 1981; Beutler, 1979; Frank, Jackson-Walker, Marks, Van Egeren, Loop, & Olson, 1998; Jahn & Lichstein, 1980; Rohrbaugh, Tennen, Press, & White, 1981).

Researchers have found that trait reactance is significantly associated with a host of personality variables that may predict resistance to persuasion (e.g., Dowd, Milne, & Wise, 1991; Dowd & Sanders, 1994; Dowd, Wallbrown, & Yesenosky, 1994). Specifically, trait reactance was "positively associated with such personality variables as autonomy, dominance, and independence, and negatively associated with such variables as affiliation, tolerance, interest in making a favorable impression, and nurturance—variables with implications for noncompliance" (Seibel & Dowd, 1999, p. 374).

The perceived threat construct in fear appeals is different from the threat construct in Reactance Theory. The former refers to perceived susceptibility and severity, whereas the latter refers to perceived threats to freedom. However, fear appeals may still be perceived as a form of a threat to behavioral freedom. Fear appeals commonly include behavioral recommendations such as dental hygiene practices (e.g., Janis & Feshbach, 1953), safe sex (e.g., Witte, 1992b), smoking cessation (e.g., Kleinot & Rogers, 1982; Rogers & Mewborn, 1976), and so on, all of which, to a varying degree, limit individuals' freedom (Cho, 2000).

Cho (2000) examined the effects of fear appeals in persuading both high- and low-reactance individuals to engage in behavior to prevent skin cancer. The results suggested that compared with low-reactance individuals, high-reactance individuals evaluate fear-appeal messages unfavorably by derogating them as a distortion of truth or mere manipulation. However, while high trait reactance may promote unfavorable evaluations, it does not appear to significantly affect compliance with fear-appeal recommendations in terms of attitudes, intentions, and behavior. In short, people high in trait reactance may not like fear appeals, but they are persuaded by them nonetheless.

Cho (2000) conjectured that there may be two possible reasons for these results. First, because behavioral recommendations are a key feature of fear appeals, fear appeals have the potential to elicit the perception of threatening the audience's behavioral freedom. However, according to Brehm (1966), one factor that determines the boomerang effects of reactance is the importance of the threatened freedom. For example, while a fear-appeal message recommending the use of sunscreen before going out in the sun in essence asks people to compromise their freedom, the reduction in freedom may be considered less important than the corresponding reduction in the risk of skin cancer. Or, the compromised freedom may be considered less serious than the risk of developing skin cancer.

A second premise of Reactance Theory is that boomerang effects of persuasion occur when individuals perceive that they have choices (Brehm, 1966). If a fear-appeal message clearly conveys to an audience that skin cancer is a serious threat and that a particular audience is vulnerable to it, members of that audience may no longer really consider going out in the sun without putting on sunscreen as a choice. Therefore, highly reactant individuals may not exhibit counterproductive attitudes, intentions, or behavior in response to the fear appeal.

A similar line of reasoning and conclusion was drawn by Bushman (1998). In his study examining the effects of warning labels on full-, reduced-, and non-fat food products, Bushman found that although subjects *preferred* full-fat cream cheese, they actually *chose to eat* reduced-fat cream cheese, because they believed that fatty foods increase a host of health risks.

More research needs to be done on the issue of reactance, because the two studies reviewed above may not have involved a great loss of behavioral freedom and therefore may have failed to produce a great deal of reactance. It could be important to examine highly reactant individuals' responses to fear appeals advocating the cessation of addictive behavior such as drinking or smoking.

Sensation Seeking

Perhaps the individual difference variable with the most significant implications for the effects of fear appeals is the trait of sensation seeking. One key aspect of sensation seeking is defiance of and a positive predisposition toward risky behaviors. Specifically, sensation seeking involves a willingness to experience consequences in order to experience sensation (Zuckerman, 1988, 1994). And sensation-arousing activities, such as drinking and drug use, tend to involve risk (Donohew, Lorch, & Palmgreen, 1991, 1998). Indeed, research to date indicates that the sensation seeker poses a special challenge to persuasion attempts using fear appeals.

Witte and Morrison (1995a) first investigated the effectiveness of fear appeals on high- and low-sensation seekers. The results of the study, advocating safe sex among high school and juvenile detention youth, indicated that high-sensation seekers were not persuaded by either high- or low-threat messages, whereas low-sensation seekers were persuaded by both high- and low-threat messages. Witte and Morrison (1995a) suspected that although high-threat messages may have captured high-sensation seekers' attention, they failed to persuade them. It appeared that adolescents' perceptions of invulnerability to risk might have worked as a barrier to persuasion.

In contrast, Berkowitz's (1998) study, in which she advocated dental hygiene practices among high- and low-sensation seekers who were college students, found that high- rather than low-threat messages were more effective for both high- and low-sensation seekers.[2] How can we explain the different results? Witte and Morrison's (1995a) study indicated that fear appeals have limited utility for persuading high-sensation seekers. However, Berkowitz's (1998) study suggests that the audience's sensation-seeking level may not influence the effects of a fear appeal.

The kind of risky and recommended behaviors presented in a fear-appeal message may play a role. Berkowitz noted, "Sensation seeking may affect attitudes, intentions, and behaviors only when the activity has high sensation value" (p. 71). Additional research is needed on topics with a high sensation value like sex, drugs, and driving fast to assess if and when fear appeals can effectively persuade high-sensation seekers. Current research suggests that without offering an equally appealing alternative to the risky behavior, the fear appeal may fail.

Stages of Behavior Change

Fear appeals have been used in a wide range of health communication contexts to bring about behavioral changes associated with risk prevention (Freimuth, Hammond, Edgar, & Monahan, 1990). Most recently, researchers noted that behavioral change is not a one time event, but rather a process involving multiple stages (Prochaska, DiClemente, & Norcross, 1992; Weinstein, 1988). Specifically, Prochaska and colleagues (1992) asserted that individuals typically go through five stages before they fully adopt and maintain a healthy behavior: precontemplation, contemplation, preparation, action, and maintenance. For example, a smoker who has no plan to quit smoking in the near future is in the precontemplation stage. However, a smoker who is thinking about quitting smoking within the next one to six months is in the contemplation/preparation stage. At the action stage, a person has refrained from smoking for more than a month, but less than six months. A person who has not smoked for more than six months is in the maintenance stage.

The results of research on fear appeals and risk communication indicate that an audience's behavioral status may be an important factor to consider in fear-appeal message design, because individuals with different behavioral statuses will respond to a fear-appeal message differently. For example, increasing susceptibility for individuals who have already been engaging in risky behaviors may produce deleterious effects. A longitudinal study found that some homosexual men exhibited "obsessive/compulsive behavior, social role impairment, and more intrusive worries about AIDS" (p. 231) as their perceived susceptibility to AIDS increased (Joseph, Montgomery, Emmons, Kirscht, Kessler, Ostrow, Wortman, O'Brien, Eller, & Eshleman, 1987). In particular, it was suspected that for individuals who have been engaging in risky behaviors, "a sense of personal risk of the development of HIV infection of AIDS is not beneficially influencing behavior" (Montgomery, Joseph, Becker, Ostrow, Kessler, & Kirscht, 1989, p. 321).

Similarly, adults who had low-quality diets were more likely to respond to the threat of food safety with fear-control responses such as defensive avoidance and fatalism than with danger-control responses of rational problem solving (Schafer, Schafer, Bultena, & Hoiberg, 1993). Somewhat similarly, in response to a message presenting heart disease risk and the role of exercise in heart health, adolescents who had engaged in exercise indicated greater danger-control responses than those who had not engaged in exercise (Fruin, Pratt, & Owen, 1991).

Thus far, a pattern of results has emerged: For the audience who has engaged in the recommended response, perceived threat may create danger-control responses. Conversely, for the audience who has not engaged in the recommended response but has engaged in the risk behavior, an increased perceived threat may produce fear-control responses. From the EPPM standpoint, individuals with different behavioral statuses respond to fear-appeal messages differently because their perceived efficacy levels are different (Cho, 1999).

Specifically, individuals in later stages of behavioral change would have strong self-efficacy perceptions because they have actually performed preventive behavior and therefore do not doubt their ability to do so. Those in earlier stages of change, however, would not be so sure of their ability to perform the behavior. By the same token, those in the later stages of change would have strong response efficacy perceptions, because by engaging in preventive behavior they have experienced benefits such as improved health. Those in earlier stages, however, have yet to experience this benefit.

What can be suspected regarding Montgomery and colleagues' (1989) study of an at-risk population is that their increasing susceptibility level was not matched by an increasing efficacy level. Because they had engaged in risky behaviors, the individuals may have believed that preventive behavior was too late to be effective (i.e., low perceived response efficacy) or that they were unable to change their long-held behavioral habit (i.e., low perceived self-efficacy).

With this premise, Cho (1999) examined unintended, adverse responses to fear appeals among individuals in different stages of behavior change delineated by Prochaska and colleagues (1992). Specifically, three types of audience were exposed to fear-appeal messages: those in the precontemplation stage (do not intend to change), those in the contemplation/preparation stage (intend to change), and those in the action/maintenance stage (engaging in preventive behavior). The results showed that individuals in the earlier stages of change exhibited greater likelihood of fear-control responses, such as defensive avoidance and fatalism, than those in the later stages of change.

In addition, the magnitude of danger-control responses was greater among individuals who had engaged in preventive behaviors than among those who thought about changing behaviors, who in turn displayed greater danger-control responses than those who had no intention of changing their behaviors. The results illustrate the relative effectiveness of persuasion in reinforcing responses rather than in creating new responses (Klapper, 1960; Stiff, 1994). Also, the results indicated the importance of designing and delivering fear appeals tailored for an audience's unique behavioral status, because individuals who did not intend to change their behavior clearly emphasized fear control over danger control.

Considering the studies reviewed above, future fear-appeal research may need to incorporate behavioral status as an important audience variable. In so doing, fear-appeal research should address the following question: How can fear appeals better persuade those who have not engaged in message recommendations to comply without creating fear-control responses?

Contexts of Exposure

Over 40 years ago, Hovland (1959) observed that an examination of the results of experiments and surveys revealed "a marked difference in the picture of communication effects obtained from each" (p. 8). One of the major factors causing such differences, according to Hovland, might be the contexts of exposure to communications.

Attempts to understand the impact of contexts of exposure on fear-appeal effects have been made by Horowitz (1969, 1972; Horowitz & Gumenik, 1970) and Berkowitz (1998). In particular, Horowitz's research focused on the role of volunteerism on fear-appeal effects. Overall, the results indicated that individuals who chose to read a fear-appeal message had more positive attitudes toward message recommendations than those who did not choose to read one.

However, Berkowitz (1998) pointed out that although Horowitz investigated the impact of choice, the choice was whether or not to participate in an experiment, not the kind of message (high or low threat). Berkowitz gave participants the option of choosing either high- or low-threat messages. The results showed that all members of the audience chose to view a low- rather than a high-threat message. However, despite the fact that their choice was unanimously in favor of the low-threat message, participants in Berkowitz's study were still more persuaded by high- rather than low-threat messages.

The implications of these studies are twofold. First, in natural settings, fear appeals, perhaps because of their arousal of strong, unpleasant emotions, may not be the message of choice from the audience's standpoint. Berkowitz's finding on message choice is even more significant considering that high-sensation-seeking participants of her study chose to view low- rather than high-threat messages, which were defined as vivid, intense, and graphic.

Second, however, the fact remains that the high-threat message was more effective than the low-threat message, despite not being the message of choice. Therefore, fear-appeal researchers may need to develop ways to bring fear appeals to their audience's attention in natural contexts. Are effective fear appeals, as a Chinese saying goes, "a good medicine which is bitter to the tongue but effective in curing a disease?" If so, research needs to focus on ways to introduce selective exposure to fear appeals in naturalistic settings. Future fear-appeal research should also incorporate the factors raised by Hovland (1959), including the impact of competing messages, delayed measurement reflecting post-communication interaction, and fear appeals without sponsorship.

Culture

Culture refers to "a set of guidelines (both explicit and implicit) which individuals inherit as members of a particular society" (Helman, 1990, p. 2). Therefore, culture determines how members of a community share meanings of verbal and nonverbal messages in their interaction (Witte & Morrison, 1995b). Consequently, what is scary in one culture may not necessarily be so in another. For example, Connors (1992) found that for intravenous drug users, being arrested for using drugs might be a more immediate and important threat than contracting HIV/AIDS. As a result, the IV drug users may continue to share needles, notwithstanding the risk of HIV infection. For fear appeals to be effective, messages should address such sociocultural contexts.

Witte's (1997) study on teen pregnancy found that teen mothers' attitudes toward the social consequences of pregnancy may not be all negative. For inner-city teen mothers, having a baby was viewed positively, but feeling "fat and bloated," "like they were all alone and that they had no one they could talk to," and "like they lost their friends and their social life and felt extremely isolated" were seen as significantly negative consequences of getting pregnant (p. 148). Economic threats or other future threats of being a teen mother did not emerge as significant threats to teen mothers. This study suggests that researchers should abandon their preconceived notions of what constitutes a health danger, and find out what a specific culture group actually finds threatening about a health issue. Thus, these findings underscore the importance of clearly understanding an audience's perceived susceptibility, an element of the EPPM introduced earlier in this chapter.

A cross-cultural study of fear appeals found that AIDS may elicit a range of threat perceptions, depending on the culture to which the target audience belongs (Witte et al., 2000). Specifically, audiences with collectivistic orientations (group-oriented) were more influenced by fear appeals threatening the collective such as the family, whereas audiences with individualistic orientations (self-oriented) were more affected by fear appeals threatening the individual. Similarly, a study on attitudes toward smoking revealed that family-related consequences such as "harming the health of their children and family criticism" were more important for Hispanic smokers than for non-Hispanics, because of Hispanics' strong family orientation and collectivism (Marin, Marin, Perez-Stable, Otero-Sabogal, & Sabogal, 1990, p. 490).

A caveat emerged from Witte and colleagues' (2000) research, which found that ethnicity does not necessarily overlap with cultural orientation. Contrary to the assumption that Taiwanese college students are more collectivistic than U.S. college students, Taiwanese college students emerged as more individualistic.

Conclusion

The overall results of recent fear-appeal research suggest that high-threat messages work better than low-threat messages—as long as perceived response and self-efficacy are high—regardless of age, trait variables, culture, and stage of change. However, individuals must truly believe they can effectively carry out a recommended response before they will do so. Similarly, it is imperative to discover what a specific target audience perceives as threatening about a specific health issue, especially in terms of young high-sensation seekers and members of different cultures. The variables of fatalism and reactance deserve more research, which should provide greater insight into the effects of fear-appeal messages.

With the emergence of remarkable technological advances that enable us to develop more and more tailored messages, it is important to consider these diverse audience variables when developing effective fear appeals. The designers of fear-appeal messages have an unprecedented opportunity to design, deliver, and engage in effective, audience-centered persuasion (Buller, Borland, & Burgoon, 1998).

Notes

1. Repressors tend to avoid potentially threatening thoughts, emotions, and experiences (Byrne, 1964). Thus, they are avoiders "who engage in perceptual defense" (Goldstein, 1959, p. 247). Sensitizers, on the other hand, are copers who "show sensitization or vigilance" in their approaches to stimuli (Goldstein, 1959, p. 247).

2. No effects of threat were found for attitude and intentions, which Berkowitz (1998) attributed to possible ceiling effect.

References

Berkowitz, J. M. (1998). *The influence of sensation seeking and message choice on responses to fear appeals.* Unpublished doctoral dissertation. Michigan State University.

Berlo, D. K. (1960). *The process of communication.* New York: Holt, Rinehart, & Winston.

Beutler, L. E. (1979). Toward specific psychological therapies for specific conditions. *Journal of Consulting and Clinical Psychology, 47,* 882–897.

Boster, F. J., & Mongeau, P. (1984). Fear-arousing persuasive messages. In R. Bostrom (Ed.), *Communication yearbook, vol. 8* (pp. 330–375). Newbury Park, CA: Sage.

Brehm, J. W. (1966). *A theory of psychological reactance.* New York: Academic Press.

Brehm, S. S., & Brehm, J. W. (1981). *Psychological reactance: A theory of freedom and control.* New York: Academic Press.

Buller, D. B., Borland, R., & Burgoon, M. (1998). Impact of behavioral intention on effectiveness of message features: Evidence from the family sun safety project. *Human Communication Research, 24,* 433–453.

Bushman, B. J. (1998). Effects of warning and information labels on consumption of full-fat, reduced-fat, and no-fat products. *Journal of Applied Psychology, 83,* 97–101.

Byrne, D. (1964). Repression-sensitization as a dimension of personality. In B. Maker (Ed.), *Progress in experimental personality research* (pp. 169–220). New York: Academic Press.

Casey, M. K. (1995). *Fatalism and the modification of the Extended Parallel Process Model.* Paper presented at the annual meeting of the Speech Communication Association, San Antonio, TX.

Cho, H. (1999). *Unintended effects of fear appeals: The role of stages of change, threat, and efficacy.* Unpublished doctoral dissertation. Michigan State University.

Cho, H. (2000). *Psychological reactance and fear appeals in health communication: Do people do the opposite when scared?* Paper presented at the annual meeting of the National Communication Association, Seattle, WA.

Connors, M. M. (1992). Risk perception, risk taking and risk management among intravenous drug users: Implications for AIDS prevention. *Social Science and Medicine, 34,* 591–601.

Dabbs, J. M., & Leventhal, H. (1966). Effects of varying the recommendations in a fear-arousing communication. *Journal of Personality and Social Psychology, 4,* 525–531.

Domino, G., Fragoso, A., & Moreno, H. (1991). Cross-cultural investigations of the imagery of cancer in Mexican nationals. *Hispanic Journal of Behavioral Sciences, 13,* 422–435.

Donohew, L., Lorch, E. P., & Palmgreen, P. (1991). Sensation seeking and targeting of televised anti-drug PSAs. In L. Donohew, H. E. Sypher, & W. J. Bukoski (Eds.), *Persuasive communication and drug abuse prevention* (pp. 209–226). Hillsdale, NJ: Erlbaum.

Donohew, L., Lorch, E. P., & Palmgreen, P. (1998). Applications of a theoretic model of information exposure to health interventions. *Human Communication Research, 24,* 433–453.

Dowd, E. T., & Sanders, D. (1994). Resistance, reactance, and the difficult client. *Canadian Journal of Counseling, 28*, 13–24.

Dowd, E. T., Milne, C. R., & Wise, S. L. (1991). The therapeutic reactance scale: A measure of psychological reactance. *Journal of Counseling and Development, 69*, 541–545.

Dowd, E. T., Wallbrown, F., Sanders, D., & Yesenosky, J. M. (1994). Psychological reactance and its relationship to normal personality variables. *Cognitive Therapy and Research, 18*, 601–612.

Dziokonski, W., & Weber, S. J. (1977). Repression-sensitization, perceived vulnerability, and the fear appeal communication. *The Journal of Social Psychology, 102*, 105–112.

Frank, S. J., Jackson-Walker, S., Marks, M., Van Egeren, L. A., Loop, K., & Olson, K. (1998). From the laboratory to the hospital, adults to adolescents, and disorders to personality: The case of psychological reactance. *Journal of Clinical Psychology, 54*, 361–381.

Freimuth, V. S., Hammond, S. L., Edgar, T., & Monahan, J. L. (1990). Reaching those at risk: A content analytic study of AIDS PSA's. *Communication Research, 17*, 775–791.

Fruin, D., Pratt, C., & Owen, N. (1991). Protection motivation theory and adolescents' perceptions of exercise. *Journal of Applied Social Psychology, 22*, 55–69.

Goldstein, M. J. (1959). The relationship between coping and avoiding behavior and response to fear-arousing propaganda. *Journal of Abnormal and Social Psychology, 58*, 247–252.

Hale, J. L., & Dillard, J. P. (1995). Fear appeals in health promotion campaigns: Too much, too little, or just right? In E. Maibach & R. L. Parrott (Eds.), *Designing health messages: Approaches from communication theory and public health practice* (pp. 65–80). Thousand Oaks, CA: Sage

Hansen, W. B., & Malotte, K. (1986). Perceived personal immunity: The development of beliefs about susceptibility to the consequences of smoking. *Preventive Medicine, 15*, 363–372.

Hardeman, W., Pierro, A., & Mannetti, L. (1997). Determinants of intentions to practice safe sex among 16–25-year-olds. *Journal of Community & Applied Social Psychology, 7*, 345–360.

Helman, C. G. (1990). *Culture, health, and illness*. London: Wright.

Hill, D., & Gardner, G. (1980). Repression-sensitization and yielding to threatening health communications, *Australian Journal of Psychology, 32*, 183–193.

Horowitz, I. A. (1969). Effects of volunteering, fear arousal, and number of communications on attitude change. *Journal of Personality and Social Psychology, 1*, 34–37.

Horowitz, I. A. (1972). Attitude change as a function of perceived arousal. *The Journal of Social Psychology, 87*, 117–226.

Horowitz, I. A., & Gumenik, W. E. (1970). Effects of the volunteer subject, choice, and fear arousal on attitude change. *Journal of Experimental Social Psychology, 6*, 293–303.

Hovland, C. I. (1959). Reconciling conflicting results derived from experimental and survey studies of attitude change. *American Psychologist, 14*, 8–17.

Hovland, C. I., Janis, I. L., & Kelly, H. H. (1953). *Communication and persuasion: Psychological studies of opinion change*. New Haven, CT: Yale University Press.

Jahn, D. L., & Lichstein, K. (1980). The resistive client. *Behavioral Modification, 4*, 303–320.

Janis, I. L., & Feshbach, S. (1953). Effects of fear-arousing communications. *The Journal of Abnormal and Social Psychology, 48*, 78–92.

Janis, I. L., & Feshbach, S. (1954). Personality differences associated with responsiveness to fear-arousing communications. *Journal of Personality, 23*, 154–166.

Jepson, C., & Chaiken, S. (1990). Chronic issue-specific fear inhibits systematic processing of persuasive communications. *Journal of Social Behavior and Personality, 5*, 61–84.

Joseph, J. G., Montgomery, S. B., Emmons, C. A., Kessler, R. C., Ostrow, D. G., Wortman, C. B., O'Brien, K., Eller, M., & Eshleman, S. (1987). Magnitude and determinants of behavioral risk reduction: Longitudinal analysis of a cohort at risk for AIDS. *Psychology and Health, 1*, 73–96.

Kalichman, S. C., Kelly, J. A., Morgan, M., & Rompa, D. (1997). Fatalism, current life satisfaction, and risk for HIV infection among gay and bisexual men. *Journal of Consulting and Clinical Psychology, 65*, 542–546.

Klapper, J. T. (1960). *The effects of mass communication*. New York: Free Press.

Kleinot, M. C., & Rogers, R. W. (1982). Identifying effective components of alcohol misuse prevention programs. *Journal of Studies on Alcohol, 43*, 802–811.

Kouabenan, D. R. (1998). Beliefs and the perception of risks and accidents. *Risk Analysis, 18,* 243–252.

Marin, B. V., Marin, G., Perez-Stable, E. J., Otero-Sabogal, R., & Sabogal, F. (1990). Cultural differences in attitudes toward smoking: Developing messages using the theory of reasoned action. *Journal of Applied Social Psychology, 20,* 478–493.

McLeod, J. M., & Becker, L. B. (1974). Testing the validity of gratification measures through political effects analysis. In J. G. Blumler & E. Katz (Eds.), *The uses of mass communications: Current perspectives on gratifications research* (pp. 137–164). Beverly Hills, CA: Sage.

McMahan, S., Witte, K., & Meyer, J. (1998). The perception of risk message regarding electromagnetic fields: Extending the extended parallel process model to an unknown risk. *Health Communication, 10,* 247–259.

Mongeau, P. A. (1998). Another look at fear-arousing persuasive appeals. In M. Allen & R. W. Preiss (Eds.), *Persuasion: Advances through meta analysis* (pp. 53–58). Cresskill, NJ: Hampton Press.

Montgomery, S. B., Joseph, J. G., Becker, M. H., Ostrow, D. G., Kessler, R. C., & Kirscht, J. P. (1989). The health belief model in understanding compliance with preventive recommendations for AIDS: How useful? *AIDS Education and Prevention, 1,* 303–323.

Prochaska, J. O., DiClemente, C. C., & Norcross, J. C. (1992). In search of how people change: Applications to addictive behaviors. *American Psychologist, 47,* 1102–1114.

Rogers, R. W. (1975). A protection motivation theory of fear appeals and attitude change. *Journal of Psychology, 91,* 93–114.

Rogers, R. W. (1983). Cognitive and physiological processes in fear appeals and attitude change: A revised theory of protection motivation. In J. Cacioppo & R. E. Petty (Eds.), *Social psychophysiology* (pp. 153–176). New York: Guilford Press.

Rogers, R. W., & Mewborn, C. R. (1976). Fear appeals and attitude change: Effects of a threat's noxiousness, probability of occurrence, and the efficacy of coping responses. *Journal of Personality and Social Psychology, 34,* 54–61.

Rohrbaugh, M., Tennen, H., Press, S., & White, L. (1981). Compliance, defiance, and therapeutic paradox. *American Journal of Orthopsychiatry, 51,* 454–467.

Schafer, R. B., Schafer, E., Bultena, G., & Hoiberg, E. (1993). Coping with a health threat: A study of food safety. *Journal of Applied Psychology, 23,* 386–394.

Schoenbachler, D. D., & Whittler, T. E. (1996). Adolescent processing of social and physical threat communications. *Journal of Advertising, 25,* 37–54.

Seibel, C. A., & Dowd, E. T. (1999). Reactance and therapeutic noncompliance. *Cognitive Therapy & Research, 23,* 373–379.

Shepherd, G. J. (1999). Advances in communication theory: A critical review. *Journal of Communication, 49,* 156–164.

Smalec, J. (1996). *Bulimia interventions via interpersonal influence: The role of threat and efficacy in persuading bulimics to seek help.* Paper presented at the annual meeting of the Speech Communication Association, San Diego, CA.

Stephenson, M. T., & Witte, K. (1998). Fear, threat, and perceptions of efficacy from frightening skin cancer messages. *Public Health Reviews, 26,* 147–174.

Straughan, P. T., & Seow, A. (1995). Barriers to mammography among Chinese women in Singapore: A focus group approach. *Health Education Research, 10,* 431–441.

Stiff, J. B. (1994). *Persuasive communication.* New York: Guilford Press.

Suchman, E. A. (1967). Preventive health behavior: A model for research on community health campaigns. *Journal of Health and Social Behavior, 8,* 197–209.

Sutton, S. R. (1982). Fear-arousing communications: A critical examination of theory and research. In J. R. Eiser (Ed.), *Social psychology and behavioral medicine,* (pp. 303–337). London, Wiley.

Weinstein, N. D. (1980). Unrealistic optimism about future life events. *Journal of Personality and Social Psychology, 39,* 806–820.

Weinstein, N. D. (1982). Unrealistic optimism about susceptibility to health problems. *Journal of Behavioral Medicine, 5,* 441–460.

Weinstein, N. D. (1988). Precaution adoption process. *Health Psychology, 7,* 355–386.

Wheatley, J. J., & Oshikawa, S. (1970). The relationship between anxiety and positive and negative advertising appeals. *Journal of Marketing Research, 7,* 85–89.

Witte, K. (1992a). The role of threat and efficacy in AIDS prevention. *International Quarterly of Community Health Education, 12,* 225–248.

Witte, K. (1992b). Putting the fear back into fear appeals: The extended parallel process model. *Communication Monographs, 59,* 330–349.

Witte, K. (1997). Preventing teen pregnancy through persuasive communications: Realities, myths, and the hard-fact truths. *Journal of Community Health, 22,* 137–154.

Witte, K. (1998). Fear as motivator, fear as inhibitor: Using the Extended Parallel Process Model to explain fear appeal successes and failures. In P. A. Andersen & L. K. Guerrero (Eds.), *The Handbook of communication and emotion: Research, theory, applications, and contexts* (pp. 423–450). San Diego, CA: Academic Press.

Witte, K., & Allen, M. (2000). A meta-analysis of fear appeals: Implications for effective public health campaigns. *Health Education & Behavior, 27,* 608–632.

Witte, K., Berkowitz, J. M., Cameron, K. A., & McKeon, J. K. (1998). Preventing the spread of genital warts: Using fear appeals to promote self-protective behaviors. *Health Education and Behavior, 25,* 571–585.

Witte, K., Cameron, K. A., McKeon, J. K., & Berkowitz, J. M. (1996). Predicting risk behaviors: Development and validation of a diagnostic scale. *Journal of Health Communication, 1,* 317–341.

Witte, K., Meyer, G., & Martell, D. (2001). *Effective health risk messages: A step-by-step guide.* Newbury Park, CA: Sage.

Witte, K., Meyer, G., & Martell, D. (in press). *Developing effective health risk messages that work.* Newbury Park, CA: Sage.

Witte, K., & Morrison, K. (1995a). The use of scare tactics in AIDS prevention: The case of juvenile detention and high school youth. *Journal of Applied Communication Research, 12,* 128–142.

Witte, K., & Morrison, K. (1995b). Intercultural and cross-cultural health communication: Understanding people and motivating healthy behaviors. *International and Intercultural Communication Annual, 19,* 216–246.

Witte, K., & Morrison, K. (2000). Examining the influence of trait anxiety/repression-sensitization on individuals' reactions to fear appeals. *Western Journal of Communication, 64,* 1–29.

Witte, K., Murray-Johnson, L., Hubbell, A. P., Liu, W. Y., Sampson, J., & Morrison, K. (2000). Addressing cultural orientations in fear appeals: Promoting AIDS-protective behaviors among Hispanic immigrant and African-American adolescents, and American and Taiwanese college students. *Journal of Health Communication, 6,* 1–23.

Witte, K., Peterson, T. R., Vallabhan, S., Stephenson, M. T., Plugge, C. D., Givens, V. K., Todd, J. D., Becktold, M. G., Hyde, M. K., & Jarrett, R. (1993). Preventing tractor-related injuries and deaths in rural populations: Using a Persuasive Health Message (PHM) framework in formative evaluation research. *International Quarterly of Community Health Education, 13,* 219–251.

Zuckerman, M. (1988). Behavior and biology: Research on sensation seeking and reactions to the media. In L. Donohew, H. E. Sypher, & E. T. Higgins (Eds.), *Communication, social cognition, and affect* (pp. 173–194). Hillsdale, NJ: Erlbaum.

Zuckerman, M. (1994). *Behavioral expressions and biosocial bases of sensation seeking.* Cambridge: Cambridge University Press.

14

Interpersonal Deception Theory

Judee K. Burgoon and David B. Buller

Introduction

Newspapers and television daily call our attention to all manner of deceptions: spies creating false identities and spinning false tales, politicians lying about their private relationships, business executives covering up fraudulent deals, foreign governments creating disinformation campaigns. But deceit is not just the stuff of sensational headlines. It is all around us, every day and in every relationship. In fact, even the most publicized cases of deceit comprise endless interpersonal encounters in which lies, exaggerations, misrepresentations and the like are created and perpetuated. An understanding of deception, then, is best realized when grounded in the interpersonal interactions that give deceit its sustenance.

Interpersonal Deception Theory (IDT) arose out of just this concern that deception should be examined within the nexus of interpersonal encounters. It was formulated to contextualize an explanation of deceptive communication in what we know about conversation. This approach stands in contrast to more psychological explanations of deceptive communication. It also draws attention to the dynamic nature of displays of deception and to the mutual influence between sender and receiver that occurs in all conversations.

This chapter outlines the assumptions on which IDT is built and discusses several key propositions of the theory. In formulating IDT, we synthesized a broad range of evidence and conceptual perspectives on conversational behavior, interpersonal influence, nonverbal communication, normative expectations, and source credibility. The most notable progenitors for IDT are the first author's research into conversational expectations and behavioral adaptation (Burgoon, 1978, 1993; Burgoon, Stern, & Dillman, 1995), the second author's research on verbal and nonverbal social influence (e.g., Buller, 1986, 1987; Buller & Aune, 1988, 1992; Buller & Burgoon, 1986), our combined functional approach to nonverbal communication (Burgoon, Buller, & Woodall, 1996), and decades of research on verbal and nonverbal factors in source credibility (see, e.g., Buller & Burgoon, 1986; Burgoon, 1976; Burgoon & Hoobler, in press). Given the broad net we cast, IDT qualifies as a mid-range theory that has multiple explanatory mechanisms within its propositions.

The remainder of the chapter is devoted to summarizing the results of our experimental tests of IDT. We present these in a largely chronological order so as to give readers a sense of how the thinking about, and testing of, IDT evolved.

Assumptions About Interpersonal Communication

The mutual influence in normal social interaction arises from the active participation of all parties to the conversation. Communicators are not involved in conversation only when encoding messages; they are dynamically engaged in reception of messages, as well. In fact, it is a misnomer in interpersonal interaction to separate senders from receivers, except in an abstract sense (which we do henceforth). In normal conversations, speakers encoding messages are simultaneously monitoring and decoding the conversational behavior of listeners (e.g., observing feedback, turn-taking cues, and overt reactions to the message—including emotional reactions). Likewise, listeners usually are not passive message recipients. While listening, they provide verbal and nonverbal feedback and turn-taking cues, manage their demeanors, and formulate their own turn at talk. All parties to deceptive episodes are likewise concerned with multiple goals such as preserving good interpersonal relationships, masking inappropriate emotions, keeping conversations running smoothly, and appearing credible. In achieving these multiple conversational functions, they must manage a host of verbal and nonverbal behaviors.

Thus, conversations are dynamic, multifunctional, multidimensional, and multimodal events in which participants must perform numerous communication tasks simultaneously in real time. Such juggling requires considerable skill to accomplish effectively. Communicators are also responding to a host of cognitive and behavioral factors that influence deliberate communication acts and in turn produce some unintended and unwitting behaviors. Although conducting social interaction is arguably a cognitively demanding activity, it appears that people are generally good at it because much of normal conversation is fairly routinized. Also, social interaction is made easier by the fact that we have learned to follow culturally prescribed rules and expectations. Some of the most important features of IDT are expectations for truthfulness, for conversational involvement, and reciprocal or matching conversation styles. How one reacts to, and interprets, the fulfillment or violation of expectations goes a long way toward determining the outcome of conversations containing deception. These features of interpersonal communication are the context in which we formulated IDT.

Assumptions About Deception

In IDT, *deception* is defined as an intentional act in which senders knowingly transmit messages intended to foster a false belief or interpretation by the receiver (Buller & Burgoon, 1996a; Ekman, 1985; Knapp & Comadena, 1979). To accomplish this, senders engage in three classes of *strategic*, or *deliberate*, activity: information, behavior, and image management. The term "management" implies that deception is a motivated behavior, undertaken for a purpose. Usually, that purpose is one that benefits the sender, although senders frequently claim that they deceive to benefit the receiver or a third party to the conversation. *Information management* refers to efforts to control the contents of a message and usually concerns verbal features of the message. *Behavior management* refers to efforts to control accompanying nonverbal behaviors that might be telltale signs that one is deceiving. It derives from the assumption that verbal and nonverbal messages are constructed as a unified whole and that nonverbal behaviors are often intended to augment and extend the meanings conveyed by verbal content. *Image management* refers to more general efforts to maintain credibility and to protect one's face, even if caught. It derives from the assumption that individuals are motivated to protect their self-image and public image. These three classes of strategic activity work hand in hand to create an overall believable message and demeanor. By way of example, a student suspected of cheating might tell her professor, "I did not look at my neighbor's exam" (information management) while crossing her arms to avoid nervous gestures or body movements (behavior management) and smiling to appear honest (image management).

This assumption that senders are active agents whose behavior reflects planning, rehearsal, editing, and other conscious or semiconscious efforts at successful deceit does not preclude deceivers from also engaging in what we refer to as *nonstrategic actions,* that is, classes of behavior that may be involuntary and uncontrolled. Nonstrategic activity may result in poor, unnatural, or embarrassing communication performances. A case in point is when a child blushes when giving a nontruthful answer to a parent's inquiry. The complexity of deceptive messages, and the knowledge that deception violates conversational rules and social prescriptions against deceit, can alter the mental state of senders. It can increase the cognitive effort needed to formulate this multifaceted conversational behavior. It may also increase arousal and provoke negative affect. All of these processes may result in inadvertent signals that something is not quite normal in the conversation, that is, nonstrategic activity, although IDT does not assume that such signals are necessarily or universally present.

Finally, because we situate deception in conversation, the actions of recipients of deceit are an object of study. As such, the most important counterparts to deceit on the part of the sender are receivers' perceptions of deceit and their suspicion (a belief held without sufficient evidence or proof to warrant certainty that a communicator may be deceiving them).

The IDT Model Summarized

With these assumptions about interpersonal communication and deception as a backdrop, we formulated a theoretical model of deception containing 18 propositions (table 14.1). They describe an iterative process of mutual influence in which the enactment of deception by one conversational participant provokes a cascade of moves and countermoves by both parties to the conversation. These moves are aimed on the one hand at adapting the deceptive message in order to maintain its apparent truthfulness (i.e., achieving deception success) and on the other at discerning the credibility of the message and the sender and

TABLE 14.1 *Propositions in Interpersonal Deception Theory*

1. Sender and receiver cognitions and behaviors vary systematically as deceptive communication contexts vary in (a) access to social cues, (b) immediacy, (c) relational engagement, (d) conversational demands, and (e) spontaneity.
2. During deceptive interchanges, sender and receiver cognitions and behaviors vary systematically as relationships vary in (a) relational familiarity (including information and behavioral familiarity) and (b) relational valence.
3. Compared with truth tellers, deceivers (a) engage in greater strategic activity designed to manage information, behavior, and image and (b) display more nonstrategic arousal cues, negative and dampened affect, noninvolvement, and performance decrements.
4. Context interactivity moderates initial deception displays so that deception in increasingly interactive contexts results in (a) greater strategic activity (information, behavior, and image management) and (b) reduced nonstrategic activity (arousal, negative or dampened affect, and performance decrements) over time relative to noninteractive contexts.
5. Senders' and receivers' initial expectations of honesty are positively related to degree of context interactivity and positivity of relationship between sender and receiver. From Buller, D. B., & Burgoon, J. K. (1996) Interpersonal deception theory. *Communication Theory, 6*, 203–242.
6. Deceivers' initial detection apprehension and associated strategic activity are inversely related to expectations of honesty (which are themselves a function of context interactivity and relationships positivity).
7. Goals and motivations moderate strategic and nonstrategic behavior displays so that (a) senders deceiving for self-gain exhibit more strategic activity and nonstrategic leakage than senders deceiving for other benefits and (b) receivers' initial behavior patterns are a function of (i) their priorities among instrumental, relational, and identity objectives and (ii) their initial intent to uncover deceit.
8. As receivers' informational, behavioral, and relational familiarity increases, deceivers not only (a) experience more detection apprehension and (b) exhibit more strategic information, behavior, and image management but also (c) engage in more nonstrategic leakage behavior.
9. Skilled senders better convey a truthful demeanor by engaging in more strategic behavior and less nonstrategic leakage than unskilled ones.
10. Initial and ongoing receiver judgments of sender credibility are positively related to (a) receiver truth biases, (b) context interactivity, and (c) sender encoding skills; they are inversely related to (d) deviations of sender communication from expected patterns.
11. Initial and ongoing receiver detection accuracy are inversely related to (a) receiver truth biases, (b) context interactivity, and (c) sender encoding skills; they are positively related to (d) informational and behavioral familiarity, (e) receiver decoding skills, and (f) deviations of sender communication from expected patterns.
12. Receiver suspicion is manifested through a combination of strategic and nonstrategic behavior.
13. Senders perceive suspicion when it is present. Deviations from expected receiver behavior increase perceptions of suspicion. Receiver behavior signaling disbelief, uncertainty, or the need for additional information increases sender perceptions of suspicion.
14. Suspicion (perceived or actual) increases senders' (a) strategic and (b) nonstrategic behavior.
15. Deception and suspicion displays change over time.

TABLE 14.1 *Continued*

16. Reciprocity is the predominant interaction adaptation pattern between senders and receivers during interpersonal deception.
17. Receiver detection accuracy, bias, and judgments of sender credibility following an interaction are a function of (a) terminal receiver cognitions (suspicion, truth biases), (b) receiver decoding skill, and (c) terminal sender behavioral displays.
18. Senders' perceived deception success is a function of (a) terminal sender cognitions (perceived suspicion) and (b) terminal receiver behavioral displays.

ultimately reaching an interpretation of the meaning (i.e., achieving detection success). Because most people know how to carry on a conversation, these actions may be "run off" with relative ease and at a low level of consciousness rather than requiring significant cognitive or physical effort. The subtlety of deceptive processes is one reason that detection is such a challenge, as we shall see. This process and its outcomes are determined by several factors discussed throughout this chapter. These include contextual factors, such as the degree of interactivity possible, senders' and receivers' preinteraction characteristics such as social skills, preexisting knowledge (called information and behavioral familiarity), the positive or negative valence of the relationship between conversational partners, and initial expectations for honesty within the exchange (see figure 14.1 for a simplified depiction of the interactive process of interpersonal deception). All of these factors should influence whether senders or receivers hold a relative advantage during deceptive episodes.

IDT has been tested in a program of experiments that address the nature of deception displays in interactive circumstances (i.e., ones in which perpetrators of deceit interact in real time with the same receivers who render judgments of sender truthfulness). To test IDT properly, the experiments had to meet a number of other criteria. They needed to be of sufficient length to capture the dynamics of interaction, including the potential for a broad range of possible strategic and nonstrategic actions to emerge. Our commitment to an interactive research design and to achieving generalizability to a broader range of discourse also led us to employ common forms of discourse, such as interviews or discussions of a particular topic, that not only situated the deception within normal conversational routines but also required far more extended talk than typical deception experiments using very brief, sometimes single-sentence, utterances. Additionally, instead of the usual practice of relying on college student samples, many studies enrolled nonstudent participants who were recruited from the jury assembly room at the county courthouse, from civic organizations, from employment centers (with training offered in exchange for participation), and from nonprofit groups (who earned money for their organization by participating). In all cases, we sought equal numbers of males and females in our sample so that our results would be applicable to both sexes. In some cases, we also included both friends and strangers so as to further increase generalizability and to uncover any relationship differences. Finally, to compare participants' perceptions with one another and with objective behavioral data, we asked participants themselves to report on their own and their partner's communication and then subjected videotaped interactions to extensive

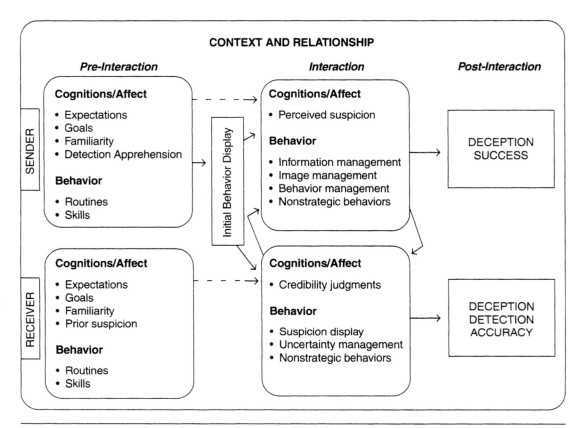

FIGURE 14.1   *Depiction of the Interactive Process of Interpersonal Deception*

coding by trained raters. Some studies also included third-party observers to test for differences due to perspective (participant versus observer).

The rest of this chapter is devoted to reviewing evidence from this program of research in support of the propositions of IDT.

Input Factors

Context Factors

A major premise of IDT setting it apart from other models of deception is that it holds that deception displays and processes differ according to whether or not the sender of deceptive messages interacts in real time with the intended recipients of those messages. This is the concept of *interactivity*. If, for example, a third party observes a videotaped interview at a later time, that third party will not have the same responses to, or assessments of, any deception by the interviewee that are available to the interviewer who asked the questions.

The observer is not "interactive" with the sender. Similarly, if two friends communicate electronically, doing so via instant messaging is more "interactive" than exchanging serial e-mail messages over the course of a week.

Interactivity is thought to make a difference in how deception plays out. One reason is that people in interpersonal interactions usually expect others to be truthful (often referred to in the deception literature as a "truth bias"), and these expectations are considered to become more pronounced as interactivity increases. Three of our studies examined this premise by comparing judgments of receivers who participated in the conversation (high interactivity) and those who merely observed it (low interactivity). In each case, participants rated senders more honest and trustworthy than observers did (Buller, Strzyzewski, & Hunsaker, 1991; Buller & Hunsaker, 1995; Dunbar, Ramirez, & Burgoon, in press). Participant-receivers also judged sender communication more favorably (rating it as more involved, pleasant, and expected) and evaluated sender credibility more leniently (judging senders as more competent, dominant, and higher in character) than observers did. Together, these studies clearly show that interactivity confers an expectation for honesty, and a bias toward lenient judgments, in receivers.

IDT suggests that interactivity should also affect senders' deception displays. Senders should increase strategic activity (e.g., briefer utterances) and decrease nonstrategic behavior (e.g., fewer pauses) in highly interactive circumstances because (1) senders have the opportunity to repair and adapt their communication as they obtain feedback from receivers on their apparent believability and (2) the rapport and trust engendered by conversational participation produces a more coordinated, smooth interaction that helps senders behave naturally in conversation (Buller & Burgoon, 1986; Burgoon, Buller, Floyd, & Grandpre, 1996). The experiments to be reviewed shortly attest to the impact of interactivity on senders' strategic and nonstrategic activity.

Finally, interactivity should affect receivers' ability to distinguish deceit from truth. Compared to observers, receivers embedded in conversations face a complex set of conversational and cognitive demands. They must interpret messages in real time while simultaneously formulating their own conversational turns at talk, providing feedback to senders, and engaging in turn management. These tasks can distract them from cues to deception. At the same time, receivers are enmeshed in relationships with senders. As such, they may commit to their expectations for honesty at the outset of the conversations and not adjust them later. These expectations can be further reinforced by the patterns of reciprocity and the maintenance of self and others' face needs during conversations (Burgoon et al., 1996).

Four out of five studies we have conducted have supported the impact of interactivity on detection accuracy (the exception being Buller & Hunsaker, 1995). Buller and colleagues (1991) showed that participants did not differentiate between truthful and deceptive messages but that observers did. A study by Burgoon and colleagues (1996) comparing sender, receiver, and observer perspectives found that observers were more attuned to behavioral differences between truthful and deceptive communications than were participant-receivers, but that neither set of receivers labeled deceptive performances as deceit. In a study comparing receivers in a dialogue (two-way communication) and monologue (one-way communication), receivers initially were less accurate at detecting deception in a dialogue than in a monologue; as conversations wore on, however, receivers in both dialogue and monologue were less accurate at detecting deception (Burgoon, Buller, & Floyd, 2001). Finally, a recent companion study that collected observer data to compare to that of dialoguing receivers found that participant-receivers were less accurate in detecting deception (Dunbar et al., in press). These studies demonstrate that interactivity reduces receivers' ability to detect deception. Two questions that arise are (1) whether losses in detection accuracy are only short-term and (2) whether any gains receivers might make in their detection acuity are offset by senders' own gains from adapting to receiver feedback. Studies summarized below partially speak to these issues.

Relationship Factors

In IDT, the nature of the relationship between sender and receiver is another input factor that influences the process and outcomes of deception (Buller & Burgoon, 1996; see also McCornack & Parks, 1986; Stiff, Kim, & Ramesh, 1989). The most important relationship features are relational familiarity and relational valence.

Relational Familiarity.   Relational familiarity can be both informational and behavioral. Compared with strangers, people in relationships clearly know more about one another and are more familiar with each other's behavior. Such informational and behavioral familiarity could improve receivers' ability to detect deception. Military intelligence specialists and law enforcement personnel routinely judge the likely validity of responses from prisoners of war or criminal suspects by asking questions to which they already know the truthful answer as a way of determining how truthful the respondent is being. The same process could be used by relational partners, either deliberately, when their suspicions are aroused, or inadvertently, when information in a deceptive message does not square with their shared history. A shared history also may make relational partners more cognizant of how each usually behaves in conversation, thus helping them better recognize deviations from normal conversational patterns. In one of our studies, novice interviewers improved their detection accuracy when asking acquaintances an unexpected question but not when asking it of a stranger (Burgoon, Buller, Ebesu, & Rockwell, 1994). Their familiarity with the source's behavior probably improved their ability to detect abnormal responses.

   Another reason detection accuracy may improve over time is that senders interacting with acquaintances, friends, and family may become worried that their deceit will be detected, precisely because of the information and behavioral familiarity these receivers possess. But this is a complex issue. On the one hand, any such concerns could be revealed by the presence of nonstrategic anxiety cues and negative affect. These telltale indicators of deception should make detecting of deception easier for the receiver. On the other hand, anxiety could also motivate senders to engage in more strategic moves to hide their deceit, making detection more difficult because there would be fewer cues for receivers to rely on. Such adjustments in turn could lead to overcontrol, reducing senders' conversational involvement and producing other performance decrements such as nonfluent speech. These additional nonstrategic behaviors should make detection easier. Thus, arousal and anxiety can have very mixed effects on deception displays and their detectability when interactants know one another.

Our research findings reflect just such a mixed bag of results. By way of illustration, in a study conducted prior to formulating IDT (Buller & Aune, 1987), intimates and friends differed from strangers in their use of eye contact, forward lean, nervous touches to the face and head, vocal nervousness, vocal pleasantness, and gestural expressivity. A recent study revealed that friends may benefit from high interactivity (dialogue) but not low interactivity (monologue). Senders dialoguing with friends were judged as managing their behavior and image better than senders dialoguing with strangers, but friends did worse than strangers when delivering a monologue (Burgoon et al., 2001). Other studies reviewed below further confirm that the nature of the interpersonal relationship between interactants influences the deception process.

Relational Valence. The degree of positivity and trust associated with a relationship may be a powerful cause of truth bias, leading receivers to overlook, discount, or misinterpret signals that the communication is not what it seems. For example, in a recent study (Burgoon et al., 2001), receivers felt that interactions with friends produced more rapport, trust, and similarity than interactions with strangers did. In another study (Burgoon et al., 1994), receivers also consistently overestimated the honesty of acquaintances. Conversely, when led to be suspicious (i.e., when receivers were induced to place a negative valence on the relationship), novice receivers (as opposed to military intelligence specialists) greatly underestimated strangers' truthfulness.

In sum, features of communication contexts and of interpersonal relationships frame deceptive encounters and must be taken into account to achieve any precision in predicting and explaining deception. Associated beliefs and expectations influence the initial judgments of sender credibility and early actions by deceptive senders within the conversation. This is just the beginning of the story of interpersonal deception. Quickly, sender and receiver begin to exert mutual influence on each other's cognitions, feelings, and behavior so that conversational patterns change over successive conversational turns. With those adjustments come changes in sender credibility and deception success. In the next section, we consider the propositions in IDT that describe the interaction processes in interpersonal deception.

Interaction Processes

Deception Displays

The prevailing wisdom prior to IDT was that the act of deception is accompanied by a number of involuntary reactions constituting telltale signs that a person is lying. Deceivers were expected to experience anxiety and negative emotions such as guilt or fear of detection, to find their cognitive workload increasing as they tried to concoct plausible lies, and to make (usually unsuccessful) efforts to suppress the signs of nervousness, discomfort, and cognitive effort—all of which would result in behavioral cues that the savvy observer could use to detect deception. Ekman and Friesen (1969) called this the leakage hypothesis. Like Sigmund Freud, they thought that people would inadvertently reveal or "leak" their deceptive intent and that these leakage cues were uncontrollable, so they would appear unbidden. All that an astute observer needed to do was tune in to the right ones to have some surefire clues that deception was occurring.

Decades of research have been dedicated to discovering the anticipated verbal and nonverbal signs of deception (see, e.g., Ekman, 1985; Zuckerman & Driver, 1985). Yet research has failed to yield many consistently reliable indicators. Pinocchio's nose is not evident in real life. Coupled with the persistent evidence that people's accuracy in detecting deception hinges on chance at best, this raised the question of whether a profile of valid indicators could be identified. An equally important question lurking in the background was whether any of the research findings would generalize to conditions in which deceivers actually interact with the intended recipients of their deceit.

This is where IDT entered the scene. Our fundamental premise that interactive and noninteractive deception differ led us to expect that deception displays would be transitory. We also predicted that deceivers (or at least, skilled ones) would make use of the communication interplay between sender and receiver to repair their performances over time, thus making detection even more difficult as time passed. We further reasoned that if deceptive performances comprise both strategic and nonstrategic elements, researchers needed to examine a broader range of associated verbal and nonverbal behaviors to see if the presence of intentional (strategic) behaviors would make deceit even less detectable. Our conviction that deceit is an active, goal-oriented activity also raised the prospect of senders employing multiple strategies for enacting deceit, each one replete with its own profile of verbal and nonverbal behaviors needing investigation. Also, our conviction that receivers are themselves active agents raised the prospect that their own communication, including overt indications of suspicion, might alter deceivers' displays.

We summarize next, in chronological order, those IDT studies that explicitly examined deception displays. In all, eight original experiments, plus secondary analyses of several of Bavelas and colleagues' experiments and follow-up analyses on our own videotaped interactions, were undertaken explicitly to test IDT propositions and hypotheses. Because experiment 1 focused on receiver suspicion and is discussed later, we begin by summarizing experiment 2, which was the first to address deception displays.

Experiment 2.   This experiment was the first to assess a wide range of perceived and coded nonverbal (Burgoon & Buller, 1994) and language behaviors (see Buller, Burgoon, Buslig, & Roiger, 1996). It built upon earlier investigations by Buller and colleagues (Buller & Aune, 1987; Buller, Comstock, Aune, & Strzyzewski, 1989) showing that deceptive performances included a mix of nonstrategic cues related to arousal and negative affect and strategic activity related to information, behavior, and image management. We hypothesized that compared to truth tellers, deceivers would manage information by obfuscating their verbal responses with vagueness, uncertainty, reticence, and nonimmediacy (avoidance language) and that this information management would be accompanied by nonverbal nonimmediacy (e.g., less gaze, greater distance) and inexpressiveness. We also hypothesized that initially, deceivers would be more nervous, negative, and nonfluent than truth tellers but that the dynamics of interactive deception would allow them to improve behavior management and image protection over time.

Our experimental methods were intended to elicit natural interactions and self-presentational concerns that would be common among friends and strangers alike, since our sample included both. Adapting procedures first used by Toris and DePaulo (1985) and Buller and Aune (1987), we framed the study as related to how people present them-selves to others during an interview and how well interviewers can detect misrepresenta-tions of true feelings and actions. Half of the participants were asked to lie after the first five questions. The first five questions thus provided a truthful baseline during which par-ticipants could acclimate to the task and familiarize themselves with the interviewees' communication style. This approach also approximated real-world circumstances in which deception and truth are intermixed. Afterward, both participants rated interviewee behav-ior, and trained coders rated assorted nonverbal behaviors from the videotaped sessions.

As hypothesized, deceivers and truth tellers behaved differently. Consistent with our contention that deceivers strategically manage what information they reveal, deceivers' statements were characterized by brevity, vagueness, uncertainty, nonimmediacy, and nonspecificity (e.g., "everybody went drinking" versus "I went drinking"). This had the effect of minimizing the amount of concrete and verifiable detail that deceivers supplied and of disassociating deceivers from what they were saying. Other linguistic patterns were contrary to predictions but also had the effect of making deceptive answers more pallid and less personal than truthful ones. Nonverbally, deceivers' initial behavioral patterns were as predicted. They displayed some strategic moves—less nonverbal immediacy, less dominance, and more formality than truth tellers—that collectively should have curtailed conversation and/or made them seem passive, polite, composed, and nonmanipulative. But their behavior also included some nonstrategic ingredients—nervousness, unpleasant-ness, and gaze avoidance—that together with the overall reduction in conversational in-volvement created an unexpected and undesirable impression. Contrary to IDT, then, deceivers did not project a more favorable image.

Had these patterns persisted throughout the course of the interaction, we might have concluded that regardless of any deliberate efforts to the contrary, deceptive performances lack credibility. However, in support of our position that deceivers actively attempt to control and repair their performances, deceivers' body language became increasingly re-laxed and pleasant over the course of these brief five-minute interactions. With more time, we might have seen even more strategic repairs. Even without major repairs, it was likely that the subdued demeanor of deceivers was effective in evading detection because, as we shall see in later investigations, deficiencies in deceptive performances need not give the deceiver away. Additionally, other results discussed shortly supported IDT's premise that deception varies by such factors as relational familiarity, partner's communication style, and suspicion.

Experiment 3.   The next experiment lengthened the interview time and replaced novice interviewers with trained interviewers who maintained a consistent interaction style across interviewees. Unacquainted participants first completed a truthful interview with a same-sex interviewer and then completed a deceptive interview with a second same-sex inter-viewer. To learn whether there might be multiple deception profiles, deceivers were instructed to use one of three types of deception—fabrication (outright lying), equivoca-tion (being vague and ambiguous), or concealment (withholding relevant information)—or, in a "general" condition, to use whatever forms of deception they wished.

As predicted, deceptive responses were seen as less conversationally complete (i.e., failed to meet usual conversational obligations), direct, relevant, clear, personalized, and veridical (honest) than truthful responses (Burgoon, Buller, Guerrero, Afifi, & Feldman,

1996). Those results related to information management confirmed that deceivers have a number of features at their disposal to effectuate deception. Senders also reported being far less truthful when fabricating answers than when concealing or equivocating, but observers failed to see differences among the three types. Linguistically, deceivers again used fewer self-references and tended to use fewer group references than truth tellers (Buller, Burgoon, Buslig, & Roiger, 1994). This stripped deceptive responses of some of their concreteness and personalization. However, as other linguistic analyses proved problematic, we made several methodological changes before the next test of deception types.

Experiment 4. Reported in Buller, Burgoon, White, and Ebesu (1994), this next experiment again employed interviews and compared three types of deceivers: falsifiers, equivocators, and concealers. To see how suspicion alters both sender and receiver behavior, we reverted to novice rather than trained interviewers, half of whom were made suspicious. Participants were civilians and military personnel from two locations and included strangers and acquaintances.

The resultant complex findings confirmed our conjecture that deception displays are highly responsive to such factors as the type of deception, degree of relational familiarity, and partner's suspicion. Information management went largely as predicted. Truthful responses were seen as more complete, veridical, direct/relevant, clear, and personalized than deceptive ones. Of the three deceptive types, falsifiers were the least truthful but also the least reticent; their answers were less vague, hesitant, and brief than those of equivocators or concealers. Equivocators were the least clear, direct, and relevant. Additionally, as predicted, deceivers tended to include distancing and ambiguous language (e.g., levelers, modifiers, and group references), but contrary to predictions they also used more present tense verbs and fewer past tense verbs. (After the fact, we conjectured that past tense verbs are more likely to sound definitive and therefore deceivers might have been expected to use present rather than past tense verbs.) As for nonverbal patterns, they failed to support a clean strategic-nonstrategic distinction, as many behaviors were opposite to predictions. For example, deceivers were expected to be less expressive than truth tellers; instead, they were more so (and yet less involved). Deceivers were hypothesized to be more formal; instead, they were less so. Further, only strangers showed the expected pattern of nondominance when deceiving; acquaintances instead became more dominant than their truth-telling counterparts.

The overall conclusion we drew from these data is that in interactive contexts, very few displays of uniform deception are likely due to deceivers adapting to audience and context and employing an array of discourse forms, each with different accompanying nonverbal cues. Still, some suggestive patterns emerged. Deceivers often seemed to opt for greater verbal reticence, withdrawal, and vagueness, which has the advantage of reducing their chances of making contradictory or implausible statements; to adopt an informal, nondominant demeanor, which might discourage others from probing too deeply and disassociates them from responsibility for their statements; to offset verbal nonimmediacy and depersonalization through more expressive body language; and to hide arousal by suppressing some, but not all, other physical activity. The net result of all these behaviors was an apparent general reduction in involvement, which was emerging as a strong telltale sign of deception, at least at the outset of conversations.

Secondary Analysis of the Equivocation Experiments. The next move in our research program (Buller et al., 1994) took us not to yet another experiment but rather to further analysis of research undertaken by Bavelas, Chovil, Black, and Mullett (1990), who had been conducting numerous experiments on equivocation. Janet Bavelas graciously made available the audiotapes and videotapes from six studies so that we could code the utterances on the same verbal and nonverbal behaviors we had measured previously. (It should be noted that Bavelas does not consider equivocation a form of deception, but her characterization of it is still quite similar to ours, namely, a form of discourse that includes truthful but indirect, irrelevant, ambiguous, or evasive information to create an impression that deviates from "the truth, the whole truth, and nothing but the truth.") Her program of research offered an excellent complement to ours because, unlike our direct instructions to subjects to be equivocal, her experiments induced equivocation by placing people in avoid-avoid conflicts (i.e., situations in which both telling the truth and lying would have negative consequences) that naturally encouraged them to equivocate. For example, in one study, people were asked to imagine that a friend had performed poorly on a task and was asking for feedback on how he or she did. Telling the truth would hurt the friend's feelings; yet people are often loath to lie outright, hence the likelihood of resorting to equivocation. Most of the experiments contrasted a conflict condition with a no-conflict condition.

Results showed that equivocators were nondominant, which would be consistent with a withdrawal response, but they were also linguistically immediate, which is an approach response. They were less expressive vocally but more expressive kinesically. They also "leaked" some tension and unpleasantness when equivocating. These combined patterns pointed to equivocation including channel discrepancies, which makes sense given that people are likely to equivocate when they are feeling ambivalent.

Further Vocal Analyses from Experiment 4. Our own and others' research had already repeatedly established that vocal behavior can be a major separator between deceptive and truthful speakers. The next investigations (Rockwell, Buller, & Burgoon, 1997a, 1997b) therefore sought to identify reliable indicators of deceit using acoustic and perceptual measures. Vocal features generally fall into one of three categories of measures (1) those related to duration or speed of utterance, (2) those related to frequency or pitch, and (3) those related to intensity. Based on the expectation that deceivers would be more reticent, withdrawn, and uncertain than truth tellers and would exercise greater control over nonverbal behaviors, we hypothesized that deceivers would exhibit shorter overall message duration, slower tempos, less fluency, and longer response latencies than truth tellers. At the same time, the voice is not as easily controlled as the body, and previous findings have shown that arousal can be leaked through higher pitch. We therefore also predicted that deceptive voices would be higher pitched. Finally, on the supposition that deceivers would try to "shrink" from discovery with a submissive demeanor, we thought they would speak more softly than truth tellers.

Trained coders rated such features as fluency, response latencies, internal pauses, pitch, vocal quality, articulatory precision, and pleasantness. Acoustic software then analyzed the recordings of the interviews, measuring such features as number of segments of sound and silence, response latency, fundamental frequency mean and variance, and intensity mean and variance. Results revealed that deceivers constructed shorter messages, spoke more slowly, were less fluent, and had longer response latencies than truth tellers did. Unlike many other deception studies, deceivers did not show elevated pitch, but the acoustic analysis revealed that they displayed more pitch variety and a wider intensity (loudness) range than truth tellers. Additionally, deceivers' voices were rated less pleasant than those of truth tellers. There are several plausible explanations for these findings. For example, deceivers may have adopted these patterns strategically so as to restrict the amount of information conveyed, to reduce their responsibility for the receiver's interpretation of what is said by being vague and uncertain, or to cover any verbal insufficiencies with an expressive voice. Alternatively, behavior patterns may have been unintended. Deception may have required greater cognitive effort that prevented rapid responses and long messages. It may have heightened arousal in a manner that impaired efficient functioning of the articulators and prevented deceivers from controlling fluctuations in intensity. The indeterminacy of whether these vocal patterns best fit a strategic or nonstrategic interpretation eventually led to the design of Experiment 6.

Experiment 5.   Meantime, this next study, reported in Burgoon, Buller, White, Afifi, and Buslig (1999), was undertaken to examine further the extent to which senders adapt their deceptive displays over time and to different receiver communication styles. Several hypotheses were tested: (1) Interactive deception displays differ from truthful ones only at the outset of interactions and approximate truthful displays over time; (2) deceivers adapt to receiver communication; (3) receiver involvement affects sender displays; (4) receiver judgments of truthfulness correlate directly with sender displays; and (5) senders' social skills affect their deceptive performance. We discuss the last hypothesis later in the chapter.

We again recruited a highly representative community sample to conduct interviews. Interviewees were instructed to alternate between telling the truth and deceiving across four blocks of three questions. Half of the interviewees started with truth, so their truth (T) and deception (D) sequence was TTTDDDTTTDDD. The other half followed a deception-first order (DDDTTTDDDTTT). Subsequently, trained coders rated the recorded sessions on verbal and nonverbal involvement.

Results were supportive of IDT generally and the hypotheses specifically. Truth tellers were initially more talkative than deceivers, but deceivers became more verbose over time and spent as much time talking by the close of the interview. Involvement followed a similar pattern. Deceivers were less involved than truth tellers initially but achieved comparable levels of involvement by the end of the interview. They also showed increases in involvement each time they shifted from truthful responses to deceptive ones, demonstrating that they were able to adjust their level of involvement upward despite the normal inclination to become subdued when deceiving. Moreover, interviewee involvement closely followed interviewer involvement levels, indicating a strong tendency for truth tellers and deceivers to adapt in a reciprocal fashion to the interviewer's communication style. The exceptions were that, as predicted, deceivers and truth tellers compensated for the interviewer's low involvement by becoming more involved. But unexpectedly, interviewees who began the interviews by deceiving also compensated for the interviewer's high involvement by becoming less involved too, possibly because they thought the high involvement conveyed suspicion and made the interview seem more like an interrogation. By contrast, interviewees who began with truthful answers reciprocated the interviewer's high involvement, probably because the interviewer's behavior remained constant when the interviewee shifted to deception, thereby making it evident that the interviewer's communication was not tied to the interviewee's behavior. These results demonstrated that both verbal and nonverbal behaviors followed IDT predictions.

Experiment 6. Up to this time, we had been making assumptions that deception includes many strategic features, and indeed we had classified entire clusters of behavioral cues as strategic. Yet we had not attempted to verify directly that deceivers intend to manage their presentations in the manner we had been hypothesizing. This next small-scale study was therefore intended to learn directly from deceivers what they thought they did to create more successful performances and to use this knowledge to refine our subsequent experiments.

Business students were recruited to participate in or observe social conversations between friends or strangers about such topics as "responsibility" and "the most unpleasant job" they had ever had to do. Participants designated as "senders" were asked to be truthful on some topics and to deceive on others. Participants designated as "receivers" were merely asked to keep the conversation flowing. Observers watched the conversations through a one- way mirror and rated senders after two target topics. Senders and receivers subsequently rated the videotaped interaction on the same target topics, and senders were personally interviewed about what they did to appear truthful.

Results provided clear evidence that deceivers intentionally manage their communication. Senders reported giving less complete information when deceiving than when telling the truth and said their deceptive answers were less clear, direct, and relevant than their truthful ones. They reported trying to achieve a normal appearance and to shift conversational responsibilities to the receiver. They thought they were as pleasant in deception as in truth. But they also thought their conversational style was less expressive, less attentive, less smooth, more anxious, and less dominant when deceiving. Participant-receivers and observers failed to detect many of these apparent changes. Receivers were particularly oblivious, seeing virtually no differences between truthful and deceptive performances. Observers were more sensitive to sender differences, seeing deceptive messages as less complete, less expressive, less other-centered, and more awkward than truthful ones. But discerning these differences made them no less willing to rate senders as believable. Thus, senders were able to escape negative judgments through their strategic machinations.

Experiment 7. A quick perusal of the IDT propositions reveals that interactivity is one of its central features; yet no experiment had tackled its role directly. This next investigation (Burgoon, Buller, & Floyd, 2001) did. One form of interactivity follows a dialogue to monologue continuum. Under dialogue (i.e., high interactivity), senders and receivers exchange turns frequently and have relatively equal turns at talk. Under monologue (i.e., low interactivity), one person holds forth for lengthy periods while the other listens. This experiment tested the effects of interactivity by having undergraduate men and women conduct social conversations while engaged in either a dialogue or a monologue. Half of the participants again became instant accomplices who deceived their partner on two of the four topics, using either a TTDD order or a DDTT order across the four topics. Afterwards, participants and trained coders rated sender communication and credibility.

Results were quite telling. Senders reported better information and speech management in a dialogue than in a monologue, both initially and over time (although these perceptions were altered somewhat by the relationship with the receiver). Behaviorally, senders felt that they appeared more dominant, involved, and pleasant when dialoguing than when monologuing, especially with friends. Coder ratings of behavior and image management behaviors showed that senders displayed more involvement, dominance, pleasantness, and adaptation when dialoguing rather than when monologuing. Finally, receivers detected deceit less accurately when the interaction was a dialogue than when it was a monologue.

Overall, these data support the IDT proposition that interactivity in the form of senders engaging in a dialogue with receivers enables better strategic management of senders' message content, nonverbal behavior, and overall image.

Experiment 8.   This next investigation entailed two studies intended to continue examination of the dynamics of senders' strategic adjustments to receiver involvement levels (White & Burgoon, 2001). The first study established participants' expectations, motivations, and typical behavior patterns under truth or deception. The second study paired students to engage in conversations similar to experiment 7, during which senders were either truthful or deceptive throughout and receivers increased or decreased their involvement level halfway through the conversation.

One research question we posed was whether attitudes before the interaction differed between deceivers and truth tellers. They did. Deceivers felt more anxious and more concerned about their self-presentations beforehand. All five hypotheses were also supported. When beginning to deceive, senders showed less involvement than their truthful counterparts, but they increased their involvement over time up to a level comparable to truth tellers. These involvement patterns are consistent with a strategic behavior management interpretation, in that senders may have initially attempted to mask their deceptiveness by suppressing behavior but eventually were able to adjust to a more normal pattern of interaction. They were thus able to satisfy competing goals of evading detection through withdrawal and creating an impression of normalcy through approach behavior. Interaction patterns were also responsive to those of the partner. If the receiver increased or decreased involvement, so did truthful senders, thus displaying the kind of reciprocal interaction patterns that characterize normal conversations. Deceivers also matched partner increases, though to a lesser extent than truth tellers. Deceivers were expected initially to compensate for partners' reduced involvement, that is, to show an offsetting increase in involvement and then to reciprocate. Results showed that they did compensate, but not immediately, and that they generally showed reciprocal decreases in involvement.

Finally, as predicted, deceivers interpreted receivers' behavior as feedback to them about their own performance. Low involvement was interpreted as possible skepticism or suspicion, something that probably motivated deceivers to try harder and consequently be less inclined to become as uninvolved as the receiver was. High involvement was interpreted as a sign of successful deception and probably reinforced deceivers' existing communication patterns, thus again leading to less adaptation by deceptive than truthful senders. We had expected deceivers to show more adjustments over time than senders, and there was definitely evidence of more variability in deceivers' responses when faced with low involvement from the partner. In retrospect, however, it makes sense that only those deceivers facing "negative feedback" might need to make adjustments. It is also possible that the demands of crafting a credible deceptive performance, combined with monitoring partner feedback and handling all the other usual conversational responsibilities, may have taxed deceivers' cognitive resources and hampered their ability to adapt. These alternative explanations warrant further investigation, because the former interpretation implies that senders had greater capacity to manage their presentations in intentional and deliberate ways, that is, to behave strategically, than does the latter.

In sum, the experiments conducted to date support many IDT propositions regarding the dynamic and adaptive properties of interpersonal deception, their responsiveness to partner behavior, and the nature of strategic and nonstrategic deceptive displays. At the same time, they have produced enough curious findings, and raised enough unresolved questions, to invite further experimentation before firm conclusions are drawn.

Suspicion Cues

A key tenet of IDT is that both sender and receiver are active participants in deceptive episodes and that senders are responsive to receiver suspicion. If this is the case, then we should be able to document that receivers exhibit overt behaviors that correlate with their suspicions. What follows is a brief review of the findings related specifically to receivers' displays of suspicion.

Experiment 1.   This first test of IDT, reported in Buller, Strzyzewski, and Comstock (1991), came upon the heels of studies by Buller and colleagues (1989) and Stiff and Miller (1986) that had investigated whether use of probing questions, which suspicious receivers might be inclined to use, elicited more detectable deception by senders. Contrary to expectations, previous studies had found that probing led receivers to judge senders as more, not less, truthful. Buller and colleagues reasoned that probing might tip senders off to receiver skepticism, leading senders to repair their performances by suppressing arousal cues and increasing immediacy and pleasantness. The result would be an honest-appearing demeanor that would defy detection as deceptive.

The current study used an interview format during which senders either lied or told the truth to friends or strangers. To induce suspicion, half the receivers were told that interviewees are often less than completely candid and truthful when interviewed face to face and that the research assistant would signal them surreptitiously if the sender's responses were not matching a previously completed version of the questionnaire. This would be their cue to ask follow-up questions about the senders' reasons for their answers to the questions, which were taken from a social desirability questionnaire. Afterward, trained coders rated the recorded interviews on a wide array of verbal and nonverbal behaviors.

Results showed that probing did elicit behavioral changes, though not all in the hypothesized direction. Senders who were subjected to probing questions gave longer answers, made more pauses and speech errors, used more illustrator gestures and body adaptor gestures (increased head nodding and shaking late in the interview), and displayed less pleasant facial expressions. The bulk of these cues suggest increased arousal accompanied by efforts to elaborate verbal answers and support them with gestures. However, when senders thought receivers were suspicious, they used fewer gestures, reduced bodily activity, laughed less, and gave shorter answers—behaviors in keeping with greater reticence and efforts to mask arousal. Overall, then, these results showed that deceptive displays are governed not solely by sender intent to be truthful or deceptive but also by how the receiver behaves and whether the receiver is thought to be suspicious.

Experiment 2.   This next experiment (described earlier) tested suspicion effects directly by creating three levels of suspicion (low, moderate, or high) based on the stated likelihood that senders misrepresent the truth. We also created separate measures of (1) receiver belief that the sender is untruthful, (2) motivation to detect sender's deceit, and (3) degree of vigilance in observing sender behavior so as to assess suspicion more thoroughly.

As Burgoon, Buller, Dillman, and Walther (1995) reported, different levels of suspicion created different behavioral profiles for both senders and deceivers. In a sampling of this very mixed set of findings, senders were vocally unpleasant and most physically active when facing moderate suspicion but pleasant and inactive when facing high suspicion. Conversely, receivers were more fluent and had smoother turn switches under moderate than under high suspicion. Deceivers thus seemed flustered under moderate suspicion, whereas receivers seemed so when they were highly suspicious. These perplexing results led us to speculate that moderate suspicion may create the highest level of uncertainty, which accounts for part of the difference in behavioral patterns.

As for the behaviors that provoked suspicion among receivers, there were quite a few. Receivers were more suspicious when senders were vague and uncertain, unpleasant vocally and kinesically, nervous and tense vocally and kinesically, nonimmediate (less eye contact, greater physical distance), and generally behaving in ways deemed undesirable. Senders who hid their demeanor allayed receiver suspicions. These findings clearly signal the importance of actual verbal and nonverbal communicative practice in perceptions of deceit.

Experiment 4.   In this next suspicion experiment, we reverted to two levels of suspicion (low or high) because of the number of other factors (three kinds of deceit, expertise, familiarity, deception, and deception order) in the design. It will be recalled that senders alternated between blocks of truthful and deceptive answers, which allowed us to look for changes across the interview and differences between truthful and deceptive responding.

The results, reported in Burgoon, Buller, Ebesu, Rockwell, and White (1996), produced a number of very interesting findings. In brief, senders' and receivers' behavior differed significantly depending on whether suspicion was present or not. Senders whose partners were not suspicious decreased their involvement levels when shifting from truth to deception, showing the typical patterns of deceit initially depressing involvement levels. If, however, partners were suspicious, senders were able to maintain a high level of involvement when shifting from truth to deception, consistent with IDT's contention that deceivers are capable of strategically adjusting involvement toward the level typical of truth tellers. An exception was concealers, who likely came across as uninvolved because they say little. Additionally, senders seemed more submissive when the interviewer was suspicious, consistent with our contention that senders will adopt avoidance and reticence strategies to reduce their conversational obligations and, hence, their likelihood of being detected. The exception was that, when they were telling outright lies, they took a more dominant tack. It seems plausible that when trying to "sell" someone on a lie, deceivers would become more assertive. This came at a price, however. Senders fabricating a lie in the face of suspicion were rated less fluent than those committing other kinds of deceit. Other behavioral changes varied according to the type of deception and relational familiarity.

As for receivers, suspicion caused them to remain more involved during deception, to be more expressive vocally but less expressive kinesically, and to be more informal. Other receiver behaviors varied depending on relational familiarity, expertise, and type of deception. These behavioral patterns reveal that suspicion creates potentially noticeable changes in receivers' nonverbal behavior, changes that can be used to tip off senders that they need to make adjustments, even when receivers' verbal behavior does not give away their suspicion. IDT posits that receivers often telegraph their suspicions to senders and that it is this cycling between deceivers' and receivers' moves and countermoves that ultimately allows deceivers to gain the upper hand through strategic adaptation of their behavior.

Experiments 5 Through 8. The remaining experiments examined suspicion indirectly by manipulating receivers' interviewing behavior. As noted previously, senders were responsive to receiver communication styles and read those styles as feedback about their own performance. Thus, whether suspicion was induced directly or "created" by having receivers act the way suspicious receivers act, deceivers altered their behavior in response to those suspicions. Ironically, because the predominant pattern was one of reciprocity— senders matching receivers' communication styles—interviewers who attempted to become more assertive in their questioning often elicited higher levels of involvement from senders, which in turn made senders look more truthful. In short, adopting an assertive interviewing style backfired because it made it easier for senders to craft a believable presentation. This may be why interviewers are often taught to create an outward appearance of neutrality so that their own style isn't "catching." Because communication is inherently a mutually influential process, when it does become "catching," it is not the sender's own internal states that govern his or her behavior but rather the receiver's external behavior. This is an important caveat in interpreting deception displays, and it becomes evident only when experiments permit sender and receiver to interact. A summary of experiments 1 through 8 is provided in table 14.2.

Outcomes of Interpersonal Deception

Initial and Ongoing Credibility Judgments

We have already discussed receivers' judgments during interpersonal deception as it relates to context and relational factors. However, in IDT, judgments of senders' credibility (i.e., honesty) are considered to be dynamic. Context and relational factors have their greatest impact on initial credibility judgments. As conversations unfold, receivers' judgments of the honesty of senders and their messages become increasingly influenced by sender performance. To the extent that senders' behavior departs from what is expected, receivers should alter their judgments accordingly. However, because senders are monitoring receivers for feedback on their success at deception in order to adjust and repair their communication, detection ability is likely to decline over time in conversations (Buller & Burgoon, 1996b; Buller, Burgoon, Afifi, White, & Buslig, 2002).

Our research has shown consistently that receivers recognize deception when it is present. However, they usually tend to judge deceptive messages as less truthful but not actually deceptive (i.e., judgments of both deceptive and truthful messages fall within the truthful portion of the continuum) (Burgoon et al., 1994). In one study, as deceivers shifted from truth to deception, receivers' judgments of honesty also shifted upward and downward correspondingly (Buller et al., 2002), indicating receivers' awareness of the shifting truth value of senders' responses. Among the factors influencing accuracy that we have confirmed are type of deception (falsification, equivocation, concealment), suspicion, and expertise (Burgoon et al., 1994). Receivers judge equivocal answers as least honest, concealments as most honest, and outright falsifications somewhere in between. Suspicion not only often fails to improve accuracy, it often hinders it. In one study, expert detectors (military intelligence specialists) were least accurate when suspicious. Receivers were especially harsh on equivocal answers when suspicious, but suspicion undermined their ability to detect concealments. Finally, suspicion led receivers to consider acquaintances more honest and strangers less honest.

Effects of Skill and Motivation on Credibility Judgments and Detection Accuracy

Given the number and complexity of tasks facing communicators in conversation, IDT holds that the ability to persuade others of one's truthfulness or to make accurate evaluations of sender credibility are skilled behaviors. Our research has bolstered others' findings that skilled senders are better able to craft an honest-appearing demeanor and so to escape detection (Burgoon, Buller, & Guerrero, 1995; Burgoon, Buller, Guerrero, & Feldman, 1994). We have been unable to determine, however, that receivers who have better social skills are better able to recognize and interpret deceit, leaving open the question of whether native abilities affect detection accuracy. Research by others has documented that with the right kind of training, receivers can improve their accuracy, which suggests that receivers may need to acquire skills through experience and training.

Sender motivation to deceive successfully is another factor that can influence receivers' abilities to make accurate assessments of sender credibility. An early conception of the motivation-accuracy relationship held that motivated senders were actually less successful at deception. This motivation impairment hypothesis held that motivation impaired nonverbal performance during deception (producing more nonstrategic behavior), even though it improved verbal performance (DePaulo & Kirkendol, 1989). This theory is similar to the proverbial "choking under pressure" notion but applied only to nonverbal behaviors and to deception (Burgoon & Floyd, 2000).

By contrast, IDT provides a different view of motivation: It is predicted to facilitate deception success (Buller & Burgoon, 1996b; Burgoon & Floyd, 2000). As we have reviewed, many nonverbal behaviors are controllable and can be strategically deployed to improve deception success. Generally speaking, then, motivation should increase strategic behavior and improve communicators' conversational performance both when telling the truth and when deceiving. (This is not to deny that extreme levels of motivation may interfere with effective production not just of some nonverbal behaviors but also of some verbal ones.) Evidence from our research program bears out these IDT predictions. In one study, deceivers who reported being more motivated were also judged more successful by observers (Burgoon et al., 1995). Another study found that motivation, measured with multiple indicators, enhanced senders' management of their behavior and image irrespective of whether they were deceiving or telling the truth. There was no evidence that any form of motivation harmed any facet of senders' verbal and nonverbal performance, and the only adverse impact on credibility occurred among truthful and deceptive senders who were overly concerned with keeping their arousal in check (Burgoon & Floyd, 2000). This evidence better fits the IDT claim that motivation facilitates strategic displays in conversations rather than the motivation impairment hypothesis.

Conclusion

In taking a communication perspective on deception, we have built a far richer and more complicated view of this all-too-common form of information management. It has forced us to reconsider some of the fundamental issues in communication such as what makes communication interactive, what multiplicity of communicator goals and responsibilities shape interpersonal interaction, and how mutual influence in conversation is enacted. These questions have complex answers, obliging us to build several explanatory mechanisms into IDT such as the distinction between strategic (goal-driven, planned) and nonstrategic (involuntary, unintended) activity, preexisting knowledge and expectations, mental shortcuts in processing deceptive messages, and conversational adaptation. Obviously, no single study can test all the propositions in IDT. Confirming evidence has had to be obtained from a multistudy research program.

To date, this research program has demonstrated that deceptive displays are highly dynamic and variable, depending, among other things, on who the deceiver is interacting with, the type of deceit being enacted, whether the receiver is suspicious or not, and the communication style of the receiver. Deceivers deliberately manage some aspects of their verbal and nonverbal behavior so as to evade detection, and those who are the most skillful communicators are very successful in appearing truthful. At the same time, receivers do recognize when something is amiss, and they often reveal their suspicions through their own communication, something that deceivers in turn recognize and use to further modify their own behavior. The net result is that more often than not, accuracy in detecting deception is low—testament, perhaps, to humans' general adeptness at creating believable deceits.

Still, much work remains to be done tilling this fertile research ground to test unresolved or untested issues. Additionally, IDT has piqued new lines of inquiry that have

TABLE 14.2 *Experiments, Variables, and Citations for Experiments Testing Interpersonal Deception Theory*

Experiment	Independent Variables	Dependent Variables	Source
pre-IDT	Relationship (intimate/friend/stranger) Sender deception (yes/no) Interaction time	Sender nonverbal behavior	Buller & Aune, 1987
pre-IDT	Sender deception (yes/no) Probing (yes/no)	Sender nonverbal behavior	Buller, Comstock, Aune, & Strzyzewski, 1989
	Participation (participant/observer) Sender nonverbal behavior	Receiver honesty Judgments Receiver accuracy	Buller, Strzyzewski, & Hunsaker, 1991
1	Sender deception (yes/no) Probing (yes/no) Suspicion (yes/no)	Sender nonverbal behavior	Buller, Strzyzewski, & Comstock, 1991
	Participation (participant/observer) Sender nonverbal behavior	Receiver honesty Judgments Receiver accuracy	Buller & Hunsaker, 1995
2	Sender deception (yes/no)	Sender nonverbal behavior	Burgoon & Buller, 1994
	Receiver suspicion (high/moderate/low)	Sender and receiver Nonverbal behavior	Burgoon, Buller, Dillman, & Walther, 1995
		Sender language	Buller, Burgoon, Buslig, & Roiger, 1996
	Sender social skills	Sender behavior	Burgoon, Buller, Guerrero, & Feldman, 1994
3	Sender deception and type (truth at time 1; fabrication/concealment/equivocation/general deception at time 2)	Sender information Management	Burgoon, Buller, Guerrero, Afifi, & Feldman, 1996
		Language	Buller, Burgoon, Buslig, & Roiger, 1996

TABLE 14.2 Continued

Experiment	Independent Variables	Dependent Variables	Source
4	Sender deception (yes/no); Deception type (fabrication/concealment/equivocation)	Sender language	Buller, Burgoon, Buslig, & Roiger, 1996
	Sender social skills	Sender behavior Receiver accuracy	Burgoon, Buller, & Guerrero, 1995
	Receiver suspicion (yes/no)	Receiver behavior	Burgoon, Buller, Ebesu, White, & Rockwell, 1996
		Receiver accuracy	Burgoon, Buller, Ebesu, & Rockwell, 1994
	Reanalysis of Bavelas et al. studies Equivocation (yes/no)	Sender information Management and language	Buller, Burgoon, Buslig, & Roiger, 1994
	Further analysis of acoustic and perceptual vocal features	Sender vocalic behavior	Rockwell, Buller, & Burgoon, 1997a, 1997b
5	Sender deception (yes/no) and order (TTTDDDTTTDDD/DDDTTTDDDTTT)	Verbal and nonverbal involvement	Burgoon, Buller, White, Afifi, & Buslig, 1999
	Receiver involvement	Same	Same
	Sender social skills	Same	Same
6	Deception (yes/no)	Sender verbal and nonverbal behavior Sender intentions	Burgoon, Buller, Floyd, & Grandpre, 1996
7	Sender deception and order (TTDD/DDTT)	Verbal and nonverbal behavior	Burgoon, Buller, & Floyd, 2001
	Sender participation (dialogue/monologue)	Same	Same
8	Deception (yes/no)	Verbal and nonverbal behavior Credibility	White & Burgoon, 2001
	Receiver involvement	Same	

applicability beyond face-to-face deception. For example, the rise of new communication technologies has moved to the foreground issues of how interactivity in various modalities (e-mail, audio- and videoconferencing) affects users' ability to discern truthful from deceptive messages due to the availability or lack of feedback and to opportunities for editing and personalizing content that facilitate greater evasion of deception detection. The number of questions deserving investigation seems endless as we peer into the cyberfuture that is close upon us. Taking a communication perspective on these and related issues should yield unique insights beyond those obtained from models that reduce deception to intrapersonal phenomena. It is hoped that by centering attention on communication practices themselves, as well as on the psychological and social factors that are their antecedents, our understanding of interpersonal deceit will be enriched and clarified.

References

Bavelas, J. B., Black, A., Chovil, N., & Mullett, J. (1990). *Equivocal communication*. Newbury Park, CA: Sage.

Buller, D. B. (1986). The effects of distraction during persuasion: A meta-analytic review. *Communication Monographs, 53*, 91–114.

Buller, D. B. (1987). Communication apprehension and reactions to proxemic violations. *Journal of Nonverbal Behavior, 11*, 13–25.

Buller, D. B., & Aune, R. K. (1987). Nonverbal cues to deception among intimates, friends, and strangers. *Journal of Nonverbal Behavior, 11*, 269–290.

Buller, D. B., & Aune, R. K. (1988). The effects of vocalics and nonverbal sensitivity on compliance: A speech accommodation theory explanation. *Human Communication Research, 14*, 301–332.

Buller, D. B., & Aune, R. K. (1992). The effects of speech rate similarity on compliance: Application of communication accommodation theory. *Western Journal of Communication, 1*, 37–53.

Buller, D. B., & Burgoon, J. K (1986). The effects of vocalics and nonverbal sensitivity on compliance: A replication and extension. *Human Communication Research, 13*, 126–144.

Buller, D. B., & Burgoon, J. K. (1996a). Another look at information management: A rejoinder to McCornack, Levine, Morrison, and Lapinski. *Communication Monographs, 63*, 92–98.

Buller, D. B., & Burgoon, J. K. (1996b). Interpersonal deception theory. *Communication Theory, 6*, 203–242.

Buller, D. B., Burgoon, J. K., Afifi, W. A., White, C., & Buslig, A. (2002). The dynamite nature of veracity judgments. Manuscript in submission.

Buller, D. B., Burgoon, J. K., Buslig, A. L. S., & Roiger, J. F. (1994). Interpersonal deception: VIII. Further analysis of nonverbal and verbal correlates of equivocation from the Bavelas et al. (1990) research. *Journal of Language and Social Psychology, 13*, 396–417.

Buller, D. B., Burgoon, J. K., Buslig, A., & Roiger, J. (1996). Testing interpersonal deception theory: The language of interpersonal deception. *Communication Theory, 6*, 268–289.

Buller, D. B., Burgoon, J. K., White, C., & Ebesu, A. S. (1994). Interpersonal deception: VII. Behavioral profiles of falsification, equivocation, and concealment. *Journal of Language and Social Psychology, 13*, 366–396.

Buller, D. B., Comstock, J., Aune, R. K., & Strzyzewski, K. D. (1989). The effect of probing on deceivers and truthtellers. *Journal of Nonverbal Behavior, 13*, 155–169.

Buller, D. B., & Hunsaker, F. (1995). Interpersonal deception: XIII. Suspicion and the truth-bias of conversational participants. In J. Aitken (Ed.), *Intrapersonal communication processes reader* (pp. 239–251). Westland, MI: McNeil.

Buller, D. B., Strzyzewski, K. D., & Comstock, J. (1991). Interpersonal deception: I. Deceivers' reactions to receivers' suspicions and probing. *Communication Monographs, 58*, 1–24.

Buller, D. B., Strzyzewski, K. D., & Hunsaker, F. G. (1991). Interpersonal deception: II. The inferiority of conversational participants as deception detectors. *Communication Monographs, 58*, 25–40.

Burgoon, J. K. (1976). The ideal source: A reexamination of source credibility measurement. *Central States Speech Journal, 27*, 200–206.

Burgoon, J. K. (1978). A communication model of personal space violations: Explication and initial test. *Human Communication Research, 4*, 129–142.

Burgoon, J. K. (1993). Interpersonal expectations, expectancy violations, and emotional communication. *Journal of Language and Social Psychology, 12*, 13–21.

Burgoon, J. K., & Buller, D. B. (1994). Interpersonal deception: III. Effects of deceit on perceived communication and nonverbal behavior dynamics. *Journal of Nonverbal Behavior, 18*, 155–184.

Burgoon, J. K., Buller, D. B., Dillman, L., & Walther, J. (1995). Interpersonal deception: IV. Effects of suspicion on perceived communication and nonverbal behavior dynamics. *Human Communication Research, 22*, 163–196.

Burgoon, J. K., Buller, D. B., Ebesu, A., & Rockwell, P. (1994). Interpersonal deception: V. Accuracy in deception detection. *Communication Monographs, 61*, 303–325.

Burgoon, J. K., Buller, D. B., Ebesu, A., Rockwell, P., & White, C. (1996). Testing interpersonal deception theory: Effects of suspicion on nonverbal behavior and relational messages. *Communication Theory, 6*, 243–267.

Burgoon, J. K., Buller, D. B., & Floyd, K. (2001). Does participation affect deception success? A test of the interactivity principle. *Human Communication Research, 27*, 503–534.

Burgoon, J. K., Buller, D. B., Floyd, K., & Grandpre, J. (1996). Deceptive realities: Sender, receiver, and observer perspectives in deceptive conversations. *Communication Research, 23*, 724–748.

Burgoon, J. K., Buller, D. B., & Guerrero, L. K. (1995). Interpersonal deception: IX. Effects of social skill and nonverbal communication on deception success and detection accuracy. *Journal of Language and Social Psychology* (special issue), *14*, 289–311.

Burgoon, J. K., Buller, D. B., Guerrero, L. K., Afifi, W., & Feldman, C. (1996). Interpersonal deception: XII. Information management dimensions underlying deceptive and truthful messages. *Communication Monographs, 63*, 50–69.

Burgoon, J. K., Buller, D. B., Guerrero, L. K., & Feldman, C. M. (1994). Interpersonal deception: VI. Viewing deception success from deceiver and observer perspectives: Effects of preinteractional and interactional factors. *Communication Studies, 45*, 263–280.

Burgoon, J. K., Buller, D. B., White, C. H., Afifi, W. A., & Buslig, A. L. S. (1999). The role of conversational involvement in deceptive interpersonal communication. *Personality and Social Psychology Bulletin, 25*, 669–685.

Burgoon, J. K., Buller, D. B., & Woodall, W. G. (1996). *Nonverbal communication: The unspoken dialogue* (2nd ed.). New York: McGraw-Hill.

Burgoon, J. K., & Floyd, K. (2000). Testing for the motivation impairment effect during deceptive and truthful interaction. *Western Journal of Communication, 64*, 243–267.

Burgoon, J. K., & Hoobler, G. (in press). Nonverbal signals. In M. L. Knapp & J. Daly (Ed.), *Handbook of interpersonal communication* (pp. 344–390). Thousand Oaks, CA: Sage.

Burgoon, J. K., Stern, L. A., & Dillman, L. (1995). *Interpersonal adaptation: Dyadic interaction patterns.* New York: Cambridge University Press.

DePaulo, B. M., & Kirkendol, S. E. (1989). The motivational impairment effect in the communication of deception. In J. Yuille (Ed.), *Credibility assessment* (pp. 51–70). Deurne, Belgium: Kluwer.

deTurck, M. A., & Miller, G. R. (1985). Deception and arousal: Isolating the behavioral correlates of deception. *Human Communication Research, 12*, 181–201.

Dunbar, N. E., Ramirez, A., Jr., & Burgoon, J. K. (in press). The effects of participation on the ability to judge deceit. *Communication Reports.*

Ekman, P. (1985). *Telling lies.* New York: Norton.

Ekman, P., & Friesen, W. V. (1969). Nonverbal leakage and clues to deception. *Psychiatry, 32*, 88–105.

Knapp, M. L., & Comadena, M. E. (1979). Telling it like it isn't: A review of theory and research on deceptive communication. *Human Communication Research, 5*, 270–285.

McCornack, S. A., & Parks, M. R. (1986). Deception detection and relationship development: The other side of trust. In M. L. McLaughlin (Ed.), *Communication Yearbook 9* (pp. 377–389). Beverly Hills, CA: Sage.

Stiff, J. B., Kim, H. J., & Ramesh, C. N. (1989, May). *Truth-biases and aroused suspicion in relational deception.* Paper presented at the annual meeting of the International Communication Association, San Francisco.

Stiff, J. B., & Miller, G. R. (1986). "Come to think of it . . .": Interrogative probes, deceptive communication, and deception detection. *Human Communication Research, 12,* 339–357.

Toris, D., & DePaulo, B. M. (1984). Effects of actual deception and suspiciousness of deception on interpersonal perceptions. *Journal of Personality and Social Psychology, 47,* 1063–1073.

Rockwell, P., Buller, D. B., & Burgoon, J. K. (1997a). The voice of deceit: Refining and expanding vocal cues to deception. *Communication Research Reports, 14,* (4), 451–459.

Rockwell, P., Buller, D. B., & Burgoon, J. K. (1997b). Measurement of deceptive voices: Comparing acoustic and perceptual data. *Applied Psycholinguistics, 18,* 471–484.

White, C. H., & Burgoon, J. K. (2001). Adaptation and communicative design: Patterns of interaction in truthful and deceptive conversations. *Human Communication Research, 27,* 9–37.

Zuckerman, M., & Driver, R. E. (1985). Telling lies: Verbal and nonverbal correlates of deception. In A. W. Siegman & S. Feldstein (Eds.), *Multichannel integrations of nonverbal behavior* (pp. 129–148). Hillsdale, NJ: Erlbaum.

15

Inoculation and Resistance to Persuasion

Michael Pfau and Erin Alison Szabo

Unlike other theories in this book, which focus on explanations of influence, *inoculation* is a theory about how to prevent influence. Inoculation, in a nutshell, is a strategy for resisting influence attempts. It motivates receivers to bolster their beliefs and attitudes, thereby rendering them less susceptible to influence.

Since the 1920s both academics, who investigate influence, and practitioners, who use it, have expended considerable time and resources to discover, understand, and perfect new and better means of persuasion. Although it has received much less emphasis than persuasion (McGuire, 1964; Miller & Burgoon, 1973), resistance to persuasion is simply the flip side of the same coin: persuasion is an exercise of influence; resistance is about protecting people against influence.

This chapter will explore one approach to resisting persuasion: McGuire's Inoculation Theory. The theory posits that *refutational* treatments, which both raise and refute counterarguments to a person's attitude, confer resistance to influence (Pfau, 1997). Inoculation Theory embodies an elaborate and systematic approach to resistance. Eagly and Chaiken call inoculation, "the grandparent theory of resistance to attitude change" (1993, p. 561).

This chapter will first trace the origins and describe the nature of Inoculation Theory and then summarize research findings on inoculation to date. Next, it will explore unresolved questions concerning inoculation and the process of resistance. Finally, the chapter will address applications of Inoculation Theory in a variety of actual contexts.

Origins and Nature of Inoculation

Inoculation traces its origins to early research on the relative superiority of one- versus two-sided messages. One-sided messages simply reinforce attitudes a person already holds. For example, a parent might tell a nonsmoking adolescent that smoking causes cancer. Two-sided messages raise arguments contrary to a person's attitudes, called *counterarguments*, and then offer arguments and evidence to refute those counterarguments. For example, in addition to the "cancer" argument, an adolescent might be told, "Your friends may tell you that you can quit smoking anytime, but nicotine addiction is extremely difficult to overcome."

In a classic experiment on message "sidedness," Lumsdaine and Janis (1953) found that one- and two-sided messages were comparable in influencing people who were not subsequently exposed to an opposing point of view. Two-sided messages, however, were superior in "producing sustained opinion changes" in people who were subsequently exposed to an opposing point of view (p. 311). That is, the two-sided message conferred lasting resistance to persuasion. The critical question was, *why?* The researchers speculated that two-sided messages may "inoculate" people, thereby making them more resistant to counterpersuasion.

It was the aftermath of the Korean conflict that provided the impetus for Inoculation Theory. During the war, some American POWs had broken, yielding to pressures from their North Korean captors to renounce their country (United States Senate, 1956). Congressional hearings following the war raised alarm about the seeming effectiveness of North Korean "brainwashing" techniques. How might such brainwashing be prevented? This question was the catalyst for McGuire's interest in ways to instill resistance to propaganda and other forms of influence (McGuire & Papageorgis, 1961).

McGuire devised Inoculation Theory as an explanation for resistance to influence. He formulated a biological analogy to explain how inoculating messages might confer resistance: "We can develop belief resistance in people as we develop disease resistance in a biologically overprotected man or animal; by exposing the person to a weak dose of the attacking material strong enough to stimulate his defenses but not strong enough to overwhelm him" (1970, p. 37). Just as injecting a person with a small dose of a flu virus can build up the person's immunity to the flu, exposing a person to weak arguments and refutation on an issue can increase the person's resistance when she or he is later exposed to stronger arguments on that issue.

Early applications of Inoculation Theory argued that these effects were particularly true for "overprotected" people. Note that, if a person has been raised in a germ-free environment, he or she will be more vulnerable when exposed to germs than someone who grew up less protected. In the same way, some beliefs, which McGuire called "cultural truisms" have never been challenged and may therefore be more vulnerable when attacked. In other words, cultural truisms are beliefs that are uncontested and therefore taken for granted. Early on in his research, McGuire focused on such truisms as the benefits of having an annual physical; the merits of penicillin; use of chest x-rays to prevent tuberculosis; and the need for regular dental hygiene (McGuire, 1970).

Although McGuire was tempted to frame Inoculation Theory much more broadly (McGuire, 1961a), research findings of the period cast doubt on whether inoculation protected beliefs other than cultural truisms (Brehm & Cohen, 1962). Thus, McGuire narrowed the boundaries of Inoculation Theory to cultural truisms (McGuire, 1970).

Later, Pryor and Steinfatt (1978) extended the theory beyond cultural truisms. They maintained that McGuire's rationale for restricting inoculation to "germ-free" (e.g., uncontested) beliefs was faulty; that the biological analogy applied to the specific arguments that might be raised in an inoculation treatment, not the topic itself. Pryor and Steinfatt's results failed to support the viability of inoculation on behalf of middle- or higher-level beliefs. However, other researchers were able to confirm that *refutational preemption*, one of the key axioms of the theory, was effective in fostering resistance to influence, even with controversial topics (Adams & Beatty, 1977; Anatol & Mandel, 1972; Burgoon, Burgoon, Riess, Butler, Montgomery, Stinnett, Miller, Long, Vaughn, & Caine, 1976; Burgoon & Chase, 1973; Burgoon, Cohen, Miller, & Montgomery, 1978; Burgoon & King, 1974; Crane, 1962; Cronen & LeFleur, 1977; Hunt, 1973; McCroskey, 1970; McCroskey, Young, & Scott, 1972; Miller & Burgoon, 1979; Sawyer, 1973; Szybillo & Heslin, 1973; Tate & Miller, 1973; Ullman & Bodaken, 1975).

Inoculation Theory posits that two components contribute to resistance: *threat* and *refutational preemption*. Threat consists of warning a person that his or her existing attitudes are likely to be challenged. For threat to work, these challenges must be sufficiently powerful to make people accept that their existing attitudes may be vulnerable. Thus, the threat serves as the *motivational trigger* in the inoculation model. It motivates the individual to strengthen his or her attitudes, setting in motion the internal process of resistance. The second element, refutational preemption, involves the process of raising, and then answering, specific objections. The refutational preemption component functions much like the two-sided message: It raises opposing arguments and then provides the arguments and evidence to refute them. These integral components, threat and refutational preemption, work in tandem: Threat motivates the individual to bolster his or her attitudes; refutational preemption offers specific content that can be used to protect and defend one's attitudes.

Of the two elements, the threat component may be the more important, because it is the "motivational effect" that boosts a person's immunity to all forms of attacks. "If the construct were limited to preemptive refutation, it would afford limited utility since communicators would need to prepare specific preemptive messages corresponding to each and every anticipated attack" (Pfau & Kenski, 1990, p. 75). However, due to the "motivational effect," inoculation unleashes a process that offers a broad umbrella of protection, extending beyond the specific arguments raised in the opposing message. Inoculation increases receivers' resistance to novel, unfamiliar counterarguments as well.

The best evidence of this broad umbrella of protection is found in the results of studies that reveal comparable efficacy for both *refutational same* and *different* inoculation treatments. Refutational "same" treatments systematically refute one or more specific counterarguments that will be encountered, whereas refutational "different" messages are more generic in nature. For example, during the 1988 presidential campaign, polling data indicated that Democrat Michael Dukakis was vulnerable to Republican attack for being soft on crime. Pfau and his colleagues (1990) prepared a refutational "same" inoculation message that raised this counterargument and preemptively refuted it. The message argued that Dukakis favored tough sentences, but that tough sentences alone did little to reduce crime. The message also argued that drugs are responsible for most crime and that Dukakis favored increased funding for drug education and enforcement. The researchers also prepared a refutational "different" message, arguing that in contrast to his opponent, Michael Dukakis believed that it was time for a change; that America can, and must, do better to extend the economic expansion to those who have been left out, provide basic health insurance for all families, and stop the pollution of America's air and water. The results of the study revealed that, following inoculation, when Dukakis supporters were confronted with a Bush message attacking Dukakis for being soft on crime, they were less persuaded by the attack than control participants who were not inoculated. The effectiveness of the refutational "same" and "different" inoculation messages was comparable. Indeed, the early laboratory research on inoculation (McGuire, 1961b, 1962, 1966; Papageorgis & McGuire, 1961), later field research (Pfau, 1992; Pfau & Burgoon, 1988; Pfau, Kenski, Nitz, & Sorenson, 1990; Pfau, Van Bockern, & Kang, 1992), and more recent experiments (Pfau, Tusing, Koerner, Lee, Godbold, Penaloza, & Yang, 1997a; Pfau, Szabo, Anderson, Morrill, Zubric, & Wan, 2000) have all indicated that refutational "same" and "different" treatments are virtually identical in their capacity to confer resistance to influence.

Additional evidence for the critical role of threat in resistance comes from two areas. First, a number of studies have confirmed a positive relationship between threat and resistance. Studies that overtly manipulated threat conditions (McGuire, 1962, 1964; McGuire & Papageorgis, 1961, 1962) or the presence of threat levels (Pfau & Burgoon, 1988; Pfau et al., 1990; Pfau et al., 1992; Pfau et al., 1997a; Pfau, Szabo et al., 2000) found that greater threat enhances resistance. Second, research findings have suggested that communication increases attitude persistence, not so much due to the specific content emphasized but by motivating people to generate their own thoughts about the topic (Love & Greenwald, 1978; Petty, 1977).

Empirical Support for Inoculation

Early research on inoculation compared the effectiveness of *supportive* (bolstering) versus *refutational* (inoculation) approaches to resistance. The supportive approach seeks to reinforce existing beliefs and attitudes. If a person believes that a ballistic missile defense system is desirable, a supportive approach would provide arguments and evidence to bolster this position. By contrast, the refutational or inoculative approach attempts to threaten people's attitudes by warning of possible challenges to attitudes and then raises and preemptively refutes these challenges. The person who supports a ballistic missile defense system would be told that she or he can expect to encounter strong arguments opposing her or his position. Then specific objections would be raised and immediately refuted.

Studies directly comparing the effectiveness of the supportive and refutational approaches have generally indicated that the refutational approach is superior (Anderson & McGuire, 1965; Crane, 1962; McGuire, 1961a, 1962, 1966; McGuire & Papageorgis, 1961, 1962; Papageorgis & McGuire, 1961; Suedfeld & Borrie, 1978; Tannenbaum, Macaulay, & Norris, 1966; Tannenbaum & Norris, 1965), although a number of these studies revealed that the use of both approaches was better than the use of either one alone (McGuire, 1961a, 1962; Tannenbaum & Norris, 1965). These studies established the viability of inoculation and in the process resolved a nagging caveat about use of inoculation, namely, whether prompting people in regard to arguments that are contrary to attitudes might unwittingly produce attitude change.

Early studies also explored the persistence of inoculation treatments over time, revealing that although treatments did deteriorate over time, refutational "different" messages decayed less than refutational "same" messages (McGuire, 1962, 1964, 1966; Pryor & Steinfatt, 1978). Also, studies explored the potential of reinforcement, or booster sessions, attempting to discover whether it was possible to prolong a resistance effect. The answer was a qualified "yes." McGuire (1961b) reported that "double defenses" provided additional reinforcement, but only with refutational "same" treatments. Tannenbaum and colleagues (1966), however, revealed that "concept-boost" messages strengthened resistance, although the effect fell short of statistical significance.

All in all, research indicates that inoculation is amazingly robust in conferring resistance to influence. Although treatments need to incorporate the core elements of threat and refutational preemption, it seems to make very little difference how else inoculation treatments are designed. Research suggests comparable efficacy for inoculation treatments whether they are written as refutational "same" or "different" (see works cited above), designed to elicit central or peripheral message processing (Pfau et al., 1997b), built to emphasize a message's content or source (Freedman & Sears, 1965; Stone, 1969), constructed as cognitive or affective positive/negative (Lee & Pfau, 1998) or affective happy/angry (Pfau, Szabo et al., 2000), or delivered via print or video (Pfau, Holbert, Zubric, Pasha, & Lin, 2000).

Questions about the Process of Resistance

Recent years have witnessed a resurgence of interest in inoculation. Some research returned to the core axioms of inoculation, seeking to uncover further nuances about the process of resistance and updating the theory on the basis of the new knowledge about social influence that has accumulated since the 1960s. This section of the chapter will focus on these efforts to understand the process of resistance.

The Core Components of Resistance

As indicated above, threat and refutational preemption are core elements of Inoculation Theory. Threat serves as the motivational catalyst for inoculation. Refutational preemption provides content that people might use in order to strengthen their attitudes and affords them an opportunity to practice defending them. Thus, the process of resistance is part motivational and part cognitive. However, much more needs to be learned about the inner workings of the process (Eagly & Chaiken, 1993).

Recent studies have focused on the role of these and other critical elements in the process of resistance. It is known, for example, that threat motivates receivers to bolster beliefs, but how? Precisely *what internal process* does threat trigger? Is the process all cognitive, causing people to come up with counterarguments to defend their attitudes, or is it both cognitive and affective? Pfau and his colleagues (1997a, 2000) tried to answer these questions by pinpointing the role and impact of threat, refutational preemption, and other potentially crucial elements in the process of resistance.

The initial study (1997a) examined a variable that Petty and Cacioppo (1979b) called *issue involvement*. People tend to display greater issue involvement when the outcome of an issue affects them personally. The question examined in the study was whether inoculation's effectiveness hinged on receiver involvement in an issue. Pfau and his colleagues (1997a) speculated that involvement might function as a prerequisite for resistance, in other words, that involvement might dictate the boundary conditions for Inoculation Theory.

Previous research had hinted that this might be the case. Studies found, for example, that for inoculation to work, the receiver must be involved in the topic or issue (Kamins & Asseal, 1987; Papageorgis, 1968; Petty & Cacioppo, 1979a; Pfau, 1992). On the other hand, the results of another study by Pfau and his colleagues (1997a) revealed that threat increased resistance, primarily with *moderately* involving topics. Specifically, with a moderately involving topic, threat accomplished two things. First, it immediately and directly strengthened the attitudes that were being threatened. Second, it caused people to come up with arguments defending their attitudes (i.e., more counterarguments), which also strengthened their resistance to attack. This effect was not nearly as pronounced with low-involving topics, and it was nonexistent with high-involving topics. Why? Pfau and his colleagues reasoned that there is an optimal level of involvement for inoculation to work. If involvement is too low, inoculation cannot generate enough threat; if it is too high, inoculation is unable to generate further threat. In other words, if an individual already cares about an issue, it is difficult to threaten her or him further. The person's high level of involvement already ensures that he or she is alert and vigilant to opposing messages.

In addition to issue involvement and the core elements of Inoculation Theory— threat and refutational preemption—Pfau and colleagues (1997a) also operationalized the process of counterarguing in terms of a person's ability to generate refutational responses to arguments contrary to existing attitudes. McGuire assumed that threat elicited "an underlying process of covert counterarguing" in inoculated receivers (Eagly & Chaiken, 1993, p. 564). Although he often employed the term *counterarguing,* to explain the process of resistance, he never operationalized it in his own research. Pfau and colleagues' (1997a) results were mixed insofar as counterarguing was concerned. With the moderately involving topic, results revealed that both inoculation treatments and issue involvement elicited threat, which in turn contributed to counterarguing and thereby to resistance to persuasive attacks. However, the results were less clear for the role of counterarguing with either low- or high-involving topics.

In addition to the role of threat, issue involvement, and receiver counterarguing in the process of resistance, results revealed that inoculation treatments make a direct, sizable contribution to resistance. This effect was evident for each of the three issues in the study. This finding suggests one of two possibilities: Either the refutational preemption component of inoculation treatments contributes independently to resistance, or there are as yet unexplained elements in the process of resistance. Insko (1967) was the first to raise the specter of unexplained elements in resistance. He noted: "Beyond these defense alerting [threat element] and defense producing [refutational preemption element] mechanisms, it is entirely possible that other mechanisms result in the creation of defenses . . ." (p. 319); "a complete explanation of resistance to persuasion will depend upon the Inoculation Theory mechanisms as well as upon . . . additional mechanisms" (p. 328). The next wave of inoculation studies will attempt to determine if attitude accessibility or priming reveal further nuances in our understanding of the process of resistance.

Role of Affect in Resistance

The next investigation to illuminate the process of resistance (Pfau, Szabo et al., 2000) examined the role and impact of *affect* on resistance. Specifically, the study examined whether making people angry or happy altered their resistance to a message that threatened their attitudes. Lee and Pfau (1998) had initially investigated the relative effectiveness of cognitive and affective (positive and negative) inoculation treatments in conferring resistance against cognitive and affective attacks. The results revealed that all three treatments (cognitive, positive affect, and negative affect) conferred resistance, but their effectiveness varied depending on the type of persuasive attack encountered. Lee and Pfau (1998) reported that cognitive inoculation treatments provided the most resistance overall. The cognitive treatments were effective with cognitive and affective positive attacks, but not affective-negative attacks. However, results for the affective inoculation treatments were obfuscated due to weak affect manipulations.

　　The Pfau and colleagues' (2000) investigation also compared the efficacy of cognitive and affective (anger and happiness) inoculation treatments. However, this study focused more broadly on the process of resistance, especially the role of elicited affect in resistance. The researchers reasoned that affect should play an instrumental role in resistance because threat functions as the motivational catalyst to resistance (Pfau, 1997) and motivation is more affective than cognitive in nature (Izard, 1993).

　　The study predicted that all three treatment types would foster resistance, since they featured both threat and refutational preemption, but that they might do so in different ways. The researchers postulated that cognitive inoculation treatments would be more effective than affective-anger treatments, which in turn would be superior to affective-happiness treatments in fostering counterarguing. However, results indicated that all three treatment types triggered counterarguing and, thereby, resistance. The reason was that *self-efficacy* moderated resistance outcomes. Self-efficacy, a measure of an individual's perceived confidence in handling environmental obstacles (Bandura, 1983), was thought to predict how a person responded to threat. Interestingly, affective-happiness messages did not work through the core resistance mechanisms of elicited threat or receiver counterarguing. The effectiveness of affective-happiness messages was also limited to receivers with low self-efficacy. Affective-anger inoculation treatments produced the greatest resistance in the high self-efficacy condition, whereas cognitive inoculation treatments produced a curvilinear effect, producing maximum resistance at moderate levels of self-efficacy.

　　Pfau and colleagues (2000) found that issue involvement triggered receiver counterarguing and contributed to resistance, providing further support for the results of Pfau et al. (1997a), especially in revealing that inoculation treatments make direct and indirect contributions to resistance. Inoculation treatments acted directly, independent of internal processes, to foster resistance. In addition, treatments worked indirectly to promote resistance. The pattern of results indicated that cognitive and affective-anger treatments elicited threat, which in turn contributed to receiver counterarguing and elicited anger, thus indirectly fostering resistance. The role and impact of elicited emotion in the process of resistance was particularly noteworthy. The results revealed that elicited anger and happiness exerted sizable, but opposite, effects: anger facilitating resistance, happiness inhibiting it.

Other Considerations in Resistance

Other important issues in resistance include the timing and persistence of inoculation and reinforcement treatments and the role and influence of communication modality in resistance.

Timing and Persistence Questions

The optimal timing of inoculation treatments has been the focus of a number of studies, but the issue remains unsettled. Because of the role of threat in resistance, some lag between treatment and attack is required in order to permit people to generate counterarguments (Miller & Baron, 1973). How much delay is unclear, especially in light of research indicating that inoculation, like any message stimulus, decays over time (McGuire, 1962; Pfau, 1997; Pfau et al., 1990; Pfau & Van Bockern, 1994; Pryor & Steinfatt, 1978).

Early inoculation scholars reasoned that the type of treatment a person receives may impact how persistent his or her attitudes will be. McGuire (1964) and Manis and Blake (1963) found that the resistance produced by inoculation "different" as opposed to "same" treatments increased following a modest delay prior to attack. In addition, McGuire (1962, 1966) and Pryor and Steinfatt (1978) reported that the decay of inoculation-induced resistance could be reduced via refutational "different," as opposed to "same," treatments. Later studies by Pfau and Burgoon (1988) and Pfau et al. (1990) indicated that the resistance conferred via inoculation "different" treatments persisted longer, at least with character attacks.

Finally, research examined the potential of reinforcement, or booster sessions, seeking to determine if the inoculation effect could be prolonged. As noted previously, two early studies of booster influence produced weak results (McGuire, 1961b; Tannenbaum et al., 1966). Further, more recent studies by Pfau and his colleagues featuring reinforcement or booster treatments (1990, 1997a, 2000) failed to clarify the matter, revealing no incremental persistence for reinforcement messages. The reason may involve timing. All studies to date have administered booster sessions within a brief interval following initial treatment (maximum of four weeks). In order to test reinforcement fairly, future research should increase the time interval between the administration of inoculation treatments and booster messages and should employ multiple reinforcements administered over time.

Role and Influence and the Communication Medium

With two exceptions (Godbold & Pfau, 2000; Pfau et al., 1992), all the inoculation research to date has employed print messages. The reason is that inoculation is supposed to be an active, cognitive process and print is perceived as the optimal medium for triggering this process. Following Medium Theory, Pfau, Holbert and colleagues (2000) reasoned that both print and visual media should function as effective vehicles for the communication of inoculation treatments, but that they might do so in different ways. Because print is considered the more effective medium for *systematic processing*, that is, actively thinking about a message (Chaiken & Eagly, 1976, 1983; Petty & Cacioppo, 1986), Pfau, Holbert, and colleagues (2000) predicted that print inoculation treatments would be superior in triggering counterarguing. Because video elevates visual over aural content (see Chesebro, 1984; Meyrowitz, 1985; Salomon, 1987), the researchers posited that video inoculation treatments would rely more heavily on source cues and less on counterarguing.

These suspicions were confirmed. Both media conferred resistance, but in markedly different ways. Video treatments worked immediately, whereas treatments using print media took more time. Video treatments fostered resistance based on the source of the message. Viewers displayed more positive perceptions of the source of the inoculating message. This in turn resulted in more negative perceptions of the credibility of the source of the counterattitudinal attacks. In contrast, print inoculation treatments worked via message content, requiring more time to foster resistance.

Applications of Inoculation Theory

Because inoculation is designed to protect people against influence, it has received increased attention in recent years in a number of applied contexts (Eagly & Chaiken, 1993). This section will focus on the applications of Inoculation Theory and research in the political, commercial, and health campaign contexts.

Political Applications

The scope and intensity of attack messages in highly visible U.S. Senate and presidential races have grown significantly in recent years (Ansolabehere & Iyengar, 1995; Jamieson, 1992; Kern, 1989; Pfau & Kenski, 1990), now comprising nearly half of all political ads (Johnson-Cartee & Copeland, 1997). Political attack messages, which seek to "create negative images" of an opposing candidate's position on issues, past record, or character (Gronbeck, 1992) are considered to be a very effective strategy to influence "leaners" and undecided voters (Ansolabehere & Iyengar, 1997; Johnson-Cartee & Copeland, 1997; Kaid & Boydston, 1987; Kern, 1989; Kern & Just, 1995; Mann & Ornstein, 1983; Newhagen & Reeves, 1991; Pfau & Kenski, 1990; Pinkleton, 1998; Sabato, 1981, 1983; Tarrance, 1980; Tinkham & Weaver-Lariscy, 1993). The question for political practitioners is, given the near certainty of facing an opponent's attacks, what can be done to deflect their influence? The standard options, refutation or response ads or news media adwatches, are after-the-fact remedies and are therefore often unable to undo the damage inflicted by the attack. By contrast, inoculation is a preemptive strategy. Inoculation seeks to make potential voters resistant to attacks before the attacks occur.

The potential of inoculation to deflect the influence of political attacks was investigated in two large field studies. The first centered on the 1986 campaign for the U.S.

Senate from South Dakota involving incumbent Republican James Abdnor and Democratic challenger Tom Daschle (Pfau & Burgoon, 1988). The other centered on the 1988 presidential campaign involving Republican George Bush and Democrat Michael Dukakis (Pfau et al., 1990).

The 1986 study included 733 potential voters and featured an intense campaign, in which the two well known and highly regarded candidates made extensive use of political advertising, spending $6.6 million, or $22 per vote cast in the election (Brokaw, 1986). The results of the 1986 study indicated that both inoculation "same" and "different" messages conferred resistance to the influence of subsequent political attacks (Pfau & Burgoon, 1988), regardless of political party, issue, and character content. Overall, inoculation effects were most pronounced among strong party identifiers, although an interaction revealed that inoculation "same" treatments were better with strong identifiers, whereas "different" treatments were better among weak identifiers (Pfau & Burgoon, 1988).

The subsequent 1988 investigation featured 314 prospective voters and was conducted in September and October of the Bush-Dukakis presidential campaign. The 1988 study featured a number of new twists. It employed direct mail to administer inoculation treatments. It featured booster sessions, and it allowed for a direct comparison of inoculation versus post hoc refutation. Inoculation is a process that intrinsically involves acknowledging vulnerabilities, based on the rationale that this is the best way to protect against counterinfluence. If there is a downside to this approach, it can only be exposed in direct comparison to post hoc approaches. Yet this has "received scant attention in the extant literature" (Pfau et al., 1990, p. 29). The only previous assessment of pre- and postrefutation treatments was conducted by Tannenbaum and colleagues and revealed a slight advantage for prerefutation (Tannenbaum & Norris, 1965; Tannenbaum et al., 1966).

Results of the 1988 investigation offered further evidence for the viability of inoculation in a political campaign context. Results confirmed previous findings, indicating that both "same" and "different" inoculation treatments increased resistance to subsequent political attacks (Pfau et al., 1990). Results did not indicate efficacy for booster sessions, perhaps due to the premature administration of the reinforcing materials.

Finally, the results indicated that a *pre-attack* approach, operationalized as inoculation and inoculation-plus-reinforcement, was superior to post hoc refutation in safeguarding voters' original attitudes about candidates. The effect was most pronounced with strong party identifiers and with nonidentifiers. With weak party identifiers, the superiority of the pre-attack over the post hoc approaches was confined to the character attack condition (Pfau et al., 1990).

The combined findings of the 1986 and 1988 studies suggest that inoculation offers "a viable approach for candidates to deflect the persuasiveness of political attack messages" (Pfau & Kenski, 1990, p. 160). Both studies used a single inoculation, injected during the final weeks of intense campaigns, conditions that should have weakened resistance effects. Inoculation would exert more impact in less intense campaigns, or, in more intense campaigns, if initiated early, prior to opponents' attacks. In today's attack oriented political campaigns, inoculation offers a viable remedy. As Republican consultant Jim

Innocenzi (cited in Ehrenhalt, 1985, p. 2563) advises, "Inoculation and preemption are what win campaigns."

The next application of inoculation in a political context was as a potential preventive to Noelle-Neumann's "spiral of silence." Noelle-Neumann (1974, 1984) posited a "dark side" of public opinion and democracy. She theorized that many people who hold opinions that deviate from majority sentiment on controversial issues become hesitant—even unwilling—to express those opinions publicly. Their reticence stems from "the fear of sanctions resulting in social isolation" (1984, p. 65). The spiral of silence sets in motion a "snowball effect," in which those in the majority continue to speak out but those in the minority fall increasingly silent.

Lin (2000) examined the potential of inoculation to break the spiral of silence in Taiwan, a fledgling democracy. He chose a highly controversial issue: Taiwan's relationship with China. The study tested the potential of inoculation treatments to boost the attitude confidence and willingness to speak out on behalf of people holding minority opinions on this issue. Results of the two-stage survey of 206 randomly sampled adults indicated that inoculation strengthened attitudes. Compared to the control group, those who were inoculated became increasingly confident in their attitudes over time. They showed more attitudinal confidence, greater willingness to speak out on behalf of attitudes, and increased likelihood of resisting the opposing positions of others (Lin, 2000). Lin concluded that inoculation can "break" the spiral of silence, potentially invigorating public deliberation of issues, a bedrock of viable democratic political systems.

Commercial Applications

Inoculation has been tested in two commercial contexts: as a strategy to mitigate the influence of comparative advertising messages, and as a strategy to protect the public image of corporations in crisis situations. In both instances, preliminary results were promising.

Five studies established a foundation for later inoculation research in commercial advertising. Two of them focused on social marketing. First, Bither, Dolich, and Nell (1971, p. 60) examined the use of inoculation to foster resistance against attacks espousing movie censorship. The study concluded that inoculation was able to reinforce attitudes. Szybillo and Heslin (1973) inoculated people's belief that airbags should be installed in automobiles, finding that refutational treatments were superior to supportive treatments. Two other studies compared the efficacy of refutational and supportive treatments in promoting resistance to Federal Trade Commission (FTC) attacks. Hunt (1973) concluded that refutational treatments were superior, but Gardner, Mitchell, and Staelin (1977) reported no differences. A fifth investigation examined the efficacy of refutational and supportive print ads on behalf of five products. Sawyer (1973) found that refutational ads were superior, with limitations based on attitude toward the product and/or the product class.

These studies employed a refutational approach, which is a necessary, but not sufficient, condition for inoculation. What they did not do was feature threat. Research on inoculation in a commercial advertising context either failed to operationalize threat and/ or failed to measure it. Since threat is one of the two core elements in inoculation, functioning as a motivational catalyst for resistance, these manipulations failed to manipulate the inoculation construct properly. What these studies have suggested is the potential for the other core element, refutational preemption, in fostering resistance.

A more recent study, which did confirm effectiveness of the threat manipulation, found that inoculation works, but with certain caveats (Pfau, 1992). The caveats are *receiver involvement* in the product class, which is viewed as an "important mediator of consumer behavior" (Mitchell, 1978, p. 195), and *comparative message format*, which involves the style and directionality of the comparison (Lamb, Pride, & Pletcher, 1978; Pride, Lamb, & Pletcher, 1977, 1979) and has been found to moderate the persuasiveness of comparative messages (Lamb, Pletcher, & Pride, 1979).

Pfau (1992) reported that inoculation treatments had a direct effect on receiver brand attitude, but that the effect of inoculation in the product class depended on receiver's level of involvement. Follow-up tests indicated that inoculation is effective in conferring resistance to comparison ads, but only for highly involving products. This finding is consistent with recent research on Inoculation Theory, which suggests that issue involvement may dictate the boundary conditions for Inoculation Theory (Pfau et al., 1997a). Scholars or practitioners interested in applications of inoculation in advertising should recognize that it may prove effective only with highly involving products (Kamins & Asseal, 1987; Pfau, 1992). This would limit its potential, since so much advertising is on behalf of goods and services that aren't highly involving.

In the context of public relations, research has focused on whether inoculation might prove to be an alternative proactive crisis communication strategy. Proactive approaches tend to be preventive in nature. The two most common proactive approaches in crisis communication are *issues management*, in which organizations try to anticipate potential problems and put in place formal plans designed to monitor and to prevent them (Heath, 1997), and *image promotion*, in which organizations strive to establish a base of goodwill to deflect damage to an organization's image should a crisis occur (Coombs, 1998).

Image promotion is a strategy that is conceptually similar to bolstering messages in the resistance literature. It seeks to foster positive attitudes about an organization, in essence building a "reservoir of goodwill" to protect an organization against attitude slippage in the event of a crisis (Fink, 1986, p. 96). In contrast, inoculation, which has not been studied in the crisis communication context, would raise an organization's potential vulnerabilities and the specter of crisis and then preemptively refute them, delineating what the organization is doing to address these concerns (Pfau & Wan, in press). Wan (2000) predicted that a combination of inoculation and image promotion would provide the best proactive approach. Wan predicted, however, that if only one approach was used, inoculation would prove superior to image promotion. This prediction is consistent with the early resistance research, indicating that refutational defenses are superior to supportive defenses (Anderson & McGuire, 1965; McGuire, 1961a, 1962, 1966; McGuire & Papageorgis, 1961, 1962; Papageorgis & McGuire, 1961; Tannenbaum et al., 1966; Tannenbaum & Norris, 1965).

To test this notion, Wan (2000) studied public attitudes toward a real petroleum company over a one-month period. Participants received an inoculation "same" treatment, an inoculation "different" message, an image-enhancing "bolstering" message, a combined "refutational-bolstering" message, or no message (control). Later, some participants assigned to crisis conditions received a counterattitudinal crisis message. The results indicated that for participants possessing positive initial attitudes toward the organization, all treatment approaches—inoculation "same" and "different," image bolstering and combination—were effective in protecting the image of the organization following exposure to the crisis scenario, but that no one approach worked best (Wan, 2000). With subjects not exposed to the crisis scenario, the bolstering approach was slightly superior to inoculation, suggesting some downside to inoculation, but a lack of power rendered this finding tentative.

Health Campaign Applications

Because inoculation is a useful approach in situations in which attitudes are vulnerable if challenged, it is receiving increased attention in the health campaign context, particularly targeting adolescent behaviors. In many areas, children's attitudes are initially formed during preadolescence but are then subject to intense pressure during adolescence. Millman and Botvin (1983) have observed this developmental pattern in a number of adolescent controversies, such as tobacco, alcohol, drugs, and sexual intercourse. Jessor and Jessor (1975) refer to these as "transition-marking behaviors." For these behaviors, inoculation would seem to be an ideal strategy because it is designed to make attitudes more resistant to change (Miller & Burgoon, 1973). In this section we will examine research on inoculation's ability to reduce the onset of adolescent smoking and drinking.

Smoking Prevention. As a result of the efforts of parents and teachers, most children develop attitudes opposing smoking early in their lives. Typically, these attitudes persist until the transition to the middle grades, when they erode due to physiological changes (Hamburg, 1979) in conjunction with intense peer pressure (Bewley & Bland, 1977; Evans & Raines, 1982; Flay, d'Avernas, Best, Kersell & Ryan, 1983; Foon, 1986; Friedman, Lichtenstein & Biglan, 1985; Goldberg & Garn, 1982; Gottlieb & Baker, 1986; Harken, 1987; Hurd, Johnson, Pechacek, Best, Jacobs, & Luepker, 1980; McAlister, Perry, & Maccoby, 1979; O'Rourke, O'Byrne, & Wilson-Davis, 1983; Pechacek & McAlister, 1980; Pederson & Lefcoe, 1982; Rosenberg, 1965; Salomon, Stein, Eisenberg, & Klein, 1984). Just before and during this period, many adolescents' antismoking attitudes soften (Elder & Stern, 1986; Evans & Raines, 1982; Hamburg, 1979; Johnson, 1982; Killen, 1985; Pfau & Van Bockern, 1994; Rokeach, 1987). Consequently, this is a high-risk period for the onset of smoking. McAlister and colleagues emphasize that, "More than half of all current young people who adopt the habit of daily smoking do so before or during their ninth grade school year" (1979, p. 651). Experts agree that a strategy of resistance is needed on or before this critical transition period; a strategy designed to protect against attitude slippage (Allegrante, O'Rourke, & Tuncalp, 1977; Bernstein & McAlister, 1976; Evans, Rozelle, & Mittlemark, 1978; Harken, 1987; McCaul, Glasgow, O'Neill, Freeborn, & Rump, 1982). The Centers for Disease Control (1998) recommended school-based prevention programs that exert maximum intensity during grades 6 through 8.

The most popular antismoking approach has been *social inoculation*, which combines one facet of Inoculation Theory, refutational preemption, with Bandura's *Social Learning Theories* (Wallack & Corbett, 1987). Despite its name, however, social inoculation is not inoculation. It doesn't operationalize the threat component, which provides the internal motivation for people to resist subsequent influence (McGuire, 1962). Instead, it features a potpourri of tactics, including teacher- and/or peer-led discussion sessions, slide and video presentations, peer modeling, schoolwide smoking prevention campaigns, and others. This smorgasbord of methods makes replication difficult, which undermines its utility. Also, it makes it impossible to isolate what elements are responsible for outcomes. Foon questioned, "If these programs are working, what special features are working and how?" (1986, p. 1025). Flay observed that, ". . . we really know very little at this time about which of these program components are necessary for program effectiveness . . ." (1985, p. 378).

The potential of inoculation, including both threat and refutational preemption elements, has been the focus of recent studies. Pfau and colleagues (1992) conducted a longitudinal field study of students making the transition from elementary school to junior high school in Sioux Falls, South Dakota, starting in fall 1990. Inoculation was accomplished via professionally prepared 12- to 25-minute videos. Students were studied for two years. Results of the first year indicated that inoculation videos instilled resistance to smoking onset, but only among adolescents with low self-esteem (Pfau et al., 1992). This interaction pattern of inoculation and receiver self-esteem dissipated by the end of the second year of the study. At this point, 84 weeks after the inoculation treatments, participants in the treatment group held less favorable attitudes toward smoking and smokers (Pfau & Van Bockern, 1994).

The next study of inoculation and smoking prevention by Szabo (2000) examined its potential with fifth- and sixth-grade nonsmokers in both a metropolitan area (163 predominantly African American students) and a rural setting (157 overwhelmingly white students in Iowa).

Szabo's study incorporated additional elements, warranted by recent research documenting a large and unexplained upsurge in adolescent smoking and by recent research on Inoculation Theory. First, Szabo posited that the surge in adolescent smoking during the 1990s, even in the face of pervasive antismoking campaigns, might in part reflect a "boomerang effect" in response to the antismoking campaigns. Using assumptions of Brehm's Psychological Reactance Theory, Szabo designed normative inoculation appeals, which stressed peer disapproval of smoking, plus more traditional health-based messages. She posited that both normative and health-based treatments, which included threat and refutational preemption elements, would instill resistance *in most* adolescents but that the normative appeals would be less likely to trigger psychological reactance *in some* adolescents. Second, to shed further light on the role of affect in resistance, Szabo designed two normative messages, one to elicit anger and one to trigger happiness. In addition, she measured affect elicited by inoculation treatments. Third, Szabo included critical individual difference variables in the design, such as self-efficacy and self-esteem, to determine their roles in the process of resistance.

Szabo's results (2000) suggested that a fine line separates antismoking messages that foster resistance from those that trigger reactance. Contrary to the prediction that all inoculation treatments would enhance resistance to smoking, the results indicated that inoculation effects were contingent on the subpopulation of interest. Inoculation elicited resistance, but only on behalf of two of the four groups targeted. The normative-anger and traditional health-based appeals achieved attitude resistance in rural sixth graders, while the normative-cognitive and health-based messages conferred attitude resistance in urban fifth graders.

Neither rural fifth graders nor urban sixth graders showed any signs of resistance; rather, they exhibited psychological reactance to all the inoculation attempts. In addition, there was some evidence of reactance in all subpopulations. For example, the health-based appeal produced reactance in rural fifth graders, the cognitive message elicited reactance in rural sixth graders, and the normative-anger treatment triggered reactance in all urban students. This study suggested that antismoking messages produce both resistance and reactance in children, depending on the message type and the subpopulation of interest. Finally, Szabo's (2000) results revealed that receiver self-efficacy was strongly associated with resistance to smoking for all students in all conditions but that self-esteem was not.

Drinking Prevention. For the same reasons that inoculation is a promising approach for smoking prevention, it offers potential for reducing the onset of adolescent alcohol use. School-based programs designed to foster resistance to alcohol use have become increasingly prevalent (Elder et al., 1987). These programs feature life skills training and are patterned after the social inoculation approach described previously. Researchers maintain that prevention is a more effective approach than trying to persuade adolescents to stop drinking once they've begun (Hansen, Graham, Wolkenstein, & Rohrbach, 1991; Kreutter, Gewirtz, Davenny, & Love, 1991; Webb, Baer, & McKelvey, 1995). To date, however, resistance efforts have yielded mixed results (Foxcroft, Lister-Sharp, & Lowe, 1997; Slater, Beauvais, Rouner, Van Leuven, Murphy, & Domenech-Rodriguez, 1996; Tobler, 1986). The reason could be "the limited application of a theoretical basis for predicting when peer-based resistance programs are effective" (Godbold & Pfau, 2000, p. 413). As with antismoking social inoculation, it is impossible to pinpoint the specific elements that are responsible for outcomes with "multicomponent" alcohol resistance programs (Kreutter et al., 1991).

Godbold and Pfau (2000) administered an inoculation study involving 417 nondrinking sixth graders. Inoculation was accomplished via three-minute informative or normative videos, designed to resemble public service announcements. Participants were exposed to attack messages either immediately after inoculation or two weeks later. Attacks consisted of actual beer commercials embedded in a series of television advertisements, made to look like a television break.

Godbold and Pfau (2000) predicted that both informative and normative inoculation approaches would be effective in conferring resistance to drinking initiation but that normative messages would be superior because research indicates that they are better suited to "judgmental tasks" (Kaplan, 1989). The results of the study indicated that normative messages produced the lowest estimates of peer acceptance of drinking. However, normative inoculation messages were no better than informative messages in instilling resistance to the beer commercials, and in fact both message strategies exerted limited influence on attitudes and behavioral intentions. The results also revealed that immediate attacks resulted in more resistant attitude and behavioral intentions than did delayed attacks.

Overall, Godbold and Pfau (2000) reported relatively weak effects involving either the normative or informative inoculation strategy. Instead, the pattern of results revealed that the key factor in resistance is adolescent perception of peer approval of drinking, which subsequently leads to threat and, finally, to resistance to alcohol use. The results suggested that practitioners should employ normative messages in order to lower the estimates of peer acceptance and peer pressure to drink in order to enhance resistance to adolescent alcohol use. Godbold and Pfau placed the blame for the weak inoculation effects on the experimental design. Results revealed that the threat manipulation was not adequate.

Conclusion

Inoculation appears to offer an effective means of bolstering receivers' resistance to opposing messages. Inoculation is particularly useful because it increases resistance not only to the specific arguments included in the inoculation treatment but also to novel arguments on the same topic or issue. Two key components of Inoculation Theory are threat and refutational preemption. Threat is the motivational trigger that prompts counterarguing. When receivers feel threatened, they are more likely to bolster their attitudes against impending attacks. Refutational preemption involves raising objections and then refuting them within an inoculating message. This approach tends to increase receivers' resistance not only to the specific objections raised but also to other, novel objections. Although a number of caveats and qualifications regarding the use of inoculation remain, the theory has been shown to work in a variety of persuasive settings.

References

Adams, W. C., & Beatty, M. J. (1977). Dogmatism, need for social approval, and the resistance to persuasion. *Communication Monographs, 44*, 321–325.

Allegrante, J. P., O'Rourke, T. W., & Tuncalp, S. (1977). A multivariate analysis of selected psychosocial variables in the development of subsequent youth smoking behavior. *Journal of Drug Education, 7*, 237–248.

Anatol, K. W. E., & Mandel, J. E. (1972). Strategies of resistance to persuasion: New subject matter for the teacher of speech communication. *Central States Speech Journal, 23*, 11–17.

Anderson, L. R., & McGuire, W. J. (1965). Prior reassurance of group consensus as a factor in producing resistance to persuasion. *Sociometry, 28*, 44–56.

Ansolabehere, S., & Iyengar, S. (1995). *Going negative: How political advertisements shrink and polarize the electorate.* New York: The Free Press.

Bandura, A. (1983). Self-efficacy determinants of anticipated fears and calamities. *Journal of Personality and Social Psychology, 45*, 464–469.

Bernstein, D. A., & McAlister, A. L. (1976). The modification of smoking behavior. *Addictive Behaviors, 1*, 89–102.

Bewley, B. R., & Bland, J. M. (1977). Academic performance and social factors related to cigarette smoking by schoolchildren. *British Journal of Preventative and Social Medicine, 31*, 18–24.

Bither, S. W., Dolich, I. J., & Nell, E. B. (1971). The application of attitude immunization techniques in marketing. *Journal of Marketing Research, 18*, 56–61.

Botvin, G. J. (1982). Broadening the focus of smoking prevention strategies. In T. J. Coates, A. C. Petersen, & C. Perry (Eds.), *Promoting adolescent health: A dialogue on research and practice* (pp. 137–147). New York: Academic Press.

Brehm, J. W., & Cohen, A. R. (1962). *Explorations in cognitive dissonance.* New York: Wiley.

Brokaw, C. (1986, December 10). Abdnor-Daschle race sets new state spending record. *Sioux Falls Argus Leader*, p. 2.

Burgoon, M., Burgoon, J. K., Riess, M., Butler, J., Montgomery, C. L., Stinnett, W. D., Miller, M., Long, M., Vaughn, D., & Caine, B. (1976). Propensity of persuasive attack and intensity of pretreatment messages as predictors of resistance to persuasion. *Journal of Psychology, 92*, 123–129.

Burgoon, M., & Chase, L. J. (1973). The effects of differential linguistic patterns in messages attempting to induce resistance to persuasion. *Speech Monographs, 40*, 1–7.

Burgoon, M., Cohen, M., Miller, M. D., & Montgomery, C. L. (1978). An empirical test of a model of resistance to persuasion. *Human Communication Research, 5*, 27–39.

Burgoon, M., & King, L. B. (1974). The mediation of resistance to persuasion strategies by language variables and active-passive participation. *Human Communication Research, 1*, 30–41.

Centers for Disease Control. (1998, April 3). Tobacco use among high school students: United States 1997. *Morbidity and Mortality Weekly Report, 47*, 229–233.

Chaiken, S., & Eagly, A. H. (1976). Communication modality as a determinant of message persuasiveness and message comprehensibility. *Journal of Personality and Social Psychology, 34*, 605–614.

Chaiken, S., & Eagly, A. H. (1983). Communication modality as a determinant of persuasion: The role of communicator salience. *Journal of Personality and Social Psychology, 45*, 241–256.

Chesebro, J. W. (1984). The media reality: Epistemological functions of media in cultural systems. *Critical Studies in Mass Communication*, 111–130.

Coombs, W. T. (1998). An analytic framework for crisis situations: Better responses from a better understanding of the situation. *Journal of Public Relations Research, 10*, 177–191.

Crane, E. (1962). Immunization—with and without use of counterarguments. *Journalism Quarterly, 39*, 445–450.

Cronen, V. E., & LaFleur, G. (1977). Inoculation against persuasive attacks: A test of alternative explanations. *Journal of Social Psychology, 102*, 255–265.

Eagly, A. H., & Chaiken, S. (1993). *The psychology of attitudes*. Orlando, FL: Harcourt Brace Jovanovich.

Ehrenhalt, A. (1985). Technology, strategy bring new campaign era. *Congressional Quarterly Weekly Report, 43*, 2559–2565.

Elder, J. P., & Stern, R. A. (1986). The ABCs of adolescent smoking prevention: An Environment and skills model. *Health Education Quarterly, 13*, 181–191.

Elder, J. P., Stern, R. A., Anderson, M., Hovell, M. F., Molgaard, C. A., & Seidman, R. L. (1987). Contingency-based strategies for preventing alcohol, drug, and tobacco use: Missing or unwanted components of adolescent health promotion. *Education and Treatment of Children, 10*, 33–47.

Evans, R. I., & Raines, B. E. (1982). Control and prevention of smoking in adolescents: A psychosocial perspective. In T. J. Coates, A. C. Petersen, & C. Perry (Eds.), *Promoting adolescent health: A dialogue on research and practice* (pp. 101–136). New York: Academic Press.

Evans, R. I., Rozelle, R. M., & Mittlemark, M. B. (1978). Deterring the onset of smoking in children. *Journal of Applied Social Psychology, 8*, 126–135.

Fink, S. (1986). *Crisis management: Planning for the inevitable*. New York: American Management Association.

Flay, B. R. (1985). Prosocial approaches to smoking prevention: A review of findings. *Health Psychology, 4*, 449–488.

Flay, B. R., d'Avernas, R. J., Best, J. A., Kersell, M. W., & Ryan, K. B. (1983). Cigarette smoking: Why young people do it and ways of preventing it. In P. J. McGrath & P. Firestone (Eds.), *Pediatric and adolescent behavioral medicine* (pp. 132–183). New York: Springer.

Foon, A. E. (1986). Smoking prevention programs for adolescents: The value of social psychological approaches. *The International Journal of the Addictions, 21*, 1017–1029.

Foxcroft, D. R., Lister-Sharp, D., & Lowe, G. (1997). Alcohol misuse prevention for young people: A systematic review reveals methodological concerns and lack of reliable evidence of effectiveness. *Addiction, 92*, 531–537.

Freedman, J. L., & Sears, D. O. (1965). Warning, distraction, and resistance to influence. *Journal of Personality and Social Psychology, 1*, 262–266.

Friedman, L. S., Lichtenstein, E., & Biglan, A. (1985). Smoking onset among teens: An empirical analysis of initial situations. *Addictive Behaviors, 10*, 1–13.

Gardner, M., Mitchell, A., & Staelin, R. (1977). The effects of attacks and inoculations in a public policy context. In B. A. Greenberg & D. N. Bellenger (Eds.), *Contemporary marketing thought: 1977 educators' proceedings* (pp. 292–297). Chicago, IL: American Marketing Association.

Goldberg, M. E., & Garn, G. J. (1982). Increasing the involvement of teenage cigarette smokers in anti-smoking campaigns. *Journal of Communication, 32*(1), 75–86.

Godbold, L. C., & Pfau, M. (2000). Conferring resistance to peer pressure among adolescents: Using inoculation theory to discourage alcohol use. *Communication Research, 27*, 411–437.

Gottlieb, N., & Baker, J. (1986). The relative influence of health beliefs, parental and peer behaviors and exercise program participation on smoking, alcohol use and physical activity. *Social Science and Medicine, 22*, 915–927.

Gronbeck, B. E. (1992). Negative narratives in 1988 presidential campaign ads. *Quarterly Journal of Speech, 78*, 333–346.

Hamburg, D. A. (1979). Disease prevention: The challenge of the future. *American Journal of Public Health, 69*, 1026–1033.

Hansen, W. B., Graham, J. W., Wolkenstein, B. H., & Rohrbach, L. A. (1991). Program integrity as a moderator of prevention program effectiveness: Results for the fifth-grade students in the adolescent alcohol prevention trial. *Journal of Studies on Alcohol, 52*, 568–579.

Harken, L. S. (1987). The prevention of adolescent smoking: A public health priority. *Evaluation & the Health Professions, 10*, 373–393.

Heath, R. L. (1997). *Strategic issues management: Organizations and public policy challenges*. Thousand Oaks, CA: Sage.

Hunt, H. K. (1973). Effects of corrective advertising. *Journal of Advertising Research, 13*, 15–22.

Hurd, P. D., Johnson, C. A., Pechacek, T., Bast, L. P., Jacobs, D. R., & Luepker, R. V. (1980). Prevention of cigarette smoking in seventh grade students. *Journal of Behavioral Medicine, 3*, 15–28.

Insko, C. A. (1967). *Theories of attitude change*. Englewood Cliffs, NJ: Prentice-Hall.

Izard, C. E. (1993). Four systems of emotion activation: Cognitive and noncognitive processes. *Psychological Review, 100*, 68–90.

Jamieson, K. H. (1992). *Dirty politics: Deception, distraction, and democracy*. New York: Oxford University Press.

Jessor, R., & Jessor, S. L. (1975). Adolescent development and the onset of drinking: A longitudinal study. *Journal of Studies on Alcohol, 36*, 27–51.

Johnson, C. A. (1982). Untested and erroneous assumptions underlying antismoking programs. In T. J. Coates, A. C. Petersen, & C. Perry (Eds.), *Promoting adolescent health: A dialogue on research and practice* (pp. 149–165). New York: Academic Press.

Johnson-Cartee, K. S., & Copeland, G. A. (1997). *Manipulating the American voter: Political campaign commercials*. New York: Praeger.

Kaid, L. L., & Boydston, J. (1987). An experimental study of the effectiveness of negative political advertisements. *Communication Quarterly, 35*, 193–201.

Kamins, M. A., & Asseal, H. (1987). Two-sided versus one-sided appeals: A cognitive perspective on argumentation, source derogation, and the effect of disconfirming trial on belief change. *Journal of Marketing Research, 24*, 29–39.

Kern, M. (1989). *Political advertising in the eighties*. New York: Praeger.

Kern, M., & Just, M. (1995). The focus group method, political advertising, campaign news, and the construction of candidate images. *Political Communication, 12*, 127–145.

Killen, J. D. (1985). Prevention of adolescent tobacco smoking: The social pressure resistance training approach. *Journal of Child Psychology and Psychiatry, 26*, 7–15.

Kreutter, K. J., Gewirtz, H., Davenny, J. E., & Love, C. (1991). Drug and alcohol prevention project for sixth graders: First-year findings. *Adolescence, 26*, 287–293.

Lamb, C. W., Pletcher, B. A., & Pride, W. M. (1979). Print readers' perceptions of various advertising formats. *Journalism Quarterly, 56*, 328–335.

Lamb, C. W., Pride, W. M., & Pletcher, B. A. (1978). A taxonomy for comparative advertising research. *Journal of Advertising, 7*, 43–47.

Lee, W., & Pfau, M. (1998, July). *The effectiveness of cognitive and affective inoculation appeals in conferring resistance against cognitive and affective attacks.* Paper presented at the annual meeting of the International Communication Association, Jerusalem, Israel.

Lin, W.-K. (2000). *Use of inoculation to combat the spiral of silence: A study of public opinion in democracy.* Unpublished doctoral dissertation, University of Wisconsin-Madison.

Love, R. E., & Greenwald, A. C. (1978). Cognitive responses to persuasion as mediators of opinion change. *Journal of Social Psychology, 104,* 231–241.

Lumsdaine, A. A., & Janis, I. L. (1953). Resistance to "counterpropaganda" produced by one-sided and two-sided "propaganda" presentations. *Public Opinion Quarterly, 17,* 311–318.

Manis, M., & Blake, J. B. (1963). Interpretation of persuasive messages as a function of prior immunization. *Journal of Abnormal and Social Psychology, 66,* 225–230.

Mann, T. E., & Ornstein, N. J. (1983). Sending a message: Voters and Congress in 1982. In T. E. Mann & N. J. Ornstein (Eds.), *The American election of 1982* (pp. 133–152). Washington, DC: American Enterprise Institute.

McAlister, A. L., Perry, C., & Maccoby, N. (1979). Adolescent smoking: Onset and prevention. *Pediatrics, 63,* 650–658.

McCaul, K. D., Glasgow, R., O'Neill, H. K., Freeborn, V., & Rump, B. S. (1982). Predicting adolescent smoking. *Journal of School Health, 52*(6), 342–346.

McCroskey, J. C. (1970). The effects of evidence as an inhibitor of counter-persuasion. *Speech Monographs, 37,* 188–194.

McCroskey, J. C., Young, T. J., & Scott, M. D. (1972). The effects of message sidedness and evidence on inoculation against counterpersuasion in small group communication. *Speech Monographs, 34,* 205–212.

McGuire, W. J. (1961a). The effectiveness of supportive and refutational defenses in immunizing and restoring beliefs against persuasion. *Sociometry, 24,* 184–197.

McGuire, W. J. (1961b). Resistance to persuasion conferred by active and passive prior refutation of the same and alternative counterarguments. *Journal of Abnormal and Social Psychology, 63,* 326–332.

McGuire, W. J. (1962). Persistence of the resistance to persuasion induced by various types of prior belief defenses. *Journal of Abnormal and Social Psychology, 64,* 241–248.

McGuire, W. J. (1964). Inducing resistance to persuasion. Some contemporary approaches. In L. Berkowitz (Ed.), *Advances in experimental social psychology* (vol. 1, pp. 191–229). New York: Academic Press.

McGuire, W. J. (1966). Persistence of the resistance to persuasion induced by various types of prior belief defenses. In C. W. Backman & P. F. Secord (Eds.), *Problems in social psychology* (pp. 128–135). New York: McGraw-Hill.

McGuire, W. J. (1970, February). A vaccine for brainwash. *Psychology Today, 3,* 36–39, 63–64.

McGuire, W. J., & Papageorgis, D. (1961). The relative efficacy of various types of prior belief-defense in producing immunity against persuasion. *Journal of Abnormal and Social Psychology, 62,* 327–337.

McGuire, W. J., & Papageorgis, D. (1962). Effectiveness of forewarning in developing resistance to persuasion. *Public Opinion Quarterly, 26,* 24–34.

Meyrowitz, J. (1985). *No sense of place.* New York: Oxford University Press.

Miller, G. R., & Burgoon, M. (1973). *New techniques of persuasion.* New York: Harper & Row.

Miller, M. D., & Burgoon, M. (1979). The relationship between violations of expectations and the induction of resistance to persuasion. *Human Communication Research, 5,* 301–313.

Miller, N., & Baron, R. S. (1973). On measuring counterarguing. *Journal for the Theory of Social Behavior, 1,* 101–118.

Millman, R. B., & Botvin, G. J. (1983). Substance use, misuse, and dependence. In M. D. Levine, W. B. Carey, A. C. Crocker, & R. T. Gross (Eds.), *Developmental-behavioral pediatrics.* Philadelphia: W. B. Saunders.

Mitchell, A. A. (1978). Involvement: A potentially important mediator of consumer behavior. In W. L. Wilkie (Ed.), *Advances in consumer research: Proceedings for the Association for Consumer Research ninth annual conference Miami Beach, Florida, October 1978* (vol. 6, pp. 191–196). Urbana, IL: Association for Consumer Research.

Newhagen, J. E., & Reeves, B. (1991). Emotion and memory responses for negative political advertising: A study of televised commercials used in the 1998 presidential election. In F. Biocca (Ed.), *Television and political advertising: Volume 1: Psychological processes* (pp. 197–220). Hillsdale, NJ: Erlbaum.

Noelle-Neumann, E. (1974). The spiral of silence: A theory of public opinion. *Journal of Communication, 24,* 43–51.

Noelle-Neumann, E. (1984). *The spiral of silence.* Chicago: University of Chicago Press.

O'Rourke, A. H., O'Byrne, D. J., & Wilson-Davis, K. (1983). Smoking among schoolchildren. *Journal of the Royal College of General Practitioners, 33,* 569–572.

Papageorgis, D. (1968). Warning and persuasion. *Psychological Bulletin, 70,* 271–282.

Papageorgis, D., & McGuire, W. J. (1961). The generality of immunity to persuasion produced by pre-exposure to weakened counterarguments. *Journal of Abnormal and Social Psychology, 62,* 475–481.

Pechacek, T. F., & McAlister, A. K. (1980). Strategies for the modification of smoking behavior: Treatment and prevention. In T. Gerguson (Ed.), *The comprehensive handbook of behavioral medicine* (vol. 3, pp. 257–298). New York: Spectrum.

Pederson, L. L., & Lefcoe, N. M. (1982). Multivariate analysis of variables related to cigarette smoking among children in grades four to six. *Canadian Journal of Public Health, 73,* 172–175.

Petty, R. E. (1977). The importance of cognitive responses in persuasion. *Advances in Consumer Research, 4,* 357–362.

Petty, R. E., & Cacioppo, J. T. (1979a). Effects of forewarning of persuasive intent and involvement on cognitive responses and persuasion. *Personality and Social Psychology Bulletin, 5,* 173–176.

Petty, R. E., & Cacioppo, J. T. (1979b). Issue involvement can increase or decrease persuasion by enhancing message-relevant cognitive responses. *Journal of Personality and Social Psychology, 37,* 1915–1926.

Petty, R. E., & Cacioppo, J. T. (1986). *Communication and persuasion: Central and peripheral routes to attitude change.* New York: Springer-Verlag.

Pfau, M. (1990). A channel approach to television influence. *Journal of Broadcasting & Electronic Media, 34,* 195–214.

Pfau, M. (1992). The potential of inoculation in promoting resistance to the effectiveness of comparative advertising messages. *Communication Quarterly, 40,* 26–44.

Pfau, M. (1997). The inoculation model of resistance to influence. In F. J. Boster & G. Barnet (Eds.), *Progress of communication sciences* (vol. 13, pp. 133–171). Norwood, NJ: Ablex Publishing Corporation.

Pfau, M., & Burgoon, M. (1988). Inoculation in political campaign communication. *Human Communication Research, 15,* 91–111.

Pfau, M., Holbert, R. L., Zubric, S. J., Pasha, N. H., & Lin, W.-K. (2000). Role and influence of communication modality in the process of resistance to persuasion. *Media Psychology, 2,* 1–33.

Pfau, M., & Kenski, H. C. (1990). *Attack politics: Strategy and defense.* New York: Praeger.

Pfau, M., Kenski, H. C., Nitz, M., & Sorenson, J. (1990). Efficacy of inoculation strategies in promoting resistance to political attack messages: Application to direct mail. *Communication Monographs, 57,* 1–12.

Pfau, M., Szabo, E. A., Anderson, J., Morrill, J., Zubric, J., & Wan, H.-H. (2000). *The role and impact of affect in the process of resistance.* Paper presented at the annual meeting of the International Communication Association, Acapulco, Mexico.

Pfau, M., Tusing, K. J., Koerner, A. F., Lee, W., Godbold, L. C., Penaloza, L. J., Yang, V. S., & Hong, Y. (1997a). Enriching the inoculation construct: The role of critical components in the process of resistance. *Human Communication Research, 24,* 187–215.

Pfau, M., Tusing, K. J., Lee, W., Godbold, L. C., Koerner, A., Penaloza, Hong, Y., & Yang, V. S. (1997b). Nuances in inoculation: The role of inoculation approach, ego-involvement, and message processing disposition in resistance. *Communication Quarterly, 45,* 461–481.

Pfau, M., & Van Bockern, S. (1994). The persistence of inoculation in conferring resistance to smoking initiation among adolescents: The second year. *Human Communication Research, 20,* 413–430.

Pfau, M., Van Bockern, S., & Kang, J. G. (1992). Use of inoculation to promote resistance to smoking initiation among adolescents. *Communication Monographs, 59,* 213–230.

Pfau, M., & Wan, H.-H. (in press). Persuasion: An intrinsic function of public relations. In C. H. Botan & V. Hazelton, Jr. (Eds.), *Public relations theory II*. Hillsdale, NJ: Erlbaum.

Pinkleton, B. E. (1998). Effects of print comparative advertising on political decision-making and participation. *Journal of Communication, 48*, 24–36.

Pride, W. M., Lamb, C. W., & Pletcher, B. A. (1977). Are comparative advertisements more informative for owners of the mentioned competing brand than for nonowners? In B. A. Greenberg & D. N. Bellenger (Eds.), *Contemporary marketing thought: 1977 educators' proceedings* (series 41, pp. 298–301). Chicago: American Marketing Association.

Pride, W. M., Lamb, C. W., & Pletcher, B. A. (1979). The informativeness of comparative advertisements: An empirical investigation. *Journal of Advertising, 8*, 29–48.

Pryor, B., & Steinfatt, T. M. (1978). The effects of initial belief level on inoculation theory and its proposed mechanisms. *Human Communication Research, 4*, 217–230.

Rokeach, M. (1987). *Health values*. Paper presented to the Institution for Health Promotion and Disease Prevention, Pasadena, CA.

Rosenberg, M. (1965). *Society and adolescent self-image*. Princeton, NJ: Princeton University Press.

Sabato, L. J. (1981). *The rise of political consultants: New ways of winning elections*. New York: Basic Books.

Sabato, L. J. (1983). Parties, PACs, and independent groups. In T. E. Mann & N. J. Ornstein (Eds.), *The American election of 1982* (pp. 72–110). Washington, DC: American Enterprise Institute.

Salomon, G., Stein, Y., Eisenberg, S., & Klein, L. (1984). Adolescent smokers and nonsmokers: Profiles and their changing structure. *Preventive Medicine, 13*, 446–461.

Salomon, G. (1987). *Interactions of media, cognition, and learning: An explanation of how symbolic forms cultivate mental skills and affect knowledge acquisition*. San Francisco: Jossey-Bass.

Sawyer, A. G. (1973). The effects of repetition of refutational and supportive advertising appeals. *Journal of Marketing Research, 10*, 23–33.

Slater, M. D., Beauvais, F., Rouner, D., Van Leuven, J., Murphy, K., & Domenech-Rodriguez, M. M. (1996). Adolescent counterarguing of TV beer advertisements: Evidence for effectiveness of alcohol education and critical viewing discussions. *Journal of Drug Education, 26*, 143–158.

Stone, V. A. (1969). Individual differences and inoculation against persuasion. *Journalism Quarterly, 46*, 267–273.

Suedfeld, P., & Borrie, R. A. (1978). Sensory deprivation, attitude change, and defense against persuasion. *Canadian Journal of Behavioral Science, 10*, 16–27.

Szabo, E. A. (2000). *Inoculation, normative appeals and emotion as strategies to promote resistance to adolescent smoking*. Unpublished doctoral dissertation, University of Wisconsin-Madison.

Szybillo, G. J., & Heslin, R. (1973). Resistance to persuasion: Inoculation theory in a marketing context. *Journal of Marketing Research, 10*, 396–403.

Tannenbaum, P. H., Macaulay, J. R., & Norris, E. L. (1966). Principle of congruity and reduction in persuasion. *Journal of Personality and Social Psychology, 2*, 223–238.

Tannenbaum, P. H., & Norris, E. L. (1965). Effects of combining congruity principle strategies for the reduction of persuasion. *Sociometry, 28*, 145–157.

Tarrance, V. L., Jr. (1980). *Negative campaigns and negative votes: The 1980 elections*. Washington, DC: Free Congress Research and Education Foundation.

Tate, E., & Miller, G. R. (1973, April). *Resistance to persuasion following counterattitudinal advocacy: Some preliminary thoughts*. Paper presented at the annual meeting of the International Communication Association, Montreal.

Tinkham, S. F., & Weaver-Lariscy, R. A. (1993). A diagnostic approach to assessing the impact of negative political television commercials. *Journal of Broadcasting & Electronic Media, 37*, 277–399.

Tobler, N. S. (1986). Meta-analysis of 143 adolescent drug prevention programs: Quantitative outcome results of program participants compared to a control or comparison group. *Journal of Drug Issues, 16*, 537–567.

Ullman, W. R., & Bodaken, E. M. (1975). Inducing resistance to persuasive attack: A test of two strategies of communication. *Western Journal of Speech Communication, 39*, 240–248.

United States Senate (1956). Committee on Government Operations, Permanent Subcommittee on Investigations (84th Congress, 2nd Session). *Communist interrogation, indoctrination and exploitation of American military and political prisoners*. Washington, DC: U.S. Government Printing Office.

Wallack, L., & Corbett, K. (1987). Alcohol, tobacco and marijuana use among youth: An overview of epidemiological, program and policy trends. *Health Education Quarterly, 14*, 223–249.

Wan, H.-H. (2000). *Inoculation and priming in the context of crisis communication.* Unpublished doctoral dissertation, University of Wisconsin-Madison.

Webb, J. A., Baer, P. E., & McKelvey, R. S. (1995). Development of a risk profile for intentions to use alcohol among fifth and sixth graders. *Journal of the American Academy of Child and Adolescent Psychiatry, 34*, 772–778.

Part IV

Contexts for Persuasion

In chapter 3 of this volume, Daniel O'Keefe discussed what he believed were three broad recent developments in the study of persuasion, social influence, and compliance gaining. Among these developments was the increasing amount of research focusing on specific contexts for persuasion. While some persuasive strategies are field invariant or context free, most are not. Even such generic strategies as fear appeals, for example, must be tailored to the specific audience, topic, and setting. Thus, a fear appeal that an attorney might use in a closing argument to a jury ("If you let the defendant go free, he will kill again.") would likely be different from a fear appeal that a car salesperson might use in trying to close a sale ("Do you really want to risk your life in a car without side air bags?"). Similarly, a political consultant who was designing campaign ads that included fear appeals ("Our opponent wants to raise taxes and cut social security.") would likely use a different approach than a police officer assigned to the D.A.R.E. program ("Drugs aren't just physically addictive, they are psychologically addictive as well."). The same applies to other persuasive strategies, principles, and processes. Persuasive strategies rarely come in a "one size fits all" variety. There probably never will be a single, unified theory of persuasion capable of encompassing all persuasive phenomena in every context. Thus, the need to study how persuasion operates in specific contexts is vital. The devil, as they say, is in the details, and the subtle nuances that can make or break a persuasive attempt lie in the particular strategies and tactics that are unique to each persuasive context. For this reason we have included this final section, which illustrates that the study and practice of social influence have many "nooks and crannies." In other words, contextual or situational factors such as the time and place of the persuasive encounter, or the nature of the relationship between the persuader and the persuadee, affect not only the types of influence strategies people use but also how effective such strategies might be.

Chapter 16, by Renee Klingle, for example, explores compliance gaining in medical contexts. In it, you will see how theories and models of persuasion have been used to identify effective and ineffective strategies in physician-patient encounters. If a husband fails to convince his wife that they should buy a big screen television, the consequences for failure aren't too dire. If a physician is unable to persuade a patient to lose weight, stop smoking, or lower his or her blood pressure, however, the patient's life may hang in the balance.

Chapter 17, by Leslie Baxter and Carma Bylund, examines persuasion in close relationships by juxtaposing three unique perspectives: the traditional, the social-meaning, and the dialogic communication approaches. The chapter illustrates not only that the nature of relationships affects the process of persuasion but also that the way in which we conceptualize and study persuasion affects our understanding of it.

Finally, the last two chapters in this volume explore social influence in traditional organizational contexts. Chapter 18, by Randy Hirokawa and Amy Wagner, examines persuasion as it occurs between superiors, subordinates, and coworkers within an organization. Specifically, it examines the nature of upward and downward influence attempts in organizational settings. Chapter 19, by John Seiter and Michael Cody, examines persuasion in retail sales contexts. Specifically, this chapter focuses on the nature of persuasion in selling contexts by exploring how buyers' and sellers' characteristics, tactics, and goals influence successful sales and buyer-seller relationships.

These are, of course, only a few of the myriad contexts in which persuasion occurs. By gaining a better understanding of how persuasion operates in these four specific contexts, you should develop a greater appreciation for the unique features of persuasion, social influence, and compliance gaining in other contexts and settings as well.

16

Compliance Gaining in Medical Contexts

Renee Storm Klingle

Introduction to Medical Compliance

Although medical adherence is generally in the best interest of the patient, patients who seek expert medical advice often fail to follow through with the prescribed or suggested treatment regimens (Eraker, Kirscht, & Becker, 1984; Pitts, 1991; Roter, Hall, Merisca, Nordstrom, Cretin, & Svarstad, 1998). In 1996, I argued that "ignoring medical advice seems to be as common as the common cold and equally difficult to cure" (Klingle, 1996, p. 206). Since that time, remedies have been advanced that are quite effective in reducing the severity and duration of the common cold. The verdict on how best to eradicate patient noncompliance, however, is still out. Even the act of defining compliance, often known as medical adherence, has been open to debate (Henson, 1997).

In the not too distant past, the term medical compliance simply referred to the degree to which patients yielded to the suggestions, orders, or recommendations given by their health care provider (Karoly, 1993). Failure to do so could take a number of forms, ranging from inability to comply, refusal to comply, overcompliance, and partial compliance with what the physician specifically recommended (Fletcher, 1989). The recent movement toward patient-centered care and away from paternalistic care (Ballard-Reisch, 1990; Jones & Phillips, 1988), however, puts a different spin on the definition of medical compliance, as well as the appropriate terminology. Consistent with this trend, authority-laden terms such as *compliance* and *adherence* have quickly begun to be replaced by words that highlight the more reciprocal nature of the physician-patient relationship such as *mutuality, concordance, cooperation,* and *therapeutic alliance* (Kyngas, Duffy, & Kroll, 2000). In turn, definitions of the phenomenon began to contain elements relating to the patient's collaboration with the health care provider and the patient's responsibility for self-care (Kyngas, 2000). Medical compliance came to mean adhering to what the physician *and* patient mutually agreed upon as the appropriate course of medical action.

289

The more politically correct names and definitions, however, could not change the fact that compliance rates, especially in the long term, often fall below 50 percent for patients of all ages, social classes, and intellectual levels, and they remain low regardless of the severity of the symptoms or the life-threatening nature of the disease (Adams, Pill, & Jones, 1997; Klopovich & Thrueworthy, 1985; Kyngas, 2000). The consequences of noncompliance or failed cooperation are often quite serious: unnecessary or dangerous diagnostic and treatment procedures (Becker & Maiman, 1980; Norell, 1980), exacerbation of the medical condition and progression of the ailment (Stewart & Cluff, 1972), inaccurate assessment regarding the value of prescribed medicines or treatment regimens (Wilson, 1973), and additional costs to the patient and the medical community (Berg, Dischler, Wagner, Raia, & Palmer-Shevlin, 1993; Weinstein, 2000). In sum, a patient's lack of adherence to medical recommendations that are either set by the physician or mutually agreed upon by the physician and patient is nothing to sneeze at. Unlike the common cold, noncompliance has the potential to be life-threatening for the patient and an economic disaster for the medical community.

For decades, social scientists have conducted studies aimed at assessing interventions linked to improved medical compliance rates. Studies in the medical field have typically focused on educational interventions such as verbal, audiovisual, and written instructions and reminders; behavioral pattern shaping and skill building; and appeals to emotions and social relationships (Roter et al., 1998). In each advocated intervention, communication between health care providers and patients is cited as playing an integral role in adherence to medical prescriptions. Medical articles (e.g., Dube, O'Donnel, & Novack, 2000; Meryn, 1998) also reiterate the need for better physician communication skills to improve adherence rates. The exact content and nature of the physician's compliance-gaining attempt, however, is generally unspecified (Klingle, 1996; Phillips & Jones, 1991). Rather, advice tends to be overly broad or general in nature. Most problematic is the fact that the vast majority of the compliance-gaining recommendations offered have been atheoretical. After an extensive review of the medical compliance literature from 1970 to 1989, Dunbar, Dunning, and Dwyer (1993) concluded that "as the absolute number of studies has increased, the proportion of studies that have been theory driven have decreased" (pp. 36–37). Little has changed since, particularly in the area of interpersonal influence messages and medical adherence (Klingle, 1996). Given the lack of theoretical guidance, it is no wonder that compliance-gaining advice is broadly stated and often limited to methods of increasing patient comprehension.

This chapter delineates effective medical compliance–gaining strategies by reviewing persuasion models and theories that uniquely address medical adherence, rather than reviewing the plethora of atheoretical research from the medical field. Additionally, the focus of this chapter is on communication as opposed to other factors that may affect compliance such as patient personality or access to medical care. An examination of three models that focus on health beliefs, the Health Belief Model, the Extended Parallel Processing Model, and the Theory of Reasoned Action and Planned Behavior, provides the starting point. These more traditional belief-adjustment models have frequently been used to guide and evaluate the "content" of health prevention campaigns and have recently been used by interpersonal researchers in their quest to develop interpersonal messages directed at increasing adherence rates. These belief change models, however, tend to ignore the role of nonverbal communication and the relational meanings attached to messages. The second part of this chapter addresses Reinforcement Expectancy Theory (RET) which addresses the relational style of the compliance-gaining message rather than its content. The final part of this chapter briefly examines the role of patient participation in the health care decision-making process.

Health Belief Perspectives and Patient Compliance

Medical compliance is often regarded as a consensual process, involving collaboration between the health care provider and patient as to medical regimens and therapeutic expectations (Anderson & Kirk, 1982; Linden, 1981). Corresponding with this viewpoint is the development of numerous compliance models espousing the importance of education and attitudinal adjustment in order to "align" expectations (Becker, 1974; Heiby & Carlson, 1986). According to a meta-analysis by Roter et al. (1998), the bulk of medical compliance–gaining studies published between 1977 and 1994 focused either exclusively on educational interventions or on combinations of both educational and behavioral interventions (e.g., skill building and behavioral modeling). Educational methods for eliciting compliance also seem to be the strategy of choice among physicians. According to empirical findings by Burgoon and colleagues (M. Burgoon, Parrott, J. K. Burgoon, Birk et al., 1990; M. Burgoon, Parrott, J. K. Burgoon, Coker et al., 1990) both patients and physicians report that health care providers are most likely to employ the use of expert power by giving simple directions or appealing to the knowledge or expertise of the physician, rather than using threats or prosocial reinforcing strategies. Schneider and Beaubien's (1996) naturalistic investigation of compliance-gaining strategies employed by doctors in medical interviews also found expertise and liking strategies to be among the most widely used compliance-gaining strategies.

However, educational programs must involve more than expert advice and instructions, since merely understanding what to do and how to do it have *not* been strongly associated with compliance (cf. Fulmer et al., 1999). The physician must make appropriate attitudinal adjustments to patients' belief systems (Becker & Maiman, 1980; Webb, 1980). Commonly used belief models and theories in the health arena such as the Health Belief Model, Extended Parallel Processing Model, the Theory of Reasoned Action, and the Theory of Planned Behavior provide recommendations for physicians by addressing specific beliefs that should form the core of educational intervention directed at improving patient compliance. It is beyond the scope of this chapter to articulate fully the complete formulations of each of these models. Instead, a summary of the central aspects of the models and theories that are most germane to the topic of message content is offered, followed by a discussion of each critical variable that should guide the content of the compliance-gaining message.

The Health Belief Model

The Health Belief Model (HBM) was originally developed to explain low compliance with preventive health behaviors (Becker & Maiman, 1975, Janz & Becker, 1984;

Rosenstock, 1974) and has been used as an organizing framework for developing and explaining a variety of preventive messages, from wearing bicycle helmets (Witte, Stokols, Ituarte, & Schneider, 1993) to having mammograms (Hyman, Baker, Ephraim, Moadel, & Phillip, 1994) to managing eating disorders (Grodner, 1991; Smalec & Klingle, 2000) to practicing safer sex (Mattson, 1999). According to the HBM model, patients will adhere to the physician's recommendations when the physician's influence message addresses several components.

The first component physicians should address includes perceptions of severity and susceptibility. According to the HBM, threatening messages must communicate to the recipient both that the effects of not complying with a health recommendation are serious (*perceived severity*) and that the recipient is personally vulnerable to the negative consequence (*perceived susceptibility*) (Becker, 1974). Health risk beliefs, or threats, are considered by many to be a vital element in persuading others to comply with health recommendations, because without threat, the danger goes unnoticed, and no action is taken (Lave, 1987).

Perceived severity reflects the individual's beliefs that not following health recommendations will result in dangerous, life threatening, and serious outcomes (Becker, 1974; Grodner, 1991). The more severe the threat appears, the more the individual will be interested in avoiding the harmful consequences (Rogers, 1983; Sutton, 1982). For instance, Klohn and Rogers (1991) found that women who were given information regarding the severe effects of osteoporosis, such as serious disfigurement, reported significantly higher perceptions of the severity and greater intention to comply with the recommended responses than did those who received only general information or no information at all. Thus, physicians attempting to gain patient cooperation must inform patients of the potentially serious consequences associated with not following through on the mutually agreed recommendations.

Patients must also feel personally at risk for contracting or developing serious effects. As an illustration of the importance of perceived susceptibility, Thurman and Franklin (1990) found that although 60 percent of the students in their study feared a campuswide spread of AIDS, less then 25 percent of them felt personally susceptible to contracting the disease and less than 50 percent changed their behaviors. Increasing patients' perceptions of susceptibility can be a major obstacle for physicians, since researchers have found that few people believe that the worst will happen to them (Perloff, 1983; Weinstein, 1983; Weinstein & Lachendro, 1982). Witte (1992a) points out that adolescents may be the most challenging audience, since young people tend to believe that they are invincible.

In addition to perceptions of threat, the HBM suggests that *self-efficacy* is an important component for physicians to address in their influence messages. In relation to health problems, self-efficacy refers to patients' own expectations that they can easily alter their own actions to enhance their well-being (Hertog, Finnegan, Rooney, Viswanath, & Potter, 1993). In the area of notoriously hard-to-change behaviors, perceptions of self-efficacy have proved particularly important in getting patients to consider as well as actually take appropriate actions (Hertog et al., 1993). Perceptions of self-efficacy have predicted alcohol abstinence (DiClementé, Carbonari, Montgomery, & Hughes, 1993; Rolnick &

Heather, 1982), smoking cessation (DiClementé, 1981), relapse of addictive behaviors in general (Marlatt & Gordon, 1980), preventive oral health behaviors (Tedesco, Keffer, & Fleck-Kandath, 1991), changes in diet to prevent cancer risks (Hertog et al., 1993), adolescents' ability to resist pressure to smoke (DeVries, Kok, & Dijkstra, 1990), and whether bulimics will seek medical help (Smalec & Klingle, 2000).

Although many studies have merely looked at the relationship between *perceived* efficacy and compliance, several studies have shown that messages can be effectively manipulated to communicate efficacy, which in turn can facilitate compliance. Rippetoe and Rogers (1987), for example, found that women who received high–self-efficacy literature on the ease of performing breast self-exams were significantly more likely to conduct self-exams than women who were given low–self-efficacy literature. Prentice-Dunn, Jones, and Floyd (1997) manipulated self-efficacy in messages regarding skin cancer prevention and found that subjects who read the high-efficacy message believed that wearing sunscreen and reducing sun exposure time would be effective, in contrast to subjects who read the low-efficacy message. Smalec and Klingle (2000) demonstrated that individuals with eating disorders were more likely to seek help for their problems if someone in their social network communicated to them that getting help would be simple and relatively effortless. Witte (1992b) manipulated the efficacy of an AIDS prevention message and found that subjects receiving the high-efficacy message as opposed to the low-efficacy message believed more strongly that they could use condoms to prevent AIDS, developed more favorable attitudes toward condoms, and were more likely to report using condoms as long as they perceived a significant AIDS threat in addition to efficacy.

According to the HBM, the third component that should be addressed in physicians' influence messages is *perceptions of benefits and costs*. Specifically, the HBM states that the benefits of complying must outweigh the costs or barriers associated with not complying. Perceived benefits in the HBM have been defined by Brown, DiClemente, and Reynolds (1991) as "the individual's beliefs regarding the effectiveness of strategies designed to decrease vulnerability or reduce the threat of illness" (p. 51). Perceived barriers are described as obstacles in the path of performing the recommended response (Leventhal & Cameron, 1987). Janz and Becker (1984) found that perceived barriers accounted for more behavior change than any of the other HBM components. Spector (2000) argues that compliance can be improved by communicating to patients the potential barriers to compliance such as side effects to medication.

Barriers can be more than just the side effects, however. They can be physical, psychological, or financial. Barriers related to quitting smoking, for instance, might include weight gain and irritability, fear of losing friends who still smoke, and financial constraints associated with buying the patch or attending a smoking cessation clinic. According to the HBM, if the barriers outweigh the benefits, noncompliance is more likely; if the benefits outweigh the barriers, compliance is more likely (Hayes, 1991; Janz & Becker, 1984).

The final component discussed by the HBM is *cues to action*. When attempting to influence threat and efficacy perceptions, the HBM states that "cues to action," such as advice from a physician, are needed to create awareness of the threat (Janz & Becker, 1984). These cues may be either internal, such as medical symptoms experienced by the patient or external, such as advice from a physician, a reminder letter, or a gruesome picture. Both internal and external cues have a direct effect on threat and an indirect effect on health-compromising behaviors. From a physician's standpoint, cues to action are the physician's messages that help bring the threat to the forefront for the patient and persuade him or her to carry out the recommended response. According to Mattson (1999), communication cues to action should be at the center of the HBM, since health beliefs, perceptions, and behavioral decisions are "socially constructed and contingent upon interaction with others" (p. 258).

Applied to the medical setting and physician compliance–gaining strategies specifically, the HBM postulates that patients will be more likely to comply if the physician communicates to them (e.g., provides "communication cues to action") that (1) the outcomes of noncompliance are severe, (2) they are vulnerable to these outcomes, and (3) the advocated health recommendation will produce positive results that outweigh the difficulties or barriers associated with noncompliance. At the same time the physician must convince patients that they have the skills to carry out the recommended action effectively. Although the HBM delineates the importance of critical message variables in shaping or altering patient health behavior, the relationships between the HBM variables are not theoretically specified in the model. The Extended Parallel Processing Model (EPPM) reconciles this problem and illustrates the relationship between threat and efficacy.

Extended Parallel Processing Model

Witte's (1992a, 1992b) EPPM (see also chapter 13 of this volume) improves upon the HBM by explaining "how" to construct fear-appeal messages efficaciously using the right combination of threat and efficacy. Although fear appeals and threats have been a primary focus of many persuasion theories, health communication scholars in the medical compliance arena have predominantly focused on interpersonal communication that produces satisfying relationships, arguing that compliance is facilitated by patient satisfaction (Cousins, 1985; DiMatteo, Prince, & Taranta, 1979; Hanson, 1986; Pendleton, 1983). Research evidence associating satisfaction with compliance, however, is often negligible (M. Burgoon, 1991; Ley, 1988). Findings that threatening communication by the physician leads to patient compliance (e.g., M. Burgoon, Birk, & Hall, 1991; Kaplan, Greenfield, & Ware, 1989; Robberson & Rogers, 1988) also appear to contradict the presumed effect of a provider's friendly bedside manner on adherence. Kaplan and colleagues (1989) examined physician communication style in a longitudinal study and found that it was physicians' negative affect, *not* their positive affect, that related to positive health status. Perhaps the "fear" of using fear appeals stems from the fact that threats have actually been known to backfire. Witte (1992a) developed the EPPM to address how to use threats without fear of a boomerang effect.

The EPPM illustrates the interdependent relationship between threat and efficacy and proposes that messages communicating threat (severity and susceptibility) and efficacy (self- and response efficacy) influence perceptions of threat and efficacy, which interact to produce either health-promoting actions or defensive actions. According to Witte's EPPM (1992a, 1998), delivery of a threatening message activates a two-appraisal process in the receiver. First, the individual evaluates the influence message to determine the degree of threat possible if the recommended response is not adopted. Similar to the HBM, the two underlying dimensions of a threatening message are susceptibility and severity. If the message doesn't adequately convey to the individual that he or she is susceptible to a severe threat, the message will not be appraised further. People are only motivated to continue message processing when a threat is relevant and serious.

If the message does adequately convey threat, the individual goes on to the second appraisal process, which involves the evaluation of efficacy. Efficacy, like threat, is a two-dimensional variable consisting of *response efficacy* and *self-efficacy*. Self-efficacy is defined in a manner consistent with the HBM's self-efficacy component, while response efficacy is defined in a manner consistent with HBM's perceived benefit component. Specifically, response efficacy is a person's belief that the advocated response will produce the desired outcome; perceived self-efficacy is a person's belief that he or she has the ability to execute the desired response.

According to EPPM, perceived efficacy interacts with threat to determine whether an individual will go into *danger control* (message acceptance) or *fear control* (message rejection). As long as efficacy perceptions are higher than threat perceptions, the individual will go into danger control, which is an adaptive response involving message acceptance and taking the recommended action to prevent the danger from happening. However, if efficacy perceptions are lower than threat perceptions, the individual will go into fear control, which is a maladaptive response involving message rejection. Rather than accepting the message, the individual who has high threat and low efficacy then attempts to control the level of fear associated with not being able to avert the threat through such methods as rationalizing away vulnerability.

Witte (1994) clearly pointed out, and has shown through a recent meta-analysis (Witte & Allen, 2000), that although threats are needed to motivate people, if perceived as too high, they can create such insurmountable levels of fear that people will respond by expending energy to rationalize away the fear (e.g., "I'm not going to get lung cancer if I smoke cigarettes for a few more years. I can quit later") rather than by taking action to avoid the danger (e.g., "I'm going to quit smoking as my doctor recommends"). Back in 1977, Bandura also theorized that high arousal states can be debilitating to performance and that individuals tend to avoid threatening situations that exceed their coping skills. Several studies addressing adherence rates in patients with chronic disease have shown that when the treatment prescribed is challenging, threat is negatively related to compliance (e.g., Bond, Aiken, & Somerville, 1992; Hartman & Becker, 1978).

Applied to the medical setting, EPPM postulates that patients will be more likely to comply with advocated health advice if the physician communicates to the patient that the outcomes of noncompliance are severe and that the patient is vulnerable to these outcomes. At the same time, the physician must clearly communicate that the patient can enact the behavior recommendations and that they will be effective. It is of critical importance, according to EPPM, that threatening messages not be used in isolation. Compliance-gaining attempts by a physician must do more than scare the patient into action. The compliance-gaining attempt must also include arguments demonstrating that the advocated response is effective at eliminating the threat and that the patient can carry out the recommended behavior.

The Theory of Reasoned Action and the
Theory of Planned Behavior

Missing from both the HBM and the EPPM is the concept of social normative beliefs, or an individual's beliefs regarding what other people think he or she should or should not do. The component of social normative beliefs, when compared to other cognitive components such as health beliefs, has been shown to be the stronger predictor of health behaviors (Seibold & Roper, 1979). Classic persuasion perspectives such as Kelman's (1961) influence processes and French and Raven's (1959) power bases provided the original foundation for the claim that individuals in our environment serve as frames of reference for making judgments about whether or not to carry out behavioral recommendations. According to Kelman's identification process, compliance is often the result of a recipient's desire to maintain a self-defined relationship with the source. Similarly, French and Raven's reference power indicated that compliance can result from a recipient's identification with the source and desire to do things to please the source. Regardless of whether one presumes that social normative beliefs influence compliance because of individuals' innate need for social approval or because of their need to maintain satisfying relationships, the power of normative beliefs in influencing compliance decisions should not be underestimated or overlooked.

Two of the most prominent theoretical models that address normative beliefs are the Theory of Reasoned Action (Ajzen & Fishbein, 1980; Fishbein & Ajzen, 1975) and the Theory of Planned Behavior (Ajzen, 1985, 1988). Both theories argue that *intention to behave* has a direct influence on actual behavior and is a function of the person's *attitude toward the behavior* and the *subjective norm* with regard to the behavior. Attitude toward the behavior is a function of the *personal consequences* expected from enacting a behavior and the *affective value* placed on those consequences. Personal consequences include the costs and benefits associated with the behavior. Thus, personal consequences encompass notions of benefits, barriers, response efficacy, susceptibility, and severity addressed in the HBM and EPPM. Subjective norm is often equated with social pressure (Friedman, Lichtenstein, & Biglan, 1985) and is defined as beliefs about what specific individuals or groups think they should do and their motivation to comply with or desire to please each of these referents.

The Theory of Planned Behavior extended the Theory of Reasoned Action by claiming that intention toward a behavior is a function of *behavioral control* in addition to attitude toward the behavior and subjective norm (Ajzen, 1985, 1988). This modification was necessary for the theory to be applied to situations in which the behavior in question was not under complete volitional control. For instance, practicing safer sex is affected by the actions of one's sexual partner and one's own ability to practice safer sex, in addition to one's attitude toward practicing safer sex and normative beliefs. Petraitis, Flay, and Miller (1995) argued that behavioral control is a concept similar to self-efficacy in that both terms are related to "perceptions of control over the successful completion of a particular behavior" (p. 69). According to the Theory of Planned Behavior, self-efficacy (i.e., behavioral control) has a direct influence on both intention and behavior. Thus, an individual may have the correct attitudes and normative beliefs but still fail to carry out the behavior because of low self-efficacy. This claim is similar to Witte's (1992a, 1994) prediction that threat beliefs are influential only to the extent that the individual believes he or she can carry out the recommended actions necessary to avert the threat. The Theory of Planned Behavior, however, adds the construct of subjective norm to the compliance equation.

Both theories have proved useful in predicting a variety of health related behaviors (Kashima, Gallois, & McCamish, 1992; Petraitis et al., 1995), and the addition of the subjective norm has turned out to be quite valuable. For instance, in adolescents, one of the best predictors of substance use among high school students is social normative beliefs regarding classmates' substance use (Johnston, O'Malley, & Bachman, 2000; Klingle & Miller, 1999). College students' decisions to use substances such as marijuana have been strongly associated with social normative beliefs regarding marijuana use (Ajzen, Timko, & White, 1982). In regards to patient compliance, Tedesco and colleagues (1991) found that intention to brush and floss was significantly associated with attitude toward the behavior and subjective norm.

Applied to the medical setting, the Theory of Reasoned Action and the Theory of Planned Behavior suggest that a physician needs to construct messages aimed at altering (1) attitudes of perceived severity, susceptibility, and efficacy toward the health behavior, (2) subjective norms, and (3) efficacy or behavioral control. Subjective norms are often equated with loved ones such as family members and friends. The physician, however, is also an important referent, and studies have found that a physician's recommendation is among the most influential factors in a patient's health care decisions (Dube et al., 2000). Kyngas (2000) showed that patients who received support from their physician were more likely to comply than patients who did not receive such support. As an important referent, the physician can modify his or her verbal and nonverbal language choices to communicate approval or disapproval of the patient's actions, which in turn should influence a patient's future behaviors. This is a central notion of Reinforcement Expectancy Theory.

Reinforcement Expectancy Theory

Although attitudinal adjustment and skill building are certainly integral to a patient's ability to follow prescribed treatment regimens, they do not guarantee that a patient will act appropriately. As Gross (1987) states, "knowing what to do and how to do it in no way insures cooperation" (p. 10). A substantial amount of research (e.g., Cummings, Becker, Kirscht, & Levin, 1982; Dunbar & Angras, 1980; Kirscht & Rosenstock, 1979; Mazzuca, 1982; Podshadley & Schweikle, 1970; Webb, 1980) has demonstrated that patients who become more knowledgeable are not necessarily more compliant. According to Altman and King (1986), these noncompliant patients who comprehend and concur with the necessity of the medical regimen are often the norm, rather than the exception, in chronic disease treatment and prevention programs. Montgomery et al. (1989) stated that chronic, lifelong diseases such as AIDS necessitate the development of more adequate theoretical frameworks than those offered by more traditional models such as the HBM.

Where the belief change approaches fall short is in not recognizing that in many situations patients have the appropriate belief structure but are confronted with a number of obstacles that affect subsequent behavior. Patients who are chronically ill or who are seeking lifestyle changes often fail to comply because of motivational shortfalls rather than as a result of misaligned belief structures. These patients visit health care profession-als on a regular basis and are often asked to comply with complex management regimens. The adherence rates for such lifelong changes are generally lower than for short-term medical regimens, and these rates decrease dramatically with time (Bloom, Cerkoney, & Hart, 1980; Epstein & Cluss, 1982).

Although the number of patients attempting difficult lifestyle changes is increasing, most strategic suggestions to improve chronic conditions and to alter patients' lifestyles are generalized from studies associated with relatively brief regimens (Klingle, 1993; Turk, Salovey, & Litt, 1986). This approach is somewhat suspect because it fails to recognize the uniqueness of long-term compliance. Long-term compliance by definition contains a time element that greatly affects the meanings attached to communication transactions, indi-viduals' expectations for future interactions (J. K. Burgoon & Le Poire, 1991), and the acceptability of communication responses (Levinger & Huesman, 1980). Additionally, situations involving long-term compliance are more likely to require time for positive con-sequences to manifest themselves, which decreases a patient's initial motivation to comply (Gross, 1987). Grounded in the notion that medical noncompliance is often related to pa-tients' motivational difficulties in adhering to long-term management programs, Klingle (1993, 1996) developed Reinforcement Expectancy Theory (RET) to address how physi-cians can use verbal and nonverbal compliance-gaining strategies to motivate patients in initial encounters as well as to increase behavioral persistence. The following sections ex-amine this theory.

Overview of RET

The logic underlying RET rests on the premise that human behavior is driven by the need to gain rewarding stimuli and eliminate aversive stimuli. To address influence messages, RET classifies verbal and nonverbal messages as either rewarding, neutral, or aversive based on the degree to which they communicate approval or disapproval for a patient; physician approval cues are assumed to be innately rewarding, and physician disapproval cues are assumed to be innately aversive to patients. The theory illustrates how approval and disapproval messages can shape patients' communication reinforcement expectations and in turn motivate and guide patients' present and future behaviors (Klingle, 1993; 1996).

To articulate the theory fully requires describing the compliance-gaining conceptu-alization scheme used by RET; explicating RET's predictions for initial encounters with a physician; comparing those predictions with those offered by Language Expectancy Theory (LET), which makes identical predictions but for different reasons; and, finally, delineating RET's unique predictions for repeated influence attempts by the physician.

Conceptualization of Verbal and Nonverbal Physician Influence Strategies

Application of reinforcement principles to human interactions must begin by conceptually defining compliance-gaining messages based on their reinforcing properties. Based on the notion that humans have a strong need for approval from others (Harre, 1980), RET classifies verbal and nonverbal strategies based on the type of approval communicated by the message (Klingle, 1993). Communication choices that signal positive feelings towards an individual or that individual's actions are considered *positive regard strategies*. Conversely, communication choices that indicate negative feelings toward an individual and/or that individual's actions are labeled *negative regard strategies*. Communication choices that are simple directives or justifications are *neutral regard strategies* that, used in isolation from other strategies, do not indicate approval or disapproval for an individual and/or an individual's actions.

The RET framework uses the relational message approach for categorizing compliance-gaining messages because of the enormous importance humans attach to the relational meanings of messages and to approval cues in general (J. Burgoon & Le Poire, 1991). In the health care context, researchers have suggested that a health care provider's relational message is much more influential than the content of the message (Buller & Buller, 1987; Street & Wiemann, 1987). Although a variety of relational messages differentiate compliance-gaining strategies (e.g., J. Burgoon & Hale, 1987), RET focuses on messages that signal the degree of approval because approval cues are universal reinforcers and are thus ideal for the application of reinforcement principles.

Conceptualizing compliance-gaining strategies based on their reinforcing properties is consistent with several communication scholars' classifications of influence attempts (Miller, 1983, Roloff & Barnicott, 1979; M. Burgoon, Parrott, J. Burgoon, Coker et al., 1990). Missing from most past conceptualizations are influence attempts that are neither rewarding nor punishing and nonverbal influence strategies. Neutral strategies used in isolation during single-episode encounters would be neither reinforcing nor aversive and would thus have little motivational utility. However, as discussed later, when used in combination with reinforcing or aversive strategies, neutral strategies can become potential influence attempts because they represent the removal of either a positive or negative state of affairs.

A second problem with previous compliance-gaining conceptualizations is that most measures of influence are based entirely on verbal utterances, which Berger (1985) states constrain researchers to studying "the tip of a very large iceberg" (p. 483). Nonverbal immediacy behaviors serve as comparable communicative indices to the proposed verbal categorization scheme, because they are associated with the degree of interpersonal warmth or approval for another. According to Mehrabian (1969), *immediacy behaviors* are approach behaviors that signal interest in, involvement with, and affect for another. Conversely, *nonimmediacy behaviors* signal hostility toward, exclusion of, and a lack of sensory engagement with another. Numerous nonverbal cues associated with immediacy have been cited in the literature, the most common being close conversational distance, direct body and facial orientation, positive reinforcers such as smiling and pleasant facial expressiveness, touching, forward body leaning, and a high degree of eye contact. Opposite behaviors, including scowls, negative facial expressions, and cold vocal tones, communicate nonimmediacy (Andersen, 1985). A substantial amount of research has shown that nonimmediacy behaviors signal disapproval or negative regard and act as aversive stimulation, whereas immediacy behaviors signal approval or positive regard (J. K. Burgoon, Buller, Hale, & deTurk, 1984; Coker & J. K. Burgoon, 1987).

Table 16.1 displays some examples of the three types of verbal and nonverbal compliance-gaining strategies used by RET: positive regard, neutral regard, and negative regard. Classifying messages based on the degree to which they communicate approval or disapproval for the patient allows a number of additional physician influence attempts to be generated that are not specifically depicted in the conceptualization scheme. The initial test of the conceptualization scheme provided empirical evidence that positive, neutral, and negative regard strategies are differentially evaluated; positive regard strategies used by physicians show the greatest amount of approval and are rewarding to patients, whereas negative regard strategies used by physicians show the least amount of approval and are aversive to patients (Klingle & Burgoon, 1995).

Initial Influence Attempts

Numerous research efforts have attempted to conceptualize and categorize compliance-gaining strategies (e.g., Boster & Stiff, 1984; M. Burgoon, Dillard, Koper, & Doran, 1984; deTurck, 1985). Such efforts, however, have rarely addressed effective strategy use. Even rarer are research efforts that have looked at effective strategy use over time. RET was specifically developed to explain strategy effectiveness in both initial and ongoing physician-patient encounters.

The predictions advanced by RET for initial physician-patient encounters coincided with those advanced by Language Expectancy Theory (LET) and were based in part on some of the basic tenets of LET. As outlined in chapter 9, LET maintains that message persuasiveness is a function of the receiver's language expectations that are grounded in sociocultural norms or standards for various speakers. According to LET, message acceptance occurs when a speaker engages in a positive violation of expectations (i.e., uses strategies that are both appropriate and more desirable than expected); message rejection occurs when a speaker engages in a negative violation of expectations (i.e., uses strategies that are socially inappropriate given what is expected for a certain communicator) (M. Burgoon, 1990; M. Burgoon & Klingle, 1998).

One characteristic that has been shown to influence receivers' judgments regarding expected language is the sex of the communicator. Numerous studies have shown that women are expected to be more emotional, less verbally aggressive, less assertive, more affiliative, and more nurturing than men in the way they communicate (Bell, 1981; M. Burgoon, Dillard, Koper et al., 1984; Fitzpatrick & Winke, 1979; Weisman & Teitelbaum, 1989). Studies testing LET (e.g., M. Burgoon, Dillard, & Doran, 1984; M. Burgoon, Dillard, Koper et al., 1984) have supported the claim that females in initial encounters are most persuasive when using affiliative or non-intense strategies, as opposed to aversive or intense strategies. On the other hand, males are most persuasive using either affiliative or aversive strategies as opposed to neutral strategies. M. Burgoon and colleagues (1991) put their theory to the test in the medical encounter and demonstrated that male physicians were most persuasive using affiliative or aggressive compliance-gaining strategies, as opposed to the neutral expertise strategies that physicians typically use. Female physicians, on the other hand, were most persuasive using affiliative, compliance-gaining strategies and least persuasive using neutral expertise strategies, followed by aggressive strategies.

One problem with applying LET to medical compliance is that LET focuses on single-episode encounters and is unable to adequately address physicians' efforts to gain

TABLE 16.1   *Strategy Definitions and Examples*

Neutral Regard Strategy Definition: Communication requests that are simple directives or justifications. These verbal strategies signal neither approval nor disapproval for the patient or the patient's actions and would be complemented with moderate nonverbal immediacy behaviors (moderate eye contact, no body lean, lack of smiling and pleasant facial expressiveness).

Types and Examples

   Direct Request: Requests that tell the patient what to do.

      "There are several dietary changes I would like you to make."

      "You need to change your eating habits."

   Justification Based on Expertise: Requests based on expertise or research.

      "In my opinion, you shouldn't put off the tests."

      "Since research indicates that diet is key, please log what you eat."

   Justification Based on Patient Condition: Requests made because of the patient's particular illness.

      "Seeing a dietitian is the best advice I can give for your situation."

      "I know from treating similar cases that these changes usually solve the problem."

Positive Regard Strategy Definition: Communication requests that are supportive, convey understanding, or stress concern for the patient. These verbal strategies signal approval of the patient and/or the patient's actions and would be complemented with high nonverbal immediacy behaviors (direct body/facial orientation, smiling, pleasant facial expressiveness, forward body leaning, and a high degree of eye contact) and altercentrism (vocal warmth/interest).

Types and Examples

   Supportive Requests: Requests that reinforce, reassure, compliment, or promise benefits for compliance.

      "You'll feel so much better about yourself because you'll know you are doing what it takes to prevent problems in the future."

      "I can tell you've been trying really hard—now just take that extra step and eliminate all the foods we discussed."

   Validation Requests: Requests that acknowledge the difficulty of the compliance act and indicate confidence in the patient following the request.

      "I know that changing one's eating habits is very difficult, but you're the kind of person who can do it."

      "If you make these changes—and I know you can—everyone will be so proud of you because we all know how difficult it is."

   Commonality of Goals: Requests that stress mutual concern, affect, or "we"ness.

      "We both want you to get better, so please eat right every day."

      "We both want to find out what could be causing you to feel so run down, so please make the appointment to have the tests."

(continued)

TABLE 16.1 *Continued*

Negative Regard Strategy Definition: Communication requests that attack or criticize the patient's past behaviors or potential future behavior, or requests that attribute primary responsibility to the patient for feeling ill. These verbal strategies signal disapproval for the patient and/or the patient's actions and would be complemented with an unpleasant and dominant nonverbal interaction style that included egocentrism (backward lean, cold vocal tones, reduced eye contact) and negative feedback (neutral or negative facial expressions, an occasional direct look).

Types and Examples

> *Nonsupportive Requests:* Requests that suggest the simplicity of the request and/or indicate disbelief in the patient's willingness to make the changes.
>
> > "It's not going to take that much of your time to see a dietitian."
> >
> > "If this is diabetes, the solution is generally quite simple—stick to your diet or spend the rest of your life wishing you had."
>
> *Invalidation Requests:* Requests that criticize or attack the patient's self-concept and/or indicate disappointment in the patient's previous actions.
>
> > "You can't keep fooling around with your diet—a responsible person would know that now is the time to take charge."
> >
> > "You have to see by now that it's absolutely irrational not to make the changes we discussed."
>
> *Negative Consequences:* Requests that suggest that noncompliant actions will lead to negative consequences.
>
> > "If you won't follow this advice, you're going to continue to feel run down and tired—it's that simple."
> >
> > "Your irregular eating habits are bound to make you overeat and gain weight."

---

ongoing compliance. RET extends LET by applying reinforcement principles, in conjunction with LET's claims regarding gender differences and language acceptability. The application of reinforcement principles allows both initial and long-term medical adherence to be addressed. RET's predictions regarding effective strategy usage by males and females in initial encounters are identical to those advanced by LET. The rationale, however, is different.

According to RET, strategy effectiveness in a patient's initial encounter with a physician is based on a *two-appraisal process* in which the patient judges first the *appropriateness of the influence message* and then its *motivational value*. Corresponding with LET, if the message is judged inappropriate by the recipient, it will be immediately rejected. Like LET, RET presumes that message appropriateness in initial encounters is influenced by physician gender in such a way that aggressive communication (i.e., negative regard strategies) by females is rejected outright and aggressive communication by males is tolerated. Although acceptable communication is necessary for an influence message to be successful, RET acknowledges that it is not a sufficient condition for increasing adherence rates for people who need motivation.

If the message is judged appropriate by the recipient, RET argues that the recipient will next evaluate its *reward potential* or *motivational value* (i.e., the degree to which the message is rewarding or aversive). Although much of the medical adherence literature has focused on material rewards such as tokens or money (see Chesney, 1984), RET focuses on the symbolic rewards in the form of verbal and nonverbal approval cues that were discussed in the previous section on strategy conceptualization. Messages that are either aversive (i.e., negative regard strategies showing disapproval) or rewarding (i.e., positive regard strategies showing approval) are stored in working memory called *reinforcement expectations* and guide the patient's future behavior. Significantly, approval cues have been shown to be more effective than material rewards in motivating humans (Greenbaum, Turner, Cook, & Melamed, 1990), and tests of mutual influence models (e.g., Andersen, 1985; J. Burgoon & Hale, 1988) have demonstrated that receivers adjust their behavior to avoid unpleasant exchanges or to maintain pleasant ones. Thus, RET's central claim is that human behavior is driven by the need to avoid aversive communication encounters and to maintain rewarding communication encounters.

In sum, RET proposes that during initial influence attempts, verbal and nonverbal messages signaling either approval or disapproval for the patient and/or the patient's actions can be used by the physician to shape a patient's reinforcement expectations. These reinforcement expectations guide the patient's future actions. The strategy chosen by the physician, however, must be viewed by the patient as socially appropriate in order for the patient to pay attention to the influence attempt. Because of sociological norms and the motivational properties of reinforcement expectations, male physicians can increase compliance in initial encounters by using either negative or positive regard strategies, whereas female physicians can increase compliance in initial encounters by using only positive regard strategies (see figure 16.1).

RET predictions for initial encounters were tested by Klingle and Burgoon (1995) using a multiple message design in which numerous different medical episodes were put to the test using positive, neutral, or negative regard strategies. The study supported the claim that message appropriateness in initial encounters is influenced by the gender of the physician; negative regard strategies were viewed by patients as more appropriate when they were used by male physicians than by female physicians. The study also clearly demonstrated the predicted physician gender by strategy type interaction on message persuasiveness. Specifically, in initial encounters patients were more persuaded when the male physician used positive or negative regard strategies than when he used neutral regard strategies. With female physicians, on the other hand, patients were most persuaded by positive regard strategies and least persuaded by negative regard strategies.

Sequential Influence Attempts

Patients who visit health care providers on a regular basis have the opportunity to continually observe the reinforcement behavior of the health care provider and formulate more elaborate reinforcement expectations (Klingle, 1993). Although the physician's frequent use of rewarding positive regard or aversive negative regard strategies would seem to establish the strongest patient expectancy for future rewarding or aversive communication, the occasional use of nonreinforcing exchanges is needed to develop motivating reinforce-

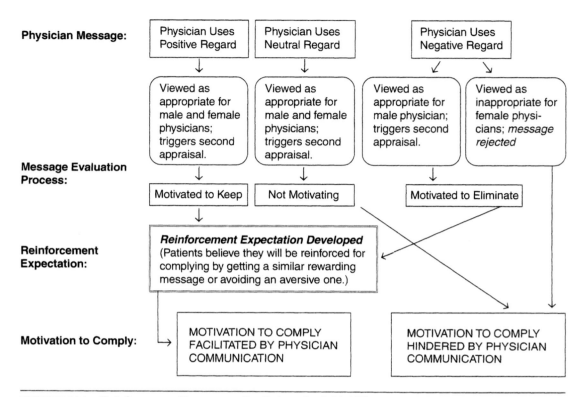

FIGURE 16.1   *Reinforcement Expectancy Predictions for Initial Physician-Patient Encounters*

ment expectations. RET predicts that patients develop motivating reinforcement expectations when the physician uses both rewarding and non-rewarding strategies, whereas nonmotivating reinforcement expectations are developed when the physician uses only one type of strategy. The theory indicates that repetitive communication patterns by the physician (i.e., all positive regard strategies, all negative regard strategies, or all neutral regard strategies) cause patients to believe that their behavior does not and cannot impact the physician's communication behavior. Thus, nonmotivating reinforcement expectations develop following repeated use of one strategy, because patients begin to expect the same type of strategy regardless of their behavioral adjustment. Physicians who use nonrepetitive communication patterns (e.g., the use of positive regard with negative regard, the use of positive regard with neutral regard, or the use of neutral regard with negative regard) assist patients in developing motivating reinforcement expectations, or expectations that the physician's behavior is a response to the patient's health-related actions. Greater motivation to comply and higher behavioral maintenance are predicted to occur following motivating reinforcement expectations than following nonmotivating reinforcement expectations (Klingle, 1996).

Klingle (1994) found that motivating reinforcement expectations following the physician's use of nonrepetitive influence strategies developed even in cases where the physician's use of reinforcement and nonreinforcement was not actually contingent on the patient's compliant action and where the ordering of the strategies (e.g., whether the order ended with a rewarding or aversive strategy) seemed to be irrelevant. Specifically, in an initial test of RET, Klingle (1994) used four sequential physician-patient sessions to create three conceptually different nonrepetitive strategy combinations (positive and neutral regard; positive and negative regard; and negative and neutral regard) and three repetitive strategy combinations (all positive; all neutral; and all negative). These episodes were the same episodes used to test the effectiveness of strategies used in the initial, one-shot encounters with the physician that were discussed earlier. The ordering of the strategy combinations was varied so that some ended with a reinforcing strategy and others with a nonreinforcing strategy; none of the strategies was directly tied to the patient's actual compliance. In all cases the nonrepetitive strategy combinations, regardless of order, produced more motivating reinforcement expectations and greater patient motivation than did the repetitive communication patterns. The fact that physicians were able to motivate patients without having to determine whether the patient complied is of critical importance given that physicians are not able to judge accurately the level of patient compliance (Norell, 1981; Rothert, 1982).

When RET was originally advanced in 1994, the assumption was made that effective strategy combinations would be influenced by sociological language norms. Thus, although nonrepetitive strategy combinations were predicted to produce the most motivating reinforcement expectations, female physicians were not predicted to be effective if using combinations involving negative regard strategies. RET predicted that female physicians would be most persuasive in ongoing exchanges with patients if they used combinations of positive and neutral regard strategies, whereas male physicians would be most persuasive using any of the nonrepetitive strategy combinations (Klingle, 1994; Klingle & Burgoon, 1995).

An initial test of the theory (Klingle, 1994; Klingle & Burgoon, 1995) showed that, as predicted by RET, nonrepetitive strategy combinations motivated patients to comply with physician recommendations more than repetitive strategy combinations did. However, the predicted gender differences did not seem to extend to established relationships, since both male and female physicians were equally successful when using each of the nonrepetitive strategy combinations. The researchers concluded that established relationships have the potential to override sex-role stereotypes present in initial relationships (Klingle, 1994; Klingle & Burgoon, 1995). This belief coincides with other researchers' claims that getting to know a person causes sex-role stereotypes to play a less significant role and that some dissatisfying communication exchanges are to be expected by both sexes as relational familiarity increases (Crocker, Fiske, & Taylor, 1984; Deaux & Lewis, 1984; Roloff, 1987).

Although not yet empirically tested, RET also argues that nonrepetitive communication patterns will facilitate behavior persistence. By applying Amsel's (1967) *frustration hypothesis*, RET states that individuals who are exposed to occasional nonreinforcement become conditioned to expect nonreinforcement in the future, whereas individuals exposed to continual reinforcement soon become frustrated when the reinforcement is taken away and quickly revert to old habits (Klingle, 1993). Klingle (1996) explained that when patients occasionally receive nonrewarding stimuli from their health care provider, they begin to build up a frustration tolerance for not being rewarded. In reinforcement expectation terms, patients realize that medical adherence will not always result in social praise. As a result, when they enter their natural environment, where social reinforcers may well be infrequent, they continue to adhere to the medical recommendations rather than becoming frustrated by the lack of reinforcement they get from their friends or family.

In sum, RET argues that long-term compliance and behavioral persistence depend on the development of motivating reinforcement expectations, which are formed when a physician uses a combination of reinforcing and nonreinforcing compliance–gaining messages. These motivating reinforcement expectations guide the patient's future actions by instilling in that patient a sense of hope that adhering to long-term health maintenance will, at some point, result in pleasant communication exchanges with the physician or others in his or her environment.

Patient Participation: A Compliance-Gaining Strategy or Just Another Compliance Problem?

One compliance-gaining technique not yet addressed in this chapter but widely advocated in the current literature as an effective tool for enlisting and maintaining patient adherence is the use of active patient participation (e.g., Kassirer, 1983; Kim, Klingle, Sharkey, Park, Smith, & Cai, 2000; Steward, 1995; Young & Klingle, 1996). In fact, current research efforts have nearly abandoned the traditional line of research on physician compliance–gaining strategies that were abundant from the late 1970s to the early 1990s and have shifted the burden of compliance to patients (Phillips & Jones, 1991), arguing that they must share responsibility for and in the medical decision-making process (Beisecker & Beisecker, 1990).

According to Kaplan (1991), active patient participation builds a sense of personal control over health matters and has a positive influence on both patient compliance and health status. The logic behind the claim that patient participation increases compliance is generally based on Festinger's (1957) Cognitive Dissonance Theory, which stated that people desire to appear consistent with what they have said and done. Decades ago, persuasion research documented that actively constructing arguments and communicating one's intentions in front of others leads to greater behavioral change and persistence than passive message reception (Greenwald & Albert, 1968; Janis & King, 1954; Slamecka & Graf, 1978). Compliance, however, is not the only outcome enhanced by active participation in the medical encounter. The health status of the patient also improves, because the very act of participating creates feelings of personal control that boost the immune system and ultimately lead to better health outcomes (Kaplan, 1991). Involved patients have also been shown to cope better with aversive results than noninvolved patients and are less likely to give in when the act of compliance results in negative outcomes (Wagener & Taylor, 1986).

Patient participation is indisputably an excellent tool for facilitating patient compliance. Unfortunately, the act of patient participation is a lot like the act of medical adherence itself. Specifically, even though patients know that active involvement is in their best interest and tend to prefer more egalitarian interactions (Beisecker & Beisecker, 1990; Ende, Kazis, Ash, & Moskowitz, 1989; Kim et al., 2000; Street & Wiemann, 1987), patient participation rates are alarmingly low (Braddock, Fign, Levinson, Jonsen, & Pearlman, 1997). Thus, it is important to remember that the physician must first of all be able to persuade the patient to comply with the request to participate actively in the decision-making process. This act in itself involves addressing barriers to patient participation and using motivational communication style.

Several researchers have advocated the use of patient-centered interviewing to increase patient participation (Levenstein, Brown, Weston, Stewart, McCracken, & McWhinney, 1989; Marshall, 1993). The physician's goal during patient-centered interviewing is to elicit patients' feelings, thoughts, and expectations through a more open-ended interviewing style, as opposed to asking traditional, closed-ended questions. Proponents of this style suggest that it leads to a more accurate exchange of information, which results in establishing the right diagnosis and treatment and enables the patient to advocate actively for his or her choice of treatment regimens. In addition to changing the physician's interviewing style, the physician may also need to communicate in a manner that dismantles some of the barriers to patient participation. Several recent studies (e.g., Kim et al., 2000; Young & Klingle, 1996) have looked at barriers to patient participation in the hopes of improving participation rates and have shown that variables such as self-efficacy (i.e., patient believes he or she has the skills to participate) and response efficacy (i.e., patient believes participating will result in positive outcomes) can have an effect on patient participation rates. Thus, many of the theories previously discussed could be applied to address how the physician should communicate to increase patients' willingness to participate.

Conclusion

Physicians attempting to alter patient health behaviors must construct influence messages and arguments that attempt to alter patients' threat, efficacy, and normative beliefs, while at the same time adapting their message style (e.g., using both reinforcing and nonreinforcing messages) to help motivate patients to enact the behaviors that correspond to those beliefs. Recent research efforts in the communication field have focused on patient participation as a viable tool for enlisting compliance and seem to have left physician-implemented influence messages by the wayside. Although patient participation is a proven motivational tool for enlisting compliance, physicians need to communicate in a manner that will convince patients to participate actively in the exchange of medical information and ideas. Rather than abandoning traditional compliance-gaining approaches, a comprehensive theory should be developed that dictates the message content and style of the physicians' influence attempts. These attempts must effectively encourage patient involvement in the medical exchange and motivate patients to adhere to mutually agreed medical regimens. Each of the theories and models reviewed in this chapter serves as a starting point. Following are specific recommendations for health care providers who wish to increase medical adherence:

1. Health care providers should develop messages that encourage patient participation by indicating that not participating may result in serious health errors that will directly affect the patient. At the same time, the health care provider must convey how easy it is to participate in the interaction (i.e., build self-efficacy) and communicate that patients are expected to participate because participation will help the medical process (i.e., build response efficacy).

2. Physician influence messages directed at enlisting adherence to mutually agreed recommendations must make the health outcome appear serious (i.e., perceived severity) and personally relevant to the patient (i.e., perceived susceptibility), while at the same time communicating to the patient that he or she can effectively overcome barriers and achieve the benefits (i.e., efficacy). Unfortunately, many of the benefits are not immediate. Thus, the style of the physician's message is of critical importance.

3. Normative beliefs influence health care decisions and can be used by the physician to motivate patients. One method of using normative beliefs would be to adapt message content to include arguments suggesting that loved ones want the patient to engage in appropriate health behaviors. A second method involves considering the health care provider as an important referent group on which patients base their decisions. Health care providers can alter the style of their communication to motivate patients, since patients are driven by the need to receive social approval from important referents, including their physician. In initial encounters, female health care providers should use verbal and nonverbal messages communicating that they approve of the patient and the patient's actions by using nonverbal immediacy behaviors and positive regard strategies that involve statements like, "I know you are the type of person who can follow through with the agreed upon regimen" (i.e., use positive regard strategies). Male health care providers can use similar messages but also have the flexibility to use messages that communicate disapproval for the patient and the patient's inability to comply (i.e., use negative regard strategies). Thus, the male physician could use nonimmediate nonverbal behaviors and sternly say, "You have to see that it would be absolutely irrational not to follow through with the agreed regimen." When communicating with patients over time, both male and female physicians must vary their language style and incorporate a variety of regard strategies to help motivate patients to stick to the agreed regimen. Physicians should use nonrepetitive strategy combinations (i.e., combinations of different regard strategies) rather than repetitive strategy combinations to keep patients motivated and promote behavioral persistence.

In sum, compliance is facilitated by communication that correctly modifies a patient's belief system and motivates patients to follow through with actions that are consistent with their beliefs. The content of the physician's message should include arguments related to severity, susceptibility, self-efficacy, response efficacy, and normative beliefs. The style of the message must involve more than just reinforcing strategies and must involve the patient in the decision-making process. Motivation to comply and behavioral persistence are enhanced through patient participation and through the physician's use of nonrepetitive strategy combinations that include messages of approval and disapproval. A comprehensive approach to medical compliance involves a combination of carefully constructed arguments by a physician that are delivered in a motivational manner and involve the patient in the decision-making process.

References

Adams, S., Pill, R., & Jones, A. (1997). Medication, chronic illness, and identity: The perspective of people with asthma. *Social Science and Medicine, 45,* 189–201.

Ajzen, I. (1985). From decisions to actions: A theory of planned behavior. In J. Kuhl & J. Beckmann (Eds.), *Action-control: From cognition to behavior* (pp. 11–39). New York: Springer.

Ajzen, I. (1988). *Attitudes, personality, and behavior.* Homewood, IL: Dorsey Press.

Ajzen, I., & Fishbein, M. (1980). *Understanding attitudes and predicting social behavior.* Englewood Cliffs, NJ: Prentice Hall.

Ajzen, I., Timko, C., & White, J. B. (1982). Self-monitoring and the attitude-behavior relation. *Journal of Personality and Social Psychology, 42,* 426–435.

Altman, D. G., & King, A. C. (1986). Approaches to compliance in primary prevention. *The Journal of Compliance in Health Care, 1,* 55–73.

Amsel, A. (1967). Partial reinforcement effects on vigor and persistence. In K. W. Spence & J. T. Spence (Eds.), *The psychology of learning and motivation: 1* (pp. 1–65). New York: Academic Press.

Andersen, P. A. (1985). Nonverbal immediacy in interpersonal communication. In A. W. Siegman & S. Feldstein (Eds.), *Multichannel integrations of nonverbal behavior* (pp. 1–36). Hillsdale, NJ: Erlbaum.

Anderson, R. J., & Kirk, L. M. (1982). Methods of improving patient compliance in chronic disease states. *Archives of Internal Medicine, 142,* 1673–1675.

Ballard-Reisch, D. S. (1990). A model of participative decision making for physician-patient interaction. *Health Communication, 2,* 91–104.

Bandura, A. (1977). *Social learning theory.* Englewood Cliffs, NJ: Prentice Hall.

Becker, M. H. (1974). The health belief model and personal health behavior. *Health Education Monographs, 2,* 324–473.

Becker, M. H., & Maiman, L. A. (1975). Sociobehavioral determinants of compliance with health and medical care recommendations. *Medical Care, 13,* 10–24.

Becker, M. H., & Maiman, L. A. (1980). Strategies for enhancing patient compliance. *Journal of Community Health, 6,* 113–135.

Beisecker, A. E., & Beisecker, T. D. (1990). Patient information-seeking behaviors when communicating with doctors. *Medical Care, 28*(1), 19–28.

Bell, R. R. (1981). Friendship of women and of men. *Psychology of Women Quarterly, 5,* 408–417.

Berg, J. Dischler, J., Wagner, D, Raia, J. J., & Palmer-Shevlin, N. (1993). Medication compliance: A healthcare problem. *Annual Pharmacotherapy, 27,* S1–S24.

Berger, C. R. (1985). Social power and interpersonal communication. In M. L. Knapp & G. R. Miller (Eds.), *Handbook of interpersonal communication* (pp. 439–499). Beverly Hills, CA: Sage.

Bloom, N., Cerkoney, K., & Hart, L. (1980). The relationship between the health beliefs model and compliance of persons with diabetes mellitus. *Diabetes Care, 33,* 490–500.

Bond, G. G., Aiken, L. S., & Somerville, S. C. (1992). The health belief model and adolescents with insulin-dependent diabetes mellitus. *Health Psychology, 11,* 190–198.

Boster, F. J., & Stiff, J. B. (1984). Compliance gaining message selection behavior. *Human Communication Research, 10,* 539–556.

Braddock, C. H., Fihn, S. D., Levinson, W., Jonsen, A. R., & Pearlman, R. A. (1997). How doctors and patients discuss routine clinical decisions: Informed decision making in the outpatient setting. *Journal of General Internal Medicine, 12,* 339–345.

Brown, L. K., DiClemente, R. J., & Reynolds, L. A. (1991). HIV prevention for adolescents: Utility of the health belief model. *AIDS Education and Prevention, 3,* 50–59.

Buller, M. K., & Buller, D. B. (1987). Physicians' communication style and patient satisfaction. *Journal of Health and Social Behavior, 28,* 375–388.

Burgoon, J. K., Buller, D. B., Hale, J. L., & deTurck, M. A. (1984). Relational messages associated with nonverbal behaviors. *Human Communication Research, 10*, 351–378.

Burgoon, J. K., & Hale, J. L. (1987). Validation and measurement of the fundamental themes of relational communication. *Communication Monographs, 54*, 19–41

Burgoon, J. K. & Hale, J. L. (1988). Nonverbal expectancy violations: Model elaboration and application to immediacy behaviors. *Communication Monographs, 55*, 58–79.

Burgoon, J. K., & Le Poire, B. A. (1991, November). *Effects of communication expectancies, actual communication, and expectancy disconfirmation on evaluation of communicators and their communication behavior.* Paper presented at the annual meeting of the Speech Communication Association, Atlanta.

Burgoon, M. (1990). Social influence. In H. Giles & P. Robinson (Eds.), *Handbook of language and social psychology* (pp. 51–72). London: John Wiley.

Burgoon, M. (1991, May). *Strangers in a strange land: The behavioral scientist in the world of the medical doctor.* Paper presented at the annual meeting of the International Communication Association Convention.

Burgoon, M., Birk, T. S., & Hall, J. R (1991). Compliance and satisfaction with physician-patient communication: An expectancy theory interpretation of gender differences. *Human Communication Research, 18*, 177–208.

Burgoon, M., Dillard, J. R., & Doran, N. (1984). Friendly or unfriendly persuasion: The effects of violations of expectations by males and females. *Human Communication Research, 10*, 283–294.

Burgoon, M., Dillard, J. P., Koper, R., & Doran, N. (1984). The impact of communication context and persuader gender on persuasive message selection. *Women's Studies in Communication, 7*, 1–12.

Burgoon, M., & Klingle, R. S. (1998). Gender differences in being influential and/or influenced: A challenge to prior explanations. In D. Canary & K. Dindia (Eds.), *Sex differences and similarities in communication* (pp. 257–285). Hillsdale, NJ: Erlbaum.

Burgoon, M., Parrott, R., Burgoon, J. K., Birk, T., Pfau, M., & Coker, R. (1990). Primary care physicians' selection of verbal compliance-gaining strategies. *Health communication, 2*, 13–27.

Burgoon, M., Parrott, R., Burgoon, J. K., Coker, R., Pfau, M., & Birk, T. (1990). Patients' severity of illness, noncompliance, and locus of control and physicians' compliance-gaining messages. *Health Communication, 2*, 29–46.

Chesney, M. A. (1984). Behavior modification and health enhancement. In J. D. Matarazzo, S. M. Weiss, J. A. Herd, N. E., Miller, & S. M. Weiss (Eds.), *Behavioral health: A handbook of health enhancement and disease prevention* (pp. 338–350). New York: John Wiley.

Coker, D. A., & Burgoon, J. K. (1987). The nature of conversational involvement and nonverbal encoding patterns. *Human Communication Research, 13*, 463–494.

Cousins, N. (1985). How patients appraise physicians. *New England Journal of Medicine, 313*, 1422–1424.

Crocker, J., Fiske, S. T., & Taylor, S. E. (1984). Schematic bases of belief change. In J. R. Eiser (Ed.), *Attitudinal judgement* (pp. 197–226). New York: Springer-Verlag.

Cummings, K. M., Becker, M. H., Kirscht, J. P., & Levin, N. W. (1982). Psychosocial factors affecting adherence to medical regimens in a group of hemodialysis patients. *Medical Care, 20*, 567–579.

Deaux, K., & Lewis, L. L. (1984). The structure of gender stereotypes: Interrelationships among components and gender label. *Journal of Personality and Social Psychology, 46*, 991–1004.

deTurck, M. A. (1985). A transactional analysis of compliance-gaining behaviors. Effects of noncompliance, relational contexts, and actors' gender. *Human Communication Research, 12*, 54–78.

DeVries, H., Kok, G., & Dijkstra, M. (1990). Self-efficacy as a determinant of the onset of smoking and interventions to prevent smoking in adolescents. *European Perspectives in Psychology, 2*, 209–222.

DiClemente, C. C. (1981). Self-efficacy and smoking cessation maintenance: A preliminary report. *Cognitive Therapy Research, 5*, 175–187.

DiClemente, C. C., Carbonari, J. P., Montgomery, R. P. G., & Hughes, S. O. (1993). The alcohol abstinence self-efficacy scale. *Journal of Studies on Alcohol, 55*, 141–148.

DiMatteo, M. R., Prince, L. M., & Taranta, A. (1979). Patients' perceptions of physicians' behavior: Determinants of patient commitment to the therapeutic relationship. *Journal of Community Health, 4*, 280–290.

Dube, C. E., O'Donnel, J. F., & Novack, D. H. (2000). Communication skills for preventive interventions. *Academy of Medicine, 75* (7), S45–54.

Dunbar, J. M., & Angras, W. S. (1980). Compliance with medical regimens. In J. M. Ferguson & C. B. Taylor (Eds.), *Comprehensive handbook of behavioral medicine* (pp. 115–145). New York: Spectrum.

Dunbar, J., Dunning, E. J., & Dwyer, K. (1993). Compliance research in pediatric and adolescent populations: Two decades of research. In N. A. Krasnegor, L. Epstein, S. B. Johnson, & S. J. Yaffe (Eds.), *Developmental aspects of health compliance behavior* (pp. 29–51). Hillsdale, NJ: Erlbaum.

Ende, J., Kazis, L., Ash, A., & Moskowitz, M. A. (1989). Measuring patients' desire for autonomy: Decision making and information seeking preferences among medical patients. *Journal of General Internal Medicine, 4,* 23–30.

Epstein, L. H., & Cluss, P. A. (1982). A behavioral medicine perspective on adherence to long-term medical regimens. *Journal of Consulting and Clinical Psychology, 50,* 950–971.

Eraker, S. A., Kirscht, J. P., & Becker, M. H. (1984). Understanding and improving patient compliance. *Annals of Internal Medicine, 100,* 258–268.

Festinger, L. A. (1957). *A theory of cognitive dissonance.* Stanford, CA: Stanford University Press.

Fishbein, M., & Ajzen, I. (1975). *Belief, attitude, intention and behavior: An introduction to theory and research.* Reading, MA: Addison-Wesley.

Fitzpatrick, M. A., & Winke, J. (1979). You always hurt the one you love: Strategies and tactics in interpersonal conflict. *Communication Quarterly, 27,* 3–11.

Fletcher, R. H. (1989). Patient compliance with therapeutic advice: A modern view. *Mount Sinai Journal of Medicine, 56* (6), 453–458.

French, J. R. P., Jr., & Raven, B. H. (1959). The bases of social power. In D. Cartwright (Ed.), *Studies in social power* (pp. 150–167). Ann Arbor, MI: University of Michigan, Institute of Social Research.

Friedman, L. S., Lichtenstein, E., & Biglan, A. (1985). Smoking onset among teens: An empirical analysis of initial situations. *Addictive Behaviors, 10,* 1–13.

Fulmer, T. T., Feldman, P. H., Kim, T. S., Carty, B., Beers, M., Molina, M., & Putnam, M. (1999). An intervention study in enhanced medication compliance in communication-dwelling elderly individuals. *Journal of Gerontological Nursing, 25,* 6–14.

Greenbaum, P. E., Turner, C., Cook, E. W., & Melamed, B. G. (1990). Dentists' voice control: Effects on children's disruptive and affective behavior. *Health Psychology, 5,* 546–558.

Greenwald, A. G., & Albert, R. D. (1968). Acceptance and recall of improvised arguments. *Journal of Experimental Psychology: Human Learning and Memory, 4,* 592–604.

Grodner, M. (1991). Using the health belief model for bulimia prevention. *College Health, 40,* 107–112.

Gross, A. M. (1987). A behavioral approach to the compliance problems of young diabetics. *The Journal of Compliance in Health Care, 2,* 7–21.

Hanson, R. W. (1986). Physician-patient communication and compliance. In K. E. Gerber & A. M. Nehemkis (Eds.), *Compliance: The dilemma of the chronically ill* (pp. 183–212). New York: Springer.

Harre, R. (1980). *Social being.* Totowa, NJ: Adams.

Hartman, P. E., & Becker, M. H. (1978). Noncompliance with prescribed regimen among chronic hemodialysis patients: A method of prediction and educational diagnosis. *Dialysis and Transplantation, 7,* 978–989.

Hayes, J. A. (1991). Psychosocial barriers to behavior change in preventing human immunodeficiency virus (HIV) infection. *Counseling Psychologist, 19,* 585–602.

Heiby, E. M., & Carlson, J. G. (1986). The health compliance model. *Journal of Compliance in Health Care, 1,* 135–152.

Henson, R. H. (1997). Analysis of the concept of mutuality. *Image—The Journal of Nursing Scholarship, 29,* 77–81.

Hertog, J. K., Finnegan, J. R., Rooney, B., Viswanath, K., & Potter, J. (1993). Self-efficacy as a target population segmentation strategy in a diet and cancer risk reduction campaign. *Health Communication, 5,* 21–40.

Hyman, R. B., Baker, S., Ephraim, R., Moadel, A., & Phillip, J. (1994). Health belief model variables as predictors of screening mammography utilization. *Journal of Behavioral Medicine, 17,* 391–406.

Janis, I. L., & King, B. T. (1954). The influence of role-playing on opinion change. *Journal of Abnormal and Social Psychology, 49*, 211–218.

Janz, N. K., & Becker, M. H. (1984). The health belief models: A decade later. *Health Education Quarterly, 11*, 1–47.

Johnston, L. D., O'Malley, P. M., & Bachman, J. G. (Dec. 2000). *National Survey Results on Drug Use from the Monitoring the Future Study, 1975–2000.* Ann Arbor: University of Michigan News and Information Services. Available online: www.monitoringthefuture.org; accessed 03/14/01.

Jones, J. A., & Phillips, G. M. (1988). *Communicating with your doctor: Rx for good medical care.* Carbondale, IL: Southern Illinois University Press.

Kaplan, R. M. (1991). Health-related quality of life in patient decision making. *Journal of Social Issues, 47*, 69–90.

Kaplan, S. H., Greenfield, S., & Ware, J. E. (1989). Assessing the effects of physician-patient interactions on the outcomes of chronic disease. *Medical Care, 27*, 110–126.

Karoly, P. (1993). Enlarging the scope of the compliance construct: Toward developmental and motivational relevance. In N. A. Krasnegor, L. Epstein, S. B. Johnson, & S. J. Yaffe (Eds.), *Developmental aspects of health compliance behavior* (pp. 11–27). Hillsdale, NJ: Erlbaum.

Kashima, Y., Gallois, C., & McCamish, M. (1992). Predicting the use of condoms: Past behavior, norms, and the sexual partner. In T. Edgar, M. A. Fitzpatrick, & V. S. Freimuth (Eds.), *AIDS: A communication perspective* (pp. 21–46). Hillsdale, NJ: Erlbaum.

Kassirer, J. P. (1983). Adding insult to injury: Usurping patients' prerogatives. *New England Journal of Medicine, 308*(15), 898–901.

Kelman, H. (1961). Processes of opinion change. *Public Opinion Quarterly, 25*, 57–78.

Kim, M. S., Klingle, R. S., Sharkey, W. F., Park, H. S., Smith, D. H., & Cai, D. (2000). A test of a cultural model of patients' motivation for verbal communication in patient-doctor interactions. *Communication Monographs, 67*, 262–283.

Kirscht, J., & Rosenstock, I. (1979). Patients' problems in following recommendations of health experts. In G. C. Stone, F. Cohen, & N. E. Adler (Eds.), *Health psychology: A handbook.* San Francisco: Jossey-Bass.

Klingle, R. S. (1993). Bringing time into physician compliance gaining research: Toward a reinforcement expectancy theory of strategy effectiveness. *Health Communication, 5*, 283–308.

Klingle, R. S. (1994). *Patient compliance and satisfaction with physician influence attempts: A reinforcement expectancy approach to compliance-gaining over time.* Doctoral dissertation.

Klingle, R. S. (1996). Physician communication as a motivational tool for long-term patient compliance: Reinforcement expectancy theory. *Communication Studies, 47*, 206–217.

Klingle, R. S., & Burgoon, M. (1995). Patient compliance and satisfaction with physician influence attempts: A reinforcement expectancy approach to compliance gaining over time. *Communication Research, 22*, 148–187.

Klingle, R. S., & Miller, M. (1999). *1998 Hawaii student alcohol and drug use study (1991–1998): Hawaii adolescent treatment needs assessment.* Honolulu, HI: Hawaii Department of Health, Alcohol and Drug Abuse Division.

Klohn, L. S., & Rogers, R. W. (1991). Dimensions of the severity of a health threat: The persuasive effects of visibility, time of onset, and rate of onset on young women's intentions to prevent osteoporosis. *Health Psychology, 10*, 23–329.

Klopovich, P. M., & Trueworthy, R. C. (1985). Adherence to chemotherapy regimens among children with cancer. *Topics in Clinical Nursing, 7*, 19–25.

Kyngas, H. (2000). Compliance of adolescents with diabetes. *Journal of Pediatric Nursing, 15*, 260–267.

Kyngas, H., Duffy, M., & Kroll, T. (2000). Conceptual analyses of concept compliance. *Journal of Clinical Nursing, 9*, 5–12.

Lave, L. B. (1987). Health and safety risk analysis: Information for better decisions. *Science, 236*, 291–295.

Levenstein, J. H., Brown, J. B., Weston, W. W., Stewart, M., McCracken, E. C., & McWhinney, I. (1989). Patient-centered clinical interviewing. In M. Stewart & D. Roter (Eds.), *Communicating with medical patients* (pp. 107–120). Newbury Park, CA: Sage.

Leventhal, H., & Cameron, L. (1987). Behavioral theories and the problem of compliance. *Patient Education Counseling*, *10*, 117–138.

Levinger, G., & Huesmann, L. R. (1980). An "incremental exchange" perspective on the pair: Interpersonal reward and level of involvement. In K. J. Gergen, M. S. Greenberg, & R. J. Willis (Eds.), *Social exchange: Advances in theory and research* (pp. 165-188). New York: Plenum.

Ley, P. (1988). *Communicating with patients*. London: Croom Helm.

Linden, M. (1981). Definition of compliance. *Journal of Therapy and Toxicology*, *19*, 86–90.

Marlatt, G. A., & Gordon, J. R. (1980). Determinants of relapse: Implications for the maintenance of behavior change. In Davidson and Davidson (Eds.), *Behavioral medicine: Changing health lifestyles*. New York: Brunner-Mazel, 410–452.

Marshall, A. A. (1993). Whose agenda is it anyway? Training medical residents in patient-centered interviewing techniques. In E. Berlin-Ray (Ed.), *Case studies in health communication* (pp. 15–30). Hillsdale, NJ: Erlbaum.

Mattson, M. (1999). Toward a reconceptualization of communication cues to action in the health belief model: HIV test counseling. *Communication Monographs*, *66*, 240–265.

Mazzuca, S. A. (1982). Does patient education in chronic disease have therapeutic value? *Journal of Chronic Disease*, *35*, 521–529.

Mehrabian, A. (1969). Significance of posture and position in the communication of attitude and status relationships. *Psychological Bulletin*, *71*, 359–372.

Meryn, S. (1998). Improving doctor-patient communication: Not an option, but a necessity. *British Medical Journal*, *316*, 1922.

Miller, G. R. (1983). On various ways of skinning symbolic cats: Recent research on persuasive message strategies. *Journal of Language and Social Psychology*, *2*, 123–140.

Montgomery, S. B., Joseph, J. G., Becker, M. H., Ostrow, D. G., Kessler, R. C., & Kirscht, J. P. (1989). The health belief model in understanding compliance with preventative recommendations for AIDS: How useful? *AIDS Education and Prevention*, *1*(4), 303–323.

Norell, S. E. (1980). Medication behavior: A study of outpatients treated with piocarpine eye drops for primary open angle glaucoma. *Acta Opthalmologica*, *14*, 1–3.

Norell, S. E. (1981). Accuracy of patient interviews and estimates by clinical staff in determining medication compliance. *Social Science Medicine*, *15*, 57–61.

Pendleton, D. (1983). Doctor-patient communication: A review. In D. Pendleton & J. Hasler (Eds.), *Doctor-patient communication* (pp. 5–56). New York: Academic Press.

Perloff, L. S. (1983). Perceptions of vulnerability to victimization. *Journal of Social Issues*, *39*, 41–61.

Phillips, G. M., & Jones, J. A. (1991). Medical compliance: Patient or physician responsibility? *American Behavioral Scientist*, *34*(6), 756–767.

Petraitis, J., Flay, B. R., & Miller, T. Q. (1995). Reviewing theories of adolescent substance use: Organizing pieces in the puzzle. *Psychological Bulletin*, *117*, 67–86.

Pitts, M. (1991). The medical consultation. In M. Pitts & K. Phillips (Eds.), *The psychology of health: An introduction* (pp. 49–63). London: Routledge.

Podshadley, A. G., & Schweikle, E. S. (1970). The effectiveness of two educational programs in changing the performance of oral hygiene by elementary school children. *Journal of Public Health Dentistry*, *30*, 17–20.

Prentice-Dunn, S., Jones, J. L., & Floyd, D. L. (1997). Persuasive appeals and the reduction of skin cancer risk: The roles of appearance concern, perceived benefits of a tan, and efficacy information. *Journal of Applied Social Psychology*, *27*, 1041–1047.

Rippetoe, P. A., & Rogers, R. W. (1987). Effects of components of protection motivation theory on adaptive and maladaptive coping with a health threat. *Journal of Personality and Social Psychology*, *52*, 596–604.

Robberson, M. R., & Rogers, R. W. (1988). Beyond fear appeals: Negative and positive persuasive appeals to health and self-esteem. *Journal of Applied Social Psychology*, *18*, 277–287.

Rogers, R. W. (1983). Cognitive and physiological processes in fear appeals and attitude change: A revised theory of protection motivation. In J. Cacioppo and R. Petty (Eds.), *Social psychophysiology*. New York: Guilford Press.

Rolnick, S., & Heather, N. (1982). The application of Bandura's self-efficacy theory to abstinence-oriented alcoholism treatment. *Addictive Behaviors, 7,* 243–250.

Roloff, M. E. (1987). Communication and reciprocity within intimate relationships. In M. E. Roloff, & G. R. Miller (Eds.), *Interpersonal processes: New directions in communication research* (pp. 11–38). Beverly Hills, CA: Sage.

Roloff, M. E., & Barnicott, E. (1979). The influence of dogmatism on the situational use of pro- and anti-social compliance-gaining strategies. *Southern Speech Communication Journal, 45,* 37–54.

Rosenstock, I. M. (1974). The health belief model and preventative health behavior. *Health Education Monographs, 2,* 354–386.

Roter, D. L., Hall, J. A., Merisca, R., Nordstrom, B., Cretin, D., & Svardstad, B. (1998). Effectiveness of Interventions to improve patient compliance: A meta-analysis. *Medical Care, 36,* 1138–1161.

Rothert, M. L. (1982). Physicians' and patients' judgments of compliance with a hypertensive regimen. *Medical Decision Making, 2,* 179–195.

Schneider, D. E., & Beaubien, R. A. (1996). A naturalistic investigation of compliance-gaining strategies employed by doctors in medical interviews. *Southern Communication Journal,* 332–341.

Seibold, D. R., & Roper, R. E. (1979). Psychosocial determinants of health care intentions: Test of the Triandis and Fishbein models. In D. Nimmo (Ed.), *Communication Yearbook 3* (pp. 627–643). New Brunswick, NJ: International Communication Association.

Slamecka, N. J., & Graf, P. (1978). The generation effect: Delineation of a phenomenon. *Journal of Experimental Psychology: Human Learning and Memory, 4,* 592–604.

Smalec, J. L., & Klingle, R. S. (2000). Bulimia intervention via interpersonal influence: The role of threat and efficacy in persuading bulimics to seek help. *Journal of Behavioral Medicine, 23,* 37–57.

Spector, S. (2000). Noncompliance with asthma therapy—Are there solutions? *Journal of Asthma, 3,* 381–388.

Steward, M. A. (1995). Effective physician-patient communication and health outcomes: A review. *Canadian Medical Association Journal, 152,* 1423–1433.

Stewart, R. B., & Cluff, L. E. (1972). A review of medication errors and compliance in ambulant patients. *Clinical Pharmacology and Therapeutics, 13,* 463–468.

Street, R. L., & Wiemann, J. M. (1987). Patient satisfaction with physicians' interpersonal involvement, expressiveness, and dominance. In M. L. McLaughlin (Ed.), *Communication Yearbook 7* (pp. 591–612). Beverly Hills, CA: Sage.

Sutton, S. R. (1982). Fear-arousing communications: A critical examination of theory and research. In J. R. Eiser (Ed.), *Social Psychology and Behavioral Medicine* (pp. 303–337). London: Wiley.

Tedesco, L. A., Keffer, M. A., & Fleck-Kandath, C. (1991). Self-efficacy, reasoned action, and oral health behavior reports: A social cognitive approach to compliance. *Journal of Behavioral Medicine, 14,* 341–353.

Thurman, Q. C., & Franklin, K. M. (1990). AIDS and college health: Knowledge, threat, and prevention at a northeastern university. *Journal of American College Health, 38,* 179–184.

Turk, D. C., Salovey, P., & Litt, M. D. (1986). Adherence: A cognitive-behavioral perspective. In K. Gerber & A. M. Nehemkis (Eds.), *Compliance: The dilemma of the chronically ill.* New York: Springer.

Wagener, J. J., & Taylor, S. E. (1986). What else could I have done? Patients' responses to failed treatment decisions. *Health Psychology, 5,* 481–496.

Webb, P. A. (1980). Effectiveness of patient education and psychosocial counseling in promoting compliance and control among hypertensive patients. *Journal of Family Practice, 10,* 1047–1055.

Weinstein, A. G. (2000). Asthma treatment and noncompliance. *Del Medical Journal, 72,* 209–213.

Weinstein, N. D. (1983). Reducing unrealistic optimism about illness susceptibility. *Health Psychology, 2,* 11–20.

Weinstein, N. D., & Lachendro, E. (1982). Egocentrism as a source of unrealistic optimism. *Personality and Social Psychology Bulletin, 8,* 195–200.

Weisman, C. S., & Teitelbaum, M. A. (1989). Women and health care communication. *Patient Education and Counseling, 13,* 183–199.

Wilson, J. T. (1973). Compliance with instructions in the evaluation of therapeutic efficacy: A common but frequently unrecognized major variable. *Clinical Pediatrics, 12,* 333.

Witte, K. (1992a). Putting the fear back into fear appeals: The extended parallel process model. *Communication Monographs, 59,* 331–349.

Witte, K. (1992b). The role of threat and efficacy in AIDS prevention. *International Quarterly of Communication Health Education, 12,* 225–249.

Witte, K. (1994). Fear control and danger control: A test of the extended parallel process model (EPPM). *Communication Monographs, 61,* 113–134.

Witte, K. (1998). Fear as motivator, fear as inhibitor: Using the EPPM to explain fear appeal successes and failures. In P. A. Andersen & L. K. Guerrero (Eds.), *The handbook of communication and emotion* (pp. 423–450). New York: Academic Press.

Witte, K., & Allen, M. (2000). A meta-analysis of fear appeals: Implications for effective public health campaigns. *Health and Education Behavior, 27,* 591–615.

Witte, K., Stokols, D., Ituarte, P., & Schneider, M. (1993). Testing the health belief model in a field study to promote bicycle safety helmets. *Communication Research, 20,* 564–586.

Young, M., & Klingle, R. S. (1996). Silent partners in medical care: A cross-cultural study of patient participation. *Health Communication, 8,* 29–53.

17

Social Influence in Close Relationships

Leslie A. Baxter and Carma L. Bylund

Kelley and his colleagues (1983) have defined a relationship as close "if the amount of mutual impact two people have on each other is great or, in other words, if there is high interdependence" (p. 13). In light of this definition, *all* of the communicative exchanges between close friends, romantic partners, spouses, and family members could be considered instances of social influence or persuasion. Such an all-encompassing approach is certainly compatible with Gass and Seiter's (2003) suggestion that any and all communicative events can be examined for their persuasive qualities. However, an exhaustive review of the research and theory surrounding all facets of communication in close relationships is beyond our scope—and our page limit. Instead, we are going to focus more narrowly on three specific perspectives on social influence between parties in close relationships.

The first perspective is more or less accepted as the *classic, or traditional, approach* in the social scientific research literature: A persuader has a goal of seeking behavioral or attitudinal change in the partner (the "target") and strategically deploys a message designed to accomplish the desired goal. The focus of attention is on the persuader's strategic choice of a tactical message. This approach hails from many disciplinary traditions, including communication, marketing, psychology, and child development. It is generally characterized by quantitative methods in which research subjects are asked to construct a single strategic message for some specified goal, or to choose a strategy among several choices presented by the researcher. This perspective has dominated the study of social influence in close relationships for over thirty years, and it has produced a large body of research findings. By contrast, the second and third perspectives discussed in this chapter are relatively recent arrivals on the social influence scene. We present them as points of contrast with the traditional perspective in order to pose alternative understandings of social influence beyond the dominant strategies approach.

The second perspective, one we label the *social-meaning approach*, also focuses on a persuader who has a goal of changing the target in some way. However, from the social-meaning perspective, the meaning of the persuasive enterprise and its execution are negotiated between the two parties to the relationship. Central to this meaning-making perspective are the identities of the parties and the rights and obligations that guide action in their relationship. From the social-meaning perspective, the target is not a passive recipient of the persuader's strategic message but an active coconstructer of meaning. From this second perspective, then, the focus of attention is on the communicative exchange between persuader and target. This second perspective, rooted in the traditions of anthropology, ethnography of communication and conversation analysis, emphasizes the qualitative study of the micro-details of naturally occurring interaction between persuader and target.

The third perspective, *dialogic communication*, suspends distinct persuader-target roles and focuses instead on those communicative episodes, called dialogic moments, in which two relationship parties jointly change each other without prior intention to do so. The focus of attention is on these occasions of dialogic communication, or genuine dialogue, between relationship parties. This third perspective, with roots in dialogism theory, feminist theory, and social constructionism, features qualitative and interpretive methods of inquiry.

The Traditional Perspective

The first section of this chapter provides an overview of literature regarding social influence strategies in two types of close relationships: intimate relationships (including friendship and romantic relationships) and family relationships (spousal and parent-child relationships). Examining influence strategies in relational contexts is important because "the relationship prescribes which strategies are proper and usual" (Poppe, van der Kloot, & Valkenberg, 1999, p. 456).

We established two guiding parameters for this section. First, the literature included had to be specific to one or more of the types of close relationships we identified. We present the literature separately in each relational context, although some studies have examined how persuasion strategies vary across different types of intimate and nonintimate relationships (e.g., Buss, 1992; Cody, McLaughlin, & Schneider, 1981; Dunn & Cowan, 1993; Poppe et al., 1999). Second, the idea of a strategy had to be present in the study to be included here. Terms such as "persuasive strategy," "compliance-gaining strategy," "influence strategy," "control strategy," "power strategy," and "manipulation tactic" are pervasive throughout this literature. We have adopted the term persuasive strategy to encompass all of these. We do not, however, include the literature on compliance resistance (e.g., Abe & Izard, 1999; Ifert, 2000; Metts, Cupach, & Imahori, 1992; White, Pearson, & Flint, 1989).

In these studies, researchers rely on different taxonomies, some developing their own for a particular context. As noted by Kellerman and Cole (1994), different classification systems have led to disorder and confusion. It is difficult to make sense of this literature because of this confusion. We do not explain each taxonomy here,[1] nor do we critique the various taxonomies used in studying relational persuasion strategies; instead, we attempt to describe and explain findings using them. We have tried to make the names of these persuasive strategies clear and to give definitions where possible, although we direct the reader to the original studies for more clarification.

Persuasive Strategies in Intimate Relationships

Intimate relationships between friends and romantic partners have been a well-studied context for persuasive strategies. These are important contexts to consider, because compliance-gaining effectiveness is related to the intimacy of the persuader and target (Boster, Rodriguez, Cruz, & Marshall, 1995; Cody et al., 1981; Guerin, 1995; Mallalieu, 1999; Miller, Boster, Roloff, & Seibold, 1977; Roloff, Janiszewski, McGrath, Burns, & Manrai, 1988). However, most of this research has been limited to college-age students and young adults (see Jones, 1985, for a study on young children's use of persuasive strategies in friendships). As Kellerman and Cole (1994) pointed out, two guiding foci of compliance-gaining research have been the types of compliance-gaining strategies available and the times when those strategies are used. We adopt the latter as a consideration for this section and add another: the effectiveness of persuasive strategies.

Conditions of Strategy Use.   Strategy use has been studied in two ways: the frequency of strategy use and the type of strategy employed. Conditions of strategy use have been operationalized as characteristics of the individual persuader or target (including sex, power, cultural background, and personality characteristics), characteristics of the relationship, and type of request.

Frequency of strategy use has received much less research attention than type of strategy. In examining frequency of strategy use, one study reported that sex alone was not the best predictor of frequency of persuasive strategy use; however, among females, interpersonal orientation (IO) predicted frequency of persuasive strategy use, with high IO females using persuasive strategies more often than low-IO females (Cataldi & Reardon, 1996).

The findings on sex as a predictor of type of strategy use are mixed. In one study, some sex differences were correlated with type of strategy use, but none was consistent across four conditions (e.g., self-report and other report in two conditions each) (Buss, Gomes, Higgins, & Lauterbach, 1987). The sex of the persuader was not shown to be a predictor of using indirect or direct strategies (Steil & Hillman, 1993) with American, Korean, or Japanese college students. In heterosexual romantic couples, however, men were more likely than women to report using bilateral and direct strategies (Falbo & Peplau, 1980). Additionally, in the context of sexual influence strategies, males have been found to be more likely than females to use pressure or manipulation as a persuasive strategy (Christopher & Frandsen, 1990).

The relative power of the persuader has also been linked to the type of strategy used. Those with more power in the relationship have reported a greater likelihood of using bilateral and direct strategies when compared to those with less power (Falbo & Peplau, 1980). In a study on married heterosexual couples and cohabiting homosexual couples, having a position of weakness in the relationship was shown to be associated with the use of weak persuasive strategies (e.g., manipulation), while a position of strength in the relationship was associated with the use of strong persuasive strategies (e.g., bullying) (Howard et al., 1986). In a study of two specific genres of persuasive strategies, synthetic benevolence (e.g., flattery) and synthetic malevolence (e.g., threat), participants reported being more likely to direct synthetic benevolence at more powerful targets and synthetic malevolence at less powerful targets (Fung, Kipnis, & Rosnow, 1987).

Another way of examining power in intimate relationships is to look at the number of people the persuader is trying to persuade. In the friendship relationship, assertiveness and exchange strategies have been shown to be used more in relationships where the power was balanced (one person influencing one friend), whereas coalition and upward appeal strategies were used more in situations in which power was not balanced (one person trying to persuade three people) (Mallalieu & Faure, 1998). Miller (1982) found that the power of the target correlated positively with the probability of the use of five of Marwell and Schmitt's (1967) strategies: debt, moral appeal, self-feeling, altercasting (positive) and altercasting (negative). We will return to the issue of power when we discuss facework in the next section.

Cultural background also appears to play a role in predicting strategy use. Korean and Japanese students report using less confrontational strategies than American students (Steil & Hillman, 1993). Further, Japanese women are more likely to use strong persuasive strategies (e.g., bullying) with their male friends than are American women, who more frequently use weak strategies (e.g., manipulation) with male friends (Dunn & Cowan, 1993). In this study, no difference was found among female friends.

Buss and colleagues (1987) also reported some association between personality characteristics and persuasive strategies. For example, participants who rated high on neuroticism were more likely to use regression (e.g., pouting or sulking until the partner complies) and the silent treatment than were those who rated low. Further, they also reported that the type of persuasive strategy used varied according to whether a target was trying to elicit behavior or terminate a behavior. Specifically, charm was used more frequently to elicit behavior, whereas silent treatment and coercion were used more frequently to terminate behavior.

Researchers have also examined characteristics of the relationship as predictors of strategy use. In looking at those in satisfied versus dissatisfied relationships, Bui, Raven, & Schwarzwald (1994) found that both men and women reported that men were likely to use strong or controlling tactics (such as coercion or obligation) in dissatisfying rather than in satisfying relationships. Women reported an equally low likelihood of using strong tactics in either satisfying or dissatisfying relationships. Romantic couples whom interviewers judged to be less similar and less well matched were more likely to use the silent treatment, debasement, and reason as persuasive strategies than were those couples judged to be more similar and better matched (Buss et al., 1987).

Effectiveness of Strategy Type.   The effectiveness of persuasive strategies has not received much attention in the literature, although a few studies have examined this topic. One study reported that direct requests are more effective than indirect requests at gaining verbal compliance when combined with high levels of relational intimacy (Jordan &

Roloff, 1990). Further, the persuasive strategies of pregiving and direct request have been shown, among friends, not to differ in effectiveness (Boster et al., 1995).

The examination of persuasive appeals regarding condom use has shown effective persuasive strategies to be appeals to caring, pleasure, and responsibility, although in one study three other strategies (health, threat, and fear) were effective but less well liked (Sheer, 1995). Additionally, the strategies of pleasure, fear, threat, and health were more effective with high- than with low-sensation seekers. Males and high-sensation seekers rated pleasure strategies as most appealing while low-sensation seekers and females rated caring and responsibility as most appealing (Sheer, 1995). Another study demonstrated that males' ratings of nine appeals for using a condom showed a strategy's persuasiveness and the likelihood of use from that strategy to be consistent. Females, however, did not rate these consistently. Although this study found only little resistance to condom use, both males and females preferred strategies that focused on health concerns (Edgar, Freimuth, Hammond, McDonald, & Fink, 1992).

Researchers have also investigated premarital sexual influence strategies. Using the Sexual Influence Tactics Scale, which they created for this research, Christopher and Frandsen (1990) determined the existence of four general influence strategies in this type of context: (1) antisocial acts, (2) pressure and manipulation, (3) emotional and physical closeness, and (4) logic and reason. The latter two were the only ones related to sexual behavior: emotional and physical closeness positively, and logic and reason negatively.

Although social influence occurs frequently in friendships and romantic relationships, opportunities also abound for social influence between different family members.

Persuasive Strategies in Families

Family Systems Theory explains that families are both made up of subsystems and nested in higher-order systems (Galvin & Brommel, 2000). The literature has focused on persuasive strategies in two of these subsystems: spouse-spouse and parent-child. We use these two subsystems as our organizing framework for this section. However, we do not focus on research examining influence strategies used in families with a history of violence (Frieze & McHugh, 1992; Oldershaw, Walters, & Hall, 1986).

Spousal. The interdependence of spouses' behaviors and lives makes the marital relationship a rich context in which to examine social influence (Witteman & Fitzpatrick, 1986).[2] Merging Kellerman and Cole's (1994) considerations and our organizational schema in the previous section, we examine the types of persuasive strategies that are used, explore how characteristics of the persuader and of the relationship affect the use of strategies, and determine which strategies are most effective.

Types of Persuasive Strategies. A basic consideration is what types of persuasive strategies spouses use. One approach to this has been to test developed taxonomies on married couples. For example, marital partners rated 12 of 16 compliance-gaining strategies (Marwell & Schmitt, 1967) as more likely to be used when trying to influence a spouse rather than a stranger; threat was the only strategy rated as more likely to be used with a stranger than a spouse (Sillars, 1980). Additionally, in a study examining only dual career couples, spouses reported using more direct strategies than indirect strategies when using Falbo and Peplau's (1980) distinctions between these strategy types (Steil & Weltman, 1992). Using cultural consensus modeling, and based on an a priori set of persuasive strategies, Mexican immigrant men and women were shown to have a shared belief system about the types of persuasive strategies both sexes use with their spouses or partners (Beckman, Harvey, Satre, & Walker, 1999).

A second approach involves using inductive techniques to create taxonomies of persuasive strategies specific to the spousal context. Research examining spousal persuasive strategies used in the context of joint purchasing decisions resulted in a taxonomy of 18 persuasive strategies, with bargaining and reason consistently reported to be the most frequently used strategies (Kirchler, 1990, 1993). Newton and Burgoon (1990) used previous research and literature to create a categorical system for verbal influence tactics used by spouses or partners in resolving disagreements. Finally, Tucker and Mueller (2000) developed a taxonomy of strategies used by husbands and wives to modify their spouses' health behaviors; those most used were engaging in health behavior together, engaging in facilitative behavior, discussing the health issue with the spouse, and requesting that the partner engage in the health behavior.

Differing Uses of Persuasive Strategies. A second area in this literature investigates differing uses of persuasive strategies by individual characteristics of the spouses and by characteristics of the spouses as a marital couple.

Many researchers have examined whether men and women use different types of strategies. For the most part, sex does not seem to be a strong predictor of the type of strategy used, with a few exceptions (Aida & Falbo, 1991; Beckman et al., 1999; Buss, 1992; Dillard & Fitzpatrick, 1985; Sagrestano, Christensen, & Heavey, 1998; Tucker & Mueller, 2000; Zvonkovic, Schmiege, & Hall, 1994; see Kirchler, 1993, for a description of husbands' and wives' different uses of persuasive strategies in purchasing decisions). As an alternative to sex as the predictor of type of persuasive strategy use, Sagrestano, Christensen, and Heavey (1998) demonstrated that it is actually the social role of the spouse in the conversation (which spouse is seeking change) that predicts the type of persuasive strategy used. Other individual characteristics that have been found to relate to type of strategy used include low confidence and wives' nurturance (Steil & Weltman, 1992) as well as wives' masculinity (Sexton & Perlman, 1989). In addition, Buss (1992) demonstrated that the Big Five personality factors (Surgency, Agreeableness, Conscientiousness, Emotional Stability, and Intellect-Openness) related to choices of spousal persuasive strategies. Finally, two studies have demonstrated that husbands' and wives' frequency of using persuasive strategies are correlated (Dillard & Fitzpatrick, 1985; Sexton & Perlman, 1989). Specifically, in looking at persuasive strategies regarding health behaviors, wives have not been shown to use these more frequently than husbands (although the sample was relatively young) (Tucker & Anders, 2001).

Fitzpatrick's three couple types have been associated with various types of persuasive strategies in spousal influence (Witteman & Fitzpatrick, 1986). First, Traditional couples (high on traditional ideology and sharing and low on conflict avoidance) rely on messages about positive or negative outcomes of the decision. Separate couples (high on traditional ideology and conflict avoidance and low on sharing) use constraining messages. The third type, Independent couples (low on traditional ideology and conflict avoidance and high on sharing) use a variety of messages, relying on more power bases than the other couple types do. In purchasing decisions, the choice of persuasive strategy is affected by the type of conflict, relationship characteristics (marital satisfaction, power patterns, and duration of the relationship), and gender (Kirchler, 1993).

Researchers have also been interested in how the employment status of spouses affects relational persuasion. One study found that career orientation (whether just the husband or both spouses work) did not predict the types of strategies used and that perceived equity did not correlate with uses of means control or credibility influence strategies by either single- or dual-career couples (Sexton & Perlman, 1989). However, results about which type of career-oriented couple uses more persuasive strategies overall seem to be mixed. Although Sexton and Perlman (1989) found that dual-career spouses use persuasive strategies more often than single-career spouses, Aida and Falbo (1991) found the opposite; equal partners (those who report it is both spouses' duty to provide income for the family) use fewer overall strategies than traditional partners (those who report it is the husband's duty to provide income for the family).

The literature reports a consistently negative relationship between marital satisfaction and use of indirect persuasive strategies. One study reported that more satisfied spouses were less likely to use indirect strategies than dissatisfied spouses (Aida & Falbo, 1991), and a second study reported that dissatisfied spouses more frequently used emotional influence, which the authors deemed to be the most indirect strategy in their study (Zvonkovic et al., 1994).

Effectiveness of Persuasive Strategies.   Only a few studies have examined which types of persuasive strategies used by spouses are more or less effective. Generally, spouses who gain compliance rely more on messages focused on the activity that is being requested rather than on power or control in the relationship. They also rely on direct statements, direct requests, and questions (Witteman & Fitzpatrick, 1986). Additionally, prosocial strategies such as content validation (e.g., agreement, explanation, problem solving) and other-support (strategies confirming or reinforcing the relationship or the other) are effective in gaining a partner's compliance, although there are some variations by sex (Newton & Burgoon, 1990). Direct requests of wives by husbands (Dillard & Fitzpatrick, 1985) have also been found to be effective.

Different types of emotional disclosures as part of a persuasive strategy have not been found to influence the objective effectiveness of requests (i.e., whether or not the spouse complies). However, these types of emotional disclosures do affect the subjective effectiveness of requests (i.e., the spouse's response to the compliance request, the spouse's attitude toward his or her spouse, the spouse's attitude toward compliance, and the spouse's attitude toward self) (Shimanoff, 1987).

Finally, the effectiveness of persuasive strategies for spouses' control of health behaviors has also been examined (Tucker & Mueller, 2000). Some strategies seem to be more effective than others for both husbands and wives, including engaging in the health behaviors with a spouse, having a spouse engage in facilitative behavior, and having a spouse provide emotional support.

Parent-Child.   The inherent imbalance of control between parent and child makes this familial subsystem interesting to examine, though it is significantly different from spousal influence. The development of the child through the stages of infancy, toddler, school age, and adolescence brings different considerations to bear in examining persuasive strategies. Here we examine the two periods in a child's life that have received the most attention in the literature: preschool and adolescence. We present an overview of literature that looks both at the persuasive strategies parents use on their children and at those that children use on their parents.

Preschool.   The majority of the literature on the persuasive strategies parents use with preschool children is based on observing or recording playtime interactions between a parent and child. Research indicates that in play situations, parents use a majority of directives (telling the child what to do) rather than prohibitory statements (telling the child what not to do) in trying to get their children to comply. Parents also tend to use more action controls (trying to influence the child's immediate physical behavior) than attention controls (trying to modify the child's perceptual activity) (McLaughlin, 1983).

The sex of the parent and the sex of the child seem to have no effect on the number of persuasive strategies used with children in play situations (McLaughlin, 1983). However, with older children fathers use more imperatives than mothers do (McLaughlin, 1983). In play situations, the total number of persuasive strategies used was indirectly associated with the child's age (McLaughlin, 1983). Additionally, American mothers used more directive strategies than did Japanese mothers during a mother-play interaction (Abe & Izard, 1999).

In one study, mothers who interacted with their children in a "responsive mother" manner, by encouraging the children to direct the interaction, received more compliance from their children than mothers who interacted with their children in a normal manner (where maternal compliance with the child was not emphasized) (Parpal & Macoby, 1985). A subsequent two-part study confirmed that positive mood was the mediating variable in this relationship. That is, children participating in responsive play had more positive moods than children participating in normal play, and children induced with positive moods were more likely to comply than their counterparts induced with negative moods (Lay, Waters, & Park, 1989). Also in play situations, child compliance was higher with attention-persuasive strategies than with action-persuasive strategies (McLaughlin, 1983) and with strategically timed persuasive strategies that attended to the child's current toy involvement (Schaeffer & Crook, 1980). Although the compliance of the child was not dependent on the sex of the parent or the sex of the child, the effectiveness of strategies did vary by the child's age (McLaughlin, 1983).

In a cross-cultural study, American mothers had more success in getting their children to comply in picking up toys during play than Japanese mothers did, when both sets of mothers gave direct commands. Perhaps this is because American mothers are more likely to use their authority and give direct commands, so American children are more accustomed to this (Abe & Izard, 1999). However, during mother-child playtime, directiveness strategies did not predict compliance in either the American or Japanese mother-child dyads (Abe & Izard, 1999).

Adolescents. The study of persuasion strategies used by parents on their adolescent children and vice versa relies on self-report data, a notable methodological difference from the studies with preschool children. Early research on parental persuasive strategies used with adolescents conceptualized these strategies into three categories: coercion, induction (obtaining voluntary compliance), and love withdrawal (deTurck & Miller, 1983). Subsequent research has shown more variance in the persuasive strategies that adolescents perceived parents using. Perceptions of strategy have been shown to be associated with adolescent gender, age, parental gender, and context (deTurck & Miller, 1983), while adolescents' reported strategy use with mothers has been associated with adolescent gender (Cowan & Avants, 1988). There is also some evidence that adolescents' use of persuasive strategies that anticipate noncompliance correlate with their mothers' use of these strategies (Cowan & Avants, 1988).

Effective strategies for gaining adolescent compliance include, for mothers, frequent maternal praise and moderate levels of attempted control; for fathers, they include moderate or high levels of attempted control. For both parents, the use of command techniques positively correlates with adolescent compliance (Smith, 1983).

One body of literature examined the consumer socialization of children (see John, 1999, for a review), including adolescents' use of persuasive strategies on their parents during consumer decision making. Unlike younger children (aged 3 to 11), who tend just to ask for products (Isler, Popper, & Ward, 1987), adolescents use a more varied range of persuasive strategies. A typology of adolescent persuasive strategies used to influence consumer decisions and parental response strategies was recently developed by Palan and Wilkes (1997). This typology includes seven types of strategies used by parents and/or adolescents. Reasoning, a substrategy of the bargaining type of strategy, was the most effective adolescent persuasive strategy named by adolescents, mothers, and fathers.

The traditional perspective has produced a sizable body of research literature for friendship, romantic, spousal, and parent-child relationships. Strategy use, particularly the type of strategy employed by the persuader, has received more research attention than strategy effectiveness. Efforts to identify patterns in findings across studies are hampered by the lack of a common strategy taxonomy.

The Social-Meaning Perspective

Two primary social-meaning approaches can be identified in existing literature: the *incremental-interactive approach* articulated by Sanders and Fitch (2001) and the *facework approach* grounded in theorizing by Goffman (1967) and by Brown and Levinson (1987). Although these two approaches are different in ways discussed below, they share a common assumption: that all interaction, including social influence, is a *social* undertaking, by which we mean that the parties' actions are guided by rules of appropriate conduct and hold implications for their identities and the nature of their relationship.

Sanders and Fitch (2001) have argued that social influence is of necessity an incremental and interactive activity in which the parties jointly negotiate the social meaning of solicitation (e.g., requesting, compliance seeking) and response (target compliance or resistance). Persuader and target engage in a subtle and complex interactional "dance" in which they jointly determine whether a persuasive attempt is necessary and allowable, how solicitations are interpreted as influence attempts rather than alternative things we can do with words, whether and how the persuader's inducements to change are appropriate and sufficient, how responses are interpreted as acts of compliance or resistance, the appropriateness of the target's responses, and the implications of the solicitation and response for the parties' identities and their relationship.

Some research from the traditional perspective has examined sequential influence attempts by the persuader when the target initially resists compliance (e.g., deTurck, 1985; Lim, 1990b; Wilson, Cruz, Marshall, & Rao, 1993). However, several crucial differences can be identified between this body of work and the incremental-interactive approach.

By way of discussing these differences, we'll work from a concrete example that fortuitously occurred between one of us and her six-year-old daughter as this chapter was being written. The conversation was prompted by the daughter's placement of her chair about six inches in front of the television screen, blocking others' view of the image:

1   Mother: "That *sounds* like an interesting television program you're watching. What is it?"

2   Daughter: "I dunno."

3   Mother: "I'd like to *watch* it too."

4   Daughter: "With me? OK!"

5   Mother: "It would be a lot easier for me to see the TV if your chair wasn't blocking the screen."

6   Daughter: "Let's both move to the couch to watch."

7   Mother: "Please move your chair back away from the screen so we can both see the program from the couch. Remember, nobody can see through the back of a chair. It's important to be "I Care" and think of others when you act."

8   Daughter: "OK." [chair is moved back]

This conversation features a particular kind of speech act known as a *directive* (Searle, 1976)—an utterance attempting to get someone to do something they otherwise would not do. The mother initially expresses the directive indirectly through hinting, first in utterance 1, then again in utterance 3, and yet again in utterance 5. In utterance 7, the directive has been expressed explicitly, along with reasons for the request.

The traditional research on sequential influence attempts presupposes that successive attempts are necessary because of target resistance; that is, the persuader-target exchange is framed as an adversarial one. However, our illustrative conversation does not appear to be characterized by target resistance. Although close-relationship parties can be engaged in an adversarial battle in which the persuader seeks to overcome target resistance, particularly in times of conflict, Sanders and Fitch (2001) have argued that everyday social influence in close relationships is far more likely to be characterized by a spirit of cooperation and agreeableness in which both parties are motivated to accommodate the needs of each other. A similar point has been made by Roloff and his colleagues (1988). In our example, the daughter does not resist the mother's request; she simply fails to understand the indirect directives of utterances 1 and 3, hearing them instead as an invitation to do something together. Although she does not take the hinted action of utterance 5, she responds in utterance 6 with a cooperative and agreeable solution to her mother's viewing difficulty—moving to a different location—a solution that also advances the child's social goal of doing something together. The mother's explicit directive of utterance 7 has accommodated to the child's desire to sit together on the couch. The child's utterance 8 accommodates to the request to move the chair.

Whereas the traditional approach views sequential attempts as necessary only under conditions of target resistance, the incremental-interactive approach presumes that all social influence is of necessity an unfolding dynamic that is enacted across multiple utterances between the persuader and the target. Sanders and Fitch (2001) have advanced two theoretical reasons why social influence is an incremental and interactive process.

The first reason, developed by Sanders (1987, 1997), is that a given utterance is understandable only as part of the larger interaction stream of preceding and subsequent utterances. Put simply, utterances do not derive their meaning in isolation. Interacting parties are busily engaged in the business of negotiating what utterances mean in, and through, their successive utterances. For example, when the mother's utterances 1 and 3 are linked together, they can be heard as a desire to see as well as hear the television. However, it is clear from the daughter's utterance 4 that the child hears this utterance stream differently—as an invitation to a joint viewing of television. In short, meaning emerges out of the "dance" between utterances. Whether and how an influence attempt is heard unfolds across the interaction. The meaning of the target's response similarly unfolds as persuader and target interact. Thus, the daughter's utterance 6 can be heard as a mere continuation of her agenda to achieve a joint viewing event, but it can also be heard as an attempt to respond cooperatively to her mother's viewing plight, as expressed in utterance 5.

The second theoretical reason social influence must of necessity be incremental and interactive is grounded in Fitch's (1994, 1998, in press) work in the cultural premises of persuasion. "Culture" refers to the premises about personhood, relationships, and communication that are shared by a community, whether that community is a society, a social network, a family, or a couple. Relationship parties are embedded in larger cultural systems and simultaneously construct their own unique culture of two, or dyadic culture (Baxter, 1987). For example, middle-class white Americans conduct their relationships in a societal culture that values individualism, and this premise serves as a backdrop against which people negotiate issues of autonomy and privacy as they relate. At the same time, each relationship pair has developed its own unique system of meanings that guides its action, for example, the circumstances in which privacy invasions are tolerated.

Cultural premises guide the process of social influence in three respects: the range of what people may appropriately be persuaded, the symbolic resources available to persuaders, and determining the pragmatic rules by which appropriate persuasion may be enacted. The range of actions and beliefs about which people may be persuaded constitute what Fitch (in press) calls *persuadables*. Each culture has a bandwidth of acceptable persuadables, bounded on one end of the continuum with actions and beliefs that are so ingrained into the social world that they require no persuasion, and on the other with actions and beliefs that are persuasion "taboos." Through their interaction, persuader and target negotiate whether the solicitation is legitimized as a persuadable. The rights and obligations of the parties that characterize their relationship are obviously important in defining whether a given solicitation is a persuadable. In the context of our mother-daughter example, it is acceptable in the societal culture and in this dyad's culture for the parental figure to make this specific request. However, we can well imagine several other kinds of encounters in which the child might challenge the parent's right to influence, particularly as the child reaches adolescence—for example, clothing preferences, friendship choices, and so on. In any social-influence interaction, the persuader and the target negotiate whether the request will be understood as a persuadable.

Cultural premises also provide a backdrop of symbolic resources available to persuader and target as they negotiate a social-influence encounter. For example, in utterance 8 above, the mother invokes the symbolic resource of "I Care," a program at the daughter's school in which children are encouraged to be thoughtful of others. Through their interaction, persuader and target jointly determine which of these symbolic resources will hold currency. This is not necessarily an easy task, as competing cultural premises can be introduced. In our mother-daughter exchange, for example, the child could have introduced individualism and her right to "do her own thing" but chose not to do so.

Last, cultural premises guide the pragmatic enactment of a social influence attempt—for example, rules of turn taking, listening to the other's position, and so forth. In our example, the mother and daughter operate on the premise that it is important to give reasons to accompany requests rather than simply ordering commands based on authority. Fitch (in press) argues that facework is one important aspect that guides the pragmatic enactment of a social-influence encounter.

The facework approach presupposes that social-influence attempts are socially meaningful in that the parties' images or identities are at stake—what Goffman (1967) referred to as "face." Brown and Levinson's (1987) Politeness Theory has been the most influential theoretical framework in understanding the implications of a persuader's request on the target's face, although several of its claims have been modified by two decades of research activity. Much of this research has employed quantitative methods in the strategies tradition, although Brown and Levinson grounded their theory in the micro-details of naturally occurring talk between interactants.

Brown and Levinson (1987) identified two kinds of face. *Negative face* is the desire to maintain one's own autonomy, that is, not having one's privacy invaded, one's resources spent, and one's actions constrained. *Positive face* is the desire to have one's attributes and actions approved of by significant others. Subsequent research has subdivided positive face into two components: fellowship face, the desire to be liked and included by others; and competence face, the desire to have one's abilities and actions respected and valued (Lim, 1990a; Lim & Bowers, 1991).

According to Brown and Levinson (1987), directives intrinsically threaten a target's negative face because an attempt is being made to constrain his or her actions in some way. However, not all directives are equally face-threatening. Brown and Levinson argued that the amount of face threat created by a directive is a function of three variables: relational distance (the more distant the parties, the greater the face threat to the target); power (the greater the power of the target relative to the persuader, the greater the face threat); and the culturally defined ranking of how much imposition is implicated in the directive (e.g., a request to borrow $100 is widely accepted as a greater imposition than a request to borrow $5). The request by the mother in our example would thus be regarded by Brown and Levinson as relatively low in its face threat to the daughter: Their relationship is close, the child has less power than the mother, and a request to move a chair is not widely regarded as involving much imposition.

Brown and Levinson (1987) articulated a hierarchy of five strategies available to persuaders who face the prospect of threatening the target's face. The lowest-level strategy is to make the request directly without any efforts to massage the target's face through politeness efforts. Second, they could express the request directly with redressive actions intended to enhance the target's positive face—for example, assurances that the target is liked and appreciated. Third, they could express the request directly with redressive actions intended to enhance the target's negative face—for example, an apology for making an imposition. Fourth, they could decide to express the request indirectly rather than directly, affording the target freedom to hear the utterance as a directive or not. Fifth, at the highest level of the hierarchy, they could decide not to seek change in the target, backing off from the face-threatening directive. According to Brown and Levinson, persuaders decide to use higher-level strategies in proportion to the amount of face threat implicated in the directive.

Two decades of politeness research suggest six primary modifications or extensions to Brown and Levinson's (1987) Politeness Theory. First, a number of scholars have argued that face threat is not a unidimensional phenomenon; instead, it is important to take into account qualitative differences in the type of face that is threatened (Craig, Tracy, Spisak, 1986; Leighty & Applegate, 1991; Lim & Bowers, 1991). Fellowship, competence, and autonomy face needs are qualitatively distinct, and a given directive could threaten these kinds of face to different degrees.

Second, and relatedly, influence acts are not all alike with respect to their face-threat implications. For example, Wilson and his colleagues (Wilson, Aleman, & Leatham, 1998; Wilson & Kunkel, 2000) have compared three different kinds of influence attempts—giving advice, requesting a favor, and enforcing an obligation—and have found that positive face threat and negative face threat vary across these types. In giving advice, for instance, the persuader may be implying a threat to the target's positive face, perhaps doubting, however indirectly, the target's competence to act. Such a threat is not implicated in the influence attempt of requesting a favor.

Third, in light of differences in types of face threat, the hierarchy of politeness strategies is problematic in placing negative-face redress at a higher level than positive-face redress (Metts, 2000). Instead, positive-face redress is viewed as responsive to positive face threats and negative-face redress is viewed as responsive to negative face threats, with no higher-lower hierarchical placement of these two politeness strategies.

Fourth, the absolute level of face imposition captured in the ranking variable has not appeared to be a very good predictor of the overall amount of face threat implicated in an act; instead, the persuader's right to make the request appears to be a more important factor (Baxter, 1984; Craig et al., 1986; Lim & Bowers, 1991). The right to make a request of another is consistent with the research finding that the more dominant the persuader, the less he or she redresses the face needs of the target (Baxter, 1984; Dillard, Wilson, Tusing, & Kinney, 1997; Leighty & Applegate, 1991; Lim & Bowers, 1991).

Fifth, Brown and Levinson's (1987) claim with respect to relational distance needs to be modified (Baxter, 1984; Lim, 1990a; Lim & Bowers, 1991; Leighty & Applegate, 1991; Roloff & Janiszewski, 1989; Roloff et al., 1988). When the directive involves a modest imposition on the target, the Brown and Levinson prediction appears to hold: Intimacy correlates negatively with face-redressive action. However, when the imposition is great, the opposite pattern appears to hold: Intimacy correlates positively with face-redressive action. In close relationships, the parties recognize that their interdependence and commitment will naturally compromise their autonomy needs; thus, modest impositions are expected and perhaps even function as an index of intimacy. However, when an imposition exceeds what would normally be expected in a committed relationship, the face threat is substantial and requires face-redressive action by the persuader.

Sixth, and last, indirectness is not necessarily regarded as more polite, or face redressive, than directness. Although some cultures view indirectness as more polite than directness, indirect hinting is regarded as rude in other cultures (e.g., Fitch & Sanders, 1994). Further, in our closest relationships, where openness and honesty are idealized, indirectness can be interpreted as a form of face threat rather than face redress (e.g., Dillard et al., 1997).

Despite their differences, the incremental-interactive and facework approaches share the view that social influence in close relationships is a social-meaning-making enterprise in which parties' rights, obligations, and identities feature prominently.

The Dialogic Communication Perspective

It is in our closest relationships that we most change and grow as individuals—what Aron and Aron (2000) refer to as *self-expansion*. In fact, Baxter and Montgomery (1996) have argued that we regard our relationships as close to the extent that they expand the parties' selves. The delicate interplay between similarities and differences between the parties provides the scaffolding for such changes in self (Aron & Aron, 2000; Baxter & Montgomery, 1996; Baxter & West, 2002; Wood, Dendy, Dordek, Germany, & Varallo, 1994). Similarities between parties are obviously important in providing the common ground upon which bonds of intimacy can be built and sustained. But equally necessary are differences. As the dialogic theorist, Mikhail Bakhtin, observed over seventy years ago, "What do I gain by having the other fuse with me? He will know and see but what I know and see. . . . Let him rather stay on the outside vantage point, and he can thus enrich essentially the event of my life" (Bakhtin, as quoted in Todorov, 1984, p. 108).

But what is the communicative process of influence by which parties change or expand? The first two perspectives would answer this question by pointing to change in the target as an outcome of intentional, goal-directed activity by the persuader. However, from the third perspective, the persuader-target distinction frames the parties' relationship as one of power and dominance in which the persuader functions to devalue the perspective of the other person. Instead, the third perspective dissolves the persuader-target distinction and examines the change that can spontaneously result when relational parties engage in genuine dialogue whose purpose is understanding rather than influence. Such change is "a result of new understanding and insights gained in the exchange of ideas" as the parties "allow diverse positions to be compared in a process of discovery and questioning that may lead to transformation for themselves" (Foss & Griffin, 1995, p. 6). The process by which this happens goes by various labels reflecting the different intellectual roots of the perspective, including "dialogue" with roots in dialogic theory (e.g., Bakhtin, 1981, 1984; Bohm, 1999; Buber, 1958; for a more complete bibliography, see Cissna & Anderson, 1998), "relational responsibility" with roots in social constructionism and feminist theory (e.g., McNamee & Gergen, 1999; Shepherd, 1992), and "invitational rhetoric" with roots in feminist theory (e.g., Foss & Griffin, 1995).

Cissna and Anderson (1994, pp. 13–15) have provided a comprehensive discussion of the characteristics that are present in the dialogic communication envisioned by the third perspective. The parties do not focus on strategic goals or outcomes but rather participate in a spontaneous, unrehearsed exchange characterized by improvisation and creativity. They refuse to assume that they already know one another's thoughts and feelings, instead displaying a willingness to recognize their "strange otherness." The parties engage one another in a spirit of authenticity and genuineness; the parties are speaking from a base of honesty, not strategy. They have a collaborative orientation in which they share their perspectives—with passion and perhaps even heated argument—not with a goal of "winning over" the other but in a spirit of sharing their views. Foss and Griffin (1995) refer to this as the discourse of offering, "the giving of expression to a perspective without advocating its support or seeking its acceptance" (p. 7). Parties sustain a vulnerability to one another's views, an openness to be changed.

Dialogic encounters are unique, fleeting moments that punctuate the everyday, mundane, task-oriented exchanges of relationship parties. But they do exist in our friendships, romantic relationships, and families and are vividly remembered by participants as emotionally intense and deeply meaningful in a variety of ways (Baxter & DeGooyer, 2001). Dialogic encounters are those occasions in which the interaction between the parties has created the opportunity for their selves to become. The parties are deeply influenced by the dialogue between them.

Conclusion

In a chapter of this length, we can do no more than provide a crude map of the forest of social influence in close relationships and examine a few specific trees along the way. We have identified three perspectives, which conceive of the influence process in radically different ways. Table 17.1 summarizes the key features of these perspectives as we have discussed them. Rather than viewing these three perspectives as either-or options by which to understand social influence between close relationship partners, we prefer to view them as complementary. Taken together, they afford us a more complete view of social influence than any single perspective can provide alone.

TABLE 17.1 *Summary of Three Perspectives on Social Influence in Close Relationships*

Feature	Perspective		
	Traditional	Social-Meaning	Dialogic
distinct persuader and target roles for the relational parties	yes	yes	no
intentional goal of seeking change in the other	yes	yes	no
communication of interest	the persuader's strategic choice of a persuasive message	the exchange between persuader and target	dialogic moments of mutuality between the parties
primary focus	target compliance-gaining	the social meaning of the influence attempt for the parties' identities	the expansion of the parties' selves
role of persuader	proactive	proactive	both parties proactive
role of target	reactive	proactive	coparticipants

Notes

1. In the section on persuasion strategies in the family, in cases in which a taxonomy was created specific to a certain relational context, we do briefly explain it.

2. In two of the studies summarized here, both unmarried and married couples were examined as one sample (Beckman et al., 1999; Newton & Burgoon, 1990).

References

Abe, J. A. A., & Izard, C. E. (1999). Compliance, noncompliance strategies, and the correlates of compliance in 5-year-old Japanese and American children. *Social Development, 8*, 1–20.

Aida, Y., & Falbo, T. (1991). Relationships between marital satisfaction, resources, and power strategies. *Sex Roles, 24*, 43–56.

Aron, A., & Aron, E. (2000). Self-expansion motivation and including other in the self. In W. Ickes & S. Duck (Eds.), *The social psychology of personal relationships* (pp. 109–128). New York: John Wiley.

Bakhtin, M. M. (1981). *The dialogic imagination: Four essays by M. M. Bakhtin* (M. Holquist, Ed.; C. Emerson & M. Holquist, Trans.). Austin, TX: University of Texas Press.

Bakhtin, M. M. (1984). *Problems of Dostoevsky's poetics* (C. Emerson, ed. and trans.). Minneapolis: University of Minnesota Press. (Original work published 1929.)

Baxter, L. A. (1984). An investigation of compliance-gaining as politeness. *Human Communication Research, 10,* 427–456.

Baxter, L. A. (1987). Symbols of relationship identity in relationship cultures. *Journal of Social and Personal Relationships, 4,* 261–280.

Baxter, L. A., & DeGooyer, D. H. (2001). Perceived aesthetic characteristics of interpersonal conversations. *Southern Communication Journal, 67,* 1–18.

Baxter, L. A., & Montgomery, B. M. (1996). *Relating: Dialogues & dialectics.* New York: Guilford Press.

Baxter, L. A., & West, L. (2002). *Couple perceptions of their similarities and differences: A dialectical perspective.* Manuscript under review.

Beckman, L. J., Harvey, S. M., Satre, S. J., & Walker, M. A. (1999). Cultural beliefs about social influence strategies of Mexican immigrant women and their heterosexual partners. *Sex Roles, 40,* 871–892.

Bohm, D. (1996). *On dialogue* (L. Nichol, Ed.). New York: Routledge.

Boster, F. J., Rodriguez, J. I., Cruz, M. G., & Marshall, L. (1995). The relative effectiveness of a direct request message and a pregiving message on friends and strangers. *Communication Research, 22,* 475–484.

Brown, P., & Levinson, S. C. (1987). *Politeness: Some universals in language usage.* Cambridge: Cambridge University Press.

Buber, M. (1958). *I and thou* (R. G. Smith, Trans.). New York: Scribner's.

Bui, K. T., Raven, B. H., & Schwarzwald, J. (1994). Influence strategies in dating relationships: The effects of relationship satisfaction, gender, and perspective. *Journal of Social Behavior and Personality, 9,* 429–442.

Buss, D. M. (1992). Manipulation in close relationships: Five personality factors in interactional context. *Journal of Personality, 60,* 477–499.

Buss, D. M., Gomes, M., Higgins, D. S., & Lauterbach, K. (1987). Tactics of manipulation. *Journal of Personality and Social Psychology, 52,* 1219–1229.

Cataldi, A. E., & Reardon, R. (1996). Gender, interpersonal orientation, and manipulation tactic use in close relationships. *Sex Roles, 35,* 205–218.

Christopher, F. S., & Frandsen, M. M. (1990). Strategies of influence in sex and dating. *Journal of Social and Personal Relationships, 7,* 89–105.

Cissna, K. N., & Anderson, R. (1994). Communication and the ground of dialogue. In R. Anderson, K. N. Cissna, & R. C. Arnett (Eds.), *The reach of dialogue: Confirmation, voice, and community* (pp. 9–30). Cresskill, NJ: Hampton Press.

Cissna, K. N., & Anderson, R. (1998). Theorizing about dialogic moments: The Buber-Rogers position and postmodern themes. *Communication Theory, 8,* 63–104.

Cody, M. J., McLaughlin, M. L., & Schneider, M. J. (1981). The impact of relational consequences and intimacy on the selection of interpersonal persuasion tactics: A reanalysis. *Communication Quarterly, 29,* 91–106.

Cowan, G., & Avants, S. K. (1988). Children's influence strategies: Structure, sex differences, and bilateral mother-child influence. *Child Development, 59,* 1303–1313.

Craig, R. T., Tracy, K., & Spisak, F. (1986). The discourse of requests: Assessment of a politeness approach. *Human Communication Research, 12,* 437–468.

de Turck, M. (1985). A transactional analysis of compliance-gaining behavior. *Human Communication Research, 12,* 54–78.

deTurck, M. A., & Miller, G. R. (1983). Adolescent perceptions of parental persuasive message strategies. *Journal of Marriage and the Family, 45,* 543–552.

Dillard, J. P., & Fitzpatrick, M. A. (1985). Compliance-gaining in marital interaction. *Personality and Social Psychology Bulletin, 11,* 419–433.

Dillard, J. P., Wilson, S. R., Tusing, K. J., & Kinney, T. A. (1997). Politeness judgments in personal relationships. *Journal of Language and Social Psychology, 16,* 297–325.

Dunn, K. F., & Cowan, G. (1993). Social influence strategies among Japanese and American college women. *Psychology of Women Quarterly, 17,* 39–52.

Edgar, T., Freimuth, V. S., Hammond, S. L., McDonald, D. A., & Fink, E. L. (1992). Strategic sexual communication: Condom use resistance and response. *Health communication, 4,* 83–104.

Falbo, T., & Peplau, L. A. (1980). Power strategies in intimate relationships. *Journal of Personality and Social Psychology, 38,* 618–628.

Fitch, K. L. (1994). A cross-cultural study of directive sequences and some implications for compliance-gaining research. *Communication Monographs, 61,* 185–209.

Fitch, K. L. (1998). *Speaking relationally: Culture, communication, and interpersonal connection.* New York: Guilford .

Fitch, K. L. (in press). Cultural persuadables. *Communication Theory.*

Fitch, K. L., & Sanders, R. E. (1994). Culture, communication, and preferences for directness in expression of directives. *Communication Theory, 4,* 219–245.

Foss, S. K., & Griffin, C. L. (1995). Beyond persuasion: A proposal for an invitational rhetoric. *Communication Monographs, 62,* 2–18.

Frieze, I. H., & McHugh, M. C. (1992). Power and influence strategies in violent and nonviolent marriages. *Psychology of Women Quarterly, 16,* 449–465.

Fung, S. S. K., Kipnis, D., & Rosnow, R. L. (1987). Synthetic benevolence and malevolence as strategies of relational compliance-gaining. *Journal of Social and Personal Relationships, 4,* 129–141.

Galvin, K. M., & Brommel, B. J. (2000). *Family Communication: Cohesion and Change* (5th ed.). New York: Addison-Wesley Longman.

Gass, R. H., & Seiter, S. J. (2003). *Persuasion, social influence, and compliance-gaining* (2nd ed.). Boston: Allyn & Bacon.

Goffman, E. (1967). *Interaction ritual: Essays on face-to-face behavior.* New York: Anchor Books.

Guerin, B. (1995). Social influence in one-to-one and group situations: Predicting influence tactics from basic group processes. *Journal of Social Psychology, 135,* 371–385.

Howard, J. A., Blumstein, P., & Schwartz, P. (1986). Sex, power, and influence tactics in intimate relationships. *Journal of Personality and Social Psychology, 51,* 102–109.

Ifert, D. E. (2000). Resistance to interpersonal requests: A summary and critique of recent research. *Communication Yearbook, 23,* 125–161.

Isler, L., Popper, T., & Ward, S. (1987). Children's purchase requests and parental responses. *Journal of Advertising Research, 27,* 28–39.

John, D. R. (1999). Consumer socialization of children: A retrospective look at twenty-five years of research. *Journal of Consumer Research, 26,* 183–213.

Jones, D. C. (1985). Persuasive appeals and responses to appeals among friends and acquaintances. *Child Development, 56,* 757–763.

Jordan, J. M., & Roloff, M. E. (1990). Acquiring assistance from others: The effect of indirect requests and relational intimacy on verbal compliance. *Human Communication Research, 16,* 519–555.

Kellerman, K., & Cole, T. (1994). Classifying compliance gaining messages: Taxonomic disorder and strategic confusion. *Communication Theory, 4,* 3–60.

Kelley, H. H., Berscheid, E., Christensen, A., Harvey, J. H., Huston, T. L., Levinger, G., McClintock, E., Peplau, L. A., & Peterson, D. R. (1983). *Close relationships.* New York: W. H. Freeman.

Kirchler, E. (1990). Spouses' influence strategies in purchase decisions as dependent on conflict type and relationship characteristics. *Journal of Economic Psychology, 11,* 101–118.

Kirchler, E. (1993). Spouses' joint purchase decisions: Determinants of influence tactics for muddling through the process. *Journal of Economic Psychology, 14,* 405–438.

Lay, K. L., Waters, E., & Park, K. A. (1989). Maternal responsiveness and child compliance: The role of mood as a mediator. *Child Development, 60,* 1405–1411.

Leighty, G., & Applegate, J. L. (1991). Social-cognitive and situational influences on the use of face-saving persuasive strategies. *Human Communication Research, 17,* 451–484.

Lim, T. S. (1990a). Politeness behavior in social influence situations. In J. P. Dillard (Ed.), *Seeking compliance: The production of interpersonal influence messages* (pp. 75–86). Scottsdale, AZ: Gorsuch Scarisbrick.

Lim, T. S. (1990b). The influence of receivers' resistance on persuaders' verbal aggressiveness. *Communication Quarterly, 38,* 170–188.

Lim, T. S., & Bowers, J. W. (1991). Facework: Solidarity, approbation, and tact. *Human Communication Research, 17*, 415–450.

Mallalieu, L. (1999). An examination of interpersonal influence in consumption and non-consumption domains. *Advances in Consumer Research, 26*, 196–202.

Mallalieu, L., & Faure, C. (1998). Toward an understanding of the choice of influence tactics: The impact of power. *Advances in Consumer Research, 25*, 407–414.

Marwell, G., & Schmitt, D. R. (1967). Dimensions of compliance-gaining behavior: An empirical analysis. *Sociometry, 30*, 350–364.

McLaughlin, B. (1983). Child compliance to parental control techniques. *Developmental Psychology, 19*, 667–673.

McNamee, S., & Gergen, K. J. (Eds.). (1999). *Relational responsibility: Resources for sustainable dialogue*. Thousand Oaks, CA: Sage.

Metts, S. (2000). Face and facework: Implications for the study of personal relationships. In K. Dindia & S. Duck (Eds.), *Communication and personal relationships* (pp. 77–94). New York: John Wiley.

Metts, S., Cupach, W. R., & Imahori, T. T. (1992). Perceptions of sexual compliance-resisting messages in three types of cross-sex relationships. *Western Journal of Communication, 56*, 1–17.

Miller, G., Boster, F., Roloff, M., & Seibold, D. (1977). Compliance-gaining message strategies: A typology and some findings concerning effects of situational differences. *Communication Monographs, 44*, 37–51.

Miller, M. D. (1982). Friendship, power, and the language of compliance-gaining. *Journal of Language and Social Psychology, 1*, 111–121.

Newton, D. A., & Burgoon, J. K. (1990). The use and consequences of verbal influence strategies during interpersonal disagreements. *Human Communication Research, 16*, 477–518.

Oldershaw, L., Walters, G. C., & Hall, D. K. (1986). Control strategies and noncompliance in abusive mother-child dyads: An observational study. *Child Development, 57*, 722–732.

Palan, K. M., & Wilkes, R. E. (1997). Adolescent-parent interaction in family decision making. *Journal of Consumer Research, 24*, 159–169.

Parpal, M., & Macoby, E. E. (1985). Maternal responsiveness and subsequent child compliance. *Child Development, 56*, 1326–1334.

Poppe, M., van der Kloot, W., & Valkenberg, H. (1999). The implicit structure of influence strategies and social relationships. *Journal of Social and Personal Relationships, 16*, 443–458.

Roloff, M. E., & Janiszewski, C. A. (1989). Overcoming obstacles to interpersonal compliance: A principle of message construction. *Human Communication Research, 16*, 33–61.

Roloff, M. E., Janiszewski, C. A., McGrath, M. A., Burns, C. S., & Manrai, L. A. (1988). Acquiring resources from intimates: When obligation substitutes for persuasion. *Human Communication Research, 14*, 364–396.

Sagrestano, L. M., Christensen, A., & Heavey, C. L. (1998). Social influence techniques during marital conflict. *Personal Relationships, 5*, 75–89.

Sanders, R. E. (1987). *Cognitive foundations of calculated speech: Controlling understandings in conversation and persuasion*. Albany, NY: SUNY Press.

Sanders, R. E. (1997). The production of symbolic objects as components of larger wholes. In J. O. Greene (Ed.), *Message production: Advances in communication theory* (pp. 245–277). Mahwah, NJ: Erlbaum.

Sanders, R. E., & Fitch, K. L. (2001). The actual practice of compliance seeking. *Communication Theory, 11*, 263–289.

Schaeffer, H. R., & Crook, C. K. (1980). Child compliance and maternal control techniques. *Developmental Psychology, 16*, 54–61.

Searle, J. (1976). A classification of illocutionary acts. *Language in Society, 5*, 1–23.

Sexton, C. S., & Perlman, D. S. (1989). Couples' career orientation, gender role orientation, and perceived equity as determinants of marital power. *Journal of Marriage and the Family, 51*, 933–941.

Sheer, V. C. (1995). Sensation seeking predispositions and susceptibility to a sexual partner's appeals for condom use. *Journal of Applied Communication Research, 23*, 212–229.

Shepherd, G. J. (1992). Communication as influence: Definitional exclusion. *Communication Studies, 43,* 203–219.

Shimanoff, S. B. (1987). Types of emotional disclosures and request compliance between spouses. *Communication Monographs, 54,* 85–100.

Sillars, A. L. (1980). The stranger and the spouse as target persons for compliance-gaining strategies: A subjective expected utility model. *Human Communication Research, 6,* 265–279.

Smith, T. E. (1983). Adolescent reactions to attempted parental control and influence techniques. *Journal of Marriage and the Family, 45,* 533–542.

Steil, J. M., & Hillman, J. L. (1993). The perceived value of direct and indirect influence strategies: A cross cultural comparison. *Psychology of Women Quarterly, 17,* 457–462.

Steil, J. M., & Weltman, K. (1992). Influence strategies at home and at work: A study of sixty dual-career couples. *Journal of Social and Personal Relationships, 9,* 65–88.

Todorov, T. (1984). *Mikhail Bakhtin: The dialogic principle* (W. Godzich, Trans.). Minneapolis: University of Minnesota Press. (Original work published 1981).

Tucker, J. S., & Anders, S. L. (2001). Social control of health behaviors in marriage. *Journal of Applied Social Psychology, 31,* 467–485.

Tucker, J. S., & Mueller, J. S. (2000). Spouses' social control of health behaviors: Use and effectiveness of specific strategies. *Personality and Social Psychology Bulletin, 26,* 1120–1130.

White, K. D., Pearson, J. C., & Flint, L. (1989). Adolescents' compliance resistance—Effects of parents' compliance strategy and gender. *Adolescence, 24,* 595–621.

Wilson, S. R., Aleman, C. G., & Leatham, G. B. (1998). Identity implications of influence goals: A revised analysis of face-threatening acts and application to seeking compliance with same-sex friends. *Human Communication Research, 25,* 64–96.

Wilson, S. R., Cruz, M., Marshall, L., & Rao, N. (1993). An attributional analysis of compliance-gaining interactions. *Communication Monographs, 60,* 352–372.

Wilson, S. R., & Kunkel, A. W. (2000). Identity implications of influence goals: Similarities in perceived face threats and facework across sex and close relationships. *Journal of Language and Social Psychology, 19,* 195–221.

Witteman, H., & Fitzpatrick, M. A. (1986). Compliance-gaining in marital interaction: Power bases, processes, and outcomes. *Communication Monographs, 53,* 130–143.

Wood, J. T., Dendy, L. L., Dordek, E., Germany, M., & Varallo, S. M. (1994). Dialectic of difference: A thematic analysis of intimates' meanings for difference. In K. Carter & M. Prisnell (Eds.), *Interpretive approaches to interpersonal communication* (pp. 115–136). New York: SUNY Press.

Zvonkovic, A. M., Schmiege, C. J., & Hall, L. D. (1994). Influence strategies used when couples make work-family decisions and their importance for marital satisfaction. *Family Relations, 43,* 182–188.

18

Superior-Subordinate Influence in Organizations

Randy Y. Hirokawa and Amy E. Wagner

Social influence is an ever-present aspect of organizational life. From formal board meetings to informal employee interactions, individuals seek to control the opinions and activities of others in the pursuit of personal and organizational goals. It is not surprising, then, that scholars from a variety of academic disciplines have pursued the study of how individuals and social units in an organizational context use verbal and nonverbal messages to modify the cognitions, beliefs, attitudes, values, and behaviors of others (Barry & Watson, 1996). This chapter takes stock of what we know about superior-subordinate influence in organizational settings and in doing so assesses the strengths and limitations of this research and suggests directions for future investigations.

Definition of Social Influence

The term "social influence" has been used rather loosely in the organizational literature. Some authors treat social influence and power more or less interchangeably (French & Raven, 1959; Mintzberg, 1983; Salanick & Pfeffer, 1977). Others equate social influence with the exercise of interpersonal control (Kipnis, Schmidt, & Wilkinson, 1980). Still others use the term synonymously with persuasion (Hirokawa & Miyahara, 1986). Because writers use the term social influence in different ways, it seems prudent to begin this chapter with a clear definition of what we mean by this term.

As used in this chapter, social influence refers to *the modification of an individual's behavior(s) through the verbal and/or nonverbal symbolic actions of another individual*. It can be thought of, and seen as, the communicative exercise of power and social control in the organization (Kipnis, Schmidt, & Wilkinson, 1980). The essence of social influence is *behavioral change*—that is, the symbolic action(s) of the influencer (agent) causes the influencee (target) to engage in behavior(s) different from what he or she would have otherwise produced. For example, an employee reports late to work on a regular basis. His supervisor tells him that he must start coming to work on time or she will fire him. Social influence is assumed to take place if the supervisor's warning or threat causes the employee to change his behavior and start reporting to work on time.

Strategies Versus Tactics

Social influence in organizations can be differentiated on the basis of strategies and tactics (see, e.g., Harper & Hirokawa, 1988; Hirokawa, Kodama, & Harper, 1990; Hirokawa, Mickey, & Miura, 1991; Hirokawa & Miyahara, 1986; Kipnis, Schmidt, & Wilkinson, 1980; Mowday, 1978; Schilit & Locke, 1982; Yukl & Falbe, 1990). *Strategies* are blueprints for goal achievement; they represent systematic plans that organizational members follow to influence the behaviors and actions of others in the organization (Berger, 1986). Frost (1987) identifies five social influence strategies that are commonly used in organizational settings:

1. *Reasoning*—the use of facts and data to support the development of a logical argument (e.g., "These charts and figures clearly indicate that X is the right thing to do").
2. *Ingratiation*—the use of impression management, flattery, and the creation of goodwill (e.g., "I know I can count on you to do X because you're one of our best employees").
3. *Assertiveness*—the use of a direct and forceful approach (e.g., "Do X right away").
4. *Sanctions*—the use of organizationally derived rewards and punishments (e.g., "If you don't do X, your promotion will be in jeopardy").
5. *Altruism*—appealing to the goodwill of others (e.g., "For the sake of the company and your colleagues, please do X").

In contrast, *tactics* are seen as "instantiations" of strategies; that is, they represent the specific verbal or nonverbal symbolic actions (messages) produced by the agent to carry out his or her strategy. Any strategy will have a number of different tactics associated with it. For example, in using an "altruism" strategy, an organizational member might choose to use a tactic such as a "favor" ("As a personal favor to me, could you please start coming to work on time?") or "duty" ("You owe it to your coworkers to report to work on time"). Similarly, in employing a "sanctions" strategy, an organizational member may choose between a "promise" ("If you start coming to work on time, I will recommend you for the promotion you have been asking for") and a "warning" ("Unless you stop being late for work, your future with this company will be in serious jeopardy").

Identifying Strategies and Tactics

Investigations of social influence in organizations have employed two contrasting methods—the so-called *deductive* and *inductive* approaches.

Deductive approach

Some researchers have drawn on interpretations of existing theories of social power and interpersonal relationships to generate a priori lists (or inventories) of influence-seeking behaviors used by organizational members. Based on the pioneering work of Marwell & Schmitt (1967), the typical study (see, e.g., Ansari, 1989; Mowday, 1978, 1979; Richmond, Davis, Saylor, & McCroskey, 1984; Vecchio & Sussman, 1989) presented respondents with a predetermined list of strategic behaviors and asked them to indicate which ones they typically employ in influence-seeking situations. Richmond and colleagues (1984), for example, used a deductive approach to examine subordinate perceptions of their own and their supervisors' use of social-influence tactics (what they called "behavior alternation techniques" or "BATs"). The participants in their study were presented with 18 different messages (e.g., "Your group needs you to do it," "If you don't, others will be hurt," "You promised to do it") associated with 18 different behavior alternation techniques (e.g., "duty," "guilt," "debt"). They were asked to rate on a five-point scale how frequently they used each of the messages to get their supervisor to change his or her behavior (5 = very often, 4 = often, 3 = occasionally, 2 = seldom, 1 = never). Using the same messages and five-point scales, the participants were then asked to indicate how often their supervisor used each message to change their behavior. The results of Richmond and colleagues' study indicated that subordinates seldom use most of the 18 BATs in their interactions with supervisors, but when they do, they favor the use of "expert" and "self-esteem" approaches. Supervisors were found to use messages associated with BATs labeled "expert," "self-esteem," "reward from behavior," "legitimate-higher authority," and "personal responsibility" (p. 85).

Critics of the deductive approach have argued that this method is of questionable value in identifying the actual influence-seeking behaviors of organizational members because it involves too much speculation on the part of respondents (Cody, McLaughlin, & Jordan, 1980; Kipnis & Schmidt, 1983). Specifically, they maintain that a priori lists enable subjects to select socially appropriate strategic behaviors and/or behaviors they would not have identified on their own (Seibold, Cantrill, & Meyers, 1985). For example, an organizational member may actually use "threats" (e.g., "Do it or else I will fire you") to influence his or her subordinates. But because "bullying others" to get one's way is not a socially acceptable behavior, that individual may indicate that she or he uses a more socially acceptable behavior like "expertise" (e.g., "From what I have learned, doing it will benefit you") even though such a tactic is never actually used by the individual.

Inductive approach

A number of researchers have argued that a better way to identify the influence-seeking behaviors of organizational members is to use an inductive method (see, e.g., Kipnis et al., 1980; Wiseman & Schenck-Hamlin, 1981). Here the researcher presents subjects with a hypothetical influence situation and then asks them to indicate what message(s) they would produce to influence the target. The researcher subsequently analyzes the constructed messages to identify the influence-seeking tactics displayed in them. For example, Hirokawa, Kodama, and Harper (1990) presented managers with the following hypothetical scenario:

One of your subordinates has been reporting to work late on a regular basis. In most cases, he is never more than 15 minutes late, but his regular tardiness is becoming an annoyance to other people in the office. What would you say to this employee to convince him to report to work on time?

The researchers analyzed the written responses of the managers and identified four general types of influence-seeking messages: "reward" strategies, involving valued resources or outcomes (e.g., "If you come to work on time, others in the office will have greater respect for you"); "punishment" strategies, involving negative sanctions or outcomes (e.g., "If you don't start coming to work on time, I will have no choice but to fire you"); "altruism" strategies, relying on the goodwill of the manager or subordinate (e.g., "Please do me a big favor and start coming to work on time"); and "rationale" strategies, involving the use of explanation or justification (e.g., "You need to come to work on time because others depend on you to perform their jobs").

Although the inductive approach appears to be favored over the deductive approach, it is not without critics. Several writers have noted that the effectiveness of this method depends on the inherent realism of the hypothetical scenario or situation presented to organizational members. That is, in order for respondents to produce influence-seeking messages that are consistent with their actual behaviors, they must be presented with scenarios that coincide with the actual or likely situations they face in the organization (see, e.g., Burleson, Waltman, Goering, Ely, & Whaley, 1988; Canary & Spitzberg, 1987; Cody & McLaughlin, 1980). If the scenario is too far removed from the respondent's range of experiences, the influence-seeking message the respondent constructs is likely to have no correlation with his or her actual behavior (Miller, Boster, Roloff, & Seibold, 1987).

Antecedents of Influence Behaviors

A number of authors have noted that the range of influence behaviors organizational members select and use is a "TPO thing," that is, it depends on *time, place,* and *occasion* (Cody & McLaughlin, 1980). In their comprehensive review of the literature, Barry and Watson (1996) organized situational determinants of influence attempts into four categories: (1) nature of relationship between superior and subordinate, (2) organizational characteristics, (3) goal(s) of the influencing agent, and (4) individual attributes of the influencing agent. We discuss each of these categories in turn.

Nature of Relationships

Relational Closeness.   Within an organization, degree of personal liking will in part determine the kind of influence strategy and tactic used by the agent on the target regardless of relative status. Several studies have shown that the level of relational closeness (liking) between the influencer (agent) and the person being influenced (target) affects the type of influence behavior used by the agent (e.g., Cody, McLaughlin, & Schneider, 1981; Fitzpatrick & Winke, 1979; Miller, Boster, Roloff & Seibold, 1977). In general, the more the agent likes the target, the more likely she or he is to use a positive strategy such as a "debt" ("I will owe you big time if you do X for me") or a "favor" ("Could you do me a favor and do X for me?"). On the other hand, the more the agent dislikes the target, the more likely she or he is to use a negative strategy such as a "threat" ("The next time you fail to do X, I will report you to management") or a "negative moral appeal" ("Only an irresponsible employee would fail to do X").

Relational Power. The kinds of influence tactics one uses in an organizational setting often depend on the balance of power in the relationship. Influence attempts can occur in three directions: (1) upward (superior/target and subordinate/agent), (2) downward (subordinate/target and superior/agent), and (3) lateral (the agent and target occupy the same space in the organizational hierarchy). Research has shown that the perceived level of subordinate power is the primary determinant of the tactic a superior will use in downward influence attempts (Tjosvold, Andrews & Struthers, 1992). For instance, a superior/agent who possesses more power than the subordinate/target will tend to use what Kipnis (1976) labeled "directive" or "power-over tactics" (e.g., "You will be fired if you do not get this report done in time"). However, when the superior and subordinate have relatively equal power the superior/agent will use "collaborative tactics" (e.g., "Let's work to get this report done on time") (Kanter, 1977). Upward influence attempts are generally marked by techniques involving rational persuasion such as logical presentations (Schilit & Locke, 1982) or reason (Chacko, 1990). It is important to note, however, that other studies have shown that rational persuasion is the tactic of choice regardless of the direction of influence (Barry & Bateman, 1992; Yukl & Falbe, 1990) and that even when differences in directional influence tactics are found, they tend to be small, indicating that relational power may not be a major determinant of strategy selection (Yukl, Falbe, & Youn, 1993).

Leadership Style. Upward influence attempts vary according to the type of leadership a superior employs. Studies show that participative leaders, those who empower their employees, are the recipients of more influence attempts (Cobb, 1986) than their authoritarian counterparts and that these influence attempts are more direct in nature (Krone, 1992). In general, the tactics used by subordinates to influence participative leaders can be characterized as direct, rational, and overt (Ansari & Kapoor, 1987; Krone, 1992). Conversely, upward influence tactics used on less participatory leaders tend to be assertive, threatening, and politically motivated (Krone, 1992). Such negative upward influence tactics can also be expected when a leader is perceived as ineffective by his or her employees (Chacko, 1990).

Subordinate Competencies. Little research has been done on the relationship between subordinate communication style, performance, and downward influence attempts. The available literature shows that superiors use assertive strategies, coalition-building strategies, appeals to higher authority, threats of sanctions, and reason with subordinates possessing an unattractive communication style (inattentive, unfriendly, and unrelaxed) but use friendliness and reason with subordinates possessing an attractive communication style (attentive, friendly, relaxed) (Garko, 1992). As might be expected, superiors use positive influence tactics such as "reward" and "exchange" (e.g., "If you stay late and work on this report I will pay you overtime") with subordinates who perform well but use negative influence tactics such as "assertion" and "sanctions" (e.g., "I do not want to hear your excuses for not having the report done") with poor performers (Ansari, 1989).

Target Resistance.   The agent's tactical choice for an influence attempt is also mediated by how much resistance is expected from the target. Wilson, Cruz, Marshall, and Rao (1993) found that agents adapt their tactics depending on the target's reason for noncompliance. Their experimental study yielded two major findings: (1) agents are more likely to use antisocial tactics (e.g., "warnings") when they believe that the target's reasons for noncompliance are within that person's control, and (2) agents are more persistent and use tactics that take issue with the target's reason for noncompliance when the target is in control of the situation but is doing something inconsistent with what the agent wants done.

Organizational Characteristics

Scholars have investigated whether organizational-level constructs such as the size, norms, climate, unionization, or type of institution influence how persons within the institution go about their selection and execution of influence attempts. Overwhelmingly, these organizational-level constructs have been shown to have little or no effect on influence tactic selection, although Schilit and Locke (1982) reported that results of much of the existing research might be confounded due to researchers' lack of vigilance in controlling for these constructs. Their analysis revealed a difference between influence tactics used in small or private organizations and those used in large or public ones, with more informal influence methods being used in the former than in the latter. Additionally, Krone (1992) found that influence agents in institutions with decentralized authority employed more open and direct tactics (e.g., "I think that we should develop a contingency plan before dedicating all our resources to a single project") than those who worked in institutions with centralized authority.

Despite the lack of evidence that situational variables have an effect on an agent's choice of influence tactics, scholars do not unilaterally accept that these variables have no effect. Instead, some scholars point to problems in the methodology and conceptualization of variables in existing studies (Burleson et al., 1988; Cody, Greene, Marston, O'Hair, Baaske & Schneider, 1986; Jackson & Backus, 1982).

Goals of the Influencing Agent

The choice of influence tactic varies according to what the influencer wishes to achieve (Dillard, 1990). For instance, an agent whose intentions have to do with the quality of the relationship or interactions with another party is likely to use compliance-gaining strategies that remind the target of the costs of noncompliance (e.g., "If you don't tell the boss you agree with me on this matter, she's going to think our department is disorganized"), whereas the agent is likely to use reason and evidence if the desired action is deemed especially important (e.g., "Based on last year's reports, I think we should make a decision immediately"). An agent who is trying to achieve an objective individually will use ingratiation tactics, but agents who have organizational objectives in mind will use a multitude of tactics—including upward appeals, blocking, and rational persuasion (Ansari &

Kapoor, 1987). Furthermore, studies have consistently found that agents wishing to promote new ideas and precipitate change employ influence strategies of reason and coalition building (Howell & Higgins, 1990; Schmidt & Kipnis, 1984) but rely on ingratiation and assertiveness when they want to change the behavior of the target (Schmidt & Kipnis, 1984).

Individual Attributes of the Influencing Agent

Sex.   Evidence regarding whether the sex of the agent affects the types of influence strategies likely to be used is mixed. Thus, it is unclear whether men and women employ different influence tactics. Yet consideration of any such differences is important in order to understand superior-subordinate interaction in organizational settings. The most consistent finding in support of sex differences indicates that males choose influence tactics that are direct and involve power, whereas females choose tactics that are indirect and collaborative (Gruber & White, 1986; Offerman & Schrier, 1985). Additionally, the goal of the agent and the reaction of his or her target may differentially impact when men and women choose to reward the target (White, 1988). Harper and Hirokawa (1988) found that male managers reported using more punishment-oriented strategies, whereas their female counterparts used more rational and altruistic methods. Specifically, 64 percent of the male but only 37 percent of the female managers surveyed in the study indicated that they would rely on punishment-based tactics such as "ultimatum" ("Shape up or find yourself another job"), "warning" ("If you don't shape up, you won't be with this company very much longer"), "threat" ("The next time you show up late, I will start docking your pay") and "negative esteem" ("Unless you are punctual, others will not view you as credible and trustworthy"). In comparison, 30 percent of the women but only 13 percent of the men indicated that they would rely on altruistic tactics such as "counsel" ("Is there anything I can do to help you?") and "duty" ("It is your obligation to report on time for work"). The remainder of the female managers reported that they would rely on rationale-based strategies like "direct request" ("I would like you to make a special effort to start coming to work on time") and "explanation" ("You need to report to work on time because . . .") (p. 164).

Notably, however, a comparable amount of empirical research suggests that there are no significant sex differences when it comes to the target's choice of influence strategy (Vecchio & Sussmann, 1991; Yukl & Falbe, 1990). Researchers have argued that the sex differences that have been found could be better explained by situational and individual difference factors such as the legitimacy of the request (Hirokawa, Mickey & Miura, 1991), personal power of the individual (Hirokawa, Kodama & Harper, 1990), or the power associated with one's position (Howard, Blumstein & Schwartz, 1986, Mainiero, 1986).

Culture.   Research shows that cultural differences affect the selection of influence tactics depending upon the values of the culture and the kind of request being issued. Fitch (1994) conducted an analysis of previous studies and found that the likelihood of a target using directive tactics was contingent upon whether directness was valued by that target's culture. Other research notes a relationship between how effective an influence tactic is perceived to be and the appropriateness of that tactic in a particular culture (Kim & Wilson, 1994). Hirokawa and Miyahara's (1986) comparison of American and Japanese managers revealed that when a request is obligatory (e.g., performing one's assigned tasks), Americans employ punishment-based strategies, whereas Japanese employ altruism or rationale. Conversely, when a request is not obligatory (e.g., staying at work late) American managers prefer rationale or reward strategies, but Japanese managers prefer altruism. Overall it appears that reason-oriented strategies are used most often in American, British, Australian (Kipnis & Schmidt, 1983), and Japanese (Sullivan & Taylor, 1991) cultures when attempting to influence a subordinate. Hirokawa and Miyahara (1986) accounted for these findings in terms of three cultural imperatives that differentiate Japanese and American managers.

1. *Japanese and American managers share different assumptions regarding the most effective way to influence others in the organization.* In Japanese organizations, managers appear to believe that the most effective way to influence employees is to take into account the circumstances involved and appeal to the personal motivations of the employee. American managers, on the other hand, appear to operate under the assumption that the most effective way to influence an employee is to use one's ability to mediate or control rewards and punishments for that individual.

2. *Japanese and American managers rely on different power bases to influence their employees.* In Japanese organizations, managers generally rely on organizational identification to bring about changes in employees' behavior, whereas American managers rely on their ability to control or mediate organizational resources to influence their employees. That is, the influence tactics used by Japanese managers depend on the fact that Japanese organizational members have embraced the goals and values of their organization. The influence tactics used by American managers, in contrast, do not reflect this fundamental assumption. Rather, they are based on the belief that employees' behaviors are tied directly to organizational resources and that manipulating those resources can therefore bring about changes in behavior.

3. *Japanese managers place a greater emphasis on corporate unity than American managers do.* Japanese managers place a greater emphasis on corporate participation and cooperation than their American counterparts. Whereas Japanese managers attempt to bring about change by getting their employees to view their role within the general scheme of the organization, American managers typically do not attempt to foster this corporate identification. Simply stated, Japanese managers appear to deal with employees in a "holistic" way (i.e., as part of the organization as a whole), whereas American managers tend to treat employees as individuals within the organization. (pp. 262–263)

Personality Variables.   Scholars have sought to understand whether certain aspects of an individual's personality will help to predict the kind of influence tactic that individual is likely to use. The personality variables that have received notable research attention include ambition, Machiavellianism, self-monitoring, locus of control, verbal aggressiveness, and dogmatism. Each of these will be considered in turn.

The *ambition* variable as it is defined here generally refers to an individual's combined desire for power and achievement. Highly ambitious individuals have been shown to be largely effective in their influence attempts, especially where upward influence is involved (Schilit, 1986). They tend to exercise influence attempts frequently and use influence tactics of reason and coalition building (Chacko, 1990) and manipulation and persuasion (Mowday, 1979).

A person who is said to be *Machiavellian* is willing to use power and deceptive or manipulative methods to achieve his or her goals (Christie & Geis, 1970). Findings regarding Machiavellianism and influence tactic selection have been mixed. O'Hair and Cody (1987) attribute this to the fact that the trait most likely represents more than one construct.

High self-monitors are concerned with how others perceive them and modify their behavior to the dictates of a given situation (Snyder, 1994). Studies reveal that high self-monitors tend to be more expressive when trying to persuade a target about an issue that is emotional or relational and use more ingratiation tactics overall (Farmer, Fedor, Goodman & Maslyn, 1993). In addition, high–self-monitoring males reported using significantly more compromise, emotional appeals, coercion, and referent influence than did their low–self-monitoring male counterparts (Smith, Cody, Lovette & Canary, 1990).

Locus of control can be defined as the extent to which individuals feel they control events in their environment. "Internals" believe they are responsible for the events that happen to them (e.g., "I get promoted at my job because I work hard"), whereas "externals" believe events that happen are outside their control (e.g., "I can't get promoted because this organization doesn't recognize hard work") (Rotter, 1966). Internal influencers have been found to rely on rationality, the manipulation of positive feelings, and relational ties in order to gain their target's compliance (Canary, Cody & Marston, 1986). Conversely, external agents avoid rational persuasion and rely on soft strategies such as requests (Farmer et al., 1993). Research has neglected to address locus of control possessed by the target; however, Wheeless, Barraclough, and Stewart (1983) hypothesize that external targets will respond more favorably to influence attempts that involve relational appeals than will internals, since the former group has a greater need for belonging.

Verbal aggressiveness (also see chapter 7) is the willingness to engage in communication that attacks or injures the self-concept of another. Agents who are highly verbally aggressive use influence tactics that include teasing, swearing, attacking the other's competence, and nonverbal expressions. Interestingly, aggressive communicators believe their behaviors are less hurtful than those of nonaggressive communicators. One study suggested that verbal aggressiveness might be a response chosen after a target has displayed unfriendly resistance to the initial influence attempt (Lim, 1990).

Tactical Considerations

In addition to the personality variables addressed above, scholars have also examined influence tactics to determine how effective they are, in what combination they are likely to be used, and what outcomes they yield. Research has shown that the effectiveness of an influence attempt depends on the nature of the relationship between the agent and target. For instance, in lateral dyads (two people belonging to the same place in an organizational hierarchy) rational tactics are effective (Barry & Bateman, 1992). Ingratiation and exchange tactics have proved successful when influence attempts are lateral or downward, yet these same strategies have been ineffective for upward influence attempts. Strategies that have been seen to be effective regardless of the direction of the influence include "consultation" (e.g., "We should screen the clients together before admitting them"), "inspirational appeals" (e.g., "This is the best idea I've had in years and it is sure to increase our profit margin"), and "rational persuasion" (e.g., "Based on the merits of the case we should sue" (Yukl & Tracey, 1992). On the other hand, "repetition" and "exaggeration" are ineffective in all directions (Barry & Bateman, 1992). Barry and Watson (1996) noted that the existing research on influence effectiveness is far from comprehensive and is limited in part due to methodological problems such as the difficulty of executing experimental manipulations and obtaining data from both the agent and target.

A complex question that has received recent research attention is how the order and combination of influence tactics affect the compliance-seeking encounter. Research shows that strategies such as "legitimizing" (validating the target's point of view), consultation (asking for the target's point of view), "ingratiation" (purposely getting into the target's good graces), and "inspirational appeals" (persuading through enthusiasm) tend to be used in combination with one another, but rational persuasion is used alone as often as it is in combination with other strategies (Yukl et al., 1993). Maslyn, Fedor, and Farmer (1994) found that the influence tactics chosen in initial and subsequent influence attempts vary with the personality of the agent and elements of the situation. In a similar vein, Kipnis and Schmidt (1988) developed a typology of agents and their associated influence strategies. The four types are (1) "shotgun" agents, who use a variety of tactics; (2) "ingratiators," who primarily rely on friendliness; (3) "tacticians," who favor rational persuasion; and (4) "bystanders," who engage in little influence-seeking behavior. Earlier work by Perreault and Miles (1978) also demonstrated that certain personalities are more likely to choose particular influence tactics. The five types they identified based on strategy use are (1) noninfluencers, (2) expert influencers, (3) referent influencers, (4) multiple strategy influencers, and (5) position power wielders.

The preceding discussion of research findings on the tactics superiors and subordinates use to gain compliance would not be complete without consideration of the outcomes these tactics yield. Job satisfaction has been found to be affected by influence tactic selection. Specifically, Vecchio and Sussmann's (1989) study revealed that subordinates are dissatisfied and have a lower quality relationship with their superior when the superior's choice of influence tactics does not match the subordinate's preference. Conversely, superiors who use coercive techniques tend to view their subordinates more negatively than those who use rational techniques, leading the scholars who conducted the study to conclude that employers may devalue employees they can easily control (O'Neal, Kipnis, & Craig, 1994). Research has shown that the influencer's strategy choice is also related to the target's job satisfaction (Roach, 1991) and satisfaction with supervision (Richmond, McCroskey, & Davis, 1986), as well as how the target evaluates the agent's communication competence (Johnson, 1992).

Other real-world outcomes are associated with influence tactic selection. For instance, Judge and Brentz (1994) found that subordinates who employed tactics with the objective of getting their supervisor to like them more were more satisfied with their jobs and received more promotions. Conversely, subordinates who used influence tactics aimed at getting their supervisors to view them as competent were less satisfied and received fewer job-related benefits. Dreher, Dougherty, and Whitely's (1989) analysis of M.B.A. salaries revealed a positive correlation between use of upward influence strategies and pay. This finding is somewhat at odds with research by Kipnis and Schmidt (1988), which concluded that male subordinates who adopted a shotgun influence style (characterized by frequent usage of a variety of influence tactics) had lower incomes and were viewed less favorably by supervisors than were subordinates who adopted the tactician style (emphasizing rational persuasion).

Conclusion

Nearly four decades of research on superior-subordinate communication in organizational settings have yielded considerable insights into the kinds of messages used by superiors and subordinates to influence and persuade one another, as well as the factors that affect their selection of persuasive messages.

These accomplishments notwithstanding, three problems exist concerning our understanding of superior-subordinate influence in organizational contexts. First, few studies of superior-subordinate influence have actually studied the communication behavior of superiors and subordinates in organizational contexts. Virtually all of the studies we reviewed in this chapter identify the influence tactics of superiors and subordinates in one of two ways: (1) asking the subjects to select from a predetermined list the behaviors they typically employ in influence-seeking situations or (2) presenting a hypothetical compliance-gaining situation to the subjects and asking them to indicate how they would attempt to influence the person in the scenario. Notably absent are studies that examine how superiors and subordinates *actually* attempt to influence one another in *real* organizational situations. Naturalistic studies of this kind are crucial in the future, because there is good reason to believe that the way we attempt to gain the compliance of someone in a hypothetical situation could differ greatly from how we actually attempt do so in a real situation. Likewise, the influence tactics we *think* we would use in an organizational context may differ greatly from the tactics we actually use in that context or situation.

A second problem with current superior-subordinate influence research is that it has generally overlooked the interactive nature of social influence in the organizational context. Rarely, if ever, does social influence occur through the use of a single message tactic. To the contrary, we often encounter resistance to our initial influence attempts, and we must respond to that resistance with an alternative influence tactic. To date, very few studies have examined how superiors and subordinates adjust or adapt their influence tactics to the resistance they encounter from those they are trying to influence. Future superior-subordinate influence studies need to look more closely at the interactive nature of social-influence processes in the organizational context.

A third problem with superior-subordinate influence studies concerns our understanding of the effectiveness of various types of tactics and strategies. In large part because we have neglected to examine actual influence processes and have failed to take into account the interactive nature of those processes, we currently do not know much about what really works. For example, we do not know whether "hard" tactics like "threats" or "warnings" achieve compliance more effectively than "soft" tactics like "reasoning" or "ingratiation." Future research should thus pay closer attention to the so-called bottom line, that is, which tactics actually succeed in bringing about desired influence.

References

Ansari, M. A. (1989). Effects of leader sex, subordinate sex, and subordinate performance on the use of influence strategies. *Sex Roles, 20,* 283–293.

Ansari, M. A., & Kapoor, A. (1987). Organizational context and upward influence tactics. *Organizational Behavior and Human Decision Processes, 40,* 39–49.

Barry, B., & Bateman, T. S. (1992). Perceptions of influence in managerial dyads: The role of hierarchy, media, and tactics. *Human Relations, 65,* 555–574.

Barry, B., & Watson, M. R. (1996). Communication aspects of dyadic social influence in organizations: A review and integration of conceptual and empirical developments. In B. Burleson (Ed.). *Communication Yearbook 19* (pp. 269–317) Thousand Oaks, CA: Sage.

Berger, C. R. (1986). Social power and interpersonal communication. In M. L. Knapp & G. R. Miller (Eds.), *Handbook of interpersonal communication* (pp. 439–499). Beverly Hills, CA: Sage.

Burleson, B. R., Wilson, S. R., Waltman, M. S., Goering, E. M., Ely, T. K., & Whaley, B. B. (1988). Item desirability effects in compliance-gaining research: Seven studies documenting artifacts in the strategy selection procedure. *Human Communication Research, 14,* 429–486.

Canary, D. J., Cody, M. J., & Marston, P. J. (1986). Goal types, compliance-gaining, and locus of control. *Journal of Language and Social Psychology, 5,* 249–269.

Canary, D. J., & Spitzberg, B. (1987). Appropriateness and effectiveness perceptions of conflict strategies. *Human Communication Research, 14,* 93–118.

Chacko, H. E. (1990). Methods of upward influence, motivational needs and administrators' perception of their supervisors' leadership styles. *Group and Organization Studies, 15,* 253–265.

Christie, R., & Geis, F. L. (1970). *Studies in Machiavellianism.* New York: Academic Press.

Cobb, A. T. (1986). Informal influence in the formal organization: Psychological and situational correlates. *Group and Organizational Studies 11,* 229–253.

Cody, M. J., & McLaughlin, M. L. (1980). Perceptions of compliance-gaining situations: A dimensional analysis. *Communication Monographs, 47,* 132–148.

Cody, M. J., McLaughlin, M. L., & Jordan, W. J. (1980). A multidimensional scaling of three sets of compliance-gaining strategies. *Communication Quarterly, 28,* 34–46.

Cody, M. J., McLaughlin, M. L., & Schneider, M. J. (1981). The impact of relational consequences and intimacy on the selection of interpersonal persuasion tactics: A reanalysis. *Communication Quarterly, 29,* 91–106.

Cody, M. J., Greene, J. O., Marston, P. J., O'Hair, H. D., Baaske, K. T., & Schneider, M. J. (1986). Situation perception and message strategy selection. In M. L. McLaughlin (Ed.), *Communication Yearbook 9* (pp. 390–420). Beverly Hills, CA: Sage.

Dillard, J. P. (1990). A goal-driven model of interpersonal influence. In J. P. Dillard (Ed.), *Seeking compliance: A production of interpersonal influence messages* (pp. 41–56). Scottsdale, AZ: Gorsuch Scarisbrick.

Dreher, G. F., Dougherty, T. W., & Whitely, W. (1989). Influence tactics and salary attainment: A gender-specific analysis. *Sex Roles, 20,* 535–550.

Farmer, S. M., Fedor, D. B., Goodman, J. S., & Maslyn, J. M. (1993). *Factors affecting the use of upward influence strategies.* Paper presented at the 53rd Annual Meeting of the Academy of Management, Atlanta, GA.

Fitch, K. L. (1994). A cross-cultural study of directive sequences and some implications for compliance-gaining research. *Communication Monographs, 61,* 185–209.

Fitzpatrick, M. A., & Winke, J. (1979). You always hurt the one you love: Strategies and tactics in interpersonal conflict. *Communication Quarterly, 27,* 3–11.

French, J., & Raven, B. H. (1959). The bases of social power. In D. Cartwright (Ed.), *Studies in social power* (pp. 150–167). Ann Arbor, MI: Institute for Social Research.

Frost, P. J. (1987). Power, politics, and influence. In F. M. Jablin, L. L. Putnam, K. H. Roberts, & L. W. Porter (Eds.), *Handbook of organizational communication* (pp. 503–548). Newbury Park, CA: Sage.

Garko, M. G. (1992). Persuading subordinates who communicate in attractive and unattractive styles. *Management Communication Quarterly, 5,* 289–315.

Gruber, K. J., & White, J. W. (1986). Gender differences in the perception of self's and others' use of power strategies. *Sex Roles, 15,* 109–118.

Harper, N. L., & Hirokawa, R. Y. (1988). A comparison of persuasive strategies used by female and male managers I: An examination of downward influence. *Communication Quarterly, 36,* 157–168.

Hirokawa, R. Y., Kodama, R. A., & Harper, N. L. (1990). Impact of managerial power on persuasive strategy selection by female and male managers. *Management Communication Quarterly, 4,* 30–50.

Hirokawa, R. Y., Mickey, J., & Miura, S. (1991). Effects of request legitimacy on the compliance-gaining tactics of male and female managers. *Communication Monographs, 58,* 421–436.

Hirokawa, R. Y., & Miyahara, A. (1986). A comparison of influence strategies utilized by managers in American and Japanese organizations. *Communication Quarterly, 34,* 250–265.

Howard, J. A., Blumstein, P., & Schwartz, P. (1986). Sex, power and influence tactics in intimate relationships. *Journal of Personality and Social Psychology, 51,* 102–109.

Howell, J. M., & Higgins, C. A. (1990). Leadership behaviors, influence tactics, and career experiences of champions of technological innovation. *Leadership Quarterly, 1,* 249–264.

Jackson, S., & Backus, D. (1982). Are compliance-gaining strategies dependent on situational variables? *Central States Speech Journal, 33,* 469–479.

Johnson, G. M. (1992). Subordinate perceptions of superior's communication competence and task attraction related to superior's use of compliance-gaining tactics. *Western Journal of Communication, 56,* 54–67.

Judge, T. A., & Brentz, R. D. (1994). Political influence behavior and career success. *Journal of Management, 20,* 43–65.

Kanter, R. M. (1977). *Men and women of the corporation.* New York: Basic Books.

Kellerman, K., & Cole, T. (1994). Classifying compliance-gaining messages: Taxonomic disorder and strategic confusion. *Communication Theory, 4,* 3–60.

Kelman, H. C., & Hamilton, V. L. (1989). *Crimes of obedience: Toward a social psychology of authority and responsibility.* New Haven, CT: Yale University Press.

Kim, M., & Wilson, S. R. (1994). A cross-cultural comparison of implicit theories of requesting. *Communication Monographs, 61,* 210–235.

Kipnis, D. (1976). *The powerholders.* Chicago: University of Chicago Press.

Kipnis, D., & Schmidt, S. M. (1983). An influence perspective on bargaining within organizations. In M. H. Bazerman & R. J. Lewicki (Eds.), *Negotiating in organizations* (pp. 303–319). Beverly Hills, CA: Sage.

Kipnis, D., & Schmidt, S. M. (1988). Upward influence styles: Relationship with performance evaluations, salary, and stress. *Administrative Science Quarterly, 33,* 528–542.

Kipnis, D., Schmidt, S. M., & Wilkinson, I. (1980). Intraorganizational influence tactics: Explorations in getting one's own way. *Journal of Applied Psychology, 65,* 440–452.

Krone, K. J. (1992). A comparison of organizational, structural, and relationship effects on subordinates' upward influence choices. *Communication Quarterly, 40,* 1–15.

Lim, T. (1990). The influences of receivers' resistance on persuader's verbal aggressiveness. *Communication Quarterly, 38,* 170–188.

Mainiero, L. (1986). Coping with powerlessness: The relationship of gender and job dependency to empowerment-strategy usage. *Administrative Science Quarterly, 31,* 633–653.

Marwell, G., & Schmitt, D. R. (1967). Dimensions of compliance-gaining behavior: An empirical analysis. *Sociometry, 30,* 350–364.

Maslyn, J. M., Fedor, D. B., & Farmer, S. M. (1994). *Predicting influence tactics: The dynamic nature of antecedents.* Paper presented at the 54th Annual Meeting of the Academy of Management, Dallas, Texas.

Miller, G. R., Boster, F. J., Roloff, M. E., & Seibold, D. R. (1987). MBRS rekindled: Some thoughts on compliance gaining in interpersonal settings. In M. E. Roloff & G. R. Miller (Eds.), *Interpersonal processes: New directions in communication research* (pp. 89–116). Newbury Park, CA: Sage.

Miller, G., Boster, F., Roloff, M., & Seibold, D. (1977). Compliance-gaining message strategies: A typology and some findings concerning effects of situational differences. *Communication Monographs, 44,* 35–71.

Mintzberg, H. (1983). *Power in and around organizations*. Englewood Cliffs, NJ: Prentice-Hall.

Mowday, R. T. (1978). The exercise of upward influence in organizations. *Administrative Science Quarterly, 23,* 137–156.

Mowday, R. T. (1979). Leader characteristics, self-confidence, and methods of upward influence in organizational decision situations. *Academy of Management Journal, 22,* 709–725.

Offerman, L. R., & Schrier, P. E. (1985). Social influence strategies: The impact of sex, role and attitudes toward power. *Personality and Social Psychology Bulletin, 11,* 286–300.

O'Hair, D., & Cody, M. J. (1987). Machiavellian beliefs and social influence. *Western Journal of Speech Communication, 51,* 279–303.

O'Neal, E. C., Kipnis, D., & Craig, K. M. (1994). Effects on the persuader of employing a coercive influence technique. *Basic and Applied Social Psychology, 15,* 225–238.

Perreault, W. D., & Miles, R. H. (1978). Influence strategy mixes in complex organizations. *Behavioral Science, 23,* 86–98.

Richmond, V. P., Davis, L. M., Saylor, K., & McCroskey, J. C. (1984). Power strategies in organizations: Communication techniques and messages. *Human Communication Research, 11,* 85–108.

Richmond, V. P., McCroskey, J. C., & Davis, L. M. (1986). The relationship of supervisor use of power and affinity-seeking strategies with subordinate satisfaction. *Communication Quarterly, 34,* 178–193.

Roach, K. D. (1991). University department chairs' use of compliance-gaining strategies. *Communication Quarterly, 39,* 75–90.

Rotter, J. B. (1966). Generalized expectancies for internal versus external control of reinforcement. *Psychological Monographs, 80* (1, Whole No. 609).

Salanick, G. R., & Pfeffer, J. (1977). Who gets power—and how they hold on to it. *Organizational Dynamics, 5,* 3–21.

Schilit, W. K. (1986). An examination of individual differences as moderators of upward influence activity in strategic decisions. *Human Relations, 39,* 933–953.

Schilit, W. K., & Locke, E. A. (1982). A study of upward influence in organizations. *Administrative Science Quarterly, 27,* 304–316.

Schmidt, S. M., & Kipnis, D. (1984) Managers' pursuit of individual and organizational goals. *Human Relations, 37,* 781–794.

Seibold, D. R., Cantrill, J. G., & Meyers, R. A. (1994). Communication and interpersonal influence. In M. L. Knapp & G. R. Miller (Eds.), *Handbook of interpersonal communication* (2nd ed., pp. 542–588). Thousand Oaks, CA: Sage.

Seibold, D. R., Cantrill, J. G., & Meyers, R. A. (1985). Communication and interpersonal influence. In M. L. Knapp & G. R. Miller (Eds.), *Handbook of interpersonal communication* (pp. 551–611). Beverly Hills, CA: Sage.

Smith, S. W., Cody, M. J., Lovette, S., & Canary, D. J. (1990). Self-monitoring, gender and compliance-gaining goals. In M. J. Cody & M. L. McLaughlin (Eds.), *The psychology of tactical communication* (pp. 91–134). Clevedon, England: Multilingual Matters.

Snyder, M. (1974). Self-monitoring of expressive behavior. *Journal of Personality and Social Psychology, 30,* 526–537.

Sullivan, J., & Taylor, S. (1991). A cross-cultural test of compliance-gaining theory. *Management Communication Quarterly, 5,* 220–239.

Tjosvold, D., Andrews, I. R., & Struthers, J. T. (1992). Leadership influence: Goal interdependence and power. *Journal of Social Psychology, 132,* 39–50.

Vecchio, R. P., & Sussman, M. (1989). Preferences for forms of supervisory social influence. *Journal of Organizational Behavior, 10,* 135–143.

Vecchio, R. P., & Sussman, M. (1991). Choice of influence tactics: Individual and organizational determinants. *Journal of Organizational Behavior, 12,* 73–80.

Wheeless, L. R., Barraclough, R., & Stewart, R. (1983). Compliance-gaining and power in persuasion. In R. N. Bostrom (Ed.), *Communication Yearbook 7* (pp. 105–145). Beverly Hills, CA: Sage.

White, J. W. (1988). Influence tactics as a function of gender, insult, and goal. *Sex Roles, 18,* 433–448.

Wilson, S. R., Cruz, M. G., Marshall, L. J., & Rao, N. (1993). An attributional analysis of compliance-gaining interactions. *Communication Monographs, 60,* 352–372.

Wiseman, R. L., & Schenck-Hamlin, W. (1981). A multidimensional scaling validation of an inductively-derived set of compliance-gaining strategies. *Communication Monographs, 48,* 251–270.

Yukl, G., & Falbe, C. M. (1990). Influence tactics and objectives in upward, downward and lateral influence attempts. *Journal of Applied Psychology, 75,* 132–140.

Yukl, G., Falbe, C. M., & Youn, J. Y. (1993). Patterns of influence behavior for managers. *Group and Organization Studies, 18,* 5–28.

Yukl, G., & Tracey, J. B. (1992). Consequences of influence tactics used with subordinates, peers, and the boss. *Journal of Applied Psychology, 77,* 525–535.

19

Social Influence in Selling Contexts

John S. Seiter and Michael J. Cody

Successful influence often entails knowing how to adapt to your audience. Some influence agents may routinely try to be "likable," while others try to be "expert." These people probably tend to be more influential than those who seem unlikable or who are lacking in expertise. However, there is evidence that adapting to one's audience pays the best dividends. This point was vividly discussed in Cialdini's (2001, pp. 198–199) observations of "Vincent," a waiter at an upscale restaurant who made the most in tips. When serving a family, Vincent was clever, friendly, even clownish with children, keeping everyone happy. When serving a couple, he would become more formal, recommending expensive items, acting even slightly "imperious." When serving an older married couple, he retained formality, acted less superior, and showed respect. When serving a large dinner party, he recommended what was best prepared that evening, and he was an expert in wines. Vincent knew what his various types of clients valued, and he gave them all what they wanted; he knew how to ensure that he would either increase the amount of the bill (on which the tip was calculated) or increase the amount tipped—or both.

This chapter suggests that such an ability to adapt to particular audiences is a key aspect of successful influence attempts, in restaurant settings and beyond. Specifically, it focuses on adaptation and other factors that lead to success in one of the most common of all persuasive encounters: the buying and selling of merchandise in retail stores. In doing so, the chapter draws upon work in a number of disciplines, including psychology, business, marketing, communication, and personal selling. Considering that volumes have been written on this topic, we must narrow our focus to a few key issues. We begin by exploring the nature of goals and how they affect selling encounters. Second, we examine the types of resources retail salespeople need in order to interact with customers successfully. Finally, we discuss the results of two of our own studies illustrating the implementation and effectiveness of several influence tactics used by different types of salesclerks in retail stores.

Multiple Goals in Selling Encounters

Chapter 11 in this volume presents a detailed account of communication as a goal-directed activity. When producing a message, goals lead people to make plans aimed at achieving those goals, and the plans in turn are used to select and guide behaviors for carrying them out (see also Dillard & Solomon, 2000; Greene, 2000). Selling merchandise, like most communication encounters, involves the same process; salespeople formulate plans for making sales, and these plans influence the strategies, tactics, and messages that they then communicate to customers.

Although at first glance, this process may seem simple, it is not. People often pursue multiple goals (see chapter 11), and their goals may change during the course of an interaction (Greene, 2000). For that reason, we suggest that effective salespeople are those who have the ability to juggle multiple goals. For example, Spitzberg and Cupach (1989) suggested that competent communicators are both effective and appropriate. We believe the same can be said of salespeople. To be effective, salesclerks must meet their instrumental goals by making sales, but if they use inappropriate or unethical tactics such as deception or intimidation, they may not succeed in cultivating "return" customers or may be perceived as manipulative. In short, salesclerks must walk a thin line between goals that have the potential of competing with one another.

Previous research has suggested that people pursue three general types of goals through communication: instrumental, self-presentation, and relational (Clark & Delia, 1979; Dillard, 1990; O'Keefe & McCornack, 1987; Tracy, Craig, Smith, & Spisak, 1984; Wilson, 1990). First we turn to a discussion of self-presentation and relational goals in selling contexts. Later in the chapter we discuss salespersons' instrumental goals and tactics for achieving them.

Self-Presentation Goals in Sales Interactions

According to Impression Management Theory, most people want to be perceived in a positive light and therefore communicate in order to create desired impressions of themselves (see Goffman, 1959). This is also true of salespeople. According to Leathers (1988), because impression management focuses on how people sell themselves, it is not surprising that impression management skills are especially important to salespeople. Previous literature has suggested that sales training is now a big business and that a large number of training courses focus on teaching salespeople how to project positive images (Leathers, 1988).

Jones and Pittman (1982) discuss five common self-presentation styles (see also Canary, Cody, & Manusov, 2000). First, the *ingratiator* wants to be liked and therefore engages in behaviors such as praise and appearing friendly, kind, helpful, and positive. Second, the *intimidator* desires to be seen as dangerous and tough and may use strategies such as threats and displays of anger. Third, the *self-promoter* wants to be perceived as competent, effective, and successful and therefore try to boost his or her credibility by attempting to appear smart or talented. Fourth, the *exemplifier* tries to appear dedicated, committed, and self-sacrificing. Finally, the *supplicator* wants to be perceived as helpless, unfortunate, and in need of nurturing.

Clearly, not all of these self-presentational styles will benefit salespeople who want to be effective. What customer, for example, wants a helpless salesclerk assisting him or her? Moreover, it is hard to imagine that threatening tactics would work well with too many customers. Having said that, we need to determine what images are most important for a salesperson to project. Though previous literature has identified a large number of characteristics desirable for salespersons (e.g., assertiveness, attractiveness, interestingness), perhaps the most important and well documented are credibility and likability. We discuss these next.

Credibility. According to Gass and Seiter (2003), although credibility may be made up of several dimensions, scholars generally agree that competence and trustworthiness are the two that are almost always relevant to the evaluation of sources (see also chapter 6). Research and theory on personal selling have confirmed that these dimensions are important for customers interacting with salespeople. For example, previous research has shown that expertise is beneficial both for establishing customer trust (Busch & Wilson, 1976) and for producing the intended behavioral response in the customer (Busch & Wilson, 1976; Jones, Moore, Stanaland, & Wyatt, 1998). Comstock and Higgins (1997) reported that trust and rapport are unequivocally the most important themes during the sales process and that customers prefer salespeople who are trustworthy over those who are similar to them. Other research has shown that when customers trust salespeople, they are more likely to engage in open and free-flowing communication (Chow & Holden, 1997), are more loyal to the company for which the salesperson works (Chow & Holden, 1997; Garbarino & Johnson, 1999), and are more cooperative with the salesclerk (Schurr, & Ozanne, 1985). Finally, in a meta-analysis, Swan, Bowers, and Richardson (1999) concluded that although trust has a moderate influence on the development of customer attitudes, intentions and behaviors, its influence is beneficial.

Given this, what characteristics lead to perceptions of expertise and trustworthiness? Retail salespersons might demonstrate expertise by claiming personal experience of a product or by being knowledgeable about fashions, designers, materials, care, and so forth. Trustworthiness might be established through nonmanipulative tactics or by pointing out possible drawbacks to certain products. Nonverbally, salespeople might project a credible image by appearing relaxed, using appropriate eye contact and vocal cues, smiling at appropriate times, and speaking fluently (Leathers, 1988). Finally, a study by Ramsey and Sohi (1997) found that when customers perceived that salespeople were listening carefully (i.e., sensing, evaluating, and responding to what they said), they not only trusted the salespeople, they expected future interaction.

Likability. In addition to projecting a credible image, effective salesclerks tend to be likable. Sales clerks may bolster their likability in several ways. First, people tend to reciprocate liking. As such, salespeople who demonstrate liking for their customers by being friendly or by doing favors are more liked themselves. According to Leathers (1988), likable salespeople tend to smile more, use a lot of eye contact, engage in affirmative head nodding, and establish an open body position. Moreover, clerks who demonstrate such positive emotions may be more persuasive. For example, Sharma (1999) found that when salespeople demonstrated positive emotions toward their customers, their customers listened to sales pitches more carefully and were more easily persuaded. Jones et al. (1998) also found that salesperson likability positively influenced customers' purchases.

Second, customers respond more positively to salesclerks when they perceive them as similar to themselves (e.g., Boles, Johnson, & Barksdale, 2000). Among other things, clerks can appear more similar by matching their customer's nonverbal behaviors (Leathers, 1988) and by conforming opinions (e.g., "I agree, that blouse looks great on you.") (Cody & Seiter, 2001). Studies have shown that customers tend to trust, be more cooperative with, follow the advice given by, and buy more from salespeople with whom they perceive they share demographics, experiences, appearances, attitudes, communication styles, and personality traits (e.g., Busch & Wilson, 1976; Dion, Easterling, & Miller, 1995; Evans, 1963; Fine & Gardial, 1990; Gadel, 1964).

Finally, salesclerks who praise their customers may be liked more than those who do not. An analysis of several studies by Gordon (1996) suggested that ingratiation is an effective tactic. But what if the ingratiator's ulterior motives are transparent? For example, what if customers suspect that salespeople are praising them just to make a sale? According to Burgoon (1994), ingratiation is most effective when the ingratiator's motives are concealed. Even so, Cialdini (2001) noted that false flattery leads to almost as much liking for the ingratiator as sincere flattery does. Not surprisingly, then, research suggests that salesclerks who praise their customers are more effective then those who do not, though Strutton, Pelton and Lumpkin (1995) suggested that if salespeople use ingratiation, they should do so only to a moderate degree to reduce the risk of mistrust on the part of customers.

Relational Goals in Sales Interactions

While salespeople pursue instrumental (making sales) and self-presentational (creating a credible and likable image) goals, they also must consider relational goals. Traditionally, building a relationship with customers has not been seen as an important goal for retail salespeople, whose interactions with customers have traditionally been characterized as one-time-only and brief. The past decade, however, has witnessed a major change in theory and practice related to personal selling and marketing. For example, Wortuba (1991) and Weitz and Bradford (1999) suggested that the nature of personal selling has evolved through four "eras"—production, sales, marketing, and partnering—and that only the last era stresses the importance of interpersonal communication and of building and maintaining long-term relationships with customers.

Nowadays, buyer-seller relationships are acknowledged as potentially important in all types of selling contexts. Indeed, recent work, including the Commitment-Trust Theory of relationship marketing (Morgan & Hunt, 1994), has suggested that although some customers have low relational orientations and are simply interested in satisfaction with a product or service, other customers have high relational orientations and as such are strongly influenced by the amount of trust or commitment they have in a company and its salespeople (see Dwyer, Schurr, & Oh, 1987; Garbarino & Johnson, 1999). For these people, salespersons are often expected to play the role of "relationship managers" (Crosby, Evans, & Cowles, 1990) between themselves and customers. Nordstrom's, for example, emphasizes not only customer-salesperson relationships but suggests that the personalized service that characterizes these interactions helps to build customer-company relations. In short, regardless of the selling context, developing buyer-seller relationships can be important. Leigh and McGraw (1989) found that in industrial sales, successful salespeople reported that their second, third, and fourth most frequent goals in initial sales calls were related to relationship development.

Reynolds and Beatty (1999a) defined a customer-salesperson relationship as existing "when there is an ongoing series of interactions between a salesperson and a customer and the parties know each other"(p. 12). Previous literature indicated that such relationships can have numerous advantages for customers. These advantages include functional benefits (e.g., saving time, convenience, fashion advice, better purchase decisions) and social benefits (e.g., enjoying another person's company, enjoying time spent with a salesperson) (Beatty, Mayer, Coleman, Reynolds, & Lee, 1996; Gwinner, Gremler, & Bitner, 1998; Reynolds & Beatty, 1999a). In addition, such relationships can have advantages for businesses. Such advantages include customer satisfaction with salespersons and companies, customer loyalty, favorable word of mouth, and increased purchases (Berry & Parasuraman, 1991; Griffin, 1995; Reynolds & Beatty, 1999a, 1999b). Finally, salespeople may also benefit from developing satisfactory relationships with clients.

Considering this, what can salesclerks do to build successful buyer-seller relationships? According to a study by Anselmi and Zemanek (1997), buyers are more satisfied when they have known the salesperson for a long period of time and when sellers have effective interpersonal skills, intensity, persistence, and enthusiasm. Dion and colleagues (1995) reported that trust and perceived similarity between buyers and sellers (see above) are positively related to relationship quality. Comstock and Higgins (1997) found that buyers like sellers whose relational messages are trustworthy and composed. Finally, Leuthesser (1997) reported that initiating a relationship, self-disclosure, and frequent interaction lead to quality relationships between buyers and sellers.

Different Types of Clerks Based on Different Goals Pursued

As we have already discussed, salesclerks have instrumental, self-presentational, and relational goals. This is not to suggest that all clerks pursue all of these goals. For example, though Ford (1999) noted that many salespeople develop a combination of service styles that include courteous, personalized, and manipulative communication behaviors, previous research has suggested that some salespeople stick to one style of selling. Different salesclerks may thus be characterized by different configurations of goals, approaching buyer-seller interactions in a variety of ways. A good deal of previous research has attempted to categorize salespeople based on their approaches to selling (e.g., see Busch & Wilson, 1976; Evans 1963; Williams & Spiro, 1985). One of our studies (Cody & Seiter, 2001) identified four different salesperson styles based on observations of buyer-seller interactions in retail stores. Many of these styles correspond to the self-presentational styles we discussed earlier in this chapter.

First, *ingratiation-style* clerks were characterized by a reliance on tactics that helped them cultivate an image that was likable and friendly. Second, *task-oriented* clerks focused on instrumental goals and tactics aimed primarily at "making the sale," efficiency, and controlling the customer. Third, *client-oriented* clerks used a variety of tactics, tried to understand customers' needs, and adapted accordingly. Finally, *passive-inactive* clerks were characterized as apathetic, using few selling tactics, approaching customers infrequently, and performing "mechanical" tasks (e.g., running the cash register). As might be expected, each of these styles influenced the outcomes in sales interactions. We examine these results later in this chapter. Now, however, we turn to a discussion of salesperson resources.

Resources and Selling

Comstock and Higgins (1997) argued that effective salespeople are competent communicators. But what makes a communicator competent? Past literature has suggested that competent communicators have the knowledge, motivation, and skills necessary to be effective and appropriate in a given context (Spitzberg & Cupach, 1989). How do salespeople come by such resources?

One approach argues that certain traits characterize successful salespeople. For example, in a review of literature, Anselmi and Zemanek (1999) noted that no one personality profile exists for the perfect salesperson but that successful salespeople tend to be well mannered, verbally skilled, punctual, enthusiastic, social, and competitive. However, research attempting to identify universally effective selling traits has also been inconsistent and equivocal (Sprowl, Carveth, & Senk, 1994; Weitz, 1978). Perhaps this is because selling encounters are interactive and thereby influenced by *both* buyer and seller characteristics (Sprowl et al., 1994). For example, Fine and Schumann (1992) found that the personality of both the salesperson and the customer influenced the outcome of sales encounters. Therefore, when specific salesperson traits influence successful sales, it may be because the traits foster involvement and interaction with customers (Boorom, Goolsby, & Ramsey, 1998).

Though we believe traits may play a role in effective sales, our position is that successful selling is primarily the result of learning. This notion is consistent with theories of message production and cognitive selling paradigms, which focus on linking behaviors (e.g., smiling while showing merchandise) to underlying knowledge that individuals learn with experience (see Dillard, 1990; Gengler, Howard, & Zolner, 1995; Greene, 2000; Leigh & McGraw, 1989; Macintosh, Anglin, Szymanski, & Gentry, 1992; Meyer, 2000; Weitz, Sujan, & Sujan, 1986). The general idea is that to maximize career effectiveness, over time salespeople abandon unsuccessful approaches while developing, refining, and remembering successful ones (Weitz et al., 1986). Meyer (2000) suggested that this process occurs unconsciously as the result of implicit learning, perhaps because of failures. For example, upon starting a job as a suit salesperson, a clerk might deal with each customer using the same approach—a simple "may I help you?"—that may often lead to watching the customer for a few minutes, commenting on the quality of the merchandise, and then waving goodbye without a sale. Eventually, though, that salesperson is likely to learn that certain customers like to be left alone and that hovering too much causes that type of customer to leave the store quickly. By experimenting with different approaches, the salesperson then learns to recognize other types of shoppers and to develop a repertoire of strategies for selling to them.

Previous research supports the view that selling skills are learned over time. For instance, a study of automobile salespeople by Gengler and colleagues (1995) found that, compared to less experienced salespeople, those with more experience used more adaptive behaviors and differentiated more between customers. VandeWalle, Brown, Cron, and Slocum (1999) found that salespeople with a *learning goal orientation* (i.e., those who would presumably seek to develop more detailed knowledge structures) were more successful than salespeople with a *performance goal orientation* (i.e., those who viewed challenging tasks as a threat and therefore failed to adapt) (see also Sujan, Weitz & Kumar, 1994). Thus, retailers should expect new salespeople to improve their performance over time. To facilitate this process, retailers should motivate and help salespeople develop detailed knowledge structures about important features in selling encounters. With that in mind, what types of knowledge are necessary for successful selling?

Previous research and theory (e.g., Sujan, Sujan, & Bettman, 1988; Weitz et al., 1986) suggests that to be successful salespeople need two types of information—declarative and procedural knowledge. Sujan and colleagues (1988) explained:

> Declarative knowledge is the set of facts used to describe the category, whereas procedural knowledge consists of the strategies or heuristics used to guide behavior. . . . The general finding is that declarative knowledge increases with skill. For salespeople, an important aspect of declarative knowledge is knowledge of traits, motives, and behaviors of the different types of customers encountered. . . . For salespeople, procedural knowledge corresponds to knowledge of sales strategies to be used with each type of customer. (p. 82)

In other words, to be effective, salespeople require knowledge not only of the selling strategies but also of the various types of customers. We discuss these issues next.

Types of Customers

Weitz (1978) argued that the process of adaptive selling occurs through several stages. First, the salesperson forms an impression of a customer. Second, the salesperson selects a goal and plans a message to achieve that goal. Third, the salesperson communicates the message. Next, the salesperson evaluates the effectiveness of the message. Finally, either the goal is achieved or the first three stages are adjusted and the process starts again. Through all of this, it is clear that forming an impression of the customer is crucial to the process of selling. To be sure, Weitz and his colleagues (Weitz, 1978, 1981; Weitz, Sujan, & Sujan, 1986) suggested that adaptive selling depends on salespeople's ability to organize their knowledge of and experiences with customers. Specifically, through experience, salespeople develop "scripts" or stereotypes about what typically unfolds during a selling encounter. These scripts contain knowledge about different types of customers. As such, these scripts or knowledge structures guide their behaviors in interactions. Moreover, the more accurate and detailed these scripts, the more successful salespeople are. For example, research has found that the accuracy with which a salesperson perceives customers and the number of ways in which a salesperson differentiates customers are related to that salesperson's effectiveness (Lambert, Marmornstein, & Sharma, 1990; Sujan et al., 1988). Not surprisingly, then, in an effort to help salespeople understand the types of customers they might encounter, a considerable amount of research has focused on developing different typologies of customers.

The most basic typologies are based on demographic characteristics. For example, Goff, Bellenger, and Stojack (1994) found that shoppers' age, gender, and whether or not they used a "purchase pal" (a shopping companion) influenced the degree to which they were persuaded by salespeople. Specifically, males were susceptible to salespeople who used relational messages, older customers were susceptible to informational and relational messages, and customers who used a purchase pal were most susceptible to recommendational strategies (Goff et al., 1994).

One of the first typologies of retail customers was developed by Stone (1954), who identified four categories of shoppers. *Economic consumers* are cautious shoppers, paying close attention to the quality and price of merchandise. *Personalizing consumers* are interested in establishing relationships with salespeople. *Ethical customers* place moral values above economic ones (e.g., they would rather help the "little guy" than save money in a big department store). Finally, the *apathetic consumer* doesn't enjoy shopping and does it only out of necessity.

Like Stone's (1954) typology, most of those that followed categorized customers on the basis of their motivation for shopping (e.g., see Dawson, Bloch, & Ridgway, 1990; Goff & Walters, 1995). According to Dawson and colleagues (1990), all of these motivations can be classified into one of three general categories: product-oriented, experiential, or a combination of both product and experiential.

> In the first case, a store visit is motivated by purchase needs or the desire to acquire product information. For instance, a consumer's need to find an anniversary gift within the next two hours will produce strong product motive. The second class of motives in the typology has a hedonic or recreational orientation. . . . Here, the attention is on store or mall visits made for the pleasure inherent in the visit itself. . . . The last motive category combines product and experiential elements, and occurs when the store visitor seeks to satisfy a purchase need as well as have a pleasurable recreational experience in the outlet. For example, a person may visit an outdoor equipment store in order to purchase hiking gear, but also to participate in enjoyable conversation about hiking experiences with a salesperson or other patron. (p. 410)

Clearly, each of these motives affects the ways shoppers respond to salespersons and influence tactics. For instance, Goff and Walters (1995) found that recreational shoppers are especially susceptible to salesperson influence, and Dawson and colleagues (1990) found that shoppers with product motives were significantly more likely to make a purchase.

While each of the above-mentioned typologies was developed by observing shoppers or asking shoppers about themselves, we find a final typology offered by Sharma and Levy (1995) especially interesting, because it was developed by going straight to the salespeople. These researchers asked 229 retail salespeople to describe the dimensions *they* use to categorize shoppers. Their responses fell into eight categories: (1) price/promotion-conscious shoppers (shoppers interested in buying products on sale), (2) need/product-based shoppers (who buy products for their own use and may need assistance), (3) gift buyers, (4) browsers (shoppers who are "just looking" and do not want to be disturbed by salespeople), (5) shoppers who need and seek sales help, (6) negatively labeled shoppers (a category that contains negative customer descriptions), (7) knowledgeable shoppers (who know what they want and don't need help), and (8) decision-style shoppers (who have their own way of making decisions).

Knowledge of Influence Tactics

In addition to developing a thorough knowledge of different types of customers, effective salespeople also have a large repertoire of influence tactics they can use to persuade their customers. The study of compliance gaining focuses on strategies and tactics aimed at getting others to do something or to act in a particular way. Traditional research in this area sought to develop typologies of compliance-gaining strategies (e.g., threat, promise, deception, and so forth) by relying on theory (French & Raven, 1959), or by asking research participants to describe the tactics they might use in a variety of situations. Whatever the method, an enormous number of tactics and typologies have been developed. Kellerman and Cole (1994), for example, identified 74 typologies of compliance-gaining messages that they integrated into a "super" typology of 64 distinct strategies

We have argued elsewhere that an alternative to this approach is to observe influence tactics that are used in actual encounters involving face-to-face interactions and to categorize the tactics on the basis of a finite set of psychological principles underlying why people comply with requests (see Cody & Seiter, 2001). One viable set of processes was presented by Cialdini (2001; see also chapter 12 in this volume). Many of these processes were also covered earlier in this chapter, particularly the importance of credibility and likability, which can be established by creating images of trust and expertise and using tactics such as appearing friendly or similar to the customer, conforming opinions, praising the customer, and rendering favors. In addition to these processes, this section briefly discusses five others: scarcity, social proof, contrast, commitment, and reciprocity.

Scarcity.   People are often surprised to learn that merchandise shortages are sometimes planned by retail stores. Indeed, retailers know what research has shown for a long time: Scarce objects are typically perceived as more desirable or unique, and as a result people are willing to pay higher prices for them (see Lynn, 1991; Verhallen & Robben, 1995). Moreover, if a product is perceived as scarce (e.g., "It's the last one in your size."), people may be more eager to buy it for fear of not having the freedom to do so in the future. Cialdini (2001) refers to this as *the principle of scarcity.*

In addition to shortages, the principle of scarcity can be used in other ways. For example, retailers often use restrictions that can assume several forms, which include limited time offers, limits on the quantity of a product that may be purchased, or a store purchase of a certain minimum dollar amount to qualify for a good price (Inman, Peter, & Raghubir, 1997). Whatever the case, when confronted with the principle of scarcity, people may perceive the product more favorably and/or purchase it in an effort to "relieve" themselves of the restrictions placed upon them. Previous research suggested that scarcity is an effective sales tactic. For example, Inman and colleagues (1997, study 1) found that sales were twice as high when a restriction was in place than when it was not.

Social Proof.   When people are trying to decide what clothes they should wear or, for that matter, what behaviors are appropriate, they often look at what other people are doing or wearing. Cialdini (2001) labeled this form of influence *social proof:*

> The tendency to see an action as more appropriate when others are doing it normally works quite well. As a rule, we will make fewer mistakes by acting in accord with social evidence than contrary to it. Usually when a lot of people are doing something, it is the right thing to do. This feature of the principle of social proof is simultaneously its major strength and its major weakness. Like the other weapons of influence, it provides a convenient shortcut for determining how to behave, but, at the same time, makes one who uses the shortcut vulnerable to the attacks of profiteers who lie in wait along its path. (p. 100)

In selling contexts, social proof is a common influence tactic. "Best-sellers" and "top ten" lists are examples of ways in which retailers try to sell products by showing that other people are also using them. Some salespeople are trained to let customers know when a particular product is "the season's hottest color," "what everyone is buying," or "the most popular." In short, social proof sells merchandise by claiming that whatever is popular is good, so customers should buy what's popular.

Contrast.   Chapter 12 of this book discusses sequential influence tactics that include the *contrast effect.* We briefly revisit the concept here to talk about how this effect operates in selling contexts. The basic idea behind this effect is that when people are exposed to some standard amount of violence, beauty, prices on commodities, temperature, happiness, and so forth, they become adjusted or adapted to that "standard" level. After this level is established, a contrast effect occurs when something is judged against the standard. For example, a lukewarm swimming pool might feel cold to someone who has just come from a hot Jacuzzi but hot to someone else who had just stepped out of a snowstorm.

The contrast effect can be implemented in selling contexts in a couple of ways. One approach, known as the *door-in-the-face tactic,* involves making a large request and following it with a smaller request. Of course, the smaller request is what the persuader wanted all along. For example, a salesperson may know that a particular customer would never consider buying a $1,000 evening gown. Even so, the salesperson might begin by showing the customer such a gown and asking if she would like to purchase it. When the customer declines, the salesperson can then show a $500 gown and ask for a sale.

A second approach is known as the *top-down sales tactic* (Donoho & Swenson, 1996). The idea is the same as before, only this time requests are not made. Instead, salespeople begin by showing the top-of-the-line or highest-priced items as a reference point and then proceed by stepping down to lower- and lower-priced items. Regardless of the approach used, the contrast effect is the underlying principle; $500-dollar items seem much less expensive when compared to $1,000 items. Compared to $100-dollar items, however, they may seem expensive.

The effectiveness of these contrast tactics has been well documented outside sales contexts, though according to Donoho and Swenson (1996), most support for the effectiveness of the top-down approach within sales contexts is anecdotal. In their study, however, Donoho and Swenson found that the top-down sales tactic was more effective than the bottom-up sales tactic (discussed below).

Commitment. The *commitment principle* suggests that the more a person is committed to a group, cause, or idea, the more likely he or she is to stick with it. For example, once a couple make a commitment to get married, buy an engagement ring, and send out wedding invitations, it becomes difficult for them to change their minds about getting married—too much cognitive dissonance. The same is true in selling contexts. Once customers become committed to the idea of making a purchase, it is difficult for them to back out.

Two commonly researched strategies that rely on the commitment principle are the *foot-in-the-door tactic* (a person agrees to a small request, which creates a commitment to an idea, and then is more likely to agree to a second, larger request) and the *low-ball tactic* (a person agrees to a request or commits to a decision and later learns there were hidden costs involved in making such a decision) (for more on these tactics, see chapter 12).

We have suggested elsewhere that in selling contexts commitment can work in a variety of other ways (Cody & Seiter, 2001). For example, once a customer becomes committed to the idea of buying a product, he or she can be shown more and more expensive items. Donoho and Swenson (1996) called this the *bottom-up sales tactic*. Second, once a customer becomes committed to buying a product, the salesperson might influence that customer to "complete" the purchase with add-on items. For example, a shopper who originally came to purchase a suit might be persuaded to complete the ensemble with the proper shirts, ties, shoes, and so forth.

Reciprocity. The expression "You scratch my back, and I'll scratch yours" epitomizes the *principle of reciprocity*. Stated simply, this principle suggests that "we should try to repay, in kind, what another person has provided us"(Cialdini, 2001, p. 20). In other words, if someone does a favor or gives a gift, the beneficiary feels indebted to him or her. As such, the beneficiary is more likely to comply with the gift giver's requests. This principle is at work when "free stuff" is given to customers. For example, Hickory Farms and See's Candies frequently give customers samples of their products. Cosmetic departments allow customers to test perfumes and often hire employees to administer the sample for added pressure. Whatever the gift, such behavior may make shoppers feel indebted. Greenberg (1980) argued that these feelings make people feel uncomfortable by threatening their sense of independence. As a result, they become motivated to repay the debt.

Adapting Tactics to Customers

A study by Sprowl and colleagues (1994) found that none of the four compliance gaining strategies reportedly used by real estate salespeople (denigration, aggrandizement, intimidation, and rational appeal) led to sales success. The researchers suggested that a possible explanation for this is that successful salespeople not only know about different strategies but also how to adapt their strategy choice to different situations. Indeed, so far we have argued that successful salespeople have detailed knowledge structures regarding types of shoppers and the types of strategies they might use to influence them. However, much research argues that detailed knowledge about customers and strategies may not be the only information necessary to be a successful salesperson. For instance Weitz and colleagues (1986) noted:

> We suggest that, to practice adaptive selling effectively, salespeople need an elaborate knowledge structure of sales situations, sales behaviors, and contingencies that link specific behaviors to situations. To utilize this knowledge, salespeople need to be skillful in collecting information about customers so that they can relate knowledge acquired in previous sales situations to the interaction in which they are currently engaged. (p. 176)

In other words, successful salespeople must be able to *join* knowledge about customers and strategies in order to adapt to specific selling situations (Sujan et al., 1988). For this reason, scholars have argued that communication is essential to the selling process (e.g., Sprowl et al., 1994; Williams & Spiro, 1985). Through communication, salespeople are not only able to develop the types of knowledge discussed earlier, they are able to elicit the needs and wants of specific customers and adapt accordingly. A large body of research and theory supports the idea that successful salespeople are those who are able to recognize different types of customers and change their behaviors to match the situation (e.g., Levy & Sharma, 1994; Sharma & Levy, 1995; Sujan et al., 1988; Weitz et al., 1986; Williams & Spiro, 1985). In light of this, a useful approach to understanding successful selling in retail contexts would be to examine the types of influence tactics that are effective for particular types of customers. In the next section, we review two studies that examine this and other issues.

Bringing It All Together: A Review of Two Studies

In order to develop a better understanding of influence processes, Cialdini (1980) advocated a strategy called "full-cycle social psychology." A central concern of this strategy is the identification of influence methods used by everyday practitioners who are undoubtedly motivated to develop and refine influence tactics in order to maximize career success. With this in mind, we published two studies (Cody & Seiter, 2001; Cody, Seiter, & Montagne-Miller, 1995) based on observations of "real life" encounters between 416 shoppers and 416 commission salesclerks in retail department stores. Both of the studies examined the use and effectiveness of Cialdini's principles of compliance discussed earlier (i.e., liking, credibility, reciprocity, commitment, contrast, social proof, and scarcity). We review these studies here because they illustrate and extend many of the issues already discussed in this chapter.

Study One

As already noted, effective salespeople not only need to know about different types of customers and the different types of influence tactics they might use but also about what types of tactics work best on which customers. Our first study (Cody et al., 1995) examined this issue by having trained students observe and record the strategies salesclerks used and how these strategies influenced different types of shoppers (for more detail on methodology, see Cody et al., 1995). Shoppers were categorized in two ways. First, we examined whether males and females were influenced differently. Second, we looked at whether a customer's motive for shopping influenced the way he or she responded to salesclerks. The three types of shoppers we included were *focused* shoppers (who knew what they wanted to buy), *recreational* shoppers (who were "just browsing"), and *gift buyers*.

Table 19.1 illustrates how various tactics influenced males and females. The results compare purchase amounts depending on whether each tactic was used or not. As can be seen, males spent more than females but were significantly influenced by fewer tactics. Although women spent significantly more in response to virtually all of the tactics, men were most influenced by reciprocity, commitment, and ingratiation tactics.

Table 19.2 illustrates how various tactics influence recreational shoppers, focused shoppers, and gift buyers. As can be seen, focused shoppers spent the most money, followed by gift buyers and then recreational shoppers. Moreover, although recreational shoppers were influenced by almost all the tactics, focused shoppers were not significantly influenced by opinion conformity, similarity, helpfulness, contrast, and scarcity tactics. Gift buyers were significantly influenced only by opinion conformity and social proof.

In general, these results indicate that the most effective tactics are those that meet customers' goals. For example, the typical male wants to buy objects as quickly and efficiently as possible, so the best approach is simply to *help* him find the desired object, *praise* his selection, and then recommend an accessory that goes with his choice. On the other hand, gift buyers want to find an object that someone besides themselves will like.

TABLE 19.1 *Average Amount (Dollars) Spent by Male and Female Shoppers When Tactics Were and Were Not Used*

Tactics	Male Shoppers		Female Shoppers	
	Not Used	Used	Not Used	Used
Liking/ingratiation	63.85	127.32*	45.95	107.39*
Praise	58.56	156.84*	44.71	122.34*
Opinion conformity	85.14	141.32	65.23	109.70*
Render favors	81.82	127.35	58.70	107.83*
Friendliness	72.67	122.83	57.82	86.35*
Similarity	93.77	117.34	65.24	110.77*
Credibility	68.62	116.70	45.82	103.16*
Helping/reciprocity	64.09	132.49*	45.67	91.82*
Commitment	74.05	161.67*	51.98	138.32*
Contrast	96.64	113.89	66.47	115.71*
Social proof	81.80	139.21	56.02	110.53*
Scarcity	90.55	139.04	64.51	105.55*

*Indicates that the tactic was significantly related to increased sales.
Source: Adapted from Cody, Seiter, & Montagne-Miller, 1995.

TABLE 19.2   *Average Amount (Dollars) Spent by Different Types of Shoppers When Tactics Were and Were Not Used*

Tactics	Recreational Shoppers (N=105)		Focused Shoppers (N=256)		Gift Buyers (N=54)	
	Not Used	Used	Not Used	Used	Not Used	Used
Liking/ingratiation						
Praise	9.21	109.42*	62.46	141.89*	75.47	91.75
Opinion conformity	18.14	132.53*	92.26	114.86	67.98	135.01*
Render favors	19.06	101.96*	84.18	121.46*	74.96	87.92
Friendliness	16.68	42.37*	73.76	125.45*	76.46	81.82
Similarity	22.92	106.43*	89.65	137.24	87.13	57.73
Credibility						
Expertise	19.95	73.34*	76.35	115.90*	69.07	91.79
Trust	26.73	96.27*	87.77	140.25*	70.70	108.97
Helping/reciprocity						
Helpfulness	4.40	31.28	98.82	96.25	75.43	79.69
Leading help	6.92	78.91*	75.03	143.76*	68.62	94.51
Commitment	19.04	124.75*	73.38	161.00*	68.10	101.26
Contrast	26.78	95.29*	92.12	133.17	79.97	75.36
Social proof	17.60	99.81*	84.43	121.83*	60.68	113.33*
Scarcity	19.71	103.69*	90.60	122.87	78.57	83.22

*Indicates that the tactic was significantly related to increased sales.
Source: Adapted from Cody, Seiter, & Montagne-Miller, 1995.

Thus, the two tactics that indicate a product is liked by others (opinion conformity and social proof) seem to be the most effective for this type of customer.

Study Two

While our first study focused on types of customers and strategies, it said nothing about the ways in which different types of salesclerks affect buyer-seller interactions. Our second study (Cody & Seiter, 2001) examined this issue.

Recall that earlier in this chapter we described the four different styles of salesperson identified in this second study: ingratiation-style clerks, task-oriented clerks, client-oriented clerks, and passive-inactive clerks. Once again, based on observations of real interactions between commission salespeople and their customers, we sought to identify the types of strategies used by clerks and how effective each clerk was. Table 19.3 illustrates our results. As can be seen, reciprocity tactics were used most often by all types of salesclerks, followed by liking or ingratiation attempts.

The table also shows that client-oriented clerks used significantly more tactics than the other clerks and that ingratiation-oriented clerks were characterized primarily by the

TABLE 19.3   *Sales Tactics Used by Four Types of Clerks*

Tactics	Client-Oriented (N=20)	Ingratiator (N=68)	Task-Oriented (N=167)	Passive/ Inactive (N=161)
Liking/ingratiation	8.45	3.48	1.96	.66
Credibility	3.70	1.38	.90	.28
Helping/reciprocity	10.35	5.94	3.40	1.81
Commitment	1.05	.46	.29	.09
Contrast	.02	.13	.13	.03
Social proof	1.00	.49	.34	.12
Scarcity	.45	.28	.14	.10
Purchase amount	$213.82	$141.07	$88.86	$20.58

Source: Adapted from Cody & Seiter, 2001.

use of friendly and helpful tactics. Interestingly, these two active styles of selling, which also resulted in the largest purchase amounts, made up only about 21 percent of all the buyer-seller interactions we observed (5 percent client-oriented and 16 percent ingratiation-oriented). Task-oriented clerks, who relied on high levels of helping tactics and moderate levels of liking tactics, made up 40 percent of our sample; passive-inactive clerks, who used minimal helping tactics and no other type of tactic, made up 39 percent of our sample. As might be expected, client-oriented clerks sold significantly more merchandise than ingratiation-oriented clerks, ingratiation-oriented clerks sold significantly more merchandise than task-oriented clerks, and task-oriented clerks sold significantly more merchandise than passive-inactive clerks.

Implications

What are the implications of these studies? For those interested in improving sales, our projects suggest that successful selling depends on clerks' ability to help shoppers achieve their goals, adapt to shoppers' needs, and foster an image of likability. If a customer is shopping for a gift, the best approach is to use social proof and opinion conformity tactics to make a sale. If the customer is a focused or recreational shopper, the best advice is to be customer-oriented, using a wide variety of tactics in order to adapt to the customer's needs (Cody & Seiter, 2001).

Conclusion

The primary theme in this review of social influence and retail sales is that in order to be effective, salespeople must be competent communicators who are able to adapt to a variety of selling situations. To this end salespeople must learn to juggle an assortment of goals, which range from making the sale in an appropriate manner to creating a credible and likable image, to building relationships with customers. We have suggested that much of this ability is learned with experience over time and that with training, salesclerks benefit from enhanced knowledge structures. These structures contain information about different influence strategies and types of customers that salespeople encounter. A key ingredient of effective sales is knowing which of these strategies work best with which type of customer. We concluded this chapter with a description of our own studies that have helped to address this issue.

Although we have covered many topics here, we freely admit that we have merely scratched the surface of the body of literature on selling. For example, most of the selling tactics we discussed (e.g., scarcity, liking, social proof) operate heuristically, influencing customers without causing them to think much about things like product quality or arguments regarding why they should or shouldn't purchase a product. Stafford (1996) suggested that many of the tactics discussed in this chapter are effective but do not represent the full range of effects that can take place in response to salesclerks' selling attempts. For example, the scarcity tactic may have a negative effect if used on shoppers with a high need for cognition (i.e., people who need to think things through carefully) (see Inman et al., 1997). Moreover, Whittler (1994) suggested that if customers interpret these tactics as manipulative selling ploys, negative effects may occur, and Stafford (1996) argued that when a buyer becomes aware that these tactics are being used, it may cause him or her to scrutinize the salesclerk's messages. Whatever the case, such research highlights the importance of ethical and appropriate behavior on the part of salesclerks and, once again, the necessity of adaptability on the part of salespeople. Indeed, effective salespeople should be able to adapt to all types of customers, even those who do not base their purchase decisions on simple heuristics.

References

Anselmi, K., & Zemanek, J. E. (1997). Relationship selling: How personal characteristics of salespeople affect buyer satisfaction. *Journal of Social Behavior and Personality, 12*, 539–550.

Beatty, S. E., Mayer, M. L., Coleman, J. E., Reynolds, K. E., & Lee, J. (1996). Customer-sales associate retail relationships. *Journal of Retailing, 72*, 223–247.

Berry, L. L., & Parasuraman, A. (1991). *Marketing services: Competing through quality.* New York: Free Press.

Boorom, M. L., Goolsby, J. R., & Ramsey, R. P. (1998). Relational communication traits and their effect on adaptiveness and sales performance. *Journal of the Academy of Marketing Science, 26*, 16–30.

Boles, J. S., Johnson, J. T., & Barksdale, H. C. (2000). How salespeople build quality relationships: A replication and extension. *Journal of Business Research, 48*, 75–81.

Burgoon, J. K. (1994). Nonverbal signals. In M. Knapp & G. M. Miller (Eds.), *Handbook of interpersonal communication* (2nd ed., pp. 229–285). Thousand Oaks, CA: Sage.

Busch, P., & Wilson, D. T. (1976). An experimental analysis of a salesman's expert and referent bases of social power in the buyer seller dyad. *Journal of Marketing, 13*, 3–11.

Canary, D. J., Cody, M. J., & Manusov, V. L. (2000). *Interpersonal communication: A goals-based approach* (2nd ed.). Boston: Bedford/St. Martin's.

Chow, S., & Holden, R. (1997). Toward an understanding of loyalty: The moderating role of trust. *Journal of Managerial Issues, 9*, 275–298.

Cialdini, R. B. (1980). Full-cycle social psychology. *Applied Social Psychology Annual, 1*, 21–45.

Cialdini, R. B. (2001). *Influence: Science and practice* (4th ed.). Boston: Allyn & Bacon.

Clark, R. A., & Delia, J. (1979). Topoi and rhetorical competence. *Quarterly Journal of Speech, 65*, 187–206.

Cody, M. J., & Seiter, J. S. (2001). Compliance principles in retail sales in the United States. In W. Wosinska, R. B. Cialdini, D. W. Barrett, & J. Reykowski (Eds.), *The practice of social influence in multiple cultures* (pp. 325–341). Mahway, NJ: Erlbaum.

Cody, M. J., Seiter, J. S., & Montagne-Miller, Y. (1995). Men and women in the market place. In P. J. Kalbfleisch and M. J. Cody (Eds.), *Gender, power, and communication in interpersonal relationships* (pp. 305–329). Mahway, NJ: Erlbaum.

Comstock, J., & Higgins, G. (1997). Appropriate relational messages in direct selling interaction: Should salespeople adapt to buyers' communicator style? *Journal of Business Communication, 34*, 401–418.

Crosby, L. A., Evans, K. R., & Cowles, D. (1990). Relationship quality in services selling: An interpersonal influence perspective. *Journal of Marketing, 54*, 68–81.

Dawson, S., Bloch, P. H., & Ridgway, N. M. (1990). Shopping motives, emotional states, and retail outcomes. *Journal of Retailing, 66*, 408–427.

Dillard, J. P. (1990). Primary and secondary goals in interpersonal influence. In M. J. Cody & M. L. McLaughlin (Eds.), *The psychology of tactical communication* (pp. 70–90). Clevedon, England: Multilingual Matters.

Dillard, J. P., & Solomon, D. H. (2000). Conceptualizing context in message production research. *Communication Theory, 10*, 167–175.

Dion, P., Easterling, D., & Miller, S. J. (1995). What is really necessary in successful buyer/seller relationships? *Journal of Marketing Management, 24*, 1–9.

Donoho, C. L., & Swenson, M. J. (1996). Top-down versus bottom-up sales tactics effects on the presentation of a product line. *Journal of Business Research, 37*, 51–61.

Dwyer, R. R., Schurr, P. H., & Oh, S. (1987). Developing buyer-seller relationships. *Journal of Marketing, 51*, 11–27.

Evans, F. (1963). Selling as a dyadic relationship: A new approach. *American Behavioral Scientist, 6*, 76–79.

Fine, S. H., & Gardial, S. F. (1990). The effects of self-monitoring and similarity on salesperson inference process. *Journal of Personal Selling and Sales Management, 10*, 7–16.

Fine, L. M., & Schumann, D. W. (1992). The nature and role of salesperson perceptions: The interactive effects of salesperson/customer personalities. *Journal of Consumer Psychology, 1*, 285–296.

Ford, W. S. Z. (1999). Communication and customer service. In M. E. Roloff (Ed.), *Communication yearbook 22* (pp. 341–376). Thousand Oaks, CA: Sage.

French, J. R. P., & Raven, B. (1959). The bases of social power. In D. Cartwright (Ed.), *Studies in social power* (pp. 150–167). Ann Arbor: University of Michigan, Institute for Social Research.

Gadel, M. S. (1964). Concentration by salesmen on congenial prospects. *Journal of Marketing, 28*, 64–66.

Garbarino, E., & Johnson, M. S. (1999). The different roles of satisfaction, trust, and commitment in customer relationships. *Journal of Marketing, 63*, 70–87.

Gass, R. H., & Seiter, J. S. (2003). *Persuasion, social influence, and compliance gaining* (2nd ed.). Boston: Allyn & Bacon.

Gengler, C. E., Howard, D. J., & Zolner, K. (1995). A personal construct analysis of adaptive selling and sales experience. *Psychology and Marketing, 12*, 287–304.

Goff, B. G., & Walters, D. L. (1995). Susceptibility to salespersons' influence and consumers' shopping orientations. *Psychological Reports, 76*, 915–928.

Goff, B. G., Bellenger, D. N., & Stojack, C. (1994). Cues to consumer susceptibility to salesperson influence: Implications for adaptive retail selling. *Journal of Personal Selling and Sales Management, 14*, 25–39.

Goffman, E. (1959). *The presentation of self in everyday life*. Garden City, NY: Doubleday.

Gordon, R. A. (1996). Impact of ingratiation on judgments and evaluations: A meta-analytic investigation. *Journal of Personality and Social Psychology, 71* (1), 54–70.

Greenberg, M. S. (1980). A theory of indebtedness. In K. Gergen, M. S. Greenberg, & R. Willis (Eds.), *Social exchange: Advances in theory and research* (pp. 3–26). New York: Plenum.

Greene, J. O. (2000). Evanescent mentation: an ameliorative conceptual foundation for research and theory on message production. *Communication Theory, 10*, 139–155.

Griffin, J. (1995). *Customer loyalty: How to earn it, how to keep it.* New York: Lexington Books.

Gwinner, K. P., Gremler, D. D., & Bitner, M. J. (1998). Relational benefits in services industries: The customer's perspective. *Journal of the Academy of Marketing Science, 26,* 101–114.

Inman, J. J., Peter, A. C., & Raghubir, P. (1997). Framing the deal: The role of restrictions in accentuating deal value. *Journal of Consumer Research, 24,* 68–79.

Jones, E., Moore, J. N., Stanland, A. J. S., & Wyatt, R. A. J. (1998). Salesperson race and gender and the access and legitimacy paradigm: Does difference make a difference? *Journal of Personal Selling and Sales Management, 18,* 71–88.

Jones, E. E., & Pittman, T. S. (1982). Toward a general theory of strategic self-presentation. In J. M. Suls (Ed.), *Psychological perspectives on the self* (pp. 231–262). Hillsdale, NJ: Erlbaum.

Kellerman, K., & Cole, T. (1994). Classifying compliance gaining messages: Taxonomic disorder and strategic confusion. *Communication Theory, 4,* 3–60.

Lambert, D. M., Marmornstein, H., & Sharma, A. (1990). The accuracy of salesperson's perceptions of their customers: Conceptual examination and an empirical study. *Journal of Personal Selling and Sales Management, 10,* 1–9.

Leathers, D. G. (1988). Impression management training: Conceptualization and application to personal selling. *Journal of Applied Communication Research, 16,* 126–145.

Leigh, T. W., & McGraw, P. F. (1989). Mapping the procedural knowledge on industrial sales personnel: A script-theoretic investigation. *Journal of Marketing, 53,* 16–34.

Leuthesser, L. (1997). Supplier relational behavior: An empirical assessment. *Industrial Marketing Management, 26,* 245–254.

Levy, M., & Sharma, A. (1994). Adaptive selling: The role of gender, age, sales experience, and education. *Journal of Business Research, 31,* 39–47.

Lynn, M. (1991). Scarcity effects on value: A qualitative review of the commodity theory literature. *Psychology and Marketing, 8,* 43–57.

Macintosh, G., Anglin, K. A., Szymanski, D. M., & Gentry, J. W. (1992). Relationship development in selling: A cognitive analysis. *Journal of Personal Selling and Sales Management, 12,* 23–34.

Meyer, J. R. (2000). Cognitive models of message production: Unanswered questions. *Communication Theory, 10,* 176–187.

Morgan, R. M., & Hunt, S. D. (1994). The commitment-trust theory of relationship marketing. *Journal of Marketing, 58,* 20–38.

O'Keefe, B. J., & McCornack, S. A. (1987). Message logic design and message goal structure: Effects on perception of message quality in regulative communication situations. *Human Communication Research, 14,* 68–92.

Ramsey, R. P., & Sohi, R. S. (1997). Listening to your customers: The impact of perceived salesperson listening behavior on relationship outcomes. *Journal of the Academy of Marketing Science, 25,* 127–137.

Reynolds, K. E., & Beatty, S. E. (1999a). Customer benefits and company consequences of customer-salesperson relationships in retailing. *Journal of Retailing, 75,* 11–32.

Reynolds, K. E., & Beatty, S. E. (1999b). A relationship customer typology. *Journal of Retailing, 75,* 509–523.

Schurr, P. H., & Ozanne, J. L. (1985). Influences on exchange processes: Buyers preconceptions of a seller's trustworthiness and bargaining toughness. *Journal of Consumer Research, 14,* 939–953.

Sharma, A. (1999). Does the salesperson like customers? A conceptual and empirical examination of the persuasive effect of perceptions of the salesperson's affect toward customers. *Psychology and Marketing, 16,* 141–162.

Sharma, A., & Levy, M. (1995). Categorization of customers by retail salespeople. *Journal of Retailing, 71,* 71–81.

Spitzberg, B. H., & Cupach, W. R. (1989). *Handbook of interpersonal competence research.* New York: Springer-Verlag.

Sprowl, J. P., Carveth, R., & Senk, M. (1994). The effect of compliance-gaining strategy choice and communicator style on sales success. *Journal of Business Communication, 31,* 291–310.

Stafford, T. F. (1996). Conscious and unconscious processing of priming cues in selling encounters. *Journal of Personal Selling and Sales Management, 16,* 37–44.

Stone, G. P. (1954). City shoppers and urban identification: observation on the social psychology of city life. *American Journal of Sociology, 60,* 36–45.

Strutton, D., Pelton, L. E., & Lumpkin, J. R. (1995). Sex differences in ingratiatory behavior: An investigation of influence tactics in the salesperson-customer dyad. *Journal of Business Research, 34,* 35–45.

Sujan, H., Sujan, M., & Bettman, J. R. (1988). Knowledge structure differences between more effective and less effective salespeople. *Journal of Marketing Research, 25,* 81–86.

Sujan, H., Weitz, B. A., & Kumar, N. (1994). Learning orientation, working smart, and effective selling. *Journal of Marketing, 58,* 39–52.

Swan, J. E., Bowers, M. R., & Richardson, L. D. (1999). Customer trust in the salesperson: An integrative review and meta-analysis of the empirical literature. *Journal of Business Research, 44,* 93–107.

Tracy, K., Craig, R. T., Smith, M., & Spisak, F. (1984). The discourse of requests: An assessment of compliance-gaining requests. *Human Communication Research, 50,* 185–199.

VandeWalle, D., Brown, S. P., Cron, W. L., & Slocum, J. W. (1999). The influence of goal orientation and self-regulation tactics on sales performance: A longitudinal field test. *Journal of Applied Psychology, 84,* 249–259.

Verhallen, T. M. M., & Robben, H. S. J. (1995). Unavailability and the evaluation of goods. *Kyklos, 48,* 369–387.

Weitz, B. A. (1978). The relationship between salesperson performance and understanding customer decision making. *Journal of Marketing Research, 15,* 501–516.

Weitz, B. A. (1981). Effectiveness in sales interactions: A contingency framework. *Journal of Marketing, 45,* 85–103.

Weitz, B. A., & Bradford, K. D. (1999). Personal selling and sales management: A relationship marketing perspective. *Journal of the Academy of Marketing Science, 27,* 241–253.

Weitz, B. A., Sujan, H., & Sujan, M. (1986). Knowledge, motivation, and adaptive behavior: A framework for improving selling effectiveness. *Journal of Marketing, 50,* 174–191.

Whittler, T. E. (1994). Eliciting consumer choice heuristics: Sales representatives' persuasion strategies. *Journal of Personal Selling and Sales Management, 14,* 41–53.

Williams, K. C., & Spiro, R. L. (1985). Communication style in the salesperson customer dyad. *Journal of Marketing Research, 22,* 434–442.

Wilson, S. R. (1990). Development and test of a cognitive rules model of interaction goals. *Communication Monographs, 57,* 81–103.

Wortuba, T. (1991). The evolution of personal selling. *Journal of Personal Selling and Sales Management, 11,* 1–12.

Author Index

Subject Index